NORTHROP
ALP

P9-EEC-594

NORTHROP
ALP

MERRILL
ECONOMICS
PRINCIPLES AND PRACTICES
CLAYTON·BROWN

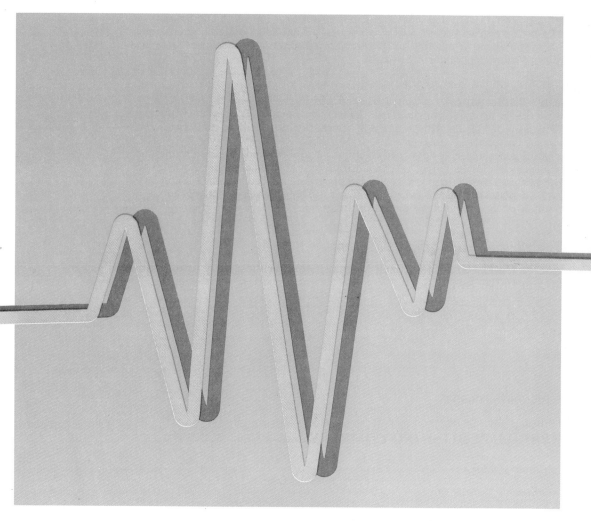

MERRILL
PUBLISHING COMPANY
Columbus, Ohio

Authors

Gary E. Clayton received his B.S. degree from Nasson College, M.A. degree from the University of New Hampshire, and Ph.D. degree from the University of Utah. He has taught business- and economics-related courses at several universities; co-authored a college text, and authored a variety of articles for educational, business, and technical journals. He has also served as a consultant to educational and community groups. At present, he teaches economics and finance at Northern Kentucky University. In 1976, he received the Outstanding Citizen Certificate of Recognition award for his work in economic education, and he received third-place recognition in the college division of the International Paper Company award sponsored by the Joint Council on Economic Education. In 1980–1981, Dr. Clayton was named in *Who's Who in the South and Southwest.* Dr. Clayton also serves as Vice President of the Kentucky Council on Economic Education and is a member of the American Economics Association and the Miami Valley Economics Association.

James E. Brown received his B.S. degree from the University of Richmond, M.A. degree from Michigan State University, and Ph.D. degree from the University of Florida. He taught economics, business policy, and finance at several universities, most recently at Northern Kentucky University; was a consulting author on an advanced economics textbook; and authored numerous articles for professional journals. In addition to serving as an economist with an international consulting firm, he headed his own firm of consulting economists. Dr. Brown also served as a consultant to several legislative committees and as a member of the President's Council on Inflation.

Contributing Authors to Program

Marsha Hafkin Greenberg, Jack Morgan, Steve Trubow, Ray Kauffman, Jo Ann Cutler Sweeney.

Cover Illustration: *graph of business activity in the United States*

ISBN 0-675-00660-0

Published by
MERRILL PUBLISHING COMPANY

Columbus, Ohio
Copyright © 1988, 1983, 1979, 1971, 1968 by Merrill Publishing Company

All rights reserved. No part of this book may be reproduced in any form, electronic or mechanical, including photocopy, recording, or any information storage or retrieval system, without permission in writing from the publisher.

Printed in the United States of America

7 8 9 10 11 12 13 14 15 VH 00 99 98 97 96 95 94 93 92 91

Preface

Economics: Principles and Practices is a practical study of the features and functions of economics and economic systems. The program develops an awareness of economic principles and theories, presenting ideas simply and developing them logically. The ideas are reinforced verbally through a readable narrative and graphically through a wide variety of precisely executed graphs, charts, tables, diagrams, and maps. The material is current, meaningful, and encourages students to recognize and interpret economic happenings in their society.

Economics: Principles and Practices is designed to inform students about the world of economics. The text is divided into seven units and 22 chapters. It begins with a Prologue that shows what economics is and ends with an Epilogue that highlights the value of economics.

Each chapter of *Economics: Principles and Practices* focuses on a topic basic to the understanding of economic systems and the economy. Concepts are reinforced with a variety of photographs and graphic art. Key economic terms appear in boldface type and are defined in context immediately after being presented. These terms are also defined in a glossary that appears in the appendix matter of the text.

Four types of special features are interspersed throughout chapters. The Profiles focus on the lives and theories of major historical and contemporary economists. Case Study: Careers introduce and describe economic- and finance-related occupations. Case Study: Issues present opposing views on current topics of debate as they relate to the American free-enterprise economy, while Understanding Sources provide students with insights on how economic data may be presented.

Each chapter of the text concludes with a review section that contains a summary of key points, a listing of economic terms, review and higher-level, thought-provoking questions, and a skill exercise. Applying Economic Understandings is designed to make the student aware of an important economic skill and to give the student practice in that skill.

Each of the units in *Economics: Principles and Practices* also concludes with a review section. In each Unit Review, key points are highlighted and comprehensive questions are asked. The review also includes a consumer skill that will help the student meet the challenges of daily life more effectively and efficiently.

Economics: Principles and Practices concludes with several special sections in the Appendix. Consumer Guidelines and Life Skills are designed to give students practical suggestions to handling typical situations faced by consumers. There are also suggested readings for the student, full-color maps of the world and the United States, a complete economic atlas that includes world demographic statistics, a glossary of key economic terms, and an index.

Reviewers

Joseph Baca
Social Studies Specialist
New Mexico Department of Education
Santa Fe, New Mexico

Edward Brennan
Social Studies Coordinator
Fairfield School District
Fairfield, Connecticut

Fred Cichon
Administrative Coordinator, Social Studies
Chatham County Schools
Savannah, Georgia

Dennis Cochran
Resource Teacher, Social Studies Department
Albert Einstein High School
Kensington, Maryland

Gail Franklin
Social Studies Teacher
Lithia Springs High School
Lithia Springs, Georgia

Nancy Lang
Director, Center for Economic Education
Northern Kentucky University
Highland Heights, Kentucky

Phillip Gonyar
Chairperson, Social Studies Department
Waterville Senior High School
Waterville, Maine

Karla McComb
Curriculum Facilitator
Clark County School District
Las Vegas, Nevada

Fred Moran
Social Studies Teacher
East Islip Senior High School
Islip Terrace, New York

Jim Sudyk
Social Studies Teacher
Henry M. Gunn High School
Palo Alto, California

Program Staff

Project Editor—Patricia Cornelius Travnicek; **Assistant Editors**—Thomas Photos, Cynthia Story Bisson, Elise Longpree, Kathy Blubaugh Tebbe, Veronica Goolsby; **Project Assistants**—Robyn Ransom, Peg MacPhearson; **Project Designer**—Patricia Cohan; **Project Artists**—Katie White; **Production Editor**—Connie Young; **Production Assistant**—Julie A. Higgins; **Graphic Illustrator**—David Germon; **Graphic Artists**—Larry Collins, Lucia Condo, Barbara White; **Photo Editor**—Mark Burnett; **Indexer**—Barbara L. Bryan; **Software Editor**—P. Morooka-Barr.

Table of Contents

Prologue

Unit 5

The Overall Economy

Unit 6

World Economy

Profiles

Understanding Sources

Case Study:

Careers

Issues

Charts, Diagrams, and Graphs

Tables

Maps

Prologue

To some people, the word *economics* means a complicated science made up of laws, statistics, mathematical formulas, hard-to-pronounce terms, and complex theories. However, to those who study economics, it is an interesting and exciting subject.

When we study economics, we study ourselves at work or at play, at home or at school, on the job, or after hours. Economics applies to almost everything, and is something that everyone can understand. While it may seem complex, economics deals with everyday problems.

The diagram below is known as a want-satisfaction chain. It is the root, the base, of economics, and all of us are part of it. We all want certain things—clothes, homes, automobiles, food, and so on. All kinds of resources—inputs—go into providing or making these things. People and machines use these inputs in different amounts and combinations to produce outputs—the things we want. More people and machines distribute the outputs to us. We buy and then use—consume—those outputs. Once we have consumed them, we are satisfied. This is what makes up economics at its simplest—the chain beginning with our wants and ending with the satisfaction of those wants.

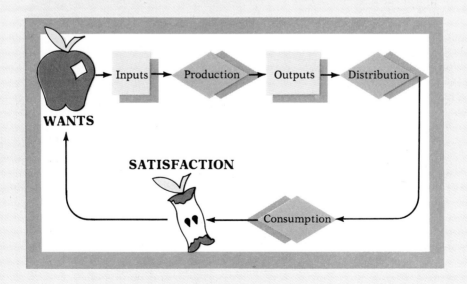

An Introduction to Economics

Economics is an old subject whose roots go back to the early days of civilization when people discovered they wanted more than they had. It involves such topics as people's needs and wants, the many different types of economic organizations that supply them, and the types of economic systems set up to meet them.

Unit 1

Contents

What is Economics?

Now, as there are many actions, arts, and sciences, their ends also are many; the
end of the medical art is health, that of shipbuilding a vessel, that of strategy
victory, that of economics wealth.

Aristotle

Chapter 1

After reading this chapter, you will be able to:

- Explain scarcity and discuss three basic questions each society must decide.

- Define economics and identify three key elements within its scope.

- Identify the key terms and concepts used to study economics.

- Give examples of each factor of production.

- Explain the decision making process and the role played by opportunity cost in that process.

- Discuss how the study of economics will help provide a better understanding of the free enterprise economy of the United States.

1.1 Economics as a Science

Many things in life seem to be "free" when, actually, they are not. For instance, you may think you are being treated to a "free" lunch—when in fact it is not free. While you may not pay for it then and there, someone had to pay the farmer for raising the food, the truck driver for delivering the food, the chef for preparing the food, and the waiter or waitress for serving the food. Who is that "someone"? Although it may come as a surprise, that someone probably is you!

For example, many schools offer "free" lunches for some children. These lunches are usually paid in part with money obtained from taxes. As long as taxpayers pay for these lunches, they are not really free. In fact, the more the government gives away "for free," the more taxes it will have to collect.

When a business buys a "free" lunch, the price of that lunch is usually buried somewhere in the price it charges for its products. The business may treat someone

These students are eating a free meal. However, the government has paid for the meal. From whom does the government get the money in order to pay for the "free" meal?

to a "free" lunch to make a sale. If the person buys, the business will recover some, if not all, of the cost of the lunch.

If the individual does not buy, then someone else will pay for the "free lunch" by paying higher prices. The business is like the government—the more it gives away "free," the more it has to charge for the items it produces and sells. In the end, someone always pays for the supposedly free lunch.

Unfortunately, most things in life are not free because someone has to pay for the production in the first place. Economic educators have a term, TINSTAAFL, which describes this concept. In short, this term means that *there is no such thing as a free lunch*. This is one of the keys to being able to understand the fundamental problem of economics.

FUNDAMENTAL ECONOMIC PROBLEM

The fundamental economic problem facing all societies is that of **scarcity**—a condition that arises because society does not have enough resources to produce all the things people would like to have. The problem of scarcity is not, as some people might think, related to a shortage of money.

For example, suppose that everyone in a society suddenly became wealthier than they ever thought possible. Even if all people became millionaires, they would still go without many of the things they want and need.

Who, for example, would want to go to work? Most people would probably try to spend their money on houses, boats, cars, vacations, and many other things. But who would actually want to take the time to produce these things?

At first, store owners would be delighted to sell their merchandise. However, the supply of items in the stores would not last long. With few people working, it would be almost impossible to order additional inventory from factories. Eventually, shelves would be empty, and there would be nothing left to buy.

The huge increase in everyone's income would not solve the economic problem. Most likely, it would have the opposite effect—the entire economy would come to

a halt until people found that their money was practically, if not totally, worthless.

Thus, the problem of scarcity is not due to a shortage of money. If everyone suddenly had an unlimited supply, they would lose the urge to work and factories would close. Rather, the problem of scarcity is a lack of resources needed to make all the things people want.

THREE BASIC QUESTIONS

When a society provides for the needs of its people, it answers three basic economic questions. In so doing, it makes decisions about the way its limited resources are going to be used.

The first question is that of WHAT to produce. Should a society, for example, devote its resources to the production of military equipment or to the production of other items such as food, clothing, or housing? Suppose the decision is to produce housing. Should its limited resources then be used for low-income, middle-income, or upper-income housing? A society cannot have everything its people want, so a choice as to WHAT to produce must be made.

The second question is that of HOW to produce. Should factory owners use assembly-line methods that require little labor, or should they use less equipment and more workers? If an area has many people unemployed, then the second method might be better. On the other hand, assembly-line methods usually have lower production costs. This would make many manufactured items less expensive and, therefore, such items could be bought by more people.

Finally, the third question deals with FOR WHOM to produce. After a society makes the decision of WHAT and HOW to

Figure 1–1

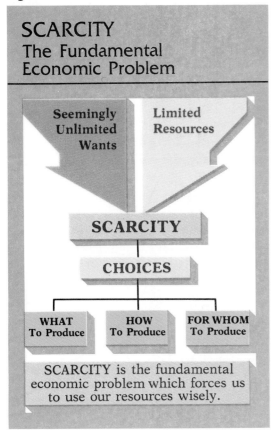

SCARCITY
The Fundamental
Economic Problem

Seemingly Unlimited Wants | Limited Resources

SCARCITY

CHOICES

WHAT To Produce | HOW To Produce | FOR WHOM To Produce

SCARCITY is the fundamental economic problem which forces us to use our resources wisely.

produce, the things produced must be allocated to someone. If the society decides to produce housing, for example, should it be distributed to workers, professional people, or government employees? Or, perhaps there is another group even more deserving. In the end, the result is the same. If there are not enough houses to go around, a choice must be made as to who will receive the existing supply.

These three choices about WHAT, HOW, and FOR WHOM to produce are not easy for any society to make. Nevertheless, a society has few options. It must answer the three basic questions as long as there are not enough resources to produce all the things people want and need. As will be shown in the next chapter, different societies answer these questions in different ways.

People consume goods and services to satisfy their wants and needs. Are the people on the roller coaster satisfying a want or a need?

Kenneth E. Boulding

1910–

Kenneth Boulding is a leading contemporary economist whose writings cover a great variety of topics. He has written more than a dozen books including *Economic Analysis, Conflict and Defense, The Meaning of the Twentieth Century,* and *Beyond Economics.*

In an early essay, "Is Economics Necessary?," Boulding argues that economics is important "not merely for the support of economists, but for the development and perhaps even the survival of science in general and the civilization that supports it." He stresses that it is significant "not merely because it investigates an important slice of life in the marketplace, but because the phenomena which emerge . . . in the marketplace are also found in virtually all other human activities."

Boulding argues that economics has evolved into a generalized theory of choice. Thus, if we study the way in which we make choices in the market, we may be better able to understand the way choices are made in other aspects of human activity.

MEANING AND SCOPE OF ECONOMICS

Economics is the study of human efforts to satisfy what seems like unlimited and competing wants through the careful use of relatively scarce resources. Along the way, economics deals with what is produced and with who gets how much of the things produced. Economics is also concerned with unemployment, inflation, international trade, the interaction of business and labor, and the effects of government spending and taxes.

Economics does not stop with the description of economic activity. It goes beyond that to discover why and how people behave as they do in making economic decisions. While the description of economic activity may be interesting, description alone leaves unanswered many important "why" and "how" questions.

PER CAPITA PERSONAL INCOME AND ITS AVERAGE ANNUAL GROWTH

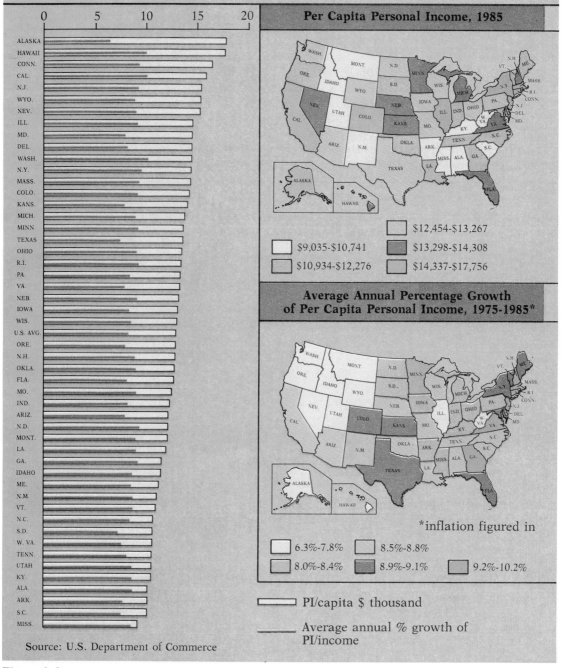

Source: U.S. Department of Commerce

Figure 1–2

For example, why are the prices of some items high while others are low? Why do some people work hard and receive low wages while others who seem to do little or no work have high incomes? Why are incomes higher in some states than in others? How does the income tax affect a person's desire to work and save? In order to answer such questions, economics goes beyond description to analyze as well as explain economic activity. In the end, the scope of economics is limited to three key elements—description, analysis, and the explanation of economic activity.

Economics is a social science. It is a systematic study of the way in which people cope with scarcity. Economists study what is, or tends to be, and how it came to be. They do not in any way pretend to tell what ought to be. In this, economists can be compared to nuclear physicists. The physicists can explain how to make a nuclear bomb and what damage the bomb can do. But, as scientists, they are not expected to judge whether or not the bomb should be used in war. People must make up their own minds about that.

In much the same way, economists can generally predict the results of different courses of action. They do not hand down economic rules for all people to obey, however. Deciding what is right and wrong is the responsibility of all citizens. The study of economics will not lead to ethical judgments for economic problems any more than the study of physics will lead to ethical decisions on the use of certain military weapons.

Section Review

1. What is the fundamental economic problem?
2. What are the three basic questions a society must answer?
3. What three elements make up the scope of economics?
4. What can economists predict?

1.2 Basic Economic Concepts

Economics, like any other social science, has its own vocabulary. To understand economics, a review of some key terms is necessary. Fortunately, most economic terms are widely used and many will already be familiar.

NEEDS, WANTS, AND DEMANDS

A **need** is a basic requirement for survival. People, for example, have basic needs such as food, clothing, and shelter. People also have higher level needs, such as com-munication, love, acceptance, knowledge, hope, and accomplishment. These needs are part of the makeup of each person.

A **want** is a means of expressing a need. Food, for example, is a basic need related to survival. To satisfy this need, a person may "want" a pizza, hamburger, taco, or other favorite food. That is, there are any number of foods that will satisfy the basic need for food.

Given a person's budget, some choices might seem reasonable while others might not. The point is that the range of things represented by the term "want" is much broader than those represented by the term "need."

Food represents a basic need related to survival, while a sports car is usually considered a want. Why do advertisers try to make wants, such as sports cars, into needs?

Sometimes the difference between a want and a need is clear; at other times, it is not. For example, some people may feel that air conditioners and automatic transmissions in automobiles are needs. However, other people may classify these things as wants. For this group, the basic need may simply be "dependable or efficient transportation."

Sometimes advertisers present wants as needs to promote their products. People are told, for example, that they "need" Brand X rather than Brand Y even though the two brands may be similar. People may be influenced by the ad, or they may decide that another brand would work just as well. Any desire they may have for Brand X, Y, or any other is only a want based on the basic need.

A basic need is reflected in a want for a particular product. By the same token, a want cannot be counted in the market-place until it becomes a **demand**—the willingness and ability to purchase a desired object. Since an individual has limited resources, only some wants will end up as measurable demands.

GOODS AND SERVICES— ECONOMIC PRODUCTS

The study of economics is concerned with **economic products**—goods and services that are useful, relatively scarce, and transferable to others. The important thing is that economic products are scarce in an economic sense. That is, one cannot get enough to satisfy individual wants and needs. The fact that economic products command a price shows that they have these characteristics.

The terms "goods" and "services" are used to describe the many things people desire. A **good** is a tangible commodity like a book, car, or stereo. A **consumer good** is intended for final use by individuals to satisfy their wants and needs. A manufactured good used to produce other goods and services is called a **capital good.** An example of a capital good would be a drill press in a factory, an oven in a bakery, or a computer in a public school.

The other type of economic product is a **service**—or work that is performed for someone. Services can include haircuts, repairs to home appliances, and forms of entertainment like rock performances. They also include the work performed by doctors, lawyers, and teachers. The difference between a good and a service is that the service is something that cannot be touched, or felt, like a good.

Many other things—sunshine, rainfall, fresh air—are known as **free products** because they are so plentiful. No one could possibly own them, nor would most people be willing to pay anything for them. In fact, some are so important that life would be impossible without them. Even so, free products are not scarce enough to be a major concern in the study of economics.

Figure 1–3

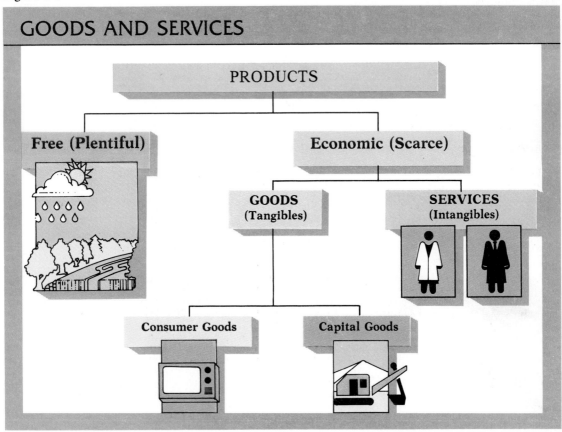

GOODS AND SERVICES

PRODUCTS

Free (Plentiful)

Economic (Scarce)

GOODS (Tangibles)

SERVICES (Intangibles)

Consumer Goods

Capital Goods

VALUE AND WEALTH

In economics, the term **value** means something has a worth that can be expressed in dollars and cents. Someone may say, for example, that he or she has a valuable coin, antique doll, or model train collection. In each case, the value is determined by the price someone would pay for the collection.

But what makes some things worth more than others? The diamond-water paradox, also known as the **paradox of value,** helps answer this question. Early economists observed that some things, like water, were essential to life yet had little monetary value. Other things, like diamonds, were not essential but had much higher value. At first, it seemed paradoxical that many essentials had little value while other items had much higher ones.

Later, economists decided that part of the reason was due to scarcity. For example, water is so plentiful in many areas that it has little or no value. On the other hand, diamonds are so scarce that they have great value. In order for something to have value, then, it has to be somewhat scarce.

Scarcity, however, is not enough. If something is to have value, it must also have **utility,** or the capacity to be useful to someone. Utility is not something that is fixed and can be measured, like weight or height. Instead, the utility of a good or service may vary from one person to the next. One person may, for example, get a great deal of enjoyment from a home computer; another may get very little. One person may enjoy a rock concert, another may not. A good or service does not have to have utility for every person, only utili-

Trees are natural resources and items of wealth. Each one is useful, scarce, transferable, as well as tangible. According to the economist, why are trees part of the national wealth?

ty for some. In the end, for something to have value, it must be scarce and have utility.

Another economic concept is **wealth**—the sum of those economic products that are tangible, scarce, useful, and transferable from one person to another. Most economic goods are counted as wealth, but services are not. The reason for this is that it is difficult to measure the value of services accurately.

For example, it is difficult to measure the contribution made by people's abilities and talents to a nation's wealth. If a country's material possessions are taken away, its people, through ability and industry, may soon restore these possessions. On the other hand, if a country's capabilities—its people—are taken away, its wealth will deteriorate.

A country's total wealth, then, is the stockpile of useful, scarce, transferable, and tangible things in existence at a given time. National wealth includes all such items as natural resources, factories, stores, houses, motels, theaters, furniture, clothing, books, video games, and even footballs.

CONSUMPTION AND CONSUMER SOVEREIGNTY

Consumers—people who use goods and services to satisfy wants and needs—play an important role in many economies. Especially in the United States, consumers often are thought of as having a certain control or power in the economy because they determine which products are ultimately produced. For example, a company may try to sell a certain item. If consumers like the product, it will sell, and the producer will be rewarded for his or her efforts. If consumers refuse to purchase,

thereby rejecting the product, the firm may go out of business.

In recent years, producers have had outstanding successes with some products—home video games, certain dolls, toy robots, and some home computers. Other products, like diesel engines for cars and gasohol, were generally rejected by consumers. The term **consumer sovereignty** describes the role of the consumer as sovereign or ruler of the market. More commonly, it is expressed in a different way by saying that "the customer is always right."

As consumers, people indulge in **consumption**—the process of using up goods and services in order to satisfy human wants. Sometimes the consumption of an economic product means that it has been destroyed as its utility is used up. For instance a meal (something useful, scarce, and transferable to others) no longer exists once it is eaten. But consumption can also mean the use of goods and services for productive purposes. For instance, a carpenter may use wood, glue, and nails while building a table. Only this time, the goods are not really used up, they are combined to make another good—one with even more usefulness and value.

Some consumers carry the process of consumption to extreme limits. **Conspicuous consumption**—the use of a good or service to impress others—is fairly common. A person may, for example, wear expensive jewelry or drive a flashy car. While that person obviously enjoys the use of these items, at least part of the enjoyment comes from showing off his or her expensive taste to others.

Consumers' wants are constantly changing as they become exposed to new ideas, products, and places. Because of advertising, children may develop absolute cravings for toys they had never seen before. Millions of consumers now want home

The miner in the picture is an important part of the economy. Without him and other workers, there would be no goods and services. What factor of production does he represent?

computers when ten years ago home computers were barely known. Modern communications and travel make people aware of things and events in other parts of the country and the world.

In the United States, for example, Americans use goods and services from every geographic area. Californians soak their waffles in maple syrup made in Vermont. New Englanders enjoy Florida orange juice. Kansans enjoy television programs produced in New York and California. Many Americans also buy Persian rugs, Japanese automobiles, and European works of art.

Thus, consumers play an important part in the economy today. They have a say in what is—and what is not—produced when they express their wants as demands in the marketplace.

FACTORS OF PRODUCTION

The reason people cannot satisfy all their wants and needs is the scarcity of productive resources. These resources, or **factors of production,** are called land, labor, and capital. They provide the means for a society to produce and distribute its goods and services.

As an economic term, **land** means the "gifts of nature," or natural resources not created by human effort. It includes deserts, fertile fields, forests, mineral deposits, rainfall, sunshine, and the climate necessary to grow crops.

Because there are only so many natural resources available at any given time, economists tend to think of land as being fixed or in limited supply. There is not enough good farmland to feed all of the earth's population, enough sandy beaches for everyone to enjoy, or enough minerals to meet people's expanding energy needs indefinitely.

In the future, the development of technology and knowledge will allow people to find and use new resources. But, for the most part, economists still treat the factor, land, as relatively fixed.

The second factor of production is **labor**—people with all their efforts and abilities. Unlike land, labor is a resource that may vary in size over time. Historically, factors such as population growth, immigration, famine, war, and disease have had a dramatic impact on both the quantity and quality of labor.

The third factor of production is **capital** —the tools, equipment, and factories used in the production of goods and services. As noted earlier, such items are also called capital goods. This is to distinguish them from **financial capital,** the money used to buy the tools and equipment used in production.

Capital is unique in that it is the result of production. A bulldozer, for example, is a capital good used in construction. At the same time, it was manufactured in a factory, which makes it the result of earlier production. Like the bulldozer, the drill press in the machine shop and the cash register in a neighborhood store are capital goods. The drill press is used to make another machine or good, while the cash register is used to speed up the record-keeping associated with the sale of merchandise.

When the three inputs—land, labor, and capital—are present, **production,** or the process of creating goods and services, can take place. Even the production of the service called education requires the presence of land, labor, and capital.

For example, the chalkboards, desks, and audio-visual equipment used in schools are capital goods. Also necessary are the services of labor, including teachers, administrators, and other school employees. Land, such as the iron ore, granite, and timber used to make the desks and building, as well as the lot where the school is located, is also needed. Therefore, it is nearly

Figure 1–4

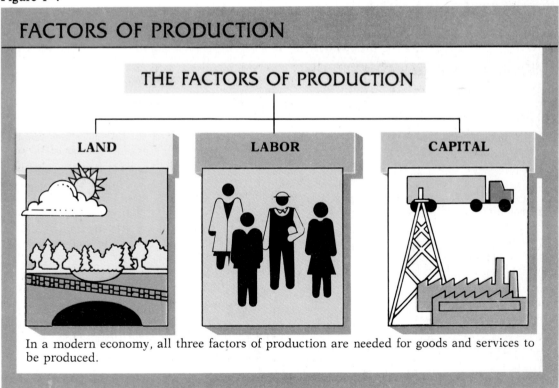

FACTORS OF PRODUCTION

THE FACTORS OF PRODUCTION

LAND LABOR CAPITAL

In a modern economy, all three factors of production are needed for goods and services to be produced.

A farmer needs capital like this harvesting machine to make food production easier and more abundant in the future. How do capital goods differ from financial capital?

impossible to provide the service of education without these three factors of production—capital, labor, and land.

▌ Section Review

1. How are needs, wants, and demands related?

2. What is the difference between free products and economic products? Goods and services?

3. How is value related to wealth?

4. What are the three major factors of production?

5. When can production take place?

1.3 *Evaluating Economic Decisions*

The process of making choices is not always easy. Still, decisions must be made by individuals, businesses, government agencies, and many other groups that try to satisfy people's wants and needs. To become a good decision maker, a person needs to know how to identify the problem; then structure the analysis in a way that carefully considers all possibilities before making the final choice.

OPPORTUNITY COST

People often think of cost in terms of dollars. To an economist, however, cost means more than the price tag placed on a good or service. Instead, economists think in terms of **opportunity cost**—the cost of the next best alternative use of money, time, or resources when one choice is made rather than another.

Suppose a person spends $12,000 on a new car. The opportunity cost of the purchase is the value of the stereo, apartment, spring vacation, or other items and activities that could have been bought with the money spent on the car.

Even time has an opportunity cost. Suppose your best friend had a chance to earn $30 for an afternoon's work. On the way, however, your friend was falsely arrested and thrown in jail. By the time the mistake was discovered, it was too late for your friend to go to work. So, the opportunity cost of the afternoon in jail was $30.

Later, suppose your friend decided to spend the evening swimming rather than playing softball. The opportunity cost of that decision was the enjoyment of the softball game, or any other activity given up because of your friend's decision to go swimming.

When economists talk in terms of costs, then, they are really talking in terms of alternatives that are given up. Thus, part of making economic decisions involves recognizing and evaluating alternatives as well as making choices from among these alternatives.

TRADE-OFFS AMONG ALTERNATIVES

Since most people cannot have everything they want, they are almost always faced with many choices when spending their income or time. While choices are not always easy to make, the decision making grid on page 20 shows one way to approach such problems. This grid summarizes a decision made by Malcolm, a newspaper carrier. His dilemma was to spend a $15 gift certificate in the best way possible.

When Malcolm visited a local store, he discovered that several alternatives seemed

These people have considered the opportunity costs of engaging in one type of activity, sports, instead of another. What do economists mean when they talk about costs?

MALCOLM'S DECISION MAKING GRID

Alternatives	CRITERIA				
	Costs $15 or Less	Durability	Parental Consent	No Other Costs	Full time Use
Airplane	+	-	+	+	+
Bow and Arrow	+	+	-	+	-
Hockey Game	+	+	+	-	+
Soccer Ball	+	+	+	+	-
Radio	+	+	+	+	+

Adapted from *Trade Offs*, © 1978 Agency for Instructional Technology (AIT).

Table 1–A

appealing—an airplane, a bow and arrow, a hockey game, a soccer ball, and a radio. At the same time, he realized that there were advantages and drawbacks to each item. For example, some items were more durable than others, some might require the consent of his parents, and some had additional costs (the batteries for the hockey game were extra, but they came with the radio).

To help with his decision, Malcolm drew a grid that listed his alternatives (the opportunity costs) and several criteria by which to judge them. Then, he used pluses and minuses to evaluate each alternative. In the end, Malcolm chose the radio because it satisfied more of his criteria than any other alternative.

Using the decision making grid is an effective way of analyzing an economic problem. Among other things, it forces one to consider a number of relevant alternatives. For another, it requires that person to identify criteria used to evaluate the alternatives. Finally, it forces one to evaluate each alternative based on the criteria.

PRODUCTION POSSIBILITIES FRONTIER

A popular model used by economists to illustrate opportunity cost is known as a **production possibilities frontier.** This diagram represents various combinations of goods and/or services that can be produced by an economy when all factors of production are fully employed.

Suppose, for example, that a mythical country called Alpha has a limited supply of land, labor, and capital. As a result, Alpha can make only two kinds of goods—guns and butter. At current production levels, Alpha produces 50 units of guns and 800 units of butter annually. This is represented by point **a** on the curve in Graph **A** on page 21.

Now, suppose that Alpha decided it did not have enough guns to protect itself. It could then shift resources from the production of butter to the production of guns. This might make the production of butter drop to 400 units, and allow the production of guns to rise to 100 units.

THE PRODUCTION POSSIBILITIES FRONTIER

(A) When resources are fully used, a country can produce anywhere along its production frontier.

(B) When all resources are not fully used, a country cannot reach its potential.

(C) Over time, resources will increase, allowing Alpha to produce more of everything.

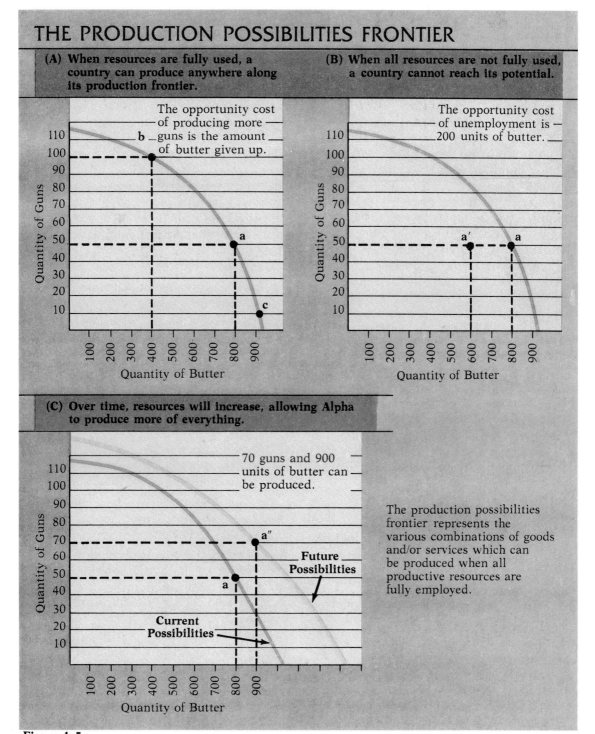

The opportunity cost of producing more guns is the amount of butter given up.

The opportunity cost of unemployment is 200 units of butter.

70 guns and 900 units of butter can be produced.

Future Possibilities

Current Possibilities

The production possibilities frontier represents the various combinations of goods and/or services which can be produced when all productive resources are fully employed.

Figure 1–5

This change is represented by point *b* in Graph *A*. The opportunity cost of producing the additional 50 units of guns is the 400 units of butter given up.

Points *a* and *b* represent only two possible mixes of output. If Alpha needed more butter, it could shift resources from guns to butter. If it shifted enough resources, it could even produce point *c* in Graph *A*.

It is also possible for Alpha to produce the mix of output shown at point *a'* in Graph *B*. In this case, all resources are not fully employed. Butter industry labor, for example, may be on strike causing the output of butter to fall to 600 units. The opportunity cost of the strike, then, is the 200 units of butter not produced because of idle resources. Production at *a'* could also be the result of other idle resources such as capital or land. As long as some resources are not used, the country cannot produce on its frontier.

Graph *C* represents the growth of Alpha's economy over time. In the long run, population can grow, new factories and equipment can be built, and natural resources can be better utilized. Therefore, Alpha may be able to produce more of both goods.

The production possibilities frontier is just one of the many tools used by economists to describe various events in the economy. Realistically, however, economies are able to produce more than two goods or services. The diagram is easier to read if only two products are examined. Even so, a simple model such as the one on page 21 is sometimes all that economists need to analyze an actual problem.

▌ Section Review

1. How do economists determine opportunity cost?

2. Why do people use a decision making grid?

3. What is a production possibilities frontier used to show?

1.4 *The Road Ahead*

The study of economics does more than explain how people deal with scarcity. It provides insight on how incomes are earned and spent, how jobs are created, and how the economy works on a daily basis. It also provides a more detailed understanding of the American **free enterprise economy**—one where privately owned businesses and consumers, rather than the government, jointly make the WHAT, HOW, and FOR WHOM decisions.

In addition, it will provide a working knowledge of the roles of property rights, competition, supply and demand, the price system, and the economic incentives that make the American economy function.

Along the way, such things as unemployment, the business cycle, inflation, and economic growth will be covered. The role of business, labor, and government in the American free enterprise economy also will be examined. Finally, the relationship of the United States economy to the international economy will also be explored.

The study of economics also helps people become better decision makers. For example, economic issues are often debated during political campaigns. Voters need to understand issues and how the candidates feel about them before deciding which candidate to support. A voter may have to decide between the candidate who favors higher taxes and more government spending and the candidate who favors lower taxes and less government spending. Or the choice may be between a candidate who favors limiting imports and one who favors free trade.

The study of economics will not provide voters with clear-cut answers to all questions. But it will help them have a better understanding of the issues involved. As such, the study of economics will help people make more intelligent choices in the voting booths.

Textbook economics can be divided into neat sections for study, but the real world is not so orderly. Most people live in dynamic societies in which things are constantly changing. New events take place daily, and the economies almost always are in a state of flux. In addition, the people of the world differ. Not everyone has the same kind or degree of ambition, strength, greed, or luck. Opinions also differ, and some issues never seem to be settled.

No matter what road people decide to take, they will not have a smooth, easy ride. In practice, the world of economics is complex and the road ahead is bumpy. But the study of economics will help make the trip more interesting and comfortable.

Section Review

1. What insights are gained from studying economics?

2. Who makes the WHAT, HOW, and FOR WHOM decisions in a free enterprise economy?

Chapter 1 Review

Summary

1. Most things in life are not free. Economic educators use the term TIN-STAAFL to describe this concept.

2. Scarcity is the fundamental economic problem and is the result of a lack of resources.

3. All societies must face the three basic questions of WHAT, HOW, and FOR WHOM to produce.

4. Economics is a social science that examines the way in which people try to satisfy seemingly unlimited wants and needs with relatively scarce resources.

5. The scope of economics is limited to description, analysis, and the explanation of economic activity.

6. All people have basic needs that come from the desire to survive, and higher-level needs such as success and love.

7. Needs and wants become demands when people in the marketplace are willing and able to buy something.

8. The study of economics deals with those goods and services that are useful, relatively scarce, and transferable to others.

9. Wealth has monetary value and includes natural resources, consumer goods, and capital goods.

10. Consumer demand helps determine which goods and services will ultimately be produced. In a free economy, the consumer is "king."

11. In order for production to take place, the factors of production—land, labor, and capital—must be used.

12. The cost of an economic decision—opportunity cost—is the alternative given up when one course of action is chosen over another.

13. Countries make trade-offs when they choose to produce some goods rather than others.

14. The study of economics helps people make informed decisions and understand the American free enterprise economy.

■ *Building an Economic Vocabulary*

scarcity
economics
need
want
demand
economic products
good
consumer good
capital good
service

free products
value
paradox of value
utility
wealth
consumers
consumer sovereignty
consumption
conspicuous consumption

factors of production
land
labor
capital
financial capital
production
opportunity cost
production possibilities frontier
free enterprise economy

■ *Reviewing the Main Ideas*

1. Why do economists say there is no such thing as a "free" lunch?

2. What effect would a large increase in each citizen's income have on the economy of a nation?

3. What causes scarcity?

4. Why is economics considered a social science?

5. What is the difference between a need and a want?

6. How do wants and needs become demands?

7. What is the relationship between goods, services, and economic products?

8. Why are services excluded when the wealth of a nation is measured?

9. Why is the consumer in the United States considered sovereign?

10. How does the efficient use of land, labor, and capital help us satisfy our wants?

11. What part does opportunity cost play in economic decision making?

12. How is the principle of opportunity cost illustrated with a production possibilities frontier?

13. In what way does the study of economics help people become better decision makers?

Practicing Critical Thinking Skills

1. Do you think that as social scientists, economists should make ethical judgments about "what ought to be"—or should they merely describe, analyze, and explain economic activity? Defend your answer.

2. Can you think of a time or place when a country or society was *not* faced with the three basic questions of WHAT, HOW, and FOR WHOM to produce?

3. Can you think of any circumstances that could change a free product to an economic one? If so, what are they, and what characteristics must the new economic products have?

4. Think of a product you have used today and then make a list of the factors of production used in its construction. Can you come up with any items that did *not* use all three factors of production?

5. If you decide to go to college after graduation from high school, what will be the opportunity cost of that decision? Use specific examples.

6. Suppose that Alpha, in Figure 1–5, was to experience a large influx of unskilled labor. How would this cause its production possibilities frontier to change? What if Alpha were to receive a large shipment of capital goods from the United States? Would the production possibilities frontier change? If so, would the change be the same one caused by the influx of unskilled labor?

Applying Economic Understandings

Making Economic Decisions

Decision making is a part of everyday life for almost everyone. One area in which we must make decisions is in spending what income we have. Refer to Malcolm's Decision Making Grid on page 20 and follow the steps listed below.

Step 1: Define in writing a problem that you as a consumer may have.

Step 2: Make a list of three to five alternatives from which you could choose to resolve the problem.

Step 3: State the criteria you feel are most important in helping you judge the alternatives you have listed.

Step 4: Evaluate each alternative in terms of your criteria. To do this, draw a simple grid like the one on page 20. In each square, indicate your evaluation with words or symbols such as the ones shown there.

Step 5: Make your decision.

Economic Systems and Decision Making

Great economic and social forces flow with a tidal sweep over communities that are only half conscious of that which is befalling them.

John Morley

Chapter 2

After reading this chapter you will be able to:

- Describe the advantages and disadvantages of a traditional, command, and market economy.

- Describe the United States economy in terms of capitalism and free enterprise.

- Discuss the economic and social goals of the American free enterprise economy.

- Discuss the role of government in the American economic system.

2.1 Economic Systems

The survival of any society depends on its ability to provide food, clothing, and shelter for its people. Since these societies are also faced with scarcity, decisions concerning WHAT, HOW, and FOR WHOM to produce must be made.

All societies have something else in common. They have an **economic system,** or an organized way of providing for the wants and needs of their people. The way in which these decisions are made will determine the type of economic system they have. There are three major kinds of economic systems—traditional, command, and market.

TRADITIONAL ECONOMY

Habit and custom are part of the tradition of many societies. Why, for example, do so many people eat turkey on Thanksgiving and Christmas? Why do families pass heirlooms on to other family members? Why are holidays such as Labor Day

A Hopi woman prepares to fire pottery much in the same way her ancestors did. Why does pottery making remain a source of income for many Hopi people living in the southwest United States?

An example of a traditional economy is the society of the polar eskimo of the last century. For generations, parents taught their children how to survive in a harsh climate, make tools, and fish and hunt. Their children, in turn, taught these skills to the next generation.

The polar eskimo was a hunter, and it was traditional to share the spoils of the hunt with other families. If a walrus or bear was taken, for example, hunters would first divide the kill evenly into as many portions as there are heads of families in the party. The hunter most responsible for the kill would have first choice, the second most responsible would choose next and so on. Later, families not represented in the hunting party would receive part of the kill, because eskimo families shared freely and generously with one another.

The hunter, then, had the "honor" of the kill and the respect the village gave to its best hunters rather than a physical claim to the entire kill itself. Because of this tradition of sharing, a village could survive harsh winters so long as there were some skilled hunters in the community. This custom has been partially responsible for the polar eskimo's survival for thousands of years.

The main advantage of the traditional economy is that everyone has a role in it. This helps keep economic life stable and community life continuous. The main disadvantage of the traditional economy is that it tends to discourage new ideas and even punishes people for breaking rules or doing things differently. So, it tends to be stagnant or fails to grow over time.

COMMAND ECONOMY

Other societies have a **command economy**—one where a central authority makes most of the WHAT, HOW, and FOR

and Memorial Day regularly observed? Or, why do people tip in restaurants? For the most part, these practices have been handed down from one generation to the next and have become tradition.

In a society with a **traditional economy,** nearly all economic activity is the result of ritual and custom. Habit and custom also prescribe most social behavior. Individuals are not free to make decisions based on what they want or would like to have. Instead, their roles are defined. They know what goods and services will be produced, how to produce them, and how such goods and services will be distributed.

WHOM decisions. Economic decisions are made at the top, and people are expected to go along with choices made by their leaders. Cuba, the Soviet Union, most Eastern European countries, and, until very recently, the People's Republic of China are examples of command economies. In the Soviet Union, for example, major economic choices are made by the government. **Gosplan,** or State Planning Commission, directs nearly all aspects of the Soviet economy. It decides goals for the economy and determines needs and production quotas for major industries.

If the Gosplan wants to stress growth of heavy manufacturing, it can shift resources from consumer goods to that sector. Or, if it wants to strengthen national defense, it can direct resources from consumer goods or heavy manufacturing to the production of military equipment and supplies.

The major advantage of a command system is that it can change direction drastically in a relatively short time. The Soviet Union, for example, went from an agricultural society to a leading industrial nation in just a few decades. It did so by emphasizing heavy industry and industrial

An important part of the command economy of the People's Republic of China is the communes, or farm cooperative. In a command economy, who makes such economic decisions as which crop to grow?

growth rather than production of consumer goods. When the country faced a shortage of male workers in the mines and on construction projects, the government put women to work in those industries. Even today, women continue to work with picks, shovels, and wheelbarrows on construction projects.

A major disadvantage of the command system is that it does not always meet the wants and needs of individuals. In the case of Soviet industrial development, for example, an entire generation was forced to give up such consumer goods as cars, home appliances, and even housing. People were often told to sacrifice for the good of the state and the benefit of future generations instead of asking for consumer products.

The wants and needs of consumers are also ignored when command economies pursue military projects that have political objectives. For example, military ventures of the Soviet Union in Afghanistan, Vietnam in Cambodia, and Cuba in Angola meant resources that could have been used for consumers were used instead for military equipment and supplies.

A second disadvantage of the command economy is the lack of incentives that encourage people to work hard. In most command economies today, workers with different degrees of responsibility receive similar wages. In addition, people seldom lose their jobs regardless of the quality of their work. As a result, there is a tendency for some to work just hard enough to fill production quotas set by planners.

Table 2–A

COMPARING ECONOMIC SYSTEMS

	TRADITIONAL	COMMAND	MARKET
Advantages:	• Sets forth certain economic roles for all members of the community.	• Is capable of dramatic change in a short time.	• Is able to adjust to change gradually. • Has economic freedom for producers and consumers. • Free from significant government intervention. • Makes a variety of consumer goods and services available.
Disadvantages:	• Stagnates and fails to grow.	• Does not always meet consumer needs. • Lacks effective incentives to get people to produce. • Requires a large bureaucracy which slows down decision making. • Does not encourage ideas.	• Rewards only productive labor.

This can have unexpected results. For example, at one time in the Soviet Union, central planners set production quotas for electrical motors in tons. Workers discovered that the easiest way to fill the quota was to add weight to the motor. As a result, Soviet workers made some of the heaviest electrical motors in the world. The Soviet Union was also famous for producing some of the heaviest chandeliers in the world for the same reason. In fact, some were so heavy that they occasionally fell from ceilings.

Another disadvantage is that the command economy requires a large decision-making bureaucracy. Many clerks, planners, and others are needed to operate the system. As a result, most decisions cannot be made until a number of people are consulted, or a large amount of paperwork is processed. This causes production costs to increase and decision-making to slow down. Thus, a command system does not have the flexibility to deal with minor, day-to-day problems.

Finally, it is difficult for people with new or unique ideas to get ahead in a command economy. In fact, there is little opportunity for individuality. Each person is expected to perform a job in a factory, in the bureaucracy, or on a farm consistent with economic decisions made by central planners.

MARKET ECONOMY

In a **market economy,** the questions of WHAT, HOW, and FOR WHOM to produce are made by individuals and firms acting in their own best interests. In economic terms, a **market** is an arrangement that allows buyers and sellers to come together to conduct transactions. A market could be in a specific location, such as a farmer's or flea market. Or it could be a list of baby sitters' phone numbers posted on a local bulletin board. As long as there is a mechanism for buyers and sellers to get together, a market can exist.

In a market economy, individual economic decisions are like votes. When consumers buy a particular product, they are casting their dollar "votes" for that product. Once the votes are counted, the manufacturers will know what people want. As such, consumer sovereignty plays a key role, because producers are continually looking for goods and services that consumers will buy.

Since consumers like products with low prices and high quality, producers in a market economy will try to supply such products. Those who make the best products for the lowest prices will make profits and stay in business. Other producers will either go out of business or switch to different products consumers will buy.

A market economy has several major advantages that traditional and command economies do not have. First, a market economy is flexible and can adjust to change over time. For example, during the gasoline shortage of the 1970's, consumers reduced their demand for large, gas guzzling automobiles and increased their demand for smaller, fuel-efficient models. Because of the shift in consumer preferences, auto makers had difficulty selling big automobiles. At the same time, they had difficulty keeping up with the demand for smaller ones. So, auto makers shifted resources from the production of large cars to small ones.

When gas prices began to level off in 1985 and then decline in 1986, the trend slowly began to reverse. Consumers began to buy large cars again and producers adjusted to meet these demands. Changes in a market economy, then, tend to be gradual. Unlike the traditional economy, change is neither stagnant nor discouraged. And, unlike the command economy, the change is neither sudden nor forced on consumers by others making decisions for them.

A second major advantage of the market economy is the freedom that exists for everyone involved. Producers are free to make whatever they think will sell. They are also free to produce their products in the most efficient manner. Consumers, on the other hand, are free to spend their money on whatever goods and services they wish to have.

A third advantage of a market economy is the lack of significant government intervention. Except for national defense, the government tries to stay out of the way so that producers and consumers can go about their business. As long as there is competition among producers, the market economy generally takes care of itself.

A fourth advantage is that the decision-making process in a market economy is decentralized. Literally billions—perhaps even trillions—of individual economic decisions are made daily. Collectively, these decisions allocate scarce resources to economic activities favored by consumers. Since these decisions are made by individuals, everyone has a voice in the way the economy is run.

A final advantage of the market economy is the incredible variety of goods and services available to consumers. In fact, almost any product can and will be produced so long as there is a buyer for it. For example, recent products include everything from wall walkers to peanut butter in squeeze containers to television

In a market economy like the United States, consumers vote with their dollars, deciding what goods and services will be produced. How has this affected the American economy automobile industry?

Profile

Adam Smith

Adam Smith was a classical Scottish economist and philosopher. His best-known work, *The Wealth of Nations*, was published in 1776.

During Smith's time, most people believed in the good of the natural order and freedom of the individual. Smith spoke out for these beliefs in the area of economics. He also championed the new middle class that was emerging as a result of the Industrial Revolution.

1723–1790

Smith felt that government should not have a large role in the economy. He believed that individuals acting naturally in their own self-interest would bring about the greatest good for society as a whole. He thought that competition among these individuals, together with the free market price system, would act as an "invisible hand" and guide resources to their most productive use. Thus, in order to yield the greatest benefits to society, private enterprise should be free of all government regulation. Business people were delighted to have their growing wealth and power supported as morally right. The doctrine of laissez faire, meaning no government intervention in economic affairs, became the watchword of the day in England.

Smith rejected the mercantilist view that money was wealth and argued instead that labor was the source of wealth. The wealth of a nation, then, amounted to all the goods and services produced by labor and available for consumption by all.

Smith's ideas about freedom extended to international trade. He felt that it was natural for people to trade with each other freely. He believed that trade would make labor more productive and increase the nation's wealth.

Smith was the first to note that labor becomes more productive as each worker becomes more skilled at a single job. He said that new machinery and the division and specialization of labor would lead to an increase in production and greater wealth for the nation.

channels devoted exclusively to music videos. In a market economy it is almost impossible to predict new or different products that will become available.

The wide range of products available in a market economy means that everyone can find something to satisfy their tastes. So, if 51 percent of the people want blue shirts, and if 49 percent want white ones, everyone gets what they want! Unlike a political election, the minority does not have to live with choices made by the majority.

The main disadvantage of the market economy is that the rewards go only to the productive resources. This may be fine in the case of land or capital, but it can be a problem with labor. Some people may be either too young or too old to support themselves. Many people would have a difficult time surviving in a pure market economy unless others are willing to care for the needy, or the government helps.

▮ Section Review

1. What determines a nation's economic system?

2. What are the three types of economic systems?

3. What are the major advantages of a market economy?

2.2 *Capitalism and Free Enterprise*

A market economy is sometimes described as being based on **capitalism,** a system in which the factors of production are owned by private citizens. It is also based on free enterprise, since businesses are allowed to compete for profit with a minimum of government interference. Both of these terms fit the United States economy reasonably well.

ECONOMIC FREEDOM

Economic freedom is a characteristic of capitalism often taken for granted. The freedom is enjoyed by individuals as well as businesses. For example, people have the freedom to choose their occupation and their employer. To a lesser extent, they can choose to work where and when they want. They may want to work on the West Coast, East Coast, or in Alaska. They may work days, nights, indoors, outdoors, in offices or in their homes.

With economic freedom, people can choose to have their own business or work for someone else. They can apply for positions and have the right to accept or reject employment if offered. Economic freedom also means that people can leave jobs and move on to others that offer greater opportunity.

Businesses also enjoy economic freedom. They are free to hire the best workers, and they have the freedom to produce the goods and services they feel will be the most profitable. They can make as many, or as few, goods and services as they want, and they can sell them wherever they please. They have the right to charge whatever price they feel is profitable, and they are free to risk success or failure.

VOLUNTARY EXCHANGE

A second characteristic of capitalism is **voluntary exchange**—the act of buyers and

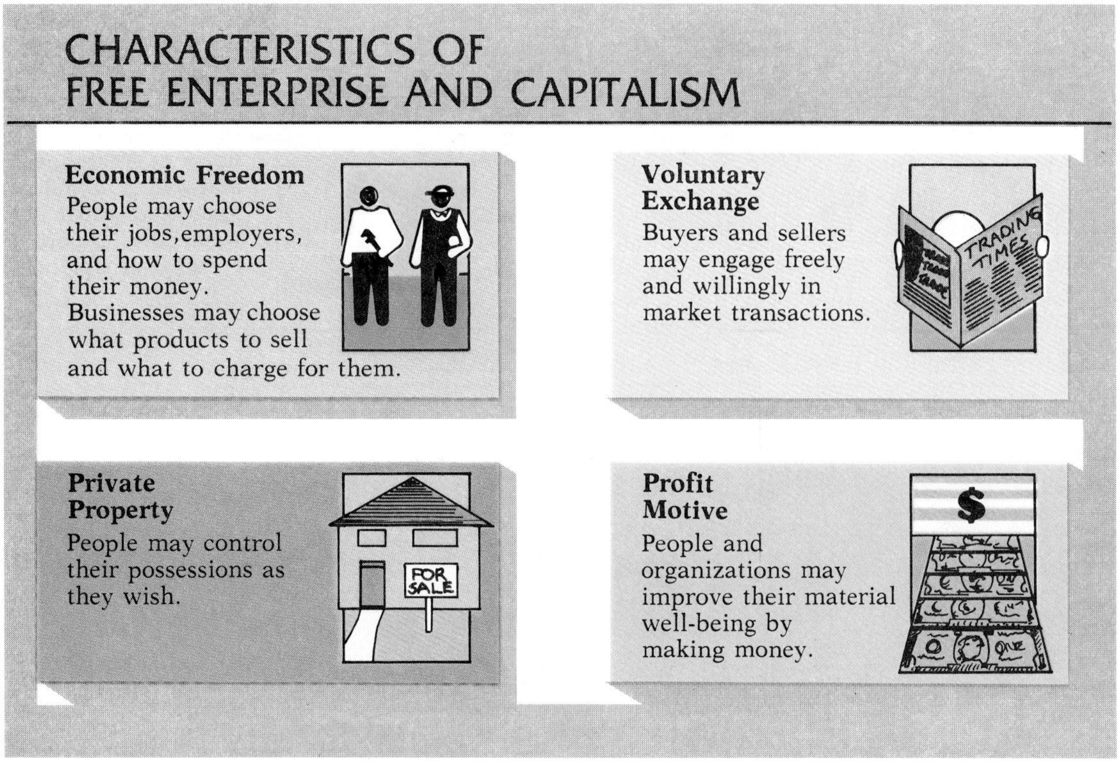

CHARACTERISTICS OF FREE ENTERPRISE AND CAPITALISM

Economic Freedom
People may choose their jobs, employers, and how to spend their money. Businesses may choose what products to sell and what to charge for them.

Voluntary Exchange
Buyers and sellers may engage freely and willingly in market transactions.

Private Property
People may control their possessions as they wish.

Profit Motive
People and organizations may improve their material well-being by making money.

Figure 2–1

sellers freely and willingly engaging in market transactions. Moreover, transactions are made in such a way that both the buyer and seller are better off after the exchange than before it occurred. Buyers, for example, can do many things with their money. They can put it in the bank, under a mattress, or exchange it for goods or services. If they spend their money on a product, they must believe that the item being purchased is of greater value to them than the money they gave up.

With voluntary exchange, sellers also have many opportunities to sell their products. If they exchange their goods and services for cash, they must feel that the money received is more valuable than the product being sold, or they would not sell in the first place. In the end, the transaction benefits both buyer and seller or it

would not have taken place. Both the buyer and the seller got something they believed had more value than the money or products given up.

PRIVATE PROPERTY

Another major feature of capitalism and free enterprise is **private property,** or the rights and privileges that allow people to control their possessions as they wish. Private property includes both the tangible and the intangible. People are free to make decisions about their property and their own abilities. They have the right to use or abuse their property so long as they do not interfere with the rights of others. They can also sell or not sell their abilities or services as they see fit.

Sanctity of contract is part of the concept of private property. A formal contract signing, such as the one shown here, usually happens when buyers and sellers do not know each other very well. What are other reasons for signing contracts?

Part of the concept of private property is a belief in the **sanctity of contract**—the freedom to enter into an agreement regarding the use of property or abilities. In the United States, this belief is so strong that some businesses make oral agreements. However, most businesses make formal contracts that describe work to be done. Formal contracts are often used when a buyer does not know a seller very well, or when one party might have difficulty obtaining corrective action if something goes wrong. If either party fails to honor the agreement, the matter can be taken to court.

Private property gives people the incentive to work, save, and invest. When people are free to do as they wish with their property, they are not afraid to use, accu-

mulate, or lend it. Private property also helps give people the incentive to get ahead. People know that if they succeed, they will be able to keep any rewards they might earn.

PROFIT MOTIVE

Under free enterprise and capitalism, people are free to risk their savings or any part of their wealth in a business venture. If it goes well for them, they will earn rewards for their efforts. If things go poorly, they could lose part or even all of their investment. The very thought of financial gain might lead someone to become an **entrepreneur,** an individual who enters

Many people, no matter what their jobs, are encouraged to work harder to earn a higher salary. What does the profit motive encourage people and organizations to improve?

business and takes a risk in hope of earning a profit.

But what, in fact, is profit? Consider, for example, the earlier case of voluntary exchange. Remember that the buyer gives up money to obtain a product, and that the seller gives up the product to obtain money. Unless both parties believe they will be better off afterward than before, neither will make the exchange. When it does take place, it does so only because both parties feel they will make a profit.

Profit, then, is the extent to which persons or organizations are better off at the end of a period than they were at the beginning. The **profit motive**—the driving force that encourages people and organizations to improve their material well-being—is largely responsible for the growth of a free enterprise system based on capitalism.

Suppose, for example, that a company wants to increase profits. One way is to be more efficient than the competition. The firm will try to lower its costs and improve the quality of its product. If successful, profits will increase because the firm

John H. Johnson started *Ebony* magazine in 1945. Today, his business empire includes four other magazines, a radio station, and Fashion Fair cosmetics. Why is Johnson considered an entrepreneur?

will be selling more of a better item for less cost. Soon, other firms will try to copy the success and, in turn, raise their own profits.

Bigger profits also generate new interest in the industry. When this happens, new firms rush in to "grab a share" of the profits. To remain competitive and stay in business, the original firms may have to cut their prices, which means that customers buy for less. In the end, the search for higher profits can lead to a chain of events that involves more production, greater competition, higher quality products, and lower prices for consumers.

Without the profit motive, manufacturers would have less incentive to improve production methods. They would be less inclined to search for new products, and

there would be less reason to compete with other manufacturers for the consumer's dollar. In the end, the products available to consumers would be of lower quality, higher price, and there would be less variety from which to choose.

SOURCE OF CAPITAL

An economic system must be able to produce the third factor of production, capital, if it is to satisfy the wants and needs of its people. Freedom and voluntary exchange, private property rights, and the profit motive are important, but they are

Figure 2–2

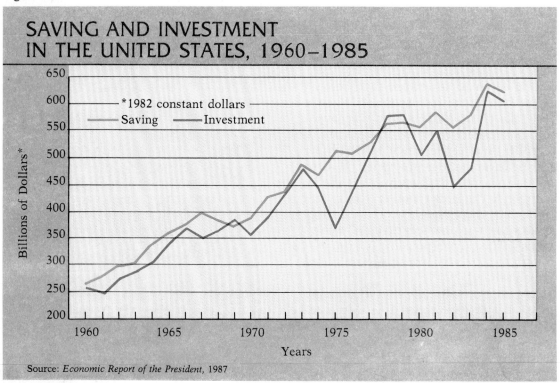

Source: *Economic Report of the President*, 1987

People save for many reasons. They save for a home, new car, or college as this student is doing. Why are savings decisions important?

not enough. People must also be willing to save if capital is to be formed. To the economist, **saving** means the absence of spending. Saving decisions are important because they make investment decisions possible.

For example, suppose someone wants to set up their own business. The first thing they might do is to put some income aside until they are ready to begin. They might keep their money in a wallet, or keep it in a bank to earn interest until they are ready to use it. When they are finally ready to begin business, they will have some funds set aside to invest.

Someone else might go right to a bank to borrow funds to begin their business. If other people have been saving rather than spending, the bank will probably have funds to lend out. However, if people have been spending rather than saving, the bank may not be able to make the loan.

For investment to take place, then, someone in the economy must save. Saving and investing can be done by the same person as noted in the first example. Or, the saving and investing can be done by different people as with the bank example. Why people save is not important. They may be saving for retirement, a vacation, or a college education. The point is that they are abstaining from consumption, which frees resources for others to borrow and use. As seen in the graph on page 38, the more people save, the more money is available to invest.

◼ Section Review

1. What two terms can be used to describe the United States economy?

2. What are the four major characteristics of capitalism?

3. What is the role of the profit motive in a free enterprise system?

4. Why are saving decisions important for capital formation?

2.3 *Evaluating Economic Performance*

Whether or not a particular economic system is best for a society depends on the ability of that system to satisfy the needs of its people. These needs are, in part, defined by the economic and social goals the society sets for itself. These goals are important because they are used to evaluate the performance of an economic system. They serve, in effect, as a series of measuring sticks that help people determine if the system meets their needs. If a system meets most, but not all of the needs, people may demand laws to change the system until their needs are met.

ECONOMIC AND SOCIAL GOALS

In the United States, people share many broad social and economic goals. While it might be difficult to find them listed in any one place, they are repeated many times in statements made by friends, relatives, community leaders, and elected officials. Seven of these major economic and social goals are described below.

ECONOMIC FREEDOM.   In the United States, people place a high value on the freedom to make their own economic deci-

sions. For instance, people like to choose their own occupation, employer, and how to spend their money. The belief in economic freedom, like political freedom, is one of the cornerstones of American society.

ECONOMIC EFFICIENCY.   Americans recognize that resources are scarce and that factors of production must be used wisely. If resources are wasted, fewer goods and services can be produced and fewer wants and needs can be satisfied. Economic decision-making also needs to be efficient so that benefits gained are greater than costs incurred.

ECONOMIC EQUITY.   Americans have a strong sense of justice, impartiality, and fairness. For example, many people feel that there should be equal pay for equal work. As a result, it is now illegal to discriminate on the basis of sex, race, or religion. In addition, laws protecting consumers against false advertising, unfair prices, and dangerous products have also been passed.

ECONOMIC SECURITY.   Americans also desire protection from such adverse economic events as layoffs and illnesses. Most states have, for example, set up funds to help workers who lose their jobs. Many employers have insurance plans to cover

Food stamps help give economic security to people with low incomes. Families that qualify for food stamps pay a fraction of the monetary value of the stamps and then spend them like money to buy food. How might inflation conflict with this form of economic security?

the injuries and illnesses of their workers. On the national level, Congress has set up **Social Security**—a federal program of disability and retirement benefits to cover most working people.

FULL EMPLOYMENT.   When people work, they earn income for themselves while they produce goods and services for use by others. When people do not have jobs, however, they cannot support themselves or their families, nor can they produce output for others. As a result, people want their economic system to provide as many jobs as possible.

PRICE STABILITY.   Another goal is to have stable prices. If there is **inflation**—a rise in the general level of prices—life becomes difficult for many people. Workers need more money to pay for food,

clothing, and shelter. People on a **fixed income**—an income that does not increase even though prices go up—find that bills are harder to pay and that planning for the future is more difficult. Price stability makes budgeting easier and adds a degree of certainty to the future.

ECONOMIC GROWTH.   The last major social and economic goal shared by most Americans is that of economic growth. Without it, people would not have more goods and services in the future than at present. Most people, for example, hope to have a better job, a newer car, better clothes, their own home, and a number of other things in the future. Since population is expected to expand, economic growth is necessary to meet everyone's future needs.

TRADE-OFFS AMONG GOALS

While most Americans seem to agree on the above set of goals, it is not always possible to satisfy everyone at the same time. Sometimes people have different ideas about how to reach a goal. At other times, the goals themselves might conflict.

For example, a policy designed to keep foreign-made shoes out of the United States would help full employment in the domestic shoe industry. But this policy would work against individual freedom because consumers would have fewer choices available. The construction of a new shopping center might stimulate economic growth in an area. But it might also threaten the stability and security of others—

possibly even other merchants—located nearby.

For the most part, individuals, businesses, and governments are usually able to resolve conflicts of goals and reach compromises. The economic system of the United States is flexible enough to allow choices, accommodate compromises, and still satisfy the majority of Americans most of the time.

▉ Section Review

1. How are goals used to evaluate the performance of economic systems?

2. What are seven major goals of the United States economy?

3. Why might goals sometimes conflict?

2.4 *The United States Economy*

The economic system of the United States is highly complex. It is based primarily on free enterprise and capitalism, but there are also elements of command and tradition. Even the role of government reflects the desires, goals, and aspirations of its people.

According to Abraham Lincoln, government should "do for the people what they wish to have done but cannot do as well or at all in their individual capacities." Basically, this describes the role of government in the American economy today. Whether it be on the federal, state, or local level, government has become a protector, provider of goods and services, consumer, regulator, and promoter of national goals.

As protector, the United States government enforces laws against false and

misleading advertising, impure food and drugs, and even unsafe automobiles. It also enforces laws against abuses of individual freedoms like discrimination because of age, sex, race, or religion.

All levels of government provide goods and services for its citizens. For example, the federal government supplies postal and national defense services. State governments provide education and public welfare. Local governments often provide parks, libraries, and bus services. In the process, government consumes the three factors of production just like any other form of business.

In its role as a regulator, the federal government is charged with preserving competition in the marketplace. It also oversees interstate commerce, communications, and even entire industries such as banking and nuclear power. Many state governments regulate insurance rates and automobile registrations. Even local governments regulate business activity with their control over the granting of building and zoning permits.

As much as anything else, however, government reflects the will of its people. In fact, many functions of government reflect the people's desire to modify the economic system to achieve the goals of freedom, efficiency, equity, security, full employment, price stability, and economic growth. Because of this, the United States is said to have a **modified private enterprise economy**—one in which people carry on their economic affairs freely but are subject to some government intervention and regulation.

Today, there is considerable debate over the "proper" role of government in the economy. Some people feel that the government does too much, others feel that it does not do enough. Americans must realize, however, that government is involved because the American people wanted it that way. It is also likely that the nation's modified free enterprise system will undergo further change as the goals and objectives of the American people change.

Section Review

1. What are the major roles of the government in the American economy today?

2. Which levels of government are involved in providing goods and services for Americans?

Chapter 2 Review

Summary

1. A society's survival depends on how well it can provide food, clothing, and shelter for its people.

2. All societies have economic systems that deal with scarcity. The three systems that have evolved over time are the traditional, command, and market economies.

3. In a traditional economy, everyone has a specific role. This can lead, however, to an economy that remains stagnant or fails to grow.

4. In command economies, the individual has little or no role in economic planning or decision making.

5. Command economies have one major advantage—the ability to change rapidly in a short time.

6. A market economy has several advantages. Among these are the ability to adjust to change over time, the lack of significant government intervention, and the large variety of goods and services available to the consumer.

7. The economic system of the United States is based on capitalism and free enterprise.

8. Capitalism has several characteristics. These include economic freedom, voluntary exchange, private property, and the profit motive.

9. Saving makes available the resources needed to produce goods and services.

10. All economic systems should satisfy the needs of its people. These needs are partially defined in economic goals a society sets for itself.

11. The United States economy today is a modified private enterprise economy where people conduct their economic affairs freely but with some government regulation.

■ Building an Economic Vocabulary

economic system
traditional economy
command economy
Gosplan
market economy
market
capitalism

voluntary exchange
private property
sanctity of contract
entrepreneur
profit
profit motive

saving
Social Security
inflation
fixed income
modified private
    enterprise economy

■ Reviewing the Main Ideas

1. On what does a society's survival depend?

2. What is the main advantage of a traditional economy? The main disadvantage?

3. How does Gosplan direct the Soviet economy?

4. What are the four major disadvantages of the command economy?

5. In what ways do consumers influence the market economy?

6. How does change in a market economy differ from change in a traditional economy? A command economy?

7. How do people and businesses benefit from economic freedom?

8. What incentives does owning private property give people?

9. Toward what can the search for higher profits lead?

10. How are saving and investment decisions related?

11. Why are economic goals important?

12. Why is it not always possible to achieve all economic goals?

13. Why is there debate over the "proper" role of government in the economy?

Practicing Critical Thinking Skills

1. How are the wants and needs of people different under each of the three types of economic systems—traditional, command, and market?

2. Some people believe the profit motive conflicts with the goals of economic security and equity. Do you agree or disagree? Why or why not?

3. In a pure command economy, do you think individuals need to know how to choose? Why or why not?

4. We tip for service in restaurants, but not for service at gas stations. Explain how this illustrates economic decision making by tradition rather than by market or by command.

Applying Economic Understandings

Taking Notes

Economists often use their research notes when preparing a report on some aspect of the economy. Taking notes involves writing information down in an orderly and brief form.

There are many different styles of note-taking. All clarify and put material in order. This order may be chronological, based on importance of events, or relationships among parts of material.

One of the most common methods of taking notes is in outline form. To do this, follow the steps in this example.

1. Read pages 27 and 28. Write the major heading of the section. In many cases, main headings form an outline of the major topics. In this example, the main headings are Economic Systems and Traditional Economy.

2. Briefly list the topics covered under each heading.

    Economic Systems
       Traditional Economy
          Definition   Advantages
          Example   Disadvantages

3. Add any additional information that is important to know about each topic. Your final notes should be similar to the following outline.

Economic Systems
I. Traditional Economy
   A. Definition
      1. ritual and custom guide activity
      2. lack of individual freedom
      3. clearly defined social roles
      4. production clearly defined
   B. Example (polar eskimo)
      1. generations pass down life skills
      2. sharing the hunt
   C. Advantages
      1. everyone knows role
      2. stable life
   D. Disadvantages
      1. discourages new ideas
      2. punishes
      3. stagnant

For further practice in this skill, take notes on the material on pages 28-34.

Economic Institutions

Some see private enterprise as a predator to be shot, others a cow to be milked, and few are those who see it as a sturdy horse pulling a wagon. **Winston Churchill**

Chapter 3

After reading this chapter, you will be able to:

- Explain the purposes of economic institutions.

- Compare the advantages and disadvantages of the three major types of business organizations.

- Describe the ways in which business in the United States can expand and grow.

- Discuss the purpose of each of the three major types of nonprofit organizations.

- Explain government's dual role as an economic institution.

3.1 Role of Economic Institutions

In the United States, many important decisions are made by **economic institutions**—persons and organizations that use, and sometimes represent, the factors of production needed to satisfy the wants and needs of consumers. Some of these include business firms, hospitals, labor unions, cooperative associations, schools, churches, and many different government agencies.

For example, an acre of land standing idle may serve no useful purpose. But when persons and organizations enter the picture, they cause the land to become productive and satisfy people's wants. When this happens, the economic institutions link the factors of production and consumers.

At times, economic institutions may simply represent the productive resources. Workers in steel, textiles, automobiles, and even farming, for example, may belong to unions that seek higher pay and better working conditions. Teachers, doctors, and other professionals may belong to other professional organizations for many of the same reasons.

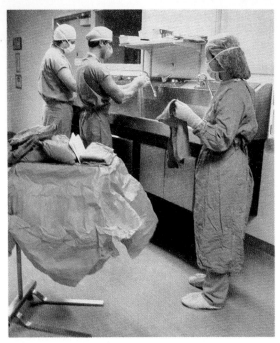

College students (left) are consumers wanting a higher education. Doctors and operating room attendants (right) provide a medical service. What economic institution links each of these consumers and services?

Even other economic institutions, such as schools, medical care facilities, and churches may be set up as **nonprofit organizations.** Like their profit-seeking counterparts, they work in a business-like way to make the best use of scarce resources while providing goods and services to consumers. The difference is that they do not seek self-enrichment. Instead they earn such emotional rewards as improving educational standards, seeing the sick become well, and helping those in need.

▌ Section Review

1. What two things do economic institutions do?

2. What are some major economic institutions in the American economy?

3.2 *Business Organizations*

One of the major economic institutions is the **business organization**—a profit-seeking enterprise that serves as the main link between scarce resources and consumer satisfactions. Most farms, corner drug stores, television manufacturers, trucking companies, and law firms fall into this category. These businesses compete with one another for the chance to satisfy people's wants.

SOLE PROPRIETORSHIPS

The most common form of business organization in the United States today is the **sole proprietorship**—a business owned and run by one person. Proprietorships are generally small. They collectively have only a fraction of the total sales of all business. Even so, they are often profitable. Today, almost one-quarter of the profits that go to all businesses are earned by sole proprietorships.

FORMING A PROPRIETORSHIP.   The sole proprietorship is the easiest form of business to start and run. Aside from certain licenses and fees that may be required by government agencies, there is almost no red tape involved. Most proprietorships are able to open for business as soon as they set up operations.

For example, someone could start a proprietorship by simply setting up a lemonade stand in their front yard. Or, someone could decide to mow lawns and do landscaping or gardening. Someone else might decide to open a grocery store, a gas station, or a restaurant.

A proprietorship may be run out of a person's home, or it may have office space in a professional building. There is no one way to set up a proprietorship. Since it is basically a business that is owned, run, and financed by a single person, many different types of businesses are represented.

ECONOMIC ADVANTAGES.   The main advantage of a sole proprietorship is that it is easy to establish and manage. If someone has an idea, or an opportunity to make a profit, he or she has only to decide to go into business and then do it. Once in business, the owner has direct control over all operations. This means that there is no co-owner, boss, or "higher-up" to consult if a decision has to be made quickly. This gives the owner considerable flexibility,

which is very important in some kinds of economic activity.

For example, suppose the owner of a small store meets a manufacturer who wants to sell something at a bargain price right away. In such a case, an immediate decision must be made. Taking the time to consult with a boss could mean that the opportunity might be missed.

Second, the sole proprietorship allows the owner to enjoy the profits of good management without having to share them. Though there is always the possibility of suffering a loss, the lure of profits makes people willing to take risks.

Third, the proprietorship does not have to pay business income taxes since the

Figure 3–1

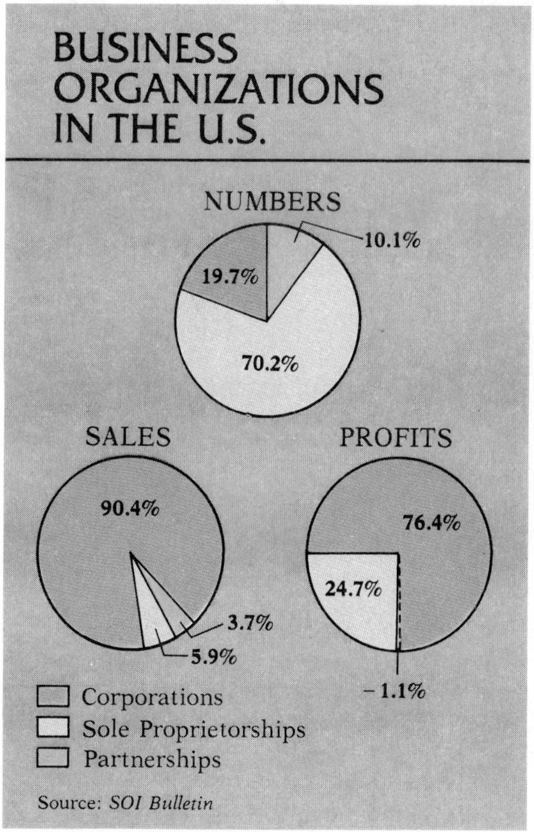

BUSINESS ORGANIZATIONS IN THE U.S.

NUMBERS

10.1%
19.7%
70.2%

SALES
90.4%
3.7%
5.9%

PROFITS
76.4%
24.7%
−1.1%

☐ Corporations
☐ Sole Proprietorships
☐ Partnerships

Source: *SOI Bulletin*

business is not recognized as a separate, legal entity. The owner must pay individual income taxes on profits taken from the proprietorship, but the business itself is tax exempt. Aside from one or two minor reports, the owner does not even have to fill out any complicated tax forms beyond those normally required for wage and salary purposes at the end of the year.

For example, suppose Mr. Smith owns and operates a small hardware store in a local shopping center, and a small auto repair business in a garage next to his home. Since neither business depends on the other, and since the only thing they have in common is ownership, the two businesses appear as separate and distinct economic activities. For tax purposes, however, everything is lumped together at the end of the year. When Mr. Smith files his personal income taxes, the profits from each business, along with wages and salaries earned from other sources, are combined. He does not pay taxes on each of the businesses separately.

A fourth advantage of sole proprietorship is psychological. Many people feel that they get a certain amount of personal freedom by being their own boss. Others feel that the satisfaction they get is worth more than a higher salary they might earn working for someone else. Also, some people have more confidence in themselves than they do in others, and believe they can succeed where others have failed. Still others have a strong desire to see their name in print, have dreams of great wealth or community status, or want to make their mark in history.

A fifth advantage is that it is easy to get out of business if the owner decides to do so. The owner simply stops offering goods and services for sale—there are no complicated legal or tax considerations, and there are no co-owners or higher-ups to consult.

ECONOMIC DISADVANTAGES.   One of the main disadvantages of a sole proprietorship is that the owner has **unlimited liability.** This means that the owner is personally and fully responsible for all losses and debts of the business. So, if the business does not do well, the owner's personal possessions may be taken away to satisfy business debts.

Consider, for example, the earlier case of Mr. Smith who owns and operates two

In the cartoon below, a sole proprietor of a small business tells why he has no profit-sharing plan for his employees. What are the economic advantages of sole proprietorships?

Profile

Thorstein Veblen

Thorstein Veblen was an American economist and social scientist who challenged the economic theories of his time. By analyzing the psychological bases of social and economic institutions, he laid the foundations for the school of institutional economics.

1857—1929

Veblen rejected the neat logic and static natural laws of most other economists and argued that the nature of the economic order was evolutionary. He felt it changed with society's values, customs, and laws and was influenced by such institutions as churches, schools, labor unions, and business organizations. He believed that along with the institutions, the prevailing attitudes of the day had a great deal of influence on economic behavior.

Veblen saw a basic conflict in corporate business structure. As he saw it, the profit-seeking "captains of industry" who owned and ran corporations knew that increased production of goods would drive prices down and lower profits. So they hired engineers, technologists, and others to increase production of the goods the consumer needed and wanted. Then, in their greed for profits, they restricted the benefits to humanity by cutting production.

In his work, *The Theory of the Leisure Class* (1899), Veblen heaped similar scorn on the wealthy. He described the higher classes as barbaric and wasteful, engaging in useless activities and conspicuous consumption, which he called "conspicuous waste." To emphasize his point, he cited such examples as the lavish parties of the 1890's—where thousands of dollars were spent on food and drink, much of which was thrown away later.

Veblen also authored other works, all written in a dry, satiric style. These include *The Theory of Business Enterprise* (1904), *The Engineers and the Price System* (1921), and *Absentee Ownership and Business Enterprise in Recent Times* (1923). Although his theories did not attract many disciples in his time, economists from that time forward have had to reckon with the influence of social institutions and values on economic behavior.

businesses. If the hardware business should fail, Mr. Smith's personal wealth, which includes the automobile repair shop, may be legally taken away to pay off debts arising from the hardware store.

A second disadvantage of a sole proprietorship is that it is usually difficult to raise financial capital. Generally, a great deal of money is needed to set up a business, and even more is required to make it expand. The problem, however, is that the personal financial resources available to most sole proprietors are limited. Even banks and other lenders usually do not want to lend money to new or very small businesses. Often the sole proprietor raises financial capital by tapping savings or borrowing from family members.

A third disadvantage is size and efficiency. Many times a business needs to be a certain size before it can operate profitably. A retail store, for example, may need to hire a minimum number of employees just to be open during normal business hours. It may also need to carry a minimum **inventory**—stock of goods in reserve—to satisfy customers. A manufacturing business may need a minimum of capital tools and equipment. This means that the proprietor will have to find the money to hire enough workers and capital to operate efficiently.

Another disadvantage is that the proprietor often has limited managerial experience. The owner-manager of a small company may, for example, be an inventor who is highly qualified as an engineer but lacks the "business sense" or time to oversee the orderly growth of the company. This owner may have to hire others to do the types of work—sales, marketing, and accounting—that he or she cannot do.

A fifth disadvantage is the difficulty of attracting qualified employees. Since proprietorships tend to be small, employees often have to be skilled in several areas. In addition, many top high-school and college graduates are more likely to be attracted to positions with larger, well-established firms than small ones. This is especially true when the larger firms offer **fringe benefits,** or employee benefits in addition to wages and salaries. Fringe benefits include paid vacations, sick leave, retirement, and insurance.

PARTNERSHIPS

A **partnership** is a business that is jointly owned by two or more persons. It shares many of the same advantages and disadvantages of a sole proprietorship and is similar in many ways. Collectively, partnerships represent about 10 percent of all business organizations in the United States, but they have only a small fraction of total business sales and profits.

The most common form of partnership is a **general partnership,** one where all partners are responsible for the management of the business. In a **limited partnership**, at least one partner is not active in the daily running of the business though he or she may have contributed funds to finance the business.

FORMING A PARTNERSHIP. Like a proprietorship, a partnership is relatively easy to set up. Because more than one owner is involved, formal legal papers are usually drawn up to specify arrangements between partners. Although not always required, these papers state ahead of time how profits—or losses—are divided.

The partnership agreement may divide the profits fifty-fifty, sixty-forty, or any other arrangement suitable to the partners. It may also state the way future partners can be taken into the business and the way the property of the business will be distributed if the partnership ends.

Partnerships, such as this bicycle shop, are important to the economy. They are easy to set up and represent about 10 percent of business organizations in the United States. What may partnership agreements contain?

ECONOMIC ADVANTAGES.   Like a sole proprietorship, a partnership is a relatively simple business to establish and manage. Generally, each partner takes care of certain parts of the business. One partner might agree to do the marketing, another the production, and so on. The partners usually agree ahead of time to consult with each other before making any major decisions.

A second advantage is that there are no special taxes on a partnership itself since it is not a separate legal entity. Like a proprietorship, the partners withdraw profits from the firm and then pay individual income taxes on them at the end of the year. The only minor difference is that each partner has to submit a special schedule to the Internal Revenue Service detailing the profits from a partnership. This is for informational purposes only and does not give a partnership any special legal status.

Third, partnerships can usually attract financial capital easier than proprietorships. They are generally a little bigger and, if established, have a better chance at getting a bank loan. If money cannot be borrowed, the existing partners can always take in new partners who bring financial capital with them as part of their price for joining the business.

A fourth advantage of a partnership is the slightly larger size, which makes efficiency easier to reach. In some areas, such as medicine and law, a relatively small firm with three or four partners may be just the right size for the market. Other partnerships, such as accounting, may have literally hundreds of partners, and the firm may offer services throughout the United States.

A final advantage is that many partnerships find it easier to attract top talent into their organizations. Since most partnerships today offer specialized services, top graduates seek out the more prestigious firms to apply their recently acquired skills in law, accounting, and other fields.

ECONOMIC DISADVANTAGES. The main disadvantage of a partnership is that each partner is fully responsible for the acts of all other partners. If, for example, one partner causes the firm to suffer a huge loss, each partner is fully and personally responsible for the loss. This is the same as the unlimited liability feature of a sole proprietorship. Nevertheless, it is more complicated because there are more owners. As a result, most people are extremely careful when they choose a business partner.

In the case of a limited partnership, the limited partner is not fully liable for the losses and debts of the business. This is known as **limited liability** and means that the owner's responsibility for the debts of the business is limited by the size of his or her investment in the firm. If the business fails, or if huge debts remain, the limited partner only loses the original investment and the other partners must make up the rest.

A second disadvantage of a partnership is that all partners share the profits. Unlike a sole proprietorship, no single person keeps all the profits. Since partnership papers usually specify the way profits are divided, the division usually stays the same over the long term.

A third disadvantage of the partnership is that it has **limited life.** This means that the firm legally stops when a partner dies, quits, or a new partner is added. A business can, however, still exist in the eyes of the public even though it goes through a legal change. For example, the partnership of A, B, and C may be known as the Widget Company. If there is a change in ownership, the new partnership may reach an agreement with the old one that allows it to use the same name.

CORPORATIONS

Although there are many sole proprietorships and partnerships in the United States today, slightly more than 90 percent of all business is done by corporations. The **corporation** is a form of business organization recognized by law as a separate legal entity. A corporation has the right to buy and sell property, enter into legal contracts, and sue and be sued.

FORMING A CORPORATION. Unlike a sole proprietorship or partnership, a corporation is a very formal and legal arrangement. People who would like to **incorporate,** or form a corporation, must file for permission in the state where the business will have its headquarters. If approved, a **charter**—a government document that gives permission to create a corporation—is granted. The charter states the name of the company, address, purpose of business, and other features of the business.

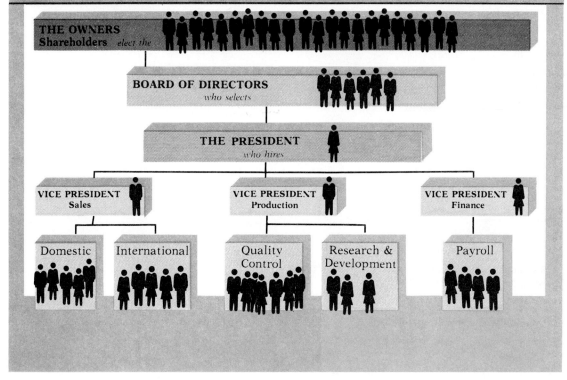

OWNERSHIP, CONTROL, AND ORGANIZATION OF THE TYPICAL CORPORATION

THE OWNERS
Shareholders *elect the*

BOARD OF DIRECTORS
who selects

THE PRESIDENT
who hires

VICE PRESIDENT
Sales

VICE PRESIDENT
Production

VICE PRESIDENT
Finance

Domestic

International

Quality Control

Research & Development

Payroll

Figure 3–2

The charter also specifies the number of shares of **stock,** or ownership parts of the firm. These shares are certificates of ownership and are sold to investors called **shareholders** or **stockholders.** The money is then used to set up the corporation. If the corporation is profitable, it will eventually issue a **dividend**—or a check representing a portion of the corporate profits—to shareholders.

CORPORATE STRUCTURE. Once an investor purchases stock, he or she becomes an owner and has certain management rights. The extent of these rights, however, depends on the type of stock purchased by the investor. The two types of stock available to the investor are common and preferred.

For example, **common stock** represents basic ownership of a corporation. The common shareholder usually receives one vote for each share of stock owned. This vote is used to elect a **board of directors** whose duty is to direct the corporation's business by setting broad policies and goals. The board also hires a professional management team to run the business on a daily basis.

On the other hand, **preferred stock** represents non-voting ownership of the corporation. Preferred shareholders receive dividends before common shareholders. In the event that the corporation goes out of business, they get their investment back before the common shareholders do. They do not, however, have the right to elect representatives to the board of directors.

In theory, a stockholder who owns a majority of a corporation's common stock can elect board members and control the company. If the corporation is very small, the shareholder might even elect himself or herself—and even other family members—to the board of directors.

In practice, however, this is not done very often, because most corporations are so large and the investment by the typical shareholder is so small. In fact, most small shareholders either do not vote, or they turn their votes over to someone else. This is done with a **proxy**—a legal document that gives a representative of the shareholder the right to cast the shareholder's vote.

ECONOMIC ADVANTAGES. The main advantage of a corporation is the ease of raising financial capital. If it needs more money, it can sell stock to investors. The revenue can then be used to finance or expand operations.

In addition to selling stock, a corporation may decide to sell **bonds.** A bond is a written promise to repay the amount borrowed at a later date. The amount borrowed is known as the **principal.** While the money is being borrowed, the corporation pays **interest,** or a fixed amount paid at regular intervals, for the use of the borrowed money.

A second advantage of a corporation is that the directors of the corporation can hire the best management available to run

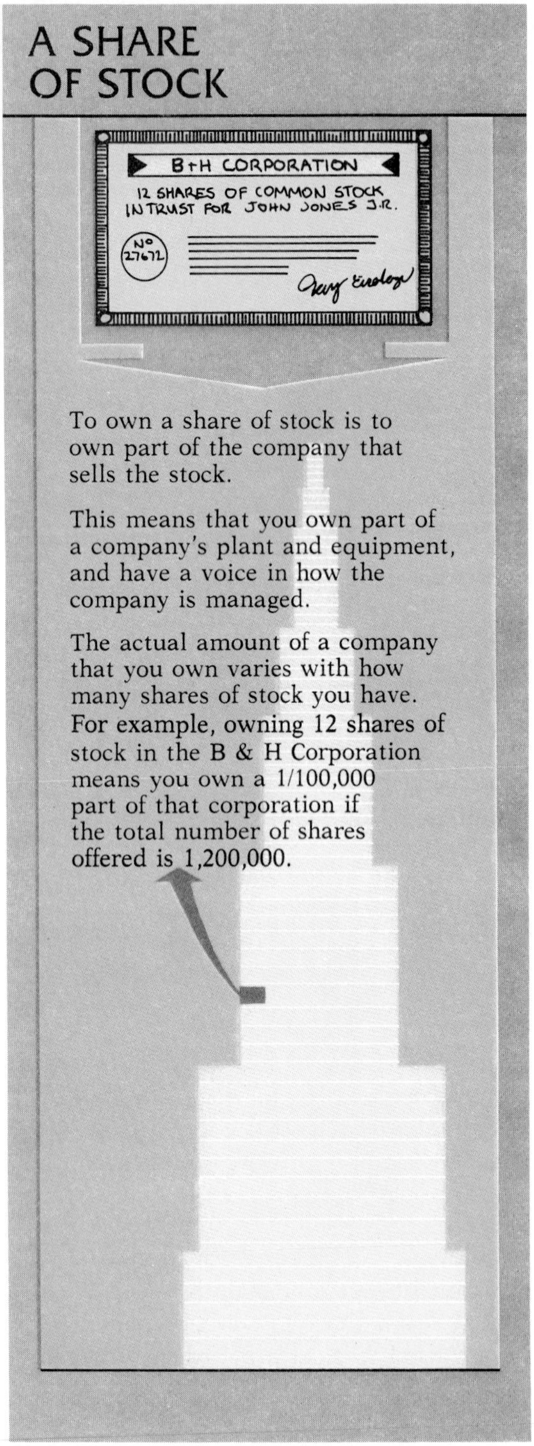

A SHARE OF STOCK
B+H CORPORATION
12 SHARES OF COMMON STOCK IN TRUST FOR JOHN JONES JR.
No 27672
To own a share of stock is to own part of the company that sells the stock.
This means that you own part of a company's plant and equipment, and have a voice in how the company is managed.
The actual amount of a company that you own varies with how many shares of stock you have. For example, owning 12 shares of stock in the B & H Corporation means you own a 1/100,000 part of that corporation if the total number of shares offered is 1,200,000.

Figure 3–3

Case Study: Career

Credit Manager

A great many people buy on credit today. As a result, many wholesale and retail businesses require a credit manager.

A credit manager's tasks vary, depending on the size and kind of firm for which he or she works. In most cases, however, the credit manager is the one who decides whether or not a person or company is extended credit. When credit to a business is involved, the manager analyzes financial reports sub-mitted by the company, checks on its management, and reviews credit agency reports on its promptness in paying bills.

Credit managers for large firms generally help draw up credit policies and set the financial standards to be met by those applying for credit. They also set up office procedures and watch over workers in the credit department who gather and analyze information and handle other general duties.

Credit managers for small firms generally interview credit applicants. Then, based on what they learn during the interview, they decide whether or not the applicant should be extended credit. They also may be responsible for contacting customers who have not paid their debts.

Credit managers must be able to analyze detailed information and then draw conclusions from their analyses. Because they often have to deal with the public, they also must be able to speak and write effectively.

A college degree is not always required for a credit manager. It is, however, becoming more important. Degrees in business administration and courses in accounting, economics, finance, computer programming, statistics, and psychology all are helpful. Most credit managers just starting out begin as management trainees and work under the supervision of a more experienced person in the credit department. This is especially true for those without college degrees.

The outlook for credit managers is good at present. As more people buy on credit, more companies will need the services of people trained to deal with credit and all it involves.

the firm. If the corporation is big enough, it can hire specialized talent in nearly all areas. So, even though some owners may know little or nothing about the business, the people who are running it do.

A third advantage of a corporation is that it provides limited liability for its owners. This is because the corporation, not the owners, is fully responsible for its debts and obligations. Suppose, for example, a court finds that a corporation owes a huge amount of money. The company might first try to work out some payment terms with the court. Or it might try to satisfy its debt by selling off some assets of the corporation. If it cannot pay off the debt, however, it can declare **bankruptcy**—meaning that a firm cannot pay its bills which forces it out of business. Under such circumstances, the investors (stockholders) would lose only their investment in the company, the amount limited to the money invested in stock. They would lose nothing else.

Because limited liability is so attractive, many firms incorporate just to take advantage of it. Suppose, for example, that Mr. Smith who owns the hardware store and the auto repair business now decides to set up each business as a corporation. If the hardware business should fail, his personal wealth, which includes the automobile repair business, is safe. Mr. Smith may lose all the money invested in the hardware business, but that would be the extent of his loss.

A final advantage of a corporation is **unlimited life.** This means that the business continues to exist even when ownership changes. The corporate organization is recognized as a legal entity, or separate unit, so long as it continues to stay in business. Even while ownership changes, the name of the company stated in its charter stays the same and the corporation continues to do business.

ECONOMIC DISADVANTAGES. One disadvantage to a corporate structure is the difficulty and expense of getting a charter. Depending on the state, expenses can run from a few hundred to several thousand dollars. Because of this, many people prefer to set up as sole proprietorships or partnerships.

Another disadvantage of the corporation is that the owners, or shareholders, have little say in how the business is run once they have voted for members of the board of directors. As a result, many investors purchase stock because they hope to receive a dividend. Others buy stock hoping that it will increase in value over time so they can sell it for profit. In most cases, however, the ability of the shareholder to influence corporate policy is limited to voting for the board of directors.

A third disadvantage of a corporation is that it has to pay taxes. This is because the corporation is recognized as a separate legal entity.

Finally, corporations are subject to more government regulation than either sole proprietorships or partnerships. For example, corporations must register with the state in which they are chartered. If a corporation wants to sell its stock to the public, it must follow regulations set forth by the federal Securities and Exchange Commission. It may also have to provide certain financial information about sales and profits. Even an attempt to take over another business may require federal government approval.

▇ Section Review

1. What part does a business organization play in the American free enterprise economy?

2. What are the advantages of each form of business organization? What are the disadvantages?

3.3 Business Growth and Expansion

In the United States, many businesses expand by joining with another business. This process is called a **merger,** or combination of two or more business enterprises to form a single firm.

BUSINESS COMBINATIONS

When one corporation merges with another, one of the two usually gives up its separate legal identity. For example, Sealtest merged with Southern Dairies when it bought Southern's common stock from investors. Southern then lost its corporate identity when its name was changed to Sealtest.

Sometimes the firm bought out keeps its name for public relations purposes. When Kraft Foods later merged with Sealtest by buying Sealtest stock, the two became one legal entity. Because Sealtest was a brand name many people trusted, however, the new company continued to use the Sealtest name on many of its products.

At other times, the name of the new company may reflect the identities of the companies that merged. When Chase National Bank and the Bank of Manhattan merged, the new organization was called the Chase Manhattan Bank of New York.

Figure 3–4

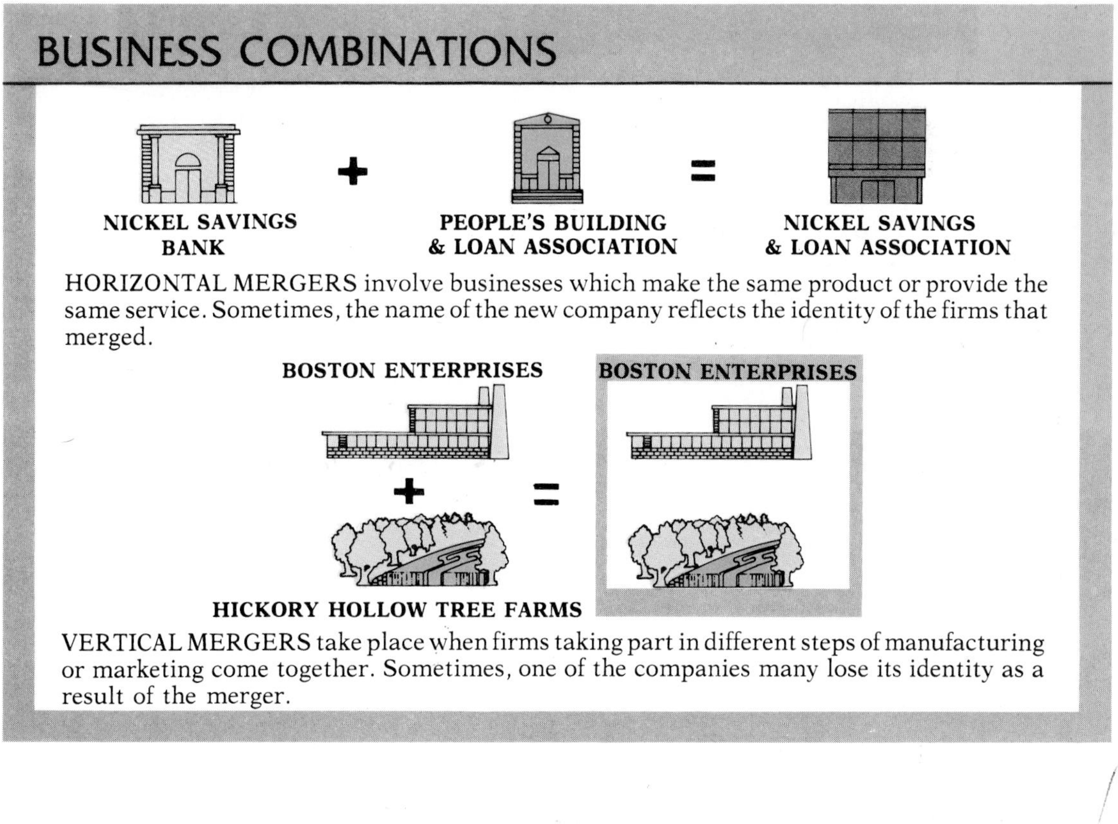

BUSINESS COMBINATIONS

NICKEL SAVINGS BANK **+** PEOPLE'S BUILDING & LOAN ASSOCIATION **=** NICKEL SAVINGS & LOAN ASSOCIATION

HORIZONTAL MERGERS involve businesses which make the same product or provide the same service. Sometimes, the name of the new company reflects the identity of the firms that merged.

BOSTON ENTERPRISES **+** HICKORY HOLLOW TREE FARMS **=** BOSTON ENTERPRISES

VERTICAL MERGERS take place when firms taking part in different steps of manufacturing or marketing come together. Sometimes, one of the companies many lose its identity as a result of the merger.

Understanding Sources

■ Mergers

The following article appeared in *U.S. News and World Report,* on June 30, 1986. Read the article and then answer the questions that follow.

FTC takes the fizz out of two soft-drink mergers

To skeptics who wonder when the government will oppose big mergers, the Federal Trade Commission has a reply—when two simultaneous buy-outs would concentrate 80 percent of an industry in the hands of just two companies. The commission voted 4-0 on June 20 to oppose the purchase of Seven-Up by PepsiCo and of Dr. Pepper by Coca-Cola.

Pepsi, with a 28 percent market share had agreed last January to buy Seven-Up from Philip Morris for $380 million. Pepsi's portion of the U.S. soft-drink business would rise to 34 percent—within hailing distance of Coca-Cola's 39 percent. A month later, Coke responded by seeking to swallow Dr. Pepper for $470 million; this combination would command 46 percent of soft-drink sales.

1. If the mergers had been approved, what percent of the market would PepsiCo and Coca-Cola have had?
2. How would such a merger, if approved, affect the level of competition in the soft-drink market?
3. How did the Federal Trade Commission rule on the proposed mergers?
4. Do you think that such mergers would be good for consumers? Why or why not?

Businesses tend to merge for different reasons. Sometimes the merger takes place because a business wants to be larger. When Kroger, a major Midwest retail food chain, merged with Dillon, another retail food chain, it became one of the largest food retailers in the country.

Another reason for a merger is efficiency. When two firms merge, they do not need two presidents, two treasurers, and two advertising agencies. This means that the new firm can have more retail outlets, or manufacturing capability, without significantly increasing management costs. In addition, the new firm can standardize its products, buy more merchandise to get better discounts, and make more effective use of its advertising.

Economists generally recognize two types of mergers. The first is a **horizontal merger.** This takes place when two firms that produce the same kind of product join forces. The merger of the Chase National and the Bank of Manhattan to form a larger entity is one example.

The second is a **vertical merger.** This takes place when firms involved in different steps of manufacturing or marketing come together. An example is USX, formerly the U.S. Steel Corporation. Through separate companies, USX mines its own ore, ships it across the Great Lakes, smelts it, and makes steel into many different products. Vertical mergers take place when companies believe that it is important to protect themselves against the loss of suppliers.

Some corporations become so large through mergers and acquisitions that they become a **conglomerate.** This is a firm that has at least four businesses, if not more, each making unrelated products, none of which is responsible for a majority of its sales.

Conglomerates are found in a number of different industries. In fact, diversification is one of the main reasons for conglomerate mergers. Firms believe that if they do not "put all their eggs in one basket," their overall sales and profits will be protected. Isolated economic happenings, such as bad weather or the sudden change of

Figure 3-5

CONGLOMERATE STRUCTURES

Book publishing:
Simon & Schuster, Pocket Books

Cigars:
Don Diego, Primo Del Rey
Don Marcos, Dutch Masters
Don Miguel, El Producto, Muriel

Insurance:
Capitol (life)
Providence
(property & casualty)

Swim and sportswear:
Cole of California, Catalina
Malibu, Bob Mackie
John Newcombe

Sports arenas:
Madison Square Garden
Roosevelt Raceway
Arlington Park

Gulf and Western (1980)
Sales: $5.3 billion
Profits: $227 million
Forbes 500 rank: 70
Rank in cigars: 1
Founded: 1958
Employees: 113,700
Headquarters: NY, NY

Auto parts:
A P S, Big A

Candy:
Schraffts, Lewis
King Kup

Sports teams:
New York Knickerbockers
New York Rangers
Washington Diplomats

Matches:
Monarch, Superior

Loan offices:
Associates

Movies:
Paramount

Paper Products:
Pert, Paper Maid
Purity towels and napkins

Hosiery:
No Nonsense, Interwoven,
Sheer Indulgence, Kayser
Esquire, Easy to Be Me

Shoes:
Bostonian, Stetson,
Jack Nicklaus, After Six
Sandler of Boston

Conglomerates, such as Gulf and Western buy and sell businesses. As a result, this short list of some of Gulf and Western's holdings will always vary.

consumer tastes, may affect some product lines at some point, but not all at one time.

MULTINATIONALS

Other corporations grow so large that they virtually become multinational in scope. A **multinational,** then, is a corporation that has manufacturing or service operations in a number of different countries. It is, in effect, a citizen of several countries at one time. As such, it is subject to the laws of, and is likely to pay taxes in, each country where it has operations.

Multinationals are important because they have the ability to move resources, goods, services, and financial capital across national borders. For example, a multinational with its headquarters in Canada is likely to sell bonds in France. The proceeds may then be used to expand a plant in Mexico that makes products for sale in the United States.

Many people welcome multinationals for three major reasons. First, multinationals help spread new technology worldwide. Second, they generate new jobs in areas where jobs are needed. Third, multinationals produce tax revenues for the host country. Many developing nations find the new technology, jobs, and revenue provided by multinationals helpful in improving their nations' economy.

Yet, there are some drawbacks to multinationals. For example, because multinationals are large and wealthy, they can influence the political life of a host nation. Other countries are concerned about economic exploitation by multinationals. This could be done either by paying low wages to workers, or exporting scarce natural resources. And workers in major industrialized nations argue that when multinationals build a plant abroad, they take away jobs at home.

Despite such drawbacks, multinationals can be a positive force in the world economy since they contribute technology, jobs, and revenue to many nations. Moreover, through buying and selling goods and services like other businesses, multinationals help integrate markets and develop the global economy.

■ Section Review

1. What are the two ways a business can merge?

2. What makes a conglomerate different from other forms of existing business organizations?

3. How is a multinational different from a conglomerate?

3.4 *Other Economic Organizations*

Sole proprietorships, partnerships, corporations, conglomerates, and multinationals are all profit-seeking business enterprises. Besides these, there are a number of other economic organizations that work to bring resources and consumers together.

Many are nonprofit organizations and are legally incorporated. They may perform many of the same functions of a profit-seeking business without issuing stock, paying dividends, or paying income taxes. Although they may earn the equivalent of a profit, such earnings are

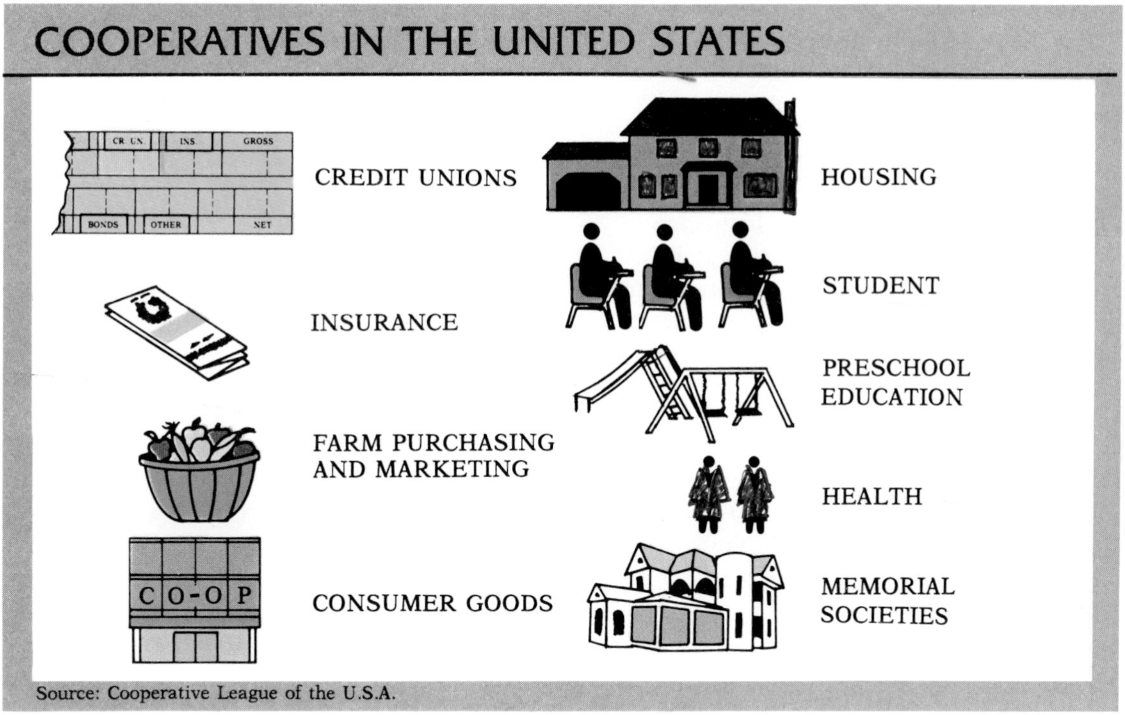

COOPERATIVES IN THE UNITED STATES

CREDIT UNIONS

INSURANCE

FARM PURCHASING AND MARKETING

CONSUMER GOODS

HOUSING

STUDENT

PRESCHOOL EDUCATION

HEALTH

MEMORIAL SOCIETIES

Source: Cooperative League of the U.S.A.

Figure 3-6

reinvested in the organization to further its goals.

For example, a church, which is an example of a nonprofit organization, may even be formally incorporated to give it the feature of unlimited life. If its weekly receipts exceed its expenses, the profit will generally be used to further the work of the church.

It is difficult to make any exact economic analysis of nonprofit organizations. They make use of the factors of production and serve many needs. Even if it is not easy to measure the value of their products, the fact that there are so many of these organizations shows that they are important links in the productive process.

COOPERATIVE ASSOCIATIONS

Another example of a nonprofit economic organization is the **cooperative,** or **co-op**—a voluntary association of persons formed to carry on some kind of economic activity that will benefit its members.

Cooperatives fall into three major classes—consumer, service, and producer. A **consumer cooperative** is one in which people join together to buy such commodities as food, clothing, and drugs in large amounts at low prices. Its aim is to offer its members products at prices lower than those charged by regular businesses.

A **service cooperative** is different from a consumer cooperative in that it deals with services rather than goods. Service cooperatives offer members insurance protection, credit, and other similar services.

One example of a service cooperative is a **credit union,** which is often begun by employees of a particular company or government agency. Credit unions receive their funds from members. In return, members earn interest on their deposits and, if needed, may borrow money from the credit union. In most cases, they can borrow at better rates and more quickly than they can from banks or commercial loan companies.

A **producer cooperative** helps members sell their products at favorable prices. In the United States, most cooperatives of this kind are made up of farmers. The co-op sells directly to central markets or to manufacturers that use the members' products. Any savings the co-op makes in marketing costs go to its members.

LABOR UNIONS

Another important economic institution is the **labor union**—an organization of workers formed to work for its members' interests in various employment matters. The union speaks for workers when disputes arise over pay, working hours, and other job-related matters. It also talks to and negotiates with management for worker benefits such as health and life insur-

These members of the 4-H are learning new farming methods. This club is part of a nonprofit education program designed to improve agriculture and home economics. What other services do nonprofit organizations provide?

Labor unions are an important economic institution in the United States. Here, union members attend a convention to hear about labor issues. What do labor unions do for their members?

ance and vacations. This negotiation between representatives of labor and management is known as **collective bargaining.**

In the early days of organized labor, most unions were local. Later, some unions joined with others to become more powerful. In time, the labor movement reached most parts of the country, spread into Canada, and became international. Today, most local unions are affiliated with a national or an international organization. Part of the dues paid by workers to their local union goes to support the activities of the national parent organization. Most local unions select delegates to attend a national convention. There they vote for national officers who make most

of the important decisions that have to do with union business. Today, the percentage of workers belonging to unions is declining. Fewer than 18 percent of the workers in the labor force in the United States belong to unions.

PROFESSIONAL AND BUSINESS ORGANIZATIONS

Although only a small part of America's workers are members of labor unions, it does not mean that other workers are not represented. Many belong to professional societies, trade associations, or academies.

Profile

John Kenneth Galbraith

John Kenneth Galbraith is a well-known and controversial economist. He has authored such books as *The Affluent Society, The New Industrial State, The Age of Uncertainty,* and *Economics and the Public Purpose.*

Galbraith believes economists failed to foresee the extent to which corporations would grow in size, dominate the market, and influence government policies. He points out that during bad times, a weak company may go bankrupt,

1908–

and during good times, it may be able to consolidate; but the end result is the same—the number of firms in the industry tends to shrink.

According to Galbraith, as corporations grow in size, they develop the ability to "manage" consumer demand and sell the quantities they desire at favorable prices by such means as advertising and withholding goods from the market. They may even be able to get governnment concessions that would protect them against competition in hard times. Ultimately, says Galbraith, "producer sovereignty" takes the place of consumer sovereignty, and the producer becomes ruler of the marketplace.

Although these groups are like unions, they do not work in quite the same way.

One such group is a **professional association**—an organization of people in a specialized occupation. It works to improve the working conditions, skill level, and public perceptions of the profession. Many college professors, for example, belong to the American Association of University Professors. Lawyers belong to the American Bar Association. Many business leaders belong to the Financial Executives Institute or the American Management Association.

Often, businesses organize to promote their collective interest. Most cities and

This inspector for the United States Food and Drug Administration enforces standards for packaged foods. What are some other examples of the direct role of government as an economic institution?

towns, for example, have a **Chamber of Commerce** that promotes the welfare of its members and the community. The typical Chamber sponsors a number of activities, ranging from educational programs to community clean-up campaigns to lobbying efforts on behalf of legislation favorable to business.

Still other business associations are formed to help protect consumers. The **Better Business Bureau,** a nonprofit organization sponsored by local businesses to provide general information on companies, is one of these. It maintains records on

consumer inquiries and complaints and offers a variety of consumer education programs.

GOVERNMENT

All levels of government play a dual role as links between consumers and resources. Sometimes, by its production of certain goods and services, government has a direct role. Other times, it has an indirect one.

DIRECT ROLE OF GOVERNMENT. Many government agencies use the factors of production to produce and distribute certain goods and services to consumers. This gives government a direct role in linking consumers and resources. For example, the federal government owns and runs the Tennessee Valley Authority (TVA). It uses land, labor, and capital to produce electric power.

The federal government also uses many of the country's scarce resources to create one service that benefits all Americans—national defense. State and local governments use land, labor, and capital to provide police and fire protection, rescue services, schools, and a system of courts. At the same time, all levels of government help develop and maintain roads, libraries, and parks. In these ways, government plays a direct part in the productive process.

INDIRECT ROLE OF GOVERNMENT. The government also plays an indirect role when it serves as an umpire to make sure the market economy operates as the rules say it should. One such case is government regulation of privately-owned electric power companies. Other **public utilities**—investor- or municipally-owned organizations that offer an important service to the public—generally are also subject to some government regulation. Because most public utilities have no competitors, government controls are needed. Without them, and without competition, these industries may not offer reasonable services at fair prices.

The government also plays an indirect role when it grants money to certain individuals. People may then enter the marketplace to buy goods and services produced by businesses, cooperatives, and government agencies. Social Security, payments to veterans, aid to dependent children, poverty grants, and unemployment compensation are some ways the government does this.

These payments give the people who receive them a power they otherwise may not have. That is the power to "vote" in the market. By casting votes in the form of dollars spent for goods and services, these people can make their demands felt in the market. This influences the production of goods and services which, in turn, affects the allocation of scarce resources.

This telephone company employee maintains service for customers. The telephone company and other public utilities offer a variety of important services. Why does government regulate public utilities?

Section Review

1. How do profit-seeking organizations differ from nonprofit organizations?
2. What are the three kinds of cooperative associations?
3. What purpose does a labor union serve?
4. Why are professional associations formed?
5. What two roles does government play in linking consumers and resources?

Chapter 3 Review

Summary

1. In the United States, different economic institutions serve as links that bring together the factors of production and the consumers who want the goods and services.

2. Economic institutions include business firms, nonprofit organizations, and government.

3. Business organizations can be organized as a sole proprietorship, a partnership, or a corporation.

4. Sole proprietorships generally are small, easy-to-manage enterprises owned by one person.

5. Some disadvantages of sole proprietorships include difficulty in raising financial capital and attracting qualified employees.

6. Partnerships are owned by two or more persons and are, most of the time, slightly larger in size than sole proprietorships.

7. The larger size of most partnerships makes it easier for them to attract financial capital and qualified workers.

8. Disadvantages of partnerships include the responsibility of each partner for the acts of the others and the limited life of the partnership.

9. Corporations are owned by individual investors called shareholders but by law can act as single individuals.

10. The type of stock owned by an investor determines that investor's management rights. Only those owning common stock vote to elect the board of directors, who in turn select a professional management team to carry out its policies.

11. Corporations not only sell preferred and common stock to raise financial capital, but they also issue bonds.

12. Corporations have certain disadvantages such as the difficulty and expense in obtaining charters and more government regulations.

13. Businesses may expand through mergers or consolidations which can be horizontal, vertical, or conglomerate. Some become multinationals.

14. Cooperative associations are major non-profit economic institutions that operate for the benefit of their members.

15. Other economic institutions include labor unions, professional associations, and government.

Building An Economic Vocabulary

economic institutions
nonprofit organizations
business organization
sole proprietorship
unlimited liability
inventory
fringe benefits
partnership
general partnership
limited partnership
limited liability
limited life
corporation
incorporate
charter

stock
shareholders
stockholders
dividend
common stock
board of directors
preferred stock
proxy
bond
principal
interest
bankruptcy
unlimited life
merger
horizontal merger

vertical merger
conglomerate
multinational
cooperative
co-op
consumer cooperative
service cooperative
credit union
producer cooperative
labor union
collective bargaining
professional association
Chamber of Commerce
Better Business Bureau
public utilities

Reviewing the Main Ideas

1. What does an economic institution do?

2. What is the most common form of business organization in the United States today?

3. Why are sole proprietorships the easiest form of business to start and run?

4. What happens to a sole proprietorship if it cannot meet its debts?

5. How are partnerships formed?

6. What enables partnerships to have a better chance at raising capital and finding good employees?

7. How do unlimited liability and limited liability differ?

8. What may corporations do because they are separate legal entities?

9. What are the differences between management rights of shareholders of common stock and preferred stock?

10. Why is limited liability attractive to owners of corporations?

11. In what different ways can business firms combine to grow and expand?

12. What are the similarities and the differences between cooperatives, labor unions, and professional associations?

13. List the differences in government's two roles as an economic institution.

Practicing Critical Thinking Skills

1. If you were planning to open your own business, which form of business organization would you prefer—sole proprietorship, partnership, or corporation? Give reasons for your answer.

2. Do you think mergers are beneficial for the United States economy? Defend your response.

3. Cite a case in your community where a cooperative would fulfill a definite economic need. Explain why you think so, and then tell what kind of cooperative you would set up.

4. Explain why labor unions are considered economic organizations.

5. Which do you think is more important when it comes to bringing resources and consumers together—the direct or indirect role of government? Defend your position.

Applying Economic Understandings

Drawing a Conclusion

Much information is presented in the study of economics. For it to be of practical use, you must be able to organize it in such a way that you can use it to draw a conclusion, or make a reasoned judgment. One way to organize your information is to make a list.

For example, there are reasons why a business organizes as a sole proprietorship, partnership, or as a corporation. Each business must decide which type best fits its individual needs. One way to arrive at such a conclusion is to list the advantages and disadvantages of each type of business organization. Then, these can be weighed against the business owner's desires and needs. An owner of a dry cleaning business might decide that having direct control and not sharing profits outweighs the difficulty of raising financial capital or attracting qualified employees. He or she might

conclude that a sole proprietorship would be the best type. For practice in drawing a conclusion, follow each of the steps below.

1. List the advantages and disadvantages of each type of business organization.

2. Share the list with the owner of a business in your community.

3. Ask the owner how his or her business is organized and if he or she considered the advantages and disadvantages listed when deciding to set up the business.

4. Ask which items on the list were the most influential in deciding how to organize the business.

5. Ask the owner if any additional items should be added to the list.

6. Do you think that the form of business organization chosen was the best for that business?

Unit 1 Review

Unit in Perspective

1. The fundamental economic problem facing all societies is that of scarcity which results from a combination of unlimited wants and limited resources.

2. The three factors of production—land, labor, and capital—used to satisfy needs are limited. As a result, careful choices on the use of such limited resources is necessary.

3. Economics is the study of WHAT to produce, HOW to produce, and FOR WHOM to produce.

4. All people have basic needs which result in wants reflected in demands.

5. Understanding basic concepts such as goods and services, wealth, value, consumption, and production is important to the study of economics.

6. Economic decisions are made on the basis of best available alternatives, or opportunity costs.

7. The tradition, command, and market economies are three ways that a so-ciety can organize itself to meet the needs of its people.

8. The market economy of the United States is based on capitalism and free enterprise. The profit motive is the driving force that motivates businesses and people and helps the economy grow.

9. Widely accepted economic and social goals have modified the basic free en-terprise economy in the United States by increasing the role of government.

10. Business and non-business economic institutions serve to bring together fac-tors of production and consumers.

11. Business organizations in the United States are organized on a for-profit basis as sole proprietorships, partner-ships, or corporations. Other organiza-tions such as cooperatives, labor unions, professional organizations, and government also serve to meet the needs of the consumers.

The Unit in Review

1. How does the term used by economic educators, TINSTAAFL, relate to the study of economics?

2. What are some key economic concepts? Why is it important to understand them?

3. How do economists think about the cost of decision-making? How is it measured? How is it illustrated?

4. Why is economic decision-making necessary? How are economic decisions made in a traditional economy? A command economy? A market economy?

5. On what is the United States economic system based? What is necessary for it to operate successfully? What does government's role in it reflect?

6. What are some key economic institutions? What role do they play in the United States?

■ *Building Consumer Skills*

Consumer Rights and Responsibilities

This skill will help you identify and classify some of the basic rights and responsibilities which you, as a consumer, have.

As a consumer, you are entitled to certain rights that are often protected by law. For example, you have the right to purchase products which are safe to use or consume. In turn, you have certain responsibilities to producers, other consumers, and the market as a whole to report gross defects in those products. You have the right to accurate billing from your creditors. On the other hand, you have the responsibility to answer all questions on a credit application form as fully and accurately as possible.

Read the examples of several hypothetical consumer situations in the paragraph below. Then, classify each of the situations that follows as a consumer right or responsibility.

1. The table and floor in an eating establishment is unusually dirty.

2. A waiter mistakenly undercharges you for a meal.

3. A birthday present has a loose and dangerous wire which may cause a shock.

4. You observe a shoplifter while shopping in a crowded mall.

5. While preparing a resume for a job interview, you consider raising your grade point just a little.

6. During a science experiment, you discover that the contents of a one pound bag of pretzels contains nineteen ounces.

7. A merchant charges you a 10 percent fee to cash a check drawn on a local bank.

8. You notice that the nutritional contents list on a locally manufactured product is misleading.

Business Behavior

A market economy is unique. In it, the forces of demand and supply interact to set market prices which serve as "signals" to allocate resources between markets, buyers, and sellers. The process is so efficient, the economy can run itself without government intervention or direction.

Unit 2

Contents

Competition
and Market Structures

People of the same trade seldom meet together, even for merriment and diversion, but the conversation ends . . . in some contrivance to raise prices.   **Adam Smith**

Chapter 4

After reading this chapter, you will be able to:

- Explain how economic markets operate and are classified in the American private enterprise economy.

- Compare market conditions that characterize pure competition, monopolistic competition, oligopoly, and monopoly.

- Discuss the monopoly problem and four solutions to it.

4.1 Capitalism, Markets, and Market Structures

Capitalism differs from other types of economic systems because it is based on the private ownership of property. This means that most factors of production are owned and operated by private individuals.

Businesses compete with each other and operate in hopes of making a profit. In the process, they do three things: First, they give the public goods and services the public wants. Second, they provide jobs.

Third, they distribute the nation's scarce resources so that the greatest benefits are brought to the most people.

In the process, the three economic choices of WHAT, HOW, and FOR WHOM to produce are made jointly by businesses and consumers. The government plays a limited role as protector and regulator in the process, but does not direct the overall decision-making mechanism in the economy.

CAPITALISM AND
PRIVATE ENTERPRISE

Until the early 1900's, the general attitude in the United States was **laissez faire**, or virtually no government intervention in economic affairs. The role of government was confined to protecting private property, enforcing contracts, settling disputes, and protecting businesses against foreign goods. Most people believed that competition among businesses for the consumer's dollar would keep the economy running smoothly. In this way, firms would come up with new and better products at lower prices. Prices would be set by the free actions of buyers and sellers. People also assumed that seeking one's self-interest

An operator of a lemonade stand provides a product the public seems to want on a hot summer day. How do consumers in a private enterprise economy encourage continued availability of a product?

would bring about the greatest common good for the economy as a whole.

This is known as a **private enterprise economy**—an economy where people are allowed to own and run their own businesses with a limited amount of government regulation. For the most part, the system worked fairly well. At times, however, mergers and takeovers reduced the number of firms and the amount of competition in selected markets. Some firms even gained so much power that they set prices to exploit consumers.

When that happened, the government stepped in to promote competition and protect the rights of the individual. Today, people in the United States still have the economic and political freedom to save, invest, and even go into business.

THE CIRCULAR FLOW OF ECONOMIC ACTIVITY

To the economist, a market is a mechanism that allows buyers and sellers to deal readily in a certain economic product. Markets may be local, regional, national, or even global. All markets are similar, however, in that their economic activity has a distinct circular flow.

For example, individuals earn their incomes in **factor markets**—the markets where productive resources are bought and sold. Here, labor is exchanged for wages and salaries, land is provided in return for rent, and money is loaned for interest or invested for a profit. When individuals receive their incomes, they spend it in **product markets**—markets where goods and services are offered for sale by producers.

In a similar way, business firms receive revenues in the product markets when they sell goods and services to individuals. This revenue pays for the land, labor, and capital bought in the factor markets. Then, these resources are used to manufacture additional products that are sold in the product markets.

All this can be seen in the diagram on page 80 which illustrates how money, resources, businesses, and consumers are linked together by economic markets. In the diagram, money circulates on the outside, while at the same time, goods, services, and factors of production flow in the opposite direction on the inside.

MARKETS AND MARKET STRUCTURES

Economists classify markets according to conditions that prevail in them. They ask questions like the following: How many suppliers are there? How large are they? Do they have any influence over price? How much competition is there between firms? What kind of economic product is involved? Are all firms in the market selling exactly the same product, or simply similar ones? Is it easy or difficult for new firms to enter the market? And, is it easy for existing ones to enter the market?

The answers to these questions help determine **market structure,** or the nature and degree of competition among firms operating in the same market. For example, one market may be highly competitive because a large number of firms produce similar products. Another may be less competitive because of fewer firms, or because the products made by each are different or unique. Yet another may have no competition at all because there is only one seller.

CIRCULAR FLOW OF ECONOMIC ACTIVITY THROUGH MARKETS

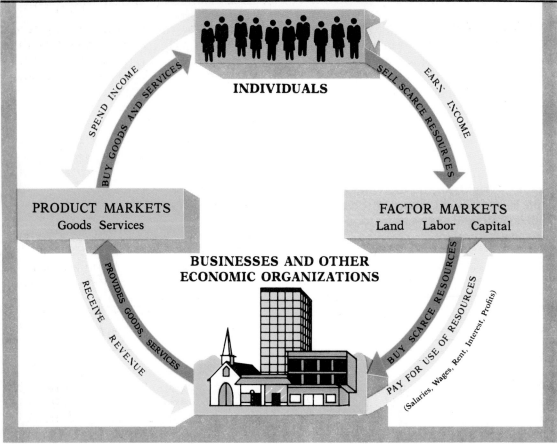

Figure 4–1

In short, markets can be classified according to certain structural characteristics that are shared by most firms in the market. Economists have names for these different market structures. They are pure competition, monopolistic competition, oligopoly, and monopoly.

▌ Section Review

1. What are three important things businesses do when competing with each other?

2. What is a private enterprise economy?

3. What does the circular flow of economic activity illustrate?

4. Who and what are the main participants in the circular flow of economic activity?

5. How does an economist classify market structures? How do they determine conditions in each?

6. What are four market structures recognized by economists?

4.2 Purely Competitive Economic Markets

An important category of economic markets is **pure competition.** This is a market situation in which there are many independent and well-informed buyers and sellers of exactly the same economic product. This market is characterized by five major conditions.

CONDITIONS FOR PURE COMPETITION

The first condition of a purely competitive market is that there be a large number of buyers and sellers. In this way, any single buyer or seller can come into or pull out of the market without affecting the price of the product.

The second condition is that buyers and sellers deal in identical economic products. Then, there is no reason for buyers to prefer one seller's merchandise over another's. There would be no difference in quality, no brand names, and no need to advertise. Table salt, for example, is always the same chemical—sodium chloride. So there is no real reason why one brand of salt should be higher in price than any other.

The third condition is that each buyer and seller act independently. They depend on forces in the market to determine price. If they are not willing to accept this price, they do not have to do business. This also means that as long as everyone acts independently, sellers compete against one another for the consumer dollar. This competition keeps prices low.

Table 4–A

ECONOMIC MARKETS IN THE UNITED STATES

	Number of Firms in Industry	Influence Over Price	Product Differentiation	Advertising	Entry Into Market	Examples
Pure Competition	Many	None	None	None	Easy	Perfect: None Near: Truck Farming
Monopolistic Competition	Many	Limited	Fair Amount	Fair Amount	Easy	Gas Stations Women's Clothing
Oligopoly	Few	Some	Fair Amount	Fair Amount	Difficult	Automobiles Rubber
Pure Monopoly	One	Fair Amount	None	None	Almost Impossible	Perfect: None Near: Electricity

The fourth condition is that buyers and sellers be reasonably well-informed about the article for sale and the market involved. They do not need to have, however, full technical knowledge of either the product or the market.

Thus, if a store offered an article for sale at a low price, most customers would know about it. And since the products offered are exactly the same, customers would have little reason to remain loyal to one seller. All sellers would be aware of other sellers' prices. And they would know that their own customers would be just as aware.

The fifth condition is that buyers and sellers be free to enter into, conduct, or get out of business. The price of an economic product would be determined by buyers and sellers operating in a free market.

A THEORETICAL SITUATION

If all five conditions for pure competition are satisfied, no one buyer or seller would be able to affect price in the market. There would be no preferred brands because all products would be identical.

No one seller would try to sell a product at a price higher than the prevailing market price because most or all of the customers would go to other sellers. There would be no restrictions or barriers to keep either buyers or sellers from doing business.

For these reasons, competition in its purest form is a theoretical situation. Few, if any, purely competitive markets truly exist. Local truck farming, however, comes close to satisfying all of the conditions. In this market, there are many sellers, and their products differ very little. The sellers do not band together to try to control prices, and both buyers and sellers have reasonable knowledge of what is being sold. There is very little restriction or regulation by government.

But even if pure competition rarely exists, it is important to understand its characteristics. In this way, it is easier to understand the market conditions which really do exist.

Section Review

1. What five conditions are needed before a market can be purely competitive?
2. Why is pure competition a theoretical situation?

4.3 Less Competitive Economic Markets

All market situations that lack one or more of the characteristics of pure competition are given the general name of **imperfect competition.** Most firms and industries in the United States fall under this broad classification. Economists generally divide it into three categories—monopolistic competition, oligopoly, and monopoly.

Profile

John Stuart Mill

John Stuart Mill was an outstanding British philosopher and noted economist who spent most of his adult life as a public servant. He held a post in the East India Company in London, England, for 36 years. He then became a member of the British Parliament.

1806—1873

In 1848, Mill's work, *Principles of Political Economy,* was published. In it, he set out to revise the earlier works of economists Adam Smith and David Ricardo. John Stuart Mill challenged the traditional idea that goods and services were distributed by natural law. He believed instead that the distribution of goods and services could be controlled. Mill thought that through technological change, the working class could have a better future and raise its standard of living.

Mill also felt that government should intervene to improve the lot of the poor. He believed that laissez faire would have to give way to a greater extension of government duties. He thought that government had to intervene to preserve competition, protect against monopolies, and safeguard the rights of the individual.

Mill believed strongly in free trade. Like Adam Smith, he was in favor of international specialization and the division of labor. Mill was the first to spell out clearly the principle of comparative advantage. The principle states that if countries produce that which they can produce most efficiently, total production will be greater.

Mill also made several important contributions in the areas of logic, ethics, philosophy, and politics. He was very much in favor of individual liberties and stressed the need for safeguards against the tyranny of the majority. He felt strongly that certain political and social reforms were needed. Among these were proportional representation, the emancipation of women, and the development of labor organizations and farm cooperatives. Many of Mill's ideas are embodied in today's laws and economic theories.

MONOPOLISTIC COMPETITION

To monopolize means to keep something for oneself. A person who monopolizes a conversation, for example, generally is trying to stand out from everyone else and thus attract attention.

A situation much like this often exists in economic markets. For example, all the conditions of pure competition may be met except that the products for sale are not exactly the same. By making its product a little different, a firm may try to attract more customers and take over the economic market. When this happens, the market situation is called **monopolistic competition.**

PRODUCT DIFFERENTIATION. The one thing that separates monopolistic competition from pure competition is **product differentiation.** That is, although the economic product being sold is very much alike from one firm to another, it is not identical. The differences among the products may be real, or the differences may be imaginary.

An example is the market for unleaded gasoline. Sellers of unleaded gasoline supply a very similar—but still a differentiated—product. Some unleaded gasolines do have small yet real differences, such as artificial coloring or special additives. But, in many cases, it is only clever advertising that leads people to believe one brand is better than others.

It is not hard to find examples of such products. Some refrigerators, for example, have metal trays while others have plastic ones. In this case, the difference between the products is real. But when it comes to different brands of aspirin, for example, the difference may be largely imaginary. Even though federal law states that all aspirin must contain certain chemicals in certain proportions, many people believe that some highly advertised brands are better than others.

EFFECT ON PRICE. If the seller can differentiate a product in the minds of the buyer, the price may be raised a little above the market price without losing many customers. If the customers really believe a brand of gasoline is different from other brands, they may be willing to pay more per gallon. But the price cannot be raised too much above the prevailing market price. If it is, customers may then switch to other brands instead.

In the case of monopolistic competition, similar products generally sell within a fairly narrow price range without greatly affecting the seller's or the competitors' total sales. The "monopolistic side" of this kind of competition is the seller's ability to raise price within this narrow range. The "competitive side" is that if sellers raise or lower price enough, customers will forget minor differences and change brands.

Most retail stores in the United States fall into the category of monopolistic competition. Not only is there some price competition, but firms also try to stress product differentiation. They advertise heavily and depend on packaging and displays to attract customers. They try to make their products seem different from everyone else's. They do this by differentiating as to location, store design, manner of payment, delivery, decorations, service, and just about everything else.

OLIGOPOLY

A market situation in which there are only a few very large sellers of a given economic product is known as **oligopoly.** The economic product of an oligopolist may be differentiated, as in the auto in-

FOOD FIGHT

	McDonald's	Burger King	Wendy's
Sales	$11.1 billion	$1.97 billion	$1.13 billion
Outlets	9000	4800	3500

Source: Annual Reports of McDonald's, Burger King, and Wendy's

Firms in the fast food franchise burger industry are oligopolistic. Changes in products offered in one franchise affect all of them. What happens when one fast food firm lowers its prices in order to attract more business?

dustry, or similar, as in the steel industry. The exact number of firms in the industry is not important. What is important is that because there are so few, any one of them may cause a change in output, sales, and prices in the industry as a whole. Because of these characteristics, oligopoly is further from pure competition than is monopolistic competition.

EFFECT ON PRICE. Oligopolists are large and powerful enough to affect the market price of their product. What they do not know, however, is how the other firms in the industry will react to price changes. Because of this, oligopolists generally do not want to engage in price competition.

Suppose, for example, that a firm decides to produce a great deal more of its product. If that firm supplies a large portion of the market, its action will mean a rather large increase in the total market

supply of that product. The oligopolist may need to charge a much lower price to increase sales, but if the other firms then decide to charge a lower price too, the result could be a full scale "price war." Since this would not benefit any of the firms, they compete in other ways.

Oligopolists may, for example, try to differentiate their products—as they do in the market for laundry soap. They also may operate in close cooperation with each other. Under most circumstances, this is against the law.

METHODS OF COOPERATION. Some oligopolists have even been known to enter into secret marketing agreements rather than compete in price or use advertising and product differentiation. This is known as **price-fixing**—agreeing to charge the same or similar prices for a product. They also might agree to divide up the market so that each firm is guaranteed to sell a certain amount. Both of these normally are against the law, and the persons can be fined heavily or sent to prison.

In the United States, many markets are already oligopolistic and many more are becoming so. For example, the soft drink market is dominated by a few large firms like Pepsi and Coke. A few years ago several personal computer companies competed. In today's personal computer market, IBM, Compaq, Tandy, and Apple dominate.

MONOPOLY

The final category of economic markets is the exact opposite of pure competition. A **monopoly** is a market situation in which there is only one seller of a particular economic product for which there is no close substitute.

There are very few cases in the American economy in which a single seller has full control of the supply of any one economic product. There are two reasons for this. First, because the American people always have viewed monopolies with suspicion, they have passed laws to prevent them from forming.

Second, in most cases, it is easy to find a reasonably close substitute for most economic products. Margarine, for example, can be used instead of butter. The private automobile can be substituted for the transportation services offered by buses, trains, and airplanes. And motorcycles can be used in place of automobiles.

While there is no perfect example of a pure monopoly, there are some, such as the local telephone company, that are fairly close. But even the telephone company faces competition from other communication companies and the post office.

For all practical purposes, a monopoly situation does not have to be completely pure to qualify as a monopoly. When economists talk about monopolies, they really are talking about near monopolies—situations that are as close to being pure as can be found in the real world.

NATURAL MONOPOLY.   There are several different kinds of monopolies. One kind in which competition is not desirable or technically possible is a **natural monopoly.**

Sometimes, the very nature of an industry dictates that society would be served best by a monopoly. For example, to have two or more competing telephone companies serving the same area could be wasteful. Such competition could lead to more telephone poles than are needed and too much other equipment.

This could happen in other areas, too. Imagine the confusion if four or five competing transit company buses raced each other to the corner to pick up waiting passengers. Think what our city streets would be like if six competing water or gas companies all kept putting in or repairing water and gas lines.

To avoid such problems, government often gives a company in the public utility industries permission to act as a natural monopoly. This arrangement is known as a **franchise.** It gives a company the exclusive right to do business in a certain area free from any competition from another company in the same industry. By accepting such franchises, the companies also accept a certain amount of government regulation.

GEOGRAPHIC MONOPOLY.   Sometimes a business has a monopoly simply because of its location. This can happen as a result of good planning or simply through good fortune. For example, a drugstore that is operating in a town that is too small to support two or more such businesses becomes a **geographic monopoly** because there is no one else who wants to compete.

Case Study: Career

Real Estate Agent

Real estate agents rent, sell, and buy property for clients. In return, they receive a percentage of the rent or sale price of the property. Their tasks include obtaining listings—owner agreements to place properties for rent or sale; arranging for advertising to promote the property; and showing the property to prospective renters and buyers. Agents spend a great deal of time talking on the telephone exploring leads, answering  inquiries about properties, and interviewing potential buyers. They often must work evenings and weekends as their schedule is determined by that of the clients.

Real estate agents, in general, must be familiar with fair market values, zoning laws, local land-use laws, housing and building codes, insurance coverages, mortgage and interest rates, and credit and loan policies. Those handling business and industrial properties also must know about leasing practices, business trends, location needs, transportation, utilities, and labor supply.

To be successful, real estate agents also must have the personality and the ability to make personal contacts and become acquainted with a large number of people. Some of these people may themselves be potential clients, while others may be able to provide an introduction to additional clients.

Although a number of colleges and universities offer two-year courses in real estate, a person does not need a college degree to become a real estate agent in most states. All states, however, require that real estate agents be licensed. To obtain a license, a person must be a high school graduate, at least 18 years old, and able to pass a written test that includes questions on basic real estate transactions and on laws relating to the sale of property. Other requirements vary from state to state.

While there almost always are job openings for real estate agents, real estate sales generally depend on the cost of housing and interest rates.

The owner of a laundromat next door to a large apartment building also has a type of geographic monopoly because the people who live in the building probably will use this laundromat rather than go to the one that is a few blocks away.

There is no assurance, however, that the business which has a geographic monopoly will be able to keep away competitors and maintain its status. If the only drugstore in a small town began to make a great deal of money, before long someone would come along and give it some competition. And if the laundromat charged much higher prices than its competitor, the laundromat would not have a monopoly for long either, no matter how convenient it was for customers.

TECHNOLOGICAL MONOPOLY.   The special privileges given to those who invent a new product or process lead to another kind of monopoly called **a technological monopoly.** This is a situation in which a firm or individual has discovered a new manufacturing technique or has invented or created something entirely new.

Many consumers complain about the high cost of heating in the winter and air conditioning in the summer. What kind of monopolies do utility companies have?

The Constitution of the United States gives Congress the power to "promote the progress of science and useful arts, by securing, for limited times, to authors and inventors, the exclusive right to their respective writings and discoveries." This may be done by granting a **patent**—an exclusive right to manufacture, use, or sell "any new and useful art, machine, manufacture, or composition of matter, or any new and useful improvement thereof." It is good for a stated number of years, after which the invention becomes "public property" available for the benefit of all.

Art and literary works are protected in much the same way by the granting of a **copyright.** It gives the author or artist the exclusive right to publish, sell, or reproduce his or her work for his or her life plus 50 years.

GOVERNMENT MONOPOLY. Still another kind of monopoly is the **government monopoly.** This is an activity which is owned and operated by the government and which may be found at all levels of government. In most cases, government monopolies deal with economic products needed for the public welfare but which people feel would not be provided adequately by private industry.

In many towns and cities, the conservation and distribution of water is a monopoly run by local government. In many others, alcoholic beverages are distributed only through state stores.

■ Section Review

1. What are the characteristics of monopolistic competition?
2. What are the important features of an oligopoly?
3. What are four kinds of monopolies found in the American economy? How are these monopolies different? How are they similar?

4.4 *Preserving Competitive Markets*

Those who favor a free enterprise system believe that competition brings about an automatic allocation of material and human resources for the benefit of the whole economy. They feel that through competition, resources are used efficiently, and consumers enjoy more and better products at lower prices.

While this is generally true, an argument can be made that the existence of a monopoly may be in everyone's best interests at times. This is especially true in such areas as national defense. In general, however, public policy often dictates an economic environment in the free market economy that encourages competition.

THE MONOPOLY PROBLEM

In the United States, the majority of economic markets tend to be some form of imperfect competition. The significance of these markets rests on their function and role as resource-allocating mechanisms.

Pressures from buyers and sellers are brought together in economic markets. Sometimes there is a rather large amount of competition. More often, however, they are brought together under controlled conditions. Product differentiation, technological innovation, and government controls are only a few of the forces that have some influence on consumer decisions.

When firms compete, the result is economic progress. This is because they try to be more efficient and make things better at a lower cost. This benefits consumers because it brings them a better product at a lower price.

Monopolists, on the other hand, are the only producers of an economic product. As such, they have full control over its supply and, therefore, can control prices on the market. If they feel they will get the greatest profits by cutting back production and thereby raising prices, they may do so. They do not have the pressures of competition to make them want to seek new and better ways of making their products.

DANGERS OF MONOPOLIES. The greatest danger of monopoly is that it denies consumers the benefit of competition. Where there is monopoly, people cannot depend on the free market system to allocate resources to bring the greatest satisfactions. Instead, they must depend on the monopolist who is, so to speak, "above the market."

When this happens, there always is the chance that too high a price will be charged. When a monopoly has gained control of an industry, it can use this position to prevent competition and restrict production. This will bring about artificial scarcities. When a product is scarce, its price generally will rise.

Another danger of monopoly has to do with resource allocation. Competition makes businesses become more efficient in the use of resources. But since monopolies are not under those pressures, they may waste and misallocate scarce resources.

A third danger of monopoly is that economic power sometimes leads to political power. In the past, some monopolists have used their huge capital resources to further their own political careers or those of their relatives and friends.

A large corporation does not have to be a monopoly for its economic power to lead to political power. However, if it is, its political influence may be even greater. For example, a corporation may want the government to give it certain considerations. To get the government to do this, it may threaten to move its plant somewhere else. If the plant moves, it could mean economic loss to the community. Since the community does not want to risk such a loss, the monopoly may pressure government officials to grant the business firm special favors.

JUSTIFICATIONS FOR MONOPOLIES. In some cases, the benefits of the monopoly are greater than its dangers. The case of public utilities, for example, may be justified on economic grounds.

At times, a monopoly also can be justified because of cost. Suppose the cost of production goes down as a business firm becomes larger and larger. It would make sense, then, for the firm to grow as much as possible to reduce the cost of production. This is called **economy of scale.** It means the larger the firm, the more efficiently the plant and equipment may be used.

If instead of one firm, there were two or more competing firms in the industry, they would be smaller and might have higher operating costs. An electric power company, for example, that serves 1 million customers generally can produce electricity at a lower cost per kilowatt hour

Profile

Paul Samuelson

Paul Samuelson is widely known as the author of the best-selling college text, *Economics*. The text, which has introduced millions of students to the study of economics, has gone through 12 editions.

In his first book, *Foundations of Economic Analysis* (1947), Samuelson developed his theory of economic equilibrium. According to it, an economic system may be thought of as a set of forces acting on the different elements of the economy. When the forces are balanced, the system is in equilibrium.

1915—

Samuelson also has written widely in the areas of international trade, welfare economics, and the theory of consumer choice. His theoretical writings were published in 1966 in the three-volume *Collected Scientific Papers of Paul Samuelson*.

In 1970, Samuelson was awarded the Nobel Prize for economics. He was the first American economist to be honored in this way.

than a smaller company which serves only 200,000 customers. Large-scale production and economic efficiency often go hand in hand.

SOLUTIONS TO THE MONOPOLY PROBLEM

Most Americans automatically view monopolies with suspicion and distrust. This has led to certain controls to restrict their power and cut back their activities.

Consumers have tried to find substitutes for the goods and services offered by monopolies. They also have demanded legislation to put a stop to unfair monopolistic practices. Government has been given the power to regulate certain monopolies which exist for the public welfare. In some cases, it has taken over certain activities and has run them as government-owned monopolies.

CONSUMER RESISTANCE. The effectiveness of a monopoly depends on the extent to which some other product can be used in place of its output. If a monopoly

Joseph Keppler drew this cartoon showing Standard Oil as a menacing octopus in the late 1800's for his humor magazine *Puck*. Why did some people feel there was a need to restrain business at that time?

sets a price which consumers believe is too high, they may try to find something else they can use in its place. And other producers constantly are trying to develop products which can be used in place of those already on the market.

The fact that there are substitutes makes it very hard for a monopoly to keep its advantage indefinitely. For example, beet sugar can take the place of cane sugar. Artificial rubber can be used instead of natural rubber. Margarine often is used in place of butter. Synthetic fibers can take the place of cotton and silk. And plastic can be used instead of wood, leather, glass, steel, and other materials. In many cases, the very threat of substitute products being developed tends to keep monopolies from emerging in the first place.

GOVERNMENT RESTRAINTS.   In the late 1800's, the United States passed laws to restrict monopolies, combinations, and **trusts**—legally formed combinations of corporations or companies. In 1890, Con-

gress passed the **Sherman Antitrust Act.** It was said to be an "act to protect trade and commerce against unlawful restraint and monopoly." The Sherman Act was the country's first significant law against monopolies. The idea behind it was to do away with restraints and monopolies which hindered competition or made it impossible.

By the early 1900's, a number of business organizations had been convicted under the Sherman Act. In 1911, for example, the Supreme Court declared that the Standard Oil Company was practicing "unreasonable" restraint of trade and ordered that it be broken up into several smaller, independent companies.

The Sherman Act laid down the broad foundations for maintaining competition. But the act was not strong enough to stop practices which restrained trade and competition. So, in 1914, to give the government greater power against monopolies, Congress passed the **Clayton Antitrust Act.**

This act outlawed **price discrimination**—charging customers different prices for the same product—in cases where it might lead to monopoly or lessen competition.

In 1936, Congress passed the **Robinson-Patman Act** in an effort to tighten up the Clayton Act, particularly the provisions that had to do with price discrimination. Under this act, companies no longer could offer special discount prices to certain customers. The new law chiefly affected national organizations and chain stores, which often were offered goods at lower prices than those paid by small independent businesses.

GOVERNMENT REGULATION. Another control is government regulation. This consists mainly of setting prices and directing the quality of services offered to the public. The object is to set up the same prices that might exist if there were competition.

For example, many cable television companies are regulated. Prices for their services are usually approved by a public commission or other government agency. If the company wants to raise rates, it must argue its case before the commission. If they win, prices will go up. If they do not, prices will not change.

Some regulatory bodies are run by state and local governments. Others, such as the ones listed in the chart on page 94, are agencies of the federal government.

GOVERNMENT OWNERSHIP. Many people feel that in some cases, government ownership of monopolies is best. It is only natural, they say, for business operations such as water and sewers to function as monopolies. In such cases, it may appear that in the best interest of the public, the government should take over.

This, however, expands the government's role beyond that for which it was originally intended. In addition, any time an economic market becomes dominated by government, economic freedom is sacrificed.

Figure 4–2

ANTI-MONOPOLY LEGISLATION

Interstate Commerce Act 1887	Established the Interstate Commerce Commission to regulate business activity between states.
Sherman Antitrust Act 1890	Outlawed all contracts "in restraint of trade" to halt the growth of trusts and monopolies.
Clayton Antitrust Act 1914	Strengthened the Sherman Act by outlawing price discrimination.
Federal Trade Commission Act 1914	Established the Federal Trade Commission to regulate unfair methods of competition in interstate commerce.
Robinson-Patman Act 1936	Forbade rebates and discounts on the sale of goods to large buyers unless the rebate and discount were available to all.

FEDERAL REGULATORY AGENCIES

Interstate Commerce Commission (ICC), 1887	Regulates rates and other aspects of commercial transportation by railroad, highway, and waterway.
Food and Drug Administration (FDA), 1906	Enforces laws to ensure purity, effectiveness, and truthful labeling of food, drugs, and cosmetics; inspects production and shipment of these products.
Federal Trade Commission (FTC), 1914	Administers antitrust laws forbidding unfair competition, price-fixing, and other deceptive practices.
Federal Home Loans Bank Board, 1932	Insures deposits in federal Savings and Loan through the Federal Savings and Loan Insurance Corporation (FSLIC); regulates federal Savings and Loan.
Federal Communications Commission (FCC), 1934	Licenses and regulates radio and television stations and regulates interstate telephone, telegraph rates and services.
Securities and Exchange Commission (SEC), 1934	Regulates and supervises the sale of listed and unlisted securities and the brokers, dealers, and bankers who sell them.
National Labor Relations Board (NLRB), 1935	Administers federal labor-management relations laws; settles labor disputes; prevents unfair labor practices.
Federal Aviation Administration (FAA), 1958	Regulates air commerce; sets standards for pilot training, aircraft maintenance, and air traffic control; controls U.S. airspace.
Equal Employment Opportunity Commission (EEOC), 1964	Investigates and rules on charges of discrimination by employers and labor unions.
Environmental Protection Agency (EPA), 1970	Coordinates federal environmental programs to fight air and water pollution.
National Highway Traffic Safety Administration (NHTSA), 1970	Sets and enforces laws to promote motor vehicle safety and to protect drivers, passengers, and pedestrians; sets safety and fuel economy standards for new motor vehicles produced or sold in the U.S.
Occupational Safety and Health Administration (OSHA), 1970	Investigates accidents at the workplace; enforces regulations to protect employees at work.
Consumer Product Safety Commission (CPSC), 1972	Sets and enforces safety standards for consumer products.
Nuclear Regulatory Commission (NRC), 1974	Licenses and regulates civilian use of nuclear materials and facilities.
Federal Energy Regulatory Commission (FERC), 1977	Fixes rates and regulates the interstate transportation and sale of electricity, oil, and natural gas; issues permits and licenses for hydroelectric projects and gas pipelines; supervises mergers and stock issues of electric power and natural gas; sets rates for interstate transportation of oil by pipeline.

Figure 4–3

GOVERNMENT AND ECONOMIC MARKETS

Concern over monopoly is one reason for government intervention in the United States economy today. Historically, the freedom to pursue self-interest led some people and businesses to seek economic gain at the expense of others. Acting under the label of competition, some larger firms used their size and power to take advantage of smaller ones. In some markets, monopoly replaced competition, and consumers suffered.

Because of such conditions, laws to prevent "evil monopolies" and to protect the rights of workers were passed. Labor unions were supported by many in the hope of getting workers more bargaining power. Food and drug laws were passed to protect people from false claims and harmful products. Some industries, such as public utilities, became subject to strict government regulation. All this led to a modification of free private enterprise.

In today's economy, people still carry on their economic affairs freely but are subject to government regulation in certain cases. Under this system, individuals supply capital to help industry grow. For the most part, they own and run the means of production and distribution. Restrictions on economic freedom are not put there to prevent the benefits of competition but to bring about more efficient use of resources.

Government takes part in economic affairs for several reasons. One is to promote and encourage competition within the rules of fair play. Another is to prevent and do away with monopolies that do not allow the public to reap the benefits of competition. A third is to regulate industries in which a monopoly is clearly for the public good. Because of this, today's modified private enterprise economy is a mixture of competition and monopoly, different kinds of business organizations, and businesses that are regulated and those that are not.

Section Review

1. What is the monopoly problem? What are four solutions to it?
2. Why are there restrictions on economic freedom?

Chapter 4 Review

Summary

1. Capitalism is an economic system based on private ownership and control of property. Under it, WHAT, HOW, and FOR WHOM to produce is decided freely by individuals and firms.

2. Under capitalism, government's role is limited.

3. In economic markets, money, goods, services, and factors of production all flow in a circular pattern. This pattern

is known as the circular flow of economic activity.

4. Economic markets allow buyers and sellers to engage in exchange. Some markets serve limited geographic areas, and others are worldwide.

5. Economic markets are classified according to such conditions as the number of producers, the degree of product differentiation, ease of entry into the market, and the ability of one or more firms to affect prices.

6. Purely competitive markets have many independent, reasonably well-informed buyers and sellers dealing with the same product. Buyers and sellers are free to enter into, conduct, or get out of business.

7. Pure competition is a theoretical ideal that rarely exists.

8. Monopolistic competition and oligopoly are forms of imperfect competition that deal with differentiated products and can influence price.

9. In a monopoly there is only one producer of a product for which there is no close substitute. There are natural, geographical, technological, and government monopolies.

10. The dangers of monopolies are: they do not allow consumers the benefits of competition, do not always use resources efficiently, and can gain and possibly abuse political power.

11. Solutions to the monopoly problem include consumer resistance, government restraints and regulations, and government ownership of some monopolies.

12. Today, the United States has an economy that mixes competition, monopoly, different types of business organizations, and regulated and nonregulated businesses.

Building an Economic Vocabulary

laissez faire	oligopoly	copyright
private enterprise economy	price-fixing	government monopoly
factor markets	monopoly	economy of scale
product markets	natural monopoly	trusts
market structure	franchise	Sherman Antitrust Act
pure competition	geographic monopoly	Clayton Antitrust Act
imperfect competition	technological monopoly	price discrimination
monopolistic competition	patent	Robinson-Patman Act
product differentiation		

Reviewing the Main Ideas

1. How are private enterprise and laissez faire economies different?

2. Why is the circular flow of economic activity helpful to an understanding of

the economy of the United States today?

3. How do economists classify markets?

4. What are the five conditions for pure competition?

5. What are the differences between pure and monopolistic competition?

6. Why would monopolistic competitors want to differentiate their product?

7. How does oligopoly differ from pure competition?

8. Why are pure monopolies rare?

9. What are the dangers of monopolies?

10. What justifications, if any, are there for having monopolies today?

11. How did the Sherman Antitrust Act, the Clayton Act, and the Robinson-Patman Act help control monopolies?

12. Why does government take part in economic affairs in the United States today?

■ *Practicing Critical Thinking Skills*

1. To what extent do you think government should be involved in a free enterprise economy? Defend your answer.

2. Do you think markets in the United States economy are less than fully competitive? Why or why not?

3. Do you think the solutions given to the monopoly problem are workable and effective? Are there other solutions?

4. Do you agree that today the United States has a modified private enterprise economy? Give reasons for your answer.

■ *Applying Economic Understandings*

Classifying Businesses

The United States has four major types of economic markets—pure competition, monopolistic competition, oligopoly, and monopoly. Classifying businesses as one of the four helps explain the production, pricing, and advertising behavior of many businesses.

Using the description of the economic markets given in this chapter, classify businesses in your area. Follow the instructions below as a guide.

1. List five businesses in your community.

2. Use the local area as the extent of the market and classify each business.

3. Change the market area to include first the region, then the state, and then the country as a whole. Explain how changing the market area affects the classification of each of the five businesses.

4. For each business, identify which geographic area is most relevant and what kinds of production, pricing, and advertising strategies you would expect the business to follow.

Demand

Although they possess enough, and more than enough, they still yearn for more.

Ovid

Chapter 5

After reading this chapter, you will be able to:

- Explain that the quantity of goods and services demanded by consumers is inversely related to price.

- Differentiate between a change in the quantity demanded and a change in demand.

- Analyze the elasticity of demand for a product.

- Discuss the four supposed exceptions to the Law of Demand.

5.1 What Is Demand?

Most people think of demand as being the desire for a certain economic product. In this sense, anyone who would like to own a swimming pool could be said to "demand" one. This, however, does not help much in the study of economics for almost everyone would like to have a swimming pool.

There is more to the definition of demand than just the desire for an economic product. That desire must be coupled with the ability and willingness to pay. Only those people with the desire and the ability and willingness to buy a product will be competing with other people with a similar desire, ability, and willingness to buy a product.

Effective demand, the kind of demand that is desire plus ability and willingness

Gasoline prices vary according to whether or not it is bought at full serve or self serve pumps, or paid for by cash or credit card. How does effective demand influence gasoline prices?

to pay, influences and helps to determine prices. When economists speak of demand, they mean effective demand.

AN ANALYSIS OF DEMAND

Knowledge of demand is essential for sound business planning. Suppose you were planning to start a television repair business. Before you even begin, you probably would want to know where the demand was, because that is where you would want to set up business. For exam-

ple, you may discover that it would be wise to open a shop in a neighborhood where there were many television sets and few repair shops. It would not be wise to open it in an area where there were few television sets and many repair shops.

Once you have decided you are going to open the shop and where it will be located, you will have to decide what to charge for your services. To do this, you will have to measure the demand for these services. But how? You could go out into other shops and do your own study of how consumers react to higher and lower prices. Or you could take a poll of consumers to see how they feel about prices and then try to measure demand from this data. Or you could study tables of data that have been compiled over past years to show the reactions of consumers to higher and lower prices.

Once you have gathered the data, you might get a general idea of the overall demand for the economic product. Still, it is not easy to gather precise data on how people behave.

In the study of economics, schedules and diagrams represent approximations of consumer behavior. Surveys aid economic analysis, and often confirm predictions about people's behavior. Surveys may not always lead to precise conclusions, but they are a valuable part of economic analysis.

DEMAND AND THE DEMAND SCHEDULE

If you were to ask business people in different industries about the demand in their own industry, you would get many different answers. A person in the oil industry might answer by saying that the demand for oil was 46 million barrels per day. Someone in agriculture might say that the daily demand for wheat was 10 million bushels. And a person in the steel industry might say that the demand for steel was 2 million tons per day.

While each person is in a different industry, they all have one thing in common. Each sees demand as measured in terms of the sales volume in his or her own industry. Each may have a general idea about current sales and perhaps can offer an educated guess as to what may happen at a later date.

Economists, however, want to know more than the amount demanded at a cer-

tain price. They also want to know how much would have been demanded at a higher or lower price. The average price of crude oil, for example, may have been $17 per barrel last year, and 16 million barrels may have been demanded at that price. But how much would have been demanded if the price had been $21 or $12 per barrel? In economic analysis, demand means that the full range of possibilities has been considered.

In order to be able to make sound economic decisions, economists must be able to see the market as a whole. They want to know the amount people will demand at each and every possible price. The result is a **demand schedule**—a listing that shows the quantity demanded at all prices that might prevail in the market at a given point in time. Viewed this way, there is no difference between the terms demand and demand schedule.

DEMAND ILLUSTRATED

To see how an economist would analyze demand for some economic product, look at the demand schedule on page 102. The data in the schedule represents an estimate of the total demand in City X for tomatoes on a certain day.

The schedule shows that if the price of tomatoes were 50¢ per pound, people would buy 1300 pounds. If the price were 40¢ per pound, they would buy 1700 pounds. If the price were 10¢ per pound, they would buy 4200 pounds.

The demand for tomatoes also can be shown graphically. To do so, the information in the schedule simply is transferred to the graph. On it, point *a* shows that at a price of 50¢ per pound, people would buy 1300 pounds. Point *b* shows the quantity demanded at 40¢ per pound, and so

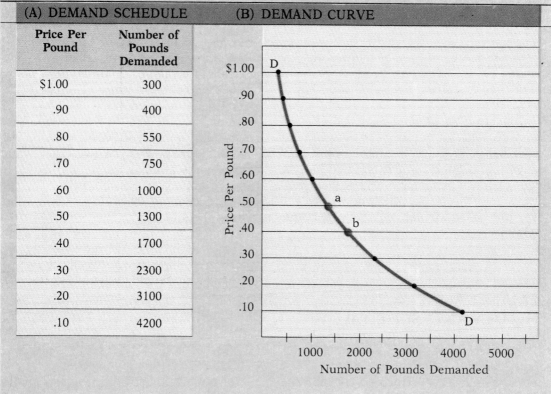

THE DEMAND FOR TOMATOES IN CITY X ON A CERTAIN DAY

(A) DEMAND SCHEDULE

Price Per Pound	Number of Pounds Demanded
$1.00	300
.90	400
.80	550
.70	750
.60	1000
.50	1300
.40	1700
.30	2300
.20	3100
.10	4200

(B) DEMAND CURVE

Figure 5–1

on. After all the price-quantity observations listed in the schedule have been transferred to the graph, the points are connected with a curve labeled **D.**

The curved line **D** is the **demand curve** for tomatoes. The curve, like the schedule, tells the amount demanded at each and every price. Both are pictures of demand. The schedule presents the information in the form of a table. The curve, which is always down-sloping, presents it in the form of a graph.

▮ Section Review

1. How do most people think of demand?
2. For what is a knowledge of demand essential?
3. What represents approximations of consumer behavior in economics?
4. Why must economists be able to see the market as a whole?
5. How are the demand schedule and demand curve different? How are they similar?

5.2 The Law of Demand

The exact prices and quantities illustrated in the demand schedule on page 102 point out an important feature of demand in general. That is, relatively high prices are associated with relatively low quantities demanded. In turn, relatively low prices are associated with relatively high quantities demanded.

In economics, this relationship of demand and price is expressed by the **Law of Demand.** It says that the demand for an economic product varies inversely with its price. In other words, if prices are high, the quantities demanded will be low. If prices are low, the quantities demanded will be high.

The correlation between demand and price does not happen by chance. Common sense and simple observation shows that the Law of Demand works. For consumers, price is an obstacle to buying, so when prices fall, the more consumers buy. We all see the Law of Demand at work when consumers flock to stores on bargain days and during special sales when prices are temporarily reduced.

A CHANGE IN THE QUANTITY DEMANDED

The table and graph on page 102 shows that 1300 pounds of tomatoes are demanded at a price of 50¢ per pound. Yet when the price falls to 40¢, 1700 pounds are demanded. This movement along the demand curve shows a **change in quantity demanded**—or the change in amount purchased in response to a change in price. An examination of the income and substitution effects explains why this happens.

THE INCOME EFFECT. When prices drop, consumers have some extra real income to spend. For example, at a price of 50¢ per pound, consumers spent $650 to buy 1300 pounds of tomatoes. But if the price drops to 40¢, they will only spend $520 on the same quantity.

Since they are $130 richer because of the drop in price, consumers may decide to spend some of it on more tomatoes. Part, but not all, of the increase from 1300 to 1700 pounds is due to the lower price. This is known as the **income effect,** or the change in quantity demanded because of a change in the consumer's real income when the price of a commodity changes.

THE SUBSTITUTION EFFECT. A lower price also means that tomatoes will be relatively less expensive than other goods. As a result, there will be a tendency to purchase more tomatoes relative to other goods. The **substitution effect** is the change in quantity demanded because of the change in the relative price of the product.

The rest of the increase from 1300 to 1700 pounds not due to the income effect is the substitution effect. Together, the income and substitution effects explain why consumers increase consumption of tomatoes to 1700 pounds when the price drops from 50¢ to 40¢.

A CHANGE IN THE LEVEL OF DEMAND

Sometimes we have **change in demand,** or change in the level of demand. This means more people are willing to buy different

A CHANGE IN THE LEVEL
OF DEMAND FOR TOMATOES

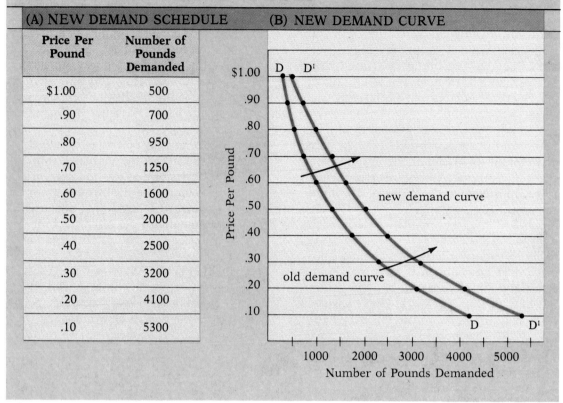

(A) NEW DEMAND SCHEDULE

Price Per Pound	Number of Pounds Demanded
$1.00	500
.90	700
.80	950
.70	1250
.60	1600
.50	2000
.40	2500
.30	3200
.20	4100
.10	5300

(B) NEW DEMAND CURVE

Figure 5–2

amounts at all prices than before. When demand changes, the entire demand curve shifts to the right to show increase in demand or to the left to show a decrease.

A change in demand, or the level of demand, is illustrated in the schedule and graph on page 104. The schedule shows that people are willing to buy more at each and every price. For example, at a price of 50¢, they are now willing to buy 2000 pounds of tomatoes instead of 1300. And at 40¢, they are willing to buy 2500 pounds instead of 1700. When this information is transferred to the graph, the demand curve has shifted to the right to show an increase in demand.

Demand can change for several reasons. It can vary because of a change in consumer income, consumer tastes, or because of a change in the price of related goods. But, whenever the level of demand changes, a new schedule must be constructed to reflect the new demand at all of the possible prevailing prices.

CONSUMER INCOME. Changes in consumer income can cause a change in demand. As incomes rise, consumers are able to buy more products at each and every price. When this happens, the demand curve shifts to the right. If incomes decline, consumers buy less of a good at each and every price. Then, the demand curve shifts to the left showing a decrease in demand.

CONSUMER TASTES.   Some products are more popular than others. Advertising a product can cause consumers to buy more of that product. If consumers want more of an item, they buy more of it at each and every price. As a result, the demand curve shifts to the right. On the other hand, if people tire of a product, they buy less at each and every price and the demand curve shifts to the left.

PRICES OF RELATED GOODS.   Finally, a change in the price of related goods can cause a change in demand. Some goods, known as **substitutes,** can be used in place of others. If the price of a good goes up, people generally shift from the consumption of that good to its substitute. For example, an increase in the price of butter would cause the demand for margarine to increase. Likewise, a decrease in the price of butter can cause the demand for margarine to decrease.

Other related goods are known as **complements,** because the use of one adds to the value of the other. Thus, an increase in the price of one good usually leads to a decrease in the demand for its complement. For example, film and cameras are two complementary goods. An increase in the price of cameras means that fewer cameras will be sold, and that the demand for film will decrease. In the same way, a decrease in the price of cameras will cause an increase in the demand for film.

For many years, Polaroid® made cameras that developed film instantly. To generate a high demand for film, camera prices were kept low. Some of the cameras were sold for about what they cost to produce. This meant that the amount of profit earned on each camera was very small. However, the film sold at very profitable prices. Thus, the company was able to use the profits on the film to recover the profits lost on the cameras. Given the complementary nature of the two products, it is unlikely that demand for film would have been as high if cameras had been more expensive.

PRINCIPLE OF DIMINISHING MARGINAL UTILITY

By selecting from among alternative ways of spending their incomes, consumers

As the price of gold drops, this shopper will be better able and more willing to buy it. The lower the price, the more he is likely to buy. How does this reflect the Law of Demand?

Tennis players quench their thirsts with lemonade after a hard game. The more they drink, the less satisfaction they get. What happens to the marginal utility of the lemonade as more is consumed?

try to get the most useful and most satisfactory combination of goods and services. In economics, this usefulness or satisfaction is called utility.

How do people decide which economic products to choose to obtain the greatest utility? One answer is found in an analysis of what economists call **marginal utility**—the extra usefulness or satisfaction a person gets from acquiring an extra unit of a product. In other words, it is the amount of satisfaction added "at the margin."

For example, how much satisfaction would you get from a single glass of ice-cold lemonade after playing a hard game of tennis on a hot summer afternoon? Whatever amount you get is the marginal

utility of that particular glass of lemonade. If you still are a little thirsty after drinking one glass of lemonade, you may decide to drink another. How much extra satisfaction will you get from the second glass? Once again, the extra satisfaction you get is the marginal utility of the second glass.

Consumers generally keep on buying a product until they reach a point where the last unit consumed gives enough, and only enough, satisfaction to justify the price. In the case of the lemonade, the marginal utility of the first glass probably is far greater than the initial amount you paid for the drink. Even the second glass may yield more satisfaction than the price. But in time, the marginal utility of still one

Profile

■ Alfred Marshall

Alfred Marshall was an English economist, philosopher, and mathematician who taught at Cambridge University for 23 years. Marshall believed that economics should be analyzed mathematically. Not long after his book, *Principles of Economics*, came out in 1890, he became recognized as the foremost economist of his time.

Marshall was concerned with theories of costs, value, and distribution. One of his greatest contributions to economic theory was the development of the concept of

1842—1924

marginal analysis. He believed that one of the most important things in economic analysis was what happened at the margin. He did not view the average revenue or average cost as important considerations. Instead, he focused on the additional revenue received from the sale of one more unit of a product compared with the additional cost incurred in making that product.

Marshall still is famous for his work in the field of demand theory. He was the first to use the term *inferior goods.* He also must be given credit for perfecting the notions of diminishing marginal utility and consumer surplus. Marshall felt that as long as the utility, or satisfaction, a person received was greater than the price of a product, the consumer enjoyed a *consumer surplus.* As long as this surplus existed, people would keep buying the product until the price of the marginal unit bought was equal to the marginal utility obtained. Marshall also pointed out that the total utility of a product increases at a diminishing rate. Thus, the price a person would be willing to pay for a product decreases as he or she gets more of it.

Marshall's theories were generally accepted until the middle 1930's. By the late 1930's, economists had come to believe that although the theories were valid, they were not complete. Marshall's influence still is felt today, however, especially in the field of microeconomics.

more glass of lemonade will be less than its price. Sooner or later, the very thought of one more glass of lemonade will make you ill. However, you probably would keep buying the lemonade as long as you got more satisfaction than the price charged. When you reach the point that the marginal utility is less than the price, you will stop buying.

This illustrates the **Principle of Diminishing Marginal Utility.** It states that the more units of a certain economic product a person acquires, the less eager that person is to buy still more. In other words, as people's wants for a particular product become more and more fully satisfied, people become less and less willing to spend their limited incomes to buy that product.

The Principle of Diminishing Marginal Utility is important to producers. According to the principle, if they want to sell more of their product, they must charge a lower price. For example, a shopper may decide to buy two sweaters at one price and three sweaters if the price is lower. The lower the price of the sweaters, the more the shopper is likely to buy. By the same token, the tired and thirsty tennis player may be willing to buy another glass or two of lemonade only if the price is much lower than before. In short, people will buy less at high prices and more when the price goes down. The Principle of Diminishing Marginal Utility provides yet another explanation of the Law of Demand.

▦ Section Review

1. How may the important relationship between demand and price be expressed in economics?

2. What happens in a demand curve when demand increases? When it decreases?

3. What are three reasons for changes in demand?

4. How does marginal utility give another view of the Law of Demand?

5. Why is the Principle of Diminishing Marginal Utility important to producers?

5.3 *Elasticity of Demand*

The Law of Demand shows that people buy more of an economic product at lower prices than at higher ones. But it does not tell how much more. If price goes down, sales will go up. But by how much? Or if a business owner is thinking about raising the price, how much will be lost in sales?

The answer to these questions is found in the concept of **demand elasticity**—a term used to indicate the extent to which changes in price cause changes in the quantity demanded.

The demand for some products is such that consumers do care about changes in price. When they buy a great many more units of a product because of a relatively small reduction in price, the demand for the product is said to be **elastic.** It also is elastic when they greatly reduce the amount they buy because of a small rise in price.

For example, the demand for T-bone steaks generally is regarded as elastic. At a regular price of $4.59 per pound, only a certain number of people will buy it. But if it is put on sale for $3.39 per pound, there may be a general rush on the supply of this kind of steak.

For other products, the demand is largely **inelastic.** This means that a change in price causes only a small change in the quantity demanded. A higher or lower price for salt, for example, probably will not bring about much change in the quantity bought because people can consume just so much salt. Even if the price were cut in half, the quantity demanded might not rise very much, if at all. Then, too, the portion of a person's yearly budget that is spent on salt is so small that even if the price were to double, it would not make much difference in the quantity demanded.

When considering the elasticity for an economic product, it is necessary to define the market being studied. For example, the demand for gasoline at a particular gas station is likely to be very elastic. If the station were to raise prices by 10 percent, there would be a large drop in the amount of gasoline sold because some customers would buy it somewhere else. If the station were to lower prices by 10 percent, the amount of gasoline sold would go up a great deal because people would go out of their way to buy "cheap" gasoline.

On the other hand, the demand for gasoline in general is likely to be inelastic. If all gas stations raised prices by 10 percent, consumers would have to pay the higher price or drive less. The law of downward-sloping demand indicates that less gasoline would be bought. But chances are that most people would not reduce their demand for gasoline by very much.

Economists, then, must be careful when discussing the elasticity of demand for a certain product. It makes a great deal of difference, for example, whether the elasticity of demand for gasoline refers to the

"Scalpel . . ."

If doctors' fees were to drop suddenly, why would there be only a small change in the quantity demanded?

gasoline a particular gas station sells or to gasoline in general.

TOTAL RECEIPTS TEST

To understand the importance of elasticity, it is useful to look at the impact of a price change on total receipts. This is sometimes called the total receipts test.

Total receipts, or total revenue, is determined by multiplying the price of a product by the quantity sold. By observing

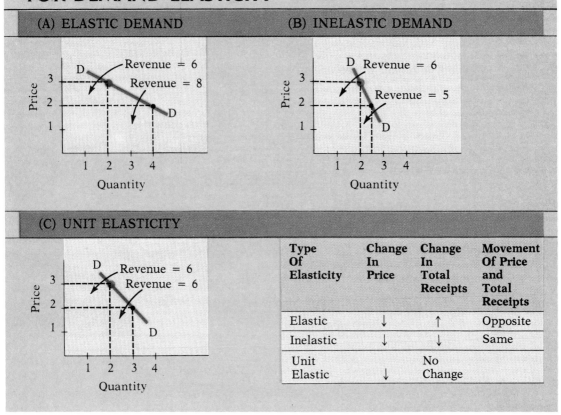

THE TOTAL RECEIPTS TEST FOR DEMAND ELASTICITY

(A) ELASTIC DEMAND

(B) INELASTIC DEMAND

(C) UNIT ELASTICITY

Type Of Elasticity	Change In Price	Change In Total Receipts	Movement Of Price and Total Receipts
Elastic	↓	↑	Opposite
Inelastic	↓	↓	Same
Unit Elastic	↓	No Change	

Figure 5–3

changes in a company's total receipts when the price changes, businesses can test for elasticity.

If demand is elastic, the total amount bought will go up sharply when the price is lowered only a little. The increase in sales means a large enough rise in total receipts to surpass the total receipts at the original price.

If demand is inelastic, a lower price would mean a small increase in the quan-

tity demanded. However, it would not be enough for total receipts to rise.

The total receipts test also works the opposite way. If demand is elastic, a higher price will mean lower total receipts because the quantity demanded will go down a great deal. Even if demand is inelastic, a higher price will cause the total amount bought to go down a little. But at the same time, total receipts will increase.

The relationship between changing prices and revenues or total receipts is summarized in the graphs and table on page 110. In each of the demand curves, the impact on total revenues of a decrease in price from $3 to $2 is shown.

Demand curve **A** is elastic. When the price drops by $1 per unit, the increase in the quantity demanded is large enough to raise total revenues from $6 to $8. Demand curve **B** is inelastic. In this case, when the price drops by $1, the increase in the quantity demanded is not enough to prevent revenues from falling below $6.

Demand curve **C** is called **unit elastic.** Now when the price drops, the quantity demanded increases barely enough to stop total revenues from either increasing or decreasing.

The three changes noted in the graphs are recorded in the table, which shows that the key to elasticity is the way in which revenues and prices change. If revenues and prices move in opposite directions, demand is elastic. If they move in the same direction, demand is inelastic. If there is no change in revenue, demand is unit elastic.

Even though all the price changes illustrated are decreases, the results would be the same if they were increases. For example, if the price rises from $2 to $3 in Graph A, receipts fall to $6. Prices and revenues still move in opposite directions as shown in the table above. The results of the summary table are also valid for the inelastic demand curve in Graph B. When the price goes up, revenues move in the same direction.

Take the demand for sugar, as shown in the demand schedule and graph on page 113. Between 60¢ and 70¢ per pound, the demand for sugar is elastic. When the price falls from 70¢ to 60¢, total receipts rise. When the price is increased from 60¢ to 70¢, total receipts go down. Prices and

revenues move in opposite directions so the demand curve is elastic in this region.

Between the prices of 40¢ to 50¢ per pound, however, the demand is inelastic. If the price were lowered within this span, the total receipts also would be lower. This is because consumers just are not responsive to changes in price below a certain level. If, however, the price is increased from 40¢ to 50¢, the total receipts would increase. Therefore, the key to the inelastic demand curve is that changes in price and changes in revenue are in the same direction.

Elasticity, then, is something that tells the way in which revenues are affected by price changes. Whether the demand for a product is elastic, inelastic, or unit elastic depends on the price range and the product being considered. The total receipts test will determine the proper classification of the product.

An understanding of elasticity helps businesses determine pricing policies that can be used to increase revenues. Physicians, for example, have an inelastic demand for their services. To raise their revenues, they simply raise their prices. On the other hand, the owner of the neighborhood gas station has an elastic demand for products. To increase revenues, prices must be lowered. If he or she tried instead to increase them, customers would go to other stations, and the gas station's total revenues would fall.

An understanding of elasticity of demand has encouraged government at all levels to tax products with relatively inelastic demands. These tax programs have worked well because people will pay almost any price, within limits, for certain products. Rather large taxes often are placed on gasoline, utility services, tobacco, and alcoholic beverages because the demand for these is relatively inelastic. The increase in price of cigarettes due to a

Case Study: *Career*

Market Researcher

Market researchers gather, record, and analyze facts about products and sales. On the basis of this, they prepare forecasts of future sales trends, offer recommendations on product design, and define the market toward which advertising should be directed. They perform these services for manufacturing companies, advertising agencies, independent research organizations, banks, the news media, university research centers, and government agencies.

Market researchers gather their information from company or government records, published materials, statistical files, and other such sources. When the information they need is not available from any of these sources, they use printed questionnaires, telephone or door-to-door surveys, or personal interviews to compile the data.

Because of the nature of their work, research analysts must be able to understand and use words effectively. They also must be able to do arithmetic quickly and accurately. Translating hundreds of thousands of symbols and figures into two or three paragraphs of analyzed information calls for a fair amount of skill. For this reason, a college degree or some other kind of advanced training generally is required. For advancement, graduate study is necessary in most cases. Courses in marketing, statistics, English composition, speech, psychology, and economics are especially helpful.

Most market researchers enter the field as research assistants or junior analysts. As such, they are required to do a great deal of clerical work and to learn how to conduct interviews and write reports on the findings of surveys. In time, they may be given responsibility for certain marketing research projects or be promoted to a supervisory position.

Today most businesses and organizations feel it is necessary to have a great deal of information about the market for their products. For this reason, market research has been in greater demand in recent years. When economic growth is slow, however, not as many new products and services are developed, and the demand for market researchers is not as great.

ELASTICITY OF DEMAND FOR GRANULATED SUGAR

(A) DEMAND SCHEDULE

Price Per Pound	Number of Pounds Demanded	Total Receipts
.80	1250	1000
.70	1500	1050
.60	2000	1200
.50	2500	1250
.40	3000	1200
.30	4000	1200
.20	5000	1000
.10	6500	650

(B) DEMAND CURVE

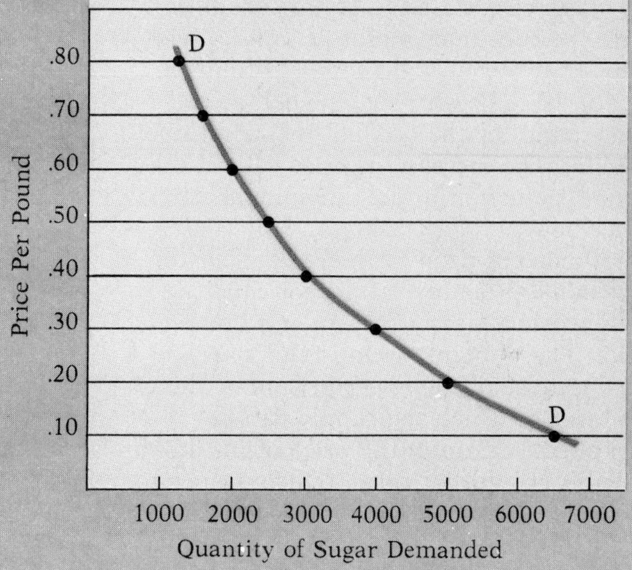

Figure 5–4

stiff tax, for example, has only a minor impact on the amount sold.

An analysis of demand elasticity has also been of value to some government agencies. One of these was the Civil Aeronautics Board (CAB). When the CAB regulated commercial air fares, it did a study on the demand for air travel, and concluded that demand was elastic. Thus, if air fares were cut, more people would fly, total revenue would increase, and everyone would benefit. Later, some carriers reduced air fares and total revenues, as predicted, went up.

Today, airlines set fares without the approval of the CAB. But because the industry is oligopolistic and price wars sometimes break out, it is difficult to predict demand elasticity.

DETERMINANTS OF DEMAND ELASTICITY

A business can determine the elasticity of demand for its products by simply considering three things: the urgency of need; the availability of adequate substitutes; and the amount of income required to buy the item.

CAN THE PURCHASE BE DELAYED? Sometimes the consumer's need for a product is urgent and cannot be put off. One example is the case of insulin. If a diabetic needs insulin, an increase in its price is not likely to make him or her put off buying the drug.

In a less extreme case, such as the need for a tank of gasoline to get to school or work, the consumer might be able to wait a day or two. But still there is a limit on the ability to go without. In such a case, the demand for the product is likely to be inelastic. The increase in price caused only a small reduction in the amount the consumer bought.

A 50 percent drop in the price of insulin or gasoline probably would not cause a sustained increase in the amount bought either. There might be an initial spurt in sales because of the lower price, but there is a limit to which the supply can be stockpiled. A drop in the price of insulin probably would not cause the consumer to actually use more. A drop in the price of gasoline probably would have more of an impact on purchases in the long run than in the short run.

If the product were tomatoes or T-bone steak instead of insulin or gasoline, people might react differently to price changes. If the price went up, they could put off buying either of these without suffering any great discomfort. They also might buy much more if the price took a significant drop.

The ability to postpone the purchase of a product, then, is one of the determinants of elasticity. If the purchase can be delayed, the demand for the product tends to be elastic. If it cannot be delayed, the demand tends to be inelastic.

ARE THERE ADEQUATE SUBSTITUTES?
If adequate substitutes are available, consumers can switch back and forth between a product and its substitute to take advantage of the best price.

If, for example, the price of steaks, butter, or gasoline from a certain gas station goes up, buyers can switch to hamburger, margarine, or gasoline from another station. With enough substitutes, even small changes in price will cause people to switch. When this happens, the amount sold will change a great deal, and there is a large impact on the total receipts, or revenue. When this is the case, the demand tends to be elastic. The fewer the substitutes for a product, the more inelastic the demand.

DOES THE PURCHASE USE A LARGE PORTION OF INCOME?
The third determinant is the amount of income required. The demand for salt, for example, is inelastic because a container costs only pennies and lasts several months. For this reason, an increase in price is not likely to be noticed by the buyer or to affect the amount bought.

The purchase of a new car, however, is another matter. Since the price of a new car is likely to be around $12,000, even a small increase can amount to several hundred extra dollars. Because of this, people tend to be more sensitive to price increases or decreases on expensive items than on less expensive ones. When the products require a large portion of income, the demand tends to be elastic. When they require a small portion of income, the demand tends to be inelastic.

The three major determinants of demand elasticity are summarized in the table on page 115. Some products, such as table salt, are rather easy to classify. Unless a salt-free diet is required for medical reasons, the consumption of salt is something that generally is not postponed. Salt is a product for which there is no real substitute, and it requires only a small portion of income. Therefore, the demand for salt is inelastic.

ESTIMATING ELASTICITY OF DEMAND

DETERMINANTS OF ELASTICITY	ECONOMIC PRODUCTS							
	Tomatoes	T-bone Steak	Table Salt	Gasoline From a Particular Station	Gasoline in General	Services of Medical Doctors	Insulin	Butter
CAN PURCHASE BE DELAYED? Yes (elastic) No (inelastic)	yes	yes	no	yes	no	no	no	yes
ARE THERE ADEQUATE SUBSTITUTES? Yes (elastic) No (inelastic)	yes	yes	no	yes	no	no	no	yes
DOES PURCHASE USE A LARGE PORTION OF INCOME? Yes (elastic) No (inelastic)	no	no	no	yes	yes	yes	no	no
Type of Elasticity:	Elastic	Elastic	Inelastic	Elastic	Inelastic	Inelastic	Inelastic	Elastic

Table 5–A

Other cases, however, are not as clear-cut. The demand for the services of doctors, for example, tends to be inelastic even though such services require a large portion of income. The lack of adequate substitutes and reluctance to put off seeing a doctor when one is sick make the demand for such services inelastic.

In the case of steak, tomatoes, and butter, the amount of income required probably is less important than the availability of substitutes and the ability to put off buying these products.

Section Review

1. What does the Law of Demand show?

2. How are total receipts determined?

3. What are the three determinants of demand elasticity?

5.4 Supposed Exceptions to the Law of Demand

The Law of Demand is one of the time-tested observations that serves as the foundation of economic reasoning. Still, there is one exception to the law, as well as several situations that appear to be exceptions but really are not.

A PARADOXICAL DEMAND CURVE

One of the first persons to point out a possible exception to the Law of Demand was the British economist Alfred Marshall

When the price of potatoes, rice, bread, and other food staples rises, there generally is more demand for them in less prosperous areas. How does this relate to the Law of Demand?

(1842–1924). Marshall talked about "bread," a term meaning so-called **inferior goods**—the "cheap and filling items" that were the main staple in the diet of low-income families.

Marshall argued that an increase in the price of "bread" would place a great drain on the resources of poor people. If they had to pay more for "bread," they would have to reduce even further the amount of meat and other more expensive foods they could eat. This, in turn, would mean they would consume more rather than less "bread" because it was still the cheapest food they could buy. In other words, when the price of "bread" rises, the incomes of the poor are reduced, and they buy more rather than less.

Is this possible? As the price of bread goes up, is more rather than less demanded? We have learned that a demand curve slopes downward. But if what Marshall says is true, the demand curve for "bread" would slope upward and contradict the Law of Demand.

For this reason, Marshall's argument is described as a **paradoxical demand curve**—a demand curve in which something appears to be contradictory. In order for this kind of curve to occur, however, the economic product in question must be an inferior good, and the consumers must be very poor. As Marshall himself observed, these cases are rare. Even today, paradoxical demand curve situations are most likely to appear only in less prosperous countries where the commodity involved is the chief article of diet.

For example, the demand for rice in many Asian countries may resemble Marshall's paradoxical demand curve. When the rice crop fails and the price of rice rises, the quantity of rice demanded also may rise, worsening the existing state of poverty.

The validity of the Law of Demand rests with how people in general react to higher or lower prices. Therefore, the attitude of only one consumer really does not disprove the law.

PERSONALIZATION FALLACY

Some people give a personal experience or attitude as an exception to the Law of Demand. How many times have you heard someone say, "I wouldn't buy that even if they cut the price in half"? While that statement seems to refute the Law of Demand, it is important to remember that not everyone may feel the same way about the product in question. This means that the particular individual speaking about the demand for the product will not be affected by any change in price. It does not mean, however, that other people will not be affected by it.

TIME-PERIOD MISUNDERSTANDING

Other people argue against the Law of Demand because they misunderstand the relationship between time and demand. They may say, for example, that while automobiles cost much more today than they did in the 1920's, the demand is greater now than it was then. This, they point out, refutes the Law of Demand, which holds that less will be sold at high prices than at low prices.

What these people have not considered is that two widely different time periods with entirely different circumstances are

As time passes, technological changes and changes in popular tastes lead to changes in a product. This can be seen in the washing machines in the photo. How is this used to argue against the Law of Demand?

involved. The population has grown, and incomes have increased about ninefold since the 1920's. Cars are more complicated and more valuable than they were 60 or 70 years ago, and they command a higher price. Streets and highways today are made to handle large volumes of traffic, while in the 1920's, roads often were no more than narrow, muddy lanes. And most cars today are thought of as necessities, while in the 1920's, they were thought of as luxuries.

At a given point in time, people will tend to buy more automobiles at low prices than at high prices. But, over time, tastes, habits, and incomes may change. It is true that the level of demand for cars is greater today than it was in the 1920's. But if today's market is considered separate from that of any other time period, the Law of Demand still holds true.

In other words, the time-period misunderstanding is due to the tendency for

people to confuse movements along a demand curve with shifts of the curve. As seen in the demand curve for tomatoes, concern generally is with the demand for a product on a certain day and in a certain market. When analyzing the demand for automobiles or other products, the Law of Demand should not be applied to more than one period of time.

PRESTIGE PURCHASES

Some people try to refute the Law of Demand by saying that so-called prestige goods will sell in greater quantities if the price is set high rather than low. They feel that the prestige and high price associated with owning a luxury car, for example, helps the manufacturer sell more cars. But if this really were true, the price of luxury cars would rise without limit. The manu-

Luxury items, such as these furs, sell at high prices because manufacturers know some people will go out of their way to buy them. Why does the prestige purchases argument not disprove the Law of Demand?

facturer would have so many orders that it no longer would be possible to produce lower-priced cars.

Such a situation clearly does not exist. The manufacturer knows that while a few people go out of their way to buy a prestige car, people in general will behave according to the Law of Demand. If the price of luxury cars rises, fewer will be sold in the total market. If the price goes down, more will be sold. This argument, like the others, does not disprove the Law of Demand which says that people buy more at low than at high prices.

Section Review

1. Under what conditions might the paradoxical demand curve occur?

2. How do the personalization fallacy and time-period misunderstanding appear to refute the Law of Demand?

3. Why do prestige purchases arguments not contradict the Law of Demand?

Chapter 5 Review

Summary

1. Economists are concerned with effective demand—the desire plus ability and willingness to pay.

2. Demand can be illustrated as a schedule that shows the amount people are willing to buy at each and every price, and graphically as a downward-sloping curve that shows the same thing.

3. The Law of Demand, which expresses the relationship of demand and price, states that people will want more products at low prices and less at high prices.

4. A change in quantity demanded means people want a different quantity at a different price. It does not mean a change in the demand schedule.

5. The income and substitution effects of a price change explain changes in quantity demanded because of that price change.

6. A change in the level of demand means people have changed their minds about the amount they would buy at each and every price. It means the demand schedule has shifted.

7. An increase in the level of demand is illustrated by shifting the demand curve to the right. A decrease in the level of demand is shown by a shift of the demand curve to the left.

8. Level of demand may change because of changes in consumer income, consumer tastes, or prices of related goods.

9. Related goods are divided into substitute and complementary groups. A change in the price of each has a different impact on the level of demand of other goods.

10. The Principle of Diminishing Marginal Utility also confirms the Law of Demand.

11. Elasticity of demand is a concept that relates changes in the quantity demanded to changes in price. If a change in price causes a great change in the quantity demanded, demand is elastic. If a change in price causes only a small change in the quantity demanded, demand is inelastic.

12. The total receipts test is used to determine demand elasticity. If prices and revenues move in opposite directions, demand is elastic. If prices and revenues move in the same direction, demand is inelastic.

13. A knowledge of demand elasticity is important to businesses because it tells them how a change in price will affect their total revenue and helps them determine pricing policies.

14. Demand elasticity is influenced by the ability to postpone a purchase, the substitutes available, and the amount of income required by the purchase.

15. A paradoxical demand curve occurs rarely and only under certain special circumstances.

16. Arguments against the Law of Demand generally are based on a personalization fallacy, a time-period misunderstanding, or prestige purchases. None refute the Law of Demand.

■ Building an Economic Vocabulary

effective demand
demand schedule
demand curve
Law of Demand
change in quantity demanded
income effect
substitution effect

change in demand
substitutes
complements
marginal utility
Principle of Diminishing
    Marginal Utility

demand elasticity
elastic
inelastic
unit elastic
inferior goods
paradoxical demand
    curve

■ Reviewing the Main Ideas

1. What does demand mean in economic analysis?

2. What is a demand schedule? A demand curve? How are they alike?

3. What is an important feature of demand in general?

4. What is meant by a change in the quantity demanded?

5. How is the income effect different from the substitution effect?

6. Together, what do the income and substitution effects explain?

7. What is the difference between a change in the quantity demanded and a change in the level of demand?

8. How is an increase in demand represented graphically? A decrease?

9. What three things cause a shift in the level of demand?

10. How do substitute and complementary goods differ? Why are they important to the study of demand?

11. What does the term "marginal" mean in economics?

12. How does the Principle of Diminishing Marginal Utility relate to the Law of Demand?

13. Why is a knowledge of elasticity important to businesses?

14. What are total receipts? How does the total receipts test reveal elasticity?

15. What is the relationship between changes in price and changes in revenue when demand is elastic? Inelastic? Unit elastic?

16. How does urgency of need affect demand elasticity? The availability of substitutes? The amount of income required?

17. Why is Marshall's argument described as a paradoxical demand curve? How often can one be found?

18. What three common situations seem to be exceptions to the Law of Demand but, in fact, are not?

Practicing Critical Thinking Skills

1. Do you think the Law of Demand accurately reflects the way most people feel about certain products? Why or why not?

2. How do you think the demand for pizza would be affected by (1) an increase in everyone's pay, (2) an increase in the cost of gas, (3) a decrease in the price of hamburger? Explain your answers.

3. What could you, as a business owner, learn about your business and product by applying the total receipts test?

4. Can you think of any case in which demand for a product will not be influenced by a price change? If you can think of one, explain how it relates to the supposed exceptions of the Law of Demand.

Applying Economic Understandings

Estimating Elasticity

Economists must be able to estimate elasticity. Without this skill, they could not predict how changes in prices affect the amount of money consumers spend on a product, or how changes in prices affect a firm's total revenue.

The following exercise will give you practice in the skill of estimating elasticity. 1. List five items you buy regularly. 2. Use the elasticity determinants in the table on page 115 to classify each and determine its overall elasticity. 3. Answer the questions below. If the price of each item were doubled, what would happen to the total amount of money you would spend on each? What would happen to the amount spent if the price of each item were cut in half? Use the total receipts test to check your conclusions.

Supply

The law of supply and demand is learned in infancy. The infant demands a clean diaper and is willing to supply peace and quiet in exchange. Mother demands peace and quiet and is willing to supply a clean diaper in exchange. The terms of trade are arranged. . . . One scream equals one diaper. The price of one diaper is one scream.

Jude Wanniski

Chapter 6

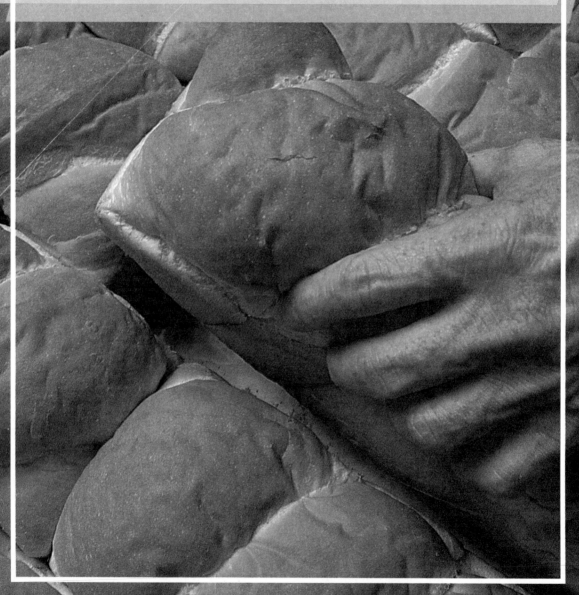

After reading this chapter, you will be able to:

- Explain that the quantity of goods and services supplied is directly related to price and elasticity of supply.

- Discuss the theory of production in terms of the Law of Variable Proportions, the production function, and the three stages of production.

- Identify the different measures of cost used by the firm when production decisions are made.

- Describe how total and marginal revenues interact with cost to determine business profits.

6.1 *What is Supply?*

Business people think of demand as the consumption of goods and services. At the same time, they think of supply as their production. As they see it, supply means the quantity of a product supplied at the price that prevailed at the time. To economists, however, it means much more.

AN ANALYSIS OF SUPPLY

Economists are concerned with the market as a whole. They want to know how much of a certain product sellers will supply at each and every possible market price. **Supply**, then, may be defined as a schedule of quantities that would be offered for sale at all of the possible prices that might prevail in the market. The supply of television sets, for example, is the number of sets manufacturers will be likely to produce if the prevailing market is $600, $400, $200, or any other price within the range of possible prices.

Everyone who offers an economic product for sale is a supplier. When you look for a job, you are offering your services for

Different models of television sets are offered for sale by a supplier. The televisions are listed at various prices. How does the price of a product affect the quantity offered for sale?

sale. You, then, are a supplier, and your service is your product. Think how you would react if you were offered a high price for your service. Most likely, you would be willing to supply more by working harder or longer hours for a high wage than you would for a low one.

A similar decision must be made by all suppliers of economic products. Each supplier must decide how much to offer for sale—a decision made according to what is best for the individual seller. What is best depends, in turn, upon the cost of producing the goods or services. Still, it is reasonable to predict that the higher the price, the greater the quantity the seller will offer for sale.

SUPPLY AND THE SUPPLY SCHEDULE

Suppose, for example, you are an army officer whose job is to obtain dress shoes for every person in uniform. Since you will need so many pairs of shoes, you will want to get the best possible buy. To do this, you could make indirect inquiries, meet with manufacturers, and then ask for bids.

The chances are that you would discover that when you offer a low price, suppliers will be willing to offer only small quantities for sale. For example, at a price of $15 a pair, they might offer only 1.6 million pairs. But if you offered a higher price, such as $21 a pair, they might be willing to offer 2.5 million pairs.

After you have gathered all the data possible, you would be able to construct a **supply schedule** such as the one on page 125. This tells the quantities offered at each and every possible market price.

The data presented in the supply schedule also can be shown graphically. The **supply curve** (S) in the graph on page 125 slopes upward and to the right to reflect the tendency of suppliers to offer greater quantities for sale at higher prices. The curve also shows that supply is the opposite of demand.

If you hold the figure in front of a mirror, you will see what looks like a demand curve. Just as the demand curve showed that greater amounts would be bought at

THE SUPPLY OF ARMY DRESS SHOES

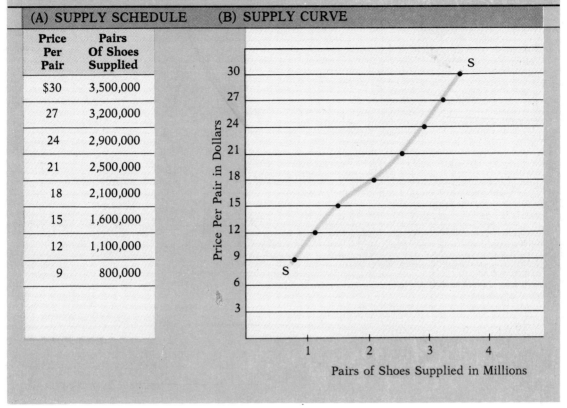

(A) SUPPLY SCHEDULE		(B) SUPPLY CURVE
Price Per Pair	**Pairs Of Shoes Supplied**	
$30	3,500,000	
27	3,200,000	
24	2,900,000	
21	2,500,000	
18	2,100,000	
15	1,600,000	
12	1,100,000	
9	800,000	

Figure 6–1

lower prices, the supply curve shows that greater amounts will be offered for sale at higher prices.

The tendency of suppliers to offer more for sale at high prices than at low prices forms the basis for the **Law of Supply.** The law states that the quantity of an economic product offered for sale varies directly with its price. In other words, if prices are high, suppliers will offer greater quantities for sale. If prices are low, they will offer smaller quantities for sale.

CHANGES IN SUPPLY

The amount that producers bring to market at any one price is called the **quantity supplied.** In the figure on page 126, 3.5 million is the quantity supplied when the price is $30. **A change in quantity supplied** takes place because of a price change. If the price decreases to $24, for example, then 2.9 million shoes or units would be supplied. A change in the quantity supplied is a movement along the supply curve.

A CHANGE IN THE LEVEL OF SUPPLY FOR SHOES

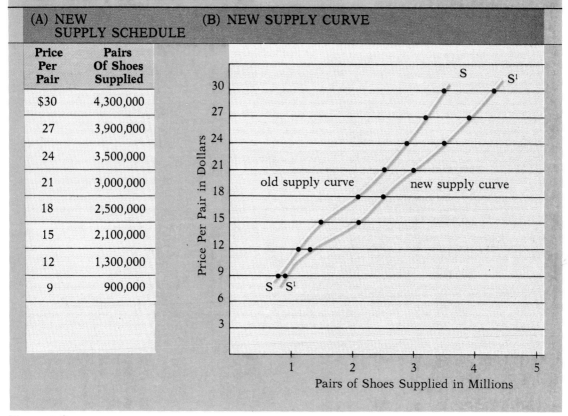

(A) NEW SUPPLY SCHEDULE

Price Per Pair	Pairs Of Shoes Supplied
$30	4,300,000
27	3,900,000
24	3,500,000
21	3,000,000
18	2,500,000
15	2,100,000
12	1,300,000
9	900,000

(B) NEW SUPPLY CURVE

Figure 6–2

The range of quantities offered at each or every point on the supply curve is called the level of supply. A change in the level of supply, or a **change in supply**, means that a different amount will be brought to market at every price.

The schedule and graph above illustrate a change in supply. The schedule shows an increase in supply—more shoes are brought to market at each and every price. For example, the schedule and graph on page 125 show that if the price per pair were $21, 2.5 million pairs of shoes would be produced. The schedule and graph above, however, show that 3 million pairs will be produced for the same price. The same is true at every price. When this happens, there is a change in, or an increase in, supply and the supply curve shifts to the right.

Changes in supply take place quite often Many times such changes come about because of a decrease in the cost of inputs. In the shoe illustration, there might have been an increase in supply because of a decline in the price of cattle, and therefore, in the cost of shoe leather. If the price of leather goes down, producers will be able to produce more pairs of shoes at each and every price.

Productivity also might affect the supply schedule. The introduction of a new machine, chemical, or industrial process might lower the cost of production and allow more pairs of shoes to be produced at each and every price.

Likewise, the supply curve might shift to the left to reflect a decrease in supply. A union, for example, might negotiate a

higher wage. This would raise the cost of inputs and cause the producer to offer fewer pairs of shoes at every price.

ELASTICITY OF SUPPLY

Just as there is elasticity of demand, there is elasticity of supply. **Supply elasticity** tells the way in which changes in the quantity supplied are affected by changes in price. For example, if a small

Figure 6–3

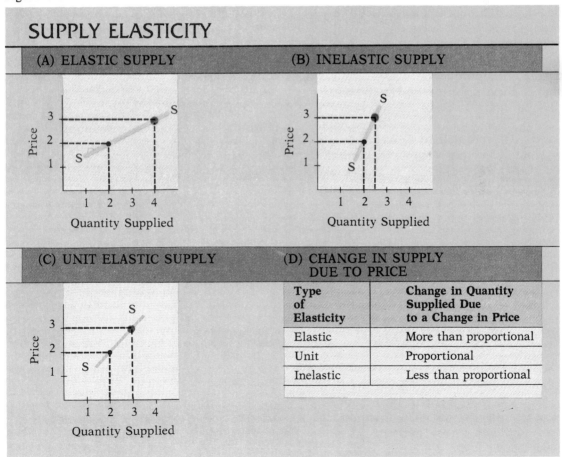

SUPPLY ELASTICITY

(A) ELASTIC SUPPLY

(B) INELASTIC SUPPLY

(C) UNIT ELASTIC SUPPLY

(D) CHANGE IN SUPPLY DUE TO PRICE

Type of Elasticity	Change in Quantity Supplied Due to a Change in Price
Elastic	More than proportional
Unit	Proportional
Inelastic	Less than proportional

increase in price causes producers to increase their output by a large amount, the supply curve is said to be elastic. If the quantity supplied changes very little, supply is inelastic.

Three kinds of supply elasticity are illustrated on page 127. In Graph **A,** supply is elastic because an increase in price from $2 to $3 causes the quantity brought to market for sale to increase a great deal. Graph **B,** on the other hand, is inelastic because the same price increase causes output to increase by only a little.

Graph **C** shows that supply also can have unit elasticity. In this case, a given change in price will cause a proportional change in the quantity supplied. The key to supply elasticity is the relationship of the change in quantity supplied to the change in price.

The extent to which a business's supply curve is elastic or inelastic depends on the nature of its production. For example, the supply curve of oil derived from shale is likely to be inelastic in the short run. No matter what price is being offered, companies will find it hard to increase output because of the huge amount of capital and technological breakthroughs needed before production can be increased very much. In the very short run, it is not likely that a doubling of the price offered per barrel of shale oil will more than double the amount brought to the market.

On the other hand, the supply curve is likely to be elastic for kites, hula hoops, and other products that can be made quickly without huge amounts of capital and skilled labor. If people are willing to pay twice the price for any of these products, producers probably will be able to gear up in a very short amount of time to increase production significantly.

Basically, there is little difference between supply elasticity and demand elasticity. If we are talking about the quantities being bought, the concept is demand elasticity. If we are concerned with the quantities being brought to market and offered for sale, the concept involved is supply elasticity.

The Law of Supply gives a general picture of how suppliers may act. The next section will look at each of the factors that influence supply.

■ Section Review

1. According to the Law of Supply, how does price affect the quantity offered for sale?

2. Why do changes in supply occur?

3. When is supply elastic? When is supply inelastic?

6.2 Theory of Production

In order to produce economic goods and services, some combinations of the factors of production are needed. When more efficient combinations of these factors are used, production goes up and costs go down. This encourages suppliers to offer greater quantities for sale. The **theory of production** deals with the relationship between the input of land, labor, and capital and the output of goods and services. It looks at how output behaves when inputs change.

The economist would not consider this advice to Al the best way to increase productivity. In general, what three things can bring about greater output?

Al, do whatever you have to do to increase productivity. Threaten, cajole, fire at will. Have fun.

LAW OF VARIABLE PROPORTIONS

The **Law of Variable Proportions** states that in the short run, output will change as one input is varied while the others are held constant. Although the law probably is new to you, the concept is not. Most likely, you are familiar with the law in action and have seen it many times.

If you prepare chili, for example, you know that one pinch of chili powder will make it taste better. Two pinches may make it taste better yet. But if you keep on adding more and more chili powder, a point soon will be reached where the chili begins to taste terrible. Basically, this is an example of the Law of Variable Proportions at work. As the amount of chili powder, which is the input, varies, so does the chili, which is the output.

This same law applies to the output of other economic products. Generally, three things can bring about greater output of the final product. The first is an increase in the amount of inputs, or the factors of production. The second is the use of higher quality factors. And the third is more skillful use of these factors through better knowledge, innovation, and new technology.

The growth in air travel illustrates this point. First, the airlines have used more factors of production such as planes, equipment, employees, and airports. Second, they have made greater use of higher quality inputs. Jets, for example, have taken the place of the smaller and slower planes. Third, there has been greater skill involved in the use of inputs. For example, safety features, scheduling, handling of reservations, and routing all have been much improved over the years.

In the economic sense, the Law of Variable Proportions deals with the relationship between the input of productive resources and the output of final products.

In most companies, managers hold regular production meetings at which they evaluate past performance and set future goals. Why is the use of the production function important in such meetings?

the Law of Variable Proportions. Suppose the manager wanted to know, given the existing machines and equipment, how the final output would be affected if one or several workers are hired. The law will help answer this question.

Of course, it is possible for all inputs to be varied at the same time. The farmer may want to know what will happen to output if not only the fertilizer but also the quantity of the other factors of production are varied. The plant manager may be interested in finding out what will happen if the company not only hires more workers but also buys several new machines and other equipment.

When more than one factor of production is varied, it becomes harder to tell what the effect on final output will be. But this does not make the law any less useful. Through this law, we can understand how final output will be affected if one factor of production is used in variable proportions while the other factors stay the same.

The law helps answer the question, "How is the output of the final product affected as more units of one variable input or resource are added to a fixed amount of other resources?"

For example, a farmer may have all the land, machines, workers, and other things needed to grow and harvest a crop. But that farmer still may need to have some questions answered about the use of fertilizer. It is important for the farmer to know, for example, how the crop yield will be affected if 100, 200, or even 300 pounds of fertilizer per acre are added to fixed amounts of the other inputs.

A plant manager who has a question about the use of labor also may turn to

PRODUCTION FUNCTION

The Law of Variable Proportions can be illustrated with the use of a **production function**—a concept that relates output to different amounts of a single input while other inputs are held constant. The production function can be illustrated in the form of a schedule such as the one on page 131, or in the form of a graph like the one on the same page.

The first two columns in the production schedule give hypothetical figures on a business's output as the number of workers is varied from one to ten. The information in these columns is used to construct the production function that appears below the schedule.

Figure 6–4

THE LAW
OF VARIABLE PROPORTIONS

(A) PRODUCTION SCHEDULE
USING VARYING AMOUNTS OF LABOR

Number Of Workers	Total Product (In Units)*	Marginal Product (In Units)*	
1	14	14	Stage I
2	42	28	
3	75	33	
4	112	37	
5	150	38	
6	180	30	Stage II
7	203	23	
8	216	13	
9	207	–9	Stage III
10	190	–17	

*All figures refer to production/productivity per worker per day.

(B) PRODUCTION FUNCTION
USING VARYING AMOUNTS OF LABOR

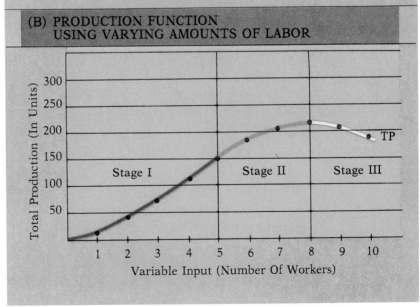

While the number of workers changes, all else remains the same. There is no change in machinery used; all workers are just as productive with each worker putting in the same number of hours. And, the same quantity of **raw materials,** or unprocessed natural products, are used in production. In other words, the only change occurs in the number of workers. Thus, any changes in output are a result of the variation in the number of workers.

TOTAL PRODUCT.   The second column in the production schedule on page 131 shows the resulting **total product,** or total output produced by the firm. With only a few workers, the plant does not operate efficiently. It may be hard for a few workers to attend the machines, keep the supply of raw materials flowing smoothly, and remove and package the finished product. These workers also have to keep up the premises and do jobs connected with normal plant operations. In fact, some of the machines may end up standing idle much of the time.

But as more workers are added, the total product rises. More machinery can be operated, and plant output is improved a great deal. Workers can specialize in certain jobs, which means that each worker's special talents can be used to the fullest. For example, one group of workers can run the machines while a second group takes care of maintenance. A third group keeps records as a forth group handles the assembly work. By working in this way—as a coordinated whole—the factory can be highly productive.

When the eighth worker is added, total product goes as high as it can. Adding the ninth and tenth workers causes total out-

As workers are added to this assembly line, output increases—but only to a certain point. What would happen if company officials doubled the number of workers in the factory shown below?

put to go down because these workers just get in the way of the others. Although the ideal number of workers to use cannot be determined until the issue of costs is considered, it is clear that the ninth and tenth workers will not be hired.

MARGINAL PRODUCT. The measure of marginal product in the third column of the production schedule on page 131 is one of the more important concepts in economics. It shows what happens at the margin as one more worker is added. The object is to find out how much additional output can be obtained from using one more unit of input. The additional output, which comes from adding one more worker or any other factor of production is known as **marginal product.**

Note that the marginal productivity of the fifth worker is 38 units, which is more than that of any preceding worker. As additional workers are hired, though, each one adds less and less to the total output. The marginal productivity of the ninth and tenth workers is less than zero. These are the workers that get in the way of production so that total output goes down. The marginal productivity of the ninth and tenth workers, then, is negative.

THREE STAGES OF PRODUCTION

An understanding of the production function and the Law of Variable Proportions helps a business decide the number of variable inputs to use in production. An examination of the three **stages of production**—increasing returns, diminishing returns, and negative returns—illustrates this. These three stages are shown in the production schedule and function on page 131.

STAGE I: INCREASING RETURNS. The first stage of the Law of Variable Proportions is illustrated by the hiring of the first five workers. Each worker hired contributes more than the worker before to total output.

In this first stage, the individual workers cannot handle the equipment efficiently because there is too much machinery and other resources per worker. In other words, there are not enough workers to handle the job well. But as the number of workers rises, the job of using the available resources is done better. The result of all this is increasing returns per worker.

As long as each new worker hired contributes more to total output than the worker before, total output rises at a faster rate. Since total output increases by larger and larger amounts every time a new worker is added, Stage I is known as the stage of increasing returns.

STAGE II: DIMINISHING RETURNS. In Stage II, the total plant production keeps growing, but by smaller and smaller amounts. Any additional workers hired may stock shelves, package parts, and do other jobs that leave the machine operators free to spend more time at the machines. But the increase in total plant production is less than it was when the other workers were hired. Marginal productivity goes down, but it still is positive. In other words, each worker makes a diminishing but positive contribution to total output.

Stage II illustrates the **Principle of Diminishing Returns.** As more and more units of a certain variable resource are applied to a constant amount of other resources, total output will keep rising but only at a diminishing rate. In the example in the figure on page 131, the addition of the seventh and eighth workers leads to increased total output. But the additional output brought about by these two workers begins to diminish. The seventh worker adds 23 units to total output, but the eighth adds only 13.

STAGE III: NEGATIVE RETURNS. Adding the ninth and tenth workers makes an even greater difference. There are too many workers, and they are getting in each other's way. Marginal productivity is negative and total plant output decreases. This means that labor service, which could be used to advantage in some other job area, is wasted.

Most companies might keep hiring if total product increased steadily. Most companies would not, however, hire workers whose addition would cause total production to go down. Therefore, the number of workers used is found only in Stage II. The number of workers actually hired, however, depends on the cost of each worker. If cost is low, eight workers might be hired. If cost is high, perhaps fewer than eight but no less than six, workers might be hired.

■ Section Review

1. How does the Law of Variable Proportions relate inputs to outputs?
2. What is the difference between total product and marginal product?
3. How are the three stages of the Law of Variable Proportions related?

6.3 Supply and the Role of Cost

An analysis of the Law of Variable Proportions tells a business it should use a combination of inputs which would put it in Stage II of production. But the exact combination of inputs in this stage cannot be determined until productivity and costs are considered.

PRODUCTIVITY AND COST

Different grades of raw materials have different productivities. There are, for example, many grades of coal, wood, steel, cotton, and glass. Businesses that use raw materials in manufacturing must decide which grade best suits their needs. Since productivity affects both cost and supply, it is important that care be taken in selecting the proper materials.

Suppose, for example, that an electric power company which uses coal to generate power can choose from among three different grades of coal. Grade A sells for $40 per ton, grade B for $33, and grade C for $30. The cost and productivities of each is shown in the chart on page 136.

Notice that grade A coal would be more productive than the other two, yielding 2500 kilowatt-hours of electric power for each ton of coal used. But when productivity is considered in terms of production cost per kilowatt-hour of electric power, grade A costs 1.6¢ per kilowatt-hour generated. Grade C also has a cost of 1.6¢ per kilowatt-hour generated.

Both grade C, which is the cheapest and least productive, and grade A, which is the most expensive and most productive, cost more per final unit than grade B. Grade B,

■ John Baptiste Say

John Baptiste Say was an early nineteenth-century French economist who was experienced in business, politics, and education. After serving first as an editor and then as editor-in-chief of a magazine dedicated to the ideas of the French Revolution, he was appointed to the French Tribunate. He held the position until he was dismissed by Napoleon. In 1807, Say started his own cotton-spinning mill, which he sold six years later. From 1817 to 1830, he was associated with the

1767–1832

Conservatoire des Arts et Métiers, where he specialized in the area of industrial economy. The last two years of his life, he was a professor of political economy at the Collège de France.

In 1803, Say published *A Treatise on Political Economy,* in which he reorganized and popularized the theories of Adam Smith. In 1821, the work was translated into English. Say also developed the concept of entrepreneur. His own career in business and as a professor of economics helped him gain a keen insight into the workings of the entrepreneur. Many economists view him as the first important economist to distinguish clearly between the entrepreneur and the capitalist.

Say is best known, however, for his theory of markets, known as Say's Law. It states that supply creates its own demand. Unlike other economists of the time, Say did not believe that periods of drastic decline in the economy were due to a lack of demand. He believed instead that the market became depressed when too much was produced for some markets while not enough was produced for others. In Say's view, this imbalance would be only temporary and in time would adjust itself automatically. Those who overproduced would have to redirect their production to go along with consumers' wants, or they would be forced out of business. By determining that supply creates its own demand, Say was affirming that there always would be a market, no matter how great output might grow. Say's Law remained central to economic thought until the Great Depression of the 1930's.

PRODUCTIVITY AND COST OF VARIOUS GRADES OF COAL

Grades Of Coal	Price Per Ton	Kilowatt Hours Of Electric Power Per Ton Of Coal Used (Estimated)	Production Cost Per Kilowatt Hour Of Electric Power
A	$40.00	2500	1.6¢
B	$33.00	2200	1.5¢
C	$30.00	1875	1.6¢

Figure 6–5

however, is the most efficient from a cost point of view.

This example shows that both productivity and cost must be kept in mind in order to make the best decision. This holds true for a person who manufactures razor blades who must consider the different grades of steel, for a person who owns a hotel who must consider the different grades of carpeting, as well as for an electric power company. In the end, the amount of output produced is a function of the quality and the quantity of inputs used.

MEASURES OF COST

It is clear that production decisions are influenced by productivity and by the cost of inputs. This means a business must analyze the issue of costs before making its decisions. To make the decision-making process easier, it helps to divide cost into several different categories.

FIXED COST. The first kind of cost is **fixed cost**—the cost that a business incurs even if the plant is idle and output is zero. It makes no difference whether the business produces nothing, very little, or a lot. Total fixed cost, or **overhead**, remains the same.

Fixed costs include salaries paid to executives, interest charges on bonds, rent payments on leased properties, and local and state property taxes. They also take in **depreciation**—the gradual wear and tear on capital goods over time and through use. A machine, for example, will not last forever. The parts will wear out slowly and, after a time, break. Then, too, as each year passes, it becomes older and less valuable because newer models are introduced. In other words, even though the machine still can function, it becomes obsolete.

The key thing to remember about fixed costs is that they do not change with changes in output. For example, consider the table on page 138, which is an extension of the production schedule on page 131. Look at the first three columns of the table. Regardless of the level of output, the

Whether this computer firm is idle (left) or producing to its full capacity (right), it still incurs fixed costs. What do these fixed costs generally include?

total fixed costs amount to $70, as shown in the fourth column of the table. Since the executive salaries, interest payments, taxes, and other overhead charges do not change with changes in output, fixed costs never vary.

VARIABLE COST.   Another kind of cost is **variable cost**—a cost that changes with changes in the business rate of operation or output. While fixed costs generally are associated with machines and other capital goods, variable costs generally are associated with labor and raw materials, which may be laid off or used again as output changes. Electric power to run the machines and freight charges on shipments of the final product also are examples of variable cost.

In the example on page 138, the assumption has been made that the only variable

cost is labor. At $46 per day, the total variable cost for one worker who produces 14 units of output is $46. Two workers, or two units of variable input, cost $92, and so on.

TOTAL COST.   The **total cost** of production is the sum of the fixed and variable costs. It takes in all the costs a business faces in the course of its operations.

For example, the business represented in the table on page 138 might employ six workers costing $46 each for a total of $276, to produce 180 units of total output. If there were no other variable costs, and if depreciation, taxes, and other fixed costs amounted to $70, then the total cost of production would be $346.

If the workers should go on strike, the total cost of production would fall to $70 even though no output is produced. The total cost of production would be equal to the fixed costs plus the variable costs, which, in this case, are zero.

MARGINAL COST.   The other measure of cost is marginal cost—the extra or additional cost incurred when a business produces one additional unit of a commodity. Since fixed costs do not change, marginal cost is the increase in variable costs, which stems from using additional factors of production.

For example, the table below shows that the addition of the first worker increased the total product by 14 units. And, since total variable costs increased by $46, each

of the additional 14 units cost $3.29. If another worker is added, 28 more units of output will be produced for an additional cost of $46. The marginal or extra cost of each unit of output is $46 divided by 28, or $1.64.

PRACTICAL APPLICATION OF COST PRINCIPLES

The combination, or mix, of inputs affects supply. If, for example, most of the costs of a certain business are fixed and only a few vary with output, total output

Table 6–A

FINDING THE PROFIT-MAXIMIZING NUMBER OF INPUTS

PRODUCTION SCHEDULE			COSTS				REVENUES		Total Profits
Number Of Workers	Total Product	Marginal Product	Total Fixed Costs	+ Total Variable Costs	= Total Costs	Marginal Costs	Total Revenue	Marginal Revenue	
0	0	0	70	0	70		0		—
1	14	14	70	46	116	3.29	28	2.00	−88
2	42	28	70	92	162	1.64	84	2.00	−78
3	75	33	70	138	208	1.39	150	2.00	−58
4	112	37	70	184	254	1.24	224	2.00	−30
5	150	38	70	230	300	1.21	300	2.00	0
6	180	30	70	276	346	1.53	360	2.00	14
7	203	23	70	322	392	2.00	406	2.00	14
8	216	13	70	368	438	3.54	432	2.00	−6
9	207	−9	70	414	484	—	414	2.00	−70
10	190	−17	70	460	530	—	380	2.00	−150

Hospitals, like many businesses, operate on a 24-hour basis. What variable costs are incurred by such businesses by operating around the clock?

could be increased with very little additional cost.

Take, for example, the case of a self-serve gas station with several pumps and a single attendant located in an enclosed booth on the lot. This operation is likely to have large fixed costs. These would include overhead expenses such as the cost of the lot—which may be located at a busy corner—the pumps and tanks, and the taxes and licensing fees paid to state and local governments.

The variable costs, on the other hand, are likely to be quite small. These would include the hourly wage paid to the employee, the cost of electricity for lights and pumps, and the cost of the gas sold. When all costs are included, however, the ratio of variable to fixed costs is small.

As a result, it does not cost much more for the owner to operate the station as many hours as possible, perhaps 24 hours a day, seven days a week. The extra cost of keeping the station open between the hours of midnight and six in the morning is minimal. The extra wages, the electricity, and other variable costs, are minor and may well be covered from the profits of the extra sales.

Another gas station may have a different mix of costs that may well determine different hours. Suppose a full-service station located nearby offers the services of a mechanic as well as several attendants to wait on customers.

If the station has been around long enough, management may even own the land. Taxes and occupational licenses may have to be paid, but fixed costs are likely to be less than those of the other gas station.

The need for the attendants and the mechanic, however, means that the variable costs are higher in comparison to fixed costs. As a result, this station is likely to operate under shorter hours and during the busiest time of the day. Thus, the mix of inputs and the nature of their costs has an impact on the amount of service offered by the owner.

A movie theater operator is faced with a similar situation. Once the decision is made to show a movie, it makes little difference as to whether ten or a thousand people come to the theater per day. The operating expenses are about the same regardless of how many customers come. Because marginal costs are low, there is little extra expense involved to show a movie in the early afternoon. In the end, the owner is concerned about recovering the large fixed costs and is more likely to schedule a number of movies at different times throughout the day.

Section Review

1. Why is it necessary for businesses to consider productivity as well as cost?

2. How do fixed costs differ from variable costs?

3. How can costs affect business decisions?

At most theaters, the price of admission depends on the time of day the film is viewed. Matinee prices are usually lower than evening prices. How do these prices affect the cost of operating the theater?

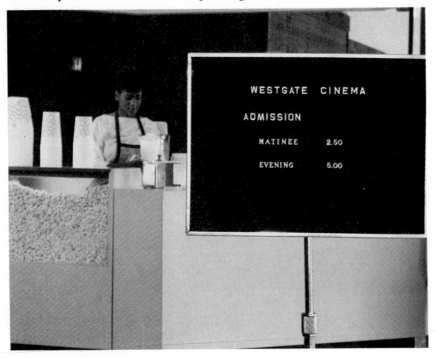

Case Study: Career

Sales Clerk

Sales clerks perform a variety of different functions, from handling stock to taking inventory to dealing directly with customers. The tasks tend to vary depending on the place of employment.

In general, however, sales clerks are expected to sell. This means they should be able to convince a customer that their product fills his or her need better than anyone else's; demonstrate the product upon request; record the sales transaction and accept payment; and, if necessary, arrange for the product's safe delivery.

Because sales clerks represent their place of employment to the public, they are expected to be neat and well-groomed, friendly, and able to get along with people of all ages. This means they must be patient and tactful. They also must be able to work under pressure—pressure from bosses who want a higher volume of goods sold and from customers who want prompt and courteous service at all times. Good sales clerks think about two sales at once—the sale in which they are engaged at the moment and the one they may be engaged in if they handle this one properly and the customer returns another time. A customer not pleased with the service probably will take his or her business somewhere else next time.

Most sales-clerk positions are open to high school graduates. Although most places of employment offer some kind of training for new clerks, additional courses in English, business math, and speech are advisable for a clerk who wants to be promoted or who wants a long-term career in sales. A sales person with a good command of the English language can describe a product and its attributes more convincingly. One with a strong working knowledge of business math can quote and calculate prices and taxes more easily and quickly. And one with the ability to speak clearly can impress the customer and sell the product more efficiently.

The number of jobs available as a sales clerk depends on the economy's performance. If the economy expands, businesses hire; if not, sales jobs are scarce.

6.4 Revenues and Profit Maximization

The final step in the analysis of supply involves revenue. When revenues are introduced, a business can gauge the benefit that will be derived from producing different amounts of output. Once the cost of the fixed and the variable inputs have been determined, the business can then estimate the rate of output that will result in the highest profits.

MEASURES OF REVENUE

Two major measures of revenue can be used by the business trying to decide what output will produce the greatest amount of profits. The first one is total revenue, and the second one is marginal revenue.

TOTAL REVENUE. The **total revenue** is the number of units sold multiplied by the average price per unit. If 42 units are sold at $2 each, the total revenue is $84.

The total revenue column in the table on page 138 is constructed on this basis. If, on the average, each of the units brings $2, then 14 units of total product generates $28 of total revenue, 75 units generates $150, and so on.

MARGINAL REVENUE. **Marginal revenue** is the extra revenue associated with the production of one additional unit of output. It is the business's and the economist's most useful measure of revenue.

The marginal revenues in the table on page 138 are determined by dividing the change in total revenue by the marginal

product. For example, when a business produces no output, it receives no revenue. But when it adds one worker, total output jumps to 14 units, and this generates $28 of total revenue. Since the $28 is earned because of the sale of 14 units of output, each unit by itself must have added $2. Therefore, the marginal, or extra, revenue brought in by each unit of output is $2.

Even if some other level of output is selected and an additional worker is added to increase production, the marginal revenue computation remains the same. If the business employs five workers, it produces 150 units of output and generates $300 of total revenue. If a sixth worker is added, output increases by 30 units, and total revenues increase to $360. To have increased total revenue by $60, each of the 30 additional units of output must have added $2.

If each unit of output sells for $2, the marginal revenue earned by the sale of one more unit is $2. For this reason, the marginal revenue column in the table on page 138 appears to be constant for every level of output. However, while this happens in this example, it will not always be the case. Businesses often find that marginal revenues start high and then decrease as more and more units are produced and sold.

The Principle of Diminishing Marginal Utility says that people get less enjoyment or satisfaction from a product as they consume more of it. It stands to reason, then, that if a business wants to expand its production, it might have to lower its market price. Another firm might, therefore, have marginal revenues that decline, rather than stay constant.

Profile

◼ William Baumol

William Baumol is a professor of economics at Princeton University and an authority in firm and industry market structure. Among his best-known works are *Economic Dynamics*, *Economic Theory and Operations Analysis*, and *The Theory of Environmental Policy*.

Baumol was the first to advance the sales maximization hypothesis—the theory that business firms tried to maximize sales rather than profits. This hypothesis is widely accepted today and helps

1922–

explain behavior in a large number of business firms.

According to Baumol, the maximization of sales is possible in large corporations today because of the separation between management and ownership. Once management has earned enough profits to keep the shareholders content, any extra profits can be used to increase sales. Because of the drive to maximize sales, firms tend to charge lower prices and produce more than they would under profit maximization.

PROFIT MAXIMIZATION

Once a business has recorded all of its costs and revenues, it can compute profit at each and every level of output. One way to do this is to subtract the total costs from the total revenues at each level.

It should be evident in the table on page 138, for example, that the business will lose a total of $30 if it uses only four workers to produce 112 units of total product. With $254 in total costs and $224 in total revenue, it will not make a profit. However, by hiring six or seven workers,

it would make the most profits. With six or seven workers, the revenues are greater than the costs, so the business earns $14 in profits. Any increase in production beyond 203 units or any amount less than 180 units would not be as profitable.

The same results hold if the marginal cost and marginal revenue columns are used. For example, the business probably would hire the fifth worker because each of the 38 additional units of output produced would cost $1.21. Since each could be sold for $2, the decision to hire the fifth worker would be profitable. The sixth

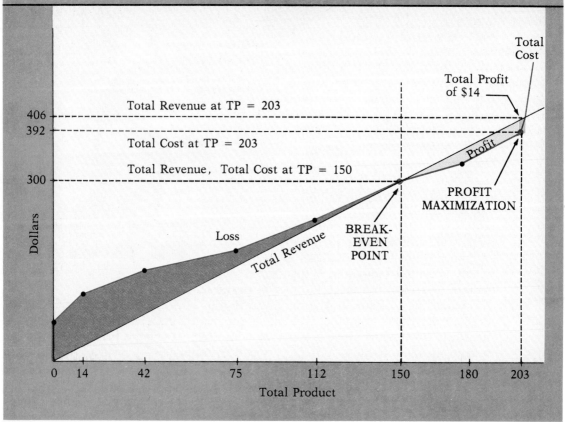

Figure 6–6

worker also would be hired since the extra output would cost only $1.53 but would generate $2 in revenues. As long as the marginal cost is less than the marginal revenue for each additional unit of output, the business will keep hiring workers.

Having made a profit on the sixth worker, most likely the business would go ahead and hire the seventh. This time, however, the cost of the additional output would equal the additional revenue earned when the product was sold. In other words, the addition of the seventh worker

neither added nor took away from total profits. However, the eighth worker would not be hired if the seventh one did not make a positive contribution toward total profits.

Economists call this type of reasoning **marginal analysis.** In other words, they examine the costs and benefits of producing one extra unit of output to see if it is profitable. If marginal cost is less than marginal revenue, output should be expanded. If marginal cost and marginal revenue are equal, the **profit-maximizing**

quantity of output has been reached, and no additional units of input will be used.

BREAK-EVEN ANALYSIS

Although businesses may not always be able to maximize their profits, they must break even if they are to avoid losing money. An important concept, then, is the **break-even point**—the amount of output a business needs to sell in order to cover its total costs.

In the graph on page 144, the break-even point of output is 150 units. If the business sells anything less than this, it will have losses. If it sells anything more than this, it will generate a profit. Of course, it would not want to produce more than 203 units of total product since that is the level of output that maximizes profits.

Section Review

1. What are the two measures of revenue?
2. How is the break-even point determined?

Chapter 6 Review

Summary

1. Supply is more than the amount of goods for sale at a given price. It includes the various quantities of output that would be offered for sale at all possible prices in the market.

2. Because producers generally are willing to offer more for sale at higher prices, the supply curve is upward-sloping.

3. A change in the quantity supplied is a movement along the supply curve and means that producers offer a different quantity for sale because of a change in price.

4. A change in the level of supply means that the supply curve or schedule has shifted and that producers offer different amounts for sale at each and every price.

5. If there is an increase in supply, the supply curve shifts to the right. If there is a decrease, the supply curve shifts to the left.

6. Supply elasticity is the change in the quantity supplied caused by a change in price.

7. Supply can be elastic, unit elastic, or inelastic. The more the quantity changes because of change in price, the more elastic the supply.

8. The theory of production deals with the way in which inputs are combined in the productive process.

9. The Law of Variable Proportions says that in the short run, output will change as one input is varied and the others remain fixed.

10. The production function illustrates the Law of Variable Proportions by relating outputs to inputs when only one input is varied.

11. Two important measures of output are total product and marginal output.

12. The three stages of production are increasing returns, diminishing returns, and negative returns.

13. Cost can be divided into four categories—fixed cost, variable cost, total cost, and marginal cost.

14. Total revenue and marginal revenue are two measures of revenue used by businesses to help decide what level of output will produce the greatest amount of profits.

15. Marginal analysis means comparing the marginal cost of production with the marginal revenue from the sale to see if it is profitable to produce an extra unit of output. If the marginal cost is bigger than the marginal revenue, the unit is not produced.

16. To avoid losing money, a business must reach a break-even point—this is the amount of output a business needs to sell in order to cover its total costs.

Building an Economic Vocabulary

supply
supply schedule
supply curve
Law of Supply
quantity supplied
change in quantity supplied
change in supply
supply elasticity
theory of production
Law of Variable Proportions

production function
raw materials
total product
marginal product
stages of production
Principle of Diminishing Returns
fixed cost
overhead
depreciation

variable cost
total cost
marginal cost
total revenue
marginal revenue
marginal analysis
profit-maximizing
    quantity of output
break-even point

Reviewing the Main Ideas

1. In what ways are supply curves and supply schedules alike?

2. What is the difference between a change in the quantity supplied and a change in supply?

3. What are three major types of supply elasticity?

4. With what does the theory of production deal?

5. How does the production function relate to the Law of Variable Proportions?

6. What are the three stages of production? What happens in each? In what stage is a firm most likely to operate?

7. What two factors must a firm consider before deciding which combination of inputs to use?

8. Which measure of revenue is most useful for business decisions? Which is least useful?

9. How does a business determine the level of output that will maximize profits?

■ *Practicing Critical Thinking Skills*

1. The Law of Supply sometimes is called "The Law of Upward-Sloping Supply." Can you give an example of a case in which this might not be true? Explain.

2. Why might production functions tend to differ from one firm to another? Give several examples that would support your answer.

3. The text states: "The measure of marginal product . . . is one of the more important concepts in economics." Why do you think this is so?

4. Give an example of a recent decision you made in which you used, perhaps without knowing it, the tools of marginal analysis.

■ *Applying Economic Understandings*

Analyzing and Classifying Costs

Fixed and variable costs are important for many businesses. The following exercise will help you develop the skill of analyzing and classifying costs.

1. Interview a local business owner or manager and explain that you are interested in learning more about that business's costs. Select a time period to analyze, such as one week or one month.

2. Make a list of all inputs used during that period of time.

3. For each type of cost, make an estimate of the dollars spent given the current rate of output or sales. Construct a matrix similar to the one given below and record this information in the first two columns. Ask how the dollar amount might change for each type of cost if output or sales were to fall by 50 percent and record this in the third column. Do the same for a doubling of sales or output and record this information in column four.

4. Based on the estimates for three different levels of output, make a judgment as to whether each cost is more likely to be fixed or variable. Discuss your findings with the owner or manager.

Costs	$ Spent per Period at Current Output Level	$ Spent per Period with Output Down 50%	$ Spent per Period with Output Doubled	Cost Classification
1.				
2.				
3.				

Prices

Everything is worth what its purchaser will pay for it.

Publius, 1st century B.C.

Chapter 7

After reading this chapter, you will be able to:

- Explain that price is the result of the interaction of supply and demand.

- Describe the process of price determination in purely competitive and less competitive markets.

- Use economic models to demonstrate how changes in supply and demand affect prices and the allocation of goods and services in the marketplace.

7.1 *The Role of Prices*

Prices play an important role in all economic markets. If there were no price system, it would be next to impossible to determine a value for any good or service. In a market economy, prices act as signals. A high price, for example, is a signal for producers to produce more and for buyers to buy less. A low price is a signal for producers to produce less and for buyers to buy more.

Prices, then, serve as a link between producers and consumers. In so doing, they help with the three basic WHAT, HOW, and FOR WHOM decisions faced by market economies. Without a system of prices to influence these decisions, the economy would not run as smoothly, and allocation decisions could end up being made by some form of government bureaucracy.

Prices, especially in a free market system, are also neutral. That is, they favor neither the producer nor the consumer. Instead, they come about as a result of competition between buyers and sellers. Thus, the more competitive the market, the more efficient the price adjustment process. If the market is less competitive, however, prices tend to favor some groups more than others.

The price system in a market economy is surprisingly flexible. Unforeseen events such as weather, strikes, natural disasters, and even wars can affect the prices for some items. When this happens, however, buyers and sellers react to the new level of prices and adjust their consumption and production accordingly. Before long, the system functions smoothly again as it had before. This flexibility to absorb unexpected "shocks" is one of the strengths of a free enterprise market economy.

THE PRICE ADJUSTMENT PROCESS

In economic markets, buyers and sellers have exactly the opposite hopes and intentions. The buyers come to the market eager to pay low prices and find good buys. The sellers come to the market hoping for high prices. For this reason, an adjustment process must take place when the two sides come together.

This process almost always leads to **market equilibrium**—a situation where prices are relatively stable, and there is neither a surplus nor a shortage in the market. A **surplus** is a situation where the quantity supplied is greater than the quantity demanded. When there is a surplus, prices fall. A **shortage** is a situation where the quantity demanded is greater than the quantity supplied. When there is a shortage, prices rise.

To better understand how the adjustment takes place, suppose, for example, that a new product called "gadgets" is introduced into a market. Since the product is new, producers cannot be sure what

Table 7–A

DEMAND AND SUPPLY SCHEDULES FOR GADGETS

Price (in dollars)	Quantity Demanded (in thousands)	Quantity Supplied (in thousands)	Shortage/ Surplus	
$ 10	600	1550	950	SURPLUS
9	720	1500	780	
8	850	1450	600	
7	990	1400	410	
6	1140	1350	210	
5	1300	1300	0	EQUILIBRIUM
4	1470	1250	−220	SHORTAGE
3	1650	1200	−450	
2	1840	1150	−690	
1	2040	1100	−940	

price to charge for it. To determine the price, they will have to experiment and see if the forces of supply and demand will help resolve the issue.

What happens can be seen in the supply and demand schedules above. The price and the consumer demand for gadgets appear in the first two columns and the quantity supplied in the third column. The demand schedule (columns 1 and 2) reflects the Law of Demand. As the price goes down, more gadgets are demanded. Likewise, the supply schedule (columns 1 and 3) reflects the Law of Supply. As the price goes up, the gadget-makers are willing to supply more. This information also can be represented in a graph where supply and demand appear in the same diagram, as shown on this page.

Once the buyers and sellers have been brought together, an **economic model** of the market emerges. It represents a set of assumptions about the market which helps economists analyze behavior and predict certain outcomes. In this case, the model helps analyze how price changes behave and what the final equilibrium price and quantity will be.

Since the market for gadgets is new, in the first trading period the suppliers might decide to produce 1400 of them to sell at $7 each. As Graph **A** on page 152 shows, only 990 of the 1400 gadgets produced are bought, leaving a surplus of 410.

The gadget-producers realize that the $7 price is too high and must be lowered. So in the second trading period, they produce 1250 gadgets and price them at $4 each. But, as Graph **B** on page 152 shows, the $4 price is too low. At this price, buyers would like to buy 1470 gadgets. Since only 1250 have been produced, there is a shortage of 220. This means the $4 price is too low and must be raised.

While the model does not show exactly how much the price must be raised, it is

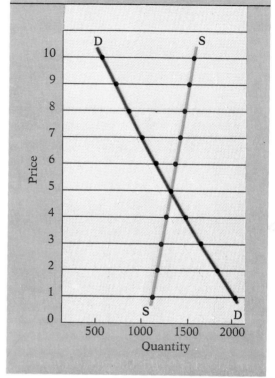

Figure 7–1

safe to assume that the shortage will drive the price up. It also is safe to assume that the price will be less than $7, which producers already know is too high. If they settle for a price of $6, there will be a surplus of 210, as seen in Graph **C** on page 153. This is because the quantity supplied is greater than that demanded. This surplus will cause the price to drop but probably not below $4, which already has proved to be too low.

As Graph **D** on page 153 shows, when the price drops to $5, the market finds its **equilibrium price.** This is the price that

DYNAMICS
OF THE PRICE ADJUSTMENT PROCESS
IN THE GADGETS INDUSTRY

(A) *DAY 1:* A price of $7 causes a surplus of 410.

(B) *DAY 2:* A surplus causes the price to drop. The new price is too low and a shortage develops.

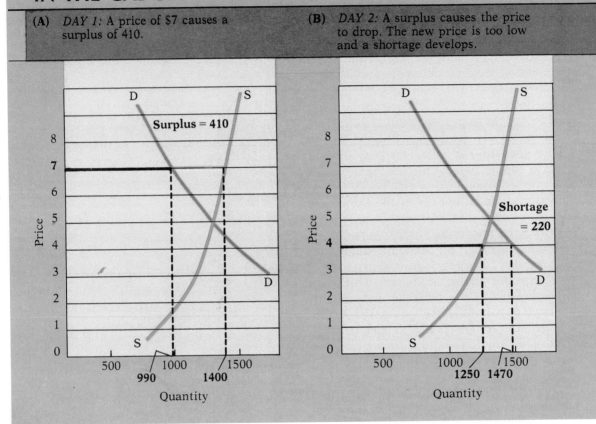

Figure 7–2

"clears the market" in the sense that after the end of the trading period, there is neither a surplus nor a shortage.

While the model of the market cannot show the exact number of trading periods needed to reach equilibrium, it does show that it will be reached. For example, the model does not show that the initial price will be $7 or the second price $4, but it does show that prices over $5 will cause a surplus. It also shows that prices less than $5 will cause a shortage.

Because of the pressure a surplus or a shortage puts on prices, the market tends to seek its own equilibrium. For instance, prices will stay at $5 and production at 1300 units in the gadget market until outside forces disturb the market.

The market also provides an important allocative function because producers receive money that they are free to spend in other markets. Those who are efficient, work hard, and are "in tune" with consumers' wants reap the benefits of compe-

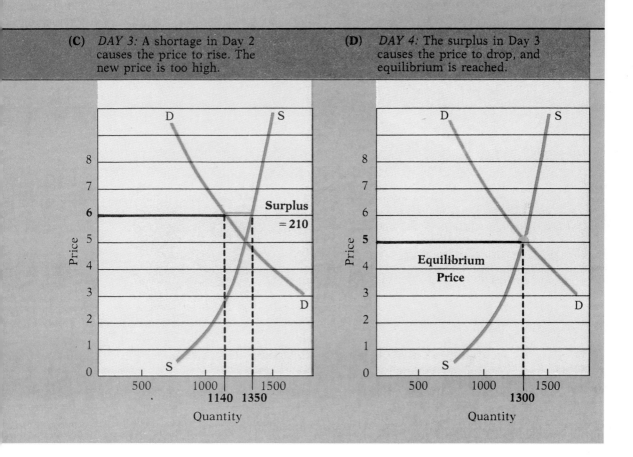

(C) *DAY 3:* A shortage in Day 2 causes the price to rise. The new price is too high.

(D) *DAY 4:* The surplus in Day 3 causes the price to drop, and equilibrium is reached.

tition. Those who are inefficient, lazy, or make products consumers do not want go out of business, releasing the factors of production to other industries.

ALLOCATIONS WITHOUT PRICES

Think what life would be like without a price system. How, for example, would a butcher allocate a limited supply of steaks? Would intelligence, or perhaps good looks, determine who could get a steak? Most people would feel that any butcher using these criteria was not fair.

Still, without a price system, some other system must be used to allocate goods and services. One such system is **rationing**—a system under which some government agency decides everyone's fair share.

A key problem with this, however, is that almost everyone feels they did not get

Understanding Sources

Commodities

A number of factors affect the price of energy. Most buyers are on the lookout for things that might change the future price of oil. The following article on energy appeared in *The Wall Street Journal*, on June 27, 1986. Read the article and then answer the questions that follow.

ENERGY: Most oil futures prices fell after rigs in the Gulf Coast area escaped damage from Hurricane Bonnie. The storm, which hit the coast yesterday, triggered minor electricity outages and wind damage, but refineries soon resumed normal operations, said Edward Dellamonte, energy analyst for Prudential-Bache Securities Inc., New York. Speculation that the storm could close refineries for a few days and disrupt supplies had spurred a rally Wednesday in oil futures.

1. According to the article, what happened to the price of oil?
2. What event affected this change?
3. How does this event affect the supply or the demand for oil?
4. Using supply and demand curves, describe the process that first drove the price in one direction and then another.
5. Is this type of situation likely to happen again? Explain.

as much as they deserved. If, for example, the government should decide to ration gas, most people would feel they did not get enough. Then, too, some would become angry about the seemingly "unnecessary" use of gas by others.

A second problem is the cost. Among other things, someone would have to pay the cost of printing gas coupons and of the salaries of the people who distributed them. In addition, no matter how much care was taken, some coupons would be stolen or counterfeited and used to consume gasoline meant for someone else.

Rationing also would have a great impact on the incentive to produce. Even if the system were set up so that everyone received an equal share, what would happen to the incentive to produce? Why should one person work harder than another when each would share equally in the stock of goods and services? In fact, what would motivate either person to do any work at all?

A system of rewards could be devised so that those who produced the most would be allowed a larger allocation of products. But then how would a person's productivity be measured? One way would be to assign a money value to productivity and give larger sums of money to those who produced more. But then how would the goods and services that these people produced be allocated? Again, a money value could be placed on things, and the people with more money could acquire more things. The more productive a person was, the more money that person would receive and the more things that person could acquire.

It is clear at this point that in trying to overcome the problem of allocating goods and services without a price system, we have gone the full cycle back to a price system. The limited supply of steaks is allocated only to people who can and will pay the price. If more people decide they would like to buy steak, the butcher could raise the price and use the higher price as a means of allocating the limited amount.

The price system operates as the allocating mechanism in every economic market.

During World War II, shoppers had to buy meat with ration coupons. Each coupon was worth a certain number of points. The point price varied for different meats. How are prices determined in a rationing system?

Case Study: Issue

Should Agricultural Price Supports be Abolished?

The government helps farmers by offering agricultural price supports, or target prices for some crops and dairy products. The system works in the following way. Farmers produce and sell a certain product at the going market price. If the market price is less than the target price for that product, farmers receive a "deficiency payment" for the government to make up the difference. For example, suppose the target price for a bushel of corn is $3.03. If the market price is $1.90 per bushel, the deficiency payment would be $1.13 per bushel.

Those who oppose price supports say that such payments waste tax dollars and encourage farmers to produce too much of certain crops. As evidence, they point out that, in 1986, federal expenditures for agriculture were over $25 billion—more than twice the original budget estimate. Finally, critics argue that price supports for farmers are unfair unless similar protection is offered to workers in other industries such as steel and textiles.

Those who favor price supports argue that agriculture differs from other industries. For one, farmers depend on the weather. They could have a surplus of crops one year and a shortage the next. For another, farmers are needed to support a growing population. If they are not helped during difficult times, there may not be enough food to supply the population. Those who favor price supports also argue that over-production of some crops may become necessary. In case of a natural disaster, such as a war, huge food supplies would be invaluable. Finally, many argue that price supports for farmers help preserve the family farm—an American tradition.

1. What are price supports?
2. Why do some people want price supports abolished?
3. For what reasons do many feel that price supports should be maintained?

But since price is determined by demand and supply, which are different in each market, the allocation of resources by the price system also will be different for each market. For this reason, the price system for each kind of market must be studied separately.

▮ Section Review

1. What is the role of prices?
2. What is the difference between a surplus and a shortage?
3. What would happen if there were no price system?

7.2 Price Determination in Purely Competitive Markets

A purely competitive market is one with a large number of independent and reasonably well-informed buyers and sellers, exactly the same economic products for sale, and free access to and from the market. The study of pricing in this market can be divided into three major time periods—the immediate period, the short run, and the long run.

In the **immediate period,** goods already have been produced, and the supply is fixed. In the **short run,** there is enough time for producers to change the amount of variable inputs used to raise or lower production within the limits of their existing capacity. In the **long run,** plant capacity can be expanded or contracted. Even the fixed costs no longer are fixed as buildings depreciate to the point where they are not worth anything and management dies, retires, or moves on to other jobs.

In real life, the three time periods overlap, and people live in all three at once. In the same way, decisions made by businesses affect all three periods at the same time. In fact, the short- and long-run competitive prices are the ones of most interest to economists because they affect the allocation of resources. The farmer, for example, may face immediate-period prices once he or she has picked the crop and carried it to market. Even so, most of his or her decisions will be made on the expectations of short- and long-run prices.

SHORT-RUN COMPETITIVE PRICES

In the short run, a business has enough time to adjust the amount of variable inputs used in the production process. If it wants to increase output, it can add more workers and raw materials and increase production. The period is not long enough to allow the business to build more manufacturing space, order new equipment, or otherwise change the "fixed" aspects of the production process.

The industry itself is made up of all the sellers who want to produce and sell the product. **Industry,** then, is the term used to represent the supply side of the market, or the collective interests of all producers.

The analysis of pricing is different for an individual firm than it is for the industry. Under conditions of pure competition, the individual firm is too small to have any influence at all on price. Therefore, the demand is viewed differently for the firm than for the industry. For example, the competitive firm can produce as much as it wishes and sell all that it produces, but only at the equilibrium price prevailing for the industry. For this reason, one price will dominate the market, and consumers will buy as much as the firm produces at that price.

The relationship between firm and industry can be seen in the graphs below. In Graph **A**, the collective supply and demand forces in the gadgets market determine the equilibrium price of $5. In Graph **B**, the gadgets firm views its demand

curve as a single horizontal line. Regardless of how many gadgets the firm makes, it receives a price, or marginal revenue, of $5 for each.

Just how many gadgets the company produces depends on its cost of production. Suppose, for example, that the marginal cost for the first gadget was $2, for the second $5, and for the third $8. Since the marginal revenue for every unit sold is $5, the firm would find the profit-maximizing quantity of output at 2. Both a lesser and a higher output than 2 would mean lower profits.

Figure 7–3

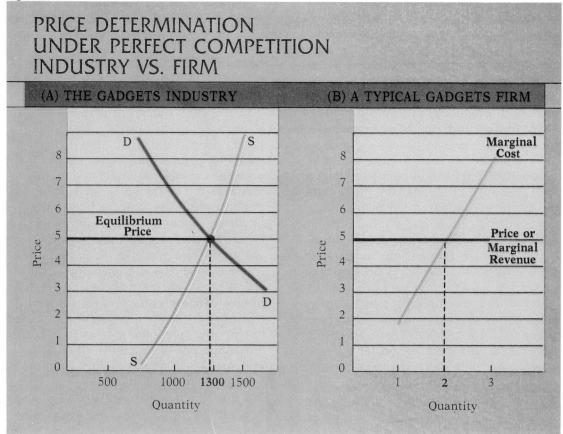

The radio on the left is an older model. The one on the right, however, is a newer model. If the prices for both radios were adjusted for 1986, the earlier model would cost more. Why do you think this is so?

LONG-RUN COMPETITIVE PRICES

The basic principles of long-run price determination in a competitive market are much the same as those of shorter time periods. The market forces of demand and supply determine the equilibrium price. The individual firm then adjusts its production to meet the market price.

The difference between the long-run and the shorter-run periods is the amount of control companies have over their production costs. In the short run, most companies are faced with some combination of fixed and variable costs. Nothing can be done about the fixed costs—they must be paid no matter how much is produced.

In the long run, however, there is enough time for companies to make their plants larger or smaller. If the long-run demand appears strong, a company may add more buildings or machinery, taking care to see that its cost of production is covered fully by the price it can receive for its final product. If the long-run demand appears weak, the company can sell some of its equipment, reducing its size and production costs. Because a company has the time in the long run to expand or contract its size, it has some control over its cost of production.

A TOUCH OF REALISM

The theory of competitive pricing represents a set of conditions and outcomes that are ideal. Because of this, it serves as a theoretical model by which to measure the performance of other less competitive market structures.

Many markets do come close to the ideal. The prices in your community of gasoline, foods, and many other items will be relatively close from one store to the next. When the prices of these items do vary, it may be because the buyers are not well informed. Or, a store may be promoting a certain item as a **loss leader**—an item specially priced to attract customers.

While there may be small differences in price even in a highly competitive market, there generally are not many large ones. Those that do exist do not last for long. How long, for example, could a store sell its apples for $1.69 a bag if other stores were selling them for 99¢? At some point, customers would become sensitive to price and change their habits.

For purposes of realistic analysis, it can be said that the competitive equilibrium price is really a small range of prices. Absolutely pure competition is not needed for the theory of price determination to be practical. The basic principles of price determination under pure competition carry over to the full range of markets and provide a foundation for describing pricing in general.

■ Section Review

1. How do the immediate period, the short run, and the long run differ?
2. What is the difference between the firm and the industry?
3. How are loss leaders used?

7.3 Price Determination in Less Competitive Markets

Price determination takes place in all markets. In the less competitive markets such as monopolistic competition, oligopoly, and monopoly, each of the firms uses marginal analysis to find the profit-maximizing quantity of output. But while the process is the same in each case, the results are different because each market structure is different.

MONOPOLISTIC COMPETITION

Examples of monopolistic competition can be found in almost every city where small independent businesses make or sell products that are very much alike or offer services that fall into the same general category. Clothing shops, dry cleaners, grocery stores, and drugstores, for example, all are monopolistic competitors.

PRODUCT DIFFERENTIATION AND PRICES. Under monopolistic competition, the equilibrium price is determined by supply and demand. But since the product may be slightly differentiated, customers may learn to favor a certain brand or become convinced that one particular product is better than others.

If a monopolistic competitor manages to convince the buyer that its product is different, it makes the market look like it

"Good heavens! Designer overalls!"

Competitors in the same market generally can produce the same product for about the same cost. Yet, prices vary greatly in the marketplace. Why are jeans producers able to charge more for designer jeans?

has fewer sellers and really is less competitive. The result of this is that the producer can charge a little higher price. If every competitor in the industry does the same, the average price in the market will be a little above the one which would prevail under pure competition.

In the market for jeans, for example, several different brands, such as Levi's, J. C. Penney, Sears, Calvin Klein, and Jordache, have been promoted heavily in the past few years. But are their products truly all that different?

Some producers have advertised that their product is just as good as the competition's. Others have spent a great deal of time, money, and effort trying to differentiate their product in the minds of the buyer. Both of these strategies generally work. Some people who would never dream of wearing plain, ordinary jeans will wear "designer jeans" almost anywhere.

The same is true for much of the clothing and fashion industry. As long as firms are able to make the buying public believe that their products are not like those of the competition, the monopolistic competitor can draw and hold customers. In this way, it creates the small degree of monopoly power that is necessary before it can raise its price.

In the long run, the monopolistic competitor faces the same conditions as the pure competitor. With nothing to stop entry into the industry, the fact that there are profits to be made will draw new firms, each of which will produce a product only a little different from the ones already on the market.

As new firms enter the field, the existing market is divided among more sellers. Each will sell smaller quantities of its particular product. If more new firms keep entering the market, it may become so crowded that some firms will not be able to sell enough to cover production costs. Before too long, some will decide to leave the industry.

In time, however, both the number of firms in the industry and the supply of the product will become fairly stable. There will be no great profits or losses. At this point, the equilibrium price for the industry will be reached.

NON-PRICE COMPETITION. When an economic product is differentiated, as it is in monopolistic competition, **non-price competition** often will take the place of price competition. This happens more in the markets for consumer goods than in those for industrial products.

Non-price competition can be divided into product and promotional competition. **Product competition** has to do with the quality of the article itself. The product is designed the way producers think buyers would want it to be so that they will develop a strong desire for it. If the design works, the seller will have a certain degree of monopoly power over the price because loyal customers will be willing to pay higher prices.

Product competition also may take in the physical aspects of the product. This includes what it looks like, of what and how well it is made, how strong it is, what color it is, and how it is packaged. It also may include the services that go with the sale, the general atmosphere of the store and how quickly it can deliver, what

the sales people are like, the kinds of credit offered, and whether or not guarantees are honored. A difference in any one of these may make a difference between two products which otherwise are exactly the same.

Promotional competition is competition designed to make buyers believe that one brand is better than any other. For the most part, this kind of competition is commercial advertising and is aimed at increasing the demand for a certain product.

Ads are run again and again using newspapers, magazines, radio, television, and outdoor billboards to convince people that one brand is better than another. Most people seem to respond to brand labels, trademarks, free samples, door-to-door promotions, and product demonstrations.

OLIGOPOLY

Oligopolistic industries like steel, automobiles, and commercial airlines face a different set of problems from those faced by monopolistic competition. With only a few firms in the industry, each is big enough to influence price. This means that an oligopolistic firm cannot afford to ignore the impact its decisions will have on others in the industry.

INTERDEPENDENT MARKET BEHAVIOR. If one oligopolistic firm does something, the others in the same industry are likely to follow through with a similar course of action. For example, if one airline announces discount fares, generally all the other airlines will try to match the lower prices.

Another example is the case of new product development. Oligopolists tend to introduce a new item at about the same time. For example, in the early 1960's in

Profile

John Bates Clark

John Bates Clark was an American economist who had a great influence on the development of economic thought in the United States. His first book was published in 1885. His well-known theoretical work, *The Distribution of Wealth*, was published 14 years later.

Clark believed that one of the chief goals of any economic system was an increase in the standard of living, which he termed "social betterment." He thought this was

1847–1938

brought about by technological change, which made labor more productive and led to higher profits for industry. In Clark's view, once industry was earning higher profits, labor would demand its share of those profits, which it would receive in the form of higher wages. The higher profits and the higher wages together would bring about increased incomes, which would mean social betterment for all.

Clark searched for some natural law for the division of national income. During the search, he developed the theory of marginal productivity for all the factors of production. According to Clark, the price a producer paid for land, labor, or capital would depend on its marginal productivity. For example, a worker would receive a wage equal to the output added by the last worker. But when the point of decreasing marginal productivity was reached, the producer would find it more profitable to replace labor with machinery. Clark firmly believed that a wage equal to the marginal productivity of labor was sound economically and fair to both the worker and the employer.

Clark's theory does not altogether reflect the real world because it ignores the influence of imperfect markets for products and factors of production. Still, his contributions have helped explain the tendencies of human economic behavior, and many present-day economists hold with his views on technological change and marginal analysis.

the automobile industry, each of the "big three" automakers—General Motors, Ford, and Chrysler—introduced competing mid-sized cars within a few months of one another. The result was that in addition to the regular line of big cars, consumers suddenly had Corvairs, Falcons, and Valiants from which to choose. Even today, automotive companies offer generally similar product lines and introduce their new models at about the same time.

In short, each oligopolist knows that the others in the industry have a lot of power and can influence the introduction of new products, prices in general, and amounts sold. And since the oligopolist is almost—but not quite—a monopolist, firms tend to act together rather than let any one upset the status quo.

PRICE DETERMINATION. The fact that oligopolistic industries are interdependent plays a part in price determination. Although price competition always is possible, price determination generally takes the form of formal price agreements, **independent pricing,** and price leadership.

A formal agreement among oligopolists to set prices is known as **collusion.** It is a conspiracy to fix prices without the public or the government knowing about it. Collusion occurs when the oligopolists in an industry agree to charge the same or like prices. In most cases, these prices are higher than those determined under competition and will bring profits to all the firms. Since collusion restrains trade, it is against the law. But neither this fact nor the threat of heavy fines and jail sentences has kept some collusion from taking place. In fact, it often is suspected that more takes place than is detected.

Some oligopolists follow a policy of independent pricing. In other words, they set their own prices based on the cost of inputs, demand, or other factors. This kind of pricing, however, does not happen very often. For an oligopolist, there always is a sense of uncertainty and insecurity about how the other firms will behave. An ambitious firm may try to steal customers by lowering its price if it is not happy with its share of the market. There always is the temptation to reach for a larger share of the market and the fear that a struggle for that share may be unleashed.

A further complication is that the firms in the industry are likely to be of different sizes and have different costs of production. When firms differ in size and costs, independent pricing can lead to more uncertainty and insecurity. A large firm may decide to remove this uncertainty by seeking a position in which it is strong enough to set prices. Or it may try to weaken smaller firms by taking part in a price war which would seriously hurt them or force them out of business. If this happens, the large firm could get a larger share of the market's total sales, increase its monopoly power, and become the leader in the market.

Price leadership takes place when one firm, perhaps the biggest and most powerful in the industry, takes the lead and initiates most changes in price. The others then follow because they fear a price war or because they believe they would be better off financially by doing so.

Price leadership often comes about quite naturally and without trouble. One firm, because it is established, experienced, and respected, may take on the task of evaluating the market. It will keep its research staff busy studying the national economy and keeping up with new technology. Then it will set an "official" price with which the others in the industry generally agree. This kind of leadership is known as **barometric price leadership.**

For example, International Business Machines (IBM) is often thought of as the

Profile

Milton Friedman

Milton Friedman is a noted American economist and leading advocate of a free enterprise economy. He was awarded the Nobel Prize in economics in 1976, and has written such works as *A Theory of the Consumption Function, Capitalism and Freedom,* and *Free to Choose.*

1912–

Friedman is in favor of competition and opposes attempts by government and special interest groups to interfere with the dynamics of the market adjustment process. He believes that minimum wages, price ceilings, agriculture price supports, and fixed interest rates keep prices from acting as signals.

According to Friedman, the United States does not have just a profit system, but a profit *and loss* system. The freedom to fail is an important feature of the American economy because failures and bankruptcies release resources for use in other industries.

---

barometric price leader in the personal computer industry. If IBM changes prices by a small amount, competitors such as Apple, AT & T, Compaq, or Tandy would quickly follow their lead.

There is no formal agreement in price leadership. For this reason, it cannot be charged with conspiracy to restrain trade and tried under the antitrust laws. Price leadership works for those who do not like the uncertainties of independent pricing yet do not want to enter into formal agreements that may be against the law.

REASONS FOR NON-PRICE COMPETITION. Among oligopolists, price competition is the most unpopular kind of competition. There are two major reasons for this. First, many businesses fear price competition because customers often are sensitive to any price differences. If one firm cuts its price, it may make a large dent in the sales of other firms, and they too will have to cut prices. This may lead to a **price war,** or a series of price cuts by all producers that may lead to unusually low prices in the industry. For a short period, the prices might even be lower than the cost of production for many of the firms.

Secondly, rival firms can match price cuts very quickly. But if instead of cutting price, a firm finds a new advertising gimmick or a way to change the product, itself, the other firms are placed at a disadvantage for a while. It takes them time to catch up and come up with some new physical attribute or advertising campaign for their own products. For these reasons, oligopolists prefer non-price competition.

Unless non-price competition increases the total sales for the industry as a whole, the division of customers among the firms may stay very much the same as it was in the first place. All the firms bring out innovations. All talk about the unique qualities of their products. All try to take business away from each other. Yet none is better off if the market share is not increased. Although all this may seem like economic waste, it appears to be the chief way an oligopolistic industry not interested in pricing competition can compete.

MONOPOLY

As a single seller or producer free from the fear of competition, a monopolist controls the supply of an economic product. While it generally cannot exercise unlimited power to set price, it can cause prices to rise by producing less. Although the monopolist and firms in a competitive market both want to earn a profit, the monopolist has an edge. It is in a position to reject a market price and set up one more favorable to itself.

MONOPOLY OUTPUT. When it comes to maximizing profits, the monopolist is the same as any other firm. It follows the logic of marginal analysis and produces the amount of output whose marginal cost of production equals the marginal revenue gained from sales.

Suppose that all the gadgets discussed earlier were supplied by a monopolist no more or no less efficient than the typical perfect competitor shown in Graph **B** on page 158. As far as production capabilities are concerned, the only difference between the two is size. While the perfect competitor had a marginal cost of $2 for the first gadget, $5 for the second, and $8 for the third, the monopolist faces a marginal cost of $2 for the thousandth gadget, $5 for the second thousandth, and so on. This means that even though the monopolist is a thousand times bigger than the perfect competitor, its cost of production is the same.

The monopolist, like the perfect competitor, uses the tools of marginal analysis to determine the quantity of output and the price that maximizes profits. There is, however, a big difference in the outcome. The perfect competitor is a **price taker** since the individual firm is too small to influence the price in the industry. Basically, the perfect competitor has to "take" the going price in the industry.

The monopolist is a **price maker,** a firm large and powerful enough to set a price favorable to itself in the market. As long as the monopolist is the only firm and supplier in the industry, then it can control price.

In the table on page 167, a column for marginal revenue was computed based on the demand schedule on page 150. A fifth column listing the marginal cost information described above is also added. According to the table, marginal cost is less than marginal revenue for the first 850 units produced by the monopolist. The monopolist would find it profitable to produce at least 850 units since each would be sold for an amount that is greater than its cost of production.

Beyond 990 units of output, marginal cost is greater than marginal revenue. If the monopolist wants to maximize profits, it will not produce more than this amount because the extra cost of production is

MARGINAL ANALYSIS: PRICE DETERMINATION BY THE MONOPOLIST IN THE GADGETS INDUSTRY

Price	Quantity Demanded	Total Revenue	Marginal Revenue		Marginal Cost
$10	600	$6000			$ .78
9	720	6480	$4.00		1.10
8	850	6800	2.46	>	1.50
7	990	6930	.93	<	1.93
	1000				2.00
6	1140	6840	− .60		2.38
5	1300	6500	− 2.13		2.98
4	1470	5880	− 3.65		3.38
	1500				3.50
3	1650	4950	− 5.17		3.92
2	1840	3680	− 6.68		4.48
	2000				5.00
1	2040	2040	− 8.20		. . . .

Table 7–B

greater than the extra revenue earned from selling the output.

If the information in the table is transferred to the graph on page 168, it looks like marginal cost is equal to marginal revenue when output is around 900 units. This means that the monopolist has found the quantity of output which will maximize its profits. Although it still could make profits at other levels of production, it never could make more than that made by producing and selling 900 units.

SHORT-RUN MONOPOLY PRICES. The graph on page 168 also shows what price the monopolist can charge with a total production of 900 units. According to the market demand curve, the price for each unit of output would be about $7.65.

Is this much too high? The answer is both "yes" and "no." The demand schedule shows that buyers would have paid $8 each for 850 units or $7 each for 990 units. Therefore, the monopoly price of $7.65 is about right for 900 units.

On the other hand, the industry produced only 900 units under monopoly as compared to 1300 units produced by the same industry under perfect competition. In this case, the monopolist found it profitable to restrict output to set a price favorable to itself. The higher price may look good as far as the monopolist is concerned, but buyers pay more and get less than they would under perfect competition.

LONG-RUN MONOPOLY PRICES. The determination of monopoly prices is almost the same in the long run as it is in the short run. The difference lies in the amount of control monopolists have over costs. In the short run, monopolists cannot change existing equipment, expand capacity to meet a strong demand, or contract operations when there is less demand. In the long run, monopolists can change the

Figure 7–4

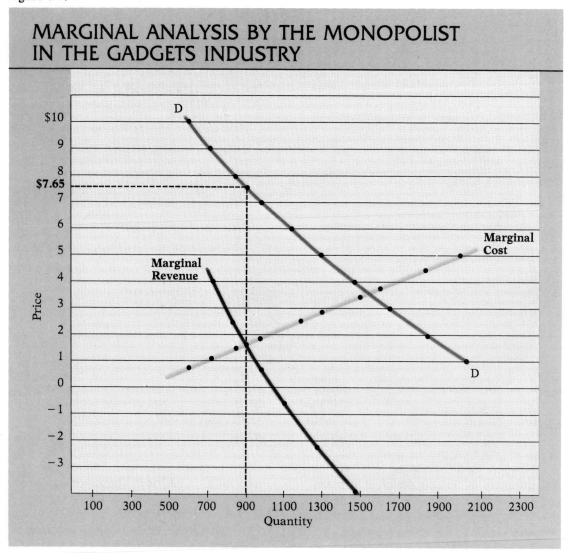

MARGINAL ANALYSIS BY THE MONOPOLIST IN THE GADGETS INDUSTRY

The owners of the motels in the photograph on the left charge similar prices for their services. The owner of the motel on the right photograph can charge more. Why?

size of their plants to meet change in long-run demand or production costs.

Since the monopolist does not have any competition, there will be no attempt to keep costs down. As a result, costs will be higher and output lower. The monopolist will still use marginal analysis to determine the best price, but the price will be higher than under competition.

Section Review

1. How does a monopolist's influence over price differ from an oligopolist's?

2. Why do oligopolists sometimes resort to collusion and price leadership?

3. What kind of price does the monopolist try to get in the short run? How is it determined?

7.4 Price System at Work

Prices are important in a market because they help producers and consumers make decisions. A market economy, however, is made up of many markets for many different products. In order to understand how the economy operates as a whole, the role of prices in this larger setting must be examined.

PRICES AS A "SYSTEM"

A price in any given market serves as a signal which helps sellers decide where to sell their resources and producers where to buy them. The same is basically true of prices collectively. In this case, they serve as signals which allocate resources between markets.

Consider, for example, the way in which higher oil prices affected producers' and consumers' decisions in the 1970's. During this time, the price of oil went from $5 a barrel to as much as $40. Since the demand for oil is basically inelastic, people had to spend a greater part of their income on energy. This left them less to spend elsewhere, a fact which affected other markets.

The market for full-size automobiles was one of the first to feel the pinch. Because most large cars did not get good gas mileage, people bought fewer big cars than before and, instead, bought more foreign-made automobiles. As the demand for big cars fell, producers ended up with unsold inventories of automobiles.

In the beginning, automakers thought the increase in gas prices might be temporary, so they were reluctant to introduce smaller, more fuel-efficient models. But as time went on, the surplus of unsold cars remained. To move their inventories, manufacturers began to offer a **rebate**—a partial refund of the original price of the product. This was the same thing as a temporary price reduction because consumers were offered a $500, $600, and even a $700 rebate on each new car they bought.

At the same time, automobile manufacturers began cutting back the production of large cars. Plants were closed, and workers were laid off. Companies used their surplus cash to change over to small car production. To keep from going bank-

rupt, some companies, such as Chrysler, cut their size by nearly half. Many of the automobile workers who lost their jobs found new ones in other industries. Although some moved to other places where they had family or friends, most went to markets where they could receive the highest pay for their skills.

The end result, then, of higher prices in the international oil market was a shift of productive resources out of the large car market into other markets. Although the process was a painful one for those involved, it was a necessary one for a market economy.

VALUE OF ECONOMIC MODELS

Economists are concerned with both explanation and prediction. They use their models of the market to explain changes in the world around them and to predict how certain events might affect the economy in the future.

Take, for example, the case of agriculture where wide swings in prices from one year to the next are fairly typical. A farmer may keep up with all the latest developments and have the best advice experts can offer. Even so, the farmer never is sure of what price to expect for the crop. A soybean farmer may put in 500 acres of beans expecting a price of $8 a bushel. At the same time, however, the farmer knows that the actual price may end up being anywhere from $5 to $12. The same is true for the cotton farmer who expects 80¢ a pound but may end up getting anywhere from 40¢ to $1.25.

This variance in prices is possible even with experience, planning, and advice from the experts for several reasons. One is that farm output is influenced by

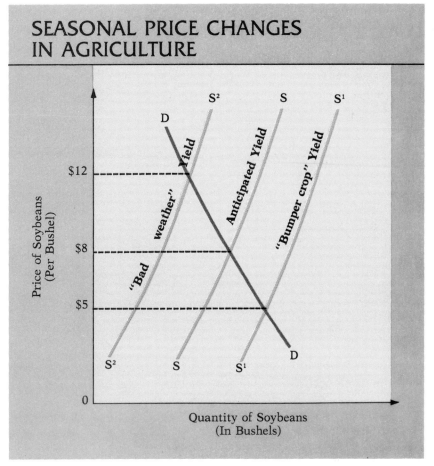

SEASONAL PRICE CHANGES IN AGRICULTURE

Figure 7–5

weather. Once the seed is in the ground, all the farmer can do is wait. If it rains too much, the seed will be washed away and the farmer must start over. If it rains too little, the seed will not germinate, and the crop will not come up. Even if the weather is perfect during the growing season, rain still can prevent the harvest from being gathered. The weather, then, can cause large changes in supply.

The result, which is shown in the graph above, is that the supply curve is likely to shift, causing the price to go up or down. The farmer may expect supply to look like

curve S. But if there is a bumper, or record, crop, it may look like S¹. Or, if there is enough bad weather, it may look like S². Since the demand for food generally is inelastic, the interaction of the two curves is enough to cause wide changes in the price.

If the demand for soybeans were highly elastic, as in Graph **A** on page 172, the results would be different. Because the demand curve is much more elastic, there would be a smaller impact on price.

Graph **B** on page 172 shows the wide price fluctuations typical of the gold

ELASTICITY AND ITS IMPACT ON PRICE CHANGES IN ECONOMIC MARKETS

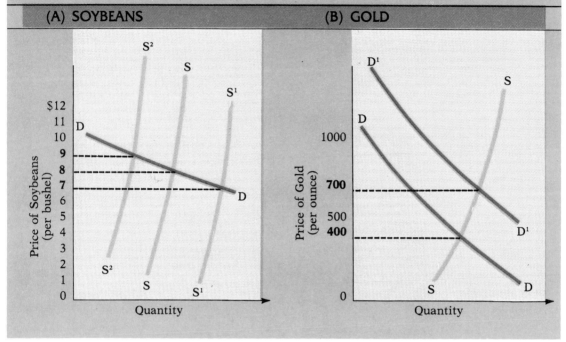

Figure 7–6

market. In this case, the price changes are due to a relatively fixed, or inelastic, supply of gold combined with frequent changes in demand. Bad news, such as reports of near-war in other countries, possible recessions, or other disasters, might cause people to suddenly increase their demand for gold to D¹. Good news, such as reports of peace agreements, growth in the economy, or a lower rate of inflation, might cause a decrease in the demand to D. The result is that the price of gold is likely to change sharply with changes in the world political and economic situation.

Changes in prices, then, can be caused by changes in supply or in demand. The elasticity of the demand and supply curves is important. If both are inelastic and

there is a change in either one, large price changes will follow. If one or both is elastic, there is likely to be less impact.

WHEN MARKETS "TALK"

Markets are highly impersonal mechanisms which serve to bring buyers and sellers together. Although markets do not "talk" in the usual sense of the word, they do "talk" in the sense that they "speak" collectively for all of the buyers and sellers who trade in them.

Suppose the government announced that to balance the federal budget it would raise taxes. If investors thought this policy would not work or that other policies might be better, they might decide to sell some of their stocks and other investments for cash and gold which could be used in case of an emergency. As the selling takes place, prices in the stock market would fall, and prices in the gold market would go up. It could be said that, in effect, "the market voiced its disapproval of the new policies."

In a sense, then, the market did "talk." Individual investors made decisions on the likely outcome of the new policies and sold stocks for cash or gold. Together, their actions were enough to influence stock prices and to send a "signal" to the government that they did not favor the policies.

If investors' feelings were divided about the new policies, some would sell and others might buy stocks. As a result, prices might not change, and the message would be that as yet "the markets have not made up their minds."

Section Review

1. How do buyers and sellers react to high prices? To low prices?

2. What is meant by the statement, "Markets have a voice"?

Chapter 7 Review

Summary

1. In a market economy, a high price signals producers to produce more and consumers to buy less. A low price signals producers to produce less and consumers to buy more.

2. A price adjustment process takes place when buyers and sellers come together in the market place. This process leads to market equilibrium.

3. A surplus in the market causes the price to fall, and a shortage causes it to rise.

4. Without a price system, some other mechanism, such as rationing, would be needed to allocate goods, services, and other resources.

5. In a purely competitive market, pricing can be divided into three major time periods—the immediate period, the short run, and the long run—all of which overlap.

6. In pure competition, supply and demand in the market set the price which affects all firms.

7. In actual practice, the competitive equilibrium price is really a narrow range of prices.

8. The average price in the market is higher under monopolistic competition than under pure competition because of product differentiation and non-price competition.

9. Because the actions one oligopolistic firm takes affects all the other firms in the industry, price competition is not popular and generally takes the form of formal price agreements, independent pricing, and price leadership.

10. As the only firm in the market, the monopolist is a price maker who can restrict output and charge a high price to maximize profits.

11. In a market economy, prices act collectively as a "system" to allocate resources between markets.

12. Economists use economic models of markets to show supply and demand, and to explain market conditions. They also use models to make predictions about the economy.

13. Since changes in supply or demand can cause changes in prices, the elasticity of the supply and demand curves is important.

14. Markets can "talk" in the sense that they reflect the collective judgments of all of the buyers and sellers in the market.

Building an Economic Vocabulary

market equilibrium
surplus
shortage
economic model
equilibrium price
rationing
immediate period
short run

long run
industry
loss leader
non-price competition
product competition
promotional competition
independent pricing

collusion
price leadership
barometric price leadership
price war
price taker
price maker
rebate

Reviewing the Main Ideas

1. How do prices play a role as signals? Who gets the signals, and how do they react to them?

2. How is the market price affected by a surplus? By a shortage?

3. What does an economic model of a market represent?

4. What happens when the market is in equilibrium?

5. Under what circumstances might rationing be needed? What are some of the problems associated with it?

6. How does the economist define industry? Why is the analysis of pricing different for it than for the individual firm under pure competition?

7. Why can a monopolistic competitor get away with charging a slightly higher price?

8. Why are oligopolists so concerned about what other firms in the industry do? How does this affect their pricing behavior?

9. Why is a monopolist a price maker?

10. How do a monopolist's output and price differ from a pure competitor's?

11. What is the collective role of prices in a market economy?

12. Of what value are economic models of markets?

13. What is meant by the statement that markets "talk"?

Practicing Critical Thinking Skills

1. Some people argue that an equilibrium price is not a fair price. Explain why you agree or disagree with this.

2. During the first Arab oil embargo, consumers found there was not enough gas to go around at the prevailing price of about 55¢ a gallon. Some people felt that the best way to deal with the shortage was to ration gas. Others felt the best way to deal with it was to allow the price to rise until equilibrium was reached. With which solution do you agree? Why?

3. Do you think there would be any advantages to making monopolies or near monopolies break up into smaller, competing firms? If so, what are they? If not, why would there not be?

Applying Economic Understandings

Constructing and Applying an Economic Model

An economic model is a tool economists use to explain everyday changes in prices and quantities observed in the marketplace and to predict future changes in the economy. Review Figures 7–1 on page 151 and 7–2 on pages 152–153. Then, follow the exercise below to practice constructing and applying an economic model.

1. Select a product manufactured in your community, and list the kinds of inputs it requires and their costs. Then, keeping in mind that elasticity is important, construct a hypothetical supply curve for the product.

2. Based on the following questions, make some judgments as to the nature of the demand elasticity of the product: Are there many substitutes for the product? Can the purchase of the product be postponed? Does the purchase of the product consume much income?

3. Combine the supply curve and the demand curve in a single graph to get a model.

4. Now that your model is constructed, ask yourself the following questions: Is something likely to happen that would cause either of the curves to shift? If so, which one would shift? If either curve shifts, what happens to prices?

5. Based on your model and the answers to the questions you have asked yourself, make some reasonable predictions about the future of your product.

Unit 2 Review

Unit in Perspective

1. America has a free private enterprise system based on the capitalistic principles of freedom, private ownership of property, and voluntary decisions.

2. Economic markets are broadly classified as purely or imperfectly competitive. Most firms and industries fall under the latter, which is divided into monopolistic competition, oligopoly, and monopoly.

3. In the free market economy, public policy dictates an economic environment that encourages competition subject to some government regulation.

4. The Law of Demand states that people are willing to buy more of a product as its price goes down. This is explained by the income and substitution affects, and principle of diminishing marginal utility.

5. The way quantity demanded responds to a price change determines if demand is elastic, inelastic, or unit elastic.

6. The Law of Supply states that producers respond to higher prices by producing more output. Supply may be elastic inelastic, or unit elastic.

7. Production deals with the relationship between the input of productive resources and final outputs.

8. To maximize profits, a firm bases its production decisions on the concept of marginal analysis, which compares marginal costs with marginal revenues.

9. Prices are determined by the interaction of supply and demand. In a market economy they function as signals to producers and consumers which allocate resources between markets.

Unit in Review

1. How does the circular flow diagram illustrate the economic activity in markets?

2. What determines how economic markets are classified? What are the characteristics of the four major markets in the American economy today?

3. How does government act to preserve competition in economic markets?

4. How is the relationship of demand and price expressed in economics? What does elasticity of demand have to do with this relationship?

5. How does the Law of Supply differ from the Law of Demand?

6. Why is the theory of production important to a business enterprise?

7. How do prices work as a "system" to allocate resources between buyers, sellers, and economic markets?

8. How do supply and demand jointly determine prices in purely competitive markets? In less competitive markets?

Building Consumer Skills

Comparative Shopping

When you compare items, you examine or note the similarities and differences between them. The number of items that you might compare in this way may range from two to twenty or more. When you go comparative shopping, you compare items to find which one best suits your needs in a particular situation, or has the best price. The following exercise will help you learn what to look for when comparative shopping.

Your math or science class needs to purchase new calculators because there are not enough for everyone. You are sent to shop for them. First, you need to find out what kinds of calculators are available in your area. Second, you need to consider the features on the calculators. Different brands will have different features such as exponential keys and constant memory; different power sources such as solar or battery; and different physical characteristics such as size, weight, and general appearance. Third, you need to consider the prices of the calculators.

After you have looked at several different models, construct a decision making grid like the one on page 20 in your text. Next, draw up a list of criteria for the calculators which you believe are important and write them across the top of the grid. Then, list the names of the calculators on the left side of the grid. Finally, using pluses and minuses, evaluate each calculator according to the criteria you have listed. When you have completed the grid, select the calculator that satisfies more of the criteria you have listed than any other.

The Role of Labor and Government

Among the economic organizations found in a free enterprise system such as the United States are organized labor and government. It is necessary to know how each functions in order to understand its role in a free enterprise economy.

Contents

Employment, Unions, and Wages

Workers do not bargain for increased wages merely because it gives them pleasure to see larger numbers on their paychecks. They are concerned . . . with what their paychecks will buy. **Leonard Woodcock**

THE PROPOSED CONTRACT

Chapter 8

After reading this chapter, you will be able to:

- Sequence events which led to the growth of organized labor in the United States.

- Describe five ways of resolving labor disputes.

- Explain the theories and factors used to determine wages.

- Discuss current employment trends and issues.

8.1 The Labor Movement

In 1986, the population of the United States was 241,489,000 people. Of these, about 48.3 percent were members of the **civilian labor force**—men and women at least 16 years of age either working or actively looking for a job. As can be seen in the graph and table on page 183, most people in the labor force were nonunion workers. About 18 percent belonged to labor unions.

Even though a small number of workers belong to unions, unions still play an important part in the economy. A major reason for this is that most unions tend to be concentrated in the heavy manufacturing industries, which have a major impact on the economy. In addition, much of the legislation that affects the pay and working conditions of many workers today came about because of past and present union actions.

Many workers want to be represented by a union because they feel they have more power that way. They believe they would be at a disadvantage if each worker had to settle job-related issues on his or her own.

Members of early labor unions were given membership certificates to show that they belonged to a particular union. What kinds of workers were accepted into early labor unions?

In their early days, most unions were local in nature. For the most part, each was made up of the workers of a given firm. Before long, however, the workers began to see the advantage of collective bargaining. Soon local unions began joining with others to become more powerful. In time, the labor movement reached all parts of the country, and spread into Canada.

Today, most local unions are affiliated with a national or international organization. Part of the dues paid by workers in the local go to support the activities of the "parent" organization. Most local unions select delegates to attend a national convention. There, they elect the national officers who make most of the important decisions that have to do with union business.

EARLY UNION DEVELOPMENT

In 1778, printers in New York City joined together to demand higher pay. This was the first time anyone had tried to organize labor in America. Before long, there were unions of shoemakers, carpenters, and tailors, each hoping to bring about new agreements covering hours, pay, and working conditions. Only a small percentage of workers belonged to these unions. Of these, most were skilled and already had strong bargaining power.

Until about 1820, most of America's work force was made up of farmers, small business owners, and people who were self-employed. Shortly after, however, immigrants began to enter the country in great numbers. Most were willing to work at any pay and under any conditions. For this reason, they often posed a threat to existing wage and labor standards. Because they provided a supply of cheap, unskilled labor, they helped maintain a wide gap between the wages of skilled and unskilled workers.

Public opinion at the time frowned on workers organizing to get higher pay, better working conditions, or job security. Most of the workers themselves believed they could negotiate best with their employers by meeting them face-to-face on a one-to-one basis. They saw no need to organize into unions to protect their rights. In fact, labor organizers were viewed by many people as troublemakers. In some parts of the country, labor unions were even against the law.

CIVIL WAR TO THE 1930'S

After the Civil War, however, things began to change. Industry started to grow, and the farm population began to fall.

THE CIVILIAN LABOR FORCE AS A PERCENTAGE OF TOTAL U.S. POPULATION, 1986

TOTAL U.S. POPULATION
238.8 million

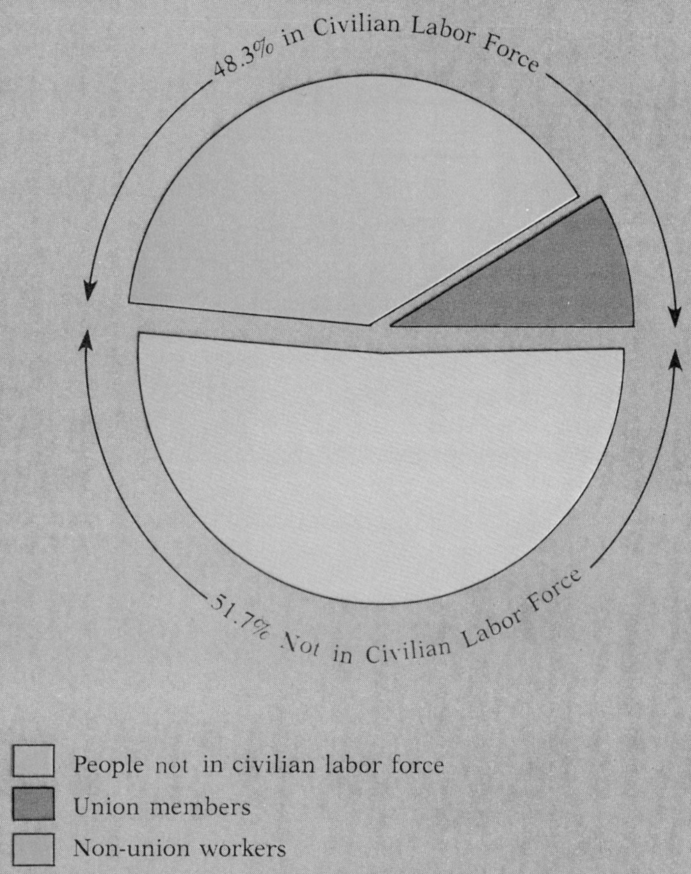

48.3% in Civilian Labor Force

51.7% Not in Civilian Labor Force

☐ People not in civilian labor force
■ Union members
☐ Non-union workers

PERCENTAGE OF CIVILIAN LABOR FORCE	PERCENTAGE OF TOTAL POPULATION	
18.0	8.7	Union Memberships
82.0	39.6	Non-union Workers
100.0	48.3	

Source: Statistical Abstract of the United States, Bureau of Labor Statistics

Figure 8–1

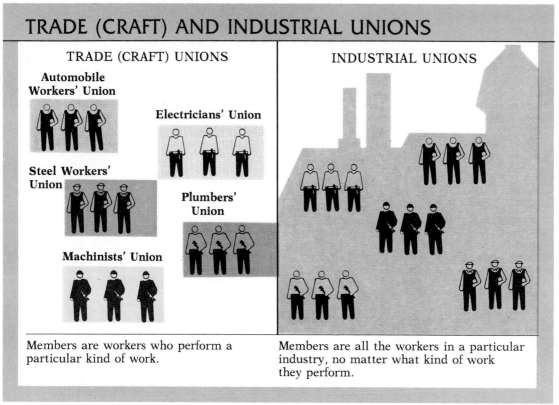

TRADE (CRAFT) AND INDUSTRIAL UNIONS

TRADE (CRAFT) UNIONS

Automobile Workers' Union

Electricians' Union

Steel Workers' Union

Plumbers' Union

Machinists' Union

Members are workers who perform a particular kind of work.

INDUSTRIAL UNIONS

Members are all the workers in a particular industry, no matter what kind of work they perform.

Figure 8–2

Hourly workers in industrial jobs made up about one fourth of the country's working population. With the Civil War came higher prices, a greater demand for goods and services, and a growing shortage of workers. The many differences between immigrants and American-born workers began to fade away, and the labor force became more unified in culture, language, and training. From all this grew a new unity among workers.

With industrialization came the unions. By now, there were two chief kinds of labor unions. One was the **craft** or **trade union**—an association of workers that performs the same kind of work. The Cigarmakers' Union, begun by union leader Samuel Gompers, is an example of this kind of union.

The other kind of union was the **industrial union**—an association made up of all workers in a given industry, no matter what kind of job each holds. The chance to organize this kind of union in such basic, mass-production industries as steel and textiles came about because of the growth of American industry. Many of the workers in these industries were unskilled and could not join trade unions. The solution to this was to organize into industrial unions.

Even though unions were making headway, times were still difficult for American workers. Because of the economy, there was little job security. During bad times, people often lost their jobs and had to struggle to survive. In addition, mechanization and mass production meant that work once performed by those in crafts could be performed by less skilled workers. With millions of unskilled immigrants arriving every year, and with many others leaving rural America for jobs in cities, high-paid or rebellious workers could easily be replaced.

Unions tried to help workers during this time. Unions would attempt to negotiate higher pay, better working conditions, and job security with employers. If an agreement could not be reached, workers would often **strike**—refuse to work until certain demands were met. Unions also placed pressure on employers by having the striking workers **picket**—parade in front of the employer's business carrying signs about the dispute. The signs might ask other workers not to seek jobs with the company. Or they might ask customers and suppliers to take their business somewhere else.

If a strike and picketing did not settle the dispute, a union could organize a **boycott.** This is a concentrated effort by workers to get others to join them in not buying products from employers involved in strikes or labor disputes. A boycott can hurt the employer's business and reduce the employer's income.

Employers fought unions a number of ways. Sometimes the owners would call for a **lockout**—refuse to let the workers work until management demands were met. At other times, management would respond to a strike or the threat of a strike by hiring all new workers. Violence often broke out when this happened and troops were sometimes brought in to keep factories open. Sometimes owners even set up **company unions**—unions organized, supported, or even run by employers—to head off efforts by others to organize workers.

During this period, public attitudes and the courts often sided with management. Even the Sherman Antitrust Act of 1890, an act aimed mainly at curbing monopolies, was used to keep labor in line.

In 1902, for example, the United Hatters Union called a strike against a Danbury, Connecticut, hat manufacturer that had turned down a union demand. The union brought pressure on store owners not to stock hats made by the Danbury firm. This led the manufacturer to bring suit against the union under the Sherman Antitrust Act. The Supreme Court held that the union was in restraint of trade and ruled against it. This court decision hurt organized labor.

The Danbury Hatters case, and several others that followed it, led organized labor to push for relief from the Sherman Antitrust Act. It was thought that relief had come in 1914 when the Clayton Antitrust Act was passed. It stated that a person's labor was not a "commodity or article of commerce." It further stated that labor unions should not be looked upon as "illegal combinations or conspiracies in restraint of trade under the antitrust laws."

The courts, however, tended to disregard the act. In 1921, for example, the Supreme Court ruled that the Machinists' Union in New York was guilty under the Sherman Antitrust Act of restraining trade. This was because the union had tried to stop the sale and installation of newspaper printing presses made by a nonunion company in Michigan. As a result of this, organized labor felt that the courts were on the side of business.

At the same time, labor unions had to deal with employer attitudes that were unfavorable to labor in general. Many employers often treated their workers as mere factory "hands" who were just another factor of production like land, equipment, or buildings.

In the automobile industry, for example, companies generally closed down completely and laid off all production workers while new model cars were being made ready for production. When the plants opened again, workers were rehired—but at a beginner's wage. In addition, workers under 35 years of age often were given preference over those who had been there longer and who had more experience.

LABOR DURING THE GREAT DEPRESSION

In 1929, the **Great Depression**—the greatest period of economic decline and stagnation in the history of the United States—began. The depression started with the collapse of the stock market in October of that year and reached bottom in 1933. It then took until 1939 for the economy to recover to the same level as in 1929.

At least 15 percent of all workers were without jobs during the entire decade of the 1930's! During the depths of the depression, one in four workers was without a job. Even those who did work, often received almost nothing for wages. In 1929, for example, the average manufacturing wage had climbed to 55¢ per hour. By 1933, wages had slipped to 5¢ per hour and many people were even glad to get that.

The Great Depression brought misery to millions, but it also brought a change in attitude toward the labor movement. Factory workers began to feel even more united by common problems. As a result, union organizers renewed efforts to unify workers.

Even federal legislation began to help labor. The **Norris-LaGuardia Act** of 1932, for example, stopped federal courts from stepping into labor disputes. The **National Labor Relations Act (NLRA)** of 1935 gave workers the right to join unions and bargain collectively through their own chosen representatives. Certain activities by employers were also defined as being unfair labor practices.

In 1937, workers at General Motors carried out a series of sit-down strikes. What act gave workers the right to join unions and bargain collectively?

The NLRA also set up the **National Labor Relations Board (NLRB).** The Board checked into workers' complaints, certified trade unions, issued certain orders, and held hearings. It also had the power to hold elections to select collective bargaining representatives.

Finally, in 1938, the **Fair Labor Standards Act** was passed. It applied to businesses which took part in or affected interstate commerce. It set a minimum wage to begin in 1939 and called for time-and-a-half pay for any hours worked over 40 a week. It also forbade labor by children under 16 years of age and the holding of hazardous jobs by anyone under 18 years of age.

LABOR SINCE WORLD WAR II

Organized labor did relatively well in the 1930's. But by the end of World War II, public opinion had shifted. Some people felt that Communists had infiltrated the unions. Others were upset by the loss of production due to strikes. In 1946 alone, more than 116 million work days were lost because of union-called strikes. People began to feel that management, not labor, was the victim.

Anti-union sentiment led to the **Taft-Hartley Act** of 1947. The act put limits on what unions could do in labor-management disputes. Among other things, it gave employers the right to sue unions for breaking contracts and prohibited them from making union membership a condition for hiring. It made it against the law for unions to give money to political campaigns and ordered them to give 60 days' notice before going out on strike.

One purpose of the Taft-Hartley Act had been to bring to an end the criminal influences that had begun to show up in the labor movement. When the act fell short of its goal, the **Landrum-Griffin Act** of 1959 was passed. It required unions to file financial reports with the government and limited the amount of money officials could borrow from the union. It also offered other measures to protect the individual union member from the unfair actions of unions and union officials.

AFL-CIO. The **American Federation of Labor (AFL)** was begun in 1886 as an organization of craft unions. Later, it added several industrial unions. The trade and industrial unions, however, did not always agree about the future of the union movement. In 1935, eight industrial unions in the AFL formed the Committee for Industrial Organization. Headed by John L. Lewis, president of the United Mine Workers of America, its goal was to bring about greater unionism in industry.

The AFL and Lewis, however, could not come to terms. In 1938, the AFL expelled the unions that made up the Committee for Industrial Organization. They then formed an independent federation called the **Congress of Industrial Organizations (CIO).** It quickly set up other industrial unions in industries that had not been unionized before, such as steel, automobile, textiles, and rubber. By the 1940's, the CIO was at it peak of power with nearly 7 million members.

As the CIO grew stronger, however, the trouble between it and the AFL also grew. Before long, the two were in a struggle for control of the labor movement. Each was trying to form unions in jobs and industries already organized by the other.

In 1955, after almost 20 years of disagreement, the AFL and CIO finally ironed out many of their differences and joined together to form the **American Federation of Labor and Congress of Industrial Organizations (AFL-CIO).**

Profile

John L. Lewis

John L. Lewis was an important labor leader of the twentieth century. The eldest son of Welsh immigrants who settled in Iowa, Lewis never attended high school.

1880–1969

Like his father, who was also a labor organizer, Lewis spent many years working as a miner, digging for copper, gold, silver, and coal. He learned firsthand the nature of mining and its dangers and the meaning of death as seen in the eyes of women whose husbands had died in the mines. This experience led him to get safety legislation passed both at the state and federal level.

Lewis's big break came when he met and came under the influence of Samuel Gompers, the founder of the American Federation of Labor (AFL). Gompers made Lewis an AFL field representative whose job was to represent the AFL at the various sessions of Congress and state legislatures. In this capacity, Lewis traveled widely throughout the United States, making contacts and learning about the strengths and weaknesses of potential friends and enemies.

In time, Lewis moved to the post of chief statistician for the United Mine Workers of America (UMW). In 1920, he became president of the union, a post that he kept until he retired in 1960.

Two ideas set Lewis apart from other labor leaders of his time. First, while Lewis respected and admired Samuel Gompers, he did not agree with Gompers that a union should be based on a single craft or trade. Lewis believed instead that there should be industrial unions made up of all unskilled workers in the new mass production industries. Lewis eventually split with the AFL over this idea and formed the Congress of Industrial Organizations (CIO).

Second, Lewis believed that unions had the right to strike even during times of war. He felt that the union was there to protect its members from unsafe work places and unfair labor practices, conditions that arise in war as well as in peace. He argued that the conditions had to be corrected even if the country was at war. Lewis won the favor of his union and the disfavor of the general public when the coal miners staged strikes during World War II.

The merger of the AFL and the CIO did not settle the basic differences between trade and industrial unions. Even today, the two may have a **jurisdictional dispute**—a disagreement over which union should perform a certain job. For example, metal workers, who are members of an industrial union, and pipe fitters, who are members of a trade union, may not agree as to which group should install a certain kind of metal pipe. This kind of dispute also could arise when two unions disagree about which has the right to organize a union at a certain company.

Even so, most labor leaders know that a conflict between the two kinds of unions that make up the AFL-CIO hurts the organized labor movement as a whole. Today, both sides generally try to settle their differences as quickly and as quietly as possible. Because of this, there is less open conflict and hostility within the movement today than there has been in the past.

INDEPENDENT UNIONS. Although the AFL-CIO is a major force in labor today, other unions are also important in the labor movement. Many are **independent unions**—unions that do not belong to the AFL-CIO. The Brotherhood of Locomotive Engineers, for one, has never been part of the AFL-CIO. The Teamsters, the Bakery Workers, the Laundry Workers, the International Longshoremen, and the United Mine Workers were once part of the AFL-CIO, but no longer are.

Section Review

1. Who makes up the civilian labor force? What percent is unionized?

2. What is the difference between a trade union and an industrial union?

3. Why do workers generally call a strike?

4. What did the Taft-Hartley Act do?

5. Who makes up the membership of the AFL-CIO?

8.2 Resolving Union and Management Differences

Over the years, many differences have arisen between labor and management. Some, such as the 1981 air traffic controllers' strike or the 1984 professional football strike make headlines. Others do not. In either case, however, labor and management generally manage to settle their differences without resorting to extreme measures. Today less than five percent of all working time is lost each year to labor disputes.

KINDS OF UNION ARRANGEMENTS

The labor movement has tried to organize workers in ways designed to help them deal more effectively with management. How the workers are organized and the way in which settlements are reached have an important impact on the entire economy. Generally speaking, there are four kinds of union arrangements.

CLOSED SHOPS. The most restrictive arrangement is the **closed shop**—an arrangement in which the employer agrees to hire only union members. The union can select who is hired by giving or denying a person union membership. Although this kind of shop was common in the 1930's and early 1940's, the Taft-Hartley Act made it illegal in companies taking part in interstate commerce. Today, since most firms in the United States are engaged in such commerce either directly or indirectly, there are few, if any, closed shops.

UNION SHOPS. The second kind of arrangement is the **union shop.** Under it, workers do not have to belong to the union to be hired; but they must join one soon after and remain a member for as long as they keep the job. No union shop agreement, however, can require membership sooner than 30 days after employment. The only exception is the construction industry, where the period is seven days. At present, union shops are outlawed in 21 states under section 14(b) of the Taft-Hartley Act. It allows states to pass **right-to-work laws**—laws that prohibit mandatory union membership.

MODIFIED UNION SHOPS. The third kind of arrangement is a **modified union shop.** Under this arrangement, workers do not have to belong to a union to be hired and cannot be made to join one to keep their job. However, should a worker voluntarily join the union, he or she must remain a member of it for as long as he or she has the job.

AGENCY SHOPS. The final arrangement is the **agency shop.** Under this arrangement, workers need not be union members to be hired or to keep their job, but they must pay dues to the union to help pay the costs of collective bargaining. Non-union workers also are subject to the contract negotiated by the union, whether or not they agree with it. In this way, non-union workers are treated almost like union members even if they did not join the union.

COLLECTIVE BARGAINING

When a union and management take part in collective bargaining, they negotiate pay and working conditions. To this end, a meeting is set up between union and management representatives. At the meeting, the workers are represented by a group of elected union officials. A union expert on collective bargaining also may be present. Management is represented by a company official in charge of labor relations. The head of the company's economic research staff and the company lawyer whose field is labor law also may be present.

During the meeting, each side will make clear its point of view and present any economic data needed. The union's economic research staff, which is paid from union dues, will present research reports and other data to back up the union's demands. The bargaining may go on for hours, days, weeks, or even months.

Collective bargaining in general calls for much give and take on the part of both parties. Before the terms of a contract can be agreed upon, every possible labor issue must be resolved. A **grievance procedure**—a provision for resolving issues that may come up later—also may be included in the issues to be resolved.

The collective bargaining process does not always work. Sometimes the disputing parties are not able to come to terms on certain points. Since there can be no contract until they do come to terms, other ways must be found to resolve the differences between the two parties.

Labor and management try to come to terms at the bargaining table. What is collective bargaining?

MEDIATION. One way to resolve differences is through **mediation**—the process of bringing in a third person or persons to help settle a dispute. The mediator's chief goal is to find a solution both parties will be willing to accept. For this reason, a mediator must be neutral and should not try to help one party at the expense of the other. A mediator must have the confidence and trust of both parties, or he or she will not be able to learn just what types of concessions each side is willing to make during bargaining.

Mediation is simply an aid to collective bargaining. Neither side has to accept a mediator's decision. Both union and management still must make their own settlements and accept full responsibility for any agreement that may be reached.

ARBITRATION. Another way differences can be cleared up is through **voluntary arbitration.** This means that both parties agree to place their differences before a third party whose decision will be accepted as final and binding. The arbitration is voluntary in the sense that both parties agree to its use. It is different from media-tion in that both parties agree ahead of time to abide by what the third-party arbitrator decides.

In some cases, such as the 1967 railroad strike, labor and management are forced to turn a dispute that has not been settled over to a third party for a binding decision. This is called **compulsory arbitration,** and, as a general rule, it is not used very often in the United States.

FACT-FINDING. A third way to resolve a dispute that cannot be settled by collective bargaining is through **fact-finding.** In such cases, labor and management agree to have an independent agency investigate the dispute and then recommend possible settlements. Neither party has to accept the recommendations. However, once the recommendations have been made public, popular sentiment may leave the parties no choice but to accept them.

INJUNCTION AND SEIZURE. A fourth way to settle labor-management disputes is through injunction or seizure. There are times when labor and management just cannot come to terms.

When vital industries are threatened, government may resort to an **injunction**—a court order not to act. This serves to keep things as they are for a short period of time. If issued against a union, it directs the union not to call a strike. If issued against a company, it directs the company not to lock out its workers. In 1978, for example, after coal miners had been off the job for more than three months, President Jimmy Carter obtained an injunction that made the coal miners return to work.

Government also may resort to **seizure**—a temporary takeover of operations. The purpose of seizure is to allow government to function as management so it can negotiate with the union. In 1946, for example, when the government seized and operated the bituminous coal industry, government officials worked out a settlement with the miners' union.

PRESIDENTIAL INFLUENCE. As a last resort, the President of the United States may step in to settle labor-management disputes. The President may do this by publicly appealing to the disputing parties to reach an early agreement. In most cases, however, this is done only when an industry that affects the national interest, such as steel, airlines, or railroads, is involved.

The President has a good deal of influence in settling labor disputes. One reason for this is that a presidential appeal generally has the support of the general public. This means that if either the union or management does not pay attention to the President's views, the general public is likely to be displeased.

In the case of federal workers who belong to a government union, the President may use an extraordinary amount of influence. The President can even fire workers. In 1981, for example, President Ronald Reagan fired striking air traffic controllers on the grounds that they were federal employees who had taken an oath not to strike.

▮ Section Review

1. What are the four kinds of union arrangements?
2. What is the purpose of collective bargaining? What is the process?
3. What methods can be used to settle labor disputes when collective bargaining does not work?

8.3 *Labor and Wages*

There are many different jobs and occupations in the United States today. In addition, wages can be different from one job or occupation to the next. In order to understand the structure of wages in the many different jobs and occupations more fully, it helps to place workers into broad groups and then study the characteristics of each.

CATEGORIES OF LABOR

There are four major categories of labor that are based on the general level of skills needed to do any kind of job. These categories are unskilled, semiskilled, skilled, and professional or managerial.

UNSKILLED LABOR. Workers who do not have the training to operate machines and equipment fall into the category of **unskilled labor.** Most of these people work chiefly with their hands at such jobs as digging ditches, picking fruit, and mopping floors.

SEMISKILLED LABOR.   Workers who have mechanical abilities fall into the category of **semiskilled labor.** They may operate power lawn mowers, electric floor polishers, or any other equipment that calls for a certain amount of skill.

SKILLED LABOR.   Workers who are able to operate complex equipment and who can do their tasks with little supervision fall into the category of **skilled labor.** Examples are carpenters, typists, tool and dye makers, and bricklayers.

PROFESSIONAL LABOR.   Workers with higher-level skills, such as doctors, lawyers, and executives of large companies, fall into the category of **professional labor.**

NONCOMPETING LABOR GRADES

While the four categories of labor are useful for classification purposes, there can be wide variation within each group. A skilled worker, for example, may have to take on some managerial responsibilities along with his or her daily duties.

Workers in one labor category generally do not compete with those in another category. For example, skilled workers do not compete with semiskilled or professional workers. For this reason, economists say that labor can be thought of as being grouped into **noncompeting labor grades.**

Generally, it is hard for members of one group of workers to qualify for occupations open to a higher group. Most unskilled workers, for example, would not find it easy to become corporate executives. To make such an upward move

Each of the workers below has different skills, and as a result, receives different wages. Into which category of labor does each of the four workers fall?

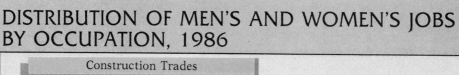

DISTRIBUTION OF MEN'S AND WOMEN'S JOBS BY OCCUPATION, 1986

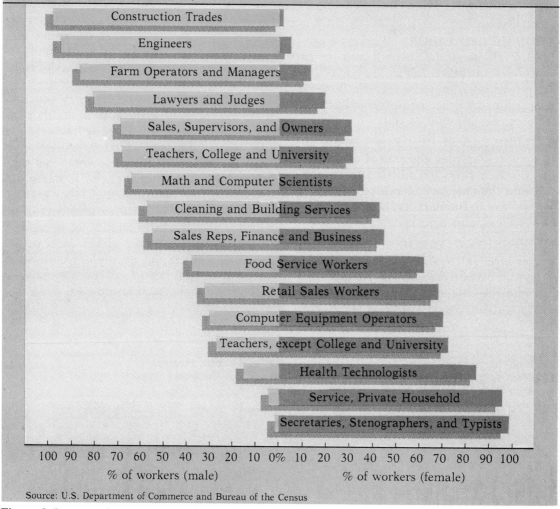

Construction Trades
Engineers
Farm Operators and Managers
Lawyers and Judges
Sales, Supervisors, and Owners
Teachers, College and University
Math and Computer Scientists
Cleaning and Building Services
Sales Reps, Finance and Business
Food Service Workers
Retail Sales Workers
Computer Equipment Operators
Teachers, except College and University
Health Technologists
Service, Private Household
Secretaries, Stenographers, and Typists

100 90 80 70 60 50 40 30 20 10 0% 10 20 30 40 50 60 70 80 90 100

% of workers (male)   % of workers (female)

Source: U.S. Department of Commerce and Bureau of the Census

Figure 8–3

would call for a higher degree of training, which may not be possible because of cost, lack of opportunity, or lack of initiative. As a result, the workers in one group tend to stay in that group.

Cost is one of the more important barriers. Many individuals, for example, may have the ability and initiative to become college professors. What some of these people may not have, however, is the financial resources needed for four-to-six years of post-college study. Others, however, may not have to worry about cost. They may have the ability and the money but lack the opportunity. For example, they may have the grades needed to get into medical school and the money to pay the fees but still not be able to get in because the schools have insufficient openings.

Other individuals do not acquire higher training or education simply because they are not willing to do what must be done to get it. Although they know they must have new skills to get a better job, they just do not want to put forth the extra effort.

WAGE DETERMINATION

Most occupations have a **wage rate**—a standard amount of pay given for work performed. How these rates are determined can be explained in two different ways. The first deals with supply and demand. The second recognizes the influence of unions on the bargaining process.

TRADITIONAL THEORY OF WAGE DETERMINATION.   The theory that uses the tools of supply and demand to explain differences in wage rates is called the **traditional theory of wage determination.** For example, many people can dig ditches or work as baby-sitters. However, fewer have the skills to become professional managers or athletes. In other words, professional managers and athletes generally are scarcer than ditchdiggers or baby-sitters.

Figure 8–4

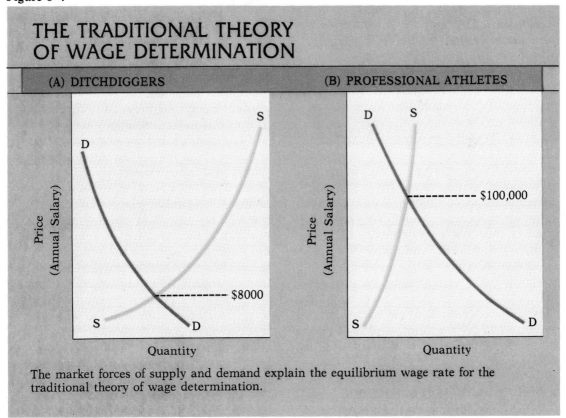

THE TRADITIONAL THEORY OF WAGE DETERMINATION

(A) DITCHDIGGERS

(B) PROFESSIONAL ATHLETES

Price (Annual Salary)

$8000

Quantity

Price (Annual Salary)

$100,000

Quantity

The market forces of supply and demand explain the equilibrium wage rate for the traditional theory of wage determination.

This can be expressed in terms of supply and demand. When the level of supply is large in relation to demand—as with ditchdiggers and baby-sitters—wages generally are low. When the level of supply is low in relation to demand—as with managers and professional athletes—wages generally are high.

The traditional theory can be illustrated with supply and demand graphs such as the ones shown on page 195. In Graph **A,** a large supply of ditchdiggers is coupled with a low level of demand. In Graph **B,** a small supply of professional athletes is paired with a high level of demand. The intersection of supply and demand determines the **equilibrium wage rate**—the wage rate that leaves neither a surplus nor a shortage in the labor markets.

In most cases, the higher the level of skills, or grade of labor, the higher the average yearly wage rate. For example, semiskilled workers will receive more, on the whole, than unskilled workers. Skilled workers will receive more than semiskilled or unskilled workers. Professional workers will receive more than any of the others.

There are, however, some cases in which the traditional theory does not explain the variations in wage rates. Some unproductive workers, for example, may receive high wages because of family ties or political influence. Some highly skilled or productive workers may receive low wages because of race, sex, or where they live.

Then, too, workers and employers do not always know what the market wage rate is or should be. A worker may accept a job that pays $4.35 an hour because he or she does not know that the firm next door is paying $4.75 for the same kind of job. Or an employer may offer to hire someone for $275 a week without knowing that the same service can be obtained for $200.

Further, businesses do not always compete for labor. In fact, they even may take steps to keep workers from seeking a better wage somewhere else. To this end, some companies offer to train workers on the job. Others promise to promote workers in the company rather than bring in new people to fill higher level jobs.

For the most part, however, these are the exceptions rather than the rule. If the forces of supply and demand operate freely, wages and the market for labor will operate as the theory suggests.

THEORY OF NEGOTIATED WAGES. At times, wages are determined not by supply and demand but by the influence of organized labor and the collective bargaining process. When this happens, economists use the **theory of negotiated wages** to explain wage rates.

In these cases, unions do not try to get higher wages for their members on the grounds that labor is in short supply relative to the demand. Nor does management push for lower wages when there is a very large supply of labor. This makes the price of labor—or wages—hard to define. In short, the labor market becomes a hazy concept open to different interpretations and to misunderstandings.

When negotiating for wages, unions want to know the wage rates in other plants and industries for the same kind of work. They also want to know what changes have taken place or will take place in the future in the cost of living. A number of factors must be kept in mind. For example, how has the productivity of labor changed? Is the company able to pay higher wages? What are the union's and the company's goals and practices? How long a period of time will the wage contract cover?

Several other factors that play no part in the traditional analysis of wages also become important when unions and collective bargaining enter the picture. One of these is **seniority**—the length of time a

Profile

■ Walter E. Williams

Walter E. Williams is a contemporary American economist who has published many articles and reports. At present, he is a professor of economics at Temple University in Philadelphia.

Williams is a strong critic of minimum wage legislation, which he believes punishes the young. He points out that every time the minimum wage increases, the number of unemployed teenagers also increases. He feels that teenage unemployment is a "national scandal"

1936–

and is a problem that must be dealt with now.

To solve this problem, Williams suggests a minimum wage for teenagers that is 30 to 40 percent lower than the adult minimum wage. He believes everyone would benefit from this. Taxpayers no longer would have to support youth-employment programs. Young people would get early work experience. New jobs would be created in cities at movie houses, hotels, restaurants, and factories.

person has been on the job. Because of seniority, some workers will receive higher wages than others for performing similar tasks. Yet, these same workers will be the last to be laid off when the company cuts back on production. Seniority is an old tradition that still is very much a part of negotiated wage contracts today.

The amount of bargaining power negotiators have is also important. Because of it, negotiated wages often are higher in some industries than in others. Strong representatives backed by the union's members often can negotiate a relatively high wage agreement. This is even more likely to happen if they are dealing with a management representative who is weak. On the other hand, management might get a relatively low wage agreement when union negotiators have weak bargaining skills or when they are not backed by their union's members.

Finally, the negotiated wage often is subject to the personal goals of those who do the negotiating. For example, the management of some companies may feel that

Understanding Sources

 ## "Psychic Income"

The following article appeared in *U.S. News & World Report* on June 23, 1986. Read the paragraph and answer the questions that follow.

> ### Money isn't everything
>
> This may be the decade of conspicuous consumption and the worship of money, but a lot of people are still taking jobs for the rewards of fighting the good fight. For them, the payoff is in "psychic income," not in bigger investment portfolios—careers that allow them to pursue a dream, perform a public service or simply spend more time with their families than at the office.
>
> Schoolteachers are a case in point. According to a recent poll by the National Center for Education Information, 90 percent of public-school teachers are satisfied with their jobs even though 55 percent feel they are underpaid.

1. What is "psychic income"?
2. Are most teachers satisfied with their work? With their salary?
3. How was this information obtained?
4. Is the title, "Money isn't everything" appropriate? Can you think of a better one?

their public image or their social responsibility to the workers is more important than making high profits. Because of this, the negotiated wage of such companies may be higher than that of other companies in the industry.

Union leaders also have been known to push for higher wages during negotiations just so that members will be pleased enough to vote for them in the next election. Then, too, there are known cases where union representatives have "sold out" to management when negotiating a wage agreement. This means they have agreed to a contract calling for fewer benefits and lower wages in return for some "favor" offered to them.

REGIONAL WAGE DIFFERENCES

No matter how wage rates are determined, they can be different for the same job from one part of the country to another. Supply and demand, labor mobility, cost of living, and attractiveness of location all can make a difference.

For example, the fact that skilled workers are scarce in some parts of the country and abundant in others can cause differences in wage rates. These differences, however, can be narrowed by **labor mobility**—the ability and willingness of workers to relocate in markets where wages are higher.

In spite of this, all workers are not mobile. Some are reluctant to move away from relatives and friends. Others may want to move, but they find that the cost is too high. Then, too, there is the inconvenience of buying a new house or renting a new apartment. Because of this, the demand for certain skills remains high in some areas and low in others, and wages tend to be different.

Another factor that affects wages is the cost of living. In most southern states, for example, there are fresh fruits and vegetables almost the year round. There is no need to buy heavy clothing or to worry about heating a home. But in Alaska, food must be brought in from thousands of miles. People must have warm clothing, and every home must be well-heated. It stands to reason, then, that the cost of living is higher in Alaska than in most

southern states. It also stands to reason that wages are considerably higher in Alaska than in most southern states.

Such differences in the cost of living—although less extreme—exist all over the United States and affect wages. For example, if it costs less to live in one area than another, a person may accept lower wages to work in the second area.

In much the same way, location can make a difference. Some locations are thought to be so attractive that lower wages can be offered there. A person who likes to hunt and fish may be willing to work for less pay in Colorado or Montana than in New York City. Another who does not like cold weather may accept the same job in Florida or New Mexico for lower pay than in Massachusetts or Wisconsin.

▌ Section Review

1. What are four major categories of labor? On what are they based?

2. What is meant by the phrase "noncompeting labor grades"?

3. What two theories can be used to explain differences in wage rates?

4. What factors contribute to regional differences in wage rates?

8.4 Current Employment Trends and Issues

There are several trends and issues in today's labor movement. These include union decline, comparable worth, renegotiating union agreements, and the minimum wage.

UNION DECLINE

A major trend in today's economy is the decline of the union movement. As recently as 1970, 30.8 percent of nonagricultural

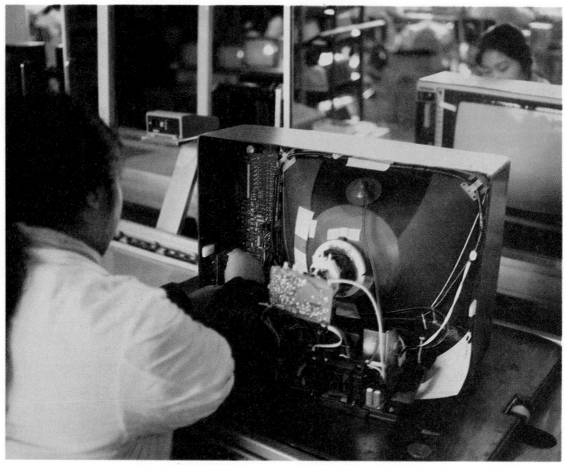

Many foreign workers earn lower wages than American workers. How does this help foreign competition and hurt American industry?

workers were members of unions. This number fell to 25.2 percent in 1980 and dropped to 18 percent in 1986.

There are several reasons for this decline. For one, unions lost members in traditionally organized industries such as steel and automobiles. For another, some employers have worked hard to keep unions out of their factories. Many hired consultants for advice on strategies to fight union efforts. Others tried to make workers feel more like "a part of the team." They added employees to the board of directors and set up profit-sharing plans that reward workers.

A third reason for union decline is that new additions to the labor force—especially women and teenagers—have little loyalty to organized labor. And, since many of these workers represent second incomes to families, there is a tendency for many of them to accept lower wages.

The last, and perhaps most important, reason for the decline is that unions seem to be the victims of their own success. Unions have been able to raise wages of their members 10 to 20 percent above the wages they would have received otherwise. As a result, union-made products, especially in the building industry, are often more expensive than nonunion ones.

Finally, American workers receive higher wages than workers in other countries. As a result, many foreign products, such as stereos, clothes, shoes, steel, ballpoint pens, and computers are priced lower than American-made ones. American industry has been hurt by such foreign competition.

COMPARABLE WORTH

One of the newer labor trends in the economy is **comparable worth.** This means that people should receive equal pay for work that is different from, but just as demanding as, other types of work. As such, it goes beyond the concept of equal pay for equal work.

Comparable worth has been mainly applied to salary discrimination cases between men and women.

During the last two decades, many efforts were made to increase the pay of women so that they received the same pay as men for the same jobs. Even so, a number of occupations such as nursing, remain typically "female." Others, such as

Figure 8–5

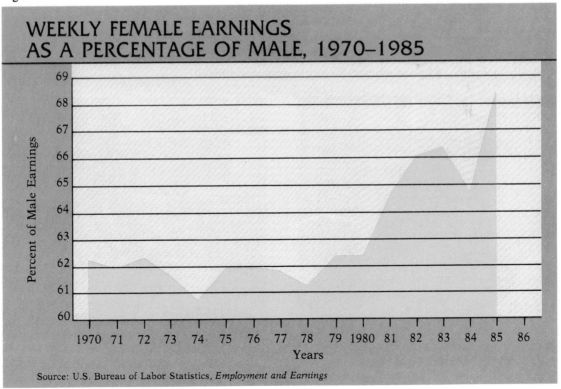

WEEKLY FEMALE EARNINGS AS A PERCENTAGE OF MALE, 1970–1985

Percent of Male Earnings

Years

Source: U.S. Bureau of Labor Statistics, *Employment and Earnings*

engineering, tend to be typically "male." Because typically female occupations pay lower wages, women overall earn less than men as shown on page 201.

In the state of Washington, a federal judge ruled that the work performed by social service workers, most of whom were female, was just as demanding as some traditionally male occupations, and ordered the state to raise wages and give workers several years' back pay. In Illinois, job evaluators trying to equate typically male occupations with typically female ones, determined that the work done by highway workers was roughly equivalent to that done by nurses. In Minnesota, the work of delivery drivers was determined roughly comparable to that of pharmacy assistants.

Today, over half the states have examined the concept of comparable worth. Several of these states, including California, Iowa, Minnesota, and Washington,

have had comparable worth laws on their books since 1984.

Comparable worth decisions are not easy to make. Many factors, such as education requirements, occupational hazards, and degree of physical difficulty, have to be considered. Because of this, some people say that comparisons of occupations not only are almost impossible to make but also are not needed as long as people are free to choose their own profession. Others argue however that comparable worth is necessary to remove sex discrimination in the marketplace.

RENEGOTIATED UNION AGREEMENTS

Another major trend in the 1980's has been that of lower wages for union workers. In some cases, lower wages were nec-

Comparable worth cases involve equating typically female occupations and typically male ones. Why are comparable worth decisions difficult?

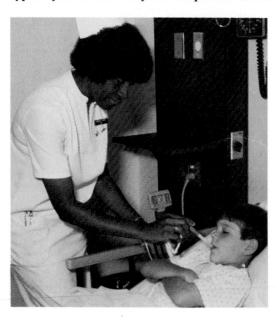

Case Study: Issue

Should Right-to-Work Laws be Abolished?

An important issue faced by unions in recent years is right-to-work laws which outlaw union shops. The debate over these laws began when some workers were forced against their wishes to join unions. As a result, the Taft-Hartley Act of 1947, contained a section, known as 14b, that permitted each state to determine if it wanted to allow union shops.

Defenders of right-to-work laws claim that people have the basic freedom to choose their own organizations. They interpret the term "right-to-work" to mean that people should have the "right to work even if they do not join a union." The laws, they say, increase a worker's freedom to choose. They also claim that workers' civil rights are violated when they are forced to join a union, especially if they themselves or their employers do not want them to join. They believe that if state right-to-work laws or Section 14b were repealed, it would allow unions to force membership, causing management to lose control over hiring and firing.

Those who oppose right-to-work laws say that anyone receiving such union benefits as improved wages and working conditions, ought to be a contributing union member. They also argue that if all employees of a company do not belong to the union, the bargaining position of the union is not as strong. Therefore, those opposed to the laws view them and Section 14b of the Taft-Hartley Act as anti-union measures. They do not agree with the laws' defenders about the increase in a worker's freedom to choose, and point out that if a state has a right-to-work law, a union shop would be prohibited even if an employer and all of the employees wanted one.

1. What do right-to-work laws prohibit? What legislation gave states the right to pass right-to-work laws?
2. What arguments do those who defend right-to-work laws offer? Those who oppose them?

essary because industries were threatened by foreign competition. In other cases, industries were simply not profitable and, therefore, could not afford expensive union contracts.

One way employers have been able to reduce union wages is by asking for a **giveback** from union workers. Givebacks are wages and fringe benefits given up when labor contracts are renegotiated.

When Chrysler faced stiff competition from foreign imports in 1981, for example, workers agreed to give up over a billion dollars in wages and fringe benefits to keep the company open. Later, the United Steelworkers Union voted to give up billions in pay and benefits to prevent lay-offs and factory closings.

Some companies have been able to get rid of labor contracts by claiming bankruptcy. When a company cannot pay its bills and is faced with going out of business, it is usually given a year to try to work out its debts. If it can show the court that wage and fringe benefits contributed significantly to its problems, the court usually allows the company to terminate its union contract and establish different wage scales.

Another way of reducing union salary scales is with a **two-tier wage system.** This system keeps the old wage for current workers, but has a much lower wage for newer workers. In 1983, for example, American Airlines won an agreement with its unions to pay all new pilots and mechanics about half what the current ones were receiving. In 1984, the United States Postal System announced that starting pay for all new employees would be cut 25 percent.

Two-tiered systems have an immediate impact on labor costs. The postal service, for example, hires about 40,000 new workers annually, so the savings are substantial. Since the savings are so large, two-tier contracts have proved popular with management. Workers, however, are less sure about the benefits of the system. They are concerned that new workers will have some hostility toward older ones. Older workers are concerned that the system might lead to problems in the future as the new and lower paid workers become a larger part of the work force.

THE MINIMUM WAGE

The **minimum wage**—the lowest wage that can be paid by law to workers in a certain job—was first set in 1939 at $.25 per hour. As Graph **A** on page 205 shows, the minimum wage increased from time to time until it reached $3.35 in 1981.

Although Graph **A** seems to indicate that the minimum wage increased considerably over time, it does not take inflation into account. For example, since prices were higher in 1986, a minimum wage of $3.35 bought more goods and services in 1981 than it did in 1986.

In order to make better comparisons over time, economists like to measure things in terms of **real** or **constant dollars.** This means that the comparison is made by using a common set of prices for all years. To do so, a **base year**—a year that serves as the basis of comparison for all other years—is selected. Next, goods and services for all years are measured in terms of the base year prices. The Department of Commerce currently uses 1982 as a base year.

The use of real or constant dollars makes it easier to look at a graph and see real changes in terms of purchasing power from one period to the next. For example, Graph **B** shows that the minimum wage had more purchasing power in 1968 than any other year. After that, the graph begins to decline. This shows that the minimum wage did not buy as many goods and services as it did earlier.

In Graph **C,** the minimum wage is expressed as a percent of the average manufacturing wage. The illustration shows that the wage has declined since the end of the 1960's to the point where it is less than 40 percent of the average manufacturing wage today.

There is always debate over the minimum wage. Some people object on the

Figure 8–6

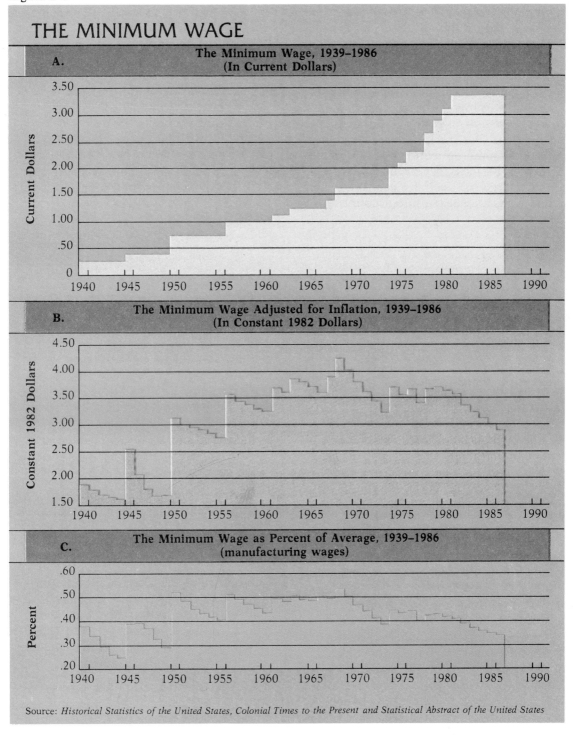

THE MINIMUM WAGE

A. **The Minimum Wage, 1939–1986**
(In Current Dollars)

Current Dollars

B. **The Minimum Wage Adjusted for Inflation, 1939–1986**
(In Constant 1982 Dollars)

Constant 1982 Dollars

C. **The Minimum Wage as Percent of Average, 1939–1986**
(manufacturing wages)

Percent

Source: *Historical Statistics of the United States, Colonial Times to the Present and Statistical Abstract of the United States*

grounds of economic freedom and argue that employers should be free to pay whatever wage they want. Others agree in principle, but think the wage is too high. This group feels that the wage discriminates against young people and is one of the reasons that many teenagers cannot find jobs.

Those who support the minimum wage do so on grounds of equity and fairness. They believe that the minimum wage gives the worker some protection against the exploitation. Besides, they argue, the wage is not very large in the first place. When historical trends are taken into account, the minimum wage gives workers less protection than at any time since 1969.

Section Review

1. What has happened to union membership since 1970?
2. Why is comparable worth an issue today?
3. What are two ways employers have been able to lower wage costs?
4. When was the minimum wage first established? What is the minimum wage today?

Chapter 8 Review

Summary

1. The civilian labor force, which accounts for about 48.3 percent of the population, is made up of men and women over the age of 16 who have jobs or are actively seeking jobs.

2. Only 18 percent of the civilian labor force belongs to unions. The rest are nonunion workers.

3. The first time workers tried to organize was in 1778. In the early 1800's, however, public opinion was against unions, and they did not show much growth.

4. Craft or trade unions represent workers who perform the same kind of job.

5. Industrial unions represent all workers in an industry, no matter what kind of job each performs.

6. During periods of labor unrest, unions would strike, picket, and boycott an employer. Employers would sometimes lock out workers from factories.

7. The Sherman Antitrust Act of 1890 was used to keep unions in line until the 1930's, when laws were passed that favored organized labor. These laws included the Norris-LaGuardia Act, the National Labor Relations Act, and the Fair Labor Standards Act.

8. After World War II, public opinion turned against labor and led to the Taft-Hartley Act of 1947, which put

limits on what unions could do in labor-management disputes.

9. The AFL, representing craft unions, and the CIO, representing industrial unions, argued for control of the labor movement until 1955, at which time they merged into the AFL-CIO.

10. Not all unions belong to the AFL-CIO. Today workers also are represented by many different independent unions.

11. There are four major kinds of union shop arrangements—closed shops, union shops, modified union shops, and agency shops.

12. The process of collective bargaining involves mediation, arbitration, fact-finding, injunction and seizure, and presidential influence.

13. There are four major categories of labor—unskilled, semiskilled, skilled, and professional. Workers in one category generally do not compete with those in another category.

14. Wage differences can be explained by the traditional theory of wage determination or by the theory of negotiated wages. Some regional differences in wages are the result of such factors as supply and demand, labor mobility, cost of living, and location.

15. In recent years, the percent of the labor force that belongs to unions has declined. Comparable worth, renegotiated labor agreements, and the minimum wage have become the subjects of debate.

■ *Building an Economic Vocabulary*

civilian labor force
craft union
trade union
industrial union
strike
picket
boycott
lockout
company unions
Great Depression
Norris-LaGuardia Act
National Labor
    Relations Act (NLRA)
National Labor
    Relations Board
    (NLRB)
Fair Labor Standards Act
Taft-Hartley Act
Landrum-Griffin Act
American Federation
    of Labor (AFL)

Congress of Industrial
    Organizations (CIO)
American Federation of
    Labor and Congress of
    Industrial Organizations
    (AFL-CIO)
jurisdictional dispute
independent unions
closed shop
union shop
right-to-work laws
modified union shop
agency shop
grievance procedure
mediation
voluntary arbitration
compulsory arbitration
fact-finding
injunction
seizure

unskilled labor
semiskilled labor
skilled labor
professional labor
noncompeting labor grades
wage rate
traditional theory of
    wage determination
equilibrium wage rate
theory of negotiated
    wages
seniority
labor mobility
comparable worth
giveback
two-tier wage system
minimum wage
real dollars
constant dollars
base year

Reviewing the Main Ideas

1. What are some factors that influenced the development of labor unions in the 1800's?

2. What was the general attitude toward workers until the 1930's? How were workers organized?

3. How did attitudes toward labor change in the 1930s?

4. What did the Norris-LaGuardia Act of 1932 do for labor? The National Labor Relations Act? The Fair Labor Standards Act?

5. What were some of the provisions of the Taft-Hartley act of 1947? The Landrum-Griffin Act of 1959?

6. What is the difference between a closed shop and a union shop?

7. In what ways are mediation and arbitration different? The same?

8. How does fact-finding differ from injunction and seizure?

9. What is the difference between an unskilled worker and a skilled worker? A skilled worker and a professional?

10. What is the traditional theory of wage determination? How is it different from the theory of negotiated wages?

11. What are some major trends and issues facing labor today?

Practicing Critical Thinking Skills

1. Given the fact that less than 18 percent of the civilian labor force belongs to unions, do you feel that unions have too much power in the United States today? Explain your answer.

2. Unions generally argue that the best interests of workers can be served when employees are members of a union. Do you agree or disagree? Defend your answer.

3. Do you think that union-management differences generally are resolved in a fair and reasonable manner? Give specific examples to support your position.

4. Some people believe that in today's economy, the theory of negotiated wages is more useful than the traditional theory of wage determination. Explain why you agree or disagree.

5. Give reasons why you agree or disagree with the following: "Unions have outlived their usefulness."

6. Present an argument for or against comparable worth.

Applying Economic Understandings

Using a Statistical Reference
  Economists, like other social scientists, analyze data to predict future trends. To do this, they often use a *statistical reference*, a summary of data gathered by government and private sources. One refer-

enc
tistica
Publishe
Commerce,
political, and
United States. O
often used by econ
Report of the Presiden
the United States Govern
lished yearly, both these p
tain statistical tables and ch
come, employment, and produc
United States.

Study the following example, whic
provide you with steps to develop the s
of using a statistical reference. In the example, the topic to be researched is that
since the mid-1970's, labor unions have
been losing members in traditionally organized industries, but have made some
gains in the service industry.

1. Define the data that is to be researched
   and analyzed. (Information on the number of workers who are members of
   labor unions in manufacturing and service industries since the mid-1970's.)

2. Decide which statistical reference you
   will use. *(Statistical Abstract of the Unit-*
   ed States because it summarizes economic data from many sources.)

3. Decide where to find the most current
   edition of the reference. (Most libraries

1
tiate
over ti

6. Write the
   the topic tha
   table tells you t
   labor union memb
   nearly all manufactu
   Labor union membersh
   such service industries as
   state, county, and municipal
   and teachers.)

For further practice in using a stati
reference, research this topic: Women
overall earn less than men.

/

often used by economists is the *Sta-* *1 Abstract of the United States.*
d yearly by the Department of
it contains data on the social,
economic organization of the
Other statistical resources
omists are the *Economic*
r and the *Budget of*
ment. Also pub-
blications con-
rts on in-
ion in the

h will
kill

have the current edition in the reference section.)

4. Acquaint yourself with the organization of the statistical reference. (The 1986 *Statistical Abstract of the United States* is divided into 33 topical sections. It also has a Table of Contents, an appendix with additional data, and an index. Each section has graphic charts of some of the data in the section, a brief discussion of the information presented in the section, and statistical tables.)

5. Look up the topic in the index or in the Table of Contents. (The index indicates that membership in labor unions is found on page 423 in a table entitled "U.S. Membership in AFL-CIO Affiliated Unions by Selected Union: 1971 to 283." It is the only table that differen-s membership in different unions ne.)

nformation that applies to
you are researching. (The
hat, from 1975 to 1983,
ership declined in
ring industries.
p increased in
firefighters;
workers;

Chapter 9

After reading this chapter, you will be able to:

- Evaluate the 1986 tax reform bill based on the criteria and major principles of taxation.

- Discuss the major categories of taxes collected by the federal government.

- List the ways in which state and local governments raise revenue.

- Describe contemporary tax issues and the economic impact of taxes.

9.1 Taxation

It takes an enormous amount of money to run the federal, state, and local governments of the United States. Collectively, all three levels of government raised nearly 1.5 trillion dollars in revenues in 1985. This figure amounted to nearly $6300 for every man, woman, and child in the United States.

To keep up with the tremendous demand for government services, total revenue collections by all levels of government have grown rapidly. The illustration on page 213 shows that total collections almost tripled between 1965 and 1985 when measured in constant dollars. On a constant per capita basis, total revenue collections more than doubled.

The single most important way governments raise revenue is through taxes. Among other items, there are taxes levied on income, sales, and property. In addition to taxes, government also raises revenue from college tuitions, unemployment insurance contributions, and even the sale of drivers' licenses.

CRITERIA FOR TAXES

In order to have an effective tax system, government must have criteria, or standards, by which to judge the merit of the taxes it imposes. One such criterion is that a tax yields enough revenue. If it does not, it may not be of much value.

A second criterion is clarity. Tax laws should be written so that both the taxpayer and the tax collector can understand them. This is not an easy task, but people seem to be more willing to pay taxes when they understand them.

A third criterion is ease of administration. A tax should be easy to collect. It should not require a large enforcement staff, and it should be designed so that citizens find it hard to avoid. This criterion also includes convenience and efficiency. That is, the tax should be administered at the lowest possible cost.

A final criterion is fairness. Taxes should be imposed impartially and justly. However, this is hard to do because people do not always agree about what is or is not fair when it comes to taxes.

PRINCIPLES OF TAXATION

The criteria of taxation afford some broad guidelines for judging tax systems. They do not, however, indicate how to select the persons or groups on which taxes

Figure 9–1

CRITERIA FOR TAXES

1. A tax must yield enough revenue.

2. A tax law must be written clearly.

3. A tax must be easy to collect.

4. A tax must be fair.

Figure 9–2

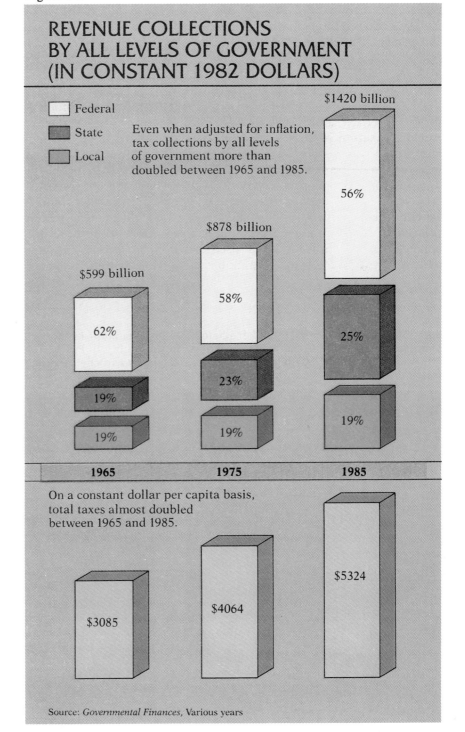

REVENUE COLLECTIONS
BY ALL LEVELS OF GOVERNMENT
(IN CONSTANT 1982 DOLLARS)

Federal

State

Local

Even when adjusted for inflation, tax collections by all levels of government more than doubled between 1965 and 1985.

$1420 billion

56%

25%

19%

$878 billion

58%

23%

19%

$599 billion

62%

19%

19%

1965   1975   1985

On a constant dollar per capita basis, total taxes almost doubled between 1965 and 1985.

$5324

$4064

$3085

Source: *Governmental Finances,* Various years

will be imposed. Since everyone pays taxes at one time or another, who will pay what is very important.

In general, taxes are based chiefly on one of two principles that have evolved over the years. These are the Benefit Principle and the Ability-to-Pay Principle.

BENEFIT PRINCIPLE.   The **Benefit Principle of Taxation** is based on two ideas. First, those who benefit from government services should be the ones to pay for them. Second, people should pay taxes in proportion to the amount of services or benefits they receive.

Gasoline taxes are a good example of the Benefit Principle. Since they are used to build streets and highways, the motorists who use streets and highways end up paying the tax. Since the tax is included in the price of the gasoline, the person who uses more gasoline will pay more tax. The person who does not buy any gasoline will not pay the tax.

The Benefit Principle has two important limitations. One is that many government services benefit most those who can least afford to pay them. In the case of welfare payments and low-income housing, for example, the people receiving the services are the ones with the lowest incomes. Even if they could pay something, they would not be able to pay taxes in proportion to the benefits received.

A second limitation of the Benefit Principle is that the benefits often are hard to

Both the teenager at work in the left photograph and the adult in the right photograph have to pay taxes. According to the Ability to Pay Principle of Taxation, how is the amount each person has to pay in taxes determined?

measure. For example, are people who drive the only ones who benefit from the roads built with gasoline taxes? What about the property owners whose property increases in value because of the roads that lead to and from it? What about the people who work in hotels and restaurants and depend on tourists who arrive by car or bus? Not all property owners or employees of hotels and restaurants buy gasoline, but they still benefit from facilities that the gasoline tax helps provide.

Another example of this limitation is school taxes. Those who favor the Benefit Principle feel that only people with school-age children should have to pay school taxes. But, in the long run, everyone benefits from public education. Directly or otherwise, all of us benefit from the education received by legislators, doctors, and others who contribute to the national well-being.

In practice, other taxes besides those on gasoline are based on the Benefit Principle. Examples are sewer taxes on water bills and garbage collection fees.

ABILITY-TO-PAY PRINCIPLE. The second is the **Ability-to-Pay Principle of Taxation.** It says that people should be taxed according to their ability to pay, no matter what benefits or services they receive. Thus, a high-income couple with no children should be just as responsible for school taxes as a low-income couple with six children.

The Ability-to-Pay Principle is based on three things. First, it is not possible to measure the benefits derived from government spending. Second, persons with higher incomes suffer less discomfort than persons with lower incomes even if they pay higher taxes. A family of four with a yearly income of $10,000, for example, needs almost every cent for the necessities of life. If the tax rate were 14 percent, this family would have to pay $1400—a huge amount for them. On the other hand, a couple with no children and a yearly income of $80,000 could afford to pay a higher tax rate of perhaps 30 percent, or $24,000, and still live very well.

Finally, the only means most people have of paying taxes is the income they earn. Since the benefits of government services to individuals are hard to measure, the other basis for distributing taxes is income.

TYPES OF TAXES

Basically, there are three types of taxes in the United States today—proportional, progressive, and regressive. Each is classified according to the way in which the tax burden changes as income changes.

PROPORTIONAL TAX. A **proportional tax** is one that imposes the same percentage rate of taxation on everyone, no matter what their income. If, for example, the income tax rate were 20 percent of all taxable income, a person with $10,000 in taxable income would pay $2000 in taxes. A person with $20,000 in taxable income would have to pay $4000. Even when income goes up, the percent of total income paid in taxes does not change.

PROGRESSIVE TAX. A **progressive tax** is one that imposes a higher percentage rate of taxation on persons with high incomes than on those with low incomes. The federal income tax rates for 1986 in the table on page 220 are an example of this. According to the tables, a single individual pays nothing on all income up to $2480, 11 percent on income between $2480 and $3670, and so on until a top rate of 50 percent is reached.

THREE TYPES OF TAXES

TYPE OF TAX	INCOME OF $10,000	INCOME OF $100,000	
Proportional	city occupational tax—$97.50 .975% of total income	city occupational tax—$975 .975 of total income	As income goes up, the percent of income paid in taxes stays the same.
Progressive	federal individual income taxes before 1987—$1000, 10% of total income	federal individual income taxes before 1987—$30,000, 30% of total income	As income goes up, the percent of income paid in taxes goes up.
Regressive	food, clothing, and medicine—$3000 taxed at 4%—$120 1.2% of total income	food, clothing, and medicine—$20,000 taxed at 4%—$800 .8% of total income	As income goes up, the percent of income paid in taxes goes down.

Table 9–A

REGRESSIVE TAX. **A regressive tax** is one that imposes a higher percentage rate of taxation on low incomes than on high incomes.

For example, a person with a yearly income of $10,000 may spend $3000 on food, clothing, and medicine, while a person with a yearly income of $100,000 may spend $20,000 on the same essentials. If the state sales tax, which is a regressive tax, were 4 percent, the person with the lower income would pay a lesser amount in dollars but a higher percentage of total income. This can be seen in the table on page 216.

1986 TAX REFORM ACT

In 1986, Congress passed the most sweeping tax reform act since income taxes were first set up in 1914. It applied to income earned in 1988 and after, with 1987 set up as a transition year. Basically, the law reduced tax brackets and closed **tax loopholes**—missing information or exceptions that allow people and businesses to avoid taxes.

While the act reformed the federal tax system, it was not designed to raise additional revenues for the federal government. Instead, the tax act was intended to be **tax neutral**—raising the same amount of revenue after the revision as before.

REASONS FOR TAX REFORM. There were a number of reasons why tax reform was passed. First, one of President Reagan's major goals was to reduce the burden of the federal tax structure on both individuals and businesses.

Second, there was a growing feeling that the tax code increasingly favored the rich and powerful. In 1983, for example, over

3000 millionaires paid no income taxes. There were also tens of thousands of others who, for one reason or another, had substantial income yet were not required to pay taxes.

Wealthy people were not the only ones who have legally avoided paying taxes. Many corporations did the same. For example, Boeing, ITT, General Dynamics, Transamerica, First Executive Corporation, and Greyhound were profitable from 1981 to 1984. But instead of paying corporate income taxes, these companies collected tax refunds during each of these four years.

A third reason for tax reform was that businesses in general were paying fewer taxes than in the past. In 1970, for example, taxes on corporate business profits amounted to 16.9 percent of the total federal revenues. By 1975, this figure had dropped to 14.5 percent and to 8.4 percent in 1985.

CONSEQUENCES OF TAX REFORM. The tax reform act did five things. First, it ended the traditionally progressive income tax paid by individuals. For years, taxpayers faced increasingly higher rates as income went up. As can be seen in the table on page 220, as recently as 1986, single individuals faced as many as 16 different brackets and rates.

For 1988 and after, however, federal income tax rates are largely proportional. Under the new law, all single individuals with taxable incomes of $17,850 or less pay a flat rate of 15 percent. If one person earns $1000, the tax rate is 15 percent. If another earns $15,000, the rate is still 15 percent. After $17,850, however, the base rate increases to 28 percent where it remains regardless of income earned. After a certain amount, higher-income taxpayers must also pay a 5 percent **surcharge**—or additional tax above and beyond the base rate. The purpose of this is to recover the

revenue lost when the first $17,850 was taxed at the lower 15 percent rate.

Second, the law made it more difficult for the very rich to avoid taxes completely. It did so by strengthening the provisions relating to the alternate 20 percent minimum tax. Corporations, like individuals, face a minimum 20 percent tax. The purpose of these provisions was to make the tax law more fair.

Third, the reform act shifted about $120 billion of taxes from individuals to businesses over a five-year period. This was

The 1986 tax reform act closed tax loopholes for many. According to the cartoon, is the married couple better or worse off after tax reform?

accompanied by removing a number of tax breaks for business that forced it to pay more. This additional revenue was then used to replace that lost when individual rates were cut.

Fourth, the tax act reversed the trend of using the tax system as a tool to promote social and economic goals. For years, for example, people could deduct consumer interest payments, including those paid on credit cards, home loans, and student educational loans. There were also tax deductions for charitable donations and tax credits for contributions to political candidates. Under the old system, then, certain kinds of activities were encouraged.

The reform law removed most exclusions and individual deductions. Except for home loans, interest payments on consumer debt—including student educational loans—are no longer deductible. Credits for contributions to political candidates have also been removed. Individual donations to charity are still allowed, but are harder to claim. The act even makes all unemployment benefits subject to taxation. Before the reform law, some unemployment payments were exempt from taxes.

Finally, the reform law helped many low-income taxpayers, the people sometimes called the "working poor." Some six million low-income taxpayers will not have to pay any taxes under the new law. Because of this, some experts feel that the tax reform law was the most important anti-poverty legislation passed in a decade.

▮ Section Review

1. How have government revenues changed in recent years?

2. What are the four criteria used to judge the merit of taxes?

3. What are the three types of taxes in the United States today? How do they differ from one another?

4. How did the 1986 tax act change rates for individuals? For businesses?

9.2 *Federal Tax System*

The federal government collects taxes from a number of sources. As shown in the graphs on page 219, the most important taxes are individual income taxes, social security taxes and contributions, and corporate income taxes.

INDIVIDUAL INCOME TAXES

In 1985, the federal government collected 45.6 percent of its total revenue in **individual income tax**—the tax on people's earnings.

In most cases, the individual income tax is paid over time through a **payroll withholding system.** Under this system, employers periodically send a portion of a worker's pay to the **Internal Revenue Service (IRS),** the branch of the Treasury Department in charge of collecting taxes.

The person who owes the taxes then files a **tax return**—a yearly report on earnings—with the IRS. The return, which is based on the previous year's earnings, gen-

FEDERAL GOVERNMENT RECEIPTS BY SOURCE

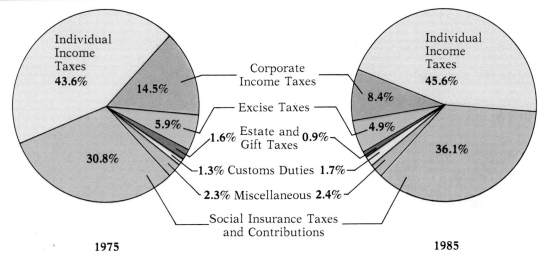

Source: *Economic Report of the President, 1976* and *1986*

Figure 9–3

erally must be filed by April 15 of each year. Any differences between the amount withheld during the year and the amount due is settled when the return is filed.

Any persons who are self-employed and do not have money withheld from their paychecks must estimate their taxes for the upcoming year and make quarterly payments of this estimate to the Internal Revenue Service. They must make a final settlement for the previous year sometime before April 15.

Generally speaking, the individual income tax is a proportional tax. In 1988, for example, single individuals paid a flat 15 percent on all income up to $17,850. After that level, a flat rate of 28 percent applied, regardless of the level of income earned.

SOCIAL SECURITY TAXES

The second kind of federal tax is social security taxes, which account for the next largest amount of federal revenue. These taxes are also called **FICA,** which stands for Federal Insurance Contributions Act. They are levied on the earnings of most salaried and self-employed people and are used to provide minimum incomes in the form of a pension to eligible retired or permanently disabled persons or their dependents or survivors. They also provide unemployment compensation; aid for the needy, the aged, the blind, and dependent children; and health care for some groups.

Social insurance taxes and contributions, also known as Social Security, are proportional up to a point and regressive from

Table 9–B

THE FEDERAL INCOME TAX

MARRIED FILING JOINTLY   **SINGLE TAXPAYERS**

1988 And Beyond

If taxable income is more than	but not more than	Tax rate is	of amount over
0	$29,750	15%	$0
$29,750		$4,463 + 28%	$29,750

If taxable income is more than	but not more than	Tax rate is	of amount over
0	$17,850	15%	$0
$17,850		$2,678 + 28%	$17,850

1987 Transition Year

If taxable income is more than	but not more than	Tax rate is	of amount over
0	$3,000	11%	$0
$3,000	$28,000	$330 + 15%	$3,000
$28,000	$45,000	$4,080 + 28%	$28,000
$45,000	$90,000	$8,840 + 35%	$45,000
$90,000		$24,590 + 38.5%	$90,000

If taxable income is more than	but not more than	Tax rate is	of amount over
0	$1,800	11%	$0
$1,800	$16,800	$198 + 15%	$1,800
$16,800	$27,000	$2,448 + 28%	$16,800
$27,000	$54,000	$5,304 + 35%	$27,000
$54,000		$14,754 + 38.5%	$54,000

1986

Taxable Income

More than	but not more than	Tax is	of amount more than
$0	$3,670		$0
$3,670	$5,940	11%	$3,670
$5,940	$8,200	$249.70 + 12%	$5,940
$8,200	$12,840	$520.90 + 14%	$8,200
$12,840	$17,270	$1,170.50 + 16%	$12,840
$17,270	$21,800	$1,879.30 + 18%	$17,270
$21,800	$26,550	$2,694.70 + 22%	$21,800
$26,550	$32,270	$3,739.70 + 25%	$26,550
$32,270	$37,980	$5,169.70 + 28%	$32,270
$37,980	$49,420	$6,768.50 + 33%	$37,980
$49,420	$64,750	$10,543.70 + 38%	$49,420
$64,750	$92,370	$16,369.10 + 42%	$64,750
$92,370	$118,050	$27,969.50 + 45%	$92,370
$118,050	$175,250	$39,525.50 + 49%	$118,050
$175,250		$67,553.50 + 50%	$175,250

Taxable income

More than	but not more than	Tax is	of amount more than
$0	$2,480		$0
$2,480	$3,670	11%	$2,480
$3,670	$4,750	$131 + 12%	$3,670
$4,750	$7,010	$260.50 + 14%	$4,750
$7,010	$9,170	$576.90 + 15%	$7,010
$9,170	$11,650	$900.90 + 16%	$9,170
$11,650	$13,920	$1,297.70 + 18%	$11,650
$13,920	$16,190	$1,706.30 + 20%	$13,920
$16,190	$19,640	$2,160.30 + 23%	$16,190
$19,640	$25,360	$2,953.80 + 26%	$19,640
$25,360	$31,080	$4,441.00 + 30%	$25,360
$31,080	$36,800	$6,157.00 + 34%	$31,080
$36,800	$44,780	$8,101.80 + 38%	$36,800
$44,780	$59,670	$11,134.20 + 42%	$44,780
$59,670	$88,270	$17,388.00 + 48%	$59,670
$88,270		$31,116.00 + 50%	$88,270

Starting in 1988, single taxpayers pay an extra 5 percent surcharge on taxable income between $43,150 and $89,560—or $71,900 and $149,000 for joint filers—or until the benefits of the personal exemption and the lower 15 percent bracket are offset.

Source: U.S. Department of the Treasury

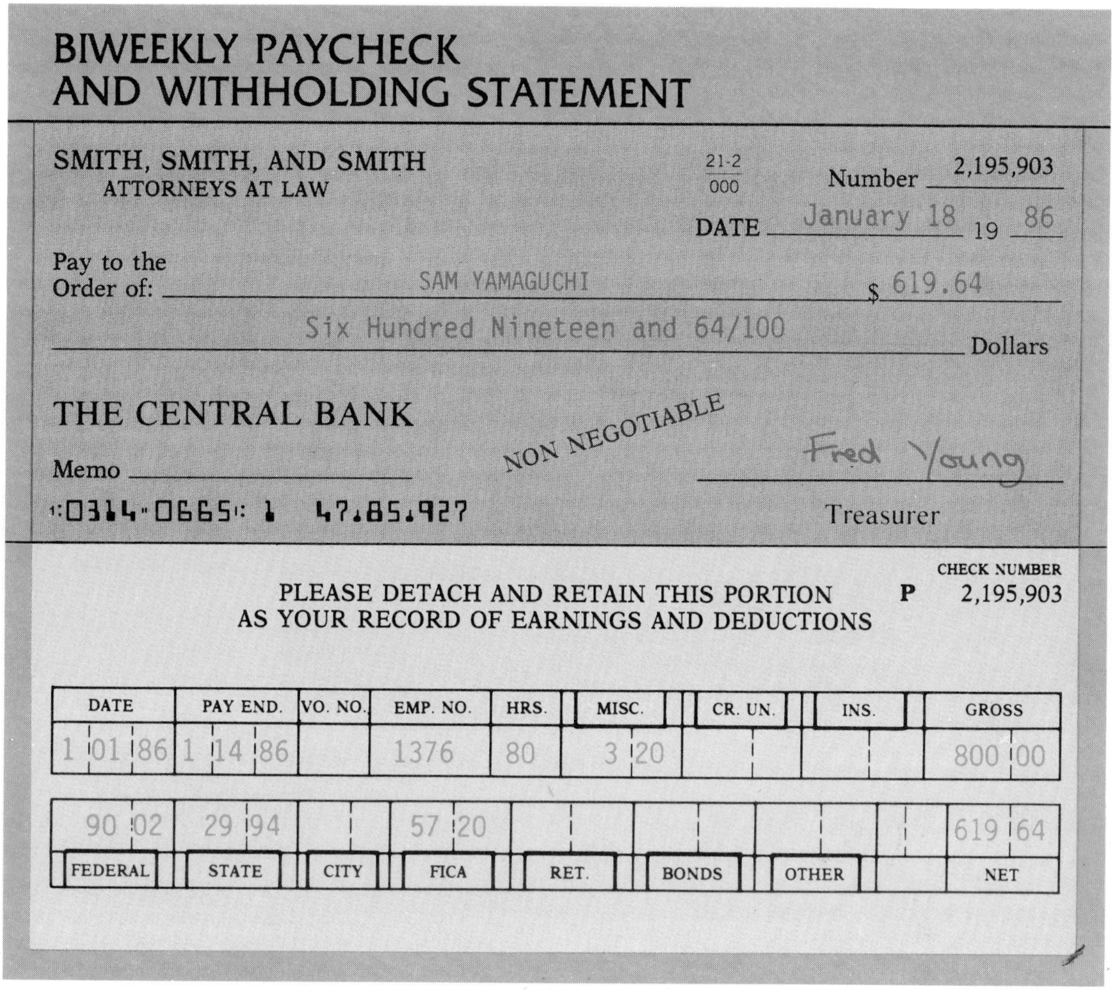

BIWEEKLY PAYCHECK AND WITHHOLDING STATEMENT

SMITH, SMITH, AND SMITH
ATTORNEYS AT LAW

$\frac{21\text{-}2}{000}$ Number ___2,195,903___

DATE ___January 18___ 19 ___86___

Pay to the
Order of: _____SAM YAMAGUCHI_____ $ 619.64

_____Six Hundred Nineteen and 64/100_____ Dollars

THE CENTRAL BANK

Memo _____

NON NEGOTIABLE

Fred Young

⑈0314⑈0665⑈ 1 47⑈85⑈927

Treasurer

PLEASE DETACH AND RETAIN THIS PORTION
AS YOUR RECORD OF EARNINGS AND DEDUCTIONS

CHECK NUMBER
P   2,195,903

DATE	PAY END.	VO. NO.	EMP. NO.	HRS.	MISC.	CR. UN.	INS.	GROSS
1 01 86	1 14 86		1376	80	3 20			800 00

FEDERAL	STATE	CITY	FICA	RET.	BONDS	OTHER	NET
90 02	29 94		57 20				619 64

Figure 9–4

then on. In 1986, any person who worked for someone else paid a tax rate of 7.15 percent on earnings up to $42,000. The employer then matched that amount. Any self-employed person paid a 14.30 percent tax rate.

After the $42,000 figure, however, the tax becomes regressive. A person who works for someone else and makes exactly $42,000 pays $3003, as do those who make $50,000, $100,000, or $250,000. Because of this upper limit, social security taxes have sometimes been called the taxes of the middle and lower classes.

Social security taxes generally are deducted directly from a person's paycheck. Examining the sample paycheck and withholding statement on page 221 will show more clearly how this works. For example, the worker to whom the check belongs,

Most major airports have customs stations. These officials are responsible for inspecting goods coming into the United States. What is a customs duty?

makes $10 an hour and receives a check every two weeks. If the length of the workweek is 40 hours, the worker's gross pay amounts to $800.

According to the 1986 tax schedule, the federal individual income tax amounts to $90.02. The FICA tax for the pay period amounts to $57.20. These two amounts plus deductions such as credit union deposits, city taxes, and savings bond purchases are subtracted from the gross pay to reach the net of $619.46 which appears on the paycheck.

tion pays on its profits. At first, the corporate income tax is progressive, but after a certain level, it becomes proportional.

There are three tax brackets for corporations. The first is 15 percent on all income under $50,000. The second is 25 percent on income from $50,000 to $75,000. The third tax bracket has a top rate of 34 percent on all income over $75,000. In addition, a company must pay a 5 percent surcharge from $75,000 to $335,000. Its purpose is to recover the revenue from taxing the first $75,000 at lower rates.

CORPORATE INCOME TAXES

The third largest category of taxes collected by the federal government is the **corporate income tax**—the tax a corpora-

EXCISE, ESTATE, AND GIFT TAXES AND CUSTOMS DUTIES

The federal government also receives some revenue in the form of excise, estate, and gift taxes and custom duties. An **excise tax** is the tax on the manufacture or sale of certain items, such as gasoline and liquor. There is, in fact, an excise tax on most of the goods almost everyone buys. Since low-income families spend more of their incomes on these goods than do high-income families, excise taxes tend to be regressive.

The **estate tax** is a tax on the estate of a person who has died. The **gift tax** is a tax on donations of money or wealth. A **customs duty** is a charge levied on goods brought in from other countries. Because these duties are fairly low, they produce little federal revenue.

Section Review

1. How do individual income, social security, and corporate income taxes differ?
2. What are the four other ways in which government can raise revenue?

9.3 *State and Local Revenue Systems*

Like the federal government, state and local governments also need to raise revenue to carry out their duties. They do this in several different ways. They receive funds from utility revenues; college and university tuitions; license taxes; insurance taxes; and taxes on tickets to theaters, sports events, and other amusements. They also receive funds in the form of **intergovernmental revenues** —these are monies received in the form of federal grants and other transfers of federal tax dollars.

State and local governments also use many of the same devices as the federal government to raise revenue. For example, many state and local governments impose income taxes, estate taxes, and gift taxes. Some also impose taxes that are like the excise taxes on gasoline and cigarettes.

In addition to these, there are a few sources of revenue available to state and local governments that are not used by the federal government. The diagram on page 225 shows two of these—the general sales tax and the property tax.

SALES TAXES

A **sales tax** is a general tax levied on consumer purchases of nearly all products. It is added to the final price paid by the consumer.

As of 1986, only five states—Alaska, Delaware, Montana, New Hampshire, and Oregon—did not have some kind of general sales tax. The tax rate varies for each of the other states, as can be seen in the map on page 224. Many individual cities also have a sales tax.

For the most part, sales taxes are collected by individual merchants at the time of the sale and are turned over weekly or monthly to the proper government agency. Most states allow merchants to keep a small portion of what they collect to compensate for their time and bookkeeping costs.

The sales tax generally is a very effective means of getting revenue for states and cities. It is hard to avoid when it is placed on such goods as cigarettes and gasoline,

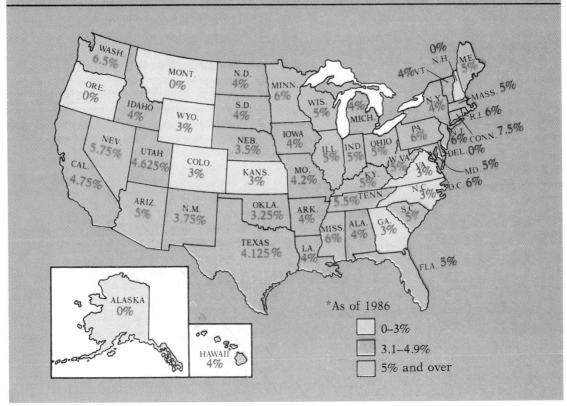

GENERAL SALES TAX BY STATE*

WASH. 6.5%
MONT. 0%
N.D. 4%
MINN. 6%
N.H. 0%
ME. 5%
ORE. 0%
IDAHO 4%
WYO. 3%
S.D. 4%
WIS. 5%
MICH. 4%
VT. 4%
N.Y. 4%
MASS. 5%
R.I. 6%
CONN. 7.5%
NEV. 5.75%
UTAH 4.625%
COLO. 3%
NEB. 3.5%
IOWA 4%
ILL. 5%
IND. 5%
OHIO 5%
PA. 6%
N.J. 6%
DEL. 0%
CAL. 4.75%
KANS. 3%
MO. 4.2%
W.VA. 5%
KY. 5%
VA. 3%
MD. 5%
D.C. 6%
ARIZ. 5%
N.M. 3.75%
OKLA. 3.25%
ARK. 4%
TENN. 5.5%
N.C. 3%
S.C. 5%
TEXAS 4.125%
LA. 4%
MISS. 6%
ALA. 4%
GA. 3%
FLA. 5%

ALASKA 0%

HAWAII 4%

*As of 1986
0–3%
3.1–4.9%
5% and over

Figure 9–5

which have an inelastic demand. Because it affects large numbers of consumers, it raises huge sums of money. The sales tax also is relatively easy to administer because it is collected at the point of sale by the merchant.

A major problem with the sales tax, however, is that it tends to be regressive. A person with a total income of $10,000 may spend $3000 on food and medicine and pay 5 percent, or $150, in taxes. But it is harder for a person with an income of $100,000 to spend $30,000 and pay 5 percent, or $1500, in taxes on the same items. For this reason, the percentage of income paid in sales tax goes down as income goes up.

To counter this regressive feature, many states do not tax such necessities as food and drugs. This makes it easier for many lower-income people as it places more of the load on those with higher incomes.

PROPERTY TAXES

A major source of revenue for local governments is the **property tax**—a tax on real property and tangible and intangible personal property. **Real property,** or real estate, includes land, buildings, and anything else permanently attached to them. This includes such things as elevators and central air-conditioning. **Tangible personal property** is all tangible items of wealth not permanently attached to land or buildings, such as furniture, automobiles, farm animals, the stock of goods in retail stores, and clothing. **Intangible personal property** includes such things as stocks, bonds, mortgages, and bank accounts.

The most important property taxes are those on real estate. With the exception of the personal property tax on automobiles, the taxes on neither tangible nor intangible property raise much money.

The main problem with personal property as a source of revenue is that many items are not always brought to the atten-

Figure 9–6

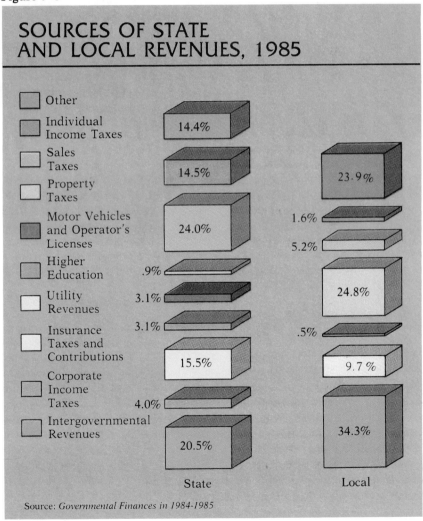

SOURCES OF STATE AND LOCAL REVENUES, 1985

Other
Individual Income Taxes — 14.4%
Sales Taxes — 14.5%
Property Taxes — 24.0%
Motor Vehicles and Operator's Licenses
Higher Education — .9%
Utility Revenues — 3.1%
Insurance Taxes and Contributions — 3.1%
Corporate Income Taxes
Intergovernmental Revenues

State: 14.4%, 14.5%, 24.0%, .9%, 3.1%, 3.1%, 15.5%, 4.0%, 20.5%

Local: 23.9%, 1.6%, 5.2%, 24.8%, .5%, 9.7%, 34.3%

State

Local

Source: *Governmental Finances in 1984-1985*

Profile

■ Martin Feldstein

Martin Feldstein is a noted conservative economist who studied at Harvard and Oxford Universities. At the age of 38, he was elected president of the National Bureau of Economic Research.

In 1977, he received the coveted John Bates Clark Award from the American Economics Association, which is given to the most outstanding economist under the age of 40. In 1982, he was appointed Chairman of President Reagan's Council of Economic Advisors. He

1939–

left this post in 1984, and currently teaches at Harvard University.

Feldstein is noted for his views relating to the impact of government on private economy. In his book—*The American Economy in Transition*—he argues that the high taxes that are needed to support retirement benefits and governmental activities hurt the economy. He believes that the expanded role of government contributes to lower rates of saving and investment, which leads to slower economic growth.

tion of the **tax assessor**—the person who places value on property for tax purposes. Because of this, many things that should be taxed never are.

Another problem is that some property is very hard to evaluate fairly. A third problem is that the rate of these taxes often is so low that it does not pay to make the effort to collect them. For these reasons, many state and local governments have decided not to tax tangible and intangible personal property.

Although large sums of money are raised by real estate and automotive property taxes, this form of taxation is not without its critics. Some people feel that the ownership of property, particularly real estate, is not a true measure of a person's ability to pay taxes. For example, the person who places a large portion of his or her income into building a very costly house will incur a rather large real estate tax. But another person who lives in a small apartment and invests the same amount of money in stocks and bonds may pay little or no property tax.

Critics of property taxes also point out that a person's income and the value of his or her home are related in a very loose way. For example, each of two people may buy a house for $80,000. One may have a high income and pay cash. The other, because of a more limited income, may only be able to pay $8000 and be forced to assume a $72,000 loan balance on the home. Although both are taxed on the basis of owning an $80,000 house, only one truly owns the home while the other owns only $8000 worth.

Some critics also say that many tax assessors are untrained, inexperienced, underpaid, or do not have the help they need to do their tasks properly. This leads to unfair assessments and taxation.

Finally, others argue that the property tax discourages home improvements. Some homeowners will not spend time and income to improve their houses to have the value—and, thus, the taxes—increase.

Section Review

1. Why is a sales tax an effective means of raising revenue?
2. How are property taxes collected? Why are some people critical of them?

9.4 Tax Issues

Many people who pay taxes feel they pay too much, while others do not pay enough. Meanwhile, government at all levels never seems to have enough revenue to satisfy its needs. For these and other reasons, there are a number of tax issues that are always a matter of debate. Five such issues are the incidence of a tax, tax breaks for businesses, the value added tax, user fees, and indexing.

INCIDENCE OF A TAX

In the United States economy, the burden of taxes can be shifted from one group to another. This makes the **incidence of a tax**—the final burden of the tax—an important issue.

For example, a city that wants to raise revenue by placing a tax on a local utility company may actually cause consumers to pay higher utility bills. Although the tax is placed on the utility company, the company may be able to shift the burden to consumers simply by raising its rates. If, however, the utility company is regulated as to the rates it can charge, the incidence of the tax might fall on others. If the company uses some of its profits to pay for the increased taxes, the burden is shifted to the shareholders who invested their money in the company. If the company's profits are not large enough to absorb the tax increase, it may not give its employees raises in pay. This shifts the burden of the tax to the employees.

Other taxes, however, such as the personal income tax, are harder to shift. If

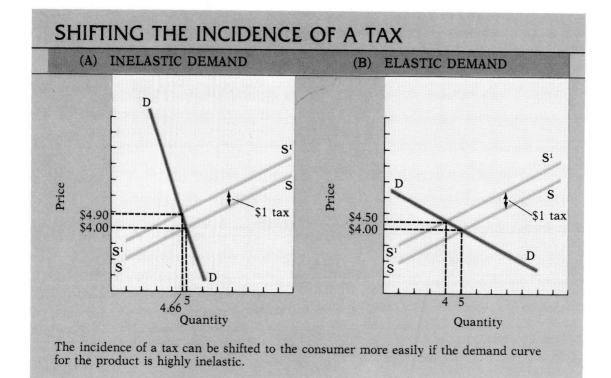

SHIFTING THE INCIDENCE OF A TAX

(A) INELASTIC DEMAND

(B) ELASTIC DEMAND

The incidence of a tax can be shifted to the consumer more easily if the demand curve for the product is highly inelastic.

Figure 9–7

the government raises these taxes, the worker simply has more taken out of his or her paycheck, and there is little that he or she can do about it.

Any government agency that wants to raise revenues through taxation must give some thought to the incidence of the tax. Although in each case the incidence is different, it can be predicted with the help of supply and demand analysis.

Generally speaking, the more elastic the demand for the product, the less likely the burden of the tax can be shifted from the producer to the consumer. This is illustrated in the supply and demand curves on page 228. Before the tax is passed, each market is in equilibrium with five units

being sold at $4 each. If the government passes a tax of $1, the cost of production rises, causing the supply curve to shift up from **S** to **S**[1]. Once the supply curve has shifted, the market must find a new equilibrium price and quantity.

Since consumers buy less at higher prices, less should be demanded. Just how much less depends on the elasticity of demand for the product. If, as in Graph **A**, the demand is very inelastic, the producer will be able to shift 90¢ of the tax to the consumer. If, as in Graph **B**, the demand is very elastic, the producer will only be able to shift 50¢ of the tax to the consumer. In both cases, however, the producer will have to absorb the rest of the tax.

The demand for such products as alcohol, tobacco, medicine, and low-cost housing tends to be inelastic. Because of this, a major portion of the tax on such items generally can be shifted directly to the consumer. If the demand happens to be elastic, as in the case of new automobiles, houses, and some luxury items, less of the tax is shifted to the consumer and more is absorbed by the producer.

TAX BREAKS FOR BUSINESSES

The 1986 tax reform bill removed many tax breaks received by businesses. On the one hand, the act raises a great amount of revenue for the federal government. On the other, the tax burden on businesses may turn out to be too great. If this happens, some of the tax breaks removed could be restored.

Two of the breaks removed by the 1986 reform law were important parts of an earlier law, the **Economic Recovery Tax Act of 1981.** This act reduced personal and business taxes in an effort to stimulate the growth of the economy.

One part of the act—**accelerated depreciation**—allowed companies to speed up depreciation of plant and equipment. It allowed a company to subtract more depreciation from income subject to the corporate income tax. This meant that the company's overall tax bill was smaller. The 1986 reform bill again lengthened the depreciation period. This means the amount of depreciation subtracted from taxable income is smaller, which makes taxes higher. Thus, companies that invest heavily in the plant and equipment pay more taxes under the new law than before.

Another section of the 1981 act was the **investment tax credit (ITC).** It allowed a company to buy tools and equipment and

then receive a credit ranging from 6 to 10 percent of the purchase price. This credit was then used to reduce the firm's total tax bill. For example, a company might purchase a $50,000 machine that qualified for a $5000 credit. If the company owed $12,000 in taxes, the credit reduced the amount to be paid to $7000. In 1986, however, the ITC was repealed in spite of its popularity with businesses.

VALUE ADDED TAX

There are many steps involved in the production of almost all goods and services. At each step along the way, some value is added to the final product. A tax called a **value added tax (VAT)** is placed on the value added at each stage of production. As such, it is a tax on consumption as opposed to one on income.

For example, consider the steps involved in the production of wooden baseball bats. First of all, trees are cut. The timber is then sold to lumber mills that process it into planks of uniform size. The planks are sold to manufacturers who turn them on a lathe to trim and shape them into baseball bats. Finally, the bats are treated, painted or varnished, and sold to a wholesaler, who, in turn, sells them to retailers. The retailers sell them to the consumer.

Any baseball bat, then, has a given amount of value. That value, however, is something that has been added bit by bit, starting when the tree was cut and ending when the retailer makes it available for purchase by the consumer.

The VAT is very much like a national sales tax that would be levied at every step of the production process. The value added by the lumber mill, for example, would be equal to the value of the lumber sold to the bat companies less the cost of

Understanding Sources

■ User Fees

The following was taken from President Reagan's *Budget of the United States Government*. Read the paragraph and then answer the questions that follow.

> Finally, user fees should be charged for services where appropriate. Those who receive special benefits and services from the federal government should be the ones to bear the costs of those services, not the general taxpayer. This budget imposes fees and premiums for federal cost recovery for meat and poultry inspection, national park and forest facilities, harbor and inland waterway use, Coast Guard and Customs inspections, and for many other services.

1. Who pays user fees?
2. How do user fees differ from taxes?
3. Do user fees tend to be regressive or progressive? Explain.

the inputs—which are the trees, labor, and capital needed to turn the raw materials into something more manageable. The size of the value added tax would be relatively small at each step; but when added up, the final tax is large enough to drive up the price of the final product.

As a way of raising revenue, the VAT has several advantages. For one, it is hard for people or companies to avoid because the tax collector simply levies it on the total amount of sales. If the company wants to reduce the size of the tax, it must prove how many inputs were used.

Secondly, the incidence of the tax has been widely spread. This makes it harder

for a single firm to shift the burden of the tax to one group or another.

Third, the tax is not visible to the final consumer because it has been built into the price before the purchase is made. Since the consumer does not know the actual amount of tax paid, he or she is less likely to become angry about it.

The United States currently does not have a VAT, although it is widely used in Europe. Even so, a number of legislators have suggested that such a tax would be a good way for the federal government to raise more revenues. Most businesses and individuals oppose tax increases on their own incomes. So, should the President decide that more tax revenue is needed, the VAT is a likely candidate.

USER FEES

Because new taxes are seldom popular, it is sometimes suggested that a **user fee**—charge levied for the use of a good or service—be required. In his *1987 Federal Budget*, President Reagan proposed that a number of such fees be charged.

The advantage of a user fee is that it shifts the burden of the cost of goods or services to the people who actually use them. For example, the small fee charged to camp in a national park does not cover the cost of operating the park and keeping it up. A larger fee would cover more expenses and lower the burden on the average taxpayer.

The disadvantage is that people would not be able to enjoy as many things if they had to pay more for everything. Many, for example, enjoy national parks because they are inexpensive recreation. Critics ask if it is really fair to charge a fee to view the Grand Canyon, or drive through the Great Smoky Mountains National Park, since these resources belong to everyone.

The user fee is not really new. People in the Northeast have been paying user fees for years when they paid tolls to use expressways and bridges. A user fee is frequently proposed as a revenue source, however, because it does not really sound like a tax. In reality, however, it is a form of benefit tax for the business or individual using the product.

INDEXING

Inflation causes many people to pay higher taxes. Suppose a worker receives a small wage increase—one just large enough to cover inflation. In real terms, the worker is no better off because the extra income offsets the increase in prices. The extra income, however, may be just enough to push the worker into a higher tax bracket. Because of this, some taxes have a provision for **indexing**—an adjustment of the tax brackets to keep up with inflation.

For example, suppose a single individual with no dependents earns $17,849 of taxable income in 1988. Now, suppose that worker receives a 6 percent raise to compensate for inflation. Without any change in the tax brackets, the person would find that the $1071 raise would be taxed at 28 percent since total income increases to $18,920. If the bracket is indexed however, the 28 percent rate does not take effect until the person earns $18,921. So, indexing means that inflation cannot push the taxpayer into a higher bracket.

Indexing of the personal income tax structure is relatively new. It first took effect in 1985 and was carried over into the 1986 tax reform bill. While it is popular with many individuals, some government officials have said that it should not be allowed. These critics argue that indexing removes a significant source of tax revenue from the federal government—revenue that could be used to provide additional government services.

◼ Section Review

1. Why is the incidence of a tax such an important taxation issue?

2. Which tax breaks for businesses were removed by the 1986 tax reform bill?

3. What are some advantages of a VAT? Why is it favored by some legislators?

4. Why do many people favor indexing? Why is it opposed by some government officials?

9.5 _Economic Impact of Taxes_

Taxes are necessary to support the operations of government. At the same time, however, they reduce the amount of income available to individuals and businesses. This, in turn, alters their spending decisions.

The key thing to remember is that taxes affect productivity and the allocation of resources in the economy. If people think that the taxes on income are too high, they may lose the incentive to work. They may see no reason to earn additional money if it means they will have to pay most of it in taxes. If taxes on businesses are too high, they will not have the incentive to expand production. This, in turn, would slow economic growth. Taxes also may affect the amount of money people save and reduce the funds available for businesses to borrow and invest.

No one can deny that taxes are necessary to support the functions of government. But no one knows the exact point at which they become so high that economic

The revenue received from tax collections is used to provide many government services. Each level of government collects taxes. Besides building and maintaining highways, what are some other services paid for by taxes?

growth suffers. To some people, of course, taxes at any level may seem too high. But this does not mean that taxation in general is bad. As long as people demand services from government, some way must be found to provide government with the revenue it needs to provide those services. At present, taxation seems to be the best way to do this.

Section Review

1. Why are taxes necessary?

2. How do taxes affect individuals?

Chapter 9 Review

Summary

1. Most of the revenue the federal, state, and local governments use to operate is raised by levying taxes.

2. There are four criteria for taxes. They must raise enough revenue, be easily understood, easily administered, and imposed impartially and justly.

3. Taxes are based chiefly on either the Benefit Principle of Taxation or the Ability-to-Pay Principle.

4. Taxes can be proportional, progressive, or regressive.

5. The 1986 tax reform bill ended the progressive income tax paid by individuals, made it more difficult for those with high incomes to avoid paying taxes, shifted billions of taxes to businesses, removed many exemptions and deductions, and eliminated tax payments for many low-income persons.

6. The individual income tax, which accounts for the largest amount of federal revenue, is generally a proportional tax paid over time through a payroll withholding system.

7. Social security taxes, or FICA, account for the second largest amount of federal revenue. They are levied on earnings of most salaried and self-employed people.

8. The taxes corporations pay on their profits represent the third largest category of federal tax revenue.

9. Excise, estate, and gift taxes and customs duties account for only a small part of total federal revenue.

10. State and local governments receive a large part of their funds in the form of intergovernmental revenue.

11. State governments receive most of their taxes from the sales tax, while local governments receive most of theirs from property taxes.

12. Five major tax issues today are the incidence of a tax, tax breaks for businesses, the value added tax, user fees, and indexing.

13. Taxes affect productivity as well as the allocation of resources in the economy.

Building an Economic Vocabulary

Benefit Principle of Taxation
Ability-to-Pay Principle
  of Taxation
proportional tax
progressive tax
regressive tax
tax loopholes
tax neutral
surcharge
individual income tax
payroll withholding
  system

Internal Revenue
  Service (IRS)
tax return
FICA
corporate income tax
excise tax
estate tax
gift tax
customs duty
intergovernmental revenues
sales tax
property tax

real property
tangible personal property
intangible personal property
tax assessor
incidence of a tax
Economic Recovery
  Tax Act of 1981
accelerated depreciation
investment tax credit (ITC)
value added tax (VAT)
user fee
indexing

Reviewing the Main Ideas

1. How do the federal, state, and local levels of government raise most of their revenue?

2. Why must the government have criteria for the taxes it imposes?

3. What are two limitations of the Benefit Principle of Taxation?

4. On what three things is the Ability-to-Pay Principle of Taxation based?

5. What are three types of taxes in the United States?

6. What are the major provisions of the 1986 tax reform bill?

7. What are the three important taxes collected by the federal government?

8. How are social security taxes paid?

9. What kind of a tax is the corporate income tax? On what is it based?

10. On what kinds of items are excise taxes levied?

11. What are two souces of revenue available to state and local governments that are not used by the federal government?

12. What are the major problems with sales and property taxes?

13. What are five major tax issues in the United States today?

14. Why is a user fee like a benefit tax?

15. How do taxes affect productivity?

Practicing Critical Thinking Skills

1. Defend or refute the following statement: "The Benefit Principle of Taxation is better for national defense than the Ability-to-Pay Principle."

2. Explain how the federal income tax does or does not satisfy each of the four criteria for taxes. Give examples to support your explanations.

3. gov
ty tax
people i
two taxes?

4. If you were an
wanted to increas

Applying Ec

Computing Federal Income Tax Using a Tax Table

Individual income taxes make up ne one-half of the federal government's reve nue. One way to determine how much tax will be deducted from a person's income is to use a tax table, a chart showing the amount of tax for different incomes. The following example will provide you with steps to develop the skill of computing federal income tax using a tax table.

Tom is a single taxpayer who made $18,500 in 1986. Compute Tom's federal income tax using Table 9–B on page 220.

1. Find the correct table to compute the tax. (Tom is a single taxpayer so he will use the 1986 table in the right half of the figure.)

2. Locate the income line that corresponds to the amount of taxable income. (Tom's taxable income is $18,500, which

4. C

$
$ 23
× 0.23
$531.30 pe
$2160.30 base t
+ 531.30 percent
$2691.60 total tax

For further practice in this sk pute Tom's federal income tax for and 1988 assuming he had the same income.

ome people object to state and local
ernments imposing sales and proper-
es. What would you say to these
your defense for the use of the

elected official who
e tax revenues, which

of the following taxes would you prefer
to use—income, sales, property, corporate income, user fees, or a VAT? Give
reasons for your decision.

5. Discuss what you think would happen if
a law were passed outlawing all federal,
state, and local taxes.

nomic Understandings

arly

'' can be located on the $16,190-
$19,640 income line.)

3. Find the amount of tax on the table.
[Tom's tax is $2160.30 (base tax) +
23% (percent) of everything over
$16,190 (base amount).]

ompute the tax.

$18,500 taxable income
16,190 base amount
2310 excess

0 excess
ercent
rcent tax
ax
tax

ill, com-
1987

Chapter 10

After reading this chapter, you will be able to:

- Discuss the growth and kinds of expenditures carried out by government.

- Explain the preparation of the federal budget and the items included in its major categories.

- Discuss the approval process and categories of expenditures at the state and local levels of government.

- Analyze the issues related to government spending.

10.1 *Government Expenditures*

If all levels of government and all tasks assigned to them are taken into consideration, it becomes clear that governments spend huge sums on goods and services. For the most part, federal, state, and local governments, which make up the **public sector** of the economy, buy their goods and services from private individuals and businesses, which make up the **private sector** of the economy. Because of the large number of goods bought and the amount of

these purchases, the public sector is very important to the private sector.

Many of the goods and services provided by government are called **public goods**—items consumed collectively rather than by single individuals. These include such things as highways, national defense, and police and fire protection.

Still, some people question how many services—and, therefore, how many expenditures—government should provide. Some people want more roads, schools, and welfare programs, while other people want fewer. People also do not seem to agree on whether government should have any role at all in such activities as the supply of electric power. Another area on which people cannot seem to agree is which services should be provided by the federal government and which services should be provided by state and local government.

No matter what their opinion, however, people in general agree that public sector spending is important to everyone, especially since more and more seems to be spent in this area each year.

GROWTH OF GOVERNMENT SPENDING

By 1985, total expenditures by federal, state, and local governments collectively amounted to $1401.2 billion—a number almost beyond comprehension!

Figure 10–1

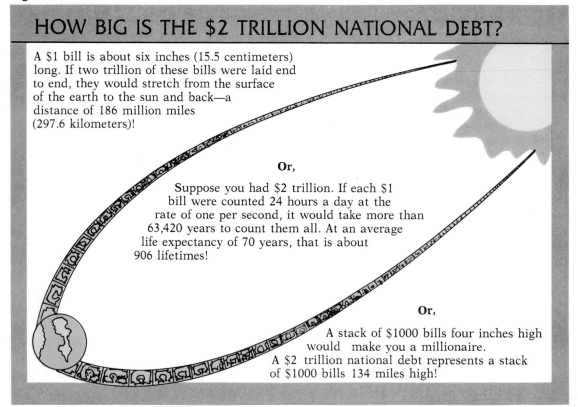

HOW BIG IS THE $2 TRILLION NATIONAL DEBT?

A $1 bill is about six inches (15.5 centimeters) long. If two trillion of these bills were laid end to end, they would stretch from the surface of the earth to the sun and back—a distance of 186 million miles (297.6 kilometers)!

Or,

Suppose you had $2 trillion. If each $1 bill were counted 24 hours a day at the rate of one per second, it would take more than 63,420 years to count them all. At an average life expectancy of 70 years, that is about 906 lifetimes!

Or,

A stack of $1000 bills four inches high would make you a millionaire. A $2 trillion national debt represents a stack of $1000 bills 134 miles high!

Profile

John M. Keynes

John Maynard Keynes was a British economist who, during his school years, was fond of the classics, mathematics, and philosophy. He became quite wealthy by speculating in the stock market and in foreign exchange.

Keynes gained fame as an economist in 1936 with a book entitled *The General Theory of Employment, Interest, and Money.* The book revolutionized the way in which the person on the street and the leader in the American White House viewed economics.

1883–1946

In his book, Keynes argued that during the Great Depression of the 1930's, not everyone who was out of work wanted to be. This was contrary to what many economists believed at the time. They felt that many able-bodied men and women were without jobs simply because they were not willing to work at the prevailing wage rate. Keynes, on the other hand, maintained that while some were not working for this reason, others had different reasons. Some did not have jobs because they had just entered the labor market and were still looking for work. Others had quit jobs with which they were not happy and had not yet found new ones. Still others did not work because private business found it unprofitable to hire them.

Keynes also argued that an economy's total spending is the sum of three groups—consumers, government, and business. If the total spending does not result in a job for everyone willing to work and the private sector of the economy feels there is no incentive for it to increase its total spending to provide enough jobs, the government must spend enough to make up the difference. Keynes felt that while private business has a right to be concerned with its rate of return on invested capital, the government must also be concerned with the well-being of all of its citizens in times of severe economic stress.

Keynes' ideas were not the traditional ones at the time. In fact, many people thought the theory that government spend in excess of its revenues—go into debt—in peacetime was quite radical. Today many people take that and other of Keynes' theories for granted.

In economic terms, the same numbers convert to a government expenditure in 1985 of nearly $5867 for every man, woman, and child in the United States. Since American taxpayers fund these expenditures, it is easy to understand why government spending is of interest and concern to most Americans.

Spending in the public sector did not begin to grow significantly until the 1940's. The growth took place at this time for two major reasons. The first was the huge increase in spending required because of World War II. The second was the change in public opinion that gave government a larger role in everyday economic affairs.

Government was called upon to regulate banks, railroads, public utilities, and many other activities. It also became involved with its citizens' economic welfare. Minimum wage laws, Social Security and welfare programs, education, highways, and transportation all began to receive greater attention. Over time, many Americans came to accept these increased government expenditures as the inevitable consequence of social and cultural change.

Today, all levels of government spend public funds for many activities. Some are services that only the government can supply. Others coexist and even compete with the private sector. Still others tend to become payoffs to special interest groups.

TWO KINDS OF GOVERNMENT SPENDING

There are, in general, two broad kinds of government expenditures. The first is for the purchase of goods and services. The government buys such goods as tanks for the army, missiles for the air force, and ships for the navy. It also buys paper clips and paper, typewriters, desks, filing cabinets, chairs, soap, and gasoline. Government also needs buildings for offices. Then there are the payments for services. These take in the wages and salaries paid to all government employees, including the President, governors, and mayors.

The second kind of government expenditure, known as a **transfer payment,** is a payment for which the government receives neither goods nor services in return. Examples of this kind of payment include Social Security, welfare, unemployment compensation, and aid to people with handicapping conditions. These people receive payments not for what they have to offer but solely because they are in need of funds.

A transfer payment made by one level of government to another is known as a **grant-in-aid.** An example of this is interstate highway construction programs in which the federal government grants money to cover the major part of the cost while the rest is paid by the states through which the roads will be built. The construction of new public schools also can be financed in part with such grants-in-aid.

Transfer payments also include the **subsidies**—payments made to individuals or entire industries to encourage or protect a certain economic activity. Farmers, for example, often are paid subsidies to build up their incomes. In the past, airlines also have received subsidies.

■ Section Review

1. How does the public sector differ from the private sector?

2. What two factors contributed to the growth in public sector spending in the 1940's?

3. What are the two broad kinds of government spending?

Alice M. Rivlin

Alice Rivlin is Director of
Economic Studies at Brookings Institution, a nonprofit organization
that studies economic, governmental, and international problems. Before she took this position in 1983,
she was Director of the Congressional Budget Office (CBO), which
analyzes taxing and spending
options in all areas of the federal
government.

Dr. Rivlin earned her doctorate
in economics at Radcliffe College.
She believes budgets must be

1931–

planned and government officials must not allow budget deficits to
continue. Dr. Rivlin argues that spending cannot be brought under
control until Congress is willing to reform the pension system,
subsidies, and other types of transfer payments.

10.2 *Federal Government*

In terms of dollars spent, the federal
government is the largest level of government. In 1985, for example, it spent $983
billion, while state and local governments
combined spent only $517 billion.

Before the federal government can spend
anything, however, Congress must estab-

lish the **federal budget**—an annual plan
outlining proposed revenues and expenditures for the coming year. If the amount of
expenditures equals the amount raised in
revenues, the government has a **balanced
budget.** If the government spends less than
it takes in in revenues, it will have a

surplus. If the government spends more than it takes in, however, it will have a deficit.

ESTABLISHING THE FEDERAL BUDGET

The federal budget is prepared for a **fiscal year**—a 12-month financial planning period. The government's fiscal year starts on October 1 of every calendar year.

The federal budget is developed within guidelines set by the President of the United States. The President is aided in the preliminary preparation by the Bureau of the Budget. Once the preliminary plans are prepared, by law they go to the House of Representatives. The House is supposed to set initial budget targets by May 15. Between this date and September 15, when the budget targets are supposed to be finalized, the House assigns appropriations bills to different House appropriations subcommittees. Each **appropriations bill** is a law that sets federal money aside for a specific purpose.

The subcommittees hold hearings on each bill and debate the measure. If it is approved, it is sent to the full House Appropriations Committee. If it passes in this committee, the bill is then sent to the House of Representatives for all members to vote on.

If the House approves the final bill, it goes to the Senate. The Senate may approve the bill as sent by the House, or it may come up with its own version. If there are any differences between the House and the Senate versions, a joint House-Senate conference committee tries to work out a compromise bill. When the bill finally is approved by both the House and the Senate, it is sent to the President, who may sign or veto it.

This process was first used in 1974 to put ceilings on expenditures and revenue. If total spending is too high, individual bills can be trimmed under the process. It also allows the House and the Senate to seek advice from several government bureaus and offices, including the **Congressional Budget Office (CBO)**—a government agency that gives projections on the impact of legislation. The CBO will let the House and the Senate know how individual bills will affect revenues and expenditures in the future.

MAJOR SPENDING CATEGORIES

The complete federal budget is hundreds of pages long and mentions thousands of individual expenditures. These, however, can be grouped into several broad categories as shown in the illustration on page 243.

NATIONAL DEFENSE.   The largest category of spending in 1985 was national defense, which accounted for 26.7 percent of all federal spending. This category included military spending by the Department of Defense, and defense-related atomic energy activities such as the development of nuclear weapons and the disposal of nuclear wastes.

SOCIAL SECURITY.   Payments to aged and disabled Americans through the Social Security program made up the second largest category of federal spending. Retired persons received benefits from the Old-Age and Survivors Insurance (OASI) program. Others unable to work received payments from disability insurance (DI) programs. In 1985, one out of every six Americans received Social Security benefits.

Figure 10–2

THE CHANGING PATTERN OF FEDERAL GOVERNMENT EXPENDITURES, 1965-1985 (BILLIONS OF 1982 $)

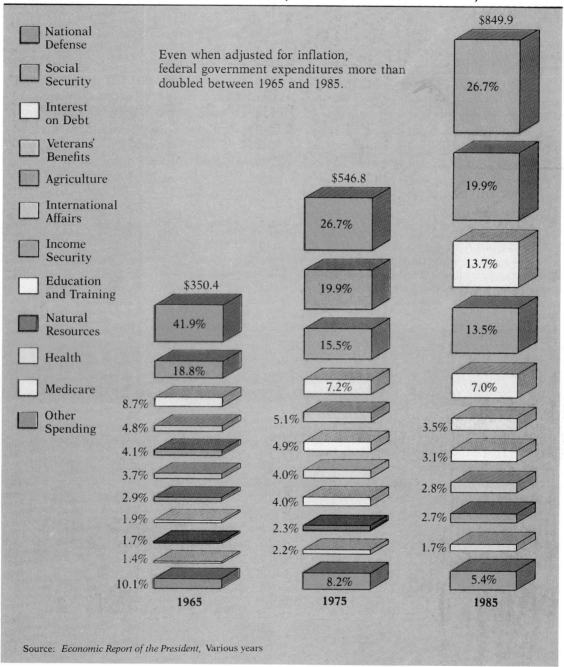

National Defense

Social Security

Interest on Debt

Veterans' Benefits

Agriculture

International Affairs

Income Security

Education and Training

Natural Resources

Health

Medicare

Other Spending

Even when adjusted for inflation, federal government expenditures more than doubled between 1965 and 1985.

$849.9
26.7%
19.9%
13.7%
13.5%
7.0%
3.5%
3.1%
2.8%
2.7%
1.7%
5.4%
1985

$546.8
26.7%
19.9%
15.5%
7.2%
5.1%
4.9%
4.0%
4.0%
2.3%
2.2%
8.2%
1975

$350.4
41.9%
18.8%
8.7%
4.8%
4.1%
3.7%
2.9%
1.9%
1.7%
1.4%
10.1%
1965

Source: *Economic Report of the President*, Various years

INTEREST ON THE FEDERAL DEBT. When the federal government spends more than it collects in taxes and other revenues, it borrows money to make up the difference. Interest on the federal debt makes up the third largest category of federal spending. Interest payments on this borrowed money amounted to 13.7 percent of total federal spending in 1985. The amount of interest tends to vary directly with changes in interest rates and the amount of money borrowed.

In the past, many believed the federal debt was war-related. Large expenditures during World War II, the Korean War, and the Vietnam War contributed to this belief. However, since 1970 the debt has continued to rise because the government spent more in other areas. As a result, people no longer think of the debt as being primarily war-related.

INCOME SECURITY. The fourth largest category of federal spending in 1985 was income security, which accounted for 13.5 percent of the budget. Included in this category were expenditures for retirement benefits to railroad workers, disabled coal miners, civil service retirement and disability programs, and retirement benefits for the military. Subsidized housing for low-income families, child nutrition, and food programs for the poor also fell under this category.

The federal government provides many services. These services—such as training those with handicapping conditions and hospital care for veterans—are paid for by federal funds. What are some other categories of federal expenditure?

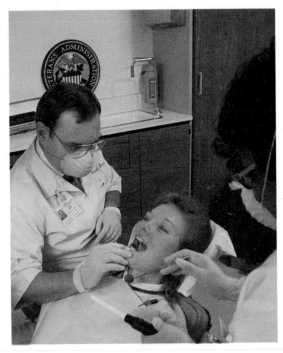

MEDICARE. **Medicare**—a health care program available to all senior citizens regardless of income—was created in 1966. In 1985, medicare payments amounted to 7.0 percent of federal spending. The program provided an insurance plan that covered major hospital costs. It also offered optional insurance that provided additional coverage for doctor and laboratory fees, out-patient services, and certain equipment costs.

HEALTH. Health care services for the poor, disease prevention and control, food and drug inspection, and consumer safety accounted for 3.5 percent of the federal budget in 1985. Federal spending for **medicaid**—a joint federal-state medical insurance program for low-income persons—made up the largest part of health spending. The **Occupational Safety and Health Administration (OSHA)**—a federal agency that monitors occupational safety and health in the work place—was also included in this category.

EDUCATION, TRAINING, EMPLOYMENT, AND SOCIAL SERVICES. This budget category amounted to 3.1 percent of federal spending in 1985. It included block grants for elementary, secondary, vocational, and adult education as well as education for those with handicapping conditions, guaranteed student loans, and summer youth employment programs. Other services such as child day-care, foster care, legal services, and care of neglected or homeless children were also part of this category.

VETERANS' BENEFITS. By 1985, federal spending for veterans amounted to 2.8 percent of the total budget. Veterans received education and training, guaranteed home loans, pensions, and hospital and medical care from these funds.

AGRICULTURE. In 1985, the federal government spent 2.7 percent of its total budget on agriculture. Nine out of ten dollars allotted for agriculture were paid to farmers in the form of price supports, crop insurance, and guaranteed loans. The government also supported the **Farmer's Home Administration (FmHA),** a type of federal bank that makes loans to those with limited financial resources who live in rural areas. Agriculture extension, 4-H youth, and animal and plant health programs consumed the remaining dollars in this category. Since most expenditures were directly related to the prices farmers received for their crops, the size of this category may vary from one year to the next.

INTERNATIONAL AFFAIRS. In 1985, 1.7 percent of the federal budget was spent on international affairs, sometimes called foreign aid. Help for other countries took the form of military, economic, and humanitarian assistance. About two thirds of all foreign aid provided funds for military supplies and training, either directly or indirectly. Over half of all indirect military aid was paid to two countries, Israel and Egypt.

OTHER SPENDING. Other miscellaneous expenditures by the federal government in 1985 accounted for only 5.7 percent of the federal budget. This category took in natural resources, commerce, energy, community and regional development, general science and space technology, and the administration of justice.

Section Review

1. When does a government have a balanced budget?
2. Who prepares the federal budget?
3. What are the four largest categories of spending in the federal budget?

10.3 State and Local Government

The federal government is not the only level of government that has expenditures. State and local levels of government also have them. Like the federal government, these levels of government also must approve spending before revenue dollars can be released.

APPROVING SPENDING

There are almost as many ways to approve spending at the state level as there are states. In most states, however, the process is loosely modeled after that of the federal government. A complicating factor is that many states have laws that prohibit them from running a deficit. Because of this, they must cut back their spending from time to time to keep it in line with their revenues.

At the local level, the approval for spending often rests with the mayor, the city council, the county judge, the board of selectmen, or some other elected representative or body. For the most part, the spending of many of these local agencies is limited by the amount of revenues they have collected from property taxes and other local sources.

At times, state and local governments are able to raise the revenue they need, at other times they cannot. As a result, they often face the problem of not being able to spend enough to please many teachers, police and fire workers, hospitals, and other local and state agencies. Because of this, they often have to try to explain why they cannot spend more money and give these groups what they want.

MAJOR SPENDING CATEGORIES

The major types of state and local government spending are generally limited to things that serve local needs. The main categories of expenditure for each level are shown in the illustration on page 247.

ELEMENTARY AND SECONDARY EDUCATION. Local governments have primary responsibility for spending in this area. In 1985, local governments spent 33.7 percent of their total budget on elementary and secondary education, while state governments spent less than .4 percent.

HIGHER EDUCATION. State governments generally have responsibility for public higher education. In 1985, state governments spent 16.5 percent of their total budget in this area. Local governments, on the other hand, spent only 2.1 percent, largely to support city colleges and universities.

PUBLIC WELFARE. The largest category of spending for state governments in 1985 was public welfare. As the illustration on page 247 shows, one of every five dollars spent at the state level was for welfare payments. Local governments, however, only spent 4.4 percent of their budget on this category.

HIGHWAYS. All states are serviced by a system of highways and roads. The federal government builds and maintains much of the interstate highway system. States, however, maintain state roads, which generally link smaller communities with larger ones. Local governments, in turn, take care of the roads and streets in their county, city, or town. In 1985, state and local governments spent 9.5 percent and

Figure 10–3

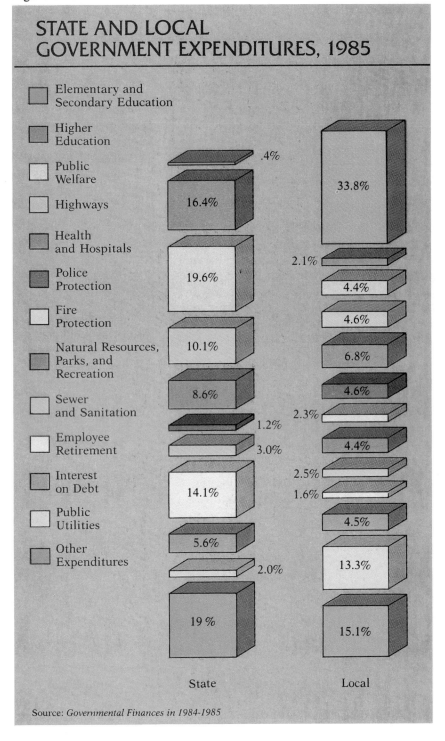

STATE AND LOCAL GOVERNMENT EXPENDITURES, 1985

Elementary and Secondary Education

Higher Education

Public Welfare

Highways

Health and Hospitals

Police Protection

Fire Protection

Natural Resources, Parks, and Recreation

Sewer and Sanitation

Employee Retirement

Interest on Debt

Public Utilities

Other Expenditures

State

.4%
16.4%
19.6%
10.1%
8.6%
1.2%
3.0%
14.1%
5.6%
2.0%
19%

Local

33.8%
2.1%
4.4%
4.6%
6.8%
4.6%
2.3%
4.4%
2.5%
1.6%
4.5%
13.3%
15.1%

Source: *Governmental Finances in 1984-1985*

4.6 percent of their budgets, respectively, on these items.

HEALTH AND HOSPITALS. Many towns and cities have their own hospitals and medical facilities. Since most do not charge enough in fees to fully recover their costs, they often turn to state and local governments for help. In 1985, state and local governments spent about the same amounts on health care and hospitals. State governments spent 8.9 percent and local governments spent 7.0 percent.

POLICE PROTECTION. Most localities have a full-time, paid, police force to protect their community. As a result, police protection is a significant cost for local governments. In 1985, local governments spent 4.6 percent of their budgets toward police protection. Since there are far fewer state than local police, state spending for police in 1985 accounted for only 1.1 percent of state budgets.

FIRE PROTECTION. Because fire equipment and personnel must be nearby at all times, fire protection is almost totally provided by local governments. Therefore, it is mainly a local expenditure category. In 1985, local governments spent 2.3 percent of their budget on this item. Unlike police protection, however, many communities have volunteer fire departments to keep the expenditure low.

SEWER AND SANITATION. Spending in this area, like that for fire and police protection, is mainly a local government responsibility. As a result, local governments spent a total of 4.5 percent of their total budget on these services during 1985.

NATURAL RESOURCES, PARKS, AND RECREATION. States generally maintain a system of parks, lakes, and other recreational facilities. Local governments main-

tain city parks, golf courses, and even some museums. Both state and local government spent less than three percent of their total budget in this area in 1985.

EMPLOYEE RETIREMENT AND UNEMPLOYMENT BENEFITS. For state governments, this is the third largest category of expenses. Retired teachers, judges, police, and many other state and municipal employees were covered by state retirement plans. Many were also eligible for state unemployment insurance. In 1985, this category amounted to 14.2 percent of the total states' budgets. Local governments only spent 1.7 percent of their budgets on this item.

INTEREST ON DEBT. State and local governments, like the federal government, sometimes borrow to cover operating costs or capital spending. Interest payments in this category were 5.4 percent of total budget for state governments and 4.4 percent for local governments. Like the federal government, interest expenses increase when rates go up and decrease when they fall.

PUBLIC UTILITIES. Many public utilities such as water serve local needs. For local governments, spending on utilities amounted to the second most important category of spending. In 1985, local governments spent 13.4 percent of their budgets in this area. Since fewer utilities serve people on a statewide basis, state governments only spent 2.0 percent of their budgets on public utilities.

OTHER SPENDING. State and local governments also have expenses for veterans' services, liquor stores, air and water transportation, libraries, correctional facilities, and various other miscellaneous items as well. State and local governments spent

18.7 and 15 percent, respectively, on these items in 1985.

Section Review

1. What factor complicates the approval of spending in many states?

2. Who has the authority to approve state spending at the state government level? At the local level?

3. What are the two largest categories of spending at the state and local levels? What does each include? 9-6

10.4 *Government Spending Issues*

Government spending is a topic that is often a matter of debate. Although there are a number of different issues, a few are debated more often and more strongly than others.

DEFICIT SPENDING

One issue most people hear about is **deficit spending**—spending more than is collected in revenues. Sometimes the government plans deficit spending. Other times it just happens because factors in the economy have reduced the amount of revenues or increased the amount of expenditures.

The illustrations on pages 250 and 251 for example, show in dollar figures and percentages the federal budget proposed by President Ronald Reagan in his budget message to Congress. That year, the federal government planned to receive $850.4 billion in revenues. At the same time, however, it planned to spend $994.0 billion. The difference of $143.6 billion was the size of the federal deficit projected for 1987.

In a sense, this is just an educated guess based on a number of assumptions about the economy for the coming year. If the economy turns out to be stronger than expected, the tax receipts—revenue—would

go up and expenditures such as unemployment compensation would go down. In a very strong economy, this might be enough to cut the deficit by 50 percent or more.

On the other hand, if the economy turns out to be weaker than expected, tax collec-

The national debt has grown continuously since 1900. What is deficit spending? How does it occur?

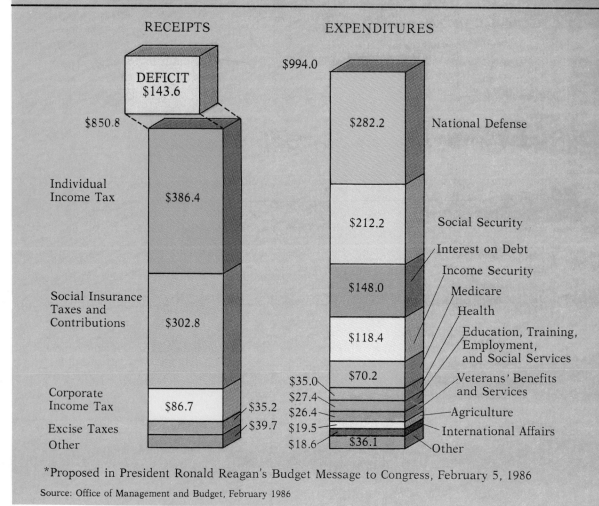

THE FEDERAL BUDGET, FISCAL YEAR 1987*

RECEIPTS

EXPENDITURES

$994.0

DEFICIT
$143.6

$850.8

$282.2 — National Defense

Individual Income Tax — $386.4

$212.2 — Social Security

Interest on Debt
Income Security
$148.0
Medicare

Social Insurance Taxes and Contributions — $302.8

Health
$118.4
Education, Training, Employment, and Social Services

$70.2

Veterans' Benefits and Services

Corporate Income Tax — $86.7

$35.0
$27.4
$26.4
$19.5
$18.6

$35.2
$39.7

Agriculture

Excise Taxes
Other

$36.1 — International Affairs
Other

*Proposed in President Ronald Reagan's Budget Message to Congress, February 5, 1986

Source: Office of Management and Budget, February 1986

Figure 10–4

tions could go down. People could lose their jobs, and unemployment compensation might rise. In that case, the deficit might be 50 percent larger than the one planned.

Recent history shows that deficits tend to appear more often than surpluses in the American economy. The graph on page 252 shows that the federal budget has been in surplus only once since 1960. It also shows that the deficits increased after 1980.

SIZE OF THE FEDERAL DEBT. There has always been a good deal of controversy over the size of the **federal debt**—the total amount borrowed from investors to

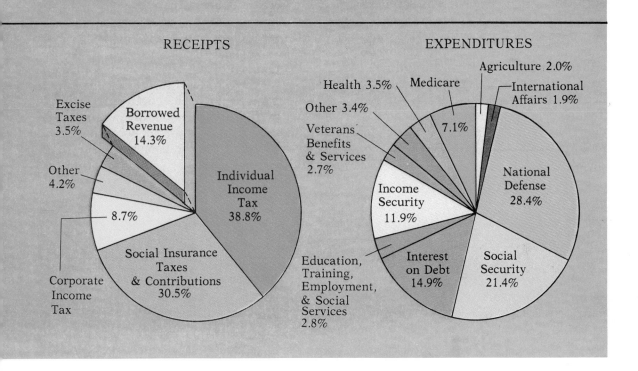

RECEIPTS

- Excise Taxes 3.5%
- Borrowed Revenue 14.3%
- Other 4.2%
- 8.7%
- Corporate Income Tax
- Individual Income Tax 38.8%
- Social Insurance Taxes & Contributions 30.5%

EXPENDITURES

- Health 3.5%
- Other 3.4%
- Veterans' Benefits & Services 2.7%
- Medicare 7.1%
- Agriculture 2.0%
- International Affairs 1.9%
- National Defense 28.4%
- Income Security 11.9%
- Education, Training, Employment, & Social Services 2.8%
- Interest on Debt 14.9%
- Social Security 21.4%

finance deficit spending by the federal government.

The size of the federal, or national, debt has grown almost continuously since 1900. That year, for example, the debt was 1.3 billion. By 1929, it had reached $16.2 billion. By 1940, it was $50.7 billion. By 1960, it had risen to $290.9 billion, and by 1970, it amounted to $382.6 billion. By 1986, the federal debt topped $2 trillion!

Simply charting the growth of the federal debt, however, does not tell the whole story. For example, the graphs on page 253 show that the debt can be measured in several different ways. In Graph **A,** it is shown first distorted by inflation. In Graph **B,** to remove the effects of inflation, it is restated in terms of constant 1982 dollars. When viewed in this light, the

debt remained relatively stable from the 1950's through the 1970's, but grew rapidly in the 1980's.

In Graph **C,** the debt is still stated in constant dollars. However, it is on a per capita basis. Since there are more people today than there were 60 years ago, the debt looks better on a per capita basis during the 1945 to 1981 period. After that, the debt began to rise sharply.

In Graph **D,** the size of the debt is stated as a percentage of **gross national product (GNP)**—the dollar value of all final goods and services during any one year. This graph shows that as a percent of the total economy, the debt began to fall after World War II and continued to fall until 1981. After that, the amount of debt, measured as a percent of GNP, rose sharply.

During the 1960's and 1970's many people thought that the debt was not a major problem. The overall dollar amount of debt rose some during this period, but, when measured in terms of constant dollars, or on some other basis it did not seem too high. Since then, however, most people have become alarmed at the sudden increase in the size of the annual deficit and the growth of the federal debt over the years.

IMPACT OF THE FEDERAL DEBT. Many people have debated the size of the federal debt. Fewer, however, have focused on an even more important aspect—its impact on the economy.

One impact of the federal debt is that it causes income to be transferred from one group to another. If the government borrows money from the wealthy, and the burden of taxes falls on the poor, money will be taken from the poor and given to

Figure 10–5

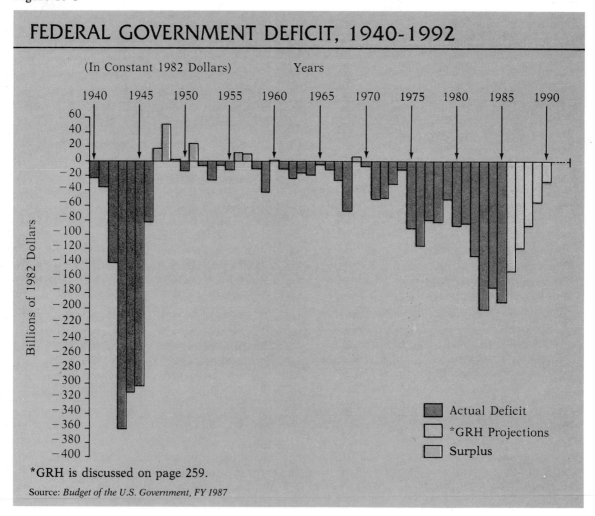

FEDERAL GOVERNMENT DEFICIT, 1940-1992

*GRH is discussed on page 259.

Source: *Budget of the U.S. Government, FY 1987*

Figure 10–6

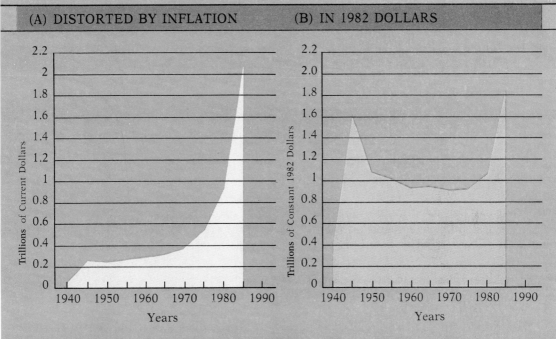

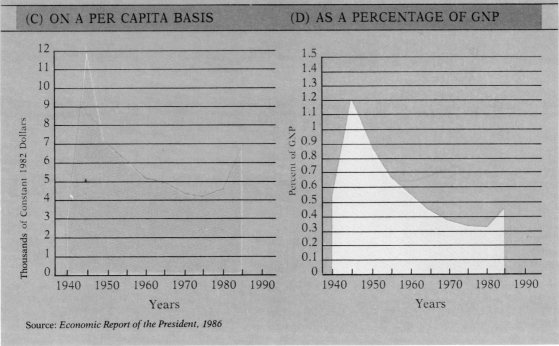

Source: *Economic Report of the President, 1986*

the rich in the form of interest payments on the debt. If the government borrows money from the middle and lower income groups, and if the burden of taxes falls on the rich, their tax money would be used to make interest payments to the middle class and the poor. The actual burden of the debt, then, is determined as much by the federal tax structure as by the size of the debt itself.

Another impact of the federal debt is that it causes a transfer of purchasing power from the private sector to the public sector. The larger the debt, the larger the interest payments and the taxes needed to pay them. When people have to pay more taxes to the government, it means they have less money to spend on their own needs. This, in turn, means that purchasing power is transferred to the government, or the public sector.

A third impact of the federal debt is that the taxes needed to pay the interest can cut down the incentive to invest. Both individuals and businesses might feel that it is not worth working harder and earning extra income if that income is to be eaten up by higher taxes.

FINANCING THE DEFICIT. When the federal government runs a deficit, it must finance the shortage of revenue by borrowing from others. It generally does this by having the Department of the Treasury sell the investing public **treasury bonds** and **treasury bills.** These are a form of I.O.U. that promises to repay borrowed money after a stated period of time. Most of these bonds have a **maturity**—a stated life for a

In 1986, the federal debt reached $2 trillion. How does the federal debt impact the economy?

One way the federal government finances its shortage of revenue is to sell savings bonds. Why are government bonds an attractive investment?

loan ranging from 1 to 15 years. Treasury bills, on the other hand, have a maturity of less than one year.

Another way the government can borrow is through the payroll-savings plan where people can buy **savings bonds**. These are registered, non-transferable, bonds issued by the United States government in amounts ranging from $25 to $1000.

Government bills and bonds are generally an attractive investment for banks, companies with extra cash, investors, and even foreign governments. There are two reasons for this. One is that the federal government will be able to pay off its old bonds when they mature by selling new bonds for cash. If the government cannot sell enough bonds, it could raise taxes to generate enough cash to pay back the old debt.

Second, the United States has a very stable political climate. This makes it likely that the government will be around to redeem its securities when they mature. For these reasons, United States government securities generally are rated the safest of all possible investments.

Although selling government bonds to finance the deficit is convenient, it does have some drawbacks. One of the greatest of these is the **crowding-out effect**—the possibility that heavy borrowing by the government will drive up interest rates and keep other borrowers out of the market. This effect is illustrated graphically on page 256.

In the graph, the demand curve for money in the money market is represented by **D** and the supply of money by **S**. If the government announces that it intends to run a deficit and tries to raise cash by selling bonds, it will cause the demand curve to shift to **D**[1]. The increased demand for money then causes the interest rate to go up. This forces other borrowers to pay higher rates or to stay out of the market.

The crowding-out effect can be a major problem for everyone, including federal budget planners and policy makers. For example, the federal deficit was large during President Reagan's first two terms in office because of tax cuts enacted during his first term and tax reform during the second term. Taxes were cut greatly, but spending cuts proved harder to make.

The result was a persistent deficit financed through the sale of treasury bills and bonds. Since government competed

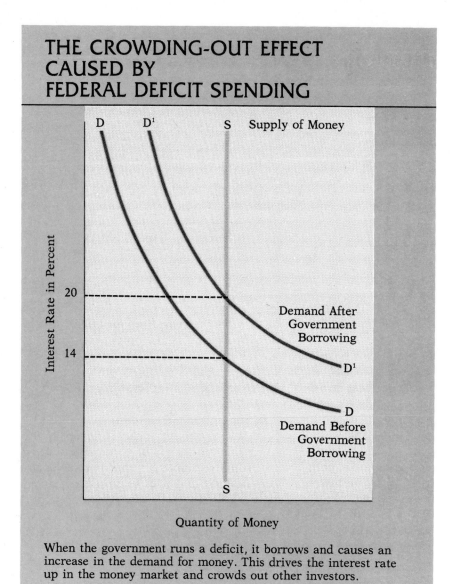

THE CROWDING-OUT EFFECT CAUSED BY FEDERAL DEFICIT SPENDING

When the government runs a deficit, it borrows and causes an increase in the demand for money. This drives the interest rate up in the money market and crowds out other investors.

Figure 10–7

with the private sector for funds, interest rates were higher than normal. Rates finally came down, but many economists still felt that they were too high when compared with the rate of inflation. During 1986, for example, many people paid 10 percent or more for mortgages and close to 22 percent on credit cards even though the rate of inflation was closer to three or four percent.

FEDERAL DEBT VERSUS PRIVATE DEBT

The size of the federal debt has led some people to believe that if it is not brought under control, the United States will go bankrupt. This, however, cannot happen so long as there are differences between the federal and the private debt.

There are, in fact, three key differences between the two kinds of debt. All three are important to any discussion of the debt and have a bearing on the argument that the country will go bankrupt if the debt gets too large.

The first difference is that, for the most part, the federal debt is owed to ourselves while the private debt is owed to others. The private borrower must make sure that he or she can repay the debt at some time in the future. The government, however, can delay this decision almost indefinitely. Although the day will come when the private debt must be paid back, it may never come for the federal debt.

There is, however, a growing exception to this in that more and more of the federal debt is owned by foreign investors and governments, many of them in the Arab world. In fact, estimates place the amount of debt now owed to others at about 30 percent. This reduces the difference between the federal and private debt.

A second difference between the private and federal debt is that the major goal of private individuals generally is to get out of debt. But there really is no reason why the government must pay off the federal debt. When the due date for existing bonds arrives, the federal government simply can issue new bonds and use the proceeds from them to pay off the old ones. As long as the nation's income is growing and is giving the government new tax revenues and new sources of borrowed funds, the federal debt can keep growing.

A third difference between the private and federal debt is that when individuals pay a debt, they are giving up some of their purchasing power. The money they used to pay the debt is gone, which means they cannot use it to buy more goods and services. On the other hand, when the federal government pays a debt, the economy as a whole does not lose purchasing power. This is because when the government pays a debt, it uses the taxes of certain individuals and organizations to pay other individuals and organizations.

BALANCING THE BUDGET

Concern over the size of the federal deficit and debt has led to suggestions for different kinds of budgets. Each of these has some merit. Each, however, also has some drawbacks.

ANNUALLY BALANCED BUDGET. Some people feel that the government should adopt an **annually balanced budget** concept. This is a budget in which the expenditures always equals the revenues generated by taxes.

While this concept has a certain amount of attraction, it also presents certain problems. For one, it can tend to make recessions worse than they would be otherwise. For example, if the economy began to decline and people began to lose their jobs, tax receipts would go down and unemployment payments would go up. To keep the budget in balance over the year, the government would have to cancel other spending plans, which would make the decline even worse.

This problem also appears in the other direction. A growing economy might mean that the federal government could collect more taxes than planned. But if it tried to

Case Study: Career

Accountant

Accountants perform different tasks according to the area in which they work. All, however, must be strong in mathematics, accurate and neat, and able to handle responsibility. Most need college degrees for entry-level jobs.

One major area of accounting is public accounting. Most public accountants have their own business or work for accounting firms. Some are auditors who specialize in examining, adjusting, and correcting the financial records or accounts of different clients. Others specialize in taxes and prepare income tax forms and advise clients on business decisions. Still others are management consultants who advise clients on their accounting systems, department organization, and equipment. Some public accountants become certified public accountants, or CPA's. To do this, they must have a certain number of years experience, pass a series of exams, be certified by a State Board of Accountancy, and be licensed or registered by the state.

A second major area of accounting is private, or management, accounting. Most management accountants handle the financial records of the firm for which they work and provide company executives with the financial information they need to make sound business decisions. Many specialize in certain areas, such as budgeting, taxation, or internal auditing. Some management accountants become certified internal auditors, or CIA's. To do this, they must have a bachelor's degree and three years experience in internal auditing. They also must pass a three-part exam and be certified by the Institute of Internal Auditors, Inc.

A third major area of accounting is government accounting. Government accountants examine the records of government agencies and audit private businesses and persons who have dealings with the government. In addition to working in regular accounting positions, they also may work as Internal Revenue Service agents, investigators, and bank examiners. Beginners, who generally are hired as trainees, must have a college degree.

spend the extra taxes, it might make the economy grow even faster and make inflation worse. Even if the government cut the tax rate, individuals and businesses would have more to spend, and the end result would be the same.

For these reasons, then, the annually balanced budget often tends to either make a good situation better or a bad one worse. It destabilizes the economy as the economy grows and shrinks from one year to the next.

FULL-EMPLOYMENT BUDGET. To get around the problem caused by the annually balanced budget, it has been proposed that the federal government adopt a **full-employment budget** concept. This is a budget that measures the surplus or deficit from the point of view of full employment.

Suppose, for example, that the federal government proposed a balanced full-employment budget for the coming year. To achieve this, it first would have to estimate the amount of taxes that would be received if everyone in the civilian labor force had a job and all factories were operating at capacity. Then it would plan its appropriations to make sure that all the tax revenues it expected to get would be spent.

Under this approach, it does not really matter whether or not the budget actually is balanced. In fact, this kind of budget is likely to produce a deficit if as much as a single worker does not have a job or a single factory is shut down.

Since a given number of workers generally are unemployed at any time, there almost always will be a deficit. The deficit, however, is created on purpose to act as a stimulant to the economy. If the economy is very depressed, the deficit will be very large. If the economy is strong, the deficit will be small.

CYCLICALLY BALANCED BUDGET. Still another kind of budget is the **cyclically ba-** **lanced budget** concept. This is a budget that averages a zero deficit over a period of years. With this kind of budget, some years may be bad and others good. During the bad years, a deficit may develop. During the good years, a surplus should appear. Because the surpluses would offset the deficits, the total amount of government debt would not grow.

While this may seem like an attractive approach to balancing the budget, it does have problems. The chief one is the difficulty of telling what the economy is going to do over the next four or five years. Then, too, because some recessions are worse than others, the past is not always the best guide to the future.

GRAMM-RUDMAN-HOLLINGS

Because attempts to control the federal deficit failed, Congress passed a law to force the federal government to have a balanced budget by 1991. The legislation was formally called the **Balanced Budget and Emergency Deficit Control Act of 1985,** or **Gramm-Rudman-Hollings (GRH)** after its sponsors. Both critics and supporters have called the act one of the most important pieces of legislation passed since the Great Depression.

The law sets a series of limits on the annual deficit, which must be met by Congress and the President. As can be seen in the figure on page 252, these limits decrease each year until the deficit reaches zero in 1991. The following excerpt, taken from President Reagan's *Budget of the United States Government—Fiscal Year 1987,* describes the process:

GRH simply requires that the President's budget meet the deficit targets. It does not impose any restrictions on how those targets are to be set. The President can propose as much or as little as he deems necessary for defense or other budget categories. GRH does not mandate the budget mix, only the minimum deficit. The same freedom exists for the Congress. It may choose to reach the target in a different way from the one the President proposes in his budget. GRH only requires that should the Congress depart from the President's proposals, it must do so in such a way that the deficit still remains at or under the targets.

If the deficit target is not met in any given year, then a series of automatic reductions take effect to reach the target. GRH requires that any forced budget reductions be split equally between defense and non-defense expenditures. However, some items are excluded from mandatory budget cuts. In addition to the interest on the national debt, several programs de-

signed to aid low income families—including care for neglected and homeless children, child nutrition, food stamps, Medicaid, and Social Security—are exempt. Several other programs, including Medicare, community and migrant health centers, Indian health services, and veterans' medical care, are not excluded, but are subject to smaller cuts.

At first, part of GRH was declared unconstitutional, so Congress amended the law to stay within Constitutional guidelines. The legislators liked the law, however, because the cuts were automatic. Thus, Congress could reduce federal spending without making voters angry by voting against individual programs.

GRH also has a safety valve that suspends the law if the economy starts to

Phil Gramm, Warren Rudman, and Ernest Hollings (left to right) are shown during a press conference following passage of the GRH amendment. What are the major provisions of this amendment?

decline. This means that the forced reductions in the deficit take place only when the economy is growing.

FUTURE DEFICITS AND SURPLUSES

With the exception of GRH, almost all of the different budget philosophies have been tried at one time or another. Yet, it still cannot be said that one approach is much better than all the others. Because of the problems of predicting the future of the economy, there are likely to be deficits and surpluses for a while no matter which philosophy is used.

In the United States, those in charge of preparing the federal budget almost always have been politicians who were elected on the basis of their campaign promises. This, plus the fact that it is easier to increase spending than to lower it and to lower taxes than to raise them, has tended to push the federal budget more toward a deficit than a surplus. Then, too, the approach taken to the federal budget tends to vary a great deal from one elected official to the next.

Section Review

1. What are four ways in which the federal debt can be measured? How can the federal debt impact the economy?

2. What does the Department of the Treasury do to help the federal government finance a deficit? What is the greatest drawback of this?

3. What are the three major differences between federal and private debt?

4. What are three different philosophies for balancing the budget? What is involved in each?

5. Why was GRH passed? Why was it popular with Congress?

10.5 *Economic Impact of Government Spending*

Government spending impacts the economy in two different ways. One, it affects the allocation of resources and two, it affects the distribution of income.

If, for example, the government decides to spend its revenues on MX missile systems rather than on social welfare programs, economic activity is stimulated in rural areas and resources are shifted to these locations. Even the smallest shifts in government spending can cause unemploy-

ment in some areas and employment shortages in others.

The same is true in agriculture. The decision to support the prices of grains, tobacco, or peanuts keeps the land, labor, and capital working. Without government support, some land would become idle, some workers would have to find new jobs, and some capital would have to be used for other purposes.

The other way government spending has an impact on the economy is by affecting the distribution of income. The incomes of such groups as the poor and the unemployed, for example, can be affected directly by increasing or decreasing transfer payments.

Incomes also can be affected indirectly if the government decides to spend its revenues for one category of the budget rather than for another. For example, by awarding contracts to industries in one area rather than in another, the government may bring about regional changes in income. Even the decision to build roads instead of libraries will affect one group's incomes more than it will another group's incomes.

The issue of spending is complex. Because of the size of the public sector, it has the potential to affect people's daily lives in many ways. For this reason, it is important to understand as completely as possible the issues relating to government spending. Spending by the public sector is very much like that of individuals and businesses. Even the problems faced by each sector are similar. In both cases, resources are scarce, and every effort must be made to make the most of the funds available.

Section Review

1. What are two ways in which government spending can affect the economy?

2. Why is it important to understand the issues relating to government spending?

Chapter 10 Review

Summary

1. Most levels of government, which make up the public sector of the economy, buy their goods and services from private individuals and businesses, which make up the private sector of the economy.

2. The government provides goods and services called public goods.

3. Government spending began to grow in the 1940's because of expenditures incurred during World War II and a shift in public opinion on government's role in the economy.

4. The government spends money to purchase goods and services.

5. In terms of dollars spent, the federal government is the largest of the three levels of government in the United States.

6. Before the federal government can spend any money, Congress must establish the federal budget.

7. National defense, Social Security, and interest on the federal debt are the three major categories of government spending.

8. State and local governments, as well as the federal government, must approve spending before revenue dollars can be released.

9. At the state level, the major category of spending is public welfare. At the local level, the major category of spending is education.

10. In recent years, deficit spending is one of the most important government spending issues.

11. Deficits appear more often than surpluses in the American economy.

12. The size of the federal debt can be measured in different ways, and people's view of the debt depends on the method used.

13. The federal debt impacts on the economy by causing income to be transferred from one group to another and purchasing power to be transferred from the private to the public sector.

It also reduces the incentive to work and to invest.

14. When the federal government runs a deficit, it must finance the shortage of revenue by borrowing from others.

15. The United States will not go bankrupt so long as there are differences between the federal and private debt.

16. There are three budget concepts: annually balanced, full-employment, and cyclically balanced.

17. The Gramm-Rudman-Hollings balanced budget amendment required that a balanced budget be reached by the federal government by 1991.

18. Because of problems predicting the future economy, there are likely to be deficits and surpluses no matter what budget concept is used.

19. Government spending affects the allocation of resources and the distribution of income.

■ *Building an Economic Vocabulary*

public sector
private sector
public goods
transfer payment
grant-in-aid
subsidies
federal budget
balanced budget
fiscal year
appropriations bill
Congressional Budget
  Office (CBO)
medicare

medicaid
Occupational Safety
  and Health
  Administration
  (OSHA)
Farmer's Home
  Administration (FmHA)
deficit spending
federal debt
gross national product
  (GNP)
treasury bonds
treasury bills

maturity
savings bond
crowding-out effect
annually balanced
  budget
full-employment budget
cyclically balanced
  budget
Balanced Budget and
  Emergency Deficit
  Control Act of 1985
Gramm-Rudman-Hollings
  (GRH)

Reviewing the Main Ideas

1. What are public goods? What do they include?

2. On what issues do people disagree regarding government spending?

3. What is a transfer payment? A grant-in-aid? A subsidy?

4. How does the Congress establish the federal budget?

5. What is the role of the Congressional Budget Office in the federal budget process?

6. To what is state and local spending limited?

7. How are highway expenses paid?

8. Why is it hard to predict the federal debt?

9. How can the size of the federal debt cut down the incentive to invest?

10. Why are government bonds attractive investments?

11. Why do some people think there is no reason to pay off the federal debt?

12. What are the drawbacks to the annually balanced budget concept?

13. How does the Gramm-Rudman-Hollings balanced budget amendment affect the annual federal deficit?

14. How does politics influence the federal debt?

Practicing Critical Thinking Skills

1. Some people argue that the role of government is too large. Do you agree? Why or why not?

2. The size of the federal debt has been a matter for debate. What is your position on the federal debt? Defend and explain your answer.

3. One major item in the federal budget is defense spending. Some people feel too much money has been spent in this area since 1960. How do you feel? Explain your answer.

4. When Ronald Reagan was elected president, he promised to balance the budget. One way he tried to do this was by cutting taxes. If you were a presidential advisor, what spending cuts would you suggest? Explain.

Applying Economic Understandings

Making A Budget

At some time, individuals, as well as the government, must be able to allocate resources. Making a budget—a plan for spending and saving income—is one way to do this.

When making a budget, a record must be kept of how much income is expected, and how much spending is expected during a given period of time. Making a budget forces people to be aware of what they have, what they have to spend, and what they need to save. The following example shows how to develop the skill of making a budget.

A student who earns $60 a week, goes through each of the following steps to set up a weekly budget.

1. Make a list of the categories into which the funds have to be divided. (gasoline, recreation and clothes, meals on the job, savings for college, auto insurance, taxes)

2. Rank the categories according to size and importance. To do this, an awareness of current needs must exist and individual priorities must be determined. (The categories are ranked in the chart below.)

3. Estimate the minimum amount of funds that will be needed for each category. (See "Minimum Funds Needed" Column.)

4. Total the estimated amount of funds needed. ($47) If the total is less than the available funds, allocate more money to some categories. (See "Final Allocation" Column.) If the total is more than the available funds, the amount allocated to some categories must be cut. (This situation does not exist in this case.)

Following these steps, construct a weekly budget of your own.

WEEKLY BUDGET

Category	Minimum Funds Needed	Final Allocation
1. Taxes	9	9
2. Savings for college	15	20
3. Gasoline	5	7
4. Auto insurance	3	3
5. Meals on the job	5	7
6. Recreation and clothes	10	14
Total =	$47	$60

Unit 3 Review

The Unit in Perspective

1. About eighteen percent of the civilian labor force of the United States belongs to labor unions, one of the largest and most influential of which is the AFL-CIO.

2. Organized labor fought for acceptance until the 1930's. From that time to the end of World War II, labor gained strength and economic power. Since then, however, its influence has diminished.

3. Labor-management disputes may be settled by various means, the most common of which is collective bargaining.

4. Workers generally fall into one of four categories based on their general level of skills. In most cases, workers in one category do not compete with those in another.

5. Wage differences among workers generally are the result of either the forces of supply and demand or the influence of organized labor and the collective bargaining process.

6. Contemporary issues facing all workers today involve comparable worth, renegotiated union agreements, and the minimum wage.

7. Most of the money with which government operates comes from proportional, progressive, or regressive taxes that affect productivity and the allocation of resources.

8. Tax reform in 1986 shifted some of the tax burden from individuals to businesses and made the tax structure more progressive.

9. Federal, state, and local budgets must be approved before any revenue can be spent. Unlike the federal government, many state governments are not permitted to run a deficit and must keep spending in line with revenues.

10. In an effort to control the growing deficit, Congress passed major legislation to cap deficit spending.

11. Government spending impacts the economy by affecting the allocation of resources and the distribution of income.

The Unit in Review

1. In what ways has the labor movement grown since the 1800's?

2. What are the major kinds of union arrangements?

3. What relation is there between categories of labor and wages?

4. What type of tax are individual income taxes? Social insurance taxes and contributions? Corporate taxes?

5. How is government spending approved at the federal level? At the state and local level?

6. What are the four major categories of federal spending in order of importance? Of state spending? Of local spending?

7. What has been the history of deficit spending since the end of World War II to the present? What has Congress been doing about it?

■ *Building Consumer Skills*

Filing Your Income Tax Form

At one time or another, almost every American must pay federal income taxes. The following exercise will help you prepare to file your taxes.

1. If you do not receive a booklet containing a federal income tax form and instructions in the mail, get one at your local post office.

2. Look in the booklet for the sections titled "Who Must File a Tax Return" and "Who Should File a Tax Return." Read the sections carefully, and determine whether you need to file.

3. Most people file either Form 1040A (short form) or Form 1040 (long form). Read the section in your booklet which explains what makes a person eligible for each.

4. If you are employed, you should have received a Wage and Tax Statement, or W-2 Form, from your employer. This form lists your yearly earnings and the amounts withheld. If you did not receive one, ask your employer for it. You will need to attach it to your income tax form.

5. The tax booklet also contains tax tables. Check the tables and find the heading which applies to you. If, for example, you plan to use Form 1040A, are not married, and have no dependents other than yourself, you must find the columns for Form 1040A, Single, 1 exemption. Find the figures in the lefthand column between which your yearly salary (as stated on your W-2 Form) falls. At a certain point, the exemption column will intersect with the row on which you found your salary. The amount at the intersection point is the amount you owe in taxes.

6. Now you are ready to fill out your income tax form.

The Role of Financial Institutions

Money is essential to a free enterprise market economy because it frees people from barter. Financial institutions are also important because they help transfer the savings dollars to investors who put them to work.

Contents

Unit 4

Chapter 11

After reading this chapter, you will be able to:

- Define the functions, evolution, and characteristics of money.

- Describe the forms of money used in the United States today.

- Trace the development of banking in the United States from the colonial period to the present.

- Discuss the operation of commercial banks and current banking issues.

11.1 Evolution of Money

Just how useful money is becomes clear if we stop to think what the world would be like without it. Consider what would happen if we lived in a **barter economy.** In this moneyless society, workers would receive various economic products instead of wages. People would have an income, but they might be surprised to find out what they could do with it.

First, without money, the exchange of goods and services among people would be greatly hindered. The individual who wanted to buy meat or gasoline or clothes would have to find someone willing to accept the particular product offered in exchange. People would find that the products they have to offer are not always acceptable or easy to divide for payment.

Second, without money, it would be difficult to measure value. One person might measure value in terms of peaches while another might use automobile tires, or catsup, or whatever other product he or she received as income.

Finally, without money, it would be difficult, if not impossible, to store value. For example, a supply of grain or nuts might keep for a time, but milk, peaches, and other perishable commodities would not last.

As the cartoon shows, a barter economy can cause problems for those
wanting to exchange goods for products they may use. How does money
function as a medium of exchange?

Money, then, is appreciated more when you consider what the world would be like without it. But what, specifically, is money?

WHAT IS MONEY?

Basically, money is what money does. This means that **money** can be any substance that functions as a medium of exchange, a measure of value, and a store of value.

As a **medium of exchange,** money is something generally accepted as payment for goods and services. In a simple barter society, trade may be carried on without using a medium of exchange. In colonial times, for example, a merchant might have accepted a chicken in exchange for some cloth, or a doctor might have exchanged medical services for potatoes. Barter may work in primitive societies, but as they become more complex, it becomes difficult to trade goods for other goods or services.

As a **measure of value,** money expresses worth in terms that most individuals understand. To say that a bicycle is worth a television set or 50 bags of onions would tend to be confusing. But if a price tag in terms of dollars is put on the bicycle, most people can assess its value. They see the dollar price of one object in relation to the dollar price of others. Thus, they are able to better estimate value because there is one single measurement of it. This enables people to measure value and trade with each other using the common denominator of money.

Finally, money also serves as a **store of value.** This means goods or services can be converted into money that is easily stored until some future time. Money, then, enables a period of time to pass between the earning and the spending of an income.

PRIMITIVE MONEY

The use of money is something that has evolved over time in many societies throughout the world. Historically, money has taken many different forms, shapes, and sizes. In almost every case, it has been used to free individuals from the time-consuming process of barter or trade.

One of the earliest forms of money was the brightly colored cowrie shells found in parts of the South Pacific and Africa. Other monies also evolved in different parts of the world, much of it things that happened to be on hand at the time.

In New Guinea, for example, dogs' teeth served as a form of currency, while in the Marshall Islands, fishhooks often were used. At Santa Cruz in the South Seas, the feathers of hundreds of honey-eating birds were attached to short sticks to make feather-stick money. In ancient China, money was tea leaves compressed into "bricks." In early Russia, cheese was compressed and used in trade. And in East Africa, the Masai people used a currency made of miniature iron spears fastened together to form a necklace.

Today, some of these monies would be classifed as **commodity money**—money that has an alternative use as a commodity. The compressed tea leaves, for example, could be made into tea when not needed for trade. Other things became **fiat money**—money by government decree. An example of this is the tiny electrum coins used in Lydia in Asia Minor in the seventh century B.C. These coins had no use as a commodity and served as money only because the government said they were money.

The use of money was something people in each society accepted because it was in everyone's best interest. In this sense, money was then—and is now—a social convention, much like the general acceptance of laws and government.

MONEY IN COLONIAL AMERICA

The money used by the early settlers in America was, in many ways, much like the money used by earlier societies. Some forms served as commodity money. In 1618, for example, the governor of colonial Virginia gave tobacco a monetary value of three English shillings, or 36 English pennies, per pound.

Other parts of colonial America established fiat monies. In 1645, for example, Connecticut set a monetary value for **wampum**—a form of currency made by the Narragansett Indians out of white conch and black mussel shells. Because both the Indians and the settlers used wampum in trade, six white or three black shells were made equal to one English penny. Later, in 1648, the General Court of Massachusetts passed a law ordering that the wampum be "suitably strung" in lengths of one, three, and 12 pennies.

As time went on, other forms of money were also used. In some cases, laws were passed that allowed individuals to print their own privately issued paper currency. Backed by gold and silver deposits in banks, it served as currency for the immediate area.

Some states passed tax-anticipation notes that could be redeemed with interest at the end of the year. The governments printed the notes and then used them to pay salaries, buy supplies, and meet other expenditures until taxes were

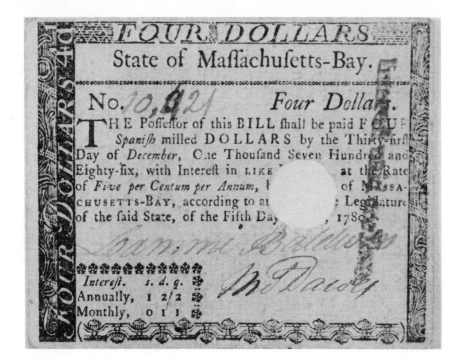

Paper currency like this bill was used during America's colonial period. Why were coins a more desirable form of money than paper?

received and the notes redeemed. The taxes, however, were collected in coins whenever possible.

Fiat money also was issued to finance the Revolutionary War. In 1775, the Continental Congress authorized the printing of **Continental Currency**—a form of paper money. By the end of the war, nearly $248 million had been printed and spent to pay those fighting and to buy materials.

Gold and silver coins also were popular. Most were English shillings sent to the colonies to pay the military and government officials. Some, however, were Spanish pesos, German talers, and other European coins brought to the New World by immigrants. The coins were the most desirable form of money because most of them contained silver. They were, however, in short supply. It was estimated that by the time of the American Revolution, there were only $12 million in coins as opposed to nearly $500 million in paper

currency, about half of which had been issued by states.

Because of the shortage of gold and silver coins and the over-issue of paper currency, people kept using commodity money after the American Revolution was over. In 1789, for example, the year George Washington became the first President of the United States, the region of Franklin, now part of the state of Tennessee, passed an act which paid the governor a yearly salary of 1000 deer skins and the Secretary of State 500 raccoon skins.

ORIGIN OF THE DOLLAR

When Washington became President, one of the first problems facing him was to set up a satisfactory money supply so the country could grow and prosper. This job was given to Benjamin Franklin and

Alexander Hamilton, the Secretary of the Treasury.

At the time, the most plentiful coin in circulation was the Spanish peso, which had come to America through piracy and trade. Long before the American Revolution had begun, silver was being mined in Central America by the Spanish. They melted the silver into **bullion**—ingots or bars of precious metals—or minted it into coins for shipment to Spain. When the Spanish treasure ships stopped in the West Indies for fresh provisions, they often were victims of Caribbean pirates who later spent the treasure they took from the ships in America's southern colonies.

The colonies also had a very profitable trade known as the triangular trade which was used to export rum and import slaves. Molasses from the West Indies was brought into New England, where much of it was made into rum. The rum was shipped across the Atlantic Ocean to Africa, where it was exchanged for slaves. The slaves were packed into ships and taken back across the Atlantic, to the West Indies. There, some would be sold for molasses and for pesos. Part of the income was used to buy more molasses, which was brought to New England.

The pesos were also known as pieces of eight because they were divided into eight

Figure 11–1

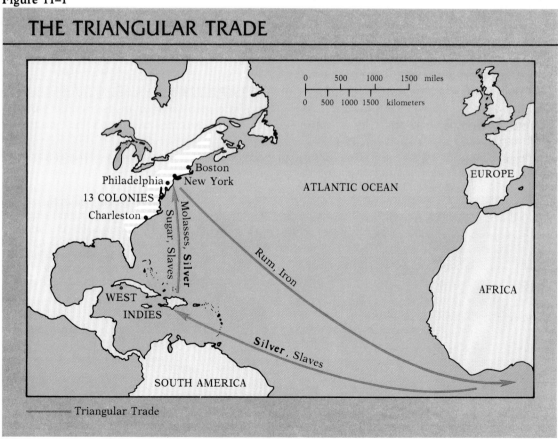

THE TRIANGULAR TRADE

——— Triangular Trade

sub-parts known as bits. Since the pesos resembled the German taler, they were nicknamed talers, which sounded like *dollars* when pronounced by the colonists. This term became so popular that Franklin and Hamilton decided to make the dollar the basic **monetary unit**—standard unit of currency in a country's money system.

Rather than divide the dollar into eighths as the Spaniards had done with the peso, Franklin and Hamilton decided to divide it into tenths, which they felt was easier to understand. Even today, some of the terminology associated with the Spanish peso remains. For example, a 25¢ coin, which is one quarter of a dollar, still is called "two bits" by many people.

CHARACTERISTICS OF MONEY

The study of primitive and colonial monies is useful because it helps determine the characteristics that give money its value. History shows, for example, that if money is to be of any real use as a me-

dium of exchange, it must be portable, durable, divisible, and stable in value.

PORTABILITY.   If money were not portable, it would be difficult to transfer from one person to another. Most primitive monies were very portable—including dogs' teeth, feather-stick money, miniature iron spear currency, and compressed blocks of tea and cheese. Even most of the stone money of the Yap Islands was portable. Much was the size of a modern plate or saucer and could be transferred easily from one owner to another.

DURABILITY.   If money were not reasonably durable, it would not last when handled. Most primitive and colonial monies were quite durable. Wampum, for example, did not require any special care when being handled and still lasted a long time. Even the fiat paper money of the colonial period was reasonably durable because it could be easily replaced by issuing new bills when old ones became worn.

DIVISIBILITY.   If money were not easily divisible into smaller units, people would not know exactly how much they might

During colonial times, animal skins were used as a medium of exchange. What characteristics made the skins a medium of exchange?

need for their next exchange. Most early monies were highly divisible. In the case of the miniature iron spear currency, the necklace was untied and some of the spears removed. The blocks of tea or cheese were cut with a knife. The bundles of tobacco leaves were just broken apart.

STABILITY IN VALUE. Finally, if something is to serve as money, it must be stable in value. This means that it must be available, but in limited supply.

The dog's teeth of New Guinea, for example, were extracted from packs of wild dogs. But since the islanders hunted the dogs for their teeth, the wild dog population never grew too large. The stones used on the Yap Islands were brought in open canoes from other islands over 400 miles (680 kilometers) away. Because navigation was primitive and the weather unpredictable, only one canoe in 20 made the round trip. This kept the supply of stone money from growing too fast.

Commodity money was the least stable in value. In Virginia, where tobacco was money, people started to grow their own. Before long there was so much tobacco that its worth fell to a penny a pound from 36 pennies a pound.

Eventually, wampum also lost some of its value. Many settlers brought industrial dyes from Europe and used them to turn the white wampum into black, which doubled its value. Because of this, and other reasons, wampum fell out of favor by the early 1700's.

■ Section Review

1. What is commodity money? How does it differ from fiat money?
2. What kinds of money were popular in colonial America?
3. How did the dollar become America's basic monetary unit?
4. What four characteristics must money have to be a medium of exchange?

11.2 Modern Money

Today, most nations use fiat money as their medium of exchange. A few, like Canada, China, South Africa, Mexico and even the United States, mint gold coins, but these generally are bought by investors. Whatever the money supply, it must be portable, durable, divisible, and stable in value in order to be useful.

MONEY IN THE UNITED STATES

The graph on page 278 shows the different forms of money in use in the United States today. Of these, however, the most familiar are coin and currency. The term **coin** refers to metallic forms of money. The term **currency** refers to paper money issued by government through an act of law.

COINS AND CURRENCY. The coins of the United States come in six denominations, starting with the penny and ranging up to the dollar. Most are made in part of copper, zinc, nickel, or silver. As can be seen in the illustration on page 279, the actual value of the metal making up each coin today is only a fraction of the coin's face value.

All the currency of the United States is issued by the **Federal Reserve System**, a

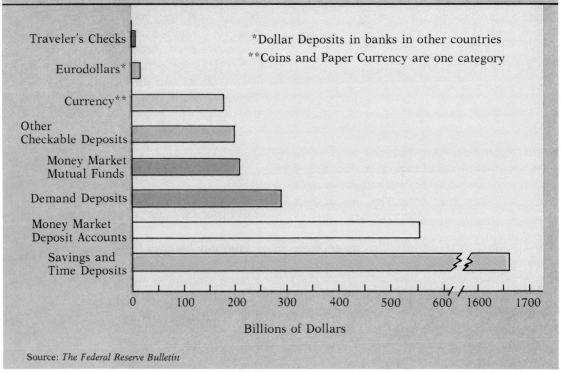

MAJOR COMPONENTS OF THE MONEY SUPPLY IN THE UNITED STATES

Traveler's Checks
Eurodollars*
Currency**
Other Checkable Deposits
Money Market Mutual Funds
Demand Deposits
Money Market Deposit Accounts
Savings and Time Deposits

*Dollar Deposits in banks in other countries
**Coins and Paper Currency are one category

0   100   200   300   400   500   600   1600   1700

Billions of Dollars

Source: *The Federal Reserve Bulletin*

Figure 11–2

central banking institution owned by banks and operated in the public interest. Today, currency is printed in denominations of $1, $2, $5, $10, $20, $50, and $100. In earlier years, however, it also was issued in amounts of $500, $1000, $10,000, and even $100,000. Although people who have the larger denomination bills still are able to spend them, the banks remove such bills from circulation when and if they find them.

DEMAND AND OTHER CHECKABLE DEPOSITS.   One of the other forms of money in the illustration above is **demand deposits.** This refers to deposits

available on demand at certain banks. These funds are available whenever the depositor wishes to have them. He or she removes them from the bank by writing a check. The bank receives no advance notice from the depositor that the money will be removed. It finds out when the check arrives to be cashed.

During the 1970's, some financial institutions began to offer different kinds of checking accounts. One of these was **money market mutual shares**—large-denomination accounts issued by large investment companies. The most popular, however, was the Negotiable Order of Withdrawal, or **NOW account.** The NOW account had a considerable effect on banking. **Commercial banks**—institutions that make short-term loans to businesses and accept demand deposits subject to withdrawal by checks—had never paid interest to the owners of demand deposits. NOW accounts, however, did pay interest. Because of this, some people began to put their money in NOW accounts instead of in commercial banks. This forced the commercial bankers to offer their own version of NOW accounts or risk losing deposits to their competitors.

Today, most depository institutions like banks, savings and loans, mutual savings banks, and credit unions offer some kind of interest-bearing demand or checkable deposits. However, in order to discourage depositors from writing too many checks, many institutions require a minimum deposit or charge an activity fee for checks drawn.

SAVINGS AND TIME DEPOSITS. Two forms of money shown in the illustration on page 278 are **savings** and **time deposits.** These are interest-earning deposits that cannot be withdrawn by check. There is one major difference between the two. Prior notice must be given to withdraw time deposits, while no prior notice is required to withdraw savings.

When people need money from these accounts, they can go to the bank and withdraw it. Generally, this does not cause a problem for the institution. If, however, the withdrawal from a savings account is very large, the institution generally can invoke a seldom-used rule that advance notice must be given before withdrawals.

Figure 11–3

THE METALLIC CONTENT OF U.S. COINS

OLD PENNY	NEW PENNY	NICKEL	DIME	QUARTER	HALF DOLLAR	SUSAN B. ANTHONY DOLLAR
95% copper	97.5% zinc	75% copper	91.7% copper	91.7% copper	91.7% copper	87.5% copper
5% zinc	2.5% copper	25% nickel	8.3% nickel	8.3% nickel	8.3% nickel	12.5% nickel
*Value** 4/10 of 1 cent	*Value* 2/10 of 1 cent	*Value* 1 cent	*Value* 4/10 of 1 cent	*Value* 1 cent	*Value* 2 cents	*Value* 1 cent

*value varies with the price of metal

Source: Bureau of the Mint

MODERN MONEY AS A MEDIUM OF EXCHANGE

While money has changed in shape, kind, or size over the years, modern money still shares many of the same characteristics of primitive money. Most importantly, to function effectively as a medium of exchange, it must satisfy the four characteristics of money.

Modern money is very portable. When people carry checkbooks, for example, they really are carrying very large sums of money since checks can be written in almost any amount.

Modern money also is very durable. Metallic coins last a long time under normal use and generally do not go out of circulation unless they are lost. Paper currency also is reasonably durable with the average life of a $1 bill being about 13 months. Checking and demand deposits never wear out.

Modern money also rates high in divisibility. The penny, which is the smallest denomination of coin, is more than small enough for almost any purchase. In addition, checks almost always can be written for the exact amount.

Modern money, however, is not as stable in value. The inflation of the 1970's indicated that money was not as scarce as it could have been. The fact that the money supply often grew at a rate of 10 to 12 percent a year was considered a major cause of inflation.

▉ Section Review

1. What different forms of money are in use in the United States today?

2. What effect did NOW accounts have on commercial banks?

3. In which of the four characteristics is modern money the weakest?

11.3 The Development of Banking

Banks fulfill two distinct needs in a community. For one, they provide a safe place for people to deposit their money. For another, they lend excess funds to individuals and businesses temporarily in need of cash. In effect, banks act as economic institutions that bring savers and borrowers together.

STATE BANKING

When the Revolutionary War came to a close, there were only four banks in the United States. This was due in part to the shortage of coin and currency and to the large use of commodity money during the colonial period. The number of banks soon began to grow, however. By 1812, the country had about 100 banks. These banks served a population of almost 8 million people.

Most of the banks were **state banks**— banks that receive their charter to operate from a state government. These banks issued their own currency. They would order several thousand notes from the local printing shop and lend them at interest to people who wanted a loan.

The state banks were supposed to keep gold and silver in the form of reserves against the notes they issued. However, most, if not all, did not do this. Some made a business of printing and then lending as much money as possible without worrying about keeping enough reserves to back their notes.

By the time of the Civil War, the United States had over 1600 banks issuing more than 10,000 different kinds of paper currency in different denominations, sizes, and colors. When a person went to the store to buy something, each of the notes offered in payment had to be checked against the latest listing of good and bad bank notes.

Bank panics and failures led to chaos in the 1800's. The development of a national banking system helped resolve the problem. What did the National Bank Act of 1863 do?

THE NATIONAL BANKING SYSTEM

In 1863, the federal government tried to bring the state banks under control by passing the National Banking Act. It set up a system of nationally chartered and inspected banks known as the **National Banking System.** State banks were invited to become **national banks** by surrendering their state charters for federal ones.

Those banks that joined the system had to fulfill certain requirements. One of these was to make public its membership in the system by using in its title the word "National" or the abbreviation "N.A.," which stood for National Association. The first bank in a community to join the system was generally called the First National Bank, the second the Second National Bank, and so on. Once there were a number of national banks in the community, new members used such titles as the People's National Bank of Commerce, Citizens' National Bank, and the Farmer's and Merchant's Trade Bank, N.A.

A second requirement was to pass stiff inspections by the **Comptroller of the Currency,** a Treasury Department official appointed by the President to supervise national banks. Because the inspections were rigorous, the people knew that national banks, as a group, were relatively safe places to keep their deposits.

Not all banks, however, wanted to join the National Banking System. Some felt comfortable as they were, and they resented inspection and regulation by federal authorities. In order to force these banks to join the system, the federal government placed a 10 percent tax on privately issued bank notes in 1863. This led most of the state banks to join. The very small number that did not decided to make loans by issuing checking accounts rather than currency.

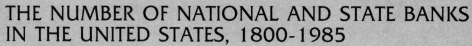

THE NUMBER OF NATIONAL AND STATE BANKS IN THE UNITED STATES, 1800-1985

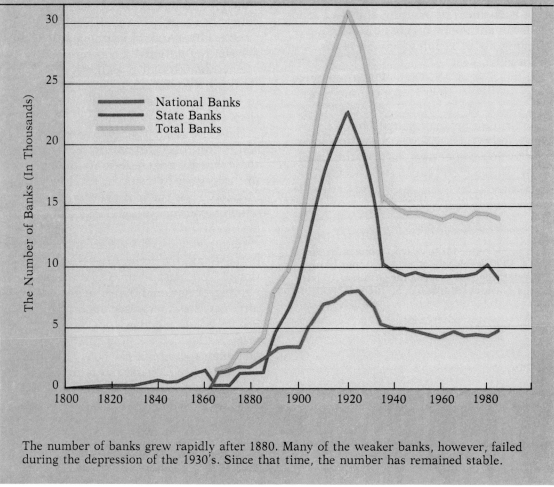

The number of banks grew rapidly after 1880. Many of the weaker banks, however, failed during the depression of the 1930's. Since that time, the number has remained stable.

Figure 11–4

Issuing checking accounts instead of currency was a relatively new idea. After a few years of experimentation, however, many people discovered that checking accounts could be used effectively in place of currency. As a result, the number of state-charted banks, after 1880, began to grow again.

As shown in the graph above, by 1887, there were as many state as national banks in the economy. By then the country had a well-established **dual banking system**—a system whereby banks can obtain charters to operate from either the state government or the federal government. This system still exists today.

Case Study: *Career*

Bank Teller

Bank tellers are responsible for carrying out various financial transactions. They receive checks and cash for deposit and also cash checks and pay out money. In the process, they examine checks for endorsements, enter deposits in passbooks or issue receipts, verify signatures, and check balances in customers' accounts. They also order the cash they need for the day's transactions and prepare cash for shipment.

There are also other tasks that bank tellers may perform. These are computing service charges, filing checks; accepting payment for certain bills; and selling travelers' checks and savings bonds. They also operate different business machines. In many banks today, tellers record deposits and withdrawals on computer terminals.

Because bank tellers are bonded employees, there must be no doubt as to their honesty and integrity. They also must have good memories, be able to work with figures, and be accurate. Since they have constant contact with bank customers, tellers are expected to be neat, friendly, tactful, and courteous. Their working hours vary and may be irregular at times. They generally are expected to stay after the bank closes to the public to count the cash they have on hand, balance their accounts for the day, and sort checks and deposit slips.

Most banks prefer that their tellers be high school graduates. Most applicants are hired as teller trainees. Some, however, begin in clerical positions and then are promoted to the position of teller. The trainees generally watch more experienced tellers perform their duties for several days before doing any tasks themselves. Tellers interested in being promoted generally have to have additional training, some of which is offered by the banking industry itself.

The job outlook for bank tellers is good. Some routine work always done by tellers is done now by machines. This, however, is not expected to affect job opportunities.

By 1910, however, banking reform was needed for several reasons. One major reason was that the National Banking System was not designed to deal with the unusually large number of checks being written.

Reform came in 1913, when an act of Congress created the Federal Reserve System, or FED, to serve as the nation's first true **central bank**—a bank that can lend to other banks in times of need.

■ Section Review

1. What two needs do banks fulfill?
2. How did state banks make loans before 1863? After 1863?
3. Why did the government set up the National Banking System? What two requirements did its members have to fulfill?
4. How does the dual banking system in the United States work?

11.4 *Commercial Banking Today*

Most business enterprises hope to make a profit, and commercial banks are no exception. Because of the nature of their business, however, banks are regulated by state and federal government agencies.

Today, as in the past, all banks must have charters before they can open. If a bank wants to be subject to state rules and regulations, it applies for a charter with the state. If it wants to be subject to federal rules and regulations, it applies to the Comptroller of the Currency in Washington, D.C.

Both of these regulatory bodies require that the owners of the bank invest a certain amount of their own funds in the bank as a protection for future depositors and owners. Since most banks are organized as corporations, the owners will contribute cash or other funds in return for which they will receive stock certificates. These certificates represent ownership and are known as **equity.**

HOW BANKS OPERATE

To gain a clear understanding of the way in which a bank operates, it helps to examine the bank's liabilities and assets. Its **liabilities** are the debts and obligations to others. Its **assets** are the properties, possessions, and claims on others. These liabilities and assets generally are put together in the form of a **balance sheet**—a condensed statement showing all assets and liabilities at a given point in time. The balance sheet also reflects **net worth**—the excess of assets over liabilities, which is a measure of the value of a business.

The illustration on page 285 represents the balance sheet for a typical commercial bank. First, the people who organized the banks as a corporation might arrange to supply, for example, $20 worth of buildings and furniture so that the bank can open its doors for business. In return for this investment, the owners receive stock that shows as net worth. To indicate that the net worth belongs to the owners of the bank, it is entered on the right side of the balance sheet.

Suppose that now a customer walks in and opens a checking account by handing $100 to the teller. This transaction is reflected on the balance sheet in two ways. First, to indicate that the money is owed to the depositor, the checking account, or

BALANCE SHEET ENTRIES FOR A TYPICAL COMMERCIAL BANK

THE NATIONAL BANK OF HIGHLAND HEIGHTS

1. When a bank is organized as a corporation, the owners contribute cash used to buy buildings and furniture. In return, the owners receive stock.

Assets *bankowner owes*		Liabilities *owes to depositors*	
Required Reserves:		Demand Deposits:	
Cash:		*Time Deposits:*	
Loans: *outstanding*		Net Worth	
Bonds: *stocks*		Equity:	$20
Buildings		*Surplus + undivided profits*	
and Furniture:	$20	*Capital stock*	
	$20		$20

2. When a customer opens an account, some of the deposit is set aside as a reserve, while the excess can be loaned out.

Assets		Liabilities	
Required Reserves:	$10	Demand Deposits:	$100
Cash:	$90		
Loans:		Net Worth	
Bonds:		Equity:	$20
Buildings			
and Furniture:	$20		
	$120		$120

3. When another person wants to borrow money, the bank can lend all cash in excess of its reserves. The bank actually swaps one asset (cash) for another (the loan or account receivable).

Assets		Liabilities	
Required Reserves:	$10	Demand Deposits:	$100
Cash:			
Loans:	$90	Net Worth	
Bonds:		Equity:	$20
Buildings			
and Furniture:	$20		
	$120		$120

Figure 11–5

demand deposit, is carried as a liability. Second, to indicate that the cash is the property of the bank, it appears as an asset on the balance sheet.

Actually, the $100 appears in two places. Ninety dollars appears as cash, and ten dollars appears as **required reserves**—the amount banks set aside according to law as a protection for depositors. The size of the reserve is determined by the **reserve requirement**—the percent of a bank's total deposits to be put aside. If the bank's reserve requirement is 10 percent, $10 would be set aside for every $100 deposited. If its requirement is 15 percent, $15 would be set aside.

Now that the bank has some cash in hand, it is in a position to make loans. In particular, it is free to offer the $90 not used to fulfill the reserve requirement in the form of a home, auto, or personal loan. If the loan were made at 10 percent, the bank would earn $9 a year in interest. This income would then be used to pay its officers and employees, utility bills, taxes, stock dividends on owner's equity, or any other business expenses.

Most of a bank's deposits return to the community in the form of loans. The bank, however, might invest some of the cash in U.S. government bonds. The bonds would be a good investment for two reasons. One is that they earn interest and, therefore, are more attractive than cash. The other is that they have a high degree of **liquidity;** that is, they can be converted into cash in a very short period of time. The liquidity adds to the bank's ability to serve its customers. When the demand for loans increases, the bonds can be sold and the cash loaned to customers.

In time, the bank would grow and prosper, diversifying its assets and liabilities in the process. It might use some of its excess funds to buy state or local bonds. It might loan some funds on a short-term basis to other banks. Then, too, a bank might use some of its assets to buy an interest in another business.

The bank also might try to attract more depositors by introducing different kinds of accounts. Once the bank attracts more funds, it can make more loans and more profits.

In order for the bank to make a profit, it must have a "spread" ranging upward from 2 percent between the rate it pays for deposits and the rate it earns on loans. If a bank pays 7 percent for the money it gets, it must make its loans at a minimum of 9 or 10 percent to make enough income to pay expenses. If it cannot maintain the spread, it will incur losses that, in time, reduce its net worth.

ISSUES IN BANKING

There are a number of issues of concern in commercial banking today. They include dual banking, branch banking, electronic banking, competition from non-bank competitors, and the regulation of interest rates.

The bank teller in the cartoon is not really telling the truth. Bank failures were a threat until the mid-1900's. How does liquidity add to a bank's ability to serve its customers?

Profile

Irving Fisher

Irving Fisher, an American economist, received his doctorate in economics from Yale. His dissertation, *Mathematical Investigations in the Theory of Value and Prices*, brought a more orderly and disciplined approach to economics. The highlight of the work was Fisher's proposal to measure the satisfaction an individual gets from the use of a good or service.

1867–1947

Fisher's reputation was established with two works, *The Nature of Capital and Income* (1906) and *The Rate of Interest* (1911). In recognition of his contributions, Fisher was elected president of the American Economic Association in 1918.

Fisher's major contributions were in two areas—capital and interest theory and monetary theory. Fisher argued that the flow of income was linked with the stock of capital by the rate of interest. If, for example, a person put $100 into a savings account for which the rate of interest was 6 percent, he or she would receive $6 of income at the end of one year. If the rate of interest increased, the income also increased.

Fisher also developed the concept known as the rate of return on investment. An individual thinking about making an investment will compare it to the current market rate of interest. If the rate of return on investment is greater than the market rate of interest, the investment will be made.

Fisher believed there were really two rates of interest—a nominal one and a real one. The nominal one is the market rate of interest. The real one is found by subtracting the current rate of interest from the nominal rate. If, for example, the nominal rate of interest were 15 percent and the current rate 10 percent, the real rate would be 5 percent.

In monetary theory, Fisher concluded that doubling the money supply would lead to doubling the general level of prices. He also introduced the idea of a compensated dollar whereby the government would lower or raise the price of gold when the general level of prices rose or fell.

DUAL BANKING. The rules and regulations federal authorities impose on national banks generally are more rigid than those states impose on state-chartered banks. For example, the amount of financial capital paid in by the owners of a new state bank is usually less than that required for national banks. In North Dakota, the owners must contribute a minimum of $50,000 before it can operate. In Maine, Iowa, Michigan, and Vermont, the amount of capital required is only $100,000. The owners of national banks, on the other hand, are required to contribute many times that amount before a bank can operate.

State-chartered banks also have more flexibility than federally chartered ones. The maximum loan allowed by national banks is usually smaller than those of state banks. Most state banks also find it easier to make certain kinds of loans or investments, especially in real estate.

For these reasons, most newly organized banks have opted for state rather than federal charters in the last few years. As a result, it has been suggested from time to time that all banks be required to join the FED, or take out national charters. These suggestions do not please state bankers who resent efforts by federal authorities to control their operations. Many bankers want to be subject only to local rules and regulations designed for local conditions.

Whether or not state banks become subject to more federal regulation remains to be seen. The history of banking in the United States suggests, however, that major changes come about only during periods of crisis. The National Banking System, for example, came out of the Civil War, and the Federal Reserve System was created because of the recession of 1907 and some major weaknesses in the National Banking System.

Dual banking, then, is likely to remain a feature of commercial banking in the United States. This might change if the banking system fails to perform well during any future crisis.

BRANCH BANKING. Most banks have found it profitable to open branches in shopping centers and other areas where their customers are likely to be. Bankers know that convenience is important to people when they select a bank. Most people want their bank to be close to their home or place of work so that they can make deposits and cash checks quickly.

Different states, however, have different requirements for branching. In many western states, banks are allowed to put a branch anywhere in the state. In many states in the Great Plains area, branching is not allowed at all. In other states—such as Kentucky, Ohio, Arkansas, Georgia, Pennsylvania, Michigan, and Iowa—branching is permitted, but only on a limited basis.

Many bankers in the states that limit or prohibit branching often favor branching restrictions to prevent competition from larger banks in nearby cities. Branching laws are slow to change because of lobbying of state legislatures by small banks.

ELECTRONIC BANKING. Today, almost any kind of banking activity not done by a customer and a teller in the lobby of a bank is considered **electronic banking.** Systems that allow people to pay their bills by phone, make deposits or cash checks 24 hours a day at an automatic-teller machine, or have a check verified in a store before it is cashed fall into this category.

Electronic banking is a natural part of the growth of the banking industry. It allows for greater convenience and flexibility, both of which work to the benefit of the consumer.

Some aspects of electronic banking have grown more slowly than most experts thought it would. This is due in part to the fears of small banks. They thought the large banks in nearby cities would use electronic banking as an inexpensive way of penetrating their local markets. When automated-teller machines became popular in the 1970's, a suit to stop their spread was filed by the Independent Banks Association of America (IBAA), the professional organization that represents small bankers in states that prohibit branching.

The IBAA argued that according to a section of the National Banking Act of 1863, the machines should be classified as branch banks. The courts agreed, and as a result, most of the banks in the states involved were not able to use the mechanical tellers as planned. Instead of putting them in shopping centers, adjoining cities, and towns in surrounding counties, the banks ended up putting them in their own lobbies.

Thus, the small banks managed to protect their local monopolies. At the same time, however, they denied consumers the benefits of competition. As a result, the legislative battle between the small and the large banks is still going on in many areas.

NON-BANK COMPETITORS. Commercial banks today are facing more and more competition from a number of non-banking institutions. Some of these—such as mutual savings banks and savings and loans—are fairly obvious; others—such as money market funds—are not.

Money market funds are funds organized by investing companies who gather small amounts from individuals. These funds, also known as money market mutual funds, are then pooled together to make large loans to banks and corporations. Since these funds are not insured, they are largely outside the control of banking authorities. Thus, bankers can pay as much interest as they want. In the early 1980's,

Most banks today offer some form of electronic banking. The banks consider this an added benefit and service for their customers. What is electronic banking?

for example, some investment companies paid 17 percent interest and higher on some money market funds.

Because the interest rates were so attractive, most depositors paid little attention to commercial bankers who pointed out that these funds were not insured. Many were willing to give up insured deposits to get returns greater than the 5¼ percent paid on savings accounts at that time. In addition, people wrote the equivalent of checks known as money market mutual shares against money they had in these money market mutual funds.

Large retailers are another source of competition facing commercial banks. Sears, for example, along with J. C. Penney, K-Mart, and Montgomery Ward, offer many financial services. All own banks and savings institutions in several states so they can issue credit cards and make loans. Some even have their own insurance companies, stock brokerages, and real estate offices. Soon, an individual will be able to deposit a weekly paycheck, get a mortgage, buy insurance, take out a loan, open a NOW or other kind of checking account, and invest in a money market fund without ever having to go to the bank.

DEREGULATION OF INTEREST RATES. To encourage competition among banks and other financial institutions, Congress, in 1980, passed the **Depository Institutions Deregulation and Monetary Control Act.** This removes several restrictions that prevented financial institutions from competing directly with one another.

One of the most important parts of the law removed the interest limits banks could pay on certain kinds of deposits. By April, 1986, **Regulation Q**—the rule that put five and one-half percent maximum interest rate on passbook savings—was removed. Today, banks may pay as much, or as little, interest as they want on savings and other deposits. As a result, banks are free to compete more effectively with each other, other financial institutions, and other firms, such as large retailers, that recently have entered the financial services market.

Unless prohibited by states, banks are also free to set their own rates for money they lend. **Usury laws**—laws regulating the maximum interest that can be charged on certain kinds of loans—are an example of this. These laws are based on judgments that say what is "fair," and they vary widely from state to state. In Kentucky, for example, the usury limit for consumer credit such as MasterCard and Visa is 21 percent. In Idaho the rate is 45 percent and in Florida the rate is 18 percent.

States, however, must also be careful when setting usury ceilings because the ceilings can cause unwanted effects. For example, Arkansas had a 10 percent usury limit written into its constitution. The law applied to all loans, including home mortgages. When interest rates rose over 10 percent in the early 1980's, banks and other lenders often lent money out of state where they could get more than a 10 percent return. The law, then, protected Arkansas residents from banks and others who would have charged more than the legal rate. At the same time, many Arkansas residents had trouble getting loans because lenders took their money elsewhere.

This situation is illustrated on page 291 of the text. The graphs show that a shortage occurs whenever the usury rate is less than the equilibrium rate. When the usury rate is above the equilibrium, however, it does not affect allocation of credit. Today, Arkansas residents no longer are faced with credit shortages caused by the usury law. The state constitution was amended in 1982 to change the usury limit.

BANKING STABILITY IN THE UNITED STATES

Because banks are important to our economy, everyone is concerned about the stability of the banking system. While not perfect, it is still safer now than at any time in our past.

FEDERAL DEPOSIT INSURANCE. Today, deposits in most banks are insured up to a maximum of $100,000 by a federal government agency known as the **Federal Deposit Insurance Corporation,** or **FDIC.** Banks ob-

STATE USURY LAWS AS PRICE CEILINGS

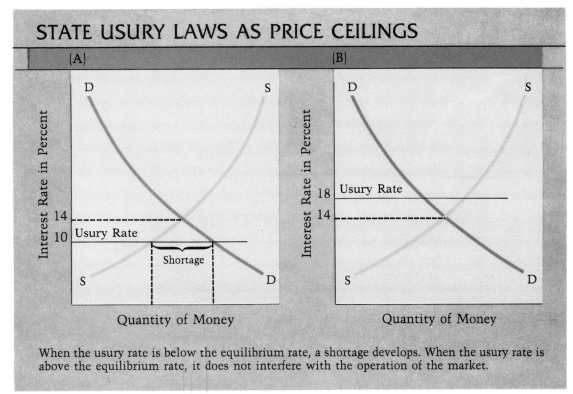

When the usury rate is below the equilibrium rate, a shortage develops. When the usury rate is above the equilibrium rate, it does not interfere with the operation of the market.

Figure 11–6

tain this insurance by paying a small fee, and agreeing to follow certain sound banking practices. Of approximately 14,500 banks in the country, fewer than 450 do not have FDIC deposit insurance.

The government started this service because of the large number of bank failures during the Great Depression—the years from 1929 to 1933, which rank as the worst economic collapse in the history of the United States. During this period, widespread concern about the safety of the deposits often caused a **run on the bank**— a rush by depositors to withdraw their funds from a bank before that bank fails. Since nearly one out of every four banks closed during the Depression, it is easy to see why people panicked.

Once the FDIC was created, however, people began to worry less about the safety of their deposits. Today, people know that their banks have passed rigid inspections and are regulated by a federal agency. Second, they know their deposits are insured. As a result, today there is little reason to have a run on a bank.

Banks that do not have FDIC insurance were generally in operation before the Great Depression, when the insurance legislation was passed. Today, FDIC insurance is required for all new banks. Most states also require FDIC insurance before a new branch office is granted or before a merger can take place. As a result, the number of non-insured banks is not expected to grow.

The Federal Deposit Insurance Corporation (FDIC) protects depositors in banks insured by it. What may the FDIC do with problem banks?

BANK FAILURES. Even though the FDIC protects depositors, bank failures continue to be a problem. As shown in the graph on page 294, the number of bank failures has increased substantially in recent years. In 1985, for example, a record 120 insured banks failed. The numbers in the table also do not reflect the number of non-FDIC insured banks that failed during the same period.

There are three reasons why bank failures are a problem. First, owners lose whatever investment they might have in a bank. This is a personal hardship for them just as the failure of any other business hurts its owners. Since most banks are incorporated, a bank failure means that the shares of stock are worthless.

Second, publicity surrounding a bank failure strains the credibility of the banking system as a whole. The failure of one bank sometimes will cause people to fear that others might fail. As a result, some depositors might try to withdraw funds or cancel other dealings they have with perfectly sound banks.

Third, depositors of a failed bank are hurt because they lose money too. The extent of damage, however, depends on whether the bank is insured and, if so, how fast the FDIC comes to the rescue. Since the FDIC inspects banks on a regular basis, it generally knows ahead of time when a bank is in trouble. If it is, the FDIC adds the bank's name to a confidential **problem bank list** that it watches closely. If things get worse, the FDIC takes control of the bank. Then, it can either sell the problem bank to a stronger one, or it can liquidate the bank and pay off the depositors. About half of the banks that fail are then sold and the other half are dissolved.

When the FDIC takes control of a bank, even the shareholders know nothing of its activities. The sale of one bank to another only takes a few days, and services are seldom interrupted. Usually people only find out about the sale when the bank opens for business under a new name. The FDIC uses such secrecy to prevent panic withdrawals and to prevent shareholders

Understanding Sources

■ Bank Failures

The following newspaper article on bank failures appeared in the *Kentucky Post* on November 8, 1986. Read the paragraph and answer the questions that follow.

> ### Most Bank Failures Since Depression
>
> Two more banks in farming and energy states failed Friday, bringing the number of bank failures to 122 this year, the highest number since the Depression. The Federal Deposit Insurance Corp. said it closed an agricultural bank in Chokio, Minn., and another bank in Baton Rouge, La. The failures topped the old post-Depression record of 120 set last year.

1. At the time of the article, how many banks had failed in 1986?
2. How did this compare with bank failures during the previous year?
3. What types of banks were they?

from selling their worthless stock to unsuspecting investors.

When the FDIC cannot find a buyer for the problem bank, it may declare the bank insolvent and close its doors. Within a few days of the bank's closure the FDIC begins to pay off depositors directly. Generally this is a speedy process, but there have been cases where it has taken several months for depositors to recover their money.

Depositors, of course, only receive payments up to the $100,000 insurance limit. If an account has more than this, the depositor must go to court as a **creditor**—a person or institution to whom money is owed—and, along with other creditors, file suit to recover the rest of the deposit. If the bank happens to be uninsured, depositors and others who have valuables stored in safe deposit boxes are simply out of luck. The chance that a depositor will go to court and recover much, if anything, from the owners of an uninsured, failed bank is quite small.

There are many reasons why banks fail, but poor management is the main one. This can happen when a bank makes loans without adequate **collateral**—property or other security used to guarantee repayment of a loan. Or the bank simply may not keep its expenses in line with its revenues. At other times, a bank may also be the victim of a weak economy.

For example, many **agricultural banks**—or banks with more than twenty-five percent of their loans in agriculture—have been hit hard recently because of falling land values and low prices for farm products. **Energy banks**—banks with more than one-quarter of their loans in gas, oil, and

other energy areas—were also hit hard when oil prices declined sharply in 1985 and 1986. Many of these banks were managed well, but were unable to avoid failure simply because too many of their loans were concentrated in a weak industry.

Despite the recent increase in the number of failed banks, the banking system is still quite sound. In fact, much of the stability of the banking system today is due to the regulation and supervision of the FDIC. By the end of 1985, the FDIC insurance fund, the account used to pay depositors of failed FDIC insured banks, had approximately 18 billion dollars. In addition, the FDIC and other federal regulatory agencies are working to better coordinate and improve the quality of their standards and inspections.

Figure 11–7

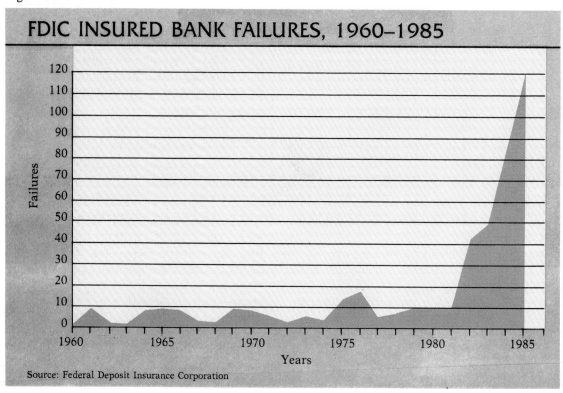

FDIC INSURED BANK FAILURES, 1960–1985

Source: Federal Deposit Insurance Corporation

1. How do bank owners receive equity?
2. In what ways are bank deposits used?
3. What are five issues in banking today?

4. Why was the Federal Deposit Insurance Corporation created?

5. What is the major reason for many bank failures?

Chapter 11 Review

Summary

1. Money is anything that serves as a medium of exchange, a measure of value, and a store of value.

2. Over time, money has taken many different forms, shapes, and sizes, and freed people from the time-consuming process of barter and trade.

3. Some early forms of money were commodity monies and fiat monies.

4. The dollar was based on the Spanish peso.

5. Money must be portable, durable, divisible, and stable in value to be useful as a medium of exchange.

6. Modern money is fiat money. Modern money in the United States includes coins, currency, demand deposits, and time and savings deposits.

7. Compared to primitive money, modern money is portable, durable, divisible, and reasonably stable in value.

8. Banks fulfill two needs. They provide a safe place for depositors' money and they lend excess funds to individuals and businesses.

9. By 1887, the United States had a dual banking system made up of state and national banks.

10. Because of a need for banking reform, the Federal Reserve System was established in 1913 as the first true central bank in the United States.

11. Today, both federal and state regulatory agencies require bank owners to invest funds in the bank to protect future owners and depositors.

12. Banks set aside some of the money received in deposits as a reserve. The rest is loaned out to be used for other investments.

13. Banks make a profit on the "spread" between the rate they pay for deposits and the rate they earn on loans.

14. Contemporary issues in banking include dual banking, branch banking, electronic banking, non-bank competitors, and deregulation of interest rates.

15. Because banks are important to our economy, the federal government tries to assure their stability through the Federal Deposit Insurance Corporation.

■ Building an Economic Vocabulary

barter economy
money
medium of exchange
measure of value
store of value
commodity money
fiat money
wampum
Continental Currency
bullion
monetary unit
coin
currency
Federal Reserve System
demand deposits
money market
   mutual shares

NOW account
commercial banks
savings deposits
time deposits
state banks
National Banking System
national banks
Comptroller of the
   Currency
dual banking system
central bank
equity
liabilities
assets
balance sheet
net worth
required reserves

reserve requirement
liquidity
electronic banking
money market funds
Depository Institutions
   Deregulation and
   Monetary Control Act
Regulation Q
usury laws
Federal Deposit Insurance
   Corporation (FDIC)
run on the bank
problem bank list
creditor
collateral
agricultural banks
energy banks

■ Reviewing the Main Ideas

1. How would the lack of money make the world a different place?

2. What are the functions of money?

3. What were some primitive monies?

4. In what ways did the American colonists satisfy their need for money?

5. How does modern money differ from primitive money? How is it similar?

6. Why does modern United States money serve satisfactorily as a medium of exchange?

7. How did authorities force state banks to join the National Banking System?

8. Why was the Federal Reserve System created?

9. How is a commercial bank like any other business? How is it different?

10. In what ways are state banks different from national banks?

11. Why is the "spread" important to bankers?

12. Why is dual banking an issue today?

13. How are the issues of branch banking and electronic banking related?

14. In what ways do non-bank competitors compete with banks?

15. How has the deregulated interest rate helped banks compete with other banks?

16. What three groups are hurt when banks fail?

1. The g
   is its la
   would you
   Why or why

2. Many bankers feel
   ing system strengthen
   giving bankers a choice
   Do you agree or disagree?
   for your answer.

Applying Economi

Making Comparisons

Economic data is compared throughout the study of economics. To *compare* means to examine in order to identify similarities or differences. Things that are very much alike or very different can be compared. For any comparison to be complete, however, at least one similarity and one difference must be noted.

Some commonly accepted words and phrases are used when making comparisons. Such words and phrases as *similarly, likewise, both,* and *as well as* indicate similarities. Such words and phrases as *however, but,* and *on the other hand* indicate differences.

To make an effective comparison, some questions must be asked. In the example below, these questions are used to compare commodity money and fiat money.

1. What do I want to compare? (commodity money and fiat money)

fo

3. On wh
   concentra

4. What similari
   mon area? (Both
   used in trade to pu
   services. Both measur

5. What differences are there
   mon area? (Commodity mone
   tea leaves or compressed chee
   used as food when not used i
   while fiat money, such as co
   pum, can only be used as m

For further practice in makin
sons, examine the similarities
ences between state banks and
banks.

Practicing Critical Thinking Skills

reatest weakness of modern money
k of stability in value. What
do to remedy this situation?
not?

hat the dual bank-
s the economy by
of regulators.
Give reasons

Understandings

3. Attack or defend the following statement: "Branching, electronic banking,
and non-bank competitors threaten
commercial banking."

4. Regulation Q went out of existence in
1986. Now, banks may pay whatever
interest they want on savings and other
deposits. In your opinion, has this
helped banks or hurt them in regard to
non-bank competitors?

2. What do the two types of money have
in common that I can compare? (origin,
rm, uses, size)

ich common area do I want to
te? (uses)

ies are there in this com-
types of money are
rchase goods and
value.)

n this com-

Chapter 12

After reading this chapter, you will be able to:

- Describe the purpose of a monetary standard and the four types that have been used in the United States.

- Discuss the structure and responsibilities of the Federal Reserve System.

- Explain how the three tools of monetary policy expand and contract the money supply.

- Analyze the effectiveness of monetary policy.

12.1 Monetary Standards

Money does more than make it easy to buy and sell things. It also frees time and other resources so that people—and the economy—are productive. Therefore, in order for a complex economy like that of the United States to run smoothly, it needs a reliable money supply. A **monetary standard**—the mechanism designed to keep the money supply portable, durable, divisible, and stable in value—helps keep the money supply reliable.

The United States has had several monetary standards over the years. Among the most important were privately issued bank notes, the gold standard, and paper currency known as the inconvertible fiat money standard.

PRIVATELY ISSUED BANK NOTES

During the Revolutionary War, nearly $250 million worth of Continental Currency was printed. Because of the problems that resulted, the framers of the Constitution were leery of the federal government printing money. Congress was granted the exclusive power to coin money, but the government refrained from printing currency well into the nineteenth century.

As a result, the major component of the money supply until the Civil War was paper currency issued by privately owned, state-chartered banks. The notes were supposed to be backed by reserves kept at the issuing bank so that people could redeem them for gold or silver.

Most banks printed only the amount of currency they could back with gold and silver. Others, however, were not content with that. They printed large amounts of currency that was spent in distant cities. Then, the banks hoped that it would take some time for the notes to return to them for redemption. Because of this, these banks often were called **wildcat banks.** People claimed that a person had to be a wildcat to get to them.

Even when the banks were honest, there were two problems. For one, each bank issued a different currency. That meant that hundreds of different kinds of notes could be in circulation in any given city. For another, there was the temptation to issue too many notes. When a bank wanted to make a loan or buy goods or services, it had only to print more currency.

GREENBACK STANDARD

After the Civil War erupted, Congress passed the **Legal Tender Act** of 1862. This law gave the federal government the right to print a new kind of currency called **United States notes.** Although these notes had no gold or silver backing, they were declared **legal tender**—fiat currency that must be accepted in payment for debts. This currency was used chiefly to finance the North's Civil War expenditures.

This one-dollar bill is but one of many printed privately in the 1800's. Such paper currency accounted for most of the money supply until the Civil War. Who issued this kind of currency?

Because they were printed with green ink to distinguish them from the state notes already in circulation, the notes soon were dubbed **greenbacks.** By 1863, they accounted for almost one half of the currency in circulation.

The government also issued **gold certificates**—paper currency backed by gold. These were printed in large denominations as early as 1863 and were used only by banks to settle differences. By 1882, however, the government began printing them in smaller denominations for general use. The National Banking System also printed currency called **national bank notes,** which was backed by U.S. government bonds.

Later, the federal government issued other kinds of paper currency as well. One was **silver certificates**—paper currency backed by silver coins—which were introduced in 1886. Silver dollars had been a part of the country's coinage long before then. By the 1880's, however, there were more coins in circulation than people would use because of their bulk and inconvenience. To please silver producers, the government agreed to buy their silver and hold it in reserve against the silver certificates. In 1890, the Treasury issued **Treasury coin notes**—paper currency redeemable in both gold and silver.

Even though there were other currencies in circulation between the Civil War and 1900, the largest number of bills were greenbacks. For this reason, the country was considered to be on a greenback standard during this period.

GOLD STANDARD

In 1900, the United States Congress passed the **Gold Standard Act** that defined the dollar as being worth 1/20.67 oz. of gold. In so doing, it put the country on a **gold standard**—a monetary standard under which the basic unit of currency is equivalent to, and can be exchanged for, a certain amount of gold.

The Gold Standard Act retired treasury coin notes, but it did little else to affect the currency at the time. People continued to use gold certificates, silver certificates, United States notes, and national bank notes. The only difference was that they could exchange their notes for gold at the Treasury whenever they wanted.

In general, a gold standard has two major advantages. For one, it makes people feel secure about their money because they know they can always convert it into gold. For another, it prevents the government from printing too much paper currency. The theory is that as long as the government has promised to redeem its paper currency in gold, it will print only small amounts. This means that the currency will remain relatively scarce and, therefore, will be more likely to keep its value.

When the United States went on the gold standard, it did not have enough gold to back all of the paper currency in circulation. This, however, is true of any country that goes on a gold standard. It needs to have only enough gold to give the *appearance* that its currency can be redeemed for gold. When the FED was established in 1913, for example, it only kept 25¢ in gold for every $1 of Federal Reserve currency printed because it was not very likely that all the notes would be redeemed at any one time.

The gold standard remained in force until the depression years of the 1930's. At that time, banks began to fail, and people had a hard time getting jobs. Since people felt safer holding gold rather than paper currency, they began to cash in their dollars for gold. Foreign governments with large holdings of dollars began to do the

Case Study: Issue

Should the United States Return to a Gold Standard?

For much of its history, the United States used gold as a form of currency or was on the gold standard. Then, in 1933, the government stopped redeeming the paper currency of U.S. citizens for gold. In 1971, President Nixon informed foreign governments that the dollar no longer would be converted into gold. This broke the last remaining link between the dollar and gold. Recently, however, there has been talk about putting the United States back on the gold standard. Some people, however, do not believe this should be done.

Those who believe the United States should return to the gold standard argue that a paper dollar not anchored by an article of real wealth is not stable. In all the years the United States was on the gold standard, prices were fairly stable except during times of war or depression. Today people do not save because they are not sure what the dollar will be able to buy in the future. The gold standard would give people confidence in the future value of the dollar. It also would stop the FED from creating money at will. In time, interest rates and prices would go down. This would reduce the cost of the government debt. It also would spur a capital-investment boom, which would mean new plants and equipment, greater demand for labor, and greater prosperity for the United States.

Those who do not favor returning to the gold standard argue that such a move would be dangerous for the world economy. There is only a limited amount of gold in the world. If it was used to back the money supply, the growth of the money supply might be restricted. This could lead to a decline in world trade and hurt the less-developed countries. For a gold standard to work, the price and output of gold must remain relatively stable. Over the last ten years or so, however, they both have fluctuated a great deal. Therefore, in today's economy, the gold standard would not work.

1. Why do some people want the United States to go back on the gold standard?
2. Why do some people not want the United States to go back on the gold standard?
3. Do you think the United States should return to the gold standard? Why or why not?

same thing. In 1933, the federal government found it no longer could honor its promise that the dollar "was as good as gold" and went off the gold standard.

INCONVERTIBLE FIAT MONEY STANDARD

Since 1933, the United States has been on what is known as the **inconvertible fiat money standard.** Under this standard, the paper currency issued by the Federal Reserve System, is fiat money. It is inconvertible because it cannot be converted into gold, silver, or anything else. Even the portion of the money supply that is in the form of demand and savings deposits and certificates of deposit can only be converted into Federal Reserve currency.

The money supply of the United States, much like those used by most other major industrialized countries today, is a "managed" money supply. In the United States, it is controlled by the FED.

■ Section Review

1. What is a monetary standard?

2. What kinds of paper currencies have been used in the United States since the Revolution?

3. What is a gold standard? Why did the United States stop using it?

4. What is an inconvertible fiat money standard?

12.2 *The Federal Reserve System*

The Federal Reserve System, or FED, was created in 1913, as America's central bank. It consists of 12 regional banks, with a headquarters in Washington, D.C. The FED serves as a clearinghouse for checks and has the power to control the money supply. In one way or another, its activities affect almost every bank in the United States.

In order to understand the responsibilities of the Federal Reserve System, something must be known about the FED's structure and its relation to its member banks. The diagram on page 305 shows the organization of the FED.

STRUCTURE OF THE FED

A little more than one third of the banks in the country are **member banks**—banks that are part of the FED. This includes all national banks, which are required to join, and about 1000 state banks, which have chosen to join.

Each member bank must contribute a small amount of financial capital upon joining. In return, each receives stock in the Federal Reserve System. Because of this, the FED is owned by commercial banks, not by the federal government.

REGIONAL STRUCTURE. The 1913 law that created the FED proposed a decentralized FED bank for each part of the country. As a result, the Federal Reserve System is divided into 12 regions, each of which has its own reserve bank and branch facilities. This can be seen in the map on page 307.

Today, the regional feature of the Federal Reserve System is less important than

Figure 12–1

PARTS OF A DOLLAR BILL

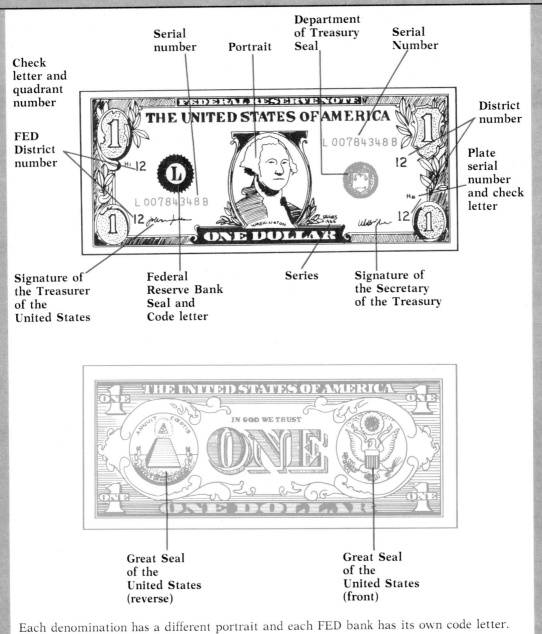

Serial number

Portrait

Department of Treasury Seal

Serial Number

Check letter and quadrant number

FED District number

District number

Plate serial number and check letter

Signature of the Treasurer of the United States

Federal Reserve Bank Seal and Code letter

Series

Signature of the Secretary of the Treasury

Great Seal of the United States (reverse)

Great Seal of the United States (front)

Each denomination has a different portrait and each FED bank has its own code letter.

it was in the past. Almost all decisions concerning monetary policy are centralized in Washington, D.C. The one responsibility left to each regional bank is the issuance of paper currency, which has a regional designation on the face of each bill.

BOARD OF GOVERNORS.   The activities of the FED are directed and controlled by the **Federal Reserve Board of Governors** in Washington, D.C. It is made up of seven members, each of which is appointed to a 14-year term by the President of the Unit-

ed States. Each appointment must be confirmed by the Senate, and the appointments are arranged so that one vacancy must be filled every two years. No member who has served a full term can be appointed again. One member is chosen by the President of the United States to be chairperson.

The Board is chiefly a regulatory and supervisory agency. It sets up general policies to be followed by Federal Reserve and member banks, watches over the 12 Federal Reserve banks, and regulates certain

Figure 12–2

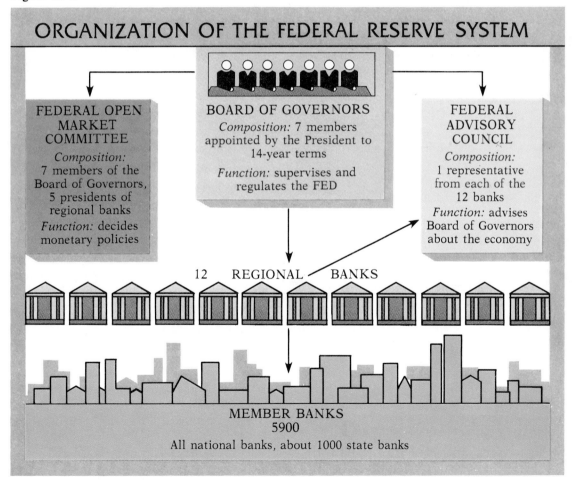

ORGANIZATION OF THE FEDERAL RESERVE SYSTEM

FEDERAL OPEN MARKET COMMITTEE

Composition: 7 members of the Board of Governors, 5 presidents of regional banks
Function: decides monetary policies

BOARD OF GOVERNORS

Composition: 7 members appointed by the President to 14-year terms

Function: supervises and regulates the FED

FEDERAL ADVISORY COUNCIL

Composition: 1 representative from each of the 12 banks
Function: advises Board of Governors about the economy

12   REGIONAL   BANKS

MEMBER BANKS
5900
All national banks, about 1000 state banks

Profile

Paul A. Volcker

Paul Volcker was the Chairman of the Board of Governors of the Federal Reserve System, a post he held from 1979 to 1987. Volcker graduated Summa Cum Laude from Princeton University and then went on to Harvard University. He later studied at the London School of Economics.

Volcker held a number of important positions in the banking community after leaving the London School. From 1969 to 1974, he was Under Secretary for Monetary

1927–

Affairs for the Department of the Treasury. While in this position, he convinced President Richard Nixon to devalue the dollar and to institute a system of floating exchange rates. In 1975, he became president of the New York Federal Reserve Bank.

Volcker believes that the only way to eliminate inflation in the United States is to have tight control over the country's money supply and the rate at which it grows.

operations of member commercial banks. It also makes a report each year to Congress and puts out a bulletin each month that reports on national and international monetary matters.

FEDERAL OPEN MARKET COMMITTEE. Decisions about the growth of the money supply and the level of interest rates are made by the **Federal Open Market Committee (FOMC).** It is made up of the seven members of the Board of Governors and five regional Reserve bank presidents who serve one-year rotating terms.

The committee meets each month in Washington, D.C., to review the country's economy and make decisions about monetary policy. Most of these are made in secret and are not revealed until six to eight weeks later.

FEDERAL ADVISORY COUNCIL. Input about the health of the economy and other matters that have to do with the FED's activities comes from the **Federal Advisory Council (FAC).** It is made up of 12 members, each of whom is elected by the member banks in the region. It has, in fact, very little impact on the daily operations of the FED.

RESPONSIBILITIES OF THE FED

As the country's central bank, the Federal Reserve System has a great many responsibilities. These include check clearing, bank regulation and supervision, consumer legislation, distributing and storing currency, and regulating the money supply.

CHECK CLEARING. One major service performed by the FED for its member banks is clearing checks. Since every bank that belongs to the FED must keep a member bank reserve (MBR) account with

Figure 12–3

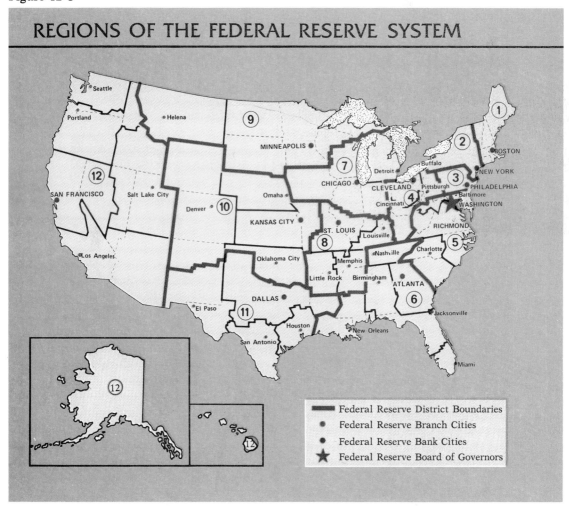

REGIONS OF THE FEDERAL RESERVE SYSTEM

it, checks can be cleared by adjusting reserve balances. The illustration on page
308 shows how this works.

The process begins with Ruth, who has
a $100 demand deposit account (DDA)
with Bank X. Ruth writes a check for $5

that she gives to Ed. At the same time, she
records the amount in her checkbook to
show a new balance of $95.

Ed, who banks at Bank Y, now has the
check. If he decides to cash it, he will have
$5 in currency in addition to his DDA of

Figure 12–4

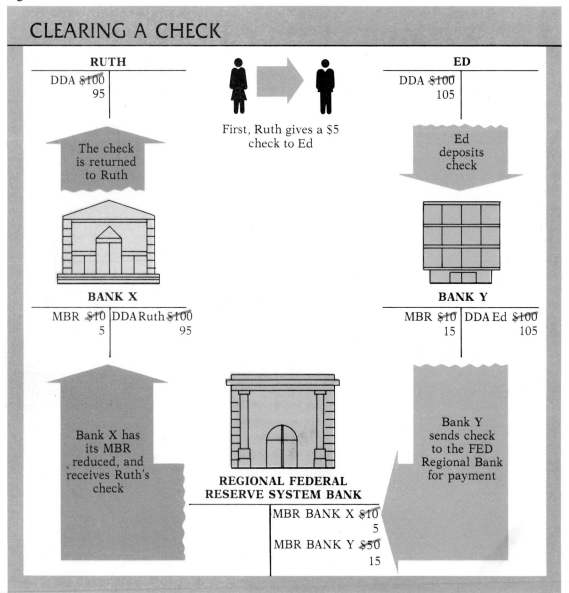

CLEARING A CHECK

RUTH
DDA ~~$100~~
95

First, Ruth gives a $5
check to Ed

ED
DDA ~~$100~~
105

The check
is returned
to Ruth

Ed
deposits
check

BANK X
MBR ~~$10~~ | DDA Ruth ~~$100~~
5 | 95

BANK Y
MBR ~~$10~~ | DDA Ed ~~$100~~
15 | 105

Bank X has
its MBR
reduced, and
receives Ruth's
check

**REGIONAL FEDERAL
RESERVE SYSTEM BANK**

MBR BANK X ~~$10~~
5
MBR BANK Y ~~$50~~
15

Bank Y
sends check
to the FED
Regional Bank
for payment

$100. If he decides to make a deposit, his DDA will rise to $105. Either way, Bank Y ends up with the check written by Ruth.

Since the check is drawn on Bank X, Bank Y gets payment for it by sending the check to the regional Federal Reserve Bank. The FED then processes the check by transferring $5 from Bank X's MBR account to Y's. The next day, the FED sends Ruth's check to Bank X.

Bank X learns of Ruth's check only when it arrives from the FED. The bank then makes up for the loss of the $5 in its MBR account by reducing Ruth's DDA by $5. Bank X then returns Ruth's check to her at the end of the month, along with any others she wrote during the same period. When Ruth gets the cancelled checks she balances her checkbook to make sure her records agree with the bank's.

Because its assets and liabilities were reduced by the same amount, Bank X is no worse off when Ruth's check cleared. And, there probably were other checks in the system going the opposite direction that offset Ruth's transaction. Except for returning checks to the customer, the entire process of clearing a check generally takes fewer than three days. At times it can be done in one day.

Millions of checks are cleared by the FED at any given time. To accomplish this, it uses the latest and most modern high-speed check-sorting machinery available to process checks around the clock. At present, it is experimenting with having banks gather the information on a check when it is deposited and then storing it on magnetic computer tape. The tape is then sent to the FED, which uses the information to adjust MBR's. In this way, the balance can be adjusted without the check having to go through the entire system.

BANK REGULATION AND SUPERVISION.   Another responsibility of the FED

is to regulate and supervise banks. Since most FED member banks are national banks, they are inspected and regulated by the Comptroller of the Currency. For this reason, the FED generally regulates and inspects the System's state-chartered member banks.

The FED does, however, have broad legislative authority over bank mergers and **bank holding companies**—a form of corporation that owns one or more banks. Mergers and acquisitions by these companies can reduce competition between banks. Congress has given the FED power to regulate this kind of activity for all banks in the country.

CONSUMER LEGISLATION.   Another responsibility of the Federal Reserve System is to set standards for some kinds of consumer legislation. This includes **truth-in-lending** legislation, laws that require sellers to make complete and accurate disclosures to people who buy on credit.

Under a provision called **Regulation Z,** truth-in-lending disclosures are extended to millions of individuals, corporations, retail stores, banks, and lending institutions.

If, for example, you buy furniture, a car, or any other item on credit, you will discover that by law, the seller must explain several things before you make the purchase. This includes the size of the down payment and the number and size of the monthly payments you must make. It also includes the total amount of interest you must pay over the life of the loan. Disclosures such as these have come about because of FED decisions on the kind of information consumers buying on credit should receive.

MAINTAINING CURRENCY.   Today's currency is made up of **Federal Reserve notes**—fiat paper money issued by Federal Reserve banks and printed at the Bureau of Engraving and Printing. This currency,

Understanding Sources

Money

The following article appeared in *U.S. News & World Report* on March 3, 1986. Read the paragraph and answer the questions that follow.

The Case of the Missing Billions

Where have all the greenbacks gone? That's what the Federal Reserve Board wants to know after completing a study showing $136 billion in U.S. currency is missing. Believe it or not, that means 88 percent of the total supposedly in circulation is missing. Based on the study, FED economists have calculated that, at any one time, individuals over age 18 keep $18 billion in U.S. coins and cash—or about $100 per person. But that accounts for only 12 percent of what's in circulation. Some of the rest is in company cash drawers, and another fraction is held by persons under age 18.

Paul Spindt, one of the authors of the FED study, suggests that much of the missing currency is being used in the cash-based "underground economy," where it is almost impossible to trace. A good chunk also is abroad, where foreigners keep American dollars in case of a political upheaval or as a hedge against inflation of their nation's currency. More missing dollars can be found in Saudi Arabia, Israel, Panama, and Bermuda, where the dollar is used side by side with local currencies in normal transactions. And in other countries, dollars are ubiquitous on local black markets.

1. What were the results of the FED's survey?

2. How much cash is kept by the average individual over the age of 18? What portion of the money supply does this represent?

issued in amounts of $1, $2, $5, $10, $20, $50, and $100, is distributed to regional banks for storage. These banks send it to member banks on request.

When tellers in banks come across currency that is mutilated or cannot be used for other reasons, they ship it to the regional FED office to be replaced. The FED then destroys it so that it cannot be put back into circulation.

REGULATING THE MONEY SUPPLY. One of the Federal Reserve System's most important responsibilities is that of **monetary policy.** This is regulating the money supply so as to influence interest rates and economic activity.

Under an **easy money policy,** the FED allows the money supply to grow and stimulate the economy. When interest rates are low, people tend to buy on credit. This stimulates sales at stores and production at factories. Businesses will borrow money to invest in new plants and equipment when money is cheap. Under a **tight money policy,** the FED restricts the growth of the money supply. When inter-est rates are high, consumers and businesses borrow and spend less, which slows economic growth.

Section Review

1. Who belongs to the FED? Who owns it?

2. Who makes up the Federal Reserve Board of Governors? What does the Board do?

3. What is the job of the FOMC? The FAC?

4. What are five major tasks of the FED? What does each involve?

12.3 *Monetary Policy*

Conducting monetary policy is not an easy job. It involves a complex and highly-structured process. In order to understand this process, a person must know something about reserve requirements and the tools the FED can use to change the money supply.

FRACTIONAL RESERVES AND MONETARY EXPANSION

In the United States today, banks oper-ate under what is known as a **fractional reserve system.** This means that by law, banks are required to keep only a fraction of their deposits in the form of reserves. The important thing about this require-ment is that it allows the money supply to grow to several times the size of the amount of reserves kept. The illustration on page 312 shows how this can happen.

In the illustration, a depositor named Fred opens a DDA on Monday by deposit-ing $1000 cash in a bank that has a 20 percent reserve requirement. By law, $200 of Fred's deposit must be set aside as a reserve in the form of vault cash or an MBR with the FED. The remaining $800 are called **excess reserves**—MBRs or bank funds not required to back existing de-mand or savings accounts. The dollar amount of these excess reserves represents the bank's lending power.

On Tuesday, the bank lends its excess reserves of $800 to Bill. Bill can either take the loan in cash or in the form of a DDA with the bank. If he decides to take the account, the money never leaves the bank. Instead, it is treated as a new depos-it, and 20 percent or $160, is set aside as a reserve. The remaining $640 are excess reserves that can be lent to someone else.

On Wednesday, Maria enters the bank and borrows $640. She can take the loan in the form of cash or a DDA. If she elects to do the latter, the bank has a new $640 deposit, 20 percent of which must be set aside as a required reserve. This leaves

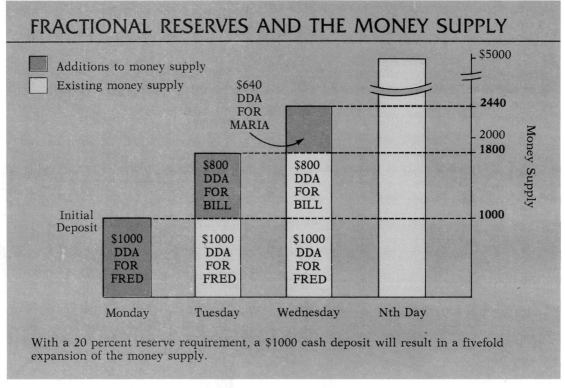

FRACTIONAL RESERVES AND THE MONEY SUPPLY

- ■ Additions to money supply
- □ Existing money supply

$640 DDA FOR MARIA

$800 DDA FOR BILL — (Tuesday)

$800 DDA FOR BILL — (Wednesday)

Initial Deposit

$1000 DDA FOR FRED — (Monday)

$1000 DDA FOR FRED — (Tuesday)

$1000 DDA FOR FRED — (Wednesday)

Monday   Tuesday   Wednesday   Nth Day

Money Supply: $5000, 2440, 2000, 1800, 1000

With a 20 percent reserve requirement, a $1000 cash deposit will result in a fivefold expansion of the money supply.

Figure 12–5

$512 of excess reserves that the bank can lend to someone else.

By Wednesday, Fred has a $1000 DDA, Bill has an $800 DDA, and Maria has either $640 in cash or a $640 DDA. This amounts to $2440 in the hands of the nonbank public by the end of the business day—a process that began on Monday with the deposit of $1000. And, as long as the bank continues to have excess reserves, the lending process can continue.

Since each new loan is smaller than the one before, the money supply will stop growing at some point. In fact, there is a formal relationship between the dollar amount of reserves, the reserve requirement, and the size of the money supply. For example, if the dollar amount of re-serves equals 20 percent of the money supply, we could write:

$$\$\text{ Reserves} = (.20)(\text{Money Supply})$$

or

$$\frac{\$\text{ Reserves}}{.20} = \text{Money Supply}$$

$$\frac{\$1000}{.20} = \$5,000$$

This shows that $1000 of reserves, given a 20 percent reserve requirement, will re-sult in a money supply of $5000. This is the final outcome of the example above when Fred makes his initial deposit.

The money supply, also, could be affect-ed by either a change in the reserve re-quirement or a change in the amount of reserves. If Maria, for example, takes the loan in the form of cash and then walks out of the bank with it, the monetary expansion process temporarily stops. Before long, however, the money will be spent and will show up in another bank. This enables the expansion process to resume. Since most bank loans are in the form of DDAs or other accounts rather than cash, the interruption to the expansion process is not that significant.

MONETARY POLICY TOOLS

The FED has three major, and several minor, tools it can use to change the money supply. Most of the tools are based on the deposit expansion process described above.

RESERVE REQUIREMENT. The first tool of monetary policy is the reserve requirement. Within limits set by Congress, the FED has the power to change this requirement for all checking, time, or savings accounts issued by every depository institution in the country. This includes credit unions, savings institutions, and nonmember banks.

This means that the FED has considerable control over the money supply. For example, suppose the FED lowers the reserve requirement in the previous example to 10 percent. Then, more money could be loaned to Bill, Maria, or others and the money supply could reach $10,000 on the Nth day. If the FED raises the reserve requirement to 40 percent, then less money would be loaned out each time and the money supply would be smaller. This is shown in the figure on page 314 where the $1000 initial deposit is loaned out under two reserve requirements.

In reality, there are many reserve requirements for banks and other depository institutions. One applies to savings accounts, another to DDAs, and other requirements to other types of deposits. Some are even structured like a progressive tax. As the deposit size increases, the reserve percentages imposed increases. Even so, the outcome of a change in the reserve requirement is the same. A higher reserve requirement on any type, or size, of deposit reduces the overall size of the money supply. A lower reserve requirement has the opposite effect.

OPEN MARKET OPERATIONS. The most popular tool of monetary policy is **open market operations**—the buying and selling of government securities in financial markets. Open market operations affect the amount of excess reserves, and, therefore, the ability of banks in general to support new loans.

Suppose, for example, that the FED decides to increase the money supply. To do so, it buys government securities from a dealer who specializes in large volume transactions of those securities. The FED pays for the securities by writing a check that is given to the dealer. The dealer then deposits the check with his or her bank. The bank forwards the check to the FED for payment. At this point, the FED "pays" the check by increasing the bank's MBR with the FED. The result is that more reserves are pumped into the banking system. Since not all reserves are needed to back existing deposits, the excess reserves can be loaned out, thus increasing the money supply.

If the FED wants to contract the money supply and drive up interest rates, it can do the opposite by selling billions of government securities back to dealers. Dealers pay for the purchase of securities with checks drawn on their own banks. The FED then processes the checks by reducing the MBRs of dealer's banks. With fewer reserves in the banking system, fewer

Figure 12–6

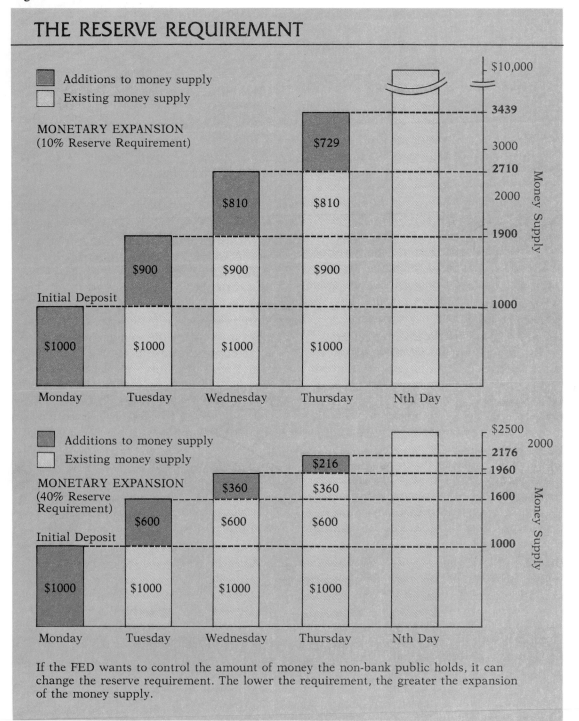

THE RESERVE REQUIREMENT

■ Additions to money supply
□ Existing money supply

MONETARY EXPANSION
(10% Reserve Requirement)

Initial Deposit

Monday — $1000
Tuesday — $1000, $900
Wednesday — $1000, $900, $810
Thursday — $1000, $900, $810, $729
Nth Day

Money Supply: $10,000 — 3439 — 3000 — 2710 — 2000 — 1900 — 1000

■ Additions to money supply
□ Existing money supply

MONETARY EXPANSION
(40% Reserve Requirement)

Initial Deposit

Monday — $1000
Tuesday — $1000, $600
Wednesday — $1000, $600, $360
Thursday — $1000, $600, $360, $216
Nth Day

Money Supply: $2500 — 2000 — 2176 — 1960 — 1600 — 1000

If the FED wants to control the amount of money the non-bank public holds, it can change the reserve requirement. The lower the requirement, the greater the expansion of the money supply.

loans are made and the money supply declines.

DISCOUNT RATE.   As a central bank, the FED makes loans to other depository institutions. The **discount rate**—the interest the FED charges on loans to financial institutions—is the third major tool of monetary policy.

A bank might obtain a loan from the FED for two reasons. First, it could have an unexpected drop in its member bank reserves. In that case, the bank would go to the FED and arrange a short-term loan to cover the shortfall. Second, a bank could be faced with seasonal demands for loans. A bank in a farming area, for example, might face a heavy demand for loans during the planting season. In that case, it would need additional MBRs to support the loans made in the spring.

The **discount window** is a teller's window at the FED that is used by depository institutions to borrow member bank reserves. Before a bank actually borrows money, however, the terms of the loan are arranged in advance over the telephone. Next, the bank delivers collateral, usually in the form of government securities, to the window. Then, when everything is complete, the loan appears as an increase in the bank's MBR account.

Changes in the discount rate affect the cost of borrowed MBRs. If the FED wants an easy money policy, it may lower the rate and/or allow more borrowing than before. When this happens, it is sometimes said that the FED is "opening" the window. The reverse is true if the FED wants to follow a tight money policy. Then, it discourages borrowing by raising the rate or by making it more difficult to borrow. When this happens, the FED is "closing" the window.

A number of financial institutions can borrow reserves from the FED. They include both member and nonmember

Member banks that borrow from the FED use the discount window. How does the FED view access to the discount window?

banks, savings institutions, and even credit unions. Access to the window, however, is viewed by the FED as a privilege rather than a right. As a result, the FED sometimes limits the number of times a borrower goes to the window.

OTHER TOOLS.   The FED may also use two other methods to control the money supply. These are moral suasion and selective credit controls.

Moral suasion is the use of some form of persuasion such as "jawboning," announcements in the form of press releases, articles in newspapers and magazines, and testimony before Congress. Moral suasion works because bankers often try to anticipate changes in monetary policy.

Suppose, for example, that the chairperson of the FED is called before Congress to give his or her views on the state of the

Moral suasion is one method the FED may use to control the money supply. Here, the Board of Governors discusses how to present their views. What are some ways that the FED uses to present its views?

economy. Assume, also, that the chair states that interest rates are somewhat low, and that it would not hurt the economy if they should rise. Bankers might well expect a tighter money policy in the next few weeks. As a result, they might be less anxious to loan their excess reserves, and they might even raise their interest rates by a small amount. In the end, the money supply might contract just slightly, even if the FED did no more than offer its views.

A second method used to control the money supply is **selective credit controls**—rules pertaining to loans for specific commodities or purposes. These controls took the form of minimum down payments on cars and other consumer goods during World War II and the Korean War. Selective credit controls during those periods were really intended to free factories to produce war materials. Because of this, selective credit controls are seldom used today.

Perhaps the best remaining example of a selective credit control is the **margin requirement**—the minimum amount of cash that must be put down by the buyer when purchasing common stock. For example, a margin requirement of 60 percent means that a person must put down 60 percent of the cash needed to buy stock. The other 40 percent can be borrowed from a banker or a stockbroker.

Section Review

1. How are fractional reserves related to the money supply?

2. What are three tools the FED can use to change the money supply? How does each work?

12.4 How Monetary Policy Affects the Economy

The impact of monetary policy on the economy is complex. In the short run, it affects interest rates and the price of credit. In the long run, it affects inflation. In addition, the time taken for the impact to be felt on the economy varies. As a result, policy makers are cautious when setting up monetary policy.

SHORT RUN IMPACT

In the short run, an increase or a decrease in the supply of money affects the interest rate, or the "price" of credit. When the FED expands the money supply, the cost of credit goes down. When the FED contracts the money supply, the cost of credit goes up.

For example, when someone borrows money to buy a car or pay college tuition, interest must be paid on the loan. The interest is the cost, or the "price," of using the money. If the FED follows a "tight" money policy, interest rates, and thus the cost of credit, will go up making car and tuition loans more expensive. An easy money policy would lower the cost of credit.

Figure 12–7

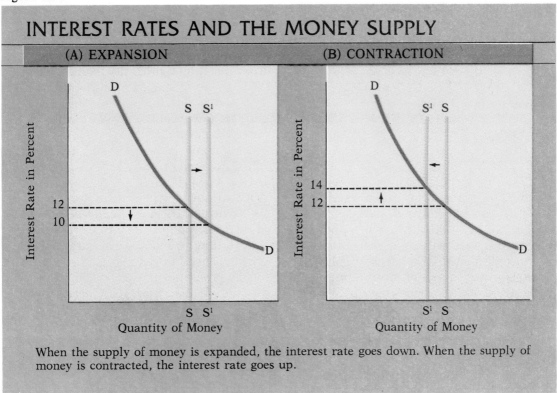

INTEREST RATES AND THE MONEY SUPPLY

(A) EXPANSION   (B) CONTRACTION

When the supply of money is expanded, the interest rate goes down. When the supply of money is contracted, the interest rate goes up.

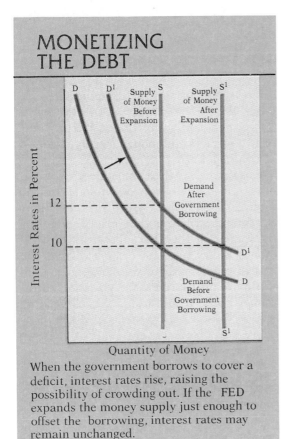

MONETIZING THE DEBT

When the government borrows to cover a deficit, interest rates rise, raising the possibility of crowding out. If the FED expands the money supply just enough to offset the borrowing, interest rates may remain unchanged.

Figure 12–8

This short run relationship between money and interest rates is shown in the graphs on page 317. The demand curve for money has the usual shape which shows that more money will be demanded when the price of money is low. The supply curve, however, does not have its usual shape. Instead, it is represented by a vertical line which indicates that the supply of money is fixed at any given time.

Before the market is disturbed, the interest rate, as shown in Graph **A**, is at 12 percent. If the FED expands the money supply to **S1,** the interest rate falls to 10

percent. Or, as shown in Graph **B**, a contraction of the money supply increases the rate from 12 to 14 percent.

Although the FED tries to do what is best for the economy, people do not always agree with its decisions. In 1981, for example, the FED was criticized for allowing interest rates to get too high. That year, the **prime rate**—the best or lowest interest rate commercial bankers charge their customers—reached 21.5 percent. Critics felt that the economy would have been better off if the FED had expanded the money supply to lower interest rates.

LONG RUN IMPACT

In the long run, changes in the supply of money affect the general level of prices. This relationship, formally known as the **quantity theory of money,** has been demonstrated over and over again in history.

For example, when the Spaniards brought gold and silver back to Spain from the New World, the increase in the money supply started an inflation that lasted for a hundred years. When the Continental Congress issued $250 million of currency during the Revolutionary War, the economy suffered a severe inflation. By 1780, five years after the first Continental Dollar was printed, the currency was worthless. Almost the same thing happened during the Civil War when nearly $500 million of greenbacks were printed.

According to many economists, history repeated itself in the 1960s when the FED let the growth of the money supply get out of hand. At that time, the federal government decided to finance the Vietnam War by borrowing in the form of deficit spending. As the government borrowed money for military expenditures, the crowding out effect threatened. To keep interest rates from going up, the FED decided to

monetize the debt—create enough extra money to offset the deficit spending.

The process of monetizing the debt is illustrated in the graph on page 318. The initial demand and supply of money is represented by *D* and *S* respectively. Now, suppose the government borrows $25 billion shifting the demand curve for money to *D1*. If the FED does not take any action, the interest rate would rise from 10 to 12 percent and crowd out some investors. If the FED wants to keep the interest rate from rising, however, it could increase the money supply to *S1* and push interest rates back to their original level.

In the short run, then, the FED can increase the money supply just enough to keep the interest rate from rising. This procedure is effective if done infrequently. However, there is always the temptation to do it again, and then again, and so on. Sooner or later, the FED discovers that repeated short-run attempts to keep rates low result in a long-term expansion of the money supply. This, in turn, makes inflation even worse.

The events in the economy from the late 1960s until the late 1970s followed this pattern. During this period, the money supply grew at rates of 12 percent or more for several years in a row. As inflation got worse, the price of most goods and services—including interest rates—also went up. Attempts by the FED to keep interest rates low by increasing the supply of money only aggravated the inflation.

By 1980, the FED seemed to realize that it had to make a choice between interest rates and inflation. As a result, it concentrated on reducing the growth of money in order to control inflation. When this happened, the prime rate in 1981 reached 21.5 percent. The dilemma for the FED, then, is the choice between lower rates today and higher inflation later on, and higher rates today and lower inflation later on.

TIMING AND BURDEN OF MONETARY POLICY

When the FED conducts monetary policy, it has two other issues to consider. The first deals with the timing of monetary policy, the second with its burden.

TIMING OF MONETARY POLICY. Sometimes a tight money policy might show results in six months. At other times, the impact might not be felt for two years. The same happens when the FED follows an easy money policy. Sometimes the policy takes effect right away, at other times it may take longer.

When money is plentiful, the interest rate is low and loans are easy to get. The opposite is true when money is scarce. What does this cartoon indicate about the money supply?

Such variations in timing make it difficult to use monetary policy to "fine tune" the economy. In other words, the FED cannot use its tools to move the economy one way or the other from one month to the next. Instead, it must take care to follow consistent policies for months at a time, even if it appears that they are not working.

BURDEN OF MONETARY POLICY. A second problem is that monetary policy has an uneven impact on the economy. If the FED follows a tight money policy to control inflation, interest rates may well increase. This hurts homebuilding and automobile sales because the cost of borrowing goes up. As a result, these industries often feel as if they have been unfairly "singled out" to bear the burden of controlling inflation.

If the FED follows a loose monetary policy, however, interest rates may go down. In this case, homebuilding and automobile sales will benefit more than other industries. As a result, the problem of uneven burden, along with the problem of timing, makes the FED cautious when it uses monetary policy.

POLITICS OF INTEREST RATES

Since the interest rate is no more than the price of credit, it tends to go down when money is plentiful and up when money is scarce. Although the interest rate is just another price, there are some differences between the price of money and such other commodities as bread, automobiles, and tickets to professional ball games.

One difference is that the price of money is much more highly publicized than that of other commodities. Another is that the FED is in a position to change the interest rate simply by using one or more of its monetary policy tools. People often expect the FED to keep interest rates low so they can buy such things as houses and cars. This is not necessarily true in the case of other commodities.

Because of the way the FED can control the interest rate, it often comes under a great deal of political pressure. A President for example, can gain some say over monetary policy by appointing certain people to the Federal Reserve Board of Governors. Once these appointments are made, however, the governors can conduct monetary policy as they wish. Some Presidents have tried to increase control further by criticizing the FED in the news media. Others have threatened to introduce legislation to make the FED less independent.

No such laws have been passed in the last 20 years. However, the threats do serve to get the FED's attention. Even so, the FED often is reluctant to accommodate most politicians because of the fear of inflation. Expanding the money supply by lowering interest rates today only means there will be more inflation later on. And unlike many politicians, especially during an election year, the FED is more concerned about the health of the economy in the long run.

Finally, people tend to use the interest rate as a measure of the overall health of the economy. In particular, they think the economy is healthy when interest rates are low. This makes it difficult for elected officials when the FED lets interest rates rise. As long as this is the case, interest rates will continue to be a political issue.

▎ Section Review

1. What three factors can reduce the effectiveness of monetary policy?

2. What are some major differences between the interest rate and price of commodities other than money?

3. In what ways can politicians put pressure on the FED? Why would they want to do so?

Chapter 12 Review

Summary

1. In order for an economy to function smoothly, it must have a reliable money supply.

2. The United States has had several monetary standards over the years, including privately issued bank notes, government-issued bank notes, the gold standard, and a managed paper currency.

3. The Federal Reserve System (FED), America's central bank, has the power to control the money supply. Its activities affect those of almost every bank in the United States.

4. Commercial banks, not the federal government, own the FED.

5. The major responsibility of the 12 regional banks in the Federal Reserve System is the issuance of paper currency.

6. All decisions about United States monetary policy are made by the Federal Reserve Board of Governors and the Federal Open Market Committee.

7. The Federal Reserve System has a great many responsibilities, the most important of which is regulating the money supply.

8. The Federal Reserve System uses three major methods to change the money supply in the United States—the reserve requirement, open market operations, and the discount rate.

9. Two other tools used by the Federal Reserve are moral suasion and selective credit controls.

10. The impact of monetary policy on the economy is different in the short run than it is in the long run.

11. Over the short run, the size of the money supply affects the interest rate. In the long run, the general level of prices is affected by the money supply.

12. The impact of monetary policy is variable, making fine-tuning difficult.

13. Unlike the prices of other commodities, the price of money is highly publicized and easily changed by the Federal Reserve System.

14. People tend to use the interest rate as a measure to determine the overall health of the economy.

Building an Economic Vocabulary

monetary standard
wildcat banks
Legal Tender Act
United States notes
legal tender
greenbacks
gold certificates
national bank notes
silver certificates
Treasury coin notes
Gold Standard Act
gold standard
inconvertible fiat
   money standard

member banks
Federal Reserve Board
   of Governors
Federal Open Market
   Committee (FOMC)
Federal Advisory
   Council (FAC)
bank holding companies
truth-in-lending
Regulation Z
Federal Reserve notes
monetary policy
easy money policy

tight money policy
fractional reserve system
excess reserves
open market operations
discount rate
discount window
moral suasion
selective credit
   controls
margin requirement
prime rate
quantity theory
   of money
monetize the debt

Reviewing the Main Ideas

1. What were two of the problems encountered by the early state-chartered banks?

2. What are the advantages of a gold standard?

3. Why is it unnecessary for a country on the gold standard to have enough gold to back its currency?

4. What are the chief responsibilities of the Federal Reserve System?

5. How can mergers affect competition in banking?

6. What happens to currency that is mutilated or otherwise not usable?

7. What happens to the economy when interest rates are low?

8. When should the FED use an easy monetary policy? A tight monetary policy?

9. What do people mean when they say that the FED has "opened" the window? "Closed" the window?

10. What is the short run impact of the FED's policy on the economy?

11. What is the quantity theory of money?

12. Why will interest rates remain a political issue?

Practicing Critical Thinking Skills

1. Some people think that the United States should return to the gold standard. What do you think? Why?

2. In your opinion, are short-run benefits of lower interest rates worth risking more inflation in the future? Why?

3. If you were on the Federal Reserve Board of Governors and could use only one method to control the money supply, which policy tool would you choose? Why?

4. Many economists feel that instead of being able to expand and contract the money supply as it sees fit, the FED should be forced to make the money supply grow at a steady rate. How do you feel about this issue? Defend your position.

5. Defend or negate the following statement: "The independence of the Federal Reserve System is essential to the health of the economy."

■ *Applying Economic Understandings*

Hypothesizing

Hypothesizing—making a logical guess about what will happen in an experiment or problem situation—is a skill economists often use to make evaluations from limited data. The guess, or hypothesis, is an assumption that may be tested to determine whether or not it is true. The guidelines used in the following example will help you develop the skill of hypothesizing.

1. Read the data provided. (Large-sized American cars decreased in sales in the mid-1970's.)

2. Determine what might be logically assumed from the data. This is the hypothesis. (The price of gasoline increased in the mid-1970's.)

3. Test the hypothesis to determine whether or not it is true. This can be done through research. (In 1973, the oil-producing countries of the Middle East placed a restriction on oil sales to the West. This embargo caused energy shortages in many parts of the world and drove up prices. During the 1970's, the price of oil went from less than $5 to more than $35 a barrel.)

4. Based on the research, determine if the hypothesis provides an explanation for or supports the data in Step 1. (The hypothesis explains one reason for the decrease in sales of large-sized American cars in the mid-1970's.)

Using these guidelines, make a hypothesis based on the following data: The impact of money on the economy is different in the short run than it is in the long run.

Financial Institutions and Markets

The greatest gambling enterprise in the United States has not been significantly touched by organized crime. That is the stock market. **Thomas Schelling**

Chapter 13

After reading this chapter, you will be able to:

- Explain the relationship between savings and growth in a free enterprise economy.

- Compare three types of non-bank depository institutions.

- Describe the contributions made by other financial institutions.

- Discuss the role of stock markets, capital and money markets, and futures markets in a free enterprise economy.

- Discuss some current issues affecting financial markets.

13.1 Savings and the Financial System

The availability of **savings**—dollars made available because of the absence of spending or consumption—is vital to the American economy. When a business borrows the savings of others to invest in plant development and equipment, new jobs are created. Whenever and wherever business invests borrowed savings, economic growth takes place.

For example, whenever the savings of others are borrowed to invest in a new house, economic activity is stimulated. People who cut trees for lumber are affected by the demand for new houses, as are people who convert the trees to lumber. Also affected are people who transport lumber to local businesses, and wholesalers who sell lumber to the contractor hired to build a house. The contractor, in turn, can hire carpenters, bricklayers, and others, who will have new income to buy other goods and services.

Thus, every time someone invests savings in the creation of something new, there is a chain reaction in the economy. This is true even if the borrowed savings are spent to buy something used, such as an older house. Even if the only new jobs created are those related to buying and selling the used item, the economy still benefits.

If, for example, someone were to buy an older house, that person simply would be trading money for what has been produced already. But the person who sold the house will have money in its place, which he or she may decide to invest in a new house. This then gives rise to increased activity once again.

The same thing happens when businesses and government use the savings accumulated by others. They may borrow different amounts of financial capital and use different methods to obtain them, but the fact remains that they could not function without access to savings.

For people to use the savings of others, an economy must have a **financial system**—a way to transfer the dollars supplied by savers to investors. This flow of activity, illustrated in the circular flow diagram below, is similar to the one in Chapter 2.

A financial system has three parts. One part supplies the savings. Households, along with some businesses and govern-

✳ **Figure 13–1**

THE FINANCIAL SYSTEM: BRINGING SAVERS AND INVESTORS TOGETHER

Savings   Savings

Financial Institutions
Banks
Savings & Loan Associations
Mutual Savings Banks
Credit Unions
Life Insurance Companies
Mutual Funds
Private Pension Funds
Government Pension Funds
REIT's
Finance Companies

Savers
Households
Businesses
Government

DDA's
CD's
Life Insurance Policies
Passbook Savings Accounts

Financial Assets

Investors
Households
Businesses
Government

Bonds
Mortgages
Commercial Loans
Installment Loans

Financial Assets

When savers transfer their dollars to financial institutions, they receive financial assets in return. When investors borrow, they create financial assets which are held by financial institutions.

ment agencies generally save. Businesses, along with governments and some households, generally borrow. Finally, financial institutions link savers with borrowers. Note that cash and financial assets flow in opposite directions as in the circular flow diagram in Chapter 2.

Households, for example, may deposit or lend excess funds to such institutions as banks, credit unions, mutual funds, or pension funds. In return, the depositors receive **financial assets**—receipts for deposits or loans that give the lender a claim on the assets and income of the borrower. These can take many forms, although DDA's, passbook savings accounts, time deposits, mortgages, and bonds are more common examples.

Many people participate in the system and there are enough financial institutions to meet almost everyone's needs. As a result, the smooth flow of funds through the system helps insure that savers will have an outlet for their savings. Borrowers, in turn, will have a source of financial capital.

Section Review

1. Why are savings important to the American economy?
2. What are the three parts of a financial system?

13.2 Non-Bank Depository Institutions

Commercial banks are not the only organizations that accept the savings of the public and make them available to individuals, business, and government. This service also is provided by **non-bank depository institutions**—organizations other than commercial banks that accept deposits and channel these savings to investors. These institutions include savings and loan associations, mutual savings banks, and credit unions.

Although some of these institutions have the term "bank" in their titles, they are neither commercial banks nor members of the Federal Reserve System. The major difference between them and commercial banks is that commercial banks create new money by loaning more than the amount of funds deposited by their customers. Non-bank depository institutions, on the other hand, make available only the funds they receive. Therefore, they do not add to the money supply.

Non-bank depository institutions are the heart of a very complex arrangement that has come about to bring together those who save and those who use savings. They make investments easier and help people borrow to pay for many things they wish to buy. They also help to raise the level of savings as a whole by providing a safe and easy-to-reach depository for the public's savings, savings from which the economy as a whole benefits.

SAVINGS AND LOAN ASSOCIATIONS

A major kind of non-bank depository institution is the **savings and loan association**—a financial institution that sells shares in the form of deposits to individuals and invests the proceeds in home mortgages. The return to investors is either in

MEMBER

FSLIC

Federal Savings & Loan Insurance Corp.

A U.S. Government Agency

Many savings and loan associations display a sticker similar to the one in the photograph in their windows. What is the FSLIC, and what is its purpose?

the form of a dividend or as interest on deposits.

Savings and loan associations began as cooperative clubs for home building called building and loan associations. In the mid-1800's, each of the association's members promised to deposit a certain sum regularly into the association. Members then took turns borrowing money to build a home. As soon as all the homes were built, the association stopped doing business.

Today, savings and loan associations actively compete for people's savings. They maintain an on-going business in which they basically make their members' savings available for the purchase of homes. Most keep some cash on hand and some on deposit with commercial banks. But loaning money for residential real estate remains their primary activity.

Deposits in savings and loan associations are insured by the **Federal Savings and Loan Insurance Corporation (FSLIC)**. This is a federal government agency much like the FDIC which serves commercial bankers.

MUTUAL SAVINGS BANKS

One of the oldest kinds of savings institutions in the United States is the **mutual savings bank**—a financial organization operated for the benefit of its depositors only. It has no stockholders or owners. It is managed by a board of trustees made up of business and professional people who serve without pay. The bank earns a return for depositors by investing the money it receives in government bonds, high-grade corporate securities, and different kinds of real estate.

Mutual savings banks are chartered by the state in which they are located. Their deposits can be insured by the FDIC, the FSLIC, or by their state's private insurance fund, when available. The major difference between mutual savings banks and savings and loan associations is that the mutuals are wholly depositor-owned.

Mutual savings banks got their start in the early 1800's. At that time, commercial banks were not interested in the accounts of small wage earners, so mutual savings banks were created to fill that need. As the country grew, they spread west following the industrial growth of the large cities.

By the mid-1800's, however, commercial banks had begun to take an interest in the savings accounts of factory workers and other wage earners. As a result, they began to compete more heavily with the mutual savings banks. They even managed to edge out the mutual savings banks in the frontier areas populated with farmers and ranchers. As a result, mutual savings banks remained strong in 17 eastern states but never really spread to other parts of the country.

Even so, mutual savings banks are a powerful influence in the economy today. In 1972, for example, the Consumer's Savings Bank of Worcester, Massachusetts, decided it would introduce its own kind of demand deposit called a Negotiable Order of Withdrawal, or NOW account. Since commercial banks were not allowed to pay interest on their checking accounts at that time, they strongly opposed NOW accounts. But the mutual savings banks had more political power than the commercial banks in the state of Massachusetts, and the NOW accounts were allowed to stay.

Before long, the NOW accounts spread to most of the New England states. Commercial bankers, however, still opposed them and, for a time, managed to contain them to the New England area. When savings and loan associations began to introduce their own version of NOW accounts in other states, the commercial bankers gave up and offered their own NOW accounts.

CREDIT UNIONS

A third kind of non-bank depository institution is the credit union. In most cases, the members use the money to buy such

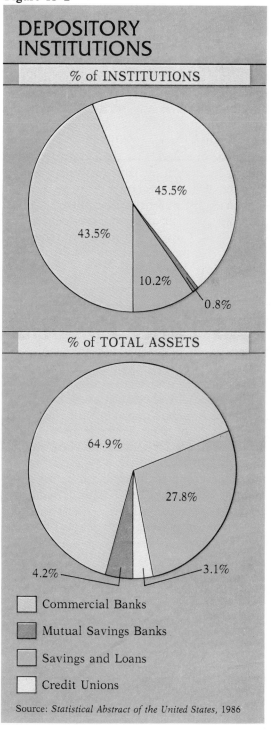

Figure 13–2

DEPOSITORY INSTITUTIONS

% of INSTITUTIONS

45.5%
43.5%
10.2%
0.8%

% of TOTAL ASSETS

64.9%
27.8%
4.2%
3.1%

☐ Commercial Banks
■ Mutual Savings Banks
☐ Savings and Loans
☐ Credit Unions

Source: *Statistical Abstract of the United States, 1986*

goods as automobiles, household appliances, and back-to-school clothes.

Credit unions are owned and operated by and for their members. But their management, help, and office facilities often are given to them by a sponsor, which may be the members' union or place of employment. Their assets are the loans they make to members. Although these assets generally are relatively small, there are more credit unions than commercial banks, savings and loans, or mutual savings banks. This is shown on page 329.

Most credit unions are organized around an employer, and contributions generally are deducted directly from a worker's paycheck. In recent years, some credit unions have followed the lead of the mutual savings banks and the savings and loans associations and have offered checking deposits. Known as **share drafts,** they look like any other check or NOW account and provide members with a way to earn interest on demand deposits.

Section Review

1. What organizations besides commercial banks accept deposits and channel savings to investors?

2. How is a mutual savings bank different from a savings and loan association?

3. How is a credit union organized?

13.3 Other Financial Institutions

Savings and loan associations, mutual savings banks, and credit unions obtain funds by having their customers or members make regular deposits as if they were dealing with a bank. There is another group of financial institutions, however, that obtains its funds in a different manner. This group includes life insurance companies, mutual funds, and private and government pension funds. It also includes real estate investment trusts and finance companies.

LIFE INSURANCE COMPANIES

One of the major financial institutions that does not get its funds through deposits is the life insurance company. Although its chief function is to provide financial protection for those persons who have survived the person insured, it also collects a great deal of cash.

The head of a family, for example, may want to leave a sum of money for a spouse and children in case of death. To do this, he or she may buy a life insurance policy. The price paid for this policy is known as a **premium,** and it must be paid at set times for the length of the protection.

If an insurance policy is cancelled, the person who took it out generally is entitled to its **cash surrender value.** This is a refund of part of the premium that already has been paid.

An insurance company often will allow its customers to borrow against the cash value of their insurance policy. In such cases, the customer generally gets a better rate of interest than he or she could obtain from a commercial bank or another lending institution.

Since insurance companies collect cash on a regular basis, they often lend surplus funds to others. They may, for example, make loans to banks in the form of large

Case Study: Career

Actuary

An actuary designs insurance and pension plans. To do this, the actuary gathers and analyzes statistics on such things as death, unemployment, and illness. This information then is used to establish how much the insured loss will be. When calculating premium rates, the actuary must make sure that the price of the insurance is high enough to cover any claims and expenses the insurance company might have to pay.

Most actuaries work for private insurance companies. Some, however, work for the government, act as consultants, or teach at colleges and universities. Those who work for private companies often are called on to explain technical points to company executives, government officials, and others. Those who work for the federal government generally handle one specific insurance or pension program. Those who work for the state government regulate insurance companies, watch over state retirement and pension programs, and handle matters related to workers' compensation and unemployment insurance.

Actuaries must have a working knowledge of subjects that can affect insurance practices. This includes general economic and social trends as well as those in health and legislation. In addition to a strong background in math and statistics and a college degree, actuaries must pass a series of exams given by professional actuarial societies. It generally takes five to ten years to complete all the tests, which are given twice a year.

In order to gain experience in as many phases of their work as possible, beginning actuaries generally rotate jobs. At first, they do such things as prepare tabulations for actuarial tables and reports. In time, they may supervise clerks, prepare reports, and do research. Job performance and the number of actuarial exams an actuary has passed determines how far he or she may advance. Because of their knowledge of math, insurance, and other related areas, actuaries often are chosen as executives in such other areas as data processing and accounting.

certificates of deposit (CD's)—formal receipts for funds left with a bank that generally are interest-bearing and payable at a given later date. They also may negotiate other arrangements with smaller consumer finance companies at certain times of the year when consumers need cash.

MUTUAL FUNDS

A second kind of financial institution is the **mutual fund.** It is a company that sells stock in itself to individual investors and then invests the money received in the securities market. Its stockholders receive any dividends or interest earned from the stock. They also receive any profits from the sale of securities.

Mutual funds allow people who do not have a lot of money to "play the market" without making analytical financial studies and without risking all they have in the stock of only one or a few companies. The size of the mutual fund makes it

possible to hire a staff of experts to analyze the securities market before buying and selling securities.

The large size of most funds also allows them to buy many different stocks and build up a more diversified portfolio than could most individual investors. Because of this, if one stock fell sharply in price, a fund's overall investment probably would not change significantly.

For all of these reasons, mutual funds have turned out to be an attractive investment for many people. From the point of view of the financial system, however, they play an important role channeling savings to investors.

PRIVATE PENSION FUNDS

A third kind of non-bank financial institution is the pension fund. A **pension** is a regular allowance intended to provide income security to someone who has worked a certain number of years, reached a cer-

Insurance companies mainly provide financial protection for family members of the person insured. What are some other functions of insurance companies?

tain age, or suffered a certain kind of injury. A **pension fund** is a fund set up to collect income and disburse payments to those persons eligible for retirement, old-age, or disability benefits.

In the case of private pension funds, employers regularly withhold a percentage of workers' salaries to deposit in the pension fund. During the 30-to-40 year lag between the time the savings are deposited and the time they generally are used by the workers, the money is usually invested in corporate stocks and bonds. Since the majority of the funds are contributed by employers, most private pension funds are regulated by the Department of Labor.

The income that some private pension plans earn on investments is **tax-exempt,** free from federal taxes. For this reason, these funds are invested in securities that have the highest rate of return. Most only have small, if any, holdings of tax-free government securities because they carry lower rates of interest.

Many retired persons receive a pension. Such funds provide income security to persons who meet certain requirements. What is a pension fund?

GOVERNMENT PENSION FUNDS

Government pension funds are very much like private ones in that the employer makes regular contributions that will be used later to pay benefits. Many of the funds in this group include state and local governments, the Civil Service, and Federal Old Age and Survivors and Federal Disability Insurance Funds. These pension funds are also tax-exempt. Generally, they are invested in corporate stocks and bonds. In recent years, however, some of these funds made loans or bought the securities of state and local governments.

For example, when New York City had its first major brush with bankruptcy in the mid-1970's, its pension funds came to the rescue. The pension funds used their assets to buy city bonds that could not be sold in the open market because of the city's poor credit rating. This, however, is the exception rather than the rule. Most pension funds prefer to keep their assets in the form of high-grade, high-yield corporate securities and government bonds.

REAL ESTATE INVESTMENT TRUSTS

Still another non-bank financial institution is the **real estate investment trust (REIT)**—a company organized chiefly to make loans to construction companies that build homes.

Although REIT's are not widely known as financial institutions, they help provide billions annually for home construction. Because of this, they are an important part of the housing market. REIT's borrow most of their funds from commercial banks and get their income from the rents and mortgage payments of the people who use their money. This income is then used to pay interest on the money originally borrowed.

FINANCE COMPANIES

A sixth kind of non-bank financial institution is the **finance company**—an organization that specializes in the buying of installment contracts from merchants who sell on the installment plan. Most contracts are issued for such consumer goods as automobiles and furniture.

Without the help of finance companies many small merchants would have a hard time doing business. Many merchants, for example, cannot afford to wait the three-to-five years it takes most consumers to pay off high-cost items on the installment plan. Instead, the merchant sells the consumer's promise to pay to a finance company in return for a single lump sum of cash. This enables the merchant to advertise "instant credit" or "easy terms" without actually carrying the loan full term, absorbing any losses for an account that does not get paid, or taking customers to court for non-payment.

Some finance companies make loans directly to consumers. These companies generally have the means to check a consumer's credit rating and will make a loan only if the individual qualifies. Because they make loans to some people banks might consider "high risks," and also because they pay more for the funds they borrow, finance companies charge more than commercial banks for loans.

One popular loan offered by many consumer finance companies is the **bill consolidation loan.** This is a loan used by a consumer to pay off all bills currently owed. The consumer must then agree to repay the loan to the finance company over a period of one or more years.

▌Section Review

1. What are six kinds of financial institutions that do not receive funds through deposits?
2. What are the functions of a life insurance company?
3. What are the advantages of a mutual fund?
4. In what does a pension fund generally invest?
5. How is an REIT different from a finance company?
6. How do finance companies help small merchants?

13.4 Major Financial Markets

The **securities market** is an economic market in which buyers and sellers of corporate and government securities are brought together. The **securities**—receipts for the savings individuals have made available to users—fall into two categories.

One is bonds or notes. The other is stock or equity. Within this broad market for securities, there are several organized **securities exchanges**—places where buyers and sellers meet to trade securities. These exchanges do not themselves buy and sell

* Securities can fall into one of two categories. They can be either bonds or notes, or stock or equity. Where are securities bought and sold?

securities. They provide a place where one holder can sell them to another.

STOCK MARKETS

The largest by far of all securities exchanges in the United States is the **New York Stock Exchange (NYSE).** It is interested chiefly in stocks with nationwide market appeal. Like most other exchanges, it decides which securities it will list, or trade. And, as the nation has developed financially, the requirements for listing have become much more strict.

For example, before a company can have its stocks listed on the New York Stock Exchange, it must give the Exchange detailed data about the corporation. It also must publish annual financial statements. Then the Exchange's Department on Stock Lists judges whether or not the company's securities meet the Exchange's standards. Finally, the Exchange's Board of Governors decides if the securities will be admitted to trading.

Not all securities are listed and traded on the NYSE. New companies and those whose owners are concentrated in a specific geographical area may not qualify for listing on a national exchange, like the New York Stock Exchange or the **American Stock Exchange (AMEX).** Instead, they may be better served by a smaller, regional stock exchange, such as the Midwest Stock Exchange, the Pacific Coast Stock Exchange, the Cincinnati Stock Exchange, or the Philadelphia Stock Exchange. All of these afford more attention to the securities of "local" firms.

Many securities are not listed or traded on any organized exchange. Instead, securities dealers buy and sell them in what is called the **over-the-counter market (O-T-C)**—an exchange for securities that are not listed or traded on any organized exchange. If you wanted to buy one or more of these unlisted securities, you would place your order with a securities person,

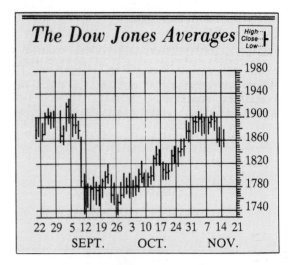

THE NEW YORK STOCK EXCHANGE

TRANSACTIONS FOR:
NOVEMBER 18, 1986

Stock	Div.	Yld %	P-E Ratio	Sales 100s	High	Low	Close	Net Chg.
AmExp	1.36	2.4	10	5156	58⅛	56¼	57⅛ +	⅝
AFaml s	.44	1.7	15	712	26⅞	26⅜	26⅝ −	½
AGnCp	1.12	3.0	10	2138	37⅞	37¼	37½	...
AGnl wt	...	...		32	17⅛	17⅛	17⅛ −	⅛
AGnl pfA	4.28e	8.0	...	37	53½	53½	53½ +	⅛
AHerit	1.32	3.4	8	27	39½	39	39 −	¼
AHoist	...	...		279	9	8⅝	8¾ −	⅜
AHoist pf	1.95	9.2	...	10	21½	21	21¼ −	¼

The Dow Jones Averages

Many investors check the **NYSE** listings and **Dow Jones** daily. In the listing above, the price of a share of stock in American Express ranged from a low of 56¼ ($56.25) to a high of 58⅛ ($58.12). The closing price was 57⅛, or 62¢, more than the closing price the day before. Each of the 515,600 shares of stock sold paid an annual dividend of $1.36. The 2.4 yield percent means that anyone who buys the stock at $57.12, would earn a 2.4 percent return on their investment. For the Dow Jones Industrial Average above, the range was from a low of 1844 to a high of 1880, closing at 1860. Why do most investors check the stock market's performance daily?

Figure 13–3

or **stock broker**—one whose job is to buy or sell securities. The broker would supply the securities from an inventory or would buy them from some other broker.

Most brokers deal in both listed and unlisted securities. But in order to make it easier to trade in ones that are listed, most brokerage houses have at least one member who owns a seat on, or is a member of, an organized exchange. Because only a limited number of seats are available, they tend to cost a good deal. For example, as long ago as 1929, a seat on the New York Stock Exchange sold for as much as $625,000. Although today's price is lower, a seat on the NYSE is still quite expensive.

The illustration on page 336 shows how prices are listed on most stock exchanges.

The price of a share of stock generally goes up and down throughout the day as the conditions of supply and demand change. As a result, three prices generally are available each day for a share of stock—the high, the low, and the closing price. In most cases, the listing also gives such additional information as the amount of annual dividend paid and the number of shares sold.

Since most investors are concerned about the performance of their stocks at the end of each day, a number of statistics are kept to indicate the market's performance. One of the most popular is the Dow Jones Industrial Average, which is shown on page 336.

↘The **Dow Jones Industrial Average** is not really an average. Historically, it is based on the sum of the closing prices of 30 selected stocks. These stocks were chosen because their performance was felt to be typical of the more than 3000 stocks listed on the New York Stock Exchange. When it is stated, for example, that the Dow Jones has dropped 4 "points," it means that the closing prices for the day of the 30 selected stocks is $4 less than it was the day before.

Another popular measure is the **Standard and Poor's 500.** It is an index that represents the price changes of 500 representative stocks on the NYSE. Since the sum of 500 stock prices would be rather large, it is reduced to an index number. Like the Dow Jones, the Standard and Poor's 500 reports on a specific market. Still, both are widely regarded as indicators of all stock price movements in the country.

CAPITAL AND MONEY MARKETS

When investors speak of the **capital market,** they mean a market where money is loaned and borrowed for periods of more than one year. Long-term CD's as well as corporate and government bonds that have more than a year to maturity all fit in this category.

When investors speak of the **money market,** they mean a market where money is loaned for periods of less than one year. Some of the legal obligations that specify the terms of the loan are known as **money market instruments.** These include certificates of deposit of one year or less, commercial paper, bankers acceptances, and Eurodollars.

Certificates of deposit in the money market are the same as those offered by many commercial banks and other lending institutions. A person who has a CD with a maturity of one year or less at a bank or some other lending institution automatically takes part in the money market. If the CD has a maturity of more than one year, the person takes part in the capital market as a supplier of funds.

Commercial paper is a corporation's short-run debt obligation which specifies that the borrowed money will be repaid after a certain period of time. Generally, it is not backed by security or collateral, but by a corporation's reputation. Most corporations prefer to borrow money directly from investors rather than from banks because it is generally cheaper.

A **bankers acceptance** is another form of short-term debt. It is a document that guarantees payment by a bank to the holders of the acceptance. It is used mostly in international trade when goods are shipped from one country to another. Exporters, who know very little about the foreign company ordering the goods, generally feel more comfortable taking a bankers acceptance rather than a check in payment.

Eurodollars are United States dollar deposits in banks in other countries. Since the U.S. dollar is used as an international currency, many loans are made in this way. Thus, Eurodollars are important short-term money market instruments. Many Eurodollar loans are also made to companies in developing countries to buy goods and services.

FUTURES MARKETS

At times, a company or an individual may decide to buy or sell **futures**—contracts to buy or sell a commodity at some point in the future at rates decided on in the present. The market where the futures

Profile

✴ Martha R. Seger

Martha Seger is presently a member of the Board of Governors of the Federal Reserve System, a post she has held since July 1984. As a member of the Board of Governors, Dr. Seger is a voting member of the Federal Open Market Committee and directly involved in formulating and executing American monetary policy. Dr. Seger graduated from the University of Michigan with an MBA in Finance and a PhD in Finance and Business Economics.

1932–

Before joining the Board of Governors, Dr. Seger taught and lectured at various universities. She also served as Commissioner of Financial Institutions for the state of Michigan and Vice President in charge of Economics and Investments at the Bank of the Commonwealth in Detroit.

✴ Dr. Seger believes that most of today's banking laws on the federal and state levels are outdated and need to be revised. She also favors the establishment of one, single bank regulatory agency, instead of several separate agencies. This single agency would then be able to examine banks more fairly.

trades take place is known as the **futures market.**

Futures grew out of the commodity markets in agriculture that were used by farmers to secure financial capital for spring plantings. A farmer could agree in May, for example, to sell a grain crop in November. A company that did not want grain until November might agree to pay the farmer in May, and the deal would be struck. This means the farmer would have the cash to plant the crop in the spring, which would later be delivered in November when it is harvested.

Financial futures can be arranged the same way. An investor can buy in the futures market gold, silver, or foreign currency based on rates decided in the present. A company might do this, for example, if it suspected that the dollar would be weaker in the future than it is at the moment and would buy more in the present than it would at some time in the future.

If, for example, a company plans to import handicrafts from India in six months, it may buy a futures contract that will convert dollars into rupees at the end of the six months. It may discover, however, that a better deal would have resulted if it had waited six months to buy the rupees. Or, on the other hand, it may find that it did the most profitable thing by not waiting. Regardless of how it works out, the advantage of the futures market is that some uncertainty has been removed.

■ Section Review

1. What is a securities market?
2. Where is the largest stock exchange?
3. How are securities traded on the over-the-counter market?
4. What are two measures kept to indicate the market's overall performance?
5. What is the difference between the capital market and the money market?
6. What are futures?

13.5 *Current Issues*

Financial markets, like other markets, work when there is competition and everyone plays by the rules. Occasionally, however, this efficiency is threatened if people act to make illegal profits or if the system becomes unsound.

INSIDER TRADING

In 1987, the stock markets had a number of scandals involving **insider trading**—the use of non-public information by individuals to make a profit on the sale or purchase of stock. Insiders generally are people who work for a company and have access to knowledge others do not have.

For example, an officer of a corporation—an insider—may know that his or her company is about to make an announcement that will drive up the price of the company's stock. The announcement may be about a new product, an upcoming merger, or an increase in profits. Or the insider may know that the company is in deep trouble, and when the public finds out, the value of the stock may fall. In either case, it is illegal for an insider to buy or sell stock in advance of the announcement, or to pass such information along to anyone outside the company.

The problem insider trading creates is that the average investor may lose faith in the stock market. If investors feel that the system is "rigged" against them, they may decide to invest their money elsewhere. This denies corporations a major source of financial capital. Yet, because insider trading is hard to detect and even harder to prove, the number of convictions for it is quite small.

SAFETY OF
NON-BANK DEPOSITS

Most deposits in commercial banks, mutual savings banks, and federally chartered savings and loans are safe because they have some type of federal insurance such as FDIC or FSLIC. But deposits in some other institutions, especially savings and loans that receive their charters from state governments, can be more risky.

What happened to the savings and loan institutions in Ohio in 1985 is an example. Until that year, every state-chartered savings and loan institution in Ohio was insured by a private insurance company. In March, 1985, it appeared that one of the largest savings and loans was about to fail, so depositors began to withdraw their deposits. Normally, the withdrawals would be covered by the insurance company, but

it had barely enough money to bail out one depository institution, let alone all 71 institutions that it insured.

When the weakness of the insurance company became public knowledge, depositors in other institutions, some of which were sound, began to withdraw their funds. To stop the spreading panic, the Governor of Ohio closed all of the state-chartered savings and loans in the state.

This was the first time since the Great Depression of the 1930's that every state-chartered savings institution in a state was closed. Many of these institutions were eventually sold to other banks or savings and loans. Others were able to reopen several weeks later. Some, however, remained closed for a year or more. While most depositors got their money back, they experienced a great deal of frustration and inconvenience until they did so.

The Ohio savings and loan crisis of 1985 caused many bank depositors to realize that charters from some private corporations or state governments can be risky. As a result of this crisis, what action are many states taking?

The problems of Ohio were extreme, but other states still have private, or state-backed insurance programs for their institutions. Because of the Ohio experience, many other states are now moving toward requiring FDIC and FSLIC insurance.

Section Review

1. What effect does insider trading have on the stock market?
2. Do all depository institutions have federal deposit insurance?

Chapter 13 Review

Summary

1. The availability of savings is vital to the American economy because savings are invested to stimulate economic activity and promote economic growth.

2. Non-bank depository institutions, which accept deposits and channel these savings to investors, do not add to the money supply because they make available only the funds they receive.

3. Three major kinds of non-bank depository institutions are the savings and loan association, the mutual savings bank, and the credit union.

4. Life insurance companies, mutual funds, private and government pension funds, real estate investment trusts, and finance companies, are non-depository financial institutions that channel savings to investors.

5. Insurance companies provide financial protection for survivors of individuals who have life insurance policies.

6. Mutual funds allow people who do not have a lot of money to invest in a wide range of securities.

7. Private and government pension funds collect income that is disbursed to workers when they are retired, elderly, or disabled.

8. A real estate investment trust (REIT) is a company that primarily makes loans to construction companies to build homes.

9. Securities are bought and sold at organized securities exchanges or in the over-the-counter market. Security prices are quoted daily in listings like the Dow Jones Industrial Average and the Standard and Poor's 500.

10. Money is loaned and borrowed for periods of more than one year in the capital market, and for one year or less in the money market.

11. Futures, which grew out of the commodity markets for agriculture, are contracts to buy or sell at some point in the future at prices that have been decided on in the present.

12. Insider trading and inadequate deposit insurance threatens some financial markets.

Building an Economic Vocabulary

savings
financial system
financial assets
non-bank depository
   institutions
savings and loan
   association
Federal Savings and
   Loan Insurance
   Corporation (FSLIC)
mutual savings bank
share drafts
premium
cash surrender value
certificates of deposit (CD's)

mutual fund
pension
pension fund
tax-exempt
real estate investment
   trust (REIT)
finance company
bill consolidation loan
securities market
securities
securities exchanges
New York Stock
   Exchange (NYSE)
American Stock
   Exchange (AMEX)

over-the-counter
   market (O-T-C)
stock broker
Dow Jones Industrial
   Average
Standard and Poor's 500
capital market
money market
money market instruments
commercial paper
bankers acceptance
Eurodollars
futures
futures market
insider trading

Reviewing the Main Ideas

1. Why are savings important?

2. What purpose do non-bank depository institutions serve?

3. What are three major kinds of non-bank depository institutions?

4. What is a premium? Cash surrender value?

5. In what does a mutual fund invest?

6. How are government pension funds different from private ones?

7. How does a finance company help merchants? Consumers?

8. What are securities?

9. What does a company have to do to get listed on the New York Stock Exchange?

10. What is the difference between commercial paper, bankers acceptances, and Eurodollars?

11. How can insider trading affect a financial market?

Practicing Critical Thinking Skills

1. Some people think that since savings and loans, mutual savings banks, and credit unions are becoming more like commercial banks, they should be governed by banking regulations. Do you agree? Why or why not?

2. Regulation Z is administered by the FED and applies to all lenders. Many non-bank lenders say that since they are not part of the banking system, they should not be subject to such regulation. From the consumer's point of view, how would you argue the case?

3. In recent years, there has been a push to unify all stock exchanges into one national organization. Do you see this as a plus or a minus for companies today? Give reasons to support your answer.

4. Defend one of the following statements: "The government should insure all savings and loan associations regardless of whether they are federally or state chartered."
"Government has not done enough to prevent abuses of insider trading."

■ *Applying Economic Understandings*

Charting Information

This chapter has provided a great deal of information on financial institutions and how they work in a free enterprise economy. To better understand a large amount of material, it may be helpful to *classify* the information—separate and arrange it into related groups. One way to do this is by placing the information into a *chart*—a graphic representation of information in tabular form.

The procedures used to set up the chart below will show you how to chart information. To complete the exercise, review the material on non-bank depository institutions on pages 327–330 of the text. Next, identify the items to be classified. List these descriptions in the appropriate categories.

For further practice in charting information, make a chart based on the information provided about major financial markets on pages 334–339.

Non-Bank Depository Institutions	Characteristics	Services
1. Savings & Loan Associations	Sells shares in the form of deposits to individuals and invests the proceeds in home mortgages.	Provides return to investors in dividends or interest on deposits.
2. Mutual Savings Banks		
3. Credit Unions		

Unit 4 Review

The Unit in Perspective

1. In colonial times, wampum and commodity monies were widely used. Later the U.S. dollar was based on the Spanish peso, or "piece of eight."

2. Money must be portable, durable, divisible, and stable in value to be useful as a medium of exchange. Modern money rates high only in the first three categories.

3. The United States has a dual banking system consisting of state and national banks which provide people with a safe place to keep their deposits and which use excess funds to make loans.

4. Banks operate under a fractional reserve requirement imposed by the Federal Reserve System. Excess reserves are lent out in the form of cash or demand deposits.

5. Before an economy can function smoothly, it must have a reliable and dependable money supply and a set of monetary standards.

6. In the United States, the money supply is controlled by the Federal Reserve System, and decisions about monetary policy are made by the Federal Reserve Board of Governors.

7. The FED can use reserve requirements, open market operations, the discount rate, and moral suasion to change the money supply.

8. The level of demand for savings is determined by ability and willingness to pay the price of money, or interest. The interest rate is determined by the forces of supply and demand.

9. The size and growth of the money supply affects interest rates in the short run and inflation over the long run. Because of this, monetary policy is often a political issue.

10. A financial system is vital because it helps transfer savings dollars to investors who put them to work.

11. Non-bank depository institutions and other lending institutions serve the American economy by accepting people's savings and making them available to investors.

12. A number of other markets including those for stocks, bonds, government securities, and foreign currencies are also part of the financial system.

The Unit in Review

1. In what ways has money changed since primitive times? In what ways has it remained the same?

2. How did the establishment of a national banking system affect U.S. bank operations? How do U.S. banks operate today?

3. What are some current issues in banking today?

4. Why was the FED first established? What is its role today?

5. What are the three major tools of monetary policy? How do they work?

6. What is the difference between the way money affects the economy in the short run and in the long run?

7. How do commercial banks, non-bank depository institutions, and lending institutions like savings and loans differ from one another?

8. What is the relationship between financial markets and savings?

9. What is the role of savings in the American economy?

■ *Building Consumer Skills*

Writing a Check

A checking account provides a safe, convenient way to pay bills and makes it easy for a person to keep orderly financial records. It is important, however, to keep a few simple rules in mind when writing checks. The following exercise will help you write checks properly.

1. Always use a pen to write a check so that it cannot be altered once you have completed it.

2. Fill in the blank for the date. Make sure you write the correct date. Most places of business will not cash a check dated later than the day it is written.

3. Fill in the amount to be paid. Start at the lefthand edge and draw a line through whatever space you do not use.

4. Write the amount of the check in numerals. Make sure the numerals are the same as the amount that is written out. Most banks and businesses will not cash a check if there is a discrepancy between the amounts.

5. Sign your name exactly as you did on the card you signed to open the account. Banks often check signatures to make sure you are who you say you are.

6. Once you have written the check, do not alter it. Write VOID across the face in large letters and tear it up into small pieces. Write a new check if desired.

7. Never sign a blank check. It is too easy for someone else to fill in an amount and cash it.

The Overall Economy

Not only do economists deal with individual components of the economy, they also deal with the economy of the nation as a whole. They use various methods to measure the health of the national economy and how it affects the lives of the American people.

Unit 5

Contents

Gross National Product

Everything should be made as simple as possible, but not more so.

Albert Einstein

Chapter 14

After reading this chapter, you will be able to:

- Explain Gross National Product and the way it is estimated.

- Describe the way GNP is broken down into sectors for use in the output-expenditure model.

- Identify four measures of national income other than GNP.

- Explain the need for price indices and their use in converting current GNP to real GNP.

14.1 Aggregate Supply

Just as economists study the amount of goods and services brought to market by a single producer, they also study the total amount of goods or services produced by the economy as a whole. Thus, they examine **aggregate supply**—the total amount of goods and services produced by the economy in a given period, usually one year.

A number of factors affect an economy's aggregate supply. Two of these are the quantity of resources used in production and the quality of those resources. For example, an economy must have an ade-

quate supply of natural resources and capital goods to be productive. It also needs a skilled and highly motivated labor force. A third factor affecting aggregate supply is the efficiency with which the resources are combined. If they are combined in a productive way, aggregate supply will increase.

In order to measure aggregate supply, statistics must be kept. To help with this task, economists use **national income accounting**—a system of statistics that keeps track of production, consumption, saving, and investment in the economy. National

The workers in the above photograph are adding to the nation's aggregate supply. How is aggregate supply measured?

income accounting also makes it possible to trace long-run trends in the economy and to form new public policies to improve the economy.

GROSS NATIONAL PRODUCT

The most important economic statistic kept in the national income accounts is Gross National Product (GNP). This is the dollar measure of the total amount of final goods and services produced in a year. It is one of the most important and comprehensive statistics kept on the economy's performance.

Although the measurement of GNP is a complicated process, the table on page 351 shows one way it may be done. In column 1 of the table, all of the individual goods and services produced in any one year are

listed. In column 2, the quantity of each good and service is noted, and in column 3, the individual price of each is given. In column 4, the dollar value of each, which is the product of the quantity and the price, is represented. The GNP, which in this case is $2.7 trillion, is then found by totaling the figures in column 4.

Because a listing like the one in the table would be far too long to compile in today's economy, government statisticians actually use other methods. The concept they use, however, is the same.

In the United States, the job of computing the country's GNP falls to the Department of Commerce. Tons of data flow into this department which then must evaluate and classify it for analysis. The people who perform this task are faced with several classification decisions that center around what should, and should not, be included in the figures that measure GNP.

One such decision has to do with the double counting of **intermediate products**—products used in making final goods. Sales of intermediate products are not counted in GNP. Replacement tires for automobiles, for example, can be counted in GNP, but tires for new cars cannot. If both the value of tires used for new automobiles and the total value of the automobiles on which the tires are used were counted, the new tires would be counted twice, and GNP would be overstated by the tires' value.

The same problem takes place with such other intermediate goods as flour, sugar, and salt. If these items are bought for final use by the consumer, they should be counted as part of the final output, which is part of GNP. But if they are used in the production of bread or any other bakery goods bought by the consumer, they should not be counted.

Another classification decision involves **secondhand sales**—the sales of used goods.

GNP FOR YEAR A

	(1) PRODUCT	(2) QUANTITY	(3) PRICE	(4) DOLLAR VALUE
Goods:	Automobiles	7 million	$10,000	$70 billion
	Replacement tires	10 million	$45	$450 million
	Toothpicks	5 million	1¢	$50,000
	...... *	......	......	......
	......	......	......	......
Services:	Haircuts	300 million	$8	$2.4 billion
	Income tax returns completed	40 million	$100	$ 4 billion
	......	......	......	......
	......	......	......	......
* ......All other goods and services				GNP = $2.7 TRILLION

Table 14–A

When used goods are transferred from one person or group to another, no new wealth is created. So while the sale of a used car or house may give others cash that they can use on new purchases, only the original sale is included in GNP.

SHORTCOMINGS OF GNP

Even though GNP is the most comprehensive measure of output for the economy, it does have some shortcomings. These do not make it any less useful as a measure of final output. Even so, the public should be aware of the fact that it does have some limits.

ACCURACY OF MEASUREMENT.   One shortcoming of GNP is the accuracy of measurement. When dealing with aggregates, or totals, in an economy as large and as complex as that of the United States, it is not always possible to be completely accurate.

Some of the figures used to arrive at GNP are based on reliable statistical estimates. Others, however, are no more than educated guesses. Imagine how hard it would be, for example, to determine the exact value of all the lawns mowed by students working part-time. At best, only a reasonable approximation of the value could be made. For this reason, then, GNP figures are accepted as being reasonably complete, if not absolutely accurate, gauges of the country's economic well-being.

Related to the accuracy of measurement is the problem of the speed at which GNP statistics are reported. Generally speaking, these figures are hard to collect and analyze. Therefore, they are reported only quarterly and then often are subject to some revision months after the quarter has ended. Because of the delays in getting current statistics on GNP, it often takes several months to find out how the economy actually performed.

COMPOSITION OF OUTPUT.   A second shortcoming of GNP is that it tells nothing about either the composition or the quality of output. For example, if GNP increases $10 million, many people may feel that the country is better off. But some of those people might not be so pleased if they knew the growth was due to the production of $10 million worth of nerve gas for use in war.

On the other hand, GNP may fall in the short run, which could be interpreted to mean that the country is not doing as well as before. Yet, would people be as upset if they knew GNP had fallen because of lower total drug sales due to a breakthrough in a patent medicine that could make other drugs on the market obsolete? In the long run, the drug might make people healthier, which would mean they could produce more.

GNP figures reflect total production, not individual welfare. For this reason, total GNP may go up without all people benefiting equally. Some people's income may rise, but others' income may remain the same or go down.

EXCLUSION OF OTHER ACTIVITIES.   A third shortcoming of GNP is the exclusion of **non-market transactions**—transactions that do not take place in the market. Some exclusions are due to a problem of measurement. GNP does not take into account the value of a person's services when he or she mows his or her own lawn, babysits brothers and sisters, or does his or her own home maintenance.

There is no doubt that all of the above transactions are productive. Yet because the services involved are not bought and sold in the market, they are hard to measure. For this reason, they are not used in computing GNP.

Other activities, however, often are excluded from GNP because they are illegal and are not reported. In the last few years, for example, it has been estimated that marijuana has taken the place of pineapples as the chief cash crop in Hawaii. It also is thought to be the largest cash crop in California. Since such crops are not reported, however, no one knows for sure.

There is a whole range of unreported activities that includes gambling, smuggling, drugs, and counterfeiting, to name a few. These unreported illegal activities, plus some legal ones that are not disclosed for tax reasons, form what is known as the **underground economy.**

Although estimates differ, economists generally agree that somewhere between 5 and 15 percent of all economic activity is part of the underground economy and is not included in GNP. Because of this, GNP actually understates the range of activity taking place in the economy.

IMPORTANCE OF GNP ANALYSIS

Even though the concept of GNP has some limits, it is generally agreed that it is a fairly good indicator of economic health. When interpreted properly, GNP analysis becomes a useful tool of economic understanding.

In a sense, GNP is a reflection of American society itself. As a society, Americans are obsessed with measurement. They measure and keep statistics on everything from professional athletes to beauty contest participants. The concept of GNP is no different. With it, Americans try to keep track of production to know how they are doing and to tell where they have been.

The narcotics officers in the photograph have siezed a marijuana crop. Growing marijuana is an example of an illegal activity that is part of the underground economy. About what percentage of all economic activity is part of the underground economy?

As a general rule, a bigger GNP is regarded as a better one. There is good reason for this. People are not concerned with output for output's sake. Nevertheless, it is the chief way in which more people can have additional goods and services to satisfy wants and raise their standard of living. Most people want a bigger slice of the "output pie" in the long run. The easiest way for everyone to succeed is to have the size of the pie grow over time. If it does not, some people can have a bigger slice only at the expense of others.

When GNP grows, people are happy because more of their wants and needs are being satisfied. If GNP does not grow, people become unhappy and strike out at society. One way they can do this is by voting Presidents and political parties out of office. In the past, this has happened in times of recession.

In addition, new economic policies often are implemented because it is believed they will stimuate GNP. Their success—or their lack of success—is measured in terms of how GNP reacts.

The importance of GNP analysis, then, is that it is widely regarded as a measure of the country's health. Even though it is not perfect, it is the single most important economic statistic compiled today.

Section Review

1. How does national income accounting relate to aggregated supply?

2. What is the most important and comprehensive statistic kept in the national income accounts?

3. What are two classification decisions faced by people who compute GNP?

4. What are some major shortcomings of GNP as a measure of the economy's output?

5. Why is GNP analysis important?

14.2 *Aggregate Demand*

An advanced country like the United States is very complex. It involves millions of individual decisionmaking units—individuals, businesses, and governments make billions of decisions daily. **Microeconomics** is the branch of economics that deals with decision making and other behavior by these individual units. Another branch of economics, known as **macroeconomics**, deals with large groups or aggregates. Because GNP deals with the output of the country as a whole, it is a macroeconomic concept.

ECONOMIC SECTORS

As a first step in understanding the macro economy of the United States, it helps to think of the economy as being made up of several different parts called sectors. These sectors represent individuals, businesses, government, and foreign markets. The sum of expenditures of these sectors is known as **aggregate demand.**

CONSUMER SECTOR.   One sector of the macro economy is the consumer sector. The basic unit in this sector is the **household,** which is made up of all persons who occupy a house, apartment, or room that constitutes separate living quarters. It includes related family members and all others—such as lodgers, foster children, and employees—who share the living quarters.

As long as the person or persons occupy a separate place of residence, a household also can consist of **unrelated individuals.**

Micro - and macroeconomics are two important branches of economics. How do they differ?

"Confound it, Merriwell! Do you mean that all this time you've been talking micro while we've been talking macro?"

Profile

David Ricardo

David Ricardo was born in London, England in 1772 into the large family of a prosperous Jewish stockbroker. He went on to become a multimillionaire, a member of Parliament, and one of the greatest economists of the early post-Adam Smith period.

Ricardo became an economist by accident. While visiting Bath, he happened to come upon a copy of Smith's *Wealth of Nations*. After reading it cover-to-cover, he became converted to ideas set forth by Smith.

1772–1823

In 1819, Ricardo's greatest work, *The Principles of Political Economy and Taxation*, was published. One of the issues analyzed in the book was why landlords, capitalists, and laborers received the share of income they did. Ricardo believed that "the distribution of the produce of the earth goes to the landlords in the form of rent, to the owners of capital in the form of profit and interest, and to the laborers as wages."

Ricardo argued that rent is the result of the ownership of land, which is a scarce natural resource. Since population tends to grow over time, the rent received by the landlords also will grow. With more people to feed, society will be forced to grow food on poorer and poorer land. The poorer land will need more preparation than the richer land, which will cause the costs of production to become higher. This, in turn, will make food prices increase. If food prices increase, the laborers will need higher wages so they can buy the higher-priced food. The factory owners can increase the wages of their laborers, but they cannot increase the price of the product those laborers produce. The only way, then, for the owners of capital to meet the increased wages is by giving up some of their profits. At the same time, however, the higher food prices result in higher revenues, or rents, for landlords who own the richer lands.

Adam Smith saw in this a harmony of society's interests. David Ricardo, on the other hand, saw a conflict over the distribution of that society's income.

United States exports make up part of what is considered the foreign sector of the macro economy. In addition to exports, what else is included in the foreign sector?

These are persons who live alone or with non-relatives even though they may have family living elsewhere. The concept of a household is somewhat broader than that of a **family**—a group of two or more persons related by blood, marriage, or adoption living together in a household.

These definitions are used by economists and the United States Bureau of the Census. Although they may seem strange at first, they suit the needs of data collectors and economic researchers.

Suppose, for example, you needed to make an estimate of the number of stoves in use today. Since a household is defined as a separate place of residence, almost every household is likely to have a stove. Thus, a simple count of households would give a reasonably close approximation of the number of stoves in use. The same is

true for such other durable goods as water heaters, furnaces, and refrigerators. In fact, many households, even when made up of persons not related by blood, marriage, or adoption, tend to behave as a single economic unit.

Although the concept of a family is familiar to almost everyone, it can cause some measurement problems. Suppose, for example, the government was taking a census. What would happen in the case of an apartment shared by four young people while they attend college?

If the census taker tries to apply the definition of a family, measurement would be difficult. The census taker would need to know the location of each of the four young people's parents so that the family size could be recorded correctly and double counting does not take place.

On the other hand, if the concept of a household is used, the measurement is much simpler. Since the apartment is a separate place of residence, the census would show one household with four unrelated individuals.

For this and other reasons, the term "household" is the basic economic unit of the consumer sector, even though "family" is a more familiar term to most people.

INVESTMENT SECTOR. A second sector of the macro economy is the business, or investment, sector. It is made up of proprietorships, partnerships, and corporations. It is the productive sector responsible for bringing the factors of production together to produce output.

GOVERNMENT SECTOR. A third sector in the macro economy is the government, or public, sector. It includes the local, state, and federal levels of government. When speaking of the government sector, then, the reference is to government in general rather than to one level.

FOREIGN SECTOR. A fourth sector of the macro economy is the foreign sector. It includes all consumers and producers external to the United States.

The United States, for example, exports computers, airplanes, and farm products to foreign buyers. It also imports a large number of different items from foreign countries. It makes no difference whether foreign buyers are governments or private investors or if purchases are made from governments or private individuals. They all are part of the foreign sector.

OUTPUT-EXPENDITURE MODEL

Economists use a macroeconomic model called an **output-expenditure model** to analyze aggregate demand. It is so named because this model describes the part of the nation's total output, or GNP, consumed by each of the four sectors of the economy.

The consumer sector, labeled C in the model, spends its income on the goods and services used by households and unrelated individuals. These expenditures, known as **personal consumption expenditures,** include groceries, rent, books, automobiles, clothes, and almost anything else people buy.

The investment, or business, sector is labeled I in the model. It spends its income on plant, equipment, and other investment goods. These expenditures, known as **gross private domestic investment,** represent the total value of capital goods created in the economy during the year. The term gross is used because purchases of all capital goods are included.

Another part of the expenditure of the investment sector has to do with inventories. These are the stocks of goods kept in reserve to satisfy consumer or producer orders. Once goods are produced, they are counted as part of the GNP. Until they are sold to the consumer sector, they are treated as if they were "purchased" by the investment sector.

The government sector, labeled G in the model, spends its income on many categories of expenditures. These include national defense, hospital care, roads, and education. The only major item of government expenditure not included in GNP is transfer payments. The reason is that this money is used by others to buy some of the goods and services that are part of the total GNP.

For example, the government may collect money by taxing the incomes of certain citizens and then use that money to pay old-age pensions or unemployment benefits. When this happens, the total output of the economy does not go up. Funds merely have been taken from one place and used in another.

The foreign sector, labeled *F* in the model, also buys a great many goods and services that make up GNP. In addition, it supplies imports of other products to be consumed at home. For this reason, the output-expenditure model is concerned with the difference between the exports and the imports.

For example, when the United States takes part in international trade, it exchanges American-made tractors, airplanes, and farm products for British woolens, Japanese cars, Korean shirts, and Brazilian shoes. The imported goods basically take the place of those sent to other countries. For this reason, the foreign sector's purchases are called **net exports of goods and services,** a term that refers to the difference between the United States' exports and its imports.

When the United States exports part of its GNP, there is less for consumption by the consumer, investment, and government sectors. This loss, however, is made up when foreign-made products are imported. In the longer run, one generally offsets the other, and the difference between the two is very small.

The consumer, investment, government, and foreign sectors together consume all of the GNP for any given year. When this is written algebraically as

$$GNP = C + I + G + F$$

the equation becomes the formal output-expenditure model used to explain and analyze the performance of the economy.

Section Review

1. How do microeconomics and macroeconomics differ?

2. What four sectors make up the macro economy of the United States?

3. What does an output-expenditure model describe? What is the algebraic equation for the formal model?

14.3 *Other Measures of Total Income*

The national income accounts provide four other measures of the nation's total income besides GNP. These measures are net national product, national income, personal income, and disposable personal income.

The illustration on page 359 is a combination of the circular flow diagram on page 80 and the output-expenditure model. It shows the relationships among the five measures of total income. In the illustration, the expenditures flow clockwise from left to right. The foreign sector (F) has been left out as it generally amounts to only a small percent of GNP expenditures for the year. The table on page 361 also shows these relationships among measures of total income.

NET NATIONAL PRODUCT

One measure of the nation's total income is **net national product (NNP)**—GNP

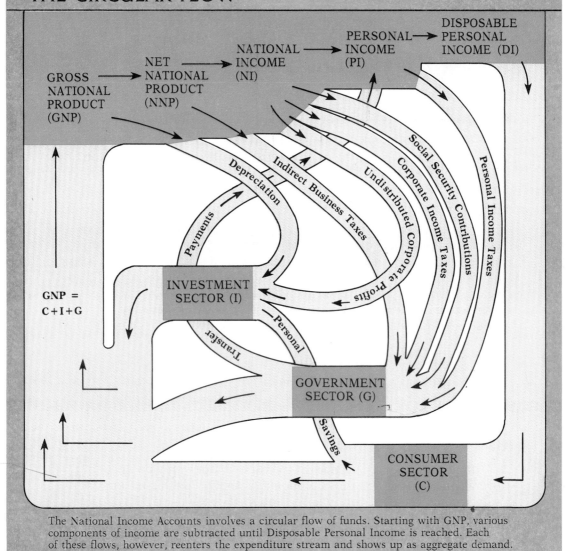

NATIONAL INCOME ACCOUNTS: THE CIRCULAR FLOW

GROSS NATIONAL PRODUCT (GNP) → NET NATIONAL PRODUCT (NNP) → NATIONAL INCOME (NI) → PERSONAL INCOME (PI) → DISPOSABLE PERSONAL INCOME (DI)

GNP = C + I + G

Payments
Depreciation
Indirect Business Taxes
Undistributed Corporate Profits
Corporate Income Taxes
Social Security Contributions
Personal Income Taxes

INVESTMENT SECTOR (I)

Transfer
Personal

GOVERNMENT SECTOR (G)

Savings

CONSUMER SECTOR (C)

The National Income Accounts involves a circular flow of funds. Starting with GNP, various components of income are subtracted until Disposable Personal Income is reached. Each of these flows, however, reenters the expenditure stream and shows up as aggregate demand.

Figure 14–1

minus depreciation. The depreciation is subtracted to give a better picture of production for the year.

For example, when the economy produces $4176 billion in goods and services in a given year, it stands to reason that some of the capital equipment is used up. If the amount of worn-out and used-up capital goods amounts to approximately $454 billion, the net amount of

Case Study: Issue

Does MEW Measure the Economy Better than GNP?

Some economists believe that a "Measure of Economic Welfare" (MEW), would provide a better measure of the economy's overall well-being than GNP. MEW would be constructed by making certain adjustments to GNP. Things such as the number of hours lost because of traffic jams, the cost of air and water pollution, and the cost of crime would be deducted from GNP. Things such as increases in leisure time, health, and services provided by homemakers would be added to GNP.

Those who favor using MEW argue that such adjustments to GNP would give a better measure of the quality of life in a nation. They argue that larger output—as measured by GNP—is not better for a nation if it contributes to pollution, traffic congestion, or general health problems. Likewise, an increase in GNP caused by the production of chemical warfare weapons or MX missiles may not mean a safer world to live in. As a result, the quality of life could go down.

Those who oppose using MEW argue that such measurements would be difficult to make. They point out, for example, the difficulty in measuring such things as traffic congestion, pollution, or leisure time. In addition, some people feel that an increase in the production of such goods as military hardware adds to the quality of life because they make the country more secure.

Although MEW is not a perfect measure, it does provide an overall measure of a nation's economic activity. For this reason, some economists will continue to support its use.

1. What is MEW? What does it measure?

2. How is GNP adjusted to obtain a "Measure of Economic Welfare"?

3. What are the main arguments against MEW?

NATIONAL INCOME ACCOUNTS (SECOND QUARTER, 1986)

GROSS NATIONAL PRODUCT	$4,176
Minus: Capital Consumption Allowances and Adjustments	−454
NET NATIONAL PRODUCT	$3,722
Minus: Indirect Business Taxes	−346
NATIONAL INCOME	$3,376
Minus: Undistributed Corporate Profits and Net Interest	−293
Social Security Contributions	−374
Plus: Transfer Payments, Misc. Items	+774
PERSONAL INCOME	$3,483
Minus: Personal Income Taxes/Non-Tax Payments	−504
DISPOSABLE PERSONAL INCOME	$2,979

Source: *Survey of Current Business*, September, 1986

Table 14–B

production—the net national product—would then be $3722 billion.

Since depreciation is considered as an expense, businesses are allowed to subtract it from their income for tax purposes. For this reason, it is treated as a source of income to the investment sector in the national income accounts. This can be seen in the illustration on page 359, which shows **capital consumption allowances,** or depreciation, flowing to the investment sector.

NATIONAL INCOME

Another measure of the nation's total income is **national income (NI)**—net national product less all taxes except the corporate profits tax businesses must pay as a cost of doing business. Examples of these taxes, also known as **indirect business taxes,** are excise taxes, property taxes, licensing fees, customs duties, and general

sales taxes. Businesses treat these taxes as costs of production because the taxes add to the final cost of goods. Indirect business taxes are treated as sources of revenue to the government sector. This fact is seen in the illustration on page 359, which shows the taxes flowing to the government sector.

PERSONAL INCOME

Still another measure of the nation's total income is **personal income (PI)**—the total amount of income going to households before taxes are subtracted. To go from national to personal income, four adjustments must be made.

First, income that does not go to the households must be subtracted from national income. One such type of income is **retained earnings,** also known as **undistributed corporate profits.** These are the profits businesses, especially corporations,

"Please, darling... just a few dollars for food?"

When prices rise in one area, they affect spending in other areas. It is difficult, for example, to cut back on essentials such as gasoline. What is the final measure of personal income?

ments from the government in the form of unemployment insurance, social security, medicaid, and several other forms of assistance. Once the transfer payments have been added, the resulting total is the final measure of personal income.

DISPOSABLE PERSONAL INCOME

The smallest measure of income is **disposable personal income (DI)**—the total amount of income households and unrelated individuals have at their disposal after taxes. This is an important measure because it reflects the actual amount of money the consumer sector is actually able to spend. For the most part, a person's disposable income is equal to the amount of money received from an employer after taxes and social security have been taken out.

In the illustration of a check on page 221, for example, the disposable personal income amounted to $619.64 after deductions were taken out. The person to whom the check is made out could choose to have more of the salary withheld to cover contributions to a credit union or a social agency like the United Way or to buy savings bonds. This would not lower the disposable personal income. The person simply has chosen to use payroll deduction features to help allocate the disposable income.

keep to reinvest in new plants and equipment. Since businesses keep these funds for their own use, they are shown as income to the investment rather than the consumer sector.

The second type of income that must be subtracted is the income taxes paid by corporations. These taxes are treated as income to the government sector since they do not go directly to individuals. The third type of income that must be subtracted is social security contributions. These, too, go to the government sector.

After these three types of income have been subtracted from national income, transfer payments must be added to it. The consumer sector receives these pay-

▍ Section Review

1. What are four measures other than GNP of the nations total income?
2. What adjustments must be made to go from national income to personal income?
3. Why is disposable personal income an important measure?

14.4 GNP and Changes in the Price Level

A major problem with GNP is that it is subject to distortions because of inflation—a rise in the general price level. With inflation, output may appear to grow from one year to the next without actually doing so.

To see how this happens, compare the GNP table on page 351 with the one on this page. Assume that the second table was compiled one year after the first one and that the inflation rate during that year was 10 percent. The second column in each table shows that the composition and quantity of output was the same both years. This means there was no real change in the amount of goods and services produced.

The third column in each table, however, is not the same. Neither is the fourth. In these columns, everything costs 10 percent more in the second table than in the first one. This makes GNP rise by 10 percent, or $270 billion. These columns, then, show the effects of inflation. The major problem is that the dollar value of the final output went up without any real underlying changes in the quantity of goods and services produced.

CONSTRUCTING A PRICE INDEX

To get around the problem of distortions by inflation, economists construct a

Table 14–C

GNP FOR YEAR *B*			
(1) PRODUCT	(2) QUANTITY	(3) PRICE	(4) DOLLAR VALUE
Goods: Automobiles	7 million	$11,000	$77 billion
Replacement tires	10 million	$49.50	$495 million
Toothpicks	5 million	1.1¢	$55,000
......*	......	......	......
......	......	......	......
Services: Haircuts	300 million	$8.80	$2.64 billion
Income tax returns completed	40 million	$110	$4.4 billion
......	......	......	......
......	......	......	......
*.... All other goods and services			GNP = $2.97 TRILLION

CONSTRUCTING A PRICE INDEX

ITEM	DESCRIPTION	PRICE BASE YEAR (1982)	PRICE SECOND PERIOD (1983)	PRICE THIRD PERIOD (1984)
1.	Toothpaste (7 oz.)	$1.40	$1.49	$1.57
2.	Milk (1 gal.)	1.29	1.29	1.39
3.	Peanut butter (2 lb. jar)	2.50	2.65	2.73
4.	Light bulbs (60 watt)	.45	.48	.55
......	......	......	......	......
......	......	......	......	......
400	Automobile engine tune-up	40.00	42.00	44.75
Total Cost of Market Basket: **Index Number:**		$179.20 100%	$189.59 105.8%	$207.87 116%

Table 14–D

price index—a statistical series that can be used to measure changes in prices over time. It can be compiled for a specific group of products or for a much broader range of items.

It is not hard to construct a price index. First of all, a base year—a year that serves as the basis of comparison for all other years—is chosen. The particular year chosen can vary. The base year is used only in a comparative sense and generally is updated as time goes by.

Second, a "typical" **market basket** of goods is selected. These are goods representative of the purchases which will be made over time. Although the number of items in the market basket is a matter of judgement, it must remain fixed once the selection is made. The advantage of this market basket concept is that it captures the overall trend in prices.

Lastly, the price of each item in the market basket is recorded and then totaled. The total represents the prices of the market basket in the base year and is assigned a value of 100 percent.

The table on this page shows how a price index can be constructed for a representative market basket containing 400 items. Because 1982 is used as the base year in the table, the prices in the base year column are lower than those today. The total of the market basket prices—$179.20—is assigned a value of 100, which is the index number for that year.

In order to see how prices change from one year to the next, the price for each of the 400 items must be recorded for the base year and then recorded again a year later. Since the total of the items for the second year—$189.59—is 5.8 percent higher than the total for the first year, the new index number is 105.8. The prices for each year that follows also must be recorded and totaled to find the new index number. This procedure is repeated until the price index is finished.

MAJOR PRICE INDICES

Price indices can be constructed for a number of different purposes. Some serve to measure the price changes of imported goods, while others do the same for agricultural products. Still others measure changes in the price of a single item. Of all these measures, three are especially important. They are the consumer price index, the producer price index, and the implicit GNP price deflator.

CONSUMER PRICE INDEX. The **consumer price index (CPI)** reports on price changes for about 400 frequently used consumer items. For a long period of time, it used a base year of 1958. This was changed to a base of 1967, however, when the index numbers became too large. The 400 goods and services it uses are taken from 85 areas around the country. Some of the items are surveyed in all the areas, while others are sampled in only a few.

The consumer price index is compiled monthly by the Bureau of Labor Statistics and is published for the economy as a whole. There also are separate indices for 28 selected areas around the country.

PRODUCER PRICE INDEX. The **producer price index,** formerly called the **wholesale price index,** measures price changes of commodities at all stages of production. It uses a sample of 3400 commodities and has a base year of 1967.

The producer price index also is reported monthly by the Bureau of Labor Statistics. Although it is compiled for all commodities, it also is broken down into subcategories that include farm products, fuels, chemicals, rubber, pulp and paper, and processed foods.

IMPLICIT GNP PRICE DEFLATOR. The **implicit GNP price deflator** measures price changes in GNP. It has a base year of 1982 and can be used to remove the effects of inflation from GNP.

Since GNP is a measure of the final output of goods and services and covers thousands of items instead of hundreds, many economists believe it is a better long-run indicator of the price changes that face consumers. Since the deflator is compiled quarterly, however, it is not as useful for measuring changes in inflation from month-to-month.

REAL VERSUS CURRENT GNP

When GNP is not adjusted for inflation, it is called **current GNP, nominal GNP,** or simply GNP. When the distortions of inflation have been removed it is called **real GNP** or **GNP in constant dollars.**

To convert current GNP to real GNP, the current GNP first is divided by the implicit GNP price deflator. This figure is then multiplied by 100 because the index number is really a percent.

For example, current GNP in 1985 dollars can be converted to real GNP in 1982 dollars by using the equation:

$$\frac{1985 \text{ GNP}}{\text{implicit price deflator}} (100) = \text{real GNP in constant dollars}$$

According to the Bureau of Labor Statistics, the implicit price deflator for 1985 was 111.7 and the GNP was $3992.5

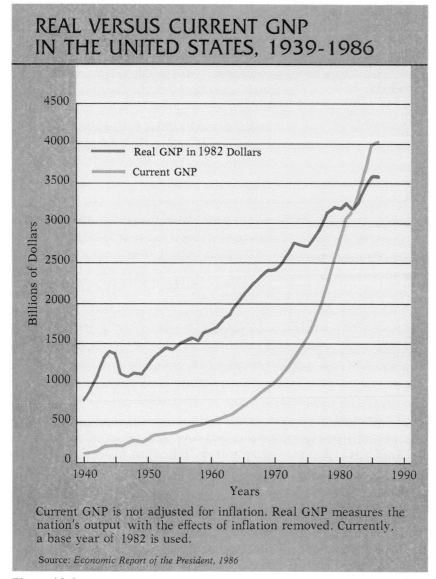

REAL VERSUS CURRENT GNP IN THE UNITED STATES, 1939-1986

Current GNP is not adjusted for inflation. Real GNP measures the nation's output with the effects of inflation removed. Currently, a base year of 1982 is used.

Source: *Economic Report of the President, 1986*

Figure 14-2

billion. Using these numbers, the equation would read as follows:

$$\frac{\$3992.5 \text{ billion}}{111.7} \ (100) \ = \ \$3574.3 \text{ billion}$$

The real GNP for 1985, then, is $3574.3 billion in terms of 1982 dollars.

Once GNP has been converted to real terms, a comparison can be made with the earlier figure. The GNP in 1982 was $3166.0 billion. In 1985, it was $3574.3 billion when measured in 1982 dollars. Therefore, the change in GNP was due to real, rather than inflationary, factors.

The advantage of real GNP is that it allows comparisons over time. The two measures of GNP in the graph on page 366 show how inflation has distorted the growth of real goods and services over the long run. Today the impact of inflation cannot be ignored. For this and other reasons, almost all modern statistics are reported in both current and real terms. To have an understanding of one without the other would be to understand only part of the picture.

Section Review

1. What is a major problem with GNP?
2. What are three major price indices used today?
3. What is the advantage of real GNP versus current GNP?

Chapter 14 Review

Summary

1. Economists use national income accounting to measure aggregate supply and to trace long-run trends in the economy.

2. Gross National Product (GNP) is one of the most important statistics of the economy's performance.

3. Shortcomings of GNP include accuracy of measurement, lack of information about the composition of output, and exclusion of non-market transactions and unreported activities.

4. Macroeconomics is the branch of economics that deals with the behavior of large groups or aggregates.

5. The U.S. macro economy is made up of four sectors—consumer, investment, government, and foreign. Together they represent the aggregate demand in the economy.

6. The basic unit of the consumer sector is the household, which is made up of all persons occupying a house, apartment, or room that constitutes separate living quarters.

7. Economists use a macroeconomic model called an output-expenditure model to describe the nation's output. The algebraic equation for the model is GNP: $= C + I + G + F$.

8. Besides GNP, the four other measures of the nation's total income are net national product, national income, personal income, and disposable personal income.

9. Disposable personal income is important because it reflects the amount of money the consumer sector is actually able to spend.

10. To remove the distortions of GNP caused by inflation, economists use price indices such as the consumer price index, producer price index, and the implicit GNP price deflator.

11. Real GNP—GNP after the distortions of inflation have been removed—has the advantage of allowing comparisons over time. Today, most modern statistics are reported in current and real terms.

■ *Building an Economic Vocabulary*

aggregate supply
national income accounting
intermediate products
secondhand sales
non-market transactions
underground economy
microeconomics
macroeconomics
aggregate demand
household
unrelated individuals
family
output-expenditure model
personal consumption
   expenditures

gross private domestic
   investment
net exports of goods and
   services
net national product (NNP)
capital consumption
   allowances
national income (NI)
indirect business taxes
personal income (PI)
retained earnings
undistributed corporate
   profits
disposable personal
   income (DI)

price index
market basket
consumer price
   index
producer price
   index
wholesale price
   index
implicit GNP price
   deflator
current GNP
nominal GNP
real GNP
GNP in constant
   dollars

■ *Reviewing the Main Ideas*

1. Why do economists use national income accounting?

2. How does the activity of the underground economy affect GNP in the United States?

3. Why is bigger GNP seen as better?

4. Why is GNP considered a macroeconomic concept?

5. How does a household differ from a family?

6. What is the investment sector's role?

7. On what does the consumer sector spend its income?

8. What is the only major item of government expenditure not included in GNP?

9. What is the algebraic expression for the output-expenditure model?

10. Why is depreciation treated as a source of income to the investment sector?

11. What is the advantage of the market-basket concept?

Practicing Critical Thinking Skills

1. Some people criticize GNP as a measure of economic well-being because it reflects output rather than individual welfare. Do you think this is a fair criticism? Why or why not?

2. Some economists believe that disposable personal income is almost as important a measure of economic performance as GNP. What do you think? Give reasons for your answer.

Applying Economic Understandings

Interpreting a Line Graph

Statistical information is displayed in many ways, a line graph being one of the most common. It often shows how a quantity changes over time. The following guidelines show how to develop the skill of interpreting a line graph.
1. Read the title of the graph.
2. Read the labels along the horizontal and vertical axes.

3. Determine what the line(s) or curve(s) symbolize.

4. Compare the line(s) in the graph to the horizontal and vertical axes.

5. Once all parts have been analyzed, determine the point being made.

6. Using the guidelines above, interpret Figure 14-2 on page 366.

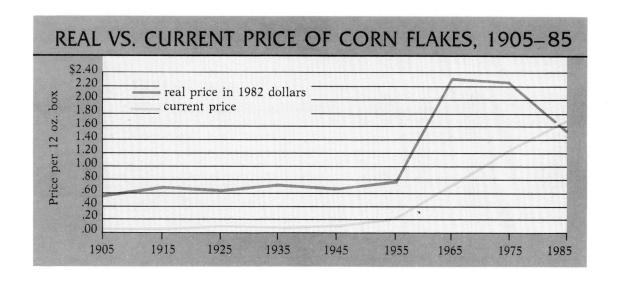

REAL VS. CURRENT PRICE OF CORN FLAKES, 1905–85

Economic Growth and Stability

A recession is when your neighbor is out of work. A depression is when you're out of work.
Harry S Truman

Chapter 15

After reading this chapter, you will be able to:

- Explain why economic growth is important and the factors that make it possible.

- Illustrate economic growth using real GNP and real GNP per capita.

- Describe the phases, causes, effects, and methods of predicting the business cycle.

- Discuss the economic and social costs of economic instability.

15.1 Economic Growth

Economic growth, which is important to everyone's well-being, is one of the seven major goals of the United States economy. When the economy of one country grows, it helps other people and other countries as well.

IMPORTANCE OF GROWTH

Economic growth benefits a country's economy and political system. It raises the standard of living, helps government carry out its work, helps solve domestic problems, helps the economies of developing countries, and helps prevent the spread of communism.

STANDARD OF LIVING. Economic growth brings about a higher **standard of living**—the quality of life based on the possession of necessities and luxuries that make life easier. A major feature of a free enterprise economy is its ability to increase real per capita output enough over

Developing nations build industry with income from the sale of their goods abroad. How do more goods help consumers in other countries?

carry out other projects for which there was no money before.

DOMESTIC PROBLEMS. Economic growth helps solve domestic problems. Like most other countries of the world, the United States is faced with a certain number of social problems. Poverty, lack of education, inadequate medical care, inequality of opportunity, and economic insecurity all are problems with which the economy must deal. Most of these stem from economic need. A greater output of goods and services means more jobs and more income for more people. This, will help cut down the economic need that is the root of many problems.

DEVELOPING NATIONS. Economic growth makes it possible to help developing nations, which, in turn, benefits the United States. Growth causes firms in the United States to increase their demand for raw materials and other products. When these are bought from developing nations, more jobs open up and income goes up in those countries.

This allows people of developing nations to buy goods and services from the United States thus generating jobs in return. It also allows the people of developing nations to build their own industry and produce additional services and goods for sale on the world market. This gives consumers in other countries, including the United States, the opportunity to choose from a greater variety of competitively priced goods and services.

In addition, when people and businesses in the United States and elsewhere purchase products made abroad, factors of production are released for use in other industries. In this way, the resources of many nations are used in the best ways possible, which, in the long run, stimulates world economic growth.

time to allow people to raise their standard of living. In the end, it also allows people to have more free time because they will not need to work as many days as before to earn the same income. With more free time, they can enjoy more hobbies and recreational, family, and cultural activities.

GOVERNMENT SPENDING. Economic growth allows government at all levels to carry out its tasks more easily. For example, at present, the burden of national defense is heavy. This means there is less money available for social welfare and other domestic items. Economic growth, however, enlarges the **tax base**—the incomes and properties that may be taxed. This gives the government greater tax revenues, which, in turn, lightens the burden of public sector spending. It also may make it possible for the government to

Case Study: Career

Systems Analyst

A systems analyst works in the field of data-processing. He or she is responsible for designing computer-based information systems, providing specifications for the equipment used in the systems, and training the people who work with the systems. To accomplish this, the analyst has to perform certain tasks. These include conducting a study to show the costs and benefits of computerization; designing the system and finding  equipment to make it work; and convincing company executives that the system is the right one for them. Then the analyst must code and implement the system, train the staff, and install the hardware.

Most systems analysts work for banks, businesses, or corporations. Those who work for a bank may be responsible for a system that handles customer deposits, withdrawals, loan requests, or the bank's investments and liabilities. Those who work for a business or corporation may be responsible for a system that keeps track of all costs so they can be assigned to the production of individual products or product lines.

Systems analysts must know a certain amount of mathematics and be thorough, logical, and precise. They also must be good salespersons, have good communications skills, and have a great deal of tact. Because they often have access to highly confidential information, they are expected to be trustworthy and reliable.

Because of the level of skills involved, most analysts being hired today have at least a college degree. Business organizations generally prefer to hire analysts with a background in accounting, business management, or economics. Scientifically oriented organizations prefer to hire analysts with a background in the physical sciences, mathematics, or engineering. Most employers in general prefer people familiar with programming languages. On-the-job experience and training in business information systems and computer sciences also may be required. At present, the demand for systems analysts is high. In fact, colleges and universities are hard-pressed to graduate enough people to meet the need.

CHALLENGE OF COMMUNISM. Economic growth helps the Free world meet the challenge of communism. In the world today, there are a number of emerging nations that have not yet formed their political and economic ideologies. Although many have a fair amount of natural resources, they do not have the capital, technology, or skilled workers they need. But with outside help, they can develop their resources and raise the standard of living of their people.

The countries of the Free world and the Communist world both are trying to influence the economic development of the emerging countries. Whenever capitalism as an economic system can prove it works better than communism, the countries of the Free world gain the respect of the emerging nations.

ESSENTIAL ELEMENTS

Economic growth depends on the ability of the economy to produce output. A number of factors are involved. Most important, however, is the quantity and the quality of the three factors of production—land, labor, and capital. Their availability, and the way in which they are organized, will determine how the economy grows.

LAND. The United States has an abundance of most natural resources needed for growth. Unlike such island nations as Great Britain and Japan, it does not depend heavily on international trade for its productive inputs. Although a number of minerals, including chromium, cobalt, crude oil, and diamonds, must be imported, the United States is a reasonably self-sufficient nation.

Even so, natural resources must be treated with care. Many of the ones most Americans take for granted, such as clean air and water, forests, and fertile land, are being used up at an alarming rate. Only some of the country's resources are **renewable resources**—resources that can be brought into being again for future use. Some forests, for example, can be reseeded for use in the near future. California redwood trees, however, take hundreds of years to grow to the size most Americans know today. Because the United States has an abundance of nature's gifts at present, it does not mean that will always be the case.

LABOR. In order for any country to grow, it must have a large and skilled labor force. Since the size of this force is related to total population, the number of people available for productive activities will grow as the population grows.

In the United States, the population has been growing, but at a decreasing rate. Between 1800 an 1900, population grew about 2.7 percent annually. This fell to 1.4 percent between 1900 and World War II, where it remained until 1980. From 1980 to 1986, the rate of growth fell to less than one percent annually.

Whether or not this trend becomes a problem remains to be seen. If the growth of population continues to decline, it will eventually affect the growth of the labor force. However, a labor shortage could be made up by workers from other countries. Or new additions to the labor force, such as women and others who traditionally have stayed at home, could offset a labor shortage.

When it comes to quality, the American labor force is thought to be more skilled today than it was in the past. This is often measured by the number of school years completed by workers, which has increased since 1940. It is estimated that by 1990, the median number of school years completed will be more than 13. This means that half of the labor force will

The quality of the American labor force today is higher than ever before. This is due, in part, to the additional schooling received by workers. What other factors besides education affect the quality of the labor force?

have a high school education plus one complete year of college or its equivalent.

A number of other factors, such as desire and motivation, also are important to the quality of the labor force. At present, however, economists do not have reliable measures for these. Even so, the quality of the American work force is considered reasonably high, especially when compared with other countries.

CAPITAL. Economists also are concerned with the quantity and quality of the capital stock. In 1986, the capital stock of the business sector amounted to more than $6 trillion. In real terms, the country's capital stock has been growing at a rate of about $100 billion a year.

Sometimes, the capital stock is divided by the number of workers in the labor

force to determine the **capital-to-labor ratio.** This measure shows the average amount of capital used by each worker in his or her productive efforts. Today the average person in the labor force has more than $60,000 of capital goods at his or her disposal.

Since capital goods are the result of production, it is possible to some extent to influence their creation. The key to this is saving. People must consume less and free the factors of production so that new capital can be produced. The money people save can go into depository institutions, which they lend to producers.

Reducing consumption and saving more, however, is not always possible. In some countries, people are so poor and their incomes so low that they must spend everything they earn just to exist. In these countries, there is very little saving and, therefore, investment in capital goods. And without capital goods, overall output remains low. People are caught in a vicious circle. They are too poor to save, and their incomes can rise only if they invest in capital goods.

PRODUCTIVITY AND GROWTH

Productivity refers to the efficient use of productive inputs to create goods and services. Because the concept of productivity deals with production, it is important to economic growth.

Although all three factors of production are used in the process, measurement is in terms of labor inputs. The result is **labor productivity**—the rate of growth of output per unit of labor input.

Since the end of World War II, productivity has grown at an average annual rate of 2.26 percent. This growth, however, has been uneven. Between 1947 and 1973, the rate was fairly constant at 2.94 percent. From 1973 to 1986, the rate dropped to an annual average of .78 percent. This change in productivity is shown in the figure on page 376.

A falling productivity rate threatens both economic growth and the general standard of living. As a result, a country can lose its competitive edge. In 1981, for example, Japan replaced the United States

Figure 15–1

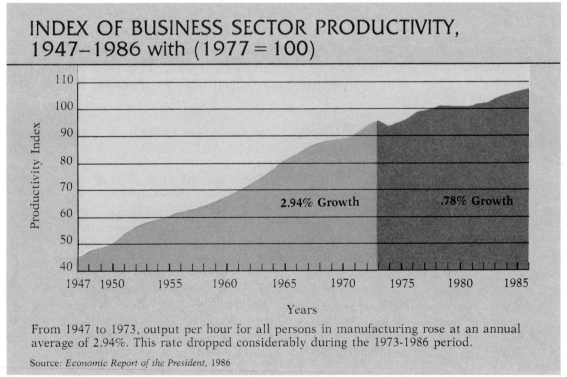

INDEX OF BUSINESS SECTOR PRODUCTIVITY, 1947–1986 with (1977 = 100)

2.94% Growth

.78% Growth

Productivity Index

1947 1950   1955   1960   1965   1970   1975   1980   1985

Years

From 1947 to 1973, output per hour for all persons in manufacturing rose at an annual average of 2.94%. This rate dropped considerably during the 1973-1986 period.

Source: *Economic Report of the President*, 1986

Today, the United States imports a great many foreign cars. This has had an adverse effect on the American auto industry. What country is the leading car manufacturer?

as the world's leading manufacturer of automobiles.

Japan is not the only country gaining on the United States. Some of the best stereo equipment comes from Norway. Lego, one of most popular toys in the world, comes from Denmark. Bic pens, which dominated the American market for ball-point pens at one time, are made in France.

The list does not stop with consumer products. Most of the high-grade plywood used in making fine furniture is imported. It is actually cheaper for firms in the United States to export logs to Japan to be turned into plywood and sent back to the United States than to have it done at home. Imported steel costs up to one-third less than steel produced in the United States. More than three-fourths of the nuts and bolts used in the United States each year are imported from abroad.

EFFECTS. When productivity falters, the entire economy suffers. When declining labor productivity in the United States is combined with a rise in the price level, the prices of goods and services become high relative to those charged by other countries. This leads people and firms to buy foreign-made products instead of American-made ones. If goods are not produced at their lowest possible cost, then, sales will be lost to others.

As other countries catch up to and surpass the United States, jobs are lost and workers are laid off. Only some of these workers will be able to find jobs in other industries. Skilled workers often find they must take jobs in other industries that do not require all the skills they used in their previous jobs. If they have to retrain or learn new skills, the economy will suffer again from a productivity decline.

CAUSES. The dynamics of productivity are not completely understood even today. Economists know how it should be measured and understand some of the essentials needed for growth. What remains unclear, however, is what is needed to make the system work.

Some people feel that productivity is down because workers are too lax in their work habits and do not really care enough about the concerns of their employer. Others say that employers are indifferent and do not care enough about the concerns of their workers. Still others charge that the tax structure discourages the reinvestment of retained earnings in new capital and equipment.

There is some truth in each of the views. The fact remains, however, that the United States has not been able to reverse the declining trend of productivity growth. For this reason, productivity is one of the major problems facing the American economy today.

Section Review

1. For what five reasons is economic growth important?
2. What is the most important factor in determining the economy's ability to produce output?
3. Why is productivity growth one of the major problems facing the American economy today?

15.2 Economic Growth in the United States

Growth is important, but just how fast does the United States economy grow? To answer this question, people first need to know how growth is measured.

MEASURING GROWTH

People usually think of economic growth as the change in real GNP from one year to the next. On this basis, the United States economy grew at an annual rate of about 3.6 percent between 1940 and 1980. Between 1980 and 1986, however, the rate was closer to 1.9 percent.

The use of real GNP, however, does not tell the whole story of growth. Because population also grows, **real GNP per capita**—the dollar amount of real GNP produced for every person in the economy—is a better measure. In fact, most economists feel that it is the single most important measure of long-term growth.

Real GNP per capita is obtained by dividing the real GNP by the population in that particular year. So if the population grows faster than real GNP, the average amount of output produced for each person in the economy falls. Or if the population grows slower than real GNP, there will be more goods and services available for everyone.

HISTORICAL RECORD

The graph on page 379 shows the relationship between real GNP and real GNP

Figure 15-2

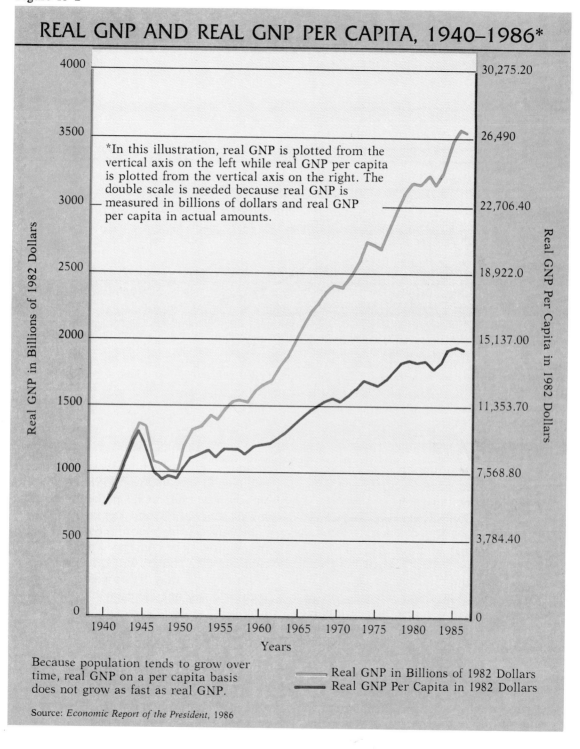

REAL GNP AND REAL GNP PER CAPITA, 1940–1986*

*In this illustration, real GNP is plotted from the vertical axis on the left while real GNP per capita is plotted from the vertical axis on the right. The double scale is needed because real GNP is measured in billions of dollars and real GNP per capita in actual amounts.

Real GNP in Billions of 1982 Dollars

Real GNP Per Capita in 1982 Dollars

Years

Because population tends to grow over time, real GNP on a per capita basis does not grow as fast as real GNP.

———— Real GNP in Billions of 1982 Dollars
———— Real GNP Per Capita in 1982 Dollars

Source: *Economic Report of the President*, 1986

REAL PER CAPITA ECONOMIC GROWTH, 1929–1985 (in percent)

Ending Year	1929	1940	1945	1950	1955	1960	1965	1970	1975	1980
1929										
1933	−9.2%									
1939	−0.6%									
1940	0.0%									
1945	3.2%	10.6%								
1950	1.5%	3.1%	−4.0%							
1955	1.7%	2.9%	−0.7%	2.6%						
1960	1.5%	2.3%	−0.3%	1.5%	0.5%					
1965	1.7%	2.5%	0.5%	2.1%	1.8%	3.1%				
1970	1.7%	2.4%	0.8%	2.0%	1.8%	2.5%	1 9%			
1975	1.7%	2.2%	0.8%	1.8%	1.6%	2.0%	1.5%	1.2%		
1980	1.7%	2.2%	1.1%	1.9%	1.8%	2.1%	1.8%	1.7%	2.3%	
1985	1.7%	2.1%	1.1%	1.8%	1.7%	2.0%	1.7%	1.6%	1.8%	1.3%

Beginning Year

To find the annual rate of real per capita growth between any two dates, find the beginning year on the horizontal axis and read up to the ending year on the vertical axis.

Figure 15–3

per capita. In the graph, both series have been constructed so as to compare the different amounts for each. In 1986, for example, real GNP in terms of constant dollars was about $3.7 trillion. Since the population in that year was 241,489 million, the amount of total output for every man, woman, and child in the country was approximately $15,000.

Rates of growth can also be represented in a **growth triangle**—a table that shows rates of growth for various periods of time—such as the one on page 380. The illustration shows, for example, that real per capita economic growth between 1929 and 1939 was −.6 percent. From 1940 to 1970, the rate of growth was 2.4 percent annually. From 1970 to 1980, it fell to 1.7 percent. From 1980 until 1985, however, the economy fell to 1.3 percent, one of the lowest since the Great Depression.

Because of this record, economists and many others are concerned about the current trend in the growth rate. If it continues, Congress may try to pass additional legislation to get the economy moving again.

Section Review

1. How do economists measure long-term economic growth?
2. What can be represented by a growth triangle?

15.3 *Business Cycles*

Some economists talk about the economy in terms of **business cycles**—regular and systematic fluctuations in the level of total output as measured in terms of real GNP. Others, however, do not care for the term business cycles and would rather talk just in terms of **fluctuations.** By fluctuations, they mean that real GNP will go up and then down from time to time, but it does not do this in a regular and predictable manner.

No matter which term is used, however, the fact remains that the American economy has a long history of economic instability, consisting of periodic ups and downs in the economy.

PHASES

As can be seen in the graph below, several terms are used to describe the state of the economy as it passes through the various phases of the business cycle. One of these terms is **recession,** which is a period of decline in the economy.

Officially, a recession is said to occur when real GNP declines for two quarters, or six months, in a row. It begins when the economy reaches a **peak**—the point where real GNP stops going up. It ends when it reaches a **trough**—the turnaround point where real GNP begins to rise again. On a graph, a recession appears shaded.

Figure 15–4

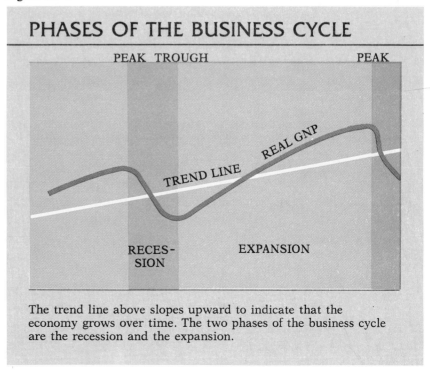

The trend line above slopes upward to indicate that the economy grows over time. The two phases of the business cycle are the recession and the expansion.

If a recession becomes very severe, it may turn into a **depression**—a state of the economy with a great many people out of work, acute shortages, and excess capacity in manufacturing plants. There is no clear-cut guide as to when a recession becomes bad enough to be called a depression.

As soon as the decline in real GNP bottoms out, **expansion**—a period of recovery from a recession—begins. It continues until a new peak is reached.

If the economy is not disturbed by alternating periods of recession and expansion, it follows a growth path called a **trend line.** By the time the economy returns to its trend line after a period of recession or expansion, it has reached the point where it would have been without having to go through the recession and recovery. If the economy is growing relatively fast by the time it regains the trend line, it may keep growing for a while and cause real GNP to

Figure 15–5

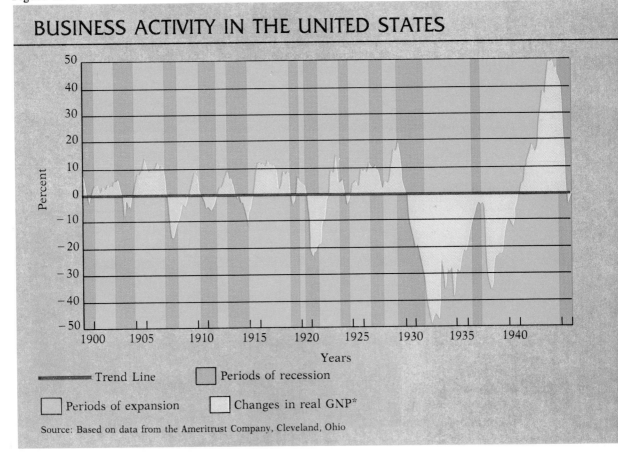

BUSINESS ACTIVITY IN THE UNITED STATES

Source: Based on data from the Ameritrust Company, Cleveland, Ohio

reach new levels. Real GNP may even decline from time to time during the expansion. If, however, it declines two quarters in a row, the economy is back in a recession.

CYCLES IN THE UNITED STATES

The graph below shows clearly that the growth of real GNP over time has been irregular in the United States. Two periods, however, stand out. One is the Great Depression of the 1930's. Another is the history of the business cycle since World War II.

THE GREAT DEPRESSION. The worst economic decline in the history of the United States—the Great Depression—took place in the 1930's. It started with the stock market crash on October 29, 1929, or

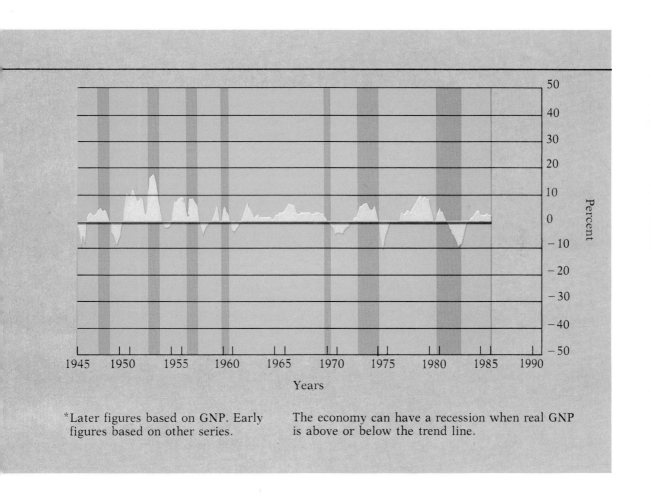

*Later figures based on GNP. Early figures based on other series.

The economy can have a recession when real GNP is above or below the trend line.

"Black Tuesday." It then took nearly ten years for the economy to fully recover.

Between 1929 and 1933, GNP fell from $103.5 to $55.6 billion—a decline of nearly 50 percent in a four-year period. At the same time, the number of people out of work rose nearly 700 percent—from 1.6 to 12.8 million. During the depths of the depression, one out of every four persons did not have a job. Even those with jobs were not much better off. The average manufacturing wage, which had reached 55¢ an hour by 1929, plunged to 5¢ an hour in many areas.

Bank deposits were not yet insured by the FDIC, so when banks went under, some families lost their entire life savings. To prevent panic withdrawals, a "bank holiday" was declared in March 1933 to close every bank in the country for several days. Some banks never reopened.

The money supply fell by one third. Currency also was in such short supply that towns, counties, Chambers of Commerce, and other civic bodies resorted to printing their own money, known as **depression scrip.** It amounted to several billion dollars and was used to pay teachers, firefighters, policemen and other municipal employees.

The exact cause of the Great Depression is hard to pinpoint, but several factors are believed to have been important. One was the inequality that appeared to exist in the way income was distributed. There were a great number of very poor people and a great number of very rich ones. The poor could not stimulate the economy with consumer spending because they did not have the income. The rich had the income, but they often used it for such non-productive purposes as stock market speculation.

The amount of credit also was believed to have been a factor. In the late 1920's, many people borrowed heavily and, as a result, were vulnerable to credit contractions, higher interest rates, and minor economic fluctuations. When the crunch came, these people had nothing on which to fall back.

Economic conditions in other parts of the world also played a part. During the 1920's, the United States made a great many foreign loans. These helped support a high level of international trade. But when the depression began in the United States, these loans were reduced greatly and exports of American products fell sharply.

At the same time, high American tariffs on imports kept many countries from selling goods to the United States. Some depended heavily on these sales, and before long, they too were faced with economic crises. As the depression spread from country to country, world trade declined and American exports dropped even further. This made conditions even worse.

BUSINESS CYCLES SINCE WORLD WAR II. By 1941, the Great Depression was over and the economy had returned to its long-run growth trend line. At the same time, the shock of World War II brought on massive spending that stimulated the economy through most of the early 1940's.

In 1945, there was a brief recession in the United States. But after the war was over, consumers went on a spending binge and again stimulated the economy. Since then, the economy has experienced several more recessions. However, each was rather short compared to the length of the recovery that followed.

A striking feature of these recessions is that with one exception, they took place on a fairly regular basis. The exception was the mid-1960's during the Vietnam War. During that time, there was no recession, probably because of the massive federal spending. As a result, the expansion that followed the April 1960 recession lasted 106 months.

Understanding Sources

◼ Index of Leading Indicators

The following report appeared in *The Wall Street Journal* of December 3, 1986. Read the paragraph and answer the questions that follow.

Economic Index Rose 0.6% in October

The government's main economic forecasting gauge increased a sharp 0.6% in October, but several analysts suggested the rise may overstate the economy's strength.

The gain in the Commerce Department's index of leading economic indicators, the largest since a 1% jump in July, partly reflects a surge in prices for sensitive materials.

The October rise followed a revised 0.2% increase in September and a revised 0.2% drop in August. The department previously reported a 0.4% rise in September and a 0.1% decline in August.

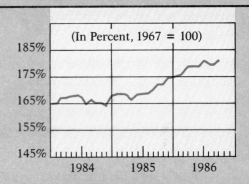

LEADING INDICATORS

(In Percent, 1967 = 100)

Composite of key indicators of future economic activity rose in October to 180.5% of the 1967 average from a revised 179.5% in September, the Commerce Department reports.

1. What happened to the index during the month of October?
2. Are the index numbers subject to frequent revision, or is the current number likely to be final?
3. If the leading indicators are index numbers, what is the base year?
4. What happened to the index during the past three months? Why is this question important?

If the war years are excluded, calculations show that the average recession lasted 10.3 months and real GNP declined at an average rate of about 2.3 percent. The average expansion, on the other hand, lasted 34 months, and the average annual real growth was close to 5 percent.

CAUSES OF BUSINESS CYCLES

Over the years, economists have offered a number of different reasons why business cycles occur. Each has some validity, but none can really be identified as the only cause. In most cases, several of the factors discussed below work together to cause a cycle.

CHANGES IN CAPITAL EXPENDITURES.   One factor that can possibly cause the business cycle is changes in capital goods expenditures. When businesses expect their future sales to be high, they invest heavily in capital goods. They may expand the capacity of the plants they have or build new ones, and they may buy new equipment and machines. With expansion, there is an increase in private investment expenditures.

But, after a time, there may no longer be a need to expand further. As a result, industry cuts back on its capital investments, and before long, a recession begins.

INVENTORY ADJUSTMENTS.   Another possible cause of the business cycle is inventory adjustments. It is not unusual for some businesses to cut back their inventories at the first sign of a slowdown in the economy or build them up at the first sign of an upturn. In either case, investment expenditures will be affected.

What happened after World War II is an example of this. At that time, businesses in

the United States invested heavily in inventories to fill the shelves that had been depleted during the long war. By 1948, the backlog of consumer demand had been largely satisfied. People stopped buying, inventories built up on the shelves, and inventory spending dropped off. This brought on a recession in 1949 that lasted for about a year.

INNOVATIONS AND IMITATIONS.   A third possible cause of the business cycle is innovations. In industry, an innovation may be a new product or a new way of performing a task. When a business innovates, it often gains an edge on its competitors because its costs go down or its sales go up. In either case, profits increase, and business grows.

If the other businesses in the industry want to keep up, they must copy what the innovator has done or come up with something even better. Generally, they must invest heavily to do this, which causes an investment boom. But once the innovation takes hold in the industry, the situation changes. Further investments are not needed, and economic activity may slow down. Meanwhile, the fluctuation of investments has produced a business cycle.

MONETARY FACTORS. A fourth possible cause of the business cycle is the credit and loan policies of the commercial banking system and the Federal Reserve.

When "easy money" policies are in effect, interest rates are low and loans are easy to get. This encourages the private sector to borrow and invest, which stimulates the economy for a short time. Then, as there is more demand for loans, interest rates rise. This, in turn, discourages new loans.

As spending slows down, the level of economic activity declines. Lenders begin to think more than once about making

©1982 BASSET FOR UNITED FEATURES SYNDICATE

"What's the matter ... Haven't you ever seen belt tightening?"

The Reagan administration opposes the FED's tight money policy. What is the relationship between a tight money policy and a business cycle?

new loans or renewing old ones. The economy keeps declining until the demand for loans falls to the point where the interest rate drops and the cycle begins all over again.

EXTERNAL SHOCKS.   A final potential cause of business cycles is external shocks that disrupt the economy, such as increases in oil prices, wars, and international conflict. Some shocks may drive the economy up; others may drive it down.

The economy may be given a boost, for example, when a new supply of natural resources is discovered unexpectedly. This happened in England in the 1970's when oil was discovered in the North Sea. When oil prices rose sharply in the 1970's, the British economy was able to earn a considerable revenue from the sale of its oil. In the United States, however, the opposite happened. The high oil prices reduced economic activity, and the economy became depressed.

In order for external shocks to cause a series of cycles such as those experienced since World War II, the shocks must take place on a regular basis. Since shocks tend to be more random than regular, most economists feel that they only add to instability rather than cause it. Noneconomists looking for a reason why a certain recession is taking place generally are the ones who believe external shocks are a major cause of the business cycle.

PREDICTING BUSINESS CYCLES

Because of the huge costs of economic instability, much work has been done in the area of forecasting business cycles. The chief focus has been on predicting peaks and troughs to determine when a recession begins and where it will end.

Economists use two methods to make their forecasts. One has to do with macroeconomic modeling, while the other makes use of statistical predictors.

ECONOMETRIC MODELS.

An **econometric model** is a macroeconomic model that uses algebraic equations to describe how the economy behaves. Most models used today are based on some adaptation of the output-expenditure model:

$$GNP = C + I + G + F$$

For example, the F for the foreign sector may be replaced with an expression that describes the difference between exports and imports. If X stands for exports and M for imports, the model would be:

$$GNP = C + I + G + (X - M)$$

Other equations in the model also may be substituted for some of the variables. Suppose, for example, that every year, households spend a amount of money along with 95 percent of their disposable personal income. In that case, $C = a + .95 (DI)$. If this were substituted for the C in the output-expenditure model, the equation would read:

$$GNP = a + .95 (DI) + I + G + (X - M)$$

Econometric models can have as few as 20 or as many as 400 equations. To get a prediction of GNP for the coming quarter, the forecasters put in the latest figures for the money supply, the interest rate, the dollar value of exports and imports, and anything else that is needed. Then, they solve for GNP. Since most econometric models are programmed to be solved by a computer, little time is needed to arrive at the solution. It takes far less time to solve the equation than to enter the latest data.

As time goes by, the model can be "tested" by checking its predictions against the actual changes in the economy. Once the model is refined and the forecasts become reasonably accurate, it can be used to help predict turning points.

Some models give reasonably good predictions for the coming six-to-nine months. After that, their accuracy goes down a great deal. Their value lies in the fact that they provide some lead time that would not be available otherwise.

INDEX OF LEADING INDICATORS.

A second method used to predict turning points is by watching for turns in the **index of leading indicators.** It is a composite of twelve statistical series that usually turn down before downturns in real GNP and turn up before upturns.

Some statistical indicators, such as the length of the average workweek, lend themselves to predicting declines or rises in real GNP. Still, no single series has proved to be completely reliable. However, when several series are combined into an overall index that closely patterns the behavior of real GNP, the index becomes a much more useful tool.

The behavior of this composite index can be seen in the graph on page 389 where the darker areas represent recessions and lighter areas expansions. The average time between the index turning down and the recession beginning is about 12 months. The average time between the index turning up and the expansion beginning is about three months.

Each time the index has turned down three months in a row, however, there has been a recession. The major problem is that the amount of advance warning varies from one recession or expansion to the next. As a result, the index by itself is not a competely reliable indicator. Therefore, the information it supplies is used along with the results of different econometric models. Together, they generally let the forecaster predict how real GNP will behave in the next six-to-nine months.

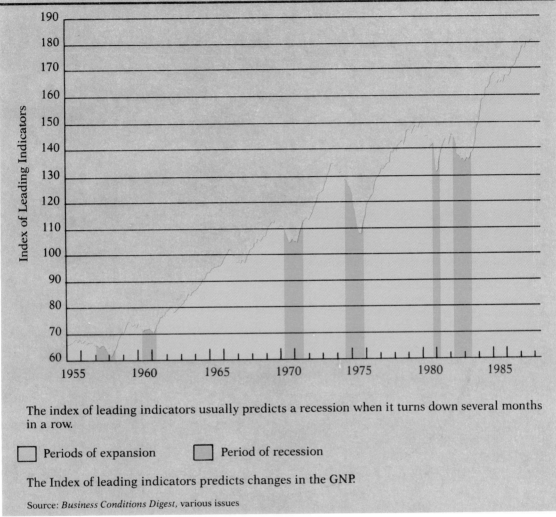

INDEX OF LEADING INDICATORS, 1955-1987

The index of leading indicators usually predicts a recession when it turns down several months in a row.

☐ Periods of expansion   ■ Period of recession

The Index of leading indicators predicts changes in the GNP.

Source: *Business Conditions Digest*, various issues

Figure 15–6

▮ Section Review

1. What are business cycles?
2. What two terms describe the state of the economy as it passes through the phases of a business cycle? How is each term defined?
3. What three factors contributed to the Great Depression?
4. What five factors are identified as possible causes of the business cycle?
5. What two tools are used to forecast business cycles?

15.4 The Economic and Social Cost of Instability

Whenever the economy is faced with cycles or fluctuations, the cost in terms of uncertainty and unemployed resources is high. If GNP declines even a fraction of a percentage point, the amount of lost production and income can be enormous.

If, for example, an economy of $4.2 trillion declines .25 percent in one year, it would lose $10.5 billion of production. This is more than the government of the United States spent on general science, space, and technology during the entire

1987 fiscal budget year. It would be equal to 500,000 workers losing jobs that paid $20,000 for an entire year. Even though in practice the effects of a decline in GNP generally are spread out over a large area rather than being concentrated in just one spot, they are no less severe.

If real GNP declines, people have less income to spend, so they put off buying some things. This causes inventories to accumulate on store shelves. This, in turn, causes stores to order fewer goods from the factories. With orders off at the factories, some workers lose their jobs, which adds to the problem of declining retail sales and unsold goods on merchants' shelves. In the end, it can become a vicious circle in which many people are hurt.

When the economy starts to recover, the process reverses itself. Orders come into the factories, and workers are hired. These workers return to the stores and buy some of the things they put off getting while they were out of work. This causes more orders to be sent to the factories, which, in turn, causes more workers to be hired.

It takes time, however, for this process to work itself out. In the meantime, there is a great deal of uncertainty. A worker may not buy something because of concern over his or her job. This hurts the economy because when purchases are not made, jobs are lost.

The worker is not the only one affected by the uncertainty. The owner of a business producing at capacity may decide against an expansion of plant and equipment though new orders are arriving daily. Instead, the producer, aware that the demand for products is greater than

The man in the cartoon is using his wallet as an indicator of the economy. What indicator would an economist use?

THE WALL STREET JOURNAL

Sauer.

"Here's a leading economic indicator—my wallet is empty!"

the supply, may try to raise prices, which adds to inflation instead of employment.

A complicating problem is that some areas of the economy are affected more than others. During hard times, for example, durable goods industries are hit harder than most because the demand for most durable goods is elastic. If they have to, people seem to be able to get a little more use out of the old car, refrigerator, washing machine, or house no matter how badly they would like new ones. They are not as likely, however, to put off buying such products as food, gasoline, medicine, and heating fuel. Since there really are no adequate substitutes for these items, they tend to have an inelastic demand. As a result, workers in these industries are less likely to be affected by any economic instability.

Other parts of society also are affected in the end. When the economy is healthy, some families make a lot of purchases, many of them on credit. When the economy turns around, they find that some of their household income is lost. Some end up declaring bankruptcy to end their debt. Others break up, with parents and children going different ways.

Even the politician cannot escape the consequences of economic instability. When times are hard, there are more complaints, which may cost a politician an election. When times are good, mediocre and even incompetent politicians stand a better chance of re-election because the voters do not look at their records as closely as they should.

In short, the social cost of economic instability is huge. The problem goes far beyond that of unused resources and postponed purchasing decisions to tear at the very fabric of society itself.

Section Review

1. What happens when real GNP declines? When it goes back up again?
2. Which industries generally are hurt most by economic instability? Why?

Chapter 15 Review

Summary

1. Economic growth in the United States brings about a higher standard of living, allows government to carry out its tasks more easily, helps solve domestic problems, makes it possible to give more help to developing nations, and helps the Free World meet the challenges of communism.

2. Economic growth depends on the ability of the economy to produce output.

3. Economic growth is determined by the quantity and the quality of land, labor, and capital.

4. Productivity generally is measured in terms of labor productivity.

5. In economics, growth means the economy's ability to increase real per capita GNP from one year to the next.

6. Real GNP per capita represents the dollar amount of real GNP produced for every person in the economy.

7. Economists use the terms recession and expansion to describe the state of the economy as it passes through the phases of the business cycle.

8. The worst economic decline in the history of the United States was the Great Depression of the 1930's.

9. Business cycles can take place because of changes in spending on capital goods expenditures; inventory adjustments; innovations and imitations; the credit and loan policies of the commercial banking system; and, external shocks.

10. Econometric models and the index of leading indicators are two tools economists use to forecast business cycles.

11. When the economy is faced with cycles or fluctuations, the cost in uncertainty and unemployed resources is high.

■ *Building an Economic Vocabulary*

standard of living
tax base
renewable resources
capital-to-labor ratio
productivity
labor productivity
real GNP per capita

growth triangle
business cycles
fluctuations
recession
peak
trough

depression
expansion
trend line
depression script
econometric model
index of leading indicators

■ *Reviewing the Main Ideas*

1. How does economic growth make it easier for government to carry out its tasks?

2. How do developing countries benefit when the U.S. economy grows?

3. Why is productivity one of the major problems facing the American economy today?

4. What is economic instability?

5. What happened in the United States during the Great Depression?

6. What are business fluctuations? How do they differ from business cycles?

7. What is the value of econometric models?

8. What is the major problem with the index of leading indicators?

9. Why are some parts of the economy affected more by economic instability?

Practicing Critical Thinking Skills

1. Some people feel that clean air and the preservation of natural resources and wildlife are more important than rapid economic growth. Do you agree or disagree with them? Why?

2. Defend or negate the following statement: "American workers don't take pride in their work anymore. All they care about is how much they make per hour and how many benefits the company will give them. No wonder productivity is down."

3. Economists devote a good deal of time and effort to predicting business cycles. What value do you see in this?

4. Do you feel that economic stability is an important key to solving some of the social ills that bother Americans today? Why or why not? Give reasons to support your answer.

Applying Economic Understandings

Identifying Trends and Making Forecasts

Many articles in newspapers and magazines are about trends—general movements in a certain direction or changes and shifts in direction. There are many kinds of trends—fashion trends, political trends, weather trends, and business trends. Some trends last a short time and then lose their popularity; other trends become accepted and remain. This second type of trend is used to make forecasts—suggestions as to future developments. Economics often use certain trends to make forecasts for the nation's economy.

1. Read the following discussion about video-cassette recorders (VCR's) and video-tapes carefully.

   VCR's are popular in the United States. If people do not wish to buy them, they may rent them for a relatively low fee. The increased number of video-tapes of old and new films, as well as television shows and rock videos, means that VCR's will stay popular for years.

2. Identify and describe the trends in the above paragraph. (The number of VCR's being used is increasing, and there are more films and shows available for use.)

3. Ask yourself what might happen in the future if the trends you have identified were to continue. (More VCR's will continue to be manufactured for rental and purchase as long as there is a large variety of films and shows for them.)

4. Ask yourself what developments could change the trends you have identified. (The quality of VCR's and video-tapes could decline a great deal, discouraging people from buying and renting machines and tapes.)

5. Based on the answers to the questions you asked yourself in steps 3 and 4, make your forecast. (Forecast: If current trends continue, and the quality of VCR's and video-tapes remains high, VCR's will remain popular.)

For practice in identifying trends in economics, refer to the graph on real GNP and real GNP per capita on page 379. Using the steps suggested, forecast the trend of real GNP per capita and real GNP.

Unemployment and Inflation

When men are employed, they are best contented.

Benjamin Franklin

Chapter 16

After reading this chapter, you will be able to:

- Explain the meaning of unemployment, how it is measured, what causes it, and in what way it relates to the concept of full employment.

- Describe the causes and effects of inflation.

- Discuss two tools used to measure the impact of unemployment and inflation on the economy.

16.1 Unemployment

The concept of **unemployment**—the state of being out of work—relates directly to an economy's ability to supply jobs for its people. Its study involves the problem of measurement, the different kinds of unemployment, as well as the concept of full employment.

MEASURES OF UNEMPLOYMENT

Two measures are used to determine the success people have in finding employment, or work. The first is the unemployment rate. The second is the employment rate. Both are affected by swings in the business cycle.

UNEMPLOYMENT RATE.   The most popular measure of unemployment is the **unemployment rate,** which is determined by dividing the number of unemployed persons by the total number of persons in the civilian labor force. It is a statistic compiled monthly by the Bureau of Labor Statistics. The Bureau tries to locate **unemployed persons**—people not working at present but who have made a specific effort to find a job within the last four weeks. It gets this information from surveys of about 55,000 households.

As can be seen in the graph on page 397, the unemployment rate tends to rise dramatically during recessions and then come down slowly afterwards. It is very sensitive to downturns in real GNP and is one of the economic costs of a recession.

During recessions, many places do not hire new workers, thus discouraging many people from looking for work. How is the unemployment rate as a statistical measure limited?

As a statistical measure, the unemployment rate does have some limitations. For one, it does not count those people who have looked for work so long that they have become discouraged and have stopped looking. During recessions, many people become so frustrated that they simply "drop out" of the labor force. The number of such dropouts has been estimated at nearly 1 million people. A person who does not have a job is not classified as "unemployed" if he or she did not make an effort to find a job within the past four weeks.

Another limitation is that the unemployment rate counts persons as fully employed even though they hold part-time jobs. According to federal definitions, **employed persons** are those who work for pay or profit a minimum of one hour a week or who work without pay in a family enterprise a minimum of 15 hours.

However, even with these limitations, the unemployment rate still is a relatively important measure. With a civilian labor force of almost 116.8 million people, even small changes in the rate are important. If the rate were to rise by just one tenth of 1 percent, nearly 116,800 additional people would be affected. That is more people than the number living in Albany, New York, or San Bernardino, California.

EMPLOYMENT RATE. Some observers do not like to use the unemployment rate because of some of the measurement problems associated with it. Instead, they prefer another measure called the **employment rate**—a measure of the people actually working as opposed to the number willing and available to work. To determine the employment rate, the number of employed persons is divided by the total population less those people in the armed forces, in such institutions as hospitals and prisons, and under the age of 16.

One advantage of this measure is that it is relatively easy to compile. For example,

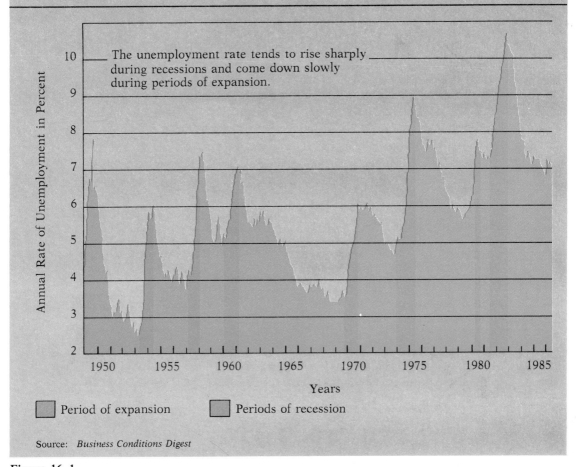

UNEMPLOYMENT AND THE BUSINESS CYCLE, 1949-1986

The unemployment rate tends to rise sharply during recessions and come down slowly during periods of expansion.

Annual Rate of Unemployment in Percent

Years

☐ Period of expansion ☐ Periods of recession

Source: *Business Conditions Digest*

Figure 16–1

it is not necessary to survey thousands of households to ask if people are willing to work and have tried to find a job within the last four weeks.

Another advantage is that it includes those people who tried to find a job, became discouraged, and have stopped looking for the time being. If enough people stop looking for work because they are discouraged, the unemployment rate goes down. The employment rate is not af-

fected, however, because these unemployed people already are counted as part of the population available for work.

KINDS OF UNEMPLOYMENT

Economists have identified several different kinds of unemployment. The nature and cause of each has a bearing on the

Profile

Wesley C. Mitchell

Wesley Clair Mitchell was an American economist known for his historical and institutional approach to economics. He believed that economics was a science of human behavior, the study of a nation and of its people in motion. For this reason, he felt that the future was to be found in the understanding of the changes that took place in the nation's economic life and institutions.

Mitchell had a long teaching career. From 1922 to 1940, he

1874–1948

taught at the University of Chicago. During his lifetime, he also taught at several other universities, including the University of California, Harvard, Columbia, and the New School for Social Research.

Mitchell authored six books, the most famous of which was *Business Cycles*, published in 1912. In these writings, he developed several important concepts. Mitchell believed that in a monetary economy, there was a division, or contradiction, between making money and making goods. Things such as national resources, machines, and the like, which were needed for the production of goods and services, would be employed only if people expected a profit from their use. Further, this profit had to be the most that could be gained from among the different ways of earning money. This meant that in most cases, self-interest would come ahead of doing what was best for the national welfare. Mitchell also determined that business cycles were self-generating. He believed that there were several reasons for this, including the relationship between the costs of production as well as the prices producers received for their products.

Mitchell's theories depended on statistical data, and he soon discovered that one person could not do all the work involved in the project. This led him to establish the National Bureau of Economic Research in 1920. He became the Bureau's first director and held the position until 1945. The Bureau is still active today and remains true to Mitchell's ideals.

level of full employment the economy can achieve.

FRICTIONAL UNEMPLOYMENT. One kind of unemployment is **frictional unemployment**—unemployment due to workers who are "between jobs" for one reason or another.

At any given moment, the economy has some workers who have left one job to look for or to take another. As long as these workers do not work for a week between jobs, they are classified as unemployed. Because of this, there is bound to be some amount of frictional unemployment as long as workers continue to change jobs.

STRUCTURAL UNEMPLOYMENT. A second—and more serious—kind of unemployment is **structural unemployment.** This takes place when people's tastes change and certain goods and services no longer are in demand or when production meth-

ods change and people's skills no longer are needed.

Structural unemployment has a long history in the United States. It existed, for example, in the South when mechanical advances in agriculture reduced the demand for unskilled labor in the cotton industry and forced some workers to move to northern cities and learn new trades and skills. In more recent years, the decline of the domestic automobile industry in Michigan and the industrial Northeast caused many of the same problems. As plants closed, many skilled workers found that the skills they used in the auto industry did not match those needed by companies looking for new workers.

In many ways, structural unemployment is one of the most severe kinds of unemployment because it tends to be concentrated in selected areas throughout the country. Many times, the problem can be remedied only by attracting new industry,

This factory is one of many factories in various industries either closed or working at reduced capacity because of a recession. What kind of unemployment is directly related to swings in the business cycle?

by giving people without jobs the chance to learn new skills, or by moving the unemployed to areas where their skills are in demand.

CYCLICAL UNEMPLOYMENT. A third kind of unemployment is **cyclical unemployment**—unemployment directly related to swings in the business cycle. During a recession, for example, many people are likely to put off buying certain durable goods. Because of this, workers in some industries are likely to experience some unemployment until inventories are worked off.

One industry which generally suffers during a recession is homebuilding. As real GNP goes down, many people hold off buying a new house. Although some houses still may be built, unemployment is likely to go up among carpenters, electricians, bricklayers, plumbers, and laborers.

Sometimes, cyclical unemployment may be mixed with other kinds of unemployment. In 1981, for example, the domestic automobile industry suffered from not only cyclical but structural unemployment as well. Some of the unemployment was due to the fact that car buyers preferred

This migrant worker has a job that often depends on the weather. Such workers move from place to place to find crops to harvest. What kind of unemployment do migrant workers experience?

"As of September 1st, I'm sorry to say, you will all be replaced by a tiny chip of silicon."

One of the major problems facing American labor today is technological unemployment. As a result, many workers find they have to learn new skills. What causes technological unemployment?

foreign cars to domestic ones—a change which led to structural unemployment. On the other hand, some of it was due to the recession which encouraged car buyers to wait before buying a new car.

Although cyclical unemployment is serious, workers affected by it generally are fairly sure their jobs will return when the economy gets better. Accordingly, many may try to "wait out" the recession by living on savings or by taking other jobs that are temporary.

SEASONAL UNEMPLOYMENT. A fourth kind of unemployment is **seasonal unemployment**—unemployment which takes place because of annual changes in the weather or changes in the demand for certain products.

Many carpenters and builders, for example, have less work during the winter than during the spring and summer because some tasks, such as replacing a roof or

digging a foundation, are harder to do when the weather is bad. Other workers, such as cashiers and clerks in retail stores, are especially in demand between the Thanksgiving and Christmas holidays when the stores register about 25 percent of their yearly sales.

The difference between seasonal and cyclical unemployment relates to the period of measurement. Cyclical unemployment takes place over the course of the business cycle, which may last three to five years. Seasonal unemployment, on the other hand, takes place every year, no matter what the general health of the economy may be.

TECHNOLOGICAL UNEMPLOYMENT. A fifth kind is **technological unemployment**—the replacement of workers who do not have the skills, talent, or education for jobs done by machines. This happens when workers face the threat of **automation**—

the operation or control of equipment, a process, or a system by mechanical or electronic devices.

Although this can happen whenever a company buys new equipment, in some cases workers are displaced in huge numbers. Japan, for example, pioneered the use of large factories operated almost exclusively by industrial robots. Entire assembly lines in industries such as automobiles and steel are being staffed by one fifth of the workers needed in a similar American plant.

Because technological unemployment is due in part to new methods of production, it is similar to structural unemployment. The major difference between the two is that structural unemployment also can

take place because of other factors that have nothing to do with more efficient means of production.

CONCEPT OF FULL EMPLOYMENT

Economists and others have long wrestled with the concept of full employment. At any given point in time, for example, there is bound to be some form of unemployment, even without the problems caused by the business cycle.

The concept of full employment, then, does not mean zero unemployment. Instead, **full employment** is the lowest possi-

Figure 16–2

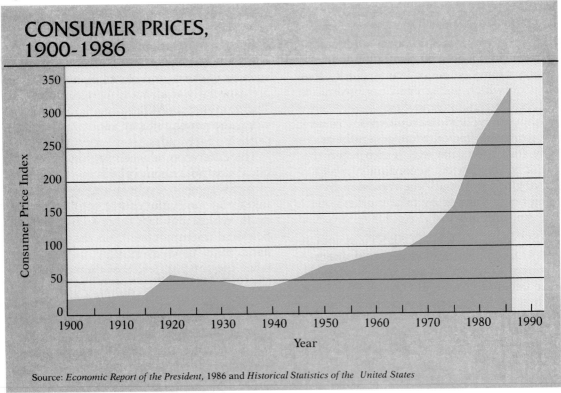

CONSUMER PRICES, 1900-1986

Source: *Economic Report of the President*, 1986 and *Historical Statistics of the United States*

ble unemployment rate with the economy growing and all factors of production being used as efficiently as possible.

Economists have long debated whether or not there is an "acceptable" level of unemployment. To date, they remain split on the issue. During the 1960's it was thought that full employment meant an unemployment rate of around 4 percent. Most believed that efforts to reduce unemployment below this figure would not be possible.

Although President Lyndon Johnson implemented many programs to try to lower the rate, it remained in the 5-to-6 percent range for most of the early 1960's. The rate finally did drop below 4 percent during the Vietnam War when the economy was stimulated by wartime spending and the ranks of the unemployed were thinned by the draft.

The unemployment rate returned to the 5-to-6 percent range when the 1970's arrived. A recession in 1975 drove the rate as high as 9 percent, but for the rest of the decade it remained in the 6-to-7 percent range. By 1980, the unemployment rate rose again and hit a peak of 10.7 percent during the recession of 1982. It dropped in 1983 and by mid-1986 it reached a low of 6.8 percent. After that, the unemployment rate began to rise again.

As a result of this experience, most economists have given up the idea of a 4 percent unemployment rate as a measure of full employment. Today, most would argue that full employment will be reached when the unemployment rate drops below 6 percent.

■ Section Review

1. How is unemployment related to the business cycle?
2. What are five kinds of unemployment?
3. What is full employment?

16.2 Inflation

Inflation is a special kind of economic instability—one which deals with changes in the level of prices rather than in employment and output. Even so, changes in prices, employment, and output are linked. Even a change in the rate of inflation can have consequences on the level of output and employment.

INFLATION IN THE UNITED STATES

The term inflation means a rise in the general price level. To get a measure of the price level, economists select a market basket of goods and construct a price index. Inflation, then, can be measured in terms of the producer price index, the consumer price index, or the implicit GNP price deflator.

From time to time, unusual circumstances have even caused the general price level to go down—a condition known as **deflation.** Only two significant deflations have taken place in the 1900's. One was during the post-World War I recession of the early 1920's. The other was during the Great Depression of the 1930's. The graph on page 402 indicates how the price level has changed since 1900.

What Dagwood really is complaining about to his boss is inflation. What are thought to be some of the major causes of inflation?

Several terms are sometimes used to describe the severity of inflation. One is **creeping inflation**—inflation in the range of 1-to-3 percent per year. Another is **galloping inflation,** which is a more intense form of inflation. It can go as high as 100-to-300 percent. Many Latin American countries have experienced rates in this range in recent years.

When inflation gets totally out of hand—in the range of 500 percent a year and up—it turns into **hyperinflation.** This, however, does not happen very often and generally is the last stage of a total monetary collapse. The all-time record for hyperinflation was set in Hungary, where huge amounts of currency were printed to pay the government's bills during World War II. Before the war, one United States dollar was equal to six Hungarian pengös. By the end of the war, one United States dollar was equal to 6.3 quintillion—or, 6,300,000,000,000,000,000—Hungarian pengös. Because of the zeros, larger notes had their amounts spelled out in words rather than numbers. Although inflation in the United States has never reached such proportions, rates during the 1970's and early 1980's ranged from 5 percent to more than 15 percent as measured by the consumer price index.

CAUSES OF INFLATION

Several explanations have been offered for the causes of inflation. Since there really is no simple test to determine which explanation is better than the others, there is some validity to each.

DEMAND-PULL. One of the more traditional explanations of inflation is known as the demand-pull explanation. According to it, the spending units in the economy try to buy more than the economy can produce.

In other words, consumers and others in the private sector converge on stores to buy goods and services, which causes shortages to develop because there is not enough to go around. This means merchants can afford to lose some customers. As a result, some merchants raise their prices. Others leave prices alone but do not offer discounts or run sales. In either case, the end result is the same—prices rise.

GOVERNMENT DEFICIT. Another explanation is that the chief cause of inflation is the deficit run by the federal government. Basically, this is a variant of the demand-pull explanation. While demand-pull blames excess demand on the private

Understanding Sources

■ Hyperinflation

The following article appeared in *The Wall Street Journal* on February 7, 1985. *Read the paragraphs and answer the questions that follow.*

When Inflation Rate Is 116,000%, Prices Change by the Hour

★★★

In Bolivia, the Pesos Paid Out Can Outweigh Purchases; No. 3 Import: More Pesos

★★★

A courier stumbles into Banco Boliviano Americano, struggling under the weight of a huge bag of money he is carrying on his back. He announces that the sack contains 32 million pesos, and a teller slaps on a notation to that effect. The courier pitches the bag into a corner.

"We don't bother counting the money anymore," explains Max Loew Stahl, a loan officer standing nearby. "We take the client's word for what's in the bag." Pointing to the courier's load, he says, "That's a small deposit."

At that moment the 32 million pesos—enough bills to stuff a mail sack—were worth only $500. Today, less than two weeks later, they are worth at least $180 less. Life's like that with quadruple-digit inflation.

A 116,000% Rate?

Bolivia's inflation rate is the highest in the world. In 1984, prices zoomed 2,700%, compared with a mere 329% the year before. Experts are predicting the inflation rate could soar as high as 40,000% this year. Even those estimates could prove conservative. The central bank last week announced January inflation of 80%; if that pace continued all year, it would mean an annual rate of 116,000%.

Prices go up by the day, the hour, or the customer. Julia Blanco Sirba, a vendor on this capital city's main street, sells a bar of chocolate for 35,000 pesos. Five minutes later, the next bar goes for 50,000 pesos. The two-inch stack of money needed to buy it far outweighs the chocolate.

Tons of paper money are printed to keep the country of 5.9 million inhabitants going. Planeloads of money arrive twice a week from printers in West Germany and Britain. Purchases of money cost Bolivia more than $20 million last year, making it the third-largest import, after wheat and mining equipment.

---

1. What country and year is described in the article?
2. What term is used to describe the inflation discussed in the article? When is that term applicable?
3. How does the inflation add to instability in the economy?

sector, this explanation blames it on the public one.

The federal deficit can contribute to inflation, especially if the Federal Reserve System expands the money supply to keep the interest rate down. If it does not monetize the debt, some borrowers will be crowded out as interest rates rise. When this happens, the federal deficit may have a greater destabilizing impact on output and employment than on the price level.

COST-PUSH. A third explanation is known as the cost-push explanation. It says inflation is caused by labor groups and others driving up prices of inputs for manufacturers.

This might take place, for example, when a strong national union wins a large wage contract, forcing producers to raise prices to consumers to recover the labor costs. An increase in the cost of non-labor inputs also could cause the price level to rise. This happened during the 1970's when oil prices went from $5 to $35 a barrel.

WAGE-PRICE SPIRAL. Still another explanation says that no single group is to blame for inflation. According to it, there is a self-perpetuated spiral of wages and prices which is hard to stop, once inflation gets started.

In other words, higher prices force workers to ask for higher wages. If they get the higher wages, producers try to recover them with higher prices. If either side tries to increase its relative position with a larger price hike than before, the rate of inflation goes up.

EXCESSIVE MONETARY GROWTH. A final explanation for inflation is that of excessive monetary growth. The monetary growth becomes excessive when the money supply grows faster than the growth in real GNP.

The longshoremen have a strong union which tries to get the best wages possible for its members. What can happen to the general level of prices when a strong national union wins a large wage contract?

According to this explanation, which may be the most popular of all, any extra money that is created will increase some group's purchasing power. When this money is spent, it causes a demand-pull effect that drives up prices.

This differs some from the traditional demand-pull approach. In the traditional version, extra spending takes place because merchants are willing to extend credit or because consumers are trying to spend the extra money since they expect to make more in the future. In the excessive money growth approach, extra spending occurs because of increases in the money supply.

Those who prefer the excess money explanation to demand-pull point out that credit alone cannot keep inflation going. At some point in time, they say, borrowers will have taken all the credit they can handle and the demand-pull effects will taper off. Therefore, for inflation to be maintained over the long run, the money supply must grow faster than the increase in real output.

DESTABILIZING EFFECT OF INFLATION

The problem of inflation is more severe than most people think and involves more than rising prices. It can have a strong destabilizing effect on an economy. There are several reasons for this.

The first reason is that inflation can cause consumers and investors to change their spending habits and disrupt the economy. Prices go up during an inflationary period, and the price of money—the interest rate—is no exception. In the early 1980's, the interest rate in the United States rose so high that consumer spending on durable goods, especially housing, fell dramatically.

What happened during the recession of 1981 is a good example of this. That year, the impact of the interest rate on housing was particularly severe. Suppose, for example, a young couple wanted to borrow $60,000 for 20 years to buy a house. At a 10 percent interest rate, their monthly mortgage payment would be $579.01. At a 12 percent rate, it would be $660.65. At a 14 percent rate, the payment would be $746.11. In 1981, some mortgage rates reached 18 percent, which meant a monthly payment of about $926. As a result of this higher rate, the housing industry almost collapsed.

Businesses also felt the pinch of inflation in 1981. Many normally order inventories months in advance so they will have goods available during the selling season. Sometimes these inventories have to be financed with borrowed money. In 1981, the interest rates on such loans often exceeded 20 percent. If businesses borrow at such high rates, they may raise prices to cover the cost of borrowing. Or, they may have to use their profits to pay the interest cost. As a result, many merchants tried instead to cut back on their purchases from factories so their inventories would be lower and, therefore, less expensive. This hurt the factories, which, in turn, tried to reduce their costs by laying off workers.

The second reason is that inflation tempts some people to speculate heavily in an attempt to take advantage of a higher price level. People who ordinarily would have put their money in reasonably safe investments began buying condominiums, diamonds and gem stones, works of art, and other exotic items in the belief that these always would increase in price. Because this diverted spending from normal ways, some structural unemployment took place.

The third reason is that inflation affects the distribution of income. During inflationary periods, lenders are hurt more than borrowers. Loans made earlier are repaid in **inflated dollars**—dollars with less purchasing power because they buy less.

Suppose, for example, a person borrowed money to buy bread selling at 50¢ a loaf. If the amount borrowed was $100, it would buy 200 loaves of bread. If, however, inflation sets in and the price doubles by the time the loan is paid back, the lender will be able to buy only 100 loaves of bread when the money is returned. Inflation, then, favors debtors over creditors.

The fourth reason is that inflation causes a decline in the value of the dollar. Since the purchasing power of the dollar falls as prices rise, a dollar loses value over time. For example, a 1986 dollar bought only 7¢ worth of goods and services it bought in 1900. This falling value is shown in the graph on page 409.

A retired person on a fixed income or pension finds that the money buys a little less each month. Since these individuals are least able to support themselves, they are hardest hit. Those who do not live on fixed incomes, such as doctors, lawyers, bankers, plumbers, and accountants, are better able to cope. They simply increase the fees for their services to have additional income.

Section Review

1. What is inflation? What terms are used to describe it?

2. What are five explanations for the causes of inflation?

3. What are three ways in which inflation can have a destabilizing effect on an economy?

Inflation can affect an economy in many different ways. One of the areas generally hardest hit is residential and industrial construction. Redevelopment of downtown areas like the one below may come to a standstill. What are some of the destabilizing effects of inflation?

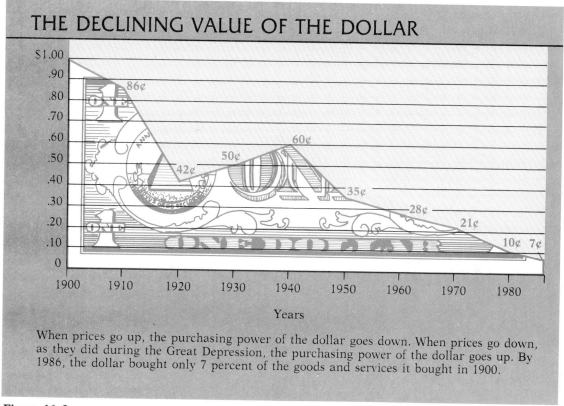

THE DECLINING VALUE OF THE DOLLAR

When prices go up, the purchasing power of the dollar goes down. When prices go down, as they did during the Great Depression, the purchasing power of the dollar goes up. By 1986, the dollar bought only 7 percent of the goods and services it bought in 1900.

Figure 16–3

16.3 Unemployment, Inflation, and Economic Growth

Unemployment and inflation are closely tied to long-run economic growth. Sometimes, the economy will have both growth and inflation. At other times, it will have neither. At even other times, the economy encounters **stagflation**—a period of stagnant growth and inflation.

One thing, however, is certain—both unemployent and inflation are types of instability which hurt economic growth. To measure the impact of unemployment and inflation, economists use two tools. One is the GNP gap, the other is the misery index.

The **GNP gap** measures the difference between the actual GNP being produced at any one time and the potential that could be produced. Since the potential is based on the amount of output that could be produced given the available amount of

THE MISERY INDEX, APRIL 1980–JULY 1986

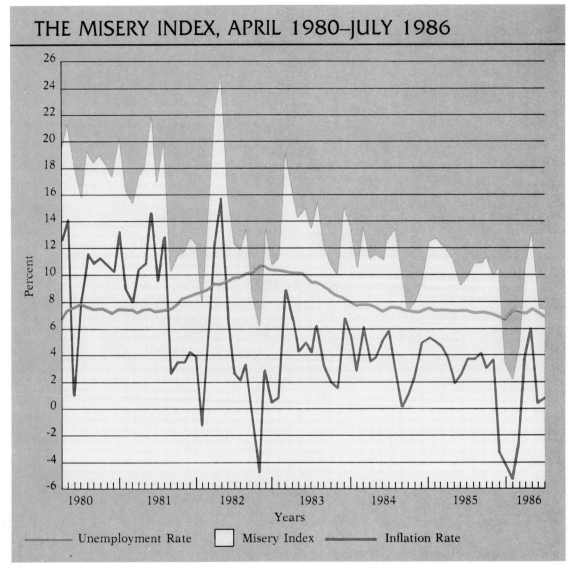

Figure 16–4

land, labor, and capital, it is a measure of the cost of unemployed resources in terms of output not produced.

The **misery index,** or the **discomfort index,** is the sum of the inflation and unemployment rates as they are reported on a monthly basis. The graph on this page shows the discomfort index for recent years. The index was first proposed as a more comprehensive measure of consumer misery during periods of high inflation and high unemployment.

Although the cost of instability can be measured in terms of dollar amounts rather easily, it is harder to measure in terms of human suffering. In those terms, the costs actually are almost beyond comprehension. During depressed times such as those in the recent past, there are unemployed workers looking for jobs; factories with idle capacity waiting to be utilized; and natural resources lying unused or going to waste.

The frustration goes beyond that of not having more goods and services that raise the standard of living. People want work and cannot find it. All this means that the economy has failed to satisfy people's wants and needs. This includes the need to be a useful and productive part of society by being employed.

Section Review

1. What is the GNP gap? For what is it used?

2. Why was the misery index first proposed?

3. What occurs in depressed times?

Chapter 16 Review

Summary

1. Unemployment relates to an economy's ability to supply jobs for people.

2. Two measures used to determine the success people have in finding work are the unemployment and the employment rates.

3. Five kinds of unemployment are frictional, structural, cyclical, seasonal, and technological.

4. Full employment is the lowest possible unemployment rate with the economy growing and all factors of production being used as efficiently as possible.

5. Inflation is a kind of instability reflected by increases in the price level.

6. Inflation can be measured in terms of the producer price index, the consumer price index, or the implicit GNP price deflator.

7. The terms creeping, galloping, and hyperinflation can be used to describe the severity of inflation.

8. Explanations for the causes of inflation include demand-pull, government deficit, cost-push, wage-price spiral, and excessive monetary growth.

9. Inflation can have a strong destabilizing effect on the economy.

10. Unemployment and inflation are closely tied to long-run economic growth.

11. Economists make use of the GNP gap and the misery index to measure the impact of unemployment and inflation.

Building an Economic Vocabulary

unemployment
unemployment rate
unemployed persons
employed persons
employment rate
frictional unemployment
structural unemployment

cyclical unemployment
seasonal unemployment
technological unemployment
automation
full employment
deflation
creeping inflation

galloping inflation
hyperinflation
inflated dollars
stagflation
GNP gap
misery index
discomfort index

Reviewing the Main Ideas

1. What is the most popular measure of unemployment? What are some of its limitations?

2. How does a recession affect the unemployment rate?

3. What is the employment rate? What are some of its advantages?

4. What is the most serious kind of unemployment?

5. What is cyclical unemployment? How does it affect consumer purchases?

6. What causes seasonal unemployment? Technological unemployment?

7. Why have most economists given up the idea of a 4 percent unemployment rate as a measure of full employment?

8. How do deflation and inflation differ?

9. How does the federal deficit contribute to inflation?

10. How do demand-pull and excessive monetary growth differ?

11. Why are people tempted to speculate heavily during periods of inflation?

12. Why does inflation hurt people on a fixed income?

Practicing Critical Thinking Skills

1. Economists have yet to define an "acceptable" level of unemployment. What rate do you think would be acceptable? Support your position.

2. The chapter describes five types of unemployment. Which ones do you think are difficult to solve? Support your choices.

3. In the past, there has been some disagreement as to a reasonable rate of inflation. What rate do you think the public would find reasonable? Why?

4. If you were one of the President's economic advisors, what advice would you give on ways in which to control inflation? Defend your answer.

■ *Applying Economic Understandings*

Making Inferences

Most people make inferences—a deduction based on facts or circumstances—every day without realizing it. For example, when you shop for a television, you consider price and quality. When you see a TV that is priced higher than others, you may infer that it is better made than the others and has more features. If one is priced a great deal lower than others, you may infer that it is not of very good quality and has fewer features. Economists also make inferences about economic activity by sifting through many facts.

The following paragraph is about retired persons living on fixed incomes, Read it and the explanation and inference that follow it:

> During periods of inflation, retired persons who live on fixed incomes or pensions find that their money buys less each month. Since these people are the ones generally least able to support themselves, they are the ones hardest hit by inflation. (The paragraph states that retired persons on fixed incomes or pensions are less able to support themselves during periods of inflation because they have less money to spend. The inference is that inflation erodes the fixed income and pensions of retired persons.)

To give you further practice in making inferences, read the paragraphs below, and for each, determine which of the statements that follow is a reasonable inference.

1. Inflation can cause consumers and investors to change their spending habits. It can lead some people to speculate heavily. It can even redistribute income.
   a. Prices go up during periods of inflation.
   b. Some people can be hurt more than others by inflation.
   c. Inflation can have a strong destabilizing effect in an economy.

2. The most popular measure of unemployment is the unemployment rate. This rate does not count workers who have dropped out of the labor force because they have become discouraged. The rate does count people who hold part-time jobs as fully employed.
   a. The employment rate is the most popular measure of unemployment
   b. The unemployment rate does not take into consideration all people who are not employed.
   c. The unemployment rate has some limitations as a statistical measure.

3. During depressed times, there are unemployed workers looking for jobs; factories with idle capacity waiting to be utilized; and natural resources lying unused or going to waste.
   a. People are frustrated during depressed times because they cannot raise their standard of living.
   b. The economy has failed to satisfy people's wants and needs.
   c. It is hard to measure output in terms of human suffering.

Achieving Economic Stability

Next, let us turn to the problems of our fiscal policy. Here the myths are legion and the truth hard to find.

John F. Kennedy

Chapter 17

After reading this chapter, you will be able to:

- Identify why economic stability is vital to the American economy.

- Compare demand-side and supply-side economics.

- Describe the theory of monetarism.

- Discuss the reasons economists differ on solutions to economic problems.

17.1 Benefits of Stability

Economic growth, full employment, and price stability are three of the seven major economic goals of the American people. In order to reach these goals, sound economic policies must be designed and implemented.

There are several ways to achieve economic stability. Some people favor policies that stimulate aggregate demand, while others favor ones that stimulate aggregate supply. Still others prefer policies that promote the growth of the money supply. Sometimes these policies are consistent with each other; but at other times, they are not.

Because of the social cost of instability, there is no disagreement on the urgency of achieving economic stability. Economists are interested not only in the production, but in the mental and social health of society as well. High crime rates, too few economic and social opportunities for minorities, the loss of individual freedoms, and the lack of stability for many Americans are all grounds for concern.

The mental and social health of society is an important concern for economists. If the economy is stable, many believe that society's social problems can be solved. What are some benefits of a healthy economy?

Many people believe that some of these social ills cannot be cured without the help of a strong and stable economy. They look to economists in hopes that they can improve the growth and performance of the American economy.

When the economy is healthy, it is easier for society to deal with its social problems. Cities and towns, for example, have higher tax collections that can be used to increase police protection and municipal services. Companies are more willing to hire the disadvantaged and provide on-the-job training.

A healthy economy also means that people will be more certain of their ability to earn an income and take care of themselves and their families. When they can do this, they are more positive about the future in general.

Section Review

1. What are three ways to achieve economic stability?

2. What is the relationship between the economy and America's social problems?

17.2 Demand-Side Economics

Economic policies designed to increase the demand for the total output of the economy are known as **demand-side economics** or **Keynesian economics.** They are based on John Maynard Keynes' theories that dealt with the need to stimulate total, or aggregate, demand to lower unemployment. These theories dominated the thinking of economists from the late 1930's until the 1970's.

CONCEPT OF AGGREGATE DEMAND

In Keynes' view, inadequate demand was the major problem during the Great Depression. In other words, not enough was spent by one or more sectors of the economy. Keynes felt that if policies could be designed to make up for the loss of spending in one part of the economy, the instability could be offset and the economy would keep growing.

Keynes suggested that the problem was not due to the spending patterns of individuals, households, or government, but to changes in investment spending by businesses. At the time Keynes presented these ideas, the United States was not gathering statistics on GNP, employment, or most other aggregate measures. All of Keynes' theorizing, therefore, had to be done without the aid of these important statistics.

Keynes, however, proved to be so persuasive that economists decided to develop measures of output useful for economic decision making. They could be used not only to check Keynes' suspicions about the instability of business spending, but for other purposes as well. As a result, the national income accounts were developed during World War II.

ROLE OF GOVERNMENT AND DEFICIT SPENDING

Keynes provided the general framework, $GNP = C + I + G + F$, now known as the output-expenditure model. According to it, changes in GNP could be traced to changes in the component parts on the right side of the equation. Since the foreign section, F, was so small, attention focused chiefly on the spending behavior of C, I, and G.

It turned out that expenditures of the consumer sector, **C**, were relatively stable. This meant that the instability of GNP had to be due to the changes in investment spending.

According to Keynes, government had a potential role to fill even though its expenditures were relatively stable. It could implement **fiscal policy**—the use of government spending and taxing policies to influence economic activity. The government had two choices. For one, it could take a direct role and set up its own spending to offset the decline in spending by businesses. Or, it could play an indirect role by lowering taxes and enacting other measures to get businesses and consumers to spend more on their own.

Suppose, for example, the government wanted to take direct steps right away to offset a $50 billion decline in business spending. To do this, it could spend $10 billion to build a dam in a rural area, give $20 billion in grants to cities to fix up poor neighborhoods, and spend another $20 billion in several other ways. In this way, the $50 billion not spent by business would be replaced by the $50 billion spent by the government. Thus, the overall sum of $C + I + G + F$ would remain unchanged.

Or, instead of spending the $50 billion, the government could reduce tax rates by that amount and give investors and consumers more purchasing power. If the $50 billion not paid in taxes were spent, the initial decline in investment spending would be offset, and the sum of $C + I + G + F$ again would remain the same.

Along the way, however, the government will likely run a deficit since it is spending money it does not have. In Keynes' view, the deficit is unfortunate, but it is needed to stop further declines in economic activity. He believed that when the economy recovered, tax collections would rise, the government would run a surplus, and the debt could be paid back.

The consequence of the Keynesian model was that temporary, short-term deficits were given legitimacy. This was a major departure from the thinking of the time. This justification for a federal deficit was one of the lasting contributions of Keynesian economics.

MULTIPLIER AND THE ACCELERATOR

Keynes also felt it was important for the government to take prompt action to offset changes in spending by the investment sector. The reason was that changes in spending could snowball if ignored for too long.

If, for example, investment spending declined by $50 billion, many workers would lose their jobs. They would spend less and pay fewer taxes. Soon, the amount of spending by all sectors in the economy would be down much more than the initial decline in investment. This effect, known as the **multiplier,** says that a change in investment spending will have a magnified effect on total income.

The multiplier is believed to be about two in today's economy. If investment spending goes down by $50 billion, there could be an overall decline of nearly $100 billion because of the multiplier effect.

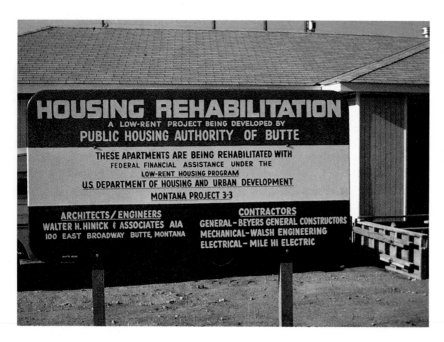

Keynesian economics states that if the federal government invests in neighborhood projects like the one in the photograph, it takes a direct role in influencing economic activity. What role do government deficits have according to this theory?

Further, conditions are likely to be made even worse by the **accelerator**—the change in investment spending caused by a change in consumer spending. Once a decline in consumer spending gets started, it causes investment spending to be reduced even further. Before long, the economy finds itself in a vicious circle. Investment spending declines because overall spending declines. This, in turn, causes more declines in investment spending.

On the other hand, the multiplier and the accelerator also can work in an upward direction. An increase in investment spending could have a multiplied effect, which would cause the economy to grow even faster. People would have more income to spend, which would lead businesses to increase their investment spending again.

The combined multiplier-accelerator effect is important because it adds to the instability of GNP. In the Keynesian model, government's role was that of an offsetting force. It was to counter declines in investment before the multiplier and the accelerator caused them to get out of hand. Although a deficit may be the result of the government spending, a small deficit would have been better than a large decline in overall GNP.

AUTOMATIC STABILIZERS

Another key part of economic philosophy since the 1930's is the role of the **automatic stabilizer.** These are fiscal policies that "automatically" trigger benefits if changes in the economy threaten people's incomes. Two important stabilizers are unemployment insurance and federal entitlement programs.

UNEMPLOYMENT INSURANCE. **Unemployment insurance** is insurance paid for by employers through payroll taxes. It can be collected by almost all American workers who lose their jobs through no fault of their own. Workers who are fired because of misconduct or who quit without good reason generally cannot collect.

Although workers generally have to wait several weeks to collect benefits, most end up getting payments equal to about one third to one half of their weekly pay. The benefits vary some from state to state. Under normal conditions, most states allow workers to collect the insurance for up to 26 weeks. At times when unemployment is high, however, they may be allowed to collect for longer.

FEDERAL ENTITLEMENT PROGRAMS. Federal entitlement programs, also known as **entitlements,** are social welfare programs designed to provide minimum health, nutritional, and income levels for

Medicare is an example of a federal entitlement program. Such programs provide benefits for certain groups of people. What are some other examples of entitlements?

selected groups of people. They take in such federal programs as welfare, government pensions, Medicare and Medicaid, and Social Security.

Congress provides the guidelines that determine who qualifies for, or is "entitled" to, these benefits. The availability of programs is a guarantee that economic instability or some other factor will not cause aggregate demand to fall below a certain level for selected groups of people.

Economists who are in favor of these programs believe they help stimulate the economy as well as offer humanitarian aid to those in need. Unemployment benefits really are a form of entitlement program,

too. However, they generally are listed separately as they are funded by state rather than federal taxes.

Section Review

1. According to Keynes, what was the major problem during the Great Depression? How did he suggest it be remedied?

2. How did the Keynesian model justify short-term deficits?

3. Why is the combined multiplier-accelerator effect important?

4. What role do automatic stabilizers play? What are two of them?

17.3 *Supply-Side Economics*

Economic policies designed to stimulate output and lower unemployment by increasing production in the economy are known as **supply-side economics.** This kind of economics became popular in the United States in 1980 when Ronald Reagan became President. Such policies formed the base of Reagan's economic program, known as **Reaganomics.** The supply-side views started to interest people in the late 1970's because demand-side policies did not seem to be able to control the country's growing unemployment and inflation.

There is less difference between supply-side economics and demand-side economics than most people think. Both policies use national income accounts to measure the economy's performance. Both policies accept the multiplier and the accelerator. In addition, both policies really have the same goal in mind—that of increased production and lower unemployment.

Supply-side economists feel, however, that the role of government has increased to the point where individual incentives to work, save, and invest are being destroyed. For this reason, they want the government to take a smaller role in the output-expenditure model. This is in contrast to the demand-siders. They want to stimulate output by generating demand with increased levels of government spending.

SMALLER ROLE FOR GOVERNMENT

A key issue for supply-siders is government's role in the economy. They feel that role must be reduced.

One way to lessen government's role is to do away with some federal agencies. During the early years of the Reagan ad-

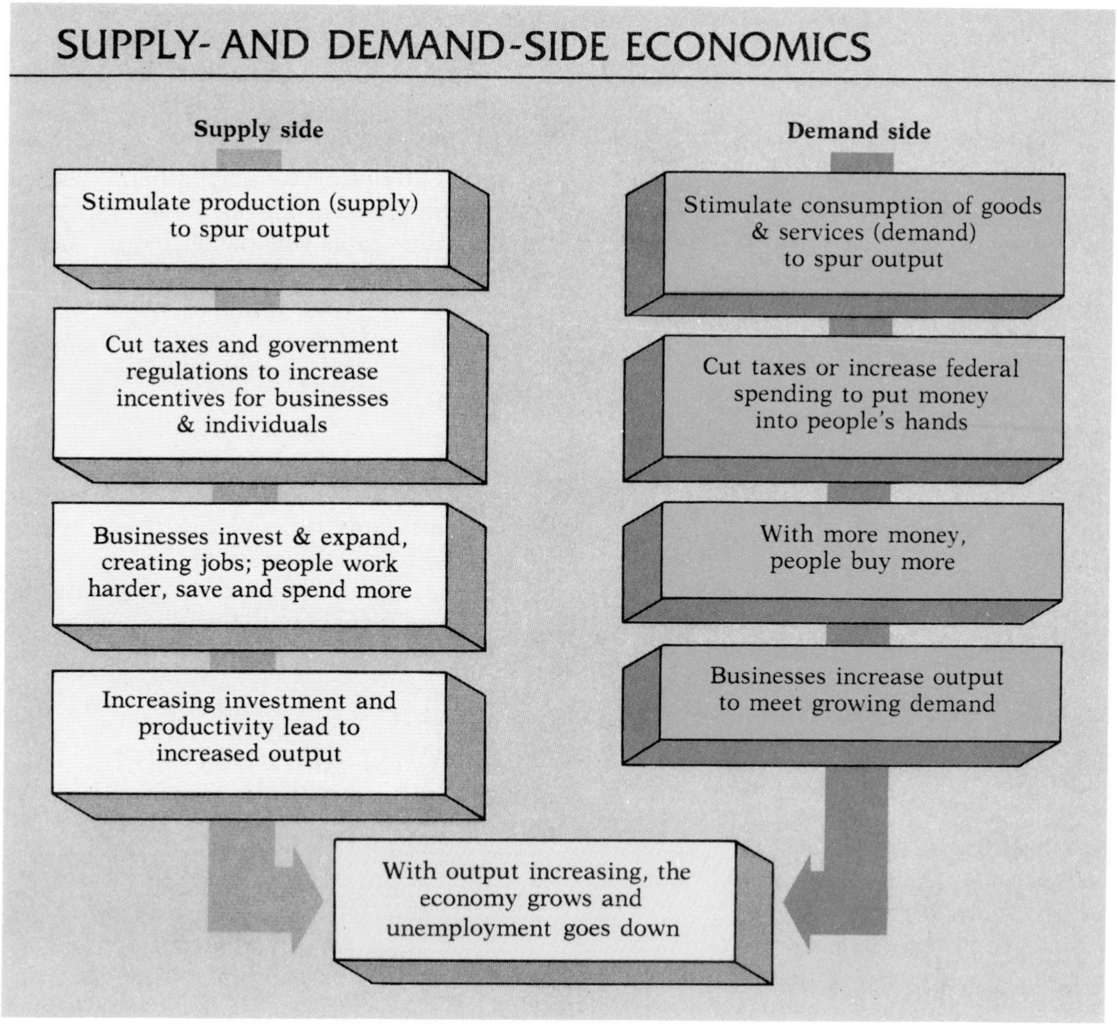

SUPPLY- AND DEMAND-SIDE ECONOMICS

Supply side	Demand side
Stimulate production (supply) to spur output	Stimulate consumption of goods & services (demand) to spur output
Cut taxes and government regulations to increase incentives for businesses & individuals	Cut taxes or increase federal spending to put money into people's hands
Businesses invest & expand, creating jobs; people work harder, save and spend more	With more money, people buy more
Increasing investment and productivity lead to increased output	Businesses increase output to meet growing demand

With output increasing, the economy grows and unemployment goes down

Figure 17–1

ministration, for example, there was talk of doing just that to the Departments of Energy and Education.

Another way to make government's role smaller is with the use of **deregulation**—the removal of established regulations with which industries must comply. This is a major target of supply-siders and also is favored by some demand-siders as well.

Under the administration of President Jimmy Carter, for example, major steps were taken in this direction in the energy, airline, and trucking industries to try to encourage competition. The Reagan administration continued the efforts—in hopes of not only bringing about more competition but of cutting down the government's role and size.

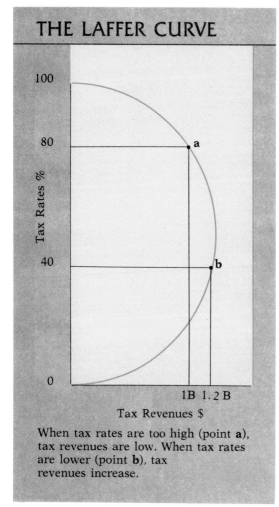

THE LAFFER CURVE

Tax Rates %

100

80 **a**

40 **b**

0

1B 1.2 B

Tax Revenues $

When tax rates are too high (point **a**),
tax revenues are low. When tax rates
are lower (point **b**), tax
revenues increase.

Figure 17–2

have more money to spend in the long
run. The government also would gain.
Even though tax rates would be lower,
total tax collections would go up because
of the extra activity.

The **Laffer Curve**—a hypothetical relationship between tax rates and tax revenues—illustrates this belief. It was the
basis for President Reagan's tax cut of
1981, which reduced income taxes 25 percent over a three-year period. The 1986 tax
reform bill, which again lowered tax
brackets for individuals and businesses, extended this philosophy. This curve is illustrated on the left of this page.

It will be several years, however, before
economists and others know if lower tax
rates will produce more tax revenues. The
reason is that the impact of a tax cut
needs to be evaluated over the course of
one, or more, complete business cycles.

GROWTH AND INSTABILITY

Basically, supply-side economic policies
are geared to restoring economic growth
rather than to dealing with economic
instability.

No matter how fast or slow the economy
grows, it seems to have a tendency to fluc-
tuate around its trend line. Demand-side
economists count on the use of automatic
stabilizers and the "safety net" features of
some social welfare programs to reduce
the fluctuations.

Supply-side policies, however, have tended to weaken the stabilizers by making the
federal tax structure less progressive and
by reducing many of the "safety net" programs. This tends to reduce the total purchasing power of those who can least afford it—which, in turn, tends to weaken
aggregate demand.

When the Reagan administration introduced its supply-side policies, it did so in

FEDERAL TAX STRUCTURE

Another target of supply-siders was the
federal tax burden on individuals and busi-
nessses. They believe that if taxes are too
high, people will not want to work, and
businesses will not produce as much as
they could. Lower tax rates would allow
individuals and businesses to keep more of
the money they earn. This would encourage them to work harder so they would

an unusual way. It cut taxes first, which gave government less to operate on and left elected officials one of two choices. They could cut spending sharply to make sure there would be no deficits. Or, they could cut spending slowly and allow large deficits to grow.

Congress, however, found that spending cuts were difficult to make. As a result, the government had huge deficits during expansions as well as recessions. Because of these deficits, many observers feel that supply-side economics never had a chance to prove itself. Instead, they argue that a better test of the effectiveness of supply-side theories will be the impact of the 1986 tax reform bill.

Section Review

1. According to supply-side economists, how can output be stimulated and the unemployment rate lowered?

2. What do supply-siders feel the government's role should be? How do they feel about taxes?

17.4 _Monetarism_

Both demand-side economics and supply-side economics are concerned with policies to stimulate production and employment. Neither of these policies assigns a great deal of importance to the money supply. There is, however, a doctrine called **monetarism** that places primary importance on the role of money and its growth. Monetarists believe the money supply can be a destabilizing element that leads to unemployment and inflation.

CONTROLLING INFLATION

The monetarists believe that if the money supply is allowed to grow at a steady rate over a long time, inflation will be controlled. The rate at which it grows would be determined by the rates of growth of real GNP and productivity.

If, for example, the rate of growth of real GNP were 3 percent, and that of productivity 1-to-2 percent, the money supply would grow at about 5 percent. At this rate, there would be just enough extra money each year to buy the additional goods and services the economy produces. Without too much money going around, inflation would slowly be reduced and, in time, would fade out altogether.

This approach to inflation control is in sharp contrast to others tried earlier. In the early 1970's, for example, President Richard Nixon tried to stop inflation by imposing **wage-price controls**—regulations that make it against the law for businesses to give workers raises or to raise prices without government permission. Most monetarists at the time said the controls would not work. In the end, the controls did little to stop inflation.

REDUCING UNEMPLOYMENT

The monetarists argue that attempts to cut unemployment by expanding the money supply will not work. The three graphs on page 424 show why they feel this way. Graph **A** shows the money stock, Graph **B** the inflation, and Graph **C** the unemployment rate.

Figure 17–3

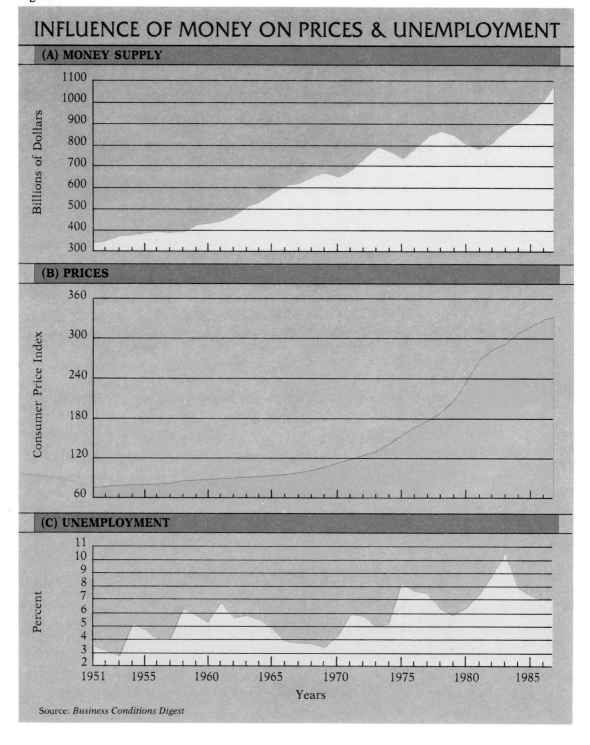

INFLUENCE OF MONEY ON PRICES & UNEMPLOYMENT

(A) MONEY SUPPLY

Billions of Dollars

1100
1000
900
800
700
600
500
400
300

(B) PRICES

Consumer Price Index

360
300
240
180
120
60

(C) UNEMPLOYMENT

Percent

11
10
9
8
7
6
5
4
3
2

1951   1955   1960   1965   1970   1975   1980   1985

Years

Source: *Business Conditions Digest*

The striking thing about the graphs is that the unemployment rate seems to go up and down regardless of the increases in the money stock. On the other hand, there does seem to be a close relationship between the price level and the money stock. Because of this, monetarists feel that in the short run, an expansion of the money supply will do little to reduce unemployment. And, in the long run, it only will make inflation worse. This, they say, adds validity to their contention that the growth of the money supply should be kept constant.

Monetarists are not really sure if a stable money supply would reduce the GNP fluctuations around the trend line. Still, they feel it would at least be of some help. Since the money supply is an important part of the economy, having it grow at a constant rate would be a stabilizing factor in the overall picture.

ROLE OF AN INDEPENDENT MONETARY AUTHORITY

An interesting feature of the American economy is that fiscal policy is in the hands of elected officials, but monetary policy is not. It is the domain of the Federal Reserve System.

For this reason, monetary and fiscal policy can—and often do—operate at cross purposes. For example, during an election year, a President may want to stimulate GNP and take credit for a growing economy. This can be done by lowering taxes, increasing Social Security payments, and approving federal spending projects.

The FED, however, might have different ideas. If there is a problem of inflation at the time, it might want to follow a tight monetary policy to slow the growth of money and reduce inflation. However, high interest rates generally go along with tight money, and they will work against the expansion hoped for by the President.

This happened in 1984 and 1986. Both times, the FED was pursuing a tighter monetary policy than the President wanted. In a move to intimidate the FED, the President threatened to introduce legislation to restrict its independent powers.

Congress, however, has never been willing to make the FED less independent. It has always believed that the power to control the creation of money should be in the hands of an independent agency rather than in those of elected officials.

▋ Section Review

1. How do monetarists think inflation can be controlled?
2. What do monetarists say will happen to unemployment if the money supply is expanded?
3. Who controls monetary policy in the United States? Why?

17.5 Historical Record

Someone looking at the economic history of the United States probably would decide that economists have not had much success coping with economic instability.

Inflation is a problem; unemployment goes up and down; recessions happen often. Despite all of this, more progress has been made than people realize.

WHY ECONOMISTS DIFFER

Someone once said that if all the economists in the world were put end-to-end, they still would not reach a conclusion. While that may be true to a certain degree, the important thing is not the differences, but why they exist.

One reason the differences exist is that most economic explanations and theories are a product of the problems of the times. Demand-side economics, for example, came about during the 1930's when the unemployment rate was nearly 25 percent. Since the government sector was so small at the time, it is not likely that supply-side policies designed to make government's role even smaller would have been of much help.

The monetarist point of view, on the other hand, emerged in the 1960's and 1970's when the country was trying to cope with inflation. Since demand-side economics were not designed to deal with inflation, new and different explanations and solutions were needed. The problem with the monetarists, however, was that they offered long-run solutions but little in the way of relief in the short run.

The supply-side explanations eventually grew out of frustrations with the economic health of the country and the solutions offered by the demand-siders and monetarists. Once again, something new and different seemed to be needed.

For the most part, economists generally do not define their position as purely demand-side, supply-side, or monetarist. Many demand-siders, for example, are monetarists when it comes to controlling inflation. Many monetarists are supply-siders when it comes to agreeing on the potential burden of the tax structure. Supply-siders and demand-siders even agree on multiplier-accelerator interactions. In short, many economists try to take a middle road that takes the best of all points of view.

Economists are caught up in the issues of the period and feel it is their duty to address them to the best of their ability. A person who grows up during a time when a lot of people are out of work, for example, is likely to be more concerned about unemployment than the person who grew up during a period when inflation was the major problem. Change has become a fact of life in the United States. As long as society keeps changing, new problems will continue to arise. From each new set of problems, new theories are bound to emerge.

ECONOMIC POLITICS

In the 1800's, the science of economics was known as "political economics." After awhile, however, the economists broke away from the political theorists and tried to establish economics as a science in its own right.

In recent years, the two fields have merged again. This time, however, they have done so in a way best described as "economic politics." Today, more than ever, politicians are concerned with the economic consequences of what they do.

For the most part, economists and politicians work together fairly closely. The President of the United States, for example, has a three-member **Council of Economic Advisors** to report on economic developments and to propose strategies. Basically, the economists are the advisors, while the politicians are at the controls.

The system, however, has two weaknesses. The first is that the politician is not always willing—or able—to follow the economists' advice. For example, a President may want a balanced budget. To

Case Study: Issue

Are Government Statistics Reliable?

Economists, business owners, politicians, and many others use statistics to help them understand how the economy performs. These statistics are often provided by the federal government and its many agencies. They include measures of Gross National Product (GNP), unemployment, the money supply, inflation, and revenue collections and tax receipts by all levels of government.

Some people, however, question the reliability of such performance statistics. Critics point out that sometimes the data is incomplete. For example, the monthly index of leading indicators is revised several times before it is final. In addition, GNP for a long time did not include the underground economy. When it was revised in 1985 to correct this oversight, the figure had increased by $111.9 billion over the previous year. Critics also point out that different government agencies sometimes publish conflicting data. In 1983, for example, the Federal Reserve reported that personal savings increased $42.6 billion from 1980 until the second quarter of 1983. Yet at the same time, the Department of Commerce reported that personal savings *decreased* $17.9 billion over the same period.

Those who defend the reliability of government statistics point out that the task is an enormous one and should be viewed in terms of what information the statistics provide, rather than what they overlook. They further argue that current estimates are still useful for purposes of analysis even though the numbers may be revised in the future. For example, new data that is subject to further revision is still useful when revealing trends in the economy. These supporters claim that we are far better off with, than without the present system, which is believed to be the best in the world.

1. Who or what is responsible for issuing most of the statistics kept on the United States economy?
2. Why are these statistics often criticized?
3. How do supporters defend the system?

Hang In There!

©1981 by Chicago Tribune-N.Y. News Synd. Inc.
All Rights Reserved

"ECONOMISTS. ONE'S A KEYNESIAN...THE OTHER ISN'T."

Although economists generally do not come to blows like the ones in this cartoon, they often do not agree on economic policies. This has been true throughout America's history. Why do economists differ in their policies?

achieve this, the economic advisors may recommend raising taxes. Yet, if one of the President's campaign pledges was to not raise taxes, there is a good chance that the advice of the economists will be ignored. Instead, the President may try to find another solution.

A second weakness is that the political system does not always react fast enough to deal with current economic problems. In 1974, for example, the American economy entered a severe recession with unemployment reaching a record high of 9 percent. At the time, this was considered the worst re-

cession since the 1930's. Nearly everyone felt that something should be done to stimulate the economy.

After the recession was well underway, Congress finally decided to give taxpayers an extra refund on their income taxes. Congress believed that this would stimulate the economy. This legislation, however, was slow to pass because many special interest groups kept trying to tack on amendments favorable to their causes.

When the bill finally passed, taxpayers received an extra $100. The refunds, however, were mailed during the second quarter of 1975, shortly after the recession ended. Thus, they were received too late to stimulate the economy in the way originally intended.

In 1982, the economy entered a worse recession, with the unemployment rate rising as high as 10.7 percent. Again, politicians were slow to deal with the problem. As a result, nothing was done in 1982 to help the economy recover.

Despite everything, economists have had a fair amount of success in the description, analysis, and explanation of economic activity. They have managed to develop many statistical measures of the economy's performance as well as models that are well-suited to economic analysis and explanation. In the process, they have helped the American people to become more aware of the workings of the economy. This has benefited everyone, from the student just starting out to the politician who must answer to the voters.

Today, economists know enough about the economy to prevent another depression like the one in the 1930's. But it is doubtful that they know enough—or can convince others that they know enough—to avoid minor recessions. They can, however, devise policies to stimulate growth and to help certain groups when unemployment rises or inflation strikes.

1. Why do economists differ in their views?

2. Why is the advice of economists not always taken?

3. What have economists accomplished?

Chapter 17 Review

Summary

1. Economists are concerned with the mental and social health of society as well as with the production of output.

2. Demand-side economic policies are designed to increase the demand for the total output of the economy.

3. John Maynard Keynes provided the general framework for aggregate demand by developing the output-expenditure model.

4. Fiscal policy is the use of government spending and taxing policies to influence economic activity.

5. One of Keynes' lasting contributions was the justification of temporary, short-term federal deficits.

6. The combined multiplier-accelerator effect adds to instability.

7. Unemployment insurance and federal entitlement programs are two automatic stabilizers.

8. Supply-side economic policies are designed to stimulate output and lower unemployment by increasing production in the economy.

9. Supply-siders want a smaller role for government in the domestic economy.

10. Monetarists believe that allowing the money supply to grow at a steady rate over a long period controls inflation.

11. In the United States, fiscal policy is determined by elected officials and monetary policy by the FED.

12. In recent years, economics and politics have merged in a way described as "economic politics."

Building an Economic Vocabulary

demand-side economics
Keynesian economics
fiscal policy
multiplier
accelerator

automatic stabilizer
unemployment insurance
entitlements
supply-side economics
Reaganomics

deregulation
Laffer Curve
monetarism
wage-price controls
Council of Economic Advisors

Reviewing the Main Ideas

1. With what did John Maynard Keynes' theories deal?

2. What is the multiplier? What is the accelerator?

3. Who is eligible to collect unemployment insurance?

4. What are federal entitlement programs and what do they provide?

5. Why did supply-side economics become popular?

6. In what ways are supply-side and demand-side economics alike? In what way are they most different?

7. What are two ways in which government's role in the economy can be made smaller?

8. What does the Laffer Curve show?

9. What are wage-price controls?

10. What do monetarists believe will happen if the money supply is allowed to grow at a steady rate for a long time?

11. Why do monetary and fiscal policies often operate at cross purposes in the United States?

12. How does the Council of Economic Advisors assist the President?

Practicing Critical Thinking Skills

1. Some economists favor policies that stimulate demand, while others favor those that stimulate the supply of goods and services. Still others prefer policies based on the growth of the money supply. With which group do you agree? Support your choice.

2. Defend or negate the following: "An increased federal deficit is a justifiable way to offset economic decline."

3. Do you believe that a larger role of the federal government destroys the incentives for individuals and businesses to invest? Why or why not?

4. Supply-side policies favor reducing "safety-net" programs. Do you agree? If not, what alternative would you suggest? Give reasons for your answer.

5. Almost every President has complained about the independence of the FED. Do you think this independence should be maintained or that elected officials should have more control over monetary policy? Support your answer.

Applying Economic Understandings

Analyzing Editorial Cartoons

Cartoons often take the place of, or accompany written material. One type of cartoon that has been popular over the years is the *editorial* or *political cartoon*. Such cartoons may comment on a topic of public interest and can be an effective way to express opinions.

To express opinions, editorial cartoonists often use symbols to represent something that their readers will recognize. For example, we often see Uncle Sam as a symbol representing the United States.

It is important to understand what an editorial cartoonist is trying to express in a drawing. This can be done by asking certain questions about the cartoon. Study the cartoon below and the questions and answers that follow. These will help you learn to analyze editorial cartoons.

1. What items or characters do you see in the cartoon? (Ziggy, a chair, and a television set)

2. What is the character doing? (sitting in a chair watching television)

3. What message is coming across from the cartoonist? (the irony that government cannot find ways to cut spending yet spends billions of dollars studying how to cut it)

4. Based on the cartoon, what do you think has been the government's history of spending? (high, if billions of dollars have been spent to study it)

For practice in this skill, analyze the editorial cartoon on page 428.

Unit 5 Review

The Unit in Perspective

1. The total output, or aggregate supply of the United States economy is measured in terms of GNP. GNP shows how the economy is producing, the rate at which output is growing, and how efficiently the economy is operating.

2. The macro economy of the United States is made up of the consumer, investment, government, and foreign sectors. Together, they represent the aggregate demand that consumes the GNP.

3. Other measures of national output include net national product, national income, and disposable income.

4. Price indices are used to remove the distortions of inflation in order to find real GNP or GNP in constant dollars.

5. When real GNP increases from one year to the next, the economy has experienced economic growth.

6. Economic growth fosters a higher standard of living, allows government to perform its functions more easily, helps solve domestic problems, permits greater assistance to developing countries, and helps the Free World meet the challenges of communism.

7. The terms recession and expansion are used to describe the state of the economy as it passes through the phases of the business cycle.

8. Swings in the business cycle can affect the success the labor force has in finding employment.

9. Other types of unemployment besides cyclical include frictional, structural, seasonal, and technological.

10. Inflation, a special type of economic instability, can be caused by excess demand, cost-push, a wage-price spiral, and excessive monetary growth.

11. Several different economic philosophies have evolved over time to help cope with economic instability. These include demand-side economics, supply-side economics, and monetarism.

12. Both demand-side and supply-side economics are concerned with policies to stimulate production and employment, while monetarism places primary importance on the role of money and the growth of the money stock.

The Unit in Review

1. What are the shortcomings of GNP? How serious are they?

2. What are the five measures of national income? How is each derived?

3. What is the value of price indices?

4. What role do the factors of production and productivity play in economic growth in the United States?

5. What has been the history of productivity growth in the United States since the end of World War II? What accounts for this record?

6. What is the difference between the unemployment and the employment rate?

7. What are several causes of inflation?

8. What effects do unemployment and inflation have on the economy?

9. How do demand-side economics, supply-side economics, and monetarism differ?

■ *Building Consumer Skills*

Using Credit Wisely

Over the years, credit cards have become a way of life for many people. Credit cards can be used today to buy a variety of items that range from gasoline for your car to furniture for your house to groceries for yourself. Because credit cards are so easy to use, it is necessary to learn to use them wisely. Follow the steps presented in the exercise below to learn how to use credit cards wisely.

1. Ask yourself: How much money do I have left to spend each month after I have paid all my expenses? Will I continue to have that amount or more each month? Since most credit card payments are due monthly, credit should be used only if you have money in your budget to pay for it.

2. When a person applies for credit, he or she generally must answer questions about employment, residence, capital, resources, and debts to show that he or she has the character and earning capacity to be eligible for credit. How would you rate yourself in each of these areas?

3. Before you open a charge account, find out what kind of credit plans are available. Most stores have three plans: a regular, or 30-day, charge which must be paid in full in 30 days; a revolving charge which allows purchases to be made up to a fixed amount and payment to be spread over several months; a time-payment plan with payments budgeted over an extended period of time. Finance charges vary according to the plan. To determine which plan is best for you, consider the kinds of purchases you plan to make, how often you plan to make them, and how much money you will have available to pay for them.

World Economy

Today, no country—even the most productive one—is totally self-sufficient. As a result, most countries have to trade with others whose economics systems may be different from their own.

Unit 6

Contents

International Trade

Our interest will be to throw open the doors of commerce, and to knock off its shackles, giving freedom to all persons for the vent of whatever they may choose to bring into our ports, and asking the same in theirs.

Thomas Jefferson

Chapter 18

After reading this chapter, you will be able to:

- Explain how absolute and comparative advantages benefit countries engaged in international trade.

- Debate the arguments for and against protectionism and free trade.

- Explain the differences between fixed and flexible exchange rates.

- Discuss the effect of trade imbalances on the United States economy.

18.1 Benefits of International Trade

The key to trade—be it among people, states, or countries—is specialization. Some people, for example, specialize in cutting hair. Others specialize in fixing television sets. These people exchange their services for money, which they then can use to buy the specialized talents and services of others.

Different areas of the United States tend to specialize in certain kinds of economic activity in much the same way. Pittsburgh, for example, is a center of the steel industry and Detroit of the automobile industry. The midwest and high plains areas are known for wheat farming, Texas for oil and cattle, and Florida and California for citrus fruit. All of these states trade with one another so that people in one area can consume the goods and services offered by people in other areas.

What can be said about specialization in the United States also can be said about specialization in other regions of the world. Each region or country generally does what it is best suited to do. As a result, international trade allows all countries the opportunity to take advantage of local production efficiencies.

AMERICAN DEPENDENCY ON TRADE: IMPORTS AS A PERCENT OF CONSUMPTION, 1984

RAW MATERIAL	IMPORTS AS A PERCENT OF CONSUMPTION	PRIMARY FOREIGN SOURCES	USE OF RAW MATERIAL
Industrial Diamonds	100	South Africa	Industrial cutting tools, Oil well drills
Columbium	100	Brazil, Canada, Thailand	Atomic energy reactors, hardened steel
Mica (sheet)	100	India, Belgium, France	Electrical insulation, ceramics
Strontium	100	Mexico, Spain	Flares, fireworks
Manganese	99	South Africa, Gabon, Australia	Stainless steel, dry cell batteries, dies
Cobalt	95	Zaire, Zambia, Canada	High temperature jet fighter engines
Tantalum	94	Thailand, Malaysia, Brazil	Surgical instruments and missile parts
Chromium	82	South Africa, Zimbabwe, Soviet Union	Chrome, ball bearings, trim on appliances and cars
Asbestos	75	Canada, South Africa	Insulation, cement, fireproof clothing

Source: *Statistical Abstract of the United States, 1986*

Table 18–A

EXTENT OF TRADE

In recent years, international trade has become increasingly important to all nations. Most of the products exchanged are goods, although some services, such as insurance and banking, are also bought and sold. For example, the United States alone imported nearly $552 billion in goods and services in 1985. This was almost $2072 for every person in the country.

The sheer magnitude of trade between nations of such different geographic, political, and religious characteristics proves that trade benefits nations. Nations freely trade for the same reason individuals do—they believe they are better off with trade than without it.

Without international trade, many products would not be available on the world market. Bananas, for example, would not leave Honduras, nor would coffee beans leave Brazil. Raw materials, such as industrial diamonds and cobalt needed for manufacturing and national defense, would not be available.

Figure 18–1

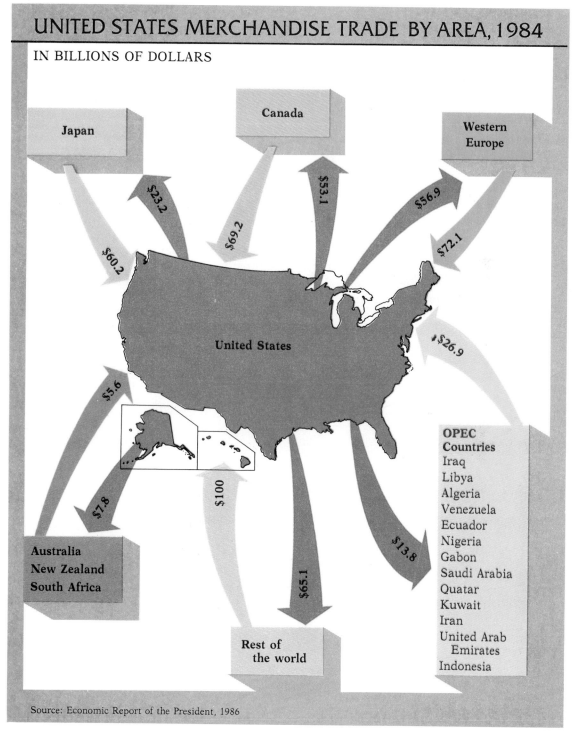

UNITED STATES MERCHANDISE TRADE BY AREA, 1984

IN BILLIONS OF DOLLARS

Japan

Canada

Western
Europe

$23.2

$69.2

$53.1

$56.9

$72.1

$60.2

United States

$26.9

$5.6

OPEC
Countries
Iraq
Libya
Algeria
Venezuela
Ecuador
Nigeria
Gabon
Saudi Arabia
Quatar
Kuwait
Iran
United Arab
    Emirates
Indonesia

$7.8

$100

$13.8

Australia
New Zealand
South Africa

$65.1

Rest of
the world

Source: Economic Report of the President, 1986

ABSOLUTE ADVANTAGE

In some cases, a country finds it cheaper to import a product than to manufacture it. The differences in the cost of production from one country to another are a basis for international trade. They are due chiefly to differences in natural resources, climate, labor force, and capital. When a country is able to produce more of a given product than another, it is said to enjoy an **absolute advantage.**

Consider, for example, the case of two countries, Alpha and Beta, which are the same size in terms of area, population, and capital stock. The only difference between the two is the climate and soil fertility. In each country, only two crops can be grown—coffee and cashew nuts.

If both countries devote all of their efforts to the production of coffee alone, Alpha can produce 40 million pounds and Beta 6 million. Alpha, then, has an absolute advantage in the production of coffee. If both countries devote all their efforts to the production of cashew nuts alone, Alpha can produce 8 million pounds and Beta 6 million. Alpha, then, also has an absolute advantage in the production of cashew nuts.

COMPARATIVE ADVANTAGE

Even when one country enjoys an absolute advantage in the production of all goods, trade between it and another country still can be of value if one of them can produce a good better than the other. A country has a **comparative advantage** if it is relatively more efficient producing a certain good.

In the case of Alpha and Beta, Alpha can produce nearly seven times as many coffee

This Latin American worker is a picker on a coffee plantation. Why do some nations specialize in the production of certain crops?

Profile

Jacob Viner

Jacob Viner was an American economist who taught at Princeton University and the University of Chicago. While at Chicago, he was a senior member of what is now known as the Chicago School. Like most of the School's other members, Viner believed in freedom from intervention by the central government. He and the other members wanted the government to have less say about banking and monetary policy. They wanted instead a money growth rule that allowed the money supply to grow at a fixed percentage rate each year. They also thought that banks should be required to keep 100 percent of all deposits in required reserves, which would do away with fractional reserve banking as most people know it today.

1892–1970

Viner made several important contributions to the theory of the firm. In 1921, he outlined the basic idea for the differentiation of products produced by firms. In 1931, in an article entitled "Cost Curves and Supply Curves," he developed much of what is considered today the standard analysis of the cost curves of the purely competitive firm.

Viner also made several contributions in the area of international trade theory. In a 1937 work, *Studies in the Theory of International Trade,* he examined the difference between opportunity costs and real costs as a basis for trade. He believed that the main cost of producing most goods was labor and that a nation might want to work less to get the same real income it had without trade.

Viner also contributed several theories about the role in international trade of the customs union—a group of countries which agree to common tariff schedules and rates. He argued that a customs union formed by competing countries would lead to an increase in the real amount of goods and services traded, while one formed by complementary countries would just mean substituting a high-cost partner for a low-cost foreigner. Viner believed that even though customs unions might lead to freer trade, they also might lead to a loss of welfare and economic well-being.

Countries should concentrate on those goods or crops that they produce best. By doing so, how does this affect world output?

beans as Beta. So, if Alpha were to specialize in the production of one good, it is likely to choose coffee beans. Alpha, then, also has a comparative advantage in the production of coffee.

On the other hand, Beta does a relatively better job of producing cashew nuts. Beta, then, has a comparative advantage in cashew nuts. For this reason, if Beta were to specialize in the production of one product, it would choose cashew nuts.

The concept of comparative advantage is based on the assumption that everyone will be better off producing the products they produce best. This concept applies to individuals, companies, states, and regions as well as to nations involved in international trade.

When nations in the real world specialize in the goods they are most efficient in producing, the total world output is greater. Take, for example, the case of the United States and Brazil. The United States has excellent supplies of iron and coal. It also has the capital and the labor that are needed to produce tractors and farm machinery efficiently. Brazil, on the other hand, does not have as much capital or skilled labor. But it does have the amount and kind of land, labor, and climate to produce coffee efficiently.

The United States, then, has a comparative advantage in the production of tractors and farm machinery. Brazil, on the other hand, has a comparative advantage in the production of coffee. Trade between the two countries would be of value to both. Each of the countries could produce its specialty at a lower cost and enjoy larger total consumption.

■ Section Review

1. Why do nations trade with one another?

2. When does a country enjoy an absolute advantage? A comparative advantage?

3. What must take place before gains can be realized from trade?

18.2 Barriers to International Trade

Although international trade can bring many benefits, some people object to it because it can displace selected industries and groups of workers. It is not unusual to hear workers say they have lost their jobs because of "unfair" foreign competition. Therefore, while people in general tend to support international trade, there are some who are very strongly against it.

RESTRICTING INTERNATIONAL TRADE

Over the years, trade has been restricted in two major ways. One is through the use of a **tariff**—a tax placed on imports to increase their price in the domestic market. The other is through the use of a **quota**—a limit placed on the amount of a product that can be imported.

TARIFFS. There are two kinds of tariffs—protective and revenue. A **protective tariff** is a tariff high enough to protect less efficient domestic industries. Suppose, for example, it costs $1 each to produce gadgets in the United States. But they can be imported from another country for 35¢ each, including transportation costs. If a tariff of 95¢ were placed on each gadget made in that country, the cost could climb to $1.30 each—more than the cost of the American-made gadget. In this way, the domestic industry would be protected from being undersold by a foreign one.

The **revenue tariff** is a tariff designed chiefly to raise money for the government. It must be high enough to generate funds when imported goods enter the country, yet not so high as to reduce imports. If, for example, the tariff on gadgets imported from abroad were 40¢, the price of the imported gadgets would be 75¢, or 25¢ less than the price of the American-made ones. The tariff, then, would be raising revenue rather than protecting domestic producers from foreign competition.

In reality, all tariffs raise some revenue and offer some protection. Before the Civil War, they were the chief source of revenue for the federal government. From the Civil War to 1913, they provided a little more than one half of the government's total revenue. In 1913, however, the federal income tax was passed. It gave the government a new and more profitable source of revenue.

QUOTAS. Sometimes, foreign goods cost so little that it is hard to place a tariff on them high enough to protect the domestic market. In such cases, the government generally uses a quota to keep foreign goods out of the country.

Quotas can be more powerful and have more of an impact on international trade than tariffs. A quota can be set as low as zero to keep a product from entering the country at all. Once the total supply of the product is restricted, domestic consumers will not be able to consume as much of it and domestic producers can charge higher prices for it. Most people just do not realize how much the total supply of products in any country can be affected by quotas.

OTHER BARRIERS. Tariffs and quotas are not the only barriers to trade. Many imported foods, for example, sometimes are subject to health inspections far more rigorous than those given to domestic foods. Another tactic is to require importers to get a license to import. If the government is slow to grant the license, or if the license fees are too high, international trade is restricted.

Profile

Bertil Ohlin

Bertil Ohlin is a Swedish economist who studied at the University of Stockholm in Sweden. He is noted for his contributions to the theory of international trade. His best-known works in this area are *The Theory of Trade* (1924), *Interregional and International Trade* (1933), and *International Economic Reconstruction* (1936).

1899–

Ohlin believes that comparative advantage results from the fact that regions are unequally endowed with productive resources. In his view, it is difficult, if not impossible, to move some of these resources from country to country. International trade, however, provides a way to do this by moving internationally the goods and services produced with those resources.

Ohlin also felt that gold bullion need not be moved from country to country to pay trade debts. Instead, when, for example, a country's imports are greater than its exports, the difference should be settled by the transfer of bank balances from one country to another.

Still another tactic is for one country to intimidate another into restricting trade voluntarily. One of the most recent cases of this involved the American automobile industry, which was losing sales to foreign manufacturers. In fact, by 1981, the United States had lost its position as the world's number one automobile producer to Japan.

One of the major reasons for Japan's success was price. Labor costs in the United States were nearly $7 to $10 an hour higher than rates in Japan. This made the Japanese-made cars cheaper than the American-made ones. Another reason was quality. Many people thought the foreign-built cars were better-made than the domestically produced ones. As a result, they bought the foreign-made ones instead of those made at home.

Domestic automobile producers found it easier to push for quotas than to lower car prices. In the end, they managed to get the Japanese to "voluntarily" restrict car exports to the amount of cars Japan had actually sold to the United States. As a result, domestic manufacturers had less competition, and Americans had fewer cars from which to choose. This made domestic prices higher than they would have been otherwise.

ARGUMENTS FOR PROTECTION

International trade has been a subject of debate for many years. Some people, known as **protectionists,** favor tariffs, quotas, and other trade barriers. Others, known as **free traders,** favor freer trade.

NATIONAL DEFENSE. One of the most important arguments against freer trade centers on national defense. Protectionists argue that without trade barriers, a country could become too specialized and end up too dependent on other countries.

In time of war, a country might not be able to get such critical supplies as food, oil, and weapons. This is the reason why today the governments of such countries as Israel and South Africa have developed large armaments industries. They want to be sure they will have a domestic source of supply if hostilities break out or other countries impose economic boycotts.

Free traders admit that this is a fair argument against free trade. They feel, however, that the value of having a reliable source of domestic supply must be weighed against the fact that the supply will be smaller and possibly less efficient than it would be with trade. There also is the problem of deciding which industries are critical to the national defense. In the past, the steel, auto, ceramic, and electronic industries all have argued that they are critical to national defense.

INFANT INDUSTRIES. Another is the **infant industries argument** that says that new and emerging industries should be protected from foreign competition. Protec-

tionists claim that these industries need to gain strength and experience before they can compete against industries in developed countries. Trade barriers would give them the time they need to develop. If they have to compete against the developed countries too soon, they might never make it.

Many people are willing to accept the infant industries argument only if protection will be eventually removed so that the industry can compete on its own. It is hard to judge, however, whether or not this will happen because of the amount of

There are several protectionist arguments. How might the issue of protectionism differ for a worker and a consumer?

"You like protectionism as a 'working man.' How about as a consumer?"

time that must pass before the industry reaches maturity.

Some developing countries of Latin America, for example, have tried to modernize by using protective tariffs to protect their infant automobile industries. Some of these tariffs went as high as several hundred percent. In many cases, this raised the price of used American-made cars to more than double the cost of new ones in the United States.

PROTECTING DOMESTIC JOBS. A third argument—and one of the ones used most often—is that tariffs and quotas protect domestic jobs from "cheap" foreign labor.

Workers in the shoe industry, for example, often protest the import of lower-cost Italian, Spanish, and Brazilian shoes. Gar-ment workers often oppose the import of lower-cost Korean, Chinese, and Indian clothing. Steel workers have even thrown up barricades to keep foreign-made cars out of company parking lots to show their displeasure with the use of foreign-made steel to produce them.

Whether limiting foreign trade really preserves American jobs is hard to prove. Over the long run, the industries that find it hard to compete are generally the less efficient ones. For this reason, many people believe it is better to allow these industries to be phased out so resources can be freed to use somewhere else. The problem, however, lies in the short run, where there is unemployment and the hardships that go along with it. Workers can hardly be blamed for wanting to keep their jobs

The workers in the photograph below believe that foreign imports cost American workers their jobs. Thus, they want imports restricted. What are some arguments protectionists use in support of trade restrictions?

or live in the communities where they grew up. The fact remains, however, that while protection can help in the short run, it does not preserve jobs for very long.

When inefficient industries are protected, the economy produces less and the standard of living goes down. Because of unnecessarily high prices, people buy less of everything, including those goods produced by protected industries. This reduces everyone's income even further. If prices get too high, substitute products will be found in time, and the economy will be in more trouble.

Free traders argue that the profit and loss system is one of the major features of the American economy. The profits are needed to reward the efficient and hard-working, while the losses are needed to eliminate the inefficient and weak.

KEEP THE MONEY HOME. Another argument, which is a variant of protecting domestic jobs, claims that limiting imports will keep American money in the United States instead of allowing it to go abroad.

Free traders, however, point out that the American dollars that go abroad generally come back again. The Japanese, for example, use the dollars they receive for their automobiles and television sets to buy American cotton, soybeans, computers, and airplanes. These purchases benefit American workers in those industries.

The same is true of the dollars used to buy OPEC oil. They come back to the United States as oil-wealthy foreigners buy American-made oil technology, Kentucky horse farms, and Hollywood mansions. In a sense, then, protectionists who want to limit imports to "keep the money home" actually are making it harder for Americans who depend on exports for their jobs.

HELPING THE BALANCE OF PAYMENTS. Another argument has to do with the **balance of payments**—the difference between the money paid to and received from other nations.

Protectionists argue that restrictions on imports will help the balance of payments. When the economy runs a **trade deficit**— a deficit in the balance of payments—it is spending more on imports than it earns on exports. As a result, money leaves the country. This means that jobs are lost and the dollar is threatened.

What protectionists overlook, however, is that the dollars will return to the United States to stimulate employment in the export industries. In the United States today, the balance of payments adjusts automatically to deficits and surpluses. For this reason, most economists do not feel that interference with free trade can be justified on the grounds of helping the balance of payments.

FREE TRADE MOVEMENT

Using trade barriers to protect domestic industries and jobs works only if other countries do not do the same in return. If they do, all countries suffer because they then have neither the benefits of efficient production, nor access to less costly inputs from other places.

This happened in 1930 when the United States passed the **Smoot-Hawley Tariff,** one of the highest in history. It set import duties so high that the price of many imported goods rose nearly 70 percent. When other countries did the same, international trade nearly came to a halt.

Since then, most countries have lowered tariffs to try to rebuild trade. In 1934, for example, the United States passed the **Reciprocal Trade Agreements Act,** which allowed it to reduce tariffs by up to 50 percent if the other countries agreed. The

Case Study: Issue

Protectionism or Free Trade: Which is Better for the United States?

In recent years, competition from foreign producers has increased. As a result, many people, including some legislators, are urging the United States to adopt some protectionist measures, including quotas and tariffs on imports.

Those who want protectionism say that protecting American workers and industries is long overdue. They point out that losses in textile, shoe, computer, steel, and auto industries are examples of industries hit hard by foreign competition. Moreover, they argue that workers are also hurt when plants are forced to close down.

Those who argue against protectionism, or those who want free trade, point out that foreign competition keeps the prices of all goods down. While some workers may suffer temporary unemployment, the overall benefit is a larger supply of high-quality, low-priced goods. Besides, businesses do not always suffer when a plant closes. They point out that if production can be moved to a less expensive location, the company makes more profits and shareholders, usually American citizens, receive bigger dividend payments. Finally, those opposed to protectionism argue that if the United States adopts such a plan, foreign countries are likely to retaliate. If so, they could hurt America by cutting off necessary raw materials imported from other countries.

1. What do protectionists believe? Why are they opposed to free trade?

2. What do free-traders believe? Why are they opposed to protectionism?

act also contained the **most favored nation clause**—a provision allowing a country to receive the benefits of a tariff reduction negotiated between the United States and another country.

Suppose, for example, the United States and Finland have a trade agreement with a most favored nation clause. If the United States then negotiates a tariff reduction with another country, it would also apply to Finland and any other nation with the most favored nation clause. This clause is very important to a foreign country because it means that its goods will sell at a lower price in the American market.

In 1947, 23 countries signed the **General Agreement on Tariffs and Trade (GATT).** This agreement extended tariff concessions and worked to do away with import quotas. It was followed by the **Trade Expansion Act** of 1962, which gave the President of the United States the power to negotiate tariff reductions another 50 percent. As a result of this legislation, there were significant tariff reductions in 1967 and 1979, with more than 100 countries agreeing to reduce the average level of tariffs. Other barriers to trade, such as quotas, unnecessary inspections, and licensing requirements were also reduced.

Because so many countries were willing to enter into agreements to reduce tariffs and quotas, international trade is flourishing today. Tariffs that once nearly doubled the price of many goods now increase the average cost by only a few percent. On many classes of goods, they have been done away with altogether. This is one of the major reasons stores and shops today are able to offer such a wide variety of industrial and consumer goods.

■ Section Review

1. In what ways can trade be restricted? Which has the greatest impact?
2. How do protectionists feel about the United States' involvement in free trade?
3. When does using trade barriers to protect domestic industries and jobs work?
4. What has been the purpose of trade legislation in the United States since 1934?

18.3 *Financing International Transactions*

Trade between nations is similar to exchange between individuals. The major difference is that each country has its own monetary system. Because of the number of different currencies used, financing of trade is much more difficult.

FOREIGN EXCHANGE

Consider the following example. An American firm wants to import suits from a company in England. Since the British firm pays its bills in the currency called pound sterling, it wants to receive payment in sterling. This means that the American firms must exchange its dollars for British pounds.

Suppose that one pound sterling—£1— is equal to $1.42. If the suits are valued at £1000 in London, the American importer can go to an American bank and, for $1420 plus a small service charge, buy a £1000 check. Once the American firm has the check, it can pay the British merchant, and the suits can be imported.

At times, American exporters also will sell goods for which they are willing to accept in return foreign currency or checks written on foreign banks. They then deposit the payments in their own banks, which helps the American banking system build a supply of foreign currency. This currency then can be sold to American firms that want to import goods from other countries. In the end, both the importer and the exporter end up with the currency of their own countries.

In the field of international finance, these foreign currencies are also known as **foreign exchange** and are bought and sold in the **foreign exchange market.** Both banks that help secure foreign currencies for importers and those that accept them from exporters are part of this market.

When the price of one country's currency is described in terms of another country's, it is known as the **foreign exchange rate.** The rate can be quoted in terms of the United States dollar equivalent—£ = $1.42—or in terms of currency per United States dollar—$1.00 = £ .70. Most often, however, it is reported in terms of the currency of both countries.

FIXED EXCHANGE RATES

Historically, there have been two major kinds of exchange rates—fixed and flexible. For most of the twentieth century, the world depended on **fixed exchange rates**— a system under which the price of one currency is fixed in terms of another so that the rate does not change.

When the world was on a gold standard, for example, all countries defined their currency in terms of a given amount of

Some banks have windows like the one in the photograph where people can exchange their currency for that of another country's. What is a foreign exchange rate?

Understanding Sources

■ Foreign Exchange

The selected listing below appeared in the financial pages of *The Wall Street Journal*, October 23, 1986. Review the data and then answer the questions that follow.

FOREIGN EXCHANGE
Thursday, October 23, 1986

The New York foreign exchange selling rates below apply to trading among banks in amounts of $1 million and more, as quoted at 3 p.m. Eastern time by Bankers Trust Co. Retail transactions provide fewer units of foreign currency per dollar.

Country	U.S. $ Equiv.		Currency per U.S. $		Country	U.S. $ Equiv.		Currency per U.S. $	
	Thurs.	Wed.	Thurs.	Wed.		Thurs.	Wed.	Thurs.	Wed.
Argentina (Austral).....	.9208	.9208	1.086	1.086	France (Franc).............	.1525	.1539	6.5580	6.4985
Australia (Dollar)........	.6475	.6382	1.5444	1.5669	30-Day Forward....	.1522	.1538	6.5700	6.5010
Brazil (Cruzado)..........	1.4245	1.4320	.7020	.6983	90-Day Forward....	.1516	.1528	6.5980	6.5425
Britian (Pound)..........	1.4245	1.4320	.7020	.6983	180-Day Forward....	.1506	.1519	6.6380	6.5825
30-Day Forward....	1.4180	1.4259	.7052	.7013	Israel (Shekel).............	.6725	.6725	1.487	1.487
90-Day Forward....	1.4040	1.4137	.7123	.7074	Japan (Yen)................	.006295	.006418	158.85	155.80
180-Day Forward....	1.3888	1.3971	.7200	.7158	30-Day Forward....	.006305	.006427	158.65	155.59
Canada (Dollar)...........	.7204	.7194	1.3881	1.3900	90-Day Forward....	.006313	.006437	158.41	155.34
30-Day Forward....	.7191	.7180	1.3907	1.3927	180-Day Forward....	.006330	.006457	157.98	154.88
90-Day Forward....	.7159	.7149	1.3969	1.3987	W. Germany (Mark)...	.4990	.5037	2.0040	1.9852
180-Day Forward....	.7109	.7098	1.4067	1.4089	30-Day Forward....	.4997	.5044	2.0013	1.9825
Chile (Official rate).....	.005111	.005111	195.66	195.66	90-Day Forward....	.5009	.5059	1.9966	1.9765
China (Yuan)...............	.2707	.2707	3.6943	3.6943	180-Day Forward....	.5024	.5073	1.9905	1.9712

1. What is the currency unit used by Britain? China? Israel?

2. What is the value of a Japanese yen in dollars?

3. What is the value of a U.S. dollar in yen?

gold. Before 1971, the United States dollar was worth 1/35 ounce of gold, the British pound 1/11.43 ounce of gold, and so on. Once the gold content was specified, the value of one country's currency could be determined in terms of the value of another country's currency. The British pound, for example, was backed by 2.8 times as much gold as the American dollar. Therefore, the British pound was worth $2.80.

Gold not only served as the common denominator that allowed comparisons to be made. It also was used to keep exchange rates in line. Suppose, for example, that a country allowed its money supply to grow too fast and then spent some of the money on imports. Under a gold standard, the other countries holding the currency would have the right to demand that it be converted into gold. Since no country wants to lose its gold, each worked to keep its money supply under control.

This, however, did not work in the 1950's and 1960's when the United States developed a huge appetite for imports. During that time, it bought large quantities of foreign goods with dollars. At first, foreign countries willingly held dollars since they were acceptable as an international currency. Year after year, dollars went to other countries to buy imports, while only a portion of these dollars came back as other countries bought American exports.

As dollars began to pile up in the rest of the world, many countries became nervous about whether or not the United States could honor its promise that the dollar was "as good as gold." As a result, France and several other countries sent their dollars back to the United States and demanded gold in return at the rate of $35 an ounce. By the late 1960's, the United States had a problem because of the huge number of foreign-held dollars that could be converted into gold.

The United States could have solved the problem in several different ways. It could have put limits on imported goods. This, however, would not help if other countries retaliated by limiting American products. It could have restricted the growth of the money supply. But this might have lead to a recession with rising unemployment and political unrest. Or, it could have decided on **devaluation**—making currency worth less in terms of gold. This, however, would not work either if other countries followed suit and reduced their gold content by as much or more. Then, too, many American politicians viewed devaluation as an admission of failure and were not in favor of such a move.

Instead, President Richard Nixon solved the problem in August 1971, by announcing that the United States no longer would redeem dollars for gold. This saved the gold stock for other purposes. At the same time, however, it angered many foreign holders of American dollars who were planning to cash them in for gold.

FLEXIBLE EXCHANGE RATES

When the United States went off the gold standard, the world monetary system went to **floating,** or **flexible exchange rates.** Under this system, the forces of supply and demand establish the value of one country's currency in terms of the value of another country's currency.

The supply and demand graphs on page 453 show how this could happen. Before 1971, for example, the price of the German mark (DM) in the United States was 25¢, and the price of the dollar in Germany was 4 DM's. In the years that followed, however, the United States imported more from Germany than it exported.

As importers in the United States sold dollars for DM's, two things happened. The sale of dollars increased the supply of dollars in the foreign currency market. This drove the value of the dollar down. At the same time, the growing demand for DM's drove up the value of the DM.

This actually happened in the early 1970's. At the time, one American dollar was worth four DM's. Therefore, if it cost 12,000 DM's to make a Volkswagen, an American importer would have had to pay $3000 to get enough DM's to buy it. Even after adding on shipping charges and other expenses, the importer still could sell the automobile at a competitive price. But as more cars were imported, the supply of dollars in the foreign exchange market increased. At the same time, the demand for DM's rose and caused the value of the dollar to drop.

FLEXIBLE EXCHANGE RATES

(A) THE MARKET FOR DOLLARS IN GERMANY	(B) THE MARKET FOR MARKS IN THE UNITED STATES

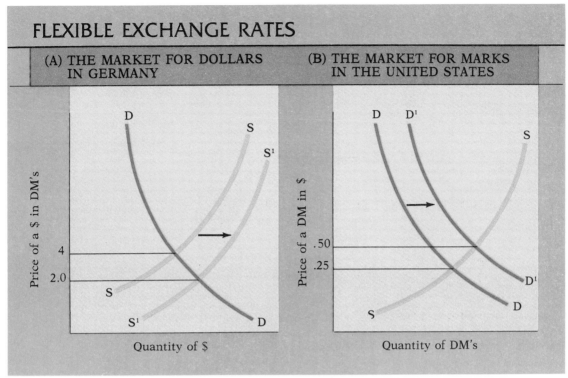

Figure 18–2

When the dollar reached a new level of 2.0 DM's, the importer had to pay more for the DM's. Although the car still cost 12,000 DM's at the factory, the new exchange rate made it cost the importer more dollars. To get the 12,000 DM's, the importer would have to give up $6000 instead of $3000. At the higher price, the car no longer was as competitive as before.

Excessive imports, then, caused the deficit in the balance of payments. This drove the value of the dollar down and made imports cost more. At the same time, however, the fact that the dollar was weak caused American exports to rise.

A German company that wanted to buy American soybeans at $6 a bushel before 1971, for example, would have given up 24

DM's for each bushel. After 1971, however, it had to give up only 12 DM's for each bushel. Because of this, soybeans were cheaper and more could be sold abroad.

When the world first went to the system of flexible rates, some people feared it might not work because of the fluctuations in exchange rates. However, the system of flexible rates worked better than most people thought it would. A company can even buy **foreign exchange futures**—currencies on the futures market—to protect against changing exchange rates. In other words, it can agree to buy currency 30, 90, or 180 days in the future at prices agreed upon in the present. More importantly, the switch to a system of flexible rates did not interrupt the growth in international trade as many people had feared. More countries

The International Monetary Fund was originally established to set up an international system of fixed exchange rates for its member nations. Today, however, it has a different role. How does its present role differ from its original purpose?

trade with one another today than ever before.

INTERNATIONAL MONETARY FUND

Today some stabilization of exchange rates is done by the **International Monetary Fund (IMF).** The fund originally was formed in 1944 by 44 countries that wanted to set up an international system of fixed exchange rates. Each country agreed to contribute a pool of currency and gold to be used to fix exchange rates at agreed-upon levels.

Under today's system of flexible rates, the IMF plays a slightly different role. Instead of using gold and currency to fix rates at a specific level, it uses them to stabilize exchange rate fluctuations. Although it may allow a country's rate to rise or fall slowly, it will step in to prevent dramatic changes.

The IMF also has de-emphasized the use of gold in international finance. In 1967, the IMF and its member nations agreed to use a **special drawing right (SDR)**—a form of "paper gold"—to add to the funds reserves. The SDR's are paper bookkeeping entries much like member bank deposits at the Federal Reserve System. They function as reserves only because the member nations of the IMF agree to use them as such to settle trade balances with one another.

■ Section Review

1. What are two major kinds of foreign exchange rates? How are they different?
2. Why did the United States go off the gold standard? What happened when it did so?
3. What is the role of the IMF in today's economy?

18.4 Trade Imbalances and the United States Economy

Since floating rates became the standard in late 1971, the Federal Reserve System has been keeping a statistic called the **trade-weighted value of the U.S. dollar.** This index shows the strength of the dollar against a group of foreign currencies. When the index falls, the dollar is "weak" in relation to other currencies. When the index rises, the dollar is "strong."

The figure on page 456 shows how the value of the trade-weighted dollar has changed from 1973 to 1986. When the dollar weakens as from 1973 to 1980, foreign goods become more expensive than American goods. As a result, exports rise, imports fall, and the balance of payments improves.

Yet, when the dollar gets stronger, as from 1981 to 1986, foreign goods become less expensive than American goods. As a result, exports fall, imports rise, and the balance of payments gets worse.

value of that country's currency on the foreign exchange markets. As a result, this causes a chain reaction that affects output and employment in that country's industries.

For example, the large deficit in the United States balance of payments since 1981 meant that the foreign exchange markets were flooded with dollars. An increase in the supply of dollars, as illustrated earlier in the graphs on page 453, means that the dollar will eventually lose some of its value on the foreign currency markets. When the dollar gets weaker, Americans have to pay more for imports, and foreigners pay less for American exports. Imports fall, exports rise, then unemployment in the import industries results. In time, the dollar will get strong again and the process reverses. This shifts demand from one industry to another, which causes changes in output and employment.

DANGERS OF A TRADE DEFICIT

Whenever a country has a large, long-lasting trade imbalance, it affects the

CORRECTING A TRADE DEFICIT

Under flexible exchange rates, trade deficits will automatically correct themselves

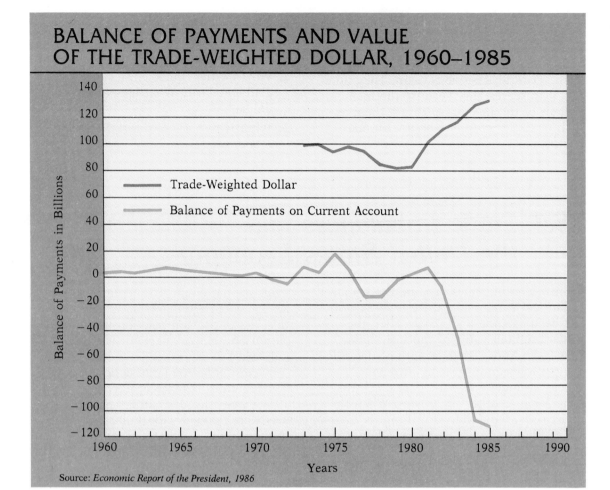

BALANCE OF PAYMENTS AND VALUE OF THE TRADE-WEIGHTED DOLLAR, 1960–1985

Source: *Economic Report of the President, 1986*

Figure 18–3

through the price system. A strong currency, for example, will probably lead to a deficit in the balance of payments. The bigger the deficit, and the longer it lasts, the more likely the value of the currency will fall. Because the length of time it takes for this to happen varies, improvement in trade balances cannot be predicted very accurately.

Sometimes trade imbalances can be improved with quotas, tariffs, or other means. But most economists believe that when legislators use these methods, threat-

ened industries only receive temporary relief. Past attempts to legislate trade flows have largely failed. As a result, many people believe that it is better for a country to adjust to change a little bit at a time, rather than all at once.

Deficits and surpluses in a country's balance of payments generally tend to be temporary. In 1978, for example, the dollar started to get weak and people worried about unemployment in the import industries. Then, in 1981, the dollar got strong again, which caused people to worry about unemployment in the export industries. Because deficits and surpluses in a country's balance of payments generally correct themselves, the United States and many other countries no longer design economic policies just to improve their balance of payments.

Section Review

1. What happened to the balance of payments in the United States in the mid-1980's?

2. What is the major danger of a trade deficit?

Chapter 18 Review

Summary

1. Goods or merchandise makes up most of the things traded between nations.

2. Differences in the cost of production from one country to another are a basis for international trade.

3. A country enjoys an absolute advantage when it is able to produce more of a given product than another country. It enjoys a comparative advantage when it is relatively more efficient in producing the product it produces best.

4. Trade has been restricted over the years through the use of tariffs, quotas, and other measures.

5. Five of the more commonly used arguments against free trade focus on national defense, infant industries, protecting domestic jobs, keeping money home, and helping the balance of payments.

6. Using trade barriers to protect domestic industries and jobs works only if other countries do not do the same in return.

7. The most favored nation clause allows a country to benefit from tariff reductions negotiated between the U.S. and other countries.

8. The foreign exchange rate describes the price of one country's currency in terms of another country's currency.

9. Fixed exchange rates were in use until 1971, at which time the United States went off the gold standard and the world monetary system went to flexible exchange rates.

10. Under flexible exchange rates, deficits in the balance of payments are self-correcting through changes in the foreign exchange rate.

11. The International Monetary Fund (IMF) uses gold and foreign currency to stabilize exchange rate fluctuations and special drawing rights (SDR's) to settle trade balances among its member nations.

12. Trade imbalances can cause problems when they shift demand between export and import industries.

Building an Economic Vocabulary

absolute advantage
comparative advantage
tariff
quota
protective tariff
revenue tariff
protectionists
free traders
infant industries
   argument
balance of payments

trade deficit
Smoot-Hawley Tariff
Reciprocal Trade
   Agreements Act
most favored nation clause
General Agreement on
   Tariffs and Trade (GATT)
Trade Expansion Act
foreign exchange
foreign exchange market

foreign exchange rate
fixed exchange rates
devaluation
floating exchange rates
flexible exchange rates
foreign exchange futures
International Monetary
   Fund (IMF)
special drawing right (SDR)
trade-weighted value of
   the U.S. dollar

Reviewing the Main Ideas

1. Why do nations trade?

2. What is the difference between absolute and comparative advantage?

3. What happens when nations specialize in the goods they are most efficient in producing?

4. What is the difference between a tariff and a quota?

5. What effect did the Smoot-Hawley Tariff have on international trade? What happened as a result of this?

6. How is international trade similar to trade between individuals? How is it different?

7. For what reasons did the world monetary system go to a system of flexible exchange rates?

8. How do deficits in the balance of payments automatically adjust under flexible exchange rates?

9. What are special drawing rights? How are they used?

Practicing Critical Thinking Skills

1. Many different industries claim they are vital to the country's defense. Which industries do you think qualify? Why?

2. It has been announced that the government has to generate additional revenue. To do this, it can raise taxes or increase tariff rates. Which do you as a consumer prefer? Give reasons to support your choice.

3. If you were a member of Congress approached by a delegation of autoworkers seeking additional tariff or quota protection, how would you respond? Defend your response.

4. Some people feel the United States should return to a system of fixed exchange rates. Defend or negate this view.

■ *Applying Economic Understandings*

Identifying Cause and Effect

To analyze economic behavior, economists must distinguish between cause and effect. The relationship between what happens and what makes it happen is known as the cause and effect relationship. The following guidelines will help develop the skill of identifying these relationships in written material.

1. Look for "clue words," certain words and phrases signifying the presence of a cause and effect relationship. Among these are *according to, because, as a result of, since, therefore*, and *if . . . then*. (For example: An increase in the price of foreign automobiles—cause—*results* in an increase in demand for American-made automobiles—effect.)

2. If no clue words are present, look for the word "and" or a comma in the sentence. These sometimes express cause and effect. (For example: The value of the trade-weighted dollar increased in 1981 *and* the U.S. balance of payments worsened.)

3. Cause and effect does not always appear in the same sentence. To determine if more than one sentence is involved in stating a cause or effect, turn one of the statements into a question by asking "why." (For example: Country *A's* currency is weak. Country *A's* imports fall and its exports rise. Reworded into a question, the relationship becomes clearer: *Why* does Country *A's* imports fall?—effect—Because Country *A's* currency is weak.—cause)

Using these guidelines, find at least six examples of cause and effect relationships stated in this chapter. In each case, identify the cause and effect, and explain what alerted you to the relationship.

Comparative Economic Systems

Many people consider the things government does for them to be social progress—but they consider the things government does for others as socialism.

Earl Warren

Chapter 19

After reading this chapter, you will be able to:

- Identify the major characteristics of capitalism, socialism, and communism.

- Discuss the economic theories of Karl Marx and their relevance today.

- Trace the history of the Soviet economy from 1917 to the present.

- Compare the economies of the Comecon countries of Eastern Europe.

- Describe the economic development of the People's Republic of China from 1949 to the present.

- Evaluate the benefits and costs of the Swedish welfare state.

- Explain the reasons for Japan's economic success.

19.1 *Spectrum of Economic Systems*

To deal with the problem of scarcity, a society can organize itself along economic lines as a traditional, market, or command economy. At the same time, it also can be organized along political lines as a monarchy, democracy, socialist state, or communist state.

COMMUNISM, SOCIALISM, AND CAPITALISM

Under pure **communism**, there is no such thing as private property. All economic goods, including factories and other means of production, are owned by society as a whole. Each person works and consumes according to his or her own abilities and needs. Goods and services have no prices, and there is no need for wages, rents, interests, or profits. There are no social classes with workers, managers, or other groups to set people apart from one another. As a result, there is no need for a central government authority.

To date, no country has achieved pure communism although Communist countries today depend extensively on government to direct economic decisions. For this reason, they are prime examples of command-type economies.

Under **socialism,** the government owns or controls some of the means of production. It also determines the distribution of some of the output. At the same time, however, there is some private ownership of goods and services. The government generally is responsible for providing such social services as free education, health care, and welfare.

Under capitalism, which generally is the economic system in a democracy, the means of production are privately owned. Wages, prices, and production are determined by the free response of people to the needs of the market. The government owns and runs only those services private enterprise cannot provide. In this market economy, the profit motive is the driving force. Decisions about WHAT to produce, HOW to produce, and FOR WHOM to produce are left to the private sector.

THE SPECTRUM

As shown in the illustration on page 463, the three types of economic systems can

Figure 19–1

CHARACTERISTICS OF THE THREE MAJOR ECONOMIC SYSTEMS

	CAPITALISM	SOCIALISM	COMMUNISM
OWNERSHIP OF RESOURCES	Productive resources are privately owned and operated.	Basic productive resources are government owned and operated; the rest are privately owned and operated.	All productive resources are government owned and operated.
ALLOCATION OF RESOURCES	Capital for production is obtained through the lure of profits in the market.	Government plans ways to allocate resources in key industries.	Government plans ways to allocate all resources.
ROLE OF GOVERNMENT IN ECONOMIC PLANNING	Government plays a limited role in the economy.	Government directs the completion of its economic plans in key industries.	Government draws up detailed orders to implement its economic plans.

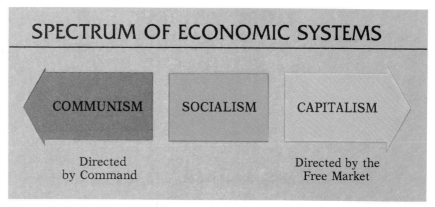

Figure 19–2

be represented in the form of a spectrum. At the far left is communism, in which a strong central government influences almost every economic decision made. In the middle is socialism, in which government owns the basic means of production and helps allocate output. At the far right is capitalism, in which government has a very limited role.

As one moves from left to right along the spectrum, the role of planning by the central government becomes less important. Under communism, there is almost total central government planning. Under socialism, only some is needed. Under capitalism, very little is needed. There is no fine line of distinction among communism, socialism, and capitalism. They appear on the spectrum as having a greater or lesser degree of direction by command and the free market. Except for the traditional economy, there is some overlap between classifications of economic societies and the political categories of communism, socialism, and democracy.

Section Review

1. What are the major characteristics of communism? Socialism? Capitalism?
2. What determines how communism, socialism, and capitalism appear on the spectrum?

19.2 Marxism

Most people today think of the nineteenth-century economic historian Karl Marx as the creator of Communist dogma. But the economist views him in a different light—as the major critic of capitalism.

Much of Marx's work was devoted to an analysis of the capitalistic system and what he saw as its failures and contradictions. **Marxists,** people who believe in Karl Marx's theories, still argue that capitalism is the cause of unemployment, inflation, and business cycles in the Free World.

THEORIES OF KARL MARX

Marx divided people into two groups. One was the **proletariat**—all people who must

Lenin, Engels, and Marx are honored at a May Day parade in Moscow. According to Marx, how would the workers take control?

work for a living because they have no means of production of their own. The other was the **capitalists,** or **bourgeoisie**— all people who own land and capital and hire labor.

Marx saw the relationship between these two groups as the most important feature of capitalism. He believed the value of any item was equal to the value of the labor used to produce it. For this reason, he felt labor should be paid the full value of the goods and services it produced. Since the wage rate paid at the time was less than the full value of the product, Marx argued that labor was exploited in a capitalist society.

Marx gave the name **surplus value** to the difference between the wage paid and the worker's output. He believed this difference became the capitalist's profit, which he felt was wrong. He thought surplus

value should go to the workers, something that never would happen under capitalism. Instead, business firms would accumulate the extra surplus value and invest it for more output.

Since workers were not being paid the full value of their labor, in time their purchasing power would fall behind production. Soon there would be a large amount of unsold goods on the market. Then production would be cut back and prices would fall. More people would be out of work and there would be less profit. Economic growth would come to a halt, and there would be a recession. Later, after the stock of unsold commodities had been disposed of, prices would rise. Profits would grow once more, and the whole cycle would begin again.

In Marx's view, this process gave rise to the recurring cycles of prosperity and depression he saw as capitalism's greatest defect. He believed that with each recurring cycle, more money and power would fall into the hands of the capitalists. At the same time, the working class would suffer more and become poorer and more the slaves of the capitalists.

In time, the working class and the capitalists would grow hostile toward one another. The workers would unite and rise up in a violent revolution to take control from the capitalists. Once workers had control, they would begin to build a classless society in which people as a whole owned everything. Everyone would work their hardest in a trade or profession, consuming only what was necessary for basic needs. There would be no crime or poverty.

At first, the proletariat would have to depend on its political power through a strong government. But once everyone became equal, no one class would have power over another. Government no longer would be needed and could be done away with completely.

Profile

Karl Marx

Karl Marx was an economic historian who earned his doctorate in philosophy and history from the University of Berlin in Germany. Because of his radical views, however, he could not get a teaching position. His writings were critical of events in Prussia and were suppressed there. This led him to wander from Cologne to Paris to Brussels to London during the 1840's.

Although Marx wrote a great many pamphlets and books, he is best known for *The Communist*

1818–1883

Manifesto (1848) and *Das Kapital,* the first volume of which was published in 1867. In these works, he argues that all history has been a class struggle. When primitive tribalism could not provide an adequate standard of living for the people, the economic relationship of slavery developed. With it came class struggle. Because slavery held the seeds of its own destruction, it evolved into feudalism, which, in turn, evolved into capitalism. In each case, one class was pitted against another: master against slave, lord against serf, capitalist against worker. In each case, it was the haves against the have-nots.

With capitalism, the means of production were available for a high standard of living, and the stage was set for the final conflict. Once the capitalists had been relieved of control over the means of production, socialism—and then communism—would evolve. Society would have come full circle. Private property no longer would matter, and everyone would have a high standard of living.

Marx believed that the value of any product was equal to the amount of labor needed to produce it. He divided the workday into two parts. In one, the worker earned his or her subsistence wage. In the other, what the worker earned went to the capitalist. This amounted to exploitation and was the reason why workers would revolt in time. Marx felt the only thing the workers had to lose by revolting was the chains that secured them to their work stations. As a result, Marx's ideas have had a profound impact all over the world.

Conditions in this Soviet rug factory are very different from those of Marx's time. What five measures did Marx suggest that would change the social order?

Since Marx knew it would be some time before the workers revolted against the system, he suggested five measures to bring change to the social order in the meantime. One was to do away entirely with the concept of private property. The second was to impose heavy progressive income taxes. The third was to do away with the right to inheritance. The fourth was to limit production to government-owned enterprises. The last was to give all children free education in public schools.

MARXISM IN PERSPECTIVE

At the time Marx was writing his theories, it was true that many workers were being exploited. In Europe, their extreme poverty contrasted sharply with the luxury enjoyed by landowners and industrialists. Capitalism was in its early stages and was to develop in a way many did not foresee.

Modern capitalism, however, is very different from that which Marx knew in the 1800's. For example, Marx believed that under capitalism, there were only two classes. People belonged to one class or the other and could not cross the line between the two. But in the United States today, members of the working class often save part of their incomes, invest what they have saved, and become capitalists.

Marx also believed that only capitalists could benefit from additional capital. But today, for example, a worker with a bulldozer is more productive than one with only a shovel and, as a result, receives higher wages.

Marx overlooked another important fact, too. A society does not have to be classless to keep one group from gaining control over another. A democratic government can place restraints on any group trying to seek an advantage that goes against the public interest. Because of this, no one group is likely to treat others unjustly.

Marx also was wrong about surplus value. A product has value not because there is labor embodied in it, but because it has utility. It is true that labor receives a wage because it is productive. Labor, however, is only one of the three factors of production—all three of which have a valid claim to a reward for producing useful products. There is, then, no such thing as surplus value to which labor alone has a right.

Many Marxists, however, are quick to point out that even today there are extremes of wealth and poverty under capitalism. This, they say, proves Marx was right when he said capitalist countries would not be able to find a permanent cure for recessions and periods of unemployment. They also feel that the fact that big business keeps growing proves that capitalists still are using surplus value to build their empires.

What the Marxists ignore, however, is that much has been done under capitalism to help the working class. Social legislation, the labor movement, and the change in business' and society's general attitude toward workers all have helped to bring about many changes for the better.

Unlike Marxists, socialists accept only some of Marx's theories and modify others. Some do not believe in the collective ownership of all industry and are not willing to give up the concept of private property completely. Most do not believe that a violent revolution is the best way to implement change. They feel that because there are more proletarians than capitalists, change can be brought about slowly through a democratic voting process.

Even countries that have nearly done away with private property do not practice pure communism, as none have done away completely with government. The most any have done is to substitute government for private capitalists.

All countries have some degree of government control. In the United States, certain functions are subject to government command. In Sweden and Great Britain, the government owns and operates certain key industries, plans part of the economy's operations, and sees that economic plans are put into practice. In the Soviet Union, government owns and controls almost all industries.

■ Section Review

1. How do most people view Karl Marx? How do economists view him?

2. Into what two classes did Marx divide society? What are the characteristics of each?

3. Why did Marx feel labor should be paid the full value of what it produced? What did he think would happen because it was not?

4. In what ways is present-day capitalism different from that which Marx knew in the 1880's?

19.3 Soviet Union

The growth of the Soviet economy shows that a command-type system can change very fast and go quite far in a short period of time. In 1917, for example, there was very little industry in Russia. Almost 90 percent of the people lived and worked on farms. Most of the good farm land, however, was owned by the nobility, who were few in number. There was a definite class distinction between the peasant farmers who worked the land and the nobles and gentry who owned it.

Since that time, the development of the Soviet economy has been dramatic. By 1985, its real GNP was about 52 percent of that of the United States. Because of the size of the Soviet population, however, real GNP on a per capita basis was only 45 percent of that of the United States.

ECONOMY UNDER LENIN AND STALIN

In 1917, a revolutionary named Vladimir Ilyich Ulyanov, or Lenin, overthrew the government of Russia. In its place, he set up a Communist government. Lenin, who was a strong believer in the theories of Karl Marx, took the large estates away from the rich, divided up the land, and gave it to the peasants. He did away with private property and turned the country's few factories over to the workers.

The workers, however, could not manage the factories. Before long, production fell and the economy began to break down. People lost faith in the money supply, and a system of barter emerged. The government sent armed forces to the farms to confiscate surplus food for the hungry city dwellers and industrial workers. The angry farmers retaliated by cutting back on their crops so there would be no surplus. The government then tried to solve the problem by assigning workers to the jobs it wanted done. Those who did not obey went to prison. As agricultural and industrial production fell sharply, internal strife spread throughout the country.

By 1921, when the situation was at its worst, Lenin decided to bring back some capitalist methods. He used an approach called the **New Economic Policy (NEP).** Now peasants could lease land and hire labor, and small, privately owned businesses could operate.

The NEP was supposed to be only a short-term measure. It was to be used only to bring productivity to the point where the government could **collectivize**—force common ownership of all agricultural, industrial, and trading enterprises. Once this happened, capitalism would be done away with and central planning put into force.

By the time the NEP came to an end in 1927, many changes had taken place. Russia had become the Soviet Union and was completely under the control of the Communists. Lenin had died, and the new leader, Joseph Stalin, wanted to change the Soviet Union from an agricultural to an industrial nation.

Under Stalin's leadership, government ownership and strong central planning were begun. In 1928, the government introduced the first **Five-Year Plan**—a comprehensive program of economic planning. It was designed to drive the economy to its limit to achieve the greatest growth rate. The government's goals were to industrialize rapidly and to collectivize farming. To do this, each sector of the economy was given a quota to fill. By 1933, industry was to increase its output 250 percent and agriculture its output 150 percent.

The government had some success with industrial growth, but it did not help the consumer. Workers were kept too busy building new factories and equipment to produce very many of the goods the people wanted and needed. Then, too, industry grew so fast that many new factories stood idle. New workers could not be trained quickly enough, and much of the usable factory equipment was ruined by unskilled labor. Industry, however, still fared better than agriculture, which suffered similar problems.

3. What is the role of the government in the Soviet economy today?

4. What three major problems must Soviet leaders resolve?

19.4 The Comecon Countries of Eastern Europe

Six other countries in Eastern Europe have Communist governments and centrally controlled economic systems. They are the **Comecon,** or Council for Mutual Economic Assistance, countries of East Germany, Poland, Czechoslovakia, Hungary, Romania, and Bulgaria. These countries are in the Soviet sphere of influence and have close ties to Moscow.

East Germany is the most successful Comecon country as shown in the chart below. Its real GNP per capita growth—3.0 percent—is higher than that of the Soviet Union—2.7 percent—and the United States—2.5 percent. Its real per capita GNP is higher than that of the Soviet Union—$7395—but lower than that of the United States—$16,716. Much of East Germany's

Table 19–A

REAL GNP PER CAPITA, 1960-1985

COUNTRY	REAL GNP PER CAPITA GROWTH 1960–1985	REAL PER CAPITA GNP, 1985
U.S.S.R.	2.7%	$7395
COMECON		
East Germany	3.0%	$10,443
Czechoslovakia	2.2%	$8748
Hungary	2.6%	$7557
Poland	2.4%	$6468
Bulgaria	3.3%	$6422
Romania	3.8%	$5449
United States	2.5%	$16,716

Source: *Handbook of Economic Statistics,1986*, Central Intelligence Agency

success is because of the drive and initiative of the people. Not only have they been able to adapt central planning to fit their own needs, but they also have speeded up the planning process through the use of computers.

Czechoslovakia and Hungary each have higher real GNP's per capita than the Soviet Union, but their growth rates are lower. Both countries are fairly small and have large agricultural sectors. In the past few years, both have stressed light industry, consumer goods, and high-technology products. Both also have been letting some free-market forces of supply and demand mix with centralized control.

Bulgaria and Poland have lower per capita GNPs than Czechoslovakia and Hungary. Although their economies are largely controlled by centralized planning, Poland is beginning to allow some free enterprise in farming. In the 1980's, Poland's economic statistics have been affected by strikes and shortages caused by the clash between the workers and the Communist government. Workers even formed a union called **Solidarity** that wanted, among other things, workers to have more say in the operation of factories.

Romania is the least successful of the Comecon countries, with the lowest per capita GNP. Its economy is tightly controlled, and there are constant shortages. As a result, many goods trade on the **black market**—a market where goods are sold illegally. In this market, eggs often cost 40¢ each and jeans as much as $180.

Section Review

1. What countries make up the Comecon countries in Eastern Europe?

2. How do the Comecon economies differ from that of the Soviet Union?

19.5 People's Republic of China

Mainland China, known as the People's Republic of China, also has had a Communist economy since 1949. That year, the Chinese Communists, under the leadership of Mao Zedong, gained control of the country.

Until that time, most of the people were poor peasants, many of whom worked the land. Most of the wealth was owned by a small percentage of the population. The Communists gained the peasants' loyalty by taking the land away from the rich and distributing it among the poor.

The new government modeled the economy on that of the Soviets and in 1953 introduced its first Five-Year Plan. In hopes of industrializing rapidly like the Soviets, the Chinese plan emphasized the development of heavy industry.

In 1958, the **Great Leap Forward**—the Second Five-Year Plan—tried to institute a system of pure communism and an industrial and agricultural revolution almost overnight. The rate of industrialization was intensified by trying to increase the capital stock at a rate of nearly 44 percent a year. At the same time, collectivization of agriculture was intensified. Farmers were forced off their land and made to live and work on large, state-owned farms. In the end, however, the Great Leap Forward turned out to be a disaster. The agricultural experiment failed, and the economy never came close to achieving the planned degree of industrialization. In addition, the gains made during the first Five-Year Plan were lost.

Three more Five-Year Plans followed. The first, begun in 1965, soon was overshadowed by a political upheaval called the Cultural Revolution. The other two also fell prey to political problems. Industry and agriculture showed little progress. Industry suffered because the political struggles had led to the removal of many capable factory managers and technicians. Agriculture suffered because collectivization did not work.

In the late 1970's, the government decided that the country no longer could follow the growth models of either the Soviet Union or the capitalist countries. Both China and its population were too large, and the communications systems too underdeveloped for large-scale centralized planning. It would be almost impossible to industrialize the cities enough to provide jobs for what amounted to nearly one-quarter of the world's population. As a result, the Chinese then tried to develop industries that were **labor-intensive.** In such industries, there is a high labor-to-capital ratio during production.

More recently, the Chinese have begun to experiment with capitalism. Some private businesses are allowed and managers of state-owned enterprises have more authority to make decisions. Although the central planners still set the over-all production goals, managers can sell their products at competitive prices and hire and fire workers. In addition, small incentives are offered to workers and managers to promote productivity.

Even the People's Bank of China plays a part in the effort to make industries more competitive. Before 1979, the Bank and its 6000 branches gave money to businesses strictly according to what was laid out in the Five-Year Plan. As long as the companies using the money acted in accordance with the plan, they did not have to pay back the money. Today, however, the Bank not only expects to be repaid, but also demands that the companies prove that the funds are needed.

The standard of living in the People's Republic still is not high when measured by Western standards. In 1985, for example, the per capita GNP was still less than $330. Even so, progress has been made in the areas of poverty and health services for the very poor. At present, the government is focusing on the major problem of population growth. Since the mid-1970's, the population has grown at a rate of 1.5

China has been working hard to modernize and increase factory output. What was the outcome of the Great Leap Forward?

percent. If it keeps growing at that rate, it will double in less than 47 years. To help solve the problem, the government is stressing family planning and offering economic incentives to those who have smaller families.

Section Review

1. What was mainland China like before 1949?

2. How did the communist government change the economy?

3. What effect did the Great Leap Forward have on the Chinese economy?

4. Why did the Chinese government change its economic tactics in the late 1970's?

5. What is one of China's major problems today?

19.6 *Sweden*

Unlike the Soviet Union, the Comecon countries, and the People's Republic of China, Sweden is a socialist state. Private enterprise exists, but the government also owns some of the means of production, including the steel mills and iron mines. In addition, it plays a major role in human services by providing free health care, education, welfare, and retirement.

Many of these benefits were instituted during the 44-year-rule of the Socialist party. During this time, wages were high, jobs were easy to find, and unemployment was in the 1-to-3 percent range. The Swedish economy, in fact, was for years thought to be the model of European socialism.

Today, Sweden is more like a welfare state. Parents receive generous maternity-care benefits, and education is free from grade school through college. Workers who are ill and cannot work are eligible for up to 90 percent of the income they would have earned at their jobs. Nearly one fourth of the population is eligible for some form of government old-age or disability pension. Recently, however, Sweden has run into some problems because of the cost of financing all of its welfare programs. The government depends heavily on tax money to pay for the programs. Because of this, tax rates are high. In 1985, for example, tax receipts were around 50 percent of GNP, almost double that of the United States. In some cases, additional income earned by Swedish citizens is taxed at an 80 percent rate. Or, a person who earns an additional $100 would keep only $20. The other $80 would go to the government for taxes.

Many Swedes object to the heavy tax burden and have come up with ways to avoid paying taxes. Some have done this by resorting to barter. A carpenter, for example, who builds some cabinets for an auto mechanic, may be "paid" not with money but with repair work on the family car. Others, like former tennis star Bjorn Borg, reside outside Sweden.

To make up for the high tax rates, Swedish workers must earn high wages. This makes Swedish goods expensive and, therefore, harder to export. All of this has contributed to a low rate of economic growth. From 1973 to 1983, for example, real per capita GNP, the standard of comparison for international growth rates, amounted to nearly 0.8 percent annually or about two-thirds that of the United States.

Even the unemployment rate is not as low as it seems. Unlike the United States, most European countries do not conduct surveys to find people who, by definition, are unemployed. Instead, a person is counted as unemployed only when he or she appears at the welfare office to collect unemployment pay. And when a factory needs more money to operate, it turns to the government to get another subsidy. So most workers, rather than being laid off, merely are reassigned to other jobs. As a result, the unemployment rate appears unrealistically low.

In the 1970's, the problem of inflation was added to the heavy tax burden and a growing federal deficit. Growing discontent with conditions finally led to the fall from power of the Socialist party in 1976.

Since then, there has been a growing revolt against socialism. Even with the high tax rate, taxes alone cannot cover the full cost of the welfare system. As welfare demands continue to grow, so does the government deficit. As a result, Sweden now has one of the highest ratios of national debt to GNP of any developed country. The burden of the debt is such that the economic growth has been reduced.

Although some Swedish people say they want a change, the government has found it hard to actually cut benefits. As a result, one of the major problems facing the Swedish economy in the years ahead is

Sweden offers its citizens a large variety of benefits. All cost a great deal. How does this affect the tax rate?

that of finding ways to either finance or control social welfare spending.

Section Review

1. What kind of economy does Sweden have?
2. Why is Sweden's unemployment rate deceptively low?
3. What is one major problem facing the Swedish economy in the future?

19.7 Japan

Japan is still a different case. Like the United States, it has a capitalist economy. Unlike the United States, however, its government is very much involved in the day-to-day activities of the private sector.

At the end of World War II, Japan was a broken country. Today, it is the third largest industrial nation in the world. Between 1950 and 1986, its per capita GNP grew by nearly 9 percent—nearly double that of any other advanced industrial nation. During that same period of time, the income of the average Japanese family nearly doubled every eight years.

One of the reasons for Japan's success is the workers' intense loyalty to their employer. Most workers join a company for life. In return, the company supplies such benefits as churches where marriage services can be performed, schools, and vacation resorts.

Another reason for the success is that Japanese workers take great pride in the quality of their work. The entire work force of a company often comes in early to prepare for the day's work by taking part in group calisthenics and meditation exercises. On the job, they often sing company songs to boost their spirits. If a worker is behind in a task, those able to help him or her get caught up will do so. Those who cannot help stay at their stations and clean their work areas, arrange their tools, or do whatever else they can to prepare for the next day. No one leaves the work

floor or goes home until every individual worker's tasks have been completed.

Another reason for the success is the ability and willingness of the Japanese to develop new technology. Because of their relatively small population, they have worked to boost productivity by developing industries that are **capital-intensive.** In such industries, a large amount of capital is used for every person employed in manufacturing. Today, the Japanese are recognized as the world leader in the area of industrial robots. As a result, most factories require only a small fraction of the workers needed by similar factories in other countries.

Japan has a relatively small public sector. The government has only a modest military capability and is not burdened with welfare spending. As a result of this, taxes are low, which allows individuals to save their money or spend it on consumer goods.

Although the Japanese have been successful, they have come under a great deal

Japan's great economic success is due in great part to its workers' loyalty and pride in their products. What other factors have contributed to Japanese success in recent years?

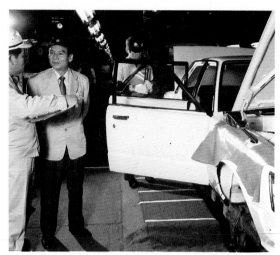

of criticism in the last few years because their economy generally is closed to the products of foreign producers. Foreign companies must have the government's permission to distribute their products in the country.

Delays in getting permission have discouraged some companies from doing business at all. At times, companies have found that while they were waiting for permission, products similar to theirs were introduced and sold by Japanese companies. Actions such as these have led many countries to accuse Japan of being discriminatory toward foreign-made products. Although the Japanese have promised to open the economy more, there has been little change.

There is, however, some question, as to whether Japan really benefits from this policy. Because few goods are supplied by foreign competitors, products generally are high-priced. Color television sets, for example, sold for 25-to-30 percent less in the United States than in Japan for years. While hard on the Japanese consumer, the practice of keeping prices high at home and selling cheaply in other countries makes it easier for foreigners to obtain high-quality goods at low prices.

If Japan wants to continue to grow, it must actively engage in international trade. As an island nation with few natural resources upon which it can depend, it must import most of its oil as well as a number of other critical materials. As a result, the Japanese are expected to aggressively develop their export markets so that they can buy more imports.

Section Review

1. What is Japan's economy like today?
2. Why have the Japanese people been so successful in their efforts to achieve economic growth?
3. Why have the Japanese come under criticism from some foreign companies?

Chapter 19 Review

Summary

1. Communism, socialism, and capitalism appear on the economic spectrum as having a greater or lesser degree of direction by command and the free market.

2. Karl Marx classified people as either proletarians or capitalists. According to Marx, the proletarians in time would defeat the capitalists and build their own classless society. Then government would not be necessary.

3. No country today practices pure communism.

4. In 1917, Lenin set up a Communist government in Russia and turned over the lands of the wealthy people to the peasants and factories to workers.

5. In 1921 Lenin introduced the New Economic Policy (NEP), a partial return to capitalism.

6. Joseph Stalin wanted to change the Soviet Union from an agricultural to an industrial country. He initiated Five-Year Plans designed to achieve growth through government ownership of agriculture and industry coupled with strong central planning.

7. In the Soviet Union today, the Communist party decides economic policy, does the actual planning, and watches over and puts into practice economic plans.

8. Worker motivation, the production of consumer goods, and the intricacies of central planning are three major problems facing Soviet leaders today.

9. The six Comecon countries of Eastern Europe have close ties with the Soviet Union but still include varying degrees of socialism and capitalism in their economies.

10. The People's Republic of China, which has had a Communist command-type economy since 1949, has made progress in the areas of poverty and health services. Recently, it has experimented with capitalism.

11. Sweden is a socialist state in which there is both private enterprise and government ownership of some means of production.

12. Japan, the third-largest industrial nation in the world, has a capitalist economy in which the government plays a protective role.

■ Building an Economic Vocabulary

communism	New Economic Policy (NEP)	Comecon
socialism	collectivize	Solidarity
Marxists	Five-Year Plan	black market
proletariat	state farms	Great Leap
capitalists	collective farms	Forward
bourgeoisie	piecework	labor-intensive
surplus value	storming	capital-intensive

■ Reviewing the Main Ideas

1. What is the role of government under communism? Under socialism? Under capitalism?

2. What are at least three of Karl Marx's ideas about capitalism?

3. What do modern Marxists ignore about capitalism today?

4. Who was Lenin? Why did he institute the NEP?

5. What was Joseph Stalin's goal for the Soviet economy?

6. How does central planning today affect Soviet factories? Soviet workers? Farmers?

7. Which Comecon countries are most successful? Least successful?

8. What economic reforms did the Chinese government adopt in the late 1970's?

9. Why is the tax rate high in Sweden?

10. How do the Japanese government's efforts to keep the economy closed affect the Japanese consumer?

◼ Practicing Critical Thinking Skills

1. The chart on page 462 notes the key features of communism, socialism, and capitalism. What advantages and disadvantages do you see in each?

2. If you were given the chance to refute Karl Marx's ideas, what arguments would you offer?

3. Do you think Five-Year Plans could work in the United States? Why or why not?

4. Why do you think worker motivation and the number, kinds, and quality of consumer goods are problems for Communist central planners? What would you propose to solve them?

5. In which of these economies do you think it would be easier to live—that of Sweden or that of Japan? Explain your answer.

◼ Applying Economic Understandings

Making Generalizations

Economists often make generalizations based on the information they find when examining information or statistics. Generalizations are broad, general conclusions drawn from a number of facts or supporting statements. In most instances, the guidelines used in the following example will help you to arrive at a generalization.

1. Read the facts or supporting statements.
   a. Under capitalism, productive resources are privately owned and operated.
   b. Under socialism, basic productive resources are government owned and operated.
   c. Under communism, all productive resources are government owned and operated.

2. Look for similarities in the facts or supporting statements. (Each statement refers to a type of economic system and uses the words "productive resources" and the phrase "owned and operated.")

3. Look for differences in the facts or supporting statements. (The owner and operator of the productive resources is different in each statement.)

4. Based on the content of each fact or supporting statement, write a logical conclusion incorporating both the similarities and differences. This is the generalization. (The ownership of productive resources varies under different economic systems.)

Using these guidelines, make a generalization based on the statements found in Figure 19-1 on page 462.

Developing Countries

*Sometimes we only eat root crops, vegetables, rats, frogs, and other wild animals.
. . . And sometimes our children only chew sugarcane to feed their hunger . . . all
the time they are chewing sugarcane.*

An advertisement from National Public Radio

Chapter 20

After reading this chapter, you will be able to:

- Discuss the reasons why the developed countries of the world are interested in the economic progress of the less-developed countries.

- Explain the conditions encountered by a country at each of the five stages of development.

- Discuss the advantages and disadvantages of three ways of financing economic development.

- Identify seven major obstacles to economic development and growth.

- Describe South Korea's economic success.

20.1 The Less-Developed Countries

Many people in the world today are concerned about the economic condition of **less-developed countries (LDC's)**—countries whose average per capita GNP is a fraction of that in more industrialized countries. Many of these countries are members of the **Third World**—developing countries of Africa, Asia, and Latin America generally not allied with any superpower.

DEVELOPING NATIONS

Today, over 30 countries in the world have a per capita GNP of less than $400

and nearly half of the world's population lives in these countries. The map on page 486 shows the contrast between the developed and the less developed nations. On the map, each country is scaled to show the size of its GNP relative to other countries. Thus, the United States, which has the largest GNP in the world, is the largest area on the map. Countries with smaller GNPs are scaled accordingly.

The map also is color coded to show countries with similar per capita GNPs. When viewed this way, the contrast is clearly shown between the developed economies of North America, Western Europe, and Japan, and the less developed countries of the Caribbean, South America, Africa, and Asia. Thus, the gap between developed and less developed countries is enormous. In the past few years, it has become even larger because many developing countries have had negative rates of growth.

Another reason for the growing gap between developed and less developed countries is the small size of the output for many countries. When Guyana grew 5.8 percent in 1983-84, only $20 was added to its real per capita GNP. In comparison, a one percent growth in the United States for the same year would have added $141 to the real per capita GNP; a 5.8 percent growth would have added $532.

Nonetheless, the less developed countries still face many of the same economic problems as the more developed countries. They still have to deal with the problem of scarcity. This means they must decide WHAT to produce, HOW to produce, and FOR WHOM to produce. They also must deal with the concepts of supply and demand, savings and investment, resource adequacy, productivity, and incentives to produce. The LDC's, then, are very much like other economies of the world. The major difference is that their problems are very much greater.

INTEREST IN DEVELOPING COUNTRIES

The more developed countries of the world have a very real interest in the future of developing countries. There are three major reasons for this. The first is humanitarian. Like many individuals, the wealthier countries of the world often feel it is their moral responsibility to help those who have less than they do. Many

Figure 20–1

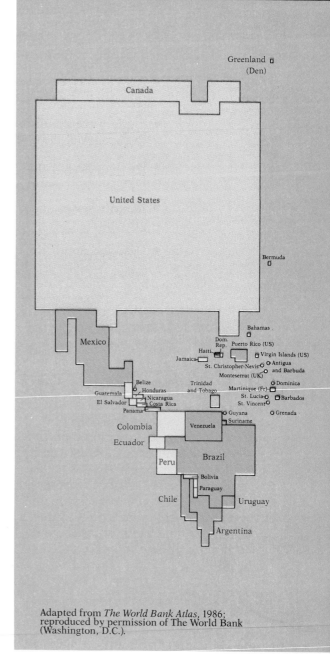

GROSS NATIONAL PRODUCT PER CAPITA, 1983

Adapted from *The World Bank Atlas*, 1986; reproduced by permission of The World Bank (Washington, D.C.).

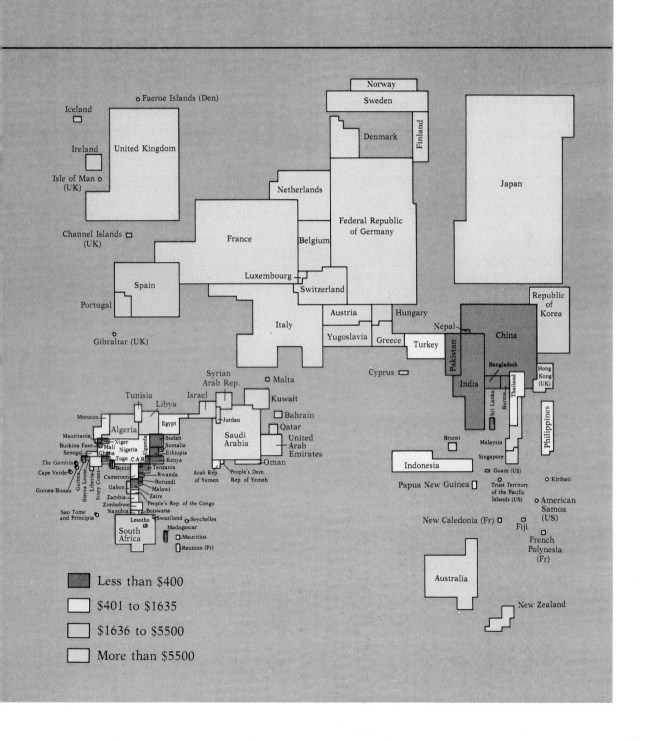

Iceland

Faeroe Islands (Den)

Ireland

United Kingdom

Isle of Man
(UK)

Channel Islands
(UK)

Norway

Sweden

Denmark

Finland

Japan

Netherlands

France

Belgium

Federal Republic
of Germany

Spain

Portugal

Luxembourg

Switzerland

Republic
of
Korea

Austria

Hungary

China

Italy

Gibraltar (UK)

Yugoslavia

Greece

Turkey

Nepal

Pakistan

Bangladesh

Hong
Kong
(UK)

India

Cyprus

Tunisia

Libya

Syrian
Arab Rep.

Israel

Malta

Kuwait

Sri Lanka

Burma

Thailand

Philippines

Morocco

Egypt

Jordan

Bahrain

Algeria

Sudan

Saudi
Arabia

Qatar

Mauritania

Niger

Somalia

United
Arab
Emirates

Brunei

Malaysia

Burkina Faso
Senegal

Mali
Ghana

Nigeria

Ethiopia

Oman

Singapore

The Gambia

Togo

C.A.R.

Kenya

Indonesia

Guam (US)

Cape Verde

Benin

Tanzania

Guinea

Sierra Leone

Liberia

Ivory Coast

Uganda

Rwanda

Burundi

Arab Rep.
of Yemen

People's Dem.
Rep. of Yemeh

Papua New Guinea

Kiribati

Trust Territory
of the Pacific
Islands (US)

Guinea-Bissau

Cameroon

Malawi

American
Samoa
(US)

Gabon

Zaire

Sao Tome
and Principia

Zambia

Zimbabwe

Namibia

People's Rep. of the Congo

Botswana

New Caledonia (Fr)

Fiji

Lesotho

Swaziland

Seychelles

French
Polynesia
(Fr)

South
Africa

Madagascar

Mauritius

Reunion (Fr)

Australia

New Zealand

Less than $400

$401 to $1635

$1636 to $5500

More than $5500

people in developing countries starve to death for lack of food or die of diseases related to inadequate diets. Under such conditions, it is hard for any country enjoying abundance to sit by without offering help.

The second reason is economic. Assistance to developing countries helps assure the wealthier industrial countries of a stable supply of certain vital raw materials. It also may provide them with important new markets for their products. Today, for example, the developing countries buy about one-third of America's exports. This is more than the combined purchases of the Common Market, Japan, and Australia. In the long run, then, international trade and all its benefits are increased by helping developing countries.

The third reason is political. Communist and non-Communist countries wage a continuing struggle for the allegiance of developing countries. Both the Communist Bloc and the Free World believe that the side that does the most will gain more allies and, as a result, greater political strength.

There always has been a gap between developed and developing countries, but never has it been so obvious or important as it is today. The growing difference in incomes has led to greater unrest and social disorder in different parts of the world. Many people in developing countries want some of the abundance enjoyed in developed countries. When these people do not achieve what they want as fast as they would like, the result can be revolution, social upheaval, and even war.

Section Review

1. With what problems do LDC's have to deal?
2. Why are the more developed countries interested in helping LDC's?
3. Why is the gap between developed and developing countries more important than ever before?

20.2 Stages of Economic Development

Some economists agree with the view that developing countries pass through several stages of economic development. These, however, actually are not fixed, definite stages of development. Instead, they are categories that describe the amount of economic growth that has taken place.

A country does not always go from one stage to the next in a logical manner. It may skip one stage altogether, or it may be in more than one stage at the same time. Stages overlap, and the boundaries between them are not always clear-cut. Even so, it is easier to think about the problems of developing countries when economic development is discussed in stages.

PRIMITIVE EQUILIBRIUM

The first and least developed stage of development is **primitive equilibrium.** It is the beginning point on the road to economic development. It is primitive only in the sense that the society has no formal economic organization. An example might be the way the polar eskimo of the last century shared the spoils of the hunt with other families in the village.

Indonesia is one Asian nation that has shown economic development over the years. These oil fields are an example of that development. To what does the term "stages of economic development" refer?

A people—or country—in primitive equilibrium may have no monetary system and may not be economically motivated. There is no real capital investment. Everything is done because of a strong sense of tradition. There is equilibrium in that nothing changes. Rules are handed down from one generation to the next, and economic decision making is directed by culture and tradition.

BREAKING WITH PRIMITIVE EQUILIBRIUM

The second stage of economic development is one of transition. It consists of a break with primitive equilibrium and a move toward real economic and cultural change. The break may be brief and sudden, or it may take many years. It generally is brought on by outside forces that show the people a different—and at times better—way of life. Missionaries and tourists, as well as war, travel, and business ventures with other countries, all show people different ways of life and of doing things.

A country does not grow economically in this transition stage, but old customs begin to crumble. People begin to question old ways and look at new patterns of living. Often there may be great deal of social unrest.

In India, agriculture is very important. Why must many developing countries depend on agriculture and mining for most of their income?

TAKEOFF

The third stage of development is the **takeoff.** It is not reached until the barriers of primitive equilibrium are overcome. A country in the takeoff stage is beginning to grow more rapidly than before. Still, that nation has not yet come close to reaching maturity or developing its greatest economic potential.

There are a number of reasons for economic growth during this stage. One is that old customs have been put aside, and people have begun to seek new and better ways of doing things. Another is that the people have begun to imitate the new or different techniques outsiders have brought into the country. Still another is that outside help from a more advanced nation may be providing financial, educational, or military aid.

During the takeoff stage, a country starts to save and invest more of its national income. New industries grow rapidly, and profits are reinvested in them. New production techniques are learned and used. Agricultural productivity is improved greatly. Although the country still is not developed, it is moving away from economic stagnation at a faster pace.

SEMI-DEVELOPED COUNTRIES

The fourth stage is semi-development. In it, the make-up of the country's economy changes, and national income grows faster than population. This leads to higher per capita income. At the same time, the core of the country's industry is built. A great deal is spent on capital investment, and technological advances are made.

As industry grows, so does transportation, communications, medicine, law, and other services. This helps the country begin to find its place in the international economy. It starts to make goods it once bought from other countries. Before long, it starts to sell goods to other countries.

HIGHLY DEVELOPED COUNTRIES

The final stage of development is that of being highly developed. In it, efforts to obtain food, shelter, and clothing are more than successful. Most people have all they need and want of the basics. Attention can be turned to services and such consumer goods as washing machines, refrigerators, and televisions.

The emphasis no longer is on industrial production. Instead, it is on increasing services and public goods. Mature service and manufacturing sectors are the sign of a highly developed economy.

Section Review

1. What are the five major stages of economic development?
2. What are the major characteristics of each stage?

20.3 Financing Economic Development

It is not always easy for a country to develop economically. Three major conditions are necessary. First, the country must overcome cultural and traditional barriers. Then it also must have political stability and responsible government. Lastly, it must obtain savings that can be turned into capital investments.

Capital is needed to develop industries in which a country has a comparative advantage. Funds may be needed, for example, to provide irrigation for farms or heavy equipment for mining. They also may be needed for roads and highways that can be used to bring products to ports to ship throughout the rest of the world.

This financial capital generally can come from three different sources. It can be generated internally; borrowed, supplied, or given by outside agencies; or obtained as a result of regional cooperation.

DEVELOPMENT WITH INTERNAL FUNDS

Since developing countries do not have much industry, they must depend on agriculture or such industries as mining and petroleum for most of their income. To develop using only internal funds, an economy must generate savings or produce more than it consumes. Goods and services left over after consumption has taken place can be used in industries still in need of development. The problem, however, is that many developing countries are so poor that there is barely enough production to take care of the consumption. Since consumption already is at the very lowest level, further reductions are not always possible.

SAVINGS IN A MARKET ECONOMY. If a developing country is modeled after a market economy, the incentive to save comes from the profit motive. Entrepreneurs in the country are free to pursue the most profitable activities. Banks, for example, pay varying interest rates that are set by the forces of supply and demand. If the demand for money is high, the rate will rise, and more saving will be encouraged. Then there will be more financial capital.

One economy developed in this way is that of Hong Kong, which has been called one of the freest market economies in the world. There is very little government interference, and people are free to pursue almost any economic activity they desire.

Although its per capita GNP is only about one third that of the United States, it is twenty times greater than that of mainland China.

SAVINGS IN A COMMAND ECONOMY.
Other developing countries, such as Cuba, the Dominican Republic, El Salvador, and Uganda, have had command economies at one time or another. In each case, a dictator tried to force saving on the economy. The governments of these countries argue that individual citizens were so poor that they did not have the incentive to save on their own. As a result, the governments felt they had to mobilize resources using command.

Unemployed people, for example, might be forced to work on farms, roads, or any other project the government thought was needed for economic development. At one point in time, the government of mainland China forced people out of the cities and factories to work on farms in an effort to boost agricultural output.

History shows that while command economies can mobilize resources, they do not always use them to promote economic growth. And when resources are mobilized for the wrong reasons, the cost in personal economic and political freedoms is higher than most people want to pay.

DEVELOPMENT WITH EXTERNAL FUNDS

No matter what system of government a poor country has, it is never easy for it to develop economically with internal funds. For this reason, some developing countries try to obtain external funds. There are three ways they can do this.

ATTRACTING PRIVATE INVESTMENT.
One way in which a country can obtain external funds is by attracting private funds from foreign investors.

Foreign investors might be attracted by a country's natural resources. This happened in the Middle East with its abundance of oil as well as in Chile with its abundance of copper. The same thing also happened in the Far East with its abundance of mahogany and teakwood.

A country that is rich in mineral resources, for example, might grant exclusive mining rights or favorable tax treatment to foreign companies or investors willing to build factories on its soil. The country also might be able to provide low-cost labor, which would make investment even more attractive.

While foreign countries often are tempted by such arrangements, there is some concern over their long-run value. Many

This installation was built with external funds. What are the sources of external funds for developing countries?

Case Study: *Career*

Peace Corps Worker

A Peace Corps worker lives in a developing country and helps the people there learn new techniques in such areas as agriculture and forestry and provides up-to-date information on such things as health care, public sanitation, and nutrition. He or she also teaches the people such trade skills as carpentry, mechanics, and welding.

At present, about 6000 Peace Corps workers are on assignment in more than 63 countries in Latin America, Africa, and the South Pacific. The tasks the workers perform vary from country to country. A worker in Kenya, for example, may help villagers plan and develop an irrigation system. Another worker in Costa Rica or Honduras may teach mechanical arts to unskilled workers in poorer urban neighborhoods. Still another worker in Chad or Nepal may explain the basics of beekeeping to farmers.

Regardless of which country members of the Peace Corps work in or what tasks they perform, the work is both challenging and demanding. Peace Corps workers must be outgoing and able to take charge. They also must be able to adapt to cultures and life-styles different from their own. Equally important, they must be patient and able to handle responsibility. In some countries, older, more mature workers are likely to gain the people's respect more easily.

To qualify for a position as a Peace Corps worker, a person must be 18 years or older, have a high school education, and be in good physical health. Once a person enters the program, he or she is expected to remain in it for at least two years. Before being assigned to a certain country, each worker receives intensive language training. Transportation to and from the assigned country is paid for by the Peace Corps. While in the field, the worker receives a monthly living allowance and free medical and dental care. At the end of service, he or she receives $175 for each month served.

Each year, there are approximately 2500 openings for Peace Corps workers. Since this number is expected to remain the same for the next few years, competition is expected to be stiff.

THE OPEC COUNTRIES

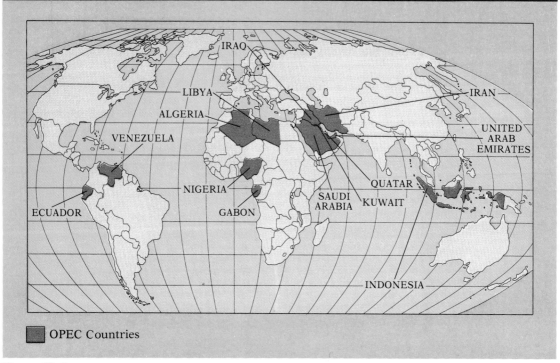

OPEC Countries

Figure 20–2

corporations have not forgotten the billions of dollars lost during the takeover of American oil facilities in Iran, copper mines in Chile, and agricultural plantations in Cuba. Because of this, many foreign investors no longer are willing to take major risks unless they are sure that the developing country is politically stable.

Developing countries which follow a policy of **expropriation**—the taking over of foreign property without some sort of payment in return—make it harder for all developing nations to attract foreign capital from developing countries.

ASSISTANCE FROM DEVELOPED COUNTRIES. Another way a country can obtain external funds is by getting grants from foreign governments or borrowing money from foreign governments.

The United States, for example, has made billions in grants to other countries since the end of World War II. About half of this amount provided military help to friendly countries. The rest was used to help Europe and the Far East rebuild after World War II and to provide economic assistance to developing countries. Other developed countries, including Canada and those in Western Europe, also grant aid to the LDC's.

The Soviet bloc also gives economic assistance to the Third World. More than 50 percent of its aid, however, goes to Ethiopia, Afghanistan, and Iraq. It is given mostly to promote political, not economic, ends.

Some economic aid also is provided by the **OPEC nations**—members of the Organization of Petroleum Exporting Countries. This aid generally is limited to only a few countries and organizations. The OPEC nation of Saudi Arabia, for example, sends most of its foreign aid to Syria, Iraq, and the Palestinian Liberation Organization. Relatively little goes to the developing countries of Africa and Latin America.

BORROWING FROM INTERNATIONAL AGENCIES. A third way a country can get external financial assistance is by obtaining a loan from an international agency. One such agency is the **International Bank for Reconstruction and Development,** which also is known as the **World Bank.** The Bank is designed to funnel funds to developing countries in the form of loans and guarantees of loans from private sources. In 1986, the bank had nearly $60 billion of loans outstanding to LDC's. It is a corporation "owned" by the member nations of the International Monetary Fund. One of the "owners" is the United States, which contributes over a billion annually.

In the past, many of the loans have been for projects such as dams, roads, and factories. In the past few years, loans have been made to developing nations in an effort to get them to change their economic policies. Rather than lend money for a certain project, such as a power plant or dam, the World Bank may grant a general loan that the borrowing country can use in any number of ways. In return, the World Bank may ask the country to lower a tariff barrier, end a budget deficit, or reduce the level of inflation.

The World Bank has several affiliates. One is the **International Finance Corporation (IFC)**—an agency that lends funds directly to private industries in developing countries. Another is the **International Development Association (IDA)**—an agency

that makes low or interest-free loans to countries that may not be able to pay them back. The IDA is the lender of last resort for many countries that could not get external financing anywhere else.

REGIONAL COOPERATION

At times, developing countries have joined together to deal with the problem of economic development. One way has been to form a **customs union**—an agreement by which two or more countries abolish tariffs and trade restrictions

Figure 20–3

THE COMMON MARKET COUNTRIES

☐ Common Market Countries

among themselves and adopt uniform tariffs for non-member countries. The advantage is that it promotes free trade among member nations. One of the most successful customs unions in the world today is the **European Economic Community (EEC), or European Common Market.** Its members, however, are industrialized countries, not developing ones. EEC members are shown in the map on page 495.

Another way developing countries have joined together is by forming a **free-trade area**—an agreement by which two or more countries reduce trade barriers and tariffs among themselves. Unlike the customs union, the free-trade area does not try to set uniform tariffs for non-members.

Neither customs unions nor free-trade areas have been that successful to date for developing countries. A third kind of joint effort, however, has had some initial, but temporary, success.

The **cartel**—a group of producers or sellers who agree to limit the production or sale of a product to control prices—was used by the OPEC nations. Formed in 1960, its members were able to take advantage of a natural monopoly and push up oil prices all over the world.

As a result of the higher prices, huge amounts of financial capital were transferred to the OPEC countries. Between 1974 and 1986, for example, OPEC earned nearly $2 trillion more as a result of the higher prices.

Even with all this financial capital, however, the growth rates of some OPEC countries were low by most standards. In Iran, for example, revolution interrupted the development of the domestic economy. In Nigeria and Venezuela, the real per capita GNP growth rate declined 1.1 percent per year from 1973 to 1983. Even Saudi Arabia, one of the largest and wealthiest OPEC members had a per capita growth rate from 1973 to 1983 lower than that of

Korea, Hong Kong, Singapore, or even Egypt.

The problem is that most of the OPEC countries were not able to absorb the oil wealth in a balanced fashion. They bought many goods and services for which they were not yet ready. At the same time, many other sectors of the economy were ignored.

Eventually, OPEC lost control of the world oil supply. After having reached a high of $34 a barrel in 1983, oil prices plunged to below $10 in 1986. OPEC had successfully controlled oil prices for nearly 12 years, but the high price finally caused developed nations to buy less, and many other nations to produce more. As a result, the supply of oil increased, and prices decreased.

Growth rates of the OPEC nations for 1973 to 1983 show that huge amounts of capital alone do not solve the problems of developing countries. To have sound economic development, countries must also address such issues as saving, investment, and the incentives that cause people to work and improve their position in life. The monopoly power created by a group as powerful as OPEC is only temporary. In the end, the forces of supply and demand and the allocations of the price system proved more powerful than OPEC. For this reason, many people today believe successful, long-term economic growth must go along with the free market forces of supply, demand, and competition.

■ Section Review

1. From what three sources can a developing country obtain financial capital?
2. What is a free-trade area? How does it differ from a customs union?
3. Why has money from OPEC countries not had more of an impact on economic development?

20.4 *Obstacles to Economic Development*

Even when countries can obtain the funds needed for development, other factors may keep them from growing. While these vary in kind and degree, some are common to many developing countries.

THIRD WORLD DEBT

A major problem facing developing nations today is the size of the **external debt**—money borrowed from foreign banks and governments. Some nations have now borrowed so much, they may never repay some loans.

According to most estimates, the total amount of external debt for all LDC's was more than $1 trillion in 1986. Two countries, Mexico and Brazil, each owe $100 billion to investors in other countries, mainly the United States. For Mexico, this amounts to roughly two-thirds of the country's GNP. For Brazil, the debt owed to others is closer to 40 percent of its total GNP.

When debts get this large, countries have trouble even paying their interest. As a result, some developing nations talk about defaulting, or simply not repaying money borrowed from some nations. Most people do not expect this to happen, however, since countries that have loaned money might retaliate. In addition, a country that defaults on its loans may never be able to borrow abroad again.

When countries get close to default, borrowers and lenders often try to work out a revised repayment schedule. Some lenders have found some very creative ways to resolve the debt crisis. Recently, for example, the Philippines was unable to repay a major loan to the Bank of America. So the Bank accepted an offer of 40 percent stock ownership in the Bank of the Philippines in place of the repayment.

CAPITAL FLIGHT

Another major problem for developing nations is **capital flight**—the legal or illegal export of currency and foreign exchange. When this happens, countries may face a cash shortage that prevents them from paying interest on their foreign debt.

For the most part, capital flight takes place when corrupt officials take money out of the country and deposit it abroad. A recent investigation by the government of Nigeria, for example, found that corrupt officials were depositing $25 million abroad daily at the peak of the oil boom

A major problem for developing countries is capital flight to foreign banks. Why is external debt another major problem?

in the 1970's. This may be one reason why Nigeria experienced a negative per capita rate of growth from 1973 to 1983, although they were an OPEC nation with rich oil reserves.

At other times, capital flight happens because people living in the borrowing countries have no faith in the policies of their government or the future of the country's economy. Business owners, for example, may take profits out of a business and deposit them abroad. When they want to expand or invest, however, they try to borrow from developed nations. For example, between 1978 and 1983, it was discovered that Argentina obtained $35.7 billion in new loans while $21 billion escaped abroad. During the same period, $27 billion left Venezuela while its borrowing from foreigners increased by $23 billion. Some estimate that as much as one-third of the money lent to LDC's in the 1970's and 1980's left the country the same month or year it arrived.

GOVERNMENT

Government also can be an obstacle to economic development. A country whose government often changes hands will have a hard time developing economically. Such constant changes make business decisions

Revolution can hurt economic development badly. This coffee grower is trying to salvage what remains of his harvest from damage caused by fighting between guerillas and government troops. How can government be an obstacle to economic development?

harder and slow long-term planning. It is even more difficult if the changes take place through violent revolution. In the process, industrial facilities may be destroyed and output reduced.

Economic development also will be slowed if a government is not honest. Corrupt officials can damage the economy in several ways. One is by depositing any savings they can squeeze out of the economy in a personal account in a foreign bank. Another is by spending huge sums meant for economic development on lavish personal living.

In either case, the people see the results of their labor being spent recklessly or going into someone else's pockets while their lives remain the same. This discourages them and reduces their incentive to save or invest. It also encourages investors from other countries to keep their money at home or invest it somewhere else.

POPULATION

One major obstacle to economic growth is population. The population of most developing countries grows at a rate more than double that of developed countries. One reason for this is the high **crude birth rate**—the number of live births per 1000 of population. The graph on page 500 shows that the countries with the highest birth rates in the world are developing countries, while the ones with the lowest birth rates are developed countries.

In some of the developing countries, the population is so large that there is barely enough fertile land and other resources to support it. When this is the case, increases in the capital stock are even more difficult to obtain.

The fact that many of the poorer countries have a large agricultural base adds to the problem. In these countries, there is actually an incentive to have children—at a time when the overall population already is growing too fast. Most farms are worked by families, and children can work in the fields at an early age. More children, then, means more workers. In addition, the more children a couple has, the more sure they are to have someone to look after them in their old age.

Another problem for the developing countries is the increasing **life expectancy**—the statistical estimate of the number of years a person is expected to live. The figure on page 590 shows, for example, the dramatic increase in life expectancy in the 16 largest developing countries between 1970 and 1983. Better education, international aid, and emphasis on health-care facilities help people live longer. This adds to the problem of a growing population due to high crude birth rates, which makes it difficult to increase their real per capita GNP.

Finally, different people have different views on what is the proper rate of population growth. Some feel that the earth is too crowded already and that societies should work for **zero population growth (ZPG)**—the condition in which the average number of births and deaths balance out so that a population stops growing. Others feel that population growth is a natural event and that efforts to disrupt it are morally and religiously wrong.

NATURAL RESOURCES

Another obstacle to economic growth is natural resources. No country can develop beyond the limits set by its potential. Poor land or a bad climate can limit economic growth. So can too few natural resources or a shortage or the lack of energy sources

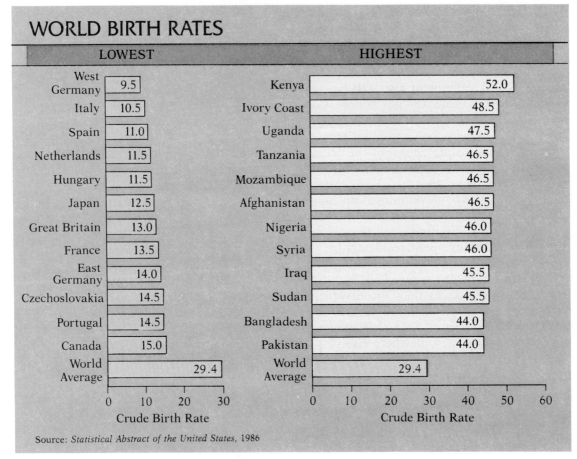

WORLD BIRTH RATES

LOWEST		HIGHEST	
West Germany	9.5	Kenya	52.0
Italy	10.5	Ivory Coast	48.5
Spain	11.0	Uganda	47.5
Netherlands	11.5	Tanzania	46.5
Hungary	11.5	Mozambique	46.5
Japan	12.5	Afghanistan	46.5
Great Britain	13.0	Nigeria	46.0
France	13.5	Syria	46.0
East Germany	14.0	Iraq	45.5
Czechoslovakia	14.5	Sudan	45.5
Portugal	14.5	Bangladesh	44.0
Canada	15.0	Pakistan	44.0
World Average	29.4	World Average	29.4

Crude Birth Rate · Crude Birth Rate

Source: *Statistical Abstract of the United States, 1986*

Figure 20–4

needed for industry. While some countries may be fortunate enough to discover oil, uranium, or some other valuable mineral, most focus on agriculture.

Many projects funded by the World Bank are in the area of agriculture. In recent years, the Bank has undertaken projects to control the desert locust in East Africa. It also has funded projects to help develop cotton, coffee, clove, sisal, cashew, tobacco, and tea crops in Tanzania and Ghana and to increase the production of millet and sorghum in northern Nigeria.

EDUCATION AND TECHNOLOGY

Still another obstacle to economic development is lack of education and technology. Many developing countries do not have the highly literate population or high level of technical skills needed to build an industrial society. Most do not have money to train engineers and scientists.

Many developing countries cannot even afford to provide free public education for school-age children. Even in those that can, not everyone can take advantage of it.

Profile

Gunnar Myrdal

Gunnar Myrdal **was** a Swedish economist, sociologist, and planner-advisor in public affairs for the Swedish government. Much of his work had been devoted to the economic problems of the developing countries and to the social problems of the more advanced or developed countries.

1898-1987

Myrdal, who believed in central planning for all countries, won international acclaim for two works—*An American Dilemma: The Negro Problem and Modern Democracy* (1944) and *Asian Drama: An Inquiry Into the Poverty of Nations* (1968). *An American Dilemma* became a classic in its field and was cited by the 1954 United States Supreme Court decision on desegregation. *Asian Drama* did much to introduce the rest of the world to the problems of the less-developed countries. In it, Myrdal argued that if these countries were to develop economically, they would have to make reforms in agriculture, land, health, education, and population. He also believed that they would need self-imposed social discipline to succeed.

In 1974, Myrdal shared the Nobel Prize in economics with Friedrich von Hayek.

In many cases, very young children must work to help feed their families. Even if school is free, it may be a luxury people cannot afford. As a result, a large part of the population does not have the basic skills needed to go on to higher levels of education when it is offered.

Although this situation can be overcome, it will take time. In countries where most of the people have a very low standard of living, many people cannot afford to wait. This puts added pressure on an already depressed economy.

CULTURE AND RELIGION

Perhaps the biggest obstacles to economic growth are the attitudes and beliefs of the people. Most people who live in advanced industrial countries are used to change and improvement. If something does not work, it is fixed or done differently. Change is a way of life to which people are accustomed.

This is not the case, however, in many of the very poor countries. They have traditional economies in which things are done certain ways because they have always been done that way. Each generation lives like the one before it, and nothing different is expected.

In some cases, religion is a barrier. In India, for example, most people are Hindu, a religion that considers cows sacred. They cannot be used for food even if the people are starving. Cows have free rein and are even allowed to raid vegetable gardens of starving peasants.

Some religions teach that the current existence is merely a test for those who seek everlasting life. Hunger, cold, discomfort, and other deprivations are a test. How they are endured helps determine a person's station in the next life. People who believe in these religions and follow their teachings, therefore, are not primarily interested in economic development or anything else that might relieve them of these many deprivations.

▪ Section Review

1. What are seven major obstacles to the economic growth of the many developing countries?
2. How does each obstacle stand in the way of economic development?

20.5 South Korea: A Study in Development

One of the most successful developing nations is the Republic of Korea, also known as South Korea. Despite its bleak prospects nearly forty years ago, it overcame overwhelming odds to become the third largest economic power in Asia today and the nineteenth largest economy in the world. From the late 1950's until the mid-1980's, South Korean exports grew at rates of 25 percent per year. In addition, its real GNP per capita growth was in the 5 to 10 percent range.

In the early 1950's, South Korea was one of the poorest nations in Asia. It had the highest **population density**—number of people per square mile of land area—in the world. It was also a war-torn economy that had to rebuild from scratch.

After the Korean War, the United States sent foreign aid to South Korea for both strategic and humanitarian reasons. However, because the South Korean economy was in such bad shape, even massive amounts of foreign aid would have done little more than maintain the country's low standard of living. Thus, for growth to take place, the South Koreans had to do more than rely on foreign aid.

As a result, the South Korean government decided to focus on labor-intensive industries and open its markets to free trade. They gave businesses incentives to encourage them to follow this strategy. In addition, they did not try to do everything at once. Instead, they focused on a few industries so that everyone could gain experience producing and exporting for world markets.

As a result of these steps, businesses in the South Korean economy first began to produce inexpensive toys and consumer goods for the world market. Next, it moved into textiles such as shirts, dresses, and sweaters. Then it moved into such heavy industry as shipbuilding and steel manufacturing. Even later, it produced consumer and electronic goods such as radios, televisions, microwave ovens, and home computers. Most recently, it has been making a strong bid as a leading producer of automobiles.

The South Korean experience shows that a country can change an underdeveloped, war-damaged economy to a well-developed, highly progressive one. This was accomplished by specialization and free trade that allowed South Korea to develop its comparative advantage. South Korea also has demonstrated that the transition from a poor, overcrowded nation to a major regional power can be achieved quicker than most people have previously thought possible.

South Korea's economic growth has made that nation an economic power. How was this growth accomplished?

Section Review

1. What were three major problems facing the South Korean economy?
2. What economic policies did the South Korean government follow?

Chapter 20 Review

Summary

1. The average per capita GNP of less developed countries is a fraction of that in more industrialized countries. The less developed countries also account for about one-half of the world's population.

2. The more developed countries of the world are interested in developing countries for humanitarian, economic, and political reasons.

3. Developing countries may pass through some or all of the five stages

of economic development: primitive equilibrium, a break with primitive equilibrium, the takeoff, semi-development, and high development.

4. To develop economically, a country must overcome cultural and traditional barriers; bring about political stability and responsible government; and obtain savings that can be turned into capital investments.

5. A country can generate financial capital internally or externally.

6. It is hard to develop economically with internal funds because the economy must produce more than it consumes.

7. A country can obtain external funds by attracting foreign investors; getting grants from foreign governments; borrowing money from foreign governments and private banks; obtaining a loan from an international agency such as the World Bank, the IFC, or the IDA; or joining with other countries to form customs unions, free-trade areas, or cartels like OPEC.

8. External debt of the Third World, along with capital flight, are major barriers to economic development. Government; population; natural resources; education and technology; and culture and religion are also obstacles to economic growth.

9. The South Korean economy developed by focusing on specialization and international trade. It is the most successful of the developing countries.

▪ *Building an Economic Vocabulary*

less-developed countries (LDC's)
Third World
primitive equilibrium
takeoff
expropriation
OPEC nations
International Bank for
   Reconstruction and Development
World Bank

International Finance
   Corporation (IFC)
International Development Association (IDA)
customs union
European Economic
   Community (EEC)
European Common Market

free-trade area
cartel
external debt
capital flight
crude birth rate
life expectancy
zero-population growth
population density

▪ *Reviewing the Main Ideas*

1. What is the Third World?

2. Why are other countries interested in the developing countries?

3. Why is there economic growth during the take-off stage of development?

4. On what is the emphasis in a highly developed country?

5. What three conditions must a country meet to develop economically?

6. Why is it hard for a poor country to generate internal funds?

7. Why does a poor country with a large agricultural base often have difficulty achieving economic growth?

8. What is perhaps the greatest obstacle to economic growth?

9. How did South Korea achieve economic growth?

Practicing Critical Thinking Skills

1. Give reasons and examples to support the statement that the United States has a highly developed economy.

2. If you were able to make a large private investment in one developing country, which would you select? Give reasons for your choice.

3. Do a study of the European Common Market and the countries that belong to it. Then explain why you would or would not join it if you were the leader of a country in the semi-developed stage of economic development.

4. Suppose you were the leader of a developing country. Describe the conditions that might exist in the country. Then draw up a detailed step-by-step plan to bring about economic growth in your country.

Applying Economic Understandings

Reading Maps

Over time, you have probably seen many kinds of maps. Some were in classrooms and textbooks, and others were used for traveling. Maps are important in the study of economics because they can help you visualize regions for economic analysis.

Look at the map on pages 486 and 487, and follow the steps outlined below to help you read maps.

1. Read the title of the map to determine the theme.
   (The title is GNP per capita, 1983. The theme is a comparison of the GNP per capita of different nations.)

2. Locate the legend, the list, and explanation of the keys that provide information related to the theme of the map.

3. Study the legend. Ask yourself such questions as, What do the colors represent?
   (The colors represent different amounts of GNP per capita.)

4. After you are familiar with the legend, determine the basic facts presented in the map. (The United States has the highest GNP per capita. The nations of Western Europe and Japan also have high GNP per capita. Additionally, many nations have $400 or less GNP per capita.)

For further practice in reading maps, turn to the maps on pages 494 and 495 and follow the steps outlined in the example above.

Unit 6 Review

The Unit in Perspective

1. By specializing in producing the products it produces best and then exchanging it with other countries, a country can realize gains from international trade.

2. Over the years, international trade has been restricted by tariffs, quotas, and other protective measures.

3. Trading with other countries means financing international transactions, which involves foreign exchange.

4. Trade deficits can cause changes in output and employment in both export and import industries. In the long run, however, trade imbalances are self-correcting.

5. The three major economic systems of the world today—communism, socialism and capitalism—appear on the economic spectrum as having a greater or lesser degree of direction by command and the free market.

6. The major critic of capitalism was Karl Marx, who was the creator of Communist dogma.

7. Today, the Soviet Union, the Comecon countries, and China have Communist command-type economies.

8. Sweden is a socialist state which combines private enterprise and government ownership of the means of production.

9. Japan has a capitalist economy in which the government plays a protective role.

10. Nearly half of the world's population lives in the less-developed countries. These countries are important to the developed nations because they provide many scarce raw materials and are an important market for the goods of the developed nations.

11. To develop economically, a country must generate financial capital and overcome such obstacles as population and lack of technology.

12. The Republic of Korea underwent rapid economic development by focusing on a program of specialization and international trade.

The Unit in Review

1. On what is international trade based?

2. What are the major arguments for protection that act as barriers to international trade? Of these, which is the most valid?

3. How is international trade financed?

4. What happens when a country imports more than it exports? How is this unbalance influenced by flexible exchange rates?

5. What characteristics differentiate the three major economic systems from one another?

6. What effects have Karl Marx's theories had on the economic and political developments of the Soviet Union?

7. How has the Soviet economy changed since 1917? What problems does it still face?

8. What are some of the problems facing Comecon countries today? The People's Republic of China? Sweden? Japan? What, if anything, is being done to solve these problems?

9. What are the stages of economic development? Why are they important?

10. What are the three ways developing nations can secure financing for economic growth and development?

11. How does culture and religion work against economic development in many countries?

■ *Building Consumer Skills*

Estimating Your Net Worth

If someone were to ask you what you are worth in dollars and cents, you probably would have difficulty answering. You should, however, know your net worth for tax purposes and future planning. In addition, banks, colleges, and universities often require net worth statements from persons requesting loans or financial assistance. The following exercise will help you estimate your net worth.

1. Make a list of your assets—what you own. Include the following: Cash and Cash Equivalents (cash on hand, in checking accounts, and in savings accounts; life insurance policies cash value; money owed you); Personal Property (furniture and other household items, cars, jewelry, etc.); Real Estate; Investments (stocks, bonds, mutual funds, etc.). Place a dollar amount on each item under Cash and Cash Equivalents and an estimated market value on each of the other items.

2. Make a list of your liabilities—what you owe. Include the following: Current Bills (rent, utilities, taxes, charge account balances, insurance premiums, taxes, etc.); Amount Owed on Loans (mortgage, auto loan, etc.); Taxes Due. Place a dollar amount on each item.

3. Total your assets and then your liabilities. Subtract your total liabilities from your total assets. The result is your net worth.

Fundamental Economic Problems

Every country, including the United States, wants to achieve economic security.
For countries to be able to do so, they must first overcome certain problems such
as large population growth, poverty, and shortages of resources.

Contents

Population, Income, and Poverty

If a free society cannot help the many who are poor, it cannot save the few who are rich.   **John F. Kennedy**

Chapter 21

After reading this chapter, you will be able to:

- Trace the rate of population growth in the United States from 1790 to the present.

- Explain how the distribution of income is analyzed and the reasons for income inequality.

- Describe some federal programs designed to end poverty.

- Debate the effects of the war on poverty.

21.1 Population

All societies are concerned about their populations. Population means people; people make things work and are responsible for the way in which things are done. People are the ones who benefit from the fruits of their efforts.

If a country's population grows too fast, it may have too many mouths to feed. This holds down output growth on a per capita basis. If, on the other hand, a country's population grows too slowly, it may not have enough productive resources to achieve economic growth.

In the United States, population data is collected every ten years by the Bureau of the Census. In addition, projections and estimates are made every year on the basis of thousands of samples taken from all over the country.

The population of the United States has grown a great deal since colonial times. In 1790, it was a little less than 4 million. Between 1790 and 1860, it grew at an average rate of 2.5 percent a year. From the Civil War until World War I, the average fell to 2.13 percent. From then until

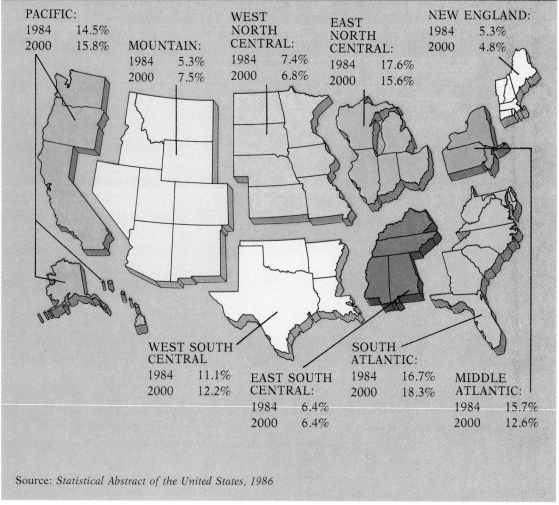

PROJECTED DISTRIBUTION AND GROWTH OF POPULATION BY REGION, 1984–2000

PACIFIC:
1984   14.5%
2000   15.8%

MOUNTAIN:
1984   5.3%
2000   7.5%

WEST NORTH CENTRAL:
1984   7.4%
2000   6.8%

EAST NORTH CENTRAL:
1984   17.6%
2000   15.6%

NEW ENGLAND:
1984   5.3%
2000   4.8%

WEST SOUTH CENTRAL
1984   11.1%
2000   12.2%

EAST SOUTH CENTRAL:
1984   6.4%
2000   6.4%

SOUTH ATLANTIC:
1984   16.7%
2000   18.3%

MIDDLE ATLANTIC:
1984   15.7%
2000   12.6%

Source: *Statistical Abstract of the United States, 1986*

Figure 21–1

today, the growth rate has been closer to 1.3 percent. In the future, it is expected to drop even further.

The census also shows that there has been a steady trend toward smaller and smaller households. During colonial times, the average household size was 5.8 people. By 1990, it will be about 2.6 people. This is consistent in part with the fact that in advanced industrial countries, children often are thought of as being a cost and families have fewer children. The other factor involved is that more individuals are living alone today than ever have before.

Each census also indicates the **center of population**—the point where the country would balance if it were flat and every American weighed the same. In 1790, the year the first census was taken, the center was east of Baltimore. Since then, it has moved slowly westward. By 1970, it was in a cornfield near Mascoutah, Illinois. According to the latest census taken in 1980, it is on a farm about 45 miles (76.5 kilometers) south of St. Louis, Missouri.

Economists also are concerned with changes in where people live as well as the make up of the population. For example, the illustration on page 512 shows the

Figure 21–2

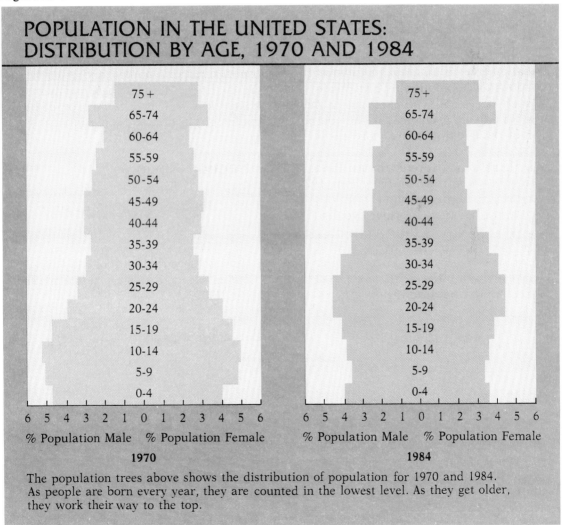

POPULATION IN THE UNITED STATES: DISTRIBUTION BY AGE, 1970 AND 1984

1970

% Population Male   % Population Female

1984

% Population Male   % Population Female

The population trees above shows the distribution of population for 1970 and 1984. As people are born every year, they are counted in the lowest level. As they get older, they work their way to the top.

projected shifts in population between 1984 and 2000. According to the map, population as a percentage of the total will drop in the Northeast and the Central Plains states, but will be offset by growth in the West and the South.

Population shifts are important to a number of groups. Political leaders, for example, are concerned about such shifts because they affect voting patterns. Community leaders are interested because population shifts impact such services as sanitation, water, and education. Businesses are concerned because they affect the location of new plants and the development and sale of new products.

Population may also be studied with a **population tree**—a diagram that shows the breakdown of population by age. When two such "trees" are compared, as in the figure on page 513, changes in the composition of the population are more easily seen.

The figure shows several things. First, the tree on the left, which represents 1970, is larger at the bottom than at the top. This means that there are more young people than elderly in the population. Second, it is a little lopsided at the top because women generally outlive men. Third, there is a bulge at the bottom of the tree. This is because the largest percentage of population is concentrated in two brackets—ages five to nine and ten to fourteen.

In the second tree, which represents 1984, the bulge is still there, but it has moved up because the people are now older. It has also gotten smaller because some of these people have died. New additions to the population are not as large as they were in the past because of the declining birth rate.

At some future time, the bulge in the middle of the tree will work its way to the top. When this happens, a larger part of the total population will be elderly. As a result, there will be greater need for welfare and retirement benefits, as well as hospitals, nursing homes, and other health care facilities. Many of these payments and services will have to be provided by a smaller proportion of people in their working years.

Section Review

1. What is the center of population? In what direction has it moved since 1790?

2. Why are households smaller today than in the past?

3. How is the population of the United States expected to shift between 1984 and 2000?

21.2 Income

In the United States, as elsewhere, everyone does not have the same income. Economists use the term **distribution of income** to describe the way in which income is distributed among individuals, families, households, and other groups.

DISTRIBUTION OF INCOME

Economists have several different ways of analyzing the distribution of income. The most common is to rank all families from highest to lowest; break them into quintiles, or fifths; and then look at the amount of income earned by each fifth.

The illustration below shows how this is done. The table shows that in 1985, the lowest fifth received 4.6 percent of the total income earned by all families. The second fifth received 10.9 percent, the middle fifth 16.9 percent, the fourth fifth 24.2 percent, and the highest fifth 43.4 percent. This information is then plotted on a **Lorenz Curve**—a curve that shows how much the actual distribution of income varies from equal distribution. In Graph

B, the percent received by the lowest quintile is plotted as point **a.** Then, the amount received cumulatively by the lowest and next-to-lowest quintiles is plotted as point **b.** This process continues until the cumulative values of all the quintiles are plotted.

Graph **B** shows that if all families received the same income, the Lorenz Curve would appear as a diagonal line running from one corner of the graph to the other. But since all families do not receive the same income, the curve showing the actual income distribution is not a diagonal. The

Figure 21–3

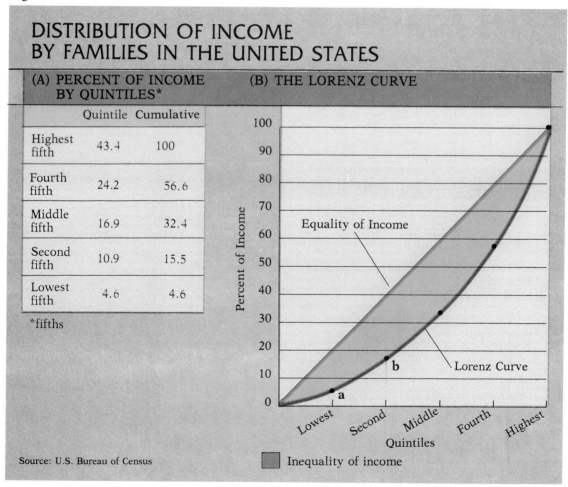

DISTRIBUTION OF INCOME BY FAMILIES IN THE UNITED STATES

(A) PERCENT OF INCOME BY QUINTILES*

	Quintile	Cumulative
Highest fifth	43.4	100
Fourth fifth	24.2	56.6
Middle fifth	16.9	32.4
Second fifth	10.9	15.5
Lowest fifth	4.6	4.6

*fifths

(B) THE LORENZ CURVE

Source: U.S. Bureau of Census

Inequality of income

area on the graph between the diagonal and the curve shows the degree of inequality that exists. The larger the area, the more unequal the income distribution.

In addition, economists look at how income is distributed between sexes and ethnic groups. In 1985, the median white family income in the United States was $29,152. Non-white families are broken into two separate categories, black and Spanish origin. Black families had a median income of $16,786; families of Spanish origin had a median income of $19,027.

REASONS FOR INCOME INEQUALITY

There are a number of reasons why the incomes of various groups may be different. They include education, wealth, discrimination, ability, and monopoly power.

EDUCATION. Some people receive higher incomes than others because they have more education. This puts them in a better position to get higher paying jobs that require a higher level of skills. Although there are exceptions to this, there generally is a strong relationship between median income and levels of education. This can be seen in the table below.

WEALTH. Income also tends to vary because some people hold more wealth than others. The distribution of wealth is, in fact, even more unequal than the distribution of income. When wealth-holders are ranked from highest to lowest, the top fifth has 75 percent of all the wealth in the country. The bottom two fifths, which is 40 percent of the people in the country, have less than 2 percent of the total wealth.

This clearly has an impact on people's ability to earn income. Wealthy families can send their children to expensive col-

Table 21–A

THE RELATIONSHIP BETWEEN INCOME & EDUCATION

LEVELS OF EDUCATION	MEDIAN INCOME IN ($)	
	Male	Female
Elementary		
Less than 8 years	7,530	4,413
8 years	10,325	5,167
High School		
1-3 years	12,529	5,559
4 years	18,825	7,839
College		
1-3 years	21,378	10,473
4 years	28,206	13,644
5 years or more	32,891	19,684

Note: Data is for persons 25 years and over.

Source: U.S. Bureau of Census

Profile

Thomas Sowell

Thomas Sowell is a noted American economist who has been associated with the University of California; Stanford University's Hoover Institute on War, Revolution and Peace; and President Reagan's Economic Policy Advisory Board.

1930–

Sowell is the author of two controversial works, *Ethnic America: A History* and *Markets and Minorities*. In these, he attacks what he believes to be myths about employment and income in the United States. He also tries to show that the free enterprise system has worked for every group, bar none. One of his principal themes is that racial prejudice is not the only cause of income differences between blacks and whites. In his view, much of the income gap can be explained by age differences, family size, and place of residence.

Sowell believes that in trying to help minorities, government has become more foe than friend. In his view, the problems of minorities can best be solved by less government and more individual effort. He also argues that quotas have harmed minorities, that the minimum wage limits choice, and that parents should be given money to spend at the school of their choice.

leges and universities. Or, they can afford to set them up in business so that they can earn a high income. Even if the wealthy choose not to work, they can invest some of their money in corporate or tax-free investments which will bring them income.

DISCRIMINATION. Another factor that has a bearing on the distribution of income is discrimination. Women, for example, may not be promoted to executive positions in certain companies because male executives believe they cannot handle the pressures of the job. Immigrants or ethnic minorities may be denied membership by certain unions on the grounds that certain ethnic groups "don't belong" in certain professions.

While discrimination of this kind is against the law today, it still takes place in some communities. When it does occur, it causes minority groups to be "crowded" into other labor markets where oversupply drives down the wages workers receive for their labor.

ABILITY. Some people earn more income because they have certain natural abilities. One of the clearest examples of this is the professional athlete who earns millions of dollars every year. Top professionals like Walter Payton, Fernando Valenzuela, and Martina Navratilova earn high incomes because they have a special ability or talent. The same is true of popular musicians, performers, or stars like Eddie Rabbitt, Stevie Wonder, Michael J. Fox, and Whitney Houston.

MONOPOLY POWER. Another important reason for differences in the distribution of income is the degree of monopoly power held by certain groups. Unions, for example, have a certain amount of power. Through the process of collective bargaining, they have been able to obtain somewhat higher wages for their members. Union carpenters, electricians, truck drivers, auto workers, and other **blue-collar workers**—industrial or factory workers who receive wages—generally are paid higher wages than those workers who are not members of unions.

Some **white-collar workers**—clerical, business, or professional workers who generally are salaried—also hold a certain amount of monopoly power. Doctors, for example, have been very successful in limiting the number of people in their profession. Medical schools can accept only a certain number of students. If they accept more than this number, they run the risk of losing accreditation by the American Medical Association. This limits the supply of doctors and affects prices.

The access to medical schools is a key part of the medical profession's monopoly power and sets it apart from most other professions. A young person who cannot get into medical school because it already is full, generally chooses another kind of school and a different profession. Without the proper education, there is no other choice.

On the other hand, a person who wants to become a lawyer or a CPA, for example, gets the education first and then worries about passing the licensing exams. If the person fails the exams, he or she can keep trying until the exams are passed. Because of this, these professions always will have a group of people ready and waiting to take available jobs. This makes it harder for those who already hold jobs in the profession to carve out a monopoly position. In the medical profession, however, there is no group waiting on the "outside."

Section Review

1. On what is the Lorenz Curve based? What does it show?
2. Why do incomes differ?

21.3 Poverty Programs

Poverty is a problem that must be faced by all societies and all countries. As long as income is not distributed equally among all people, someone has to be at the bottom of the income scale. That "someone" may be too old, too young, or too ill to work. On the other hand, that someone may be willing to work but can-

This family of five in Arkansas is typical of many other families across the nation whose only income is from welfare. What kinds of help do social welfare net programs provide?

not find a job. Or, that person may be content to depend on others to provide for his or her needs. Generally, however, that "someone" is a combination of all of these people.

Poverty is a relative measure that depends on the level of prices, the general standard of living, and the incomes earned by others. What may seem like poverty to one person may, on the other hand, seem like riches to another. For this reason, governments define poverty by a **poverty level**—a minimum income below which a person or family lacks the means to provide even the basic needs.

In 1986, the poverty level in the United States, excluding Alaska and Hawaii, for a family of four was $11,000. The poverty level for a family of four in Hawaii was $12,650 and $13,750 for Alaska. Normally, about 12 to 14 percent of the total United States population have incomes below poverty levels in any given year.

Wiping out poverty has proved to be a difficult task. Many poor people are too young or too old to find jobs or have obligations in the home that make it impossible for them to work. Many others simply live in the wrong place. Companies often build new plants on the outskirts of town because the land costs less and they have better access to major highways. But, at the same time, much of the potential labor force may live miles away in the central city. If the city does not have an adequate transportation system to provide service to the new plants, they will draw workers from suburbs, and those in the central city will remain unemployed.

Over the years, the government of the United States has instituted a number of programs to help the needy. Most come under the general heading of welfare and are part of the broad **social welfare net programs**—programs designed to help the needy, but place a limit on the ability of poor families to buy and consume. These programs provide three basic kinds of help—income assistance, general assistance, and assistance in the form of social service programs. A fourth kind of help is based on the market and tries to incorporate the incentives of the market system.

INCOME ASSISTANCE

Programs that provide direct cash assistance to those in need fall into the category of income assistance. One such program is **Aid to Families with Dependent Children (AFDC).** Under it, a family in need because of the death, continuous absence, or permanent disability of a parent can receive cash payments.

Although the program is subject to broad guidelines, individual states can determine whether a family is eligible for benefits and how large the benefits should be. For this reason, benefits vary widely from state to state.

Another income assistance program is the **Supplemental Security Income (SSI),** which makes cash payments to blind or disabled persons over the age of 65. The program was administered originally by the states. But, because benefits varied so much from state to state, the federal government took it over in 1979.

GENERAL ASSISTANCE

Programs that do not provide direct cash assistance fall into the category of general assistance. One example of this is the food stamp program, which serves millions of Americans. **Food stamps** are government-issued coupons that can be redeemed for food. They may be given or sold to eligible low-income persons. If, for example, a person pays 40¢ for a $1 food coupon, that person is getting a dollar's worth of food for a fraction of its cost. The program, which began in 1961 and became law in 1964, is different from other programs because it is based solely on income. Age, race, and physical condition play no part in determining eligibility.

Another general assistance program is Medicaid—a joint federal-state medical insurance program. Under the program, the federal government pays about 60 percent of health-care costs, and the state pays the rest. Medicaid also serves millions of Americans. Most of these are children, blind, disabled, and/or persons over the age of 65.

SOCIAL SERVICE PROGRAMS

Over the years, the individual states have developed a wide variety of social service programs to help the needy. These include such areas as child abuse, foster care, family planning, job training, child welfare, and day care.

Although the states control the kinds of services provided by the programs, the federal government matches part of the cost. To be eligible for matching funds, a state must file an annual service plan. If the plan is approved, the state is free to select the social issues it wishes to address, set the eligibility requirements, and

Case Study: *Career*

Statistician

A statistician works with numerical data that generally is obtained from experiments and surveys. This often means being involved in the design, execution, and interpretation of a sample. This is a survey of a small portion of the population that reveals certain characteristics of the population in general. The statistician must be able to make decisions about where to obtain the needed data, the size and structure of the sample group, and how workers should tabulate the returns.

A statistician's tasks vary according to the area in which he or she works. Most statisticians work in private industry. Others, however, work for the government or teach at colleges and universities. Those in private industry might work for manufacturing firms and develop surveys to determine consumer acceptance of a new product. They also might design sampling procedures to measure the quality of products coming off the assembly line. Or they might work for a public opinion agency like a television rating service and use a sample of a few thousand homes to make predictions about the size of the national audience watching certain shows each week. These projections often are used to determine the rates major networks charge advertisers. Those who work for the federal government might gather and interpret data on which estimates of gross national product, unemployment, and inflation can be based.

No matter in which area a statistician works, he or she must deal with the collection, organization, and interpretation of numerical data. Therefore, he or she must be good in mathematics and able to analyze problems in a logical and organized fashion. Most statisticians are required to have the equivalent of a college degree in statistics or mathematics. In some cases, graduate study in either of these areas is helpful, as are courses in physics, political science, biology, or economics. More recently, familiarity with computers, which are used extensively to analyze data, also is recommended.

Food stamps are government-issued coupons that can be redeemed by low-income people to purchase food. How is eligibility for this program determined?

decide how the program is to be carried out.

MARKET INCENTIVES

Some approaches proposed to reduce poverty focus on ways to use the incentive of the market to help those in need. One such approach is the negative income tax. Another is through enterprise zones.

NEGATIVE INCOME TAX.   The **negative income tax** is a type of tax that would make cash payments to certain low-income groups below the poverty line. For this reason, it is called a "negative" income tax. For example, the federal government might set an income level below which people did not have to pay taxes. Then, the federal government would pay a

certain amount of money to any person who earned less than the level.

For example, a person who earned no income during a year might receive $3000. That person's total income for the year would then be $3000. Another person who actually earned $3000 might receive $1500 from the government. This would bring that person's income to $4500 for the year. A third person who made $6000 for the year would receive nothing from the government. But, because the income was not over the set level, that person still would not have to pay taxes.

A fourth person, however, who earned more than $6000 would have to pay some taxes. In addition, as income got higher, so would the taxes. For example, a person with an income of $10,000 might pay a tax of $1500, while a person with an income of $15,000 might pay $3000.

Case Study: Issue

Is Workfare a Good Idea?

Because of rising welfare costs, many state and local governments require those who receive welfare to provide labor as a condition for receiving welfare. When welfare recipients provide labor in exchange for benefits, this is known as *workfare*. These people are often required to assist police, fire, sanitation, and highway crews, or perform other types of community-service work. Such work is required of almost everyone except for those with young children, the disabled, and elderly persons.

Those who favor workfare believe that those who are able to work, should do so. In addition, they argue that many on workfare receive on-the-job training and employment skills necessary for them to join the workforce. These supporters say that many people would not be on welfare roles if they knew they had to work for benefits.

Those who oppose workfare believe that such a system exploits those who need public assistance. An unemployed accountant, for example, may feel embarrassed collecting garbage, raking leaves, or sweeping floors. Many on workfare claim that the jobs assigned to them are ones they dislike in the first place, and would never take even if they learned the required skills. And, the amount of hours worked is closely tied to the benefits received. Yet, they often must work at near minimum wage levels. Thus, many say they are made to feel as if they are being punished because they need public assistance.

1. Why is workfare popular with many state and local governments? Who is required to participate?
2. Why do many people support the concept of workfare?
3. Why do some on workfare oppose the concept?

The negative income tax would be cost-effective because it could be used in place of existing welfare programs. It would eliminate costly welfare programs yet still allow people to have money that they could spend as they saw fit. Government would save because it would have fewer administrative costs. The tax also would prevent those who are not truly needy from depending on government support. Even though the tax is not used today, many people feel it would be a reasonable alternative to the existing social welfare net programs.

ENTERPRISE ZONES. Special **enterprise zones** are areas where companies can locate free of certain local, state, and federal tax laws and operating restrictions. This would benefit not only businesses, but area residents as well. People without jobs could find work without worrying about transportation, and run-down areas would begin to grow again.

▎ Section Review

1. Why is poverty hard to measure?

2. What three kinds of help does the government provide for the needy? What does each involve?

3. What are two approaches to poverty that focus on ways to use market incentives to help the needy? What are the characteristics of each?

21.4 *Progress Against Poverty*

Over the years, debate has continued about whether the war on poverty is being won or lost. One reason is the way in which the poverty level is defined. In 1986, for example, the poverty level for a non-farm family of four was $11,000. Some people believed that a family would have had a hard time making ends meet at that

Many have debated whether government has done enough to fight back against poverty. Why is there so much disagreement on this subject?

Understanding Sources

Poverty Levels

The following article appeared in the August 27, 1986 edition of *The Wall Street Journal.* Read the article and answer the questions that follow.

WASHINGTON—The nation's poverty rate edged down to 14% last year from 14.4% in 1984, but represented the fifth consecutive year of relatively high poverty levels, the Census Bureau said.

In 1985, 33.1 million Americans lived below the poverty threshold, a statistically insignificant decrease of 600,000 from the year before, the bureau said. Their numbers shrank 1.6 million in 1984, but between 1981 and 1983, 3.5 million people joined the ranks of the poor.

The poverty threshold for a family of four rose to $10,989 in annual cash income last year from $10,609 in 1984.

The report is based on a nationwide survey last March of about 60,000 households.

1. How did the poverty rate change between 1984 and 1985?
2. According to the article, is the poverty rate considered high or low from a historical viewpoint?

level. Others argued that the figure was too high because families were receiving more transfer payments and other forms of governmental assistance than in the past. Many argued that a poverty-level family in the 1980's was much better off than a poverty-level family in the 1950's.

Before a good deal of headway can be made on the war on poverty, incomes of families in the lowest income brackets need to be raised. The 1986 tax reform act benefited some families since nearly 6 million low-income persons were taken off the tax rolls. These families now have more real income to spend. The reform bill alone, however, will not boost all families out of poverty and into higher income brackets.

Nearly everyone agrees that one of the best weapons in the fight against poverty is a healthy and growing economy. If the economy is stable, more employment opportunities are available for all Americans, enabling everyone the chance to work. This, in turn, puts more people above the poverty line. They then are better able to pay taxes and to support those who are less fortunate than themselves.

Section Review

1. In 1986, what was the poverty level for a family of four?

2. Why is there debate about whether progress has been made in the war on poverty?

Chapter 21 Review

Summary

1. Since colonial times, the population of the United States has grown considerably, households have become smaller, and the center of population has moved westward.

2. The term distribution of income is used to describe how income is distributed among individuals, families, households, and other groups.

3. The Lorenz Curve shows how much the actual distribution of income varies from equal distribution.

4. Income differences from one group to another may be due to education, wealth, discrimination, ability, or monopoly power.

5. Government programs designed to help the needy fall into three categories—income assistance, general assistance, and social service.

6. The negative income tax uses the incentive of the market to help the needy by making cash payments to those with incomes below the poverty level.

7. To make headway on the war against poverty, more of the country's income must be diverted to people in the lowest income bracket.

Building an Economic Vocabulary

center of population
population tree
distribution of income
Lorenz Curve
blue-collar workers

white-collar workers
poverty level
social welfare net programs
Aid to Families with
    Dependent Children (AFDC)

Supplemental Security
    Income (SSI)
food stamps
negative income tax
enterprise zones

Reviewing the Main Ideas

1. What is the most common way of analyzing the distribution of income?

2. How do discrimination and ability affect the distribution of income?

3. What can happen to the income of a group with high monopoly power?

4. For what reason is poverty a relative measure?

5. Why do many people think a negative income tax would be a reasonable alternative to the existing social welfare net programs?

Practicing Critical Thinking Skills

1. A philosopher once said, "Poverty is a state of mind." As an economist, how would you refute this statement?

2. Do you think the negative income tax is a reasonable alternative to social welfare net programs? Why or why not?

3. How do you define poverty? Do you think progress has been made in the fight against poverty?

Applying Economic Understandings

Verifying a Theory

Economists often have to **verify** or determine the truth of a theory. There are several steps that can be taken to do this.

1. Gather evidence to support or disprove the theory. Then, organize the evidence to make a comparison.

2. Analyze the evidence. Study each point to make sure it relates to the topic and to other points.

3. Weigh the evidence. Then, determine if your evidence supports or disproves the theory by asking questions.

One way to verify or disprove the theory; "Some people receive higher incomes than others because they have more education," would be to first choose some occupations. Then, classify each according to the level of education required. Estimate the income earned by each and examine the results using the chart given.

To examine the results of the investigation, the following questions were asked and then answered about the occupations listed in the chart.

Occupation	Education Required	Annual Salary
accounts payable clerk	2 years college	$15,600
computer operator trainee	high school	11,000
teacher	4 years college	17,500
engineer	5 years or more college	28,000
fast food clerk	8 years	7,176
typist	1-3 years high school	10,400

1. Which occupations require the most education? The least?

2. Which occupations pay the best salary? The least?

3. As the educational level increases, do the salaries increase?

The result of the analysis supports the theory that some people receive higher incomes than others because they have more education.

For further practice in this skill, follow the steps given above (choosing different occupations and using your local classified advertisements) to determine if you can verify the same theory.

The Resource Challenge

. . . the view of earth from space dramatizes the image of man as inhabiting a small, closed spaceship, destination unknown and resources limited.
Kenneth Boulding

Chapter 22

After reading this chapter, you will be able to:

- Recognize that the depletion of vital resources is a major global problem.

- Explain the ways in which economic incentives influence the usage, abuse, and conservation of vital resources.

- Discuss the reasons for pollution and two ways in which it can be controlled.

22.1 *Demand for Resources*

One of the major problems facing countries today is that the demand for many vital resources is outrunning the supply. Concern for resource shortages is not new. It can be traced back to the eighteenth-century economist Thomas Malthus, who argued that population would grow faster than its ability to feed itself. Malthus feared that if remedies were not found, in time the world's population would be reduced to a condition of **subsistence**—the state in which the population produces barely enough to support itself.

Malthus, however, did not foresee the huge advances in productivity that allowed an increasing standard of living to accompany a growing population. He also did not foresee the fact that families might choose to have fewer children. As a result, his predictions were not entirely accurate for the advanced industrial countries. They may have been closer to correct, however,

Profile

■ Thomas Malthus

Thomas Malthus was an English economist, sociologist, and member of the clergy who pioneered modern population study. He believed that the major reason for the extreme poverty of some people was that the world's population was growing faster than the food supply.

1766–1834

In 1798, Malthus published his ideas about population and the food supply in *An Essay on the Principles of Population*. In it, he argued that poverty and distress could not be avoided because population increases at a geometric rate (1, 2, 4, 8, 16, ...), while food supplies increase at an arithmetic rate (1, 2, 3, 4, . . .). In other words, both population and the food supply would double in 25 years. In the next 25 years, population would double again to four times its original size, but the food supply would increase to only three times what it was originally. At the end of a 100-year period, then, population will have increased 16 times and the food supply only 5 times.

At first, Malthus saw only three things that could check the growth of population—war, famine, and disease. Several years later, he revised this line of thinking and added a fourth check—"moral restraint." Singly or together, these factors could raise the death rate and/or lower the birthrate. In Malthus' view, however, these restraints on population growth would not be enough to prevent the standard of living for most of the world from remaining at the subsistence level forever. The increases in the food supply would eventually be offset by population growth, and the great mass of humanity never could improve its lot.

One of Malthus' other theories was that of diminishing returns, which has become an important tool of economic analysis. He argued that additions of labor and fertilizer would increase the yield per acre of land only up to a certain point. Once that point was reached, the increases would become smaller and smaller. Eventually, they would not be worth the cost of the extra labor and fertilizer. Later, the same reasoning was applied to industry.

This child is one of many all over the world who suffer from hunger. What effect does population have on the food supply?

In many of these countries, poverty is widespread, especially in the larger cities. The Indian city of Calcutta, for example, is home to 8 million people. It is one of the most crowded and poorest cities in the world. It is estimated that hundreds of thousands of "street dwellers" beg or search for food in the city dumps and refuse piles by day. At night they sleep on the sidewalks.

At present, the world population is growing at about 1.7 percent a year. While this may not seem like a very large increase, the consequences can be enormous over time. In 1986, for example, the world population was estimated to be about 5 billion people. If the population keeps growing at this rate, the world population will be over 6 billion by the end of the century and nearly 15 billion by 2050. Stated differently, the population of the world will more than double from the time a high school senior graduates in 1990 until he or she retires at age 65.

Section Review

1. What is one of the major problems facing most countries today?
2. Who was Thomas Malthus? What was his theory about population?

for many of the developing countries, which tend to have larger families and greater populations.

22.2 Resources and Economic Incentives

Population is not the only pressure on resources. Some important resources are being depleted with no effort being made to replace them for the generations to come. Others are being polluted at an alarming rate. Gas, water, land, and food all are important resources that have been threatened. The degree to which each is used or abused, however, often depends on economic incentives.

ENERGY

Energy is a precious resource for any country. As a factor of production, energy belongs to the "land" category and is, therefore, needed before production can take place. In one form or another, it makes life more comfortable. In the form of gas, it powers cars. In the form of electricity, it heats and cools homes.

In the past, the price of energy was relatively low, demand was high, and consumption tended to grow rapidly. Between 1900 and 1970, for example, energy consumption in the United States doubled almost every 14 years. Because prices were relatively low, automobiles tended to be big and heavy and got poor gas mileage. Houses tended to be large, spacious, and poorly insulated. People tended to live some distance from where they worked and spent hours traveling to and from their jobs.

All this came to a halt, however, in 1973 when the oil-producing countries of the Middle East placed an **embargo**—a restriction on the export or import of a commodity in trade—on oil sales to the West. The embargo caused energy shortages in many parts of the world and drove up prices. Shortly after, the OPEC nations agreed among themselves to set even higher

Figure 22–1

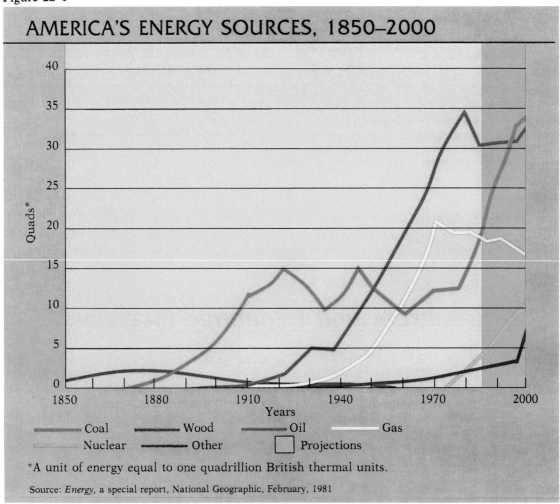

AMERICA'S ENERGY SOURCES, 1850–2000

Quads*

Years

Coal — Wood — Oil — Gas
Nuclear — Other — Projections

*A unit of energy equal to one quadrillion British thermal units.

Source: *Energy*, a special report, National Geographic, February, 1981

Understanding Sources

 Oil Prices, Production, and Reserves

The following report appeared in *The Wall Street Journal* on November 3, 1986. Read the paragraph and answer the questions that follow.

Even $18-a-Barrel Oil Won't Halt Plunging U.S. Output

The decline in U.S. petroleum production triggered by this year's oil-price collapse is accelerating. Battered domestic producers say even an $18-a-barrel price won't turn things around.

At 8.7 million barrels a day, domestic output of crude oil is down 300,000 barrels a day since the start of 1986, reversing four consecutive years of increase. The stage is set for further and bigger drops. The gap has to be filled with foreign oil imports, which are rising at a fast rate because of increased petroleum demand.

Oil industry executives say that an increase in oil prices from the current average of $14-a-barrel—half that of a year ago—might slow the erosion in U.S. petroleum production. Eventually, they say, the production slide could even be halted—if oil prices were to rise high enough to spur a resurgence of exploration in the U.S.

---

1. What happened to the production of crude oil in the United States between 1985 and 1986?
2. What accounted for the change in production?
3. Why does the textbook state that "the amount of energy reserves are a function of price"?

prices for their oil exports. During the 1970's, the price of oil went from less than $5 to more than $35 a barrel.

During this period, oil was bought directly from agencies representing OPEC. Some oil, however, was traded on the Amsterdam **spot market**—a cash market where oil is openly bought and sold at prices set freely by supply and demand. Sometimes, the spot market prices were as much as $10-to-$12 a barrel higher than the OPEC price. Other times, they were lower than the OPEC price.

In 1981, prices began to fall because of a worldwide **glut**—substantial oversupply of oil. There were several major causes. One was a recession that was taking place in most countries. With fewer goods being produced, less energy was needed in production, and the demand for oil and gas

The Americans in this cartoon have no sympathy for the OPEC representatives drowning in a sea of oil. Many Americans felt OPEC had taken advantage of the oil shortage. What did OPEC do during the shortage?

declined in industry. Another was that people had learned to conserve energy. Still another was the alternatives many countries had found to high-priced oil. The major reason, however, was that the high price of oil encouraged all nations to produce more. Finally, by 1986, OPEC lost the ability to control the supply of oil. As a result, the price of oil dropped briefly to under $10 a barrel.

RENEWABLE ENERGY SOURCES. Before 1973, there was very little incentive to develop renewable energy sources such as solar, hydroelectric, or wind power. The oil embargo and soaring oil prices, however, provided the incentive. Americans became concerned about cost and about their dependence on foreign countries for energy. As a result, they began to look for alternatives.

One alternative was solar power, which, until recently, had been of interest mostly to inventors and scientists. After the embargo, however, the federal government began issuing grants to researchers to help them find ways to bring down the cost of solar energy. Congress passed laws giving taxpayers credits for installing energy-saving devices in their homes. This encouraged many homeowners to insulate, install storm windows, and equip their homes with solar-powered water heaters.

Another alternative was hydropower, which, in the past, had been used to power the mills and factories of the Northeast. The power was reliable, and, at the time, its source—water—was free. The drawback was that most dams were small and could not distribute power very efficiently to other locations. Later, when oil could be obtained cheaply from the Middle

East, water power became less important. As a result, by the late 1950's most of the commercial power dams in the United States had been abandoned. When oil became more expensive, however, steps were taken to bring some of the dams back into use. Today, it is estimated that hydropower could reduce imported oil usage by close to 20 percent.

A third alternative was electricity generated by wind. In the early 1980's, sales of wind-driven equipment for electrical generation amounted to hundreds of millions of dollars. Many "wind farms" were built, and produced enough electricity to power a medium-size city.

Other alternatives included wood for use in stoves and **gasohol**—a fuel that is a

Figure 22–2

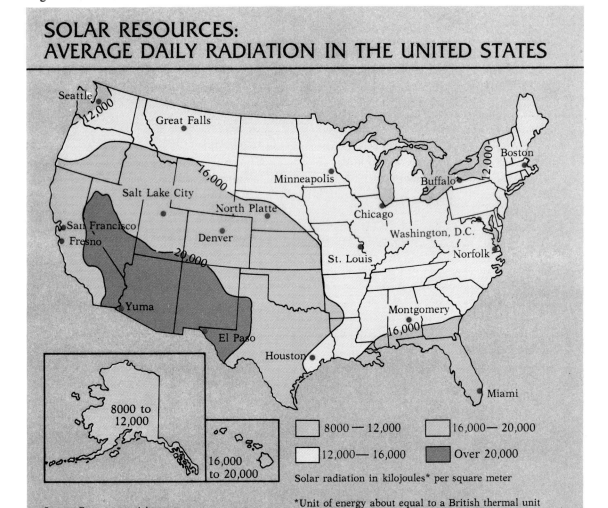

SOLAR RESOURCES: AVERAGE DAILY RADIATION IN THE UNITED STATES

8000 — 12,000	16,000 — 20,000
12,000 — 16,000	Over 20,000

Solar radiation in kilojoules* per square meter

*Unit of energy about equal to a British thermal unit

Source: *Energy*, a special report, National Geographic, February 1981

Profile

■ Sylvia Porter

Sylvia Porter is an economist and journalist who is known to many Americans for her clear and timely advice on money matters.

She has published more than a dozen books including *How to Live Within Your Income, Sylvia Porter's Money Book for the 80's, Your Own Money,* and her annual *Sylvia Porter's Income Tax Guide.* In addition, she has authored numerous articles and columns on nearly every topic of interest to consumers.

1913–

In her writings, she has always sought to give consumers the information, tips, and advice necessary to make wise choices. She was a leading spokesperson of the consumer movement before it became a popular cause. Her advice often went beyond financial information and frequently included such tips as how to write a resumé and look for a job.

She was named "Woman of the Decade" by the *Ladies Home Journal* in 1979 and one of America's 25 most influential women in the 1982 *World Almanac.* Her columns, books, and other writings continue to inspire and guide consumers in a variety of areas.

---

mixture of 90 percent unleaded gasoline and 10 percent grain alcohol. Although gasohol has not caught on as fast as supporters first hoped, it still has a small share of the market in some areas. Wood and coal stoves, on the other hand, have grown rapidly in popularity, especially in high-cost energy areas like the industrial Northeast. Other less-known alternatives also have been developed by private industry. Major food firms like Kroger, for example, have made progress in converting chicken waste to fuel in the form of methane gas that can be recycled for industrial and commercial use.

NONRENEWABLE ENERGY SOURCES. The high price of oil also increased interest in such nonrenewable energy sources as natural gas, oil from shale and tar sands, coal, and nuclear power. During the 1960's, for example, there was little interest in the natural gas locked deep in the earth. Deep wells were expensive to dig. Since the federal government was keeping the price of gas very low to protect consumers, there was little incentive for producers to drill for it. For this reason, much less natural gas was recovered than could have been.

Congress tried to stimulate gas discovery and production by lifting the price controls on **deep gas**—pockets of natural gas 15,000 feet or more below the earth's surface. This increased its price to three or four times that of gas found above 15,000 feet. As a result, much of the recent exploration for gas has been devoted chiefly to deep gas.

The lack of interest on the part of oil and gas producers in drilling for shallow gas is consistent with the Law of Supply, which maintains that the lower the price paid to producers, the less will be brought to market. Also consistent with the law is the effort by producers to produce the higher-priced deep gas.

In the end, the efforts to keep gas prices low to help the consumer had significant side effects. As long as gas was cheap, people found many ways to use it. They heated their homes and swimming pools with gas and built their factories and technology around it. This was fine as long as the price of gas remained low. Once the prices began to rise, however, people found they were locked into using a product they would prefer to abandon. The high price of oil, along with the rising price of gas, forced consumers and industry to look for alternative energy sources. Oil companies began experimenting with ways to extract oil from shale deposits in the western United States and from hydrocarbon deposits, or tar sands, in Canada.

Interest was renewed in coal, which was the major source of energy in the United States until the late 1940's. At that time, it became cheaper and easier to transport oil and gas than coal. Today, nearly two thirds of the world's known coal reserves are in the United States, the Soviet Union,

and China. It is estimated that at the present rate of consumption, the reserves could last more than 200 years.

Interest also grew in nuclear energy, which today generates about 10 percent of the commercial electricity used in the United States. The future of nuclear power, however, is not certain for several reasons. For one, nuclear energy produces highly hazardous by-products, the safe disposal of which poses a major problem. For another, construction costs of nuclear reactors are staggering. Lastly, many people are not yet convinced that nuclear power does not present a danger to health and the environment. The 1986 melt down of the reactor in Chernobyl reminded the world of the hazards of nuclear power.

In practice, then, the amount of energy reserves is a function of price. Not long ago, for example, it was thought that the reserves of natural gas in the United States would last only another 30 years or so. That prediction, however, was made when the price of natural gas was low. If the price were higher, less would be bought, and the given reserves would stretch further. At the same time, the higher price would encourage more exploration, and more reserves would be found. As a result, the supplies would last even longer.

OTHER RESOURCES

There has been a growing awareness in recent years that resources besides those used to generate energy may be in trouble. These include water, land, and food.

WATER.   In the recent past, American concern with water focused chiefly on the pollution of the country's waterways. Today, however, the focus is on the availability of water and the fact that it is in

Nuclear energy is considered an alternative energy source. Its future, however, is uncertain especially after the meltdown at Chernobyl in May 1986. What other reasons make the future of nuclear power uncertain?

critical supply in many parts of the country. Recently, for example, it was estimated that more than 80 percent of the water consumed in the United States was used in agriculture. Most of this was used in the form of surface irrigation, which has a high evaporation rate. As a result, much of it is lost into the atmosphere rather than being consumed by the crop.

Farmers have been able to tap large sources of water from rivers, streams, ponds, and **aquifers**—underground water-bearing rock formations. The aquifers supply nearly 40 percent of the water used by farmers and are the source of fresh water for many communities. One of the largest aquifers in the country is the Ogallala aquifer, which supplies water to the High Plains states from Texas to Nebraska. The pumping is so heavy, however, that the aquifer's water table has been dropping at a rate of about three feet a year. Some experts have gone so far as to predict that it will run out of water within the next 40 or 50 years.

The shortage of water also is a problem in California. Southern California hoped to solve its problem by using a canal to bring in water from the Sacramento River, which is in the northern part of the state. Northern Californians, however, were not pleased with this idea. They feared they would end up with too little water for their own needs causing them to pay more for the water they already use.

Like energy, water was an inexpensive resource until recently. When it was available in large amounts and at very low prices, farmers used a great deal of it in areas not suitable for farming otherwise. Consumers also tended to use it freely. They watered their lawns; washed cars; used large-capacity washing machines; filled bathtubs; and ran showers for long periods of time. When water became scarce and its price went up, however, consumers began to wash their cars less often, install water-saving devices in the bathroom, and reduced other usage of water around the home.

Farmers also are affected by the water shortage—even when they take most of their water out of the ground. Often, this is done with pumps driven by electricity or natural gas. When water tables fall because of pumping, it costs more to pump the water. As long as farmers continue to make a profit on their crops, they probably will be willing to pay the higher price for the water.

In time, the falling water table will make some of the shallow wells useless, and deeper, more costly ones will have to be drilled in their place. When this happens, the price system will come into play again. Deeper wells will be dug for profitable crops, while unprofitable crops will be abandoned.

In the end, the price system will work to help establish an equilibrium between the rising cost of recovering water and the depleted water tables. Although some crops and fields will be abandoned, they are likely to be the ones that were the least productive in the first place. As a result, the actual amount of agricultural output will not be much less than it is at present.

LAND. Another valuable natural resource subject to the demands of a growing world population is land. Land, however, is different from other resources primarily because it is immobile and cannot be moved from one place to another. It also is fixed in supply.

A growing population often tends to occupy some of the best farmland, which means it cannot be used for farming. In the early days, for example, many of the settlers located in river valleys because the land was fertile enough to farm and the river provided transportation. As time went on, however, the population grew. Towns and cities took the place of the early river settlements. As communities grew, factories, roads, and houses were built on the fertile land near the river. This forced the farmers to move to the outskirts.

Irrigating sprayers such as this one are fairly common in the United States. Why is water an important resource?

As this pattern of growth repeated itself many times all over the country, some of the finest farmland ended up beneath expressways, shopping centers, and housing developments. This is especially true today in the fertile river basin areas of California. Since many farmers willingly sold their land to the industrial and housing interests, this trend would be hard to reverse today.

When the farmers sold their land, they often relocated in areas where the land was less fertile but, at the same time, cost less. Since the proper combination of inputs depends on both the cost and the productivity of inputs, the decisions to relocate where they did made sense. Since then, the development and availability of fertilizers, pesticides, herbicides, and other technology advances have kept the farmers far ahead of other sectors of the economy as far as productivity is concerned.

FOOD.   There is a critical shortage of food on a global scale today. Many Americans, however, find this hard to believe because the United States is not suffering from such shortages.

One of the reasons for this is that in the United States, the federal government has instituted **target prices** or **support prices**— legal floor prices that producers are entitled to receive by law. When market prices fall below the support levels, the government either buys the crops outright or makes a cash payment for the difference.

In May, 1986, the target or support price, for example, for wheat was $4.38 a bushel. The demand and supply of wheat on the market set the price closer to $3.38 a bushel. Even so, farmers received the target price. They sold wheat in the market for $3.38 and then received the additional $1.00 a bushel, or a "deficiency payment," from the government.

This is an underground storage facility in Missouri. The cost of storing dairy surpluses and other items is a matter of debate in the U.S. Why does the U.S. have such surpluses?

Dairy products are handled a little differently. The government sets a certain price and then buys any surplus that cannot be sold at that price. For the most part, production is in the form of milk, which then is processed into cheese, dry milk, and butter so it can be preserved longer. By the end of March, 1986, the government owned 248 million pounds of butter, 607 million pounds of cheese, and 953 million pounds of non-fat, or powdered, milk. On a per capita basis, this amounted to nearly 7.5 pounds of butter, cheese, or powdered milk for every person in the country.

Storing the surplus is an expense and a problem. Today, it costs the government over $1 million a day for storage. It leases warehouse space around the country and even uses underground caverns. Wheat has even been stored in the holds of old battleships and on open ground near Palo Alto, California.

All the surplus is not stored. Some is redistributed to schools in the form of low-cost lunches. Some is used to feed the armed forces. Most of the surplus, however, is allowed to spoil or is destroyed. The Department of Agriculture has opposed efforts to give away any of the surplus in the belief that giving it away would reduce the consumer demand for agricultural products. Although the Department has sold crops to foreign countries at reduced prices, it will not sell them in the United States for less because it might drive agricultural prices down.

Price supports have proven to be so attractive that farmers often try to increase production. In order to restrict output, Congress authorizes **allotments**—quotas on the number of acres that can be devoted to a certain crop. The allotments are particularly important in the tobacco and peanut industries in which price supports have had a long history of congres-

sional support. Many farmers are required to have allotments to qualify for the price supports. Without the price supports, there is little reason to grow the crop.

By taking advantage of modern methods, American farmers today can produce more output per capita than ever before. This extra output has driven prices down. Price supports were instituted to help keep farmers' incomes up. Even today, many farmers will argue that the problem with farming is that there are too many farmers. Many would like to see an end to price supports in certain crops so that prices could be established by the forces of supply and demand. These prices, they feel, would reflect more accurately the true value of farm output.

The problem of an adequate food supply in the United States, then, is one of distribution rather than production. Quite simply, people who cannot afford to buy food do not get as much as they need, even if a surplus lies rotting in government warehouses. In the rest of the world, however, the problem is one of both distribution and production.

Section Review

1. What was the oil embargo? What effect did it have on the United States?
2. What are three renewable energy sources that serve as an alternative to oil?
3. What is deep gas? Why has much of the recent gas exploration been devoted to it?
4. On what is the American concern with water focused today? Why?
5. Why is land different from other resources? What effect has this had on farming?
6. What are price supports? How do they affect farmers?

22.3 Pollution

Pollution is the contamination of air, water, or soil by the discharge of poisonous or noxious substances. It is a problem that most countries today must face. It is important to understand why pollution exists and to determine what can be done about it.

INCENTIVE TO POLLUTE

For years, factories have located along the banks of rivers so they could dump their refuse into the moving waters. Some factories, which generated smoke and other air pollutants, located further away from the water, but their tall smokestacks still blew the pollutants far and wide.

Others tried to avoid the problem by digging refuse pits on their property and burying their toxic wastes.

In all three cases, factory owners simply were trying to lower production costs by using the environment as a giant waste-disposal system. From an economic point of view, the reasoning was sound. Firms get an edge when they lower production costs. Those who produce for the least cost make the most profits. Pollution, then, from the point of view of the firm makes sense. It may even mean the difference between survival and failure.

The costs of pollution to society as a whole, however, are huge. For example, **acid rain**—a mixture of water and sulphur dioxide that makes a mild form of sulphu-

This lake in Michigan has been severely polluted. Why are many American waterways polluted?

ric acid—falls over much of North America stripping countless rivers and streams of aquatic life. Other areas are choking from fertilizer and raw sewage that disrupt the ecology.

There is no argument about the fact that the costs of pollution are high. What many people cannot agree on, however, is what is the best way to solve the problem.

CONTROLLING POLLUTION

Basically, there are two ways by which pollution can be controlled. One is with legislated standards, and the other is through tax incentives.

Legislated standards include laws that specify the minimum standards of purity for air, water, and auto emissions. For example, Congress has declared that all automobiles sold in the United States must meet certain pollution standards. If they do not meet the standards, the Environmental Protection Agency will not certify them, and they cannot be sold domestically.

Even though affected industries have objected to them, some legislated standards have worked quite well. The auto industry, for example, complained loudly for years that it could not meet the standards. Yet, when pressed to do so, most auto manufacturers managed to meet them. Some other companies, however, did not fare as well. They decided to close down rather than to spend the money needed to upgrade their aging capital stock.

An alternative to legislated standards is to have companies pay tax on the amount of pollutants they release. The size of the tax would depend on the severity of the pollution and the quantity of toxic substances being released.

Suppose, for example, a community is trying to reduce air pollution caused chief-

Despite legislation, air pollution is still a problem in many parts of the United States. How can tax incentives help solve the problem?

ly by four factories, each of which releases large quantities of coal dust into the air. A tax of $50 for every ton of coal dust released into the air could be applied to each factory. The total tax each paid over the course of the year would depend on the number of tons of dust discharged. Devices attached to the top of the factory's smokestacks during a one-week period could be used to measure the amount of discharge. Once the average rate of discharge is established, the factory could be billed accordingly.

Each company would have the choice of paying the tax bill or removing the pollutants themselves. Suppose two factories

Case Study: Career

Economic Geographer

An economic geographer combines the skills of a geographer and an economist. He or she deals with the geographic distribution of such economic activities as manufacturing, mining, agriculture, trade, and communications.

In other words, the economic geographer uses his or her knowledge of land forms, climate, human resources, and other geographical features to help determine and analyze what economic activity is best-suited to a particular area. The knowledge also may be used to determine and analyze why an economic activity takes place where it does. To help in this task, the economic geographer uses maps, aerial photographs, census reports, and statistics.

Economic geographers may work for local, state, or federal government; private industry; or colleges and universities. In government or industry, they can offer valuable information and advice to planners who want to attract a certain kind of economic activity to a particular area. They can do the same for firms that want to know where to set up new plants or businesses.

Economic geographers must have formal training in both economics and geography. As a result, they generally have the background to work as climatologists, community development specialists, land economists, regional planners, site researchers, and transportation planners. No matter what job title they hold, however, they should enjoy reading, studying, and research. They also should be able to work on their own and to communicate ideas clearly both orally and in writing. Since they may have to do some field work in areas that are not fully developed, they also must be willing and able to adapt to different social and cultural environments.

In most cases, a bachelor's degree is required for entry level positions. For those wishing to teach or to advance to senior or administrative positions in government or business, a master's degree or Ph.D. is becoming essential. At present, the number of positions open to economic geographers still is limited.

find that if they install scrubbers, they can remove the coal dust for $40 a ton—$10 a ton less than the tax would cost them. Most likely, they would choose to install the scrubbers rather than have to pay the tax. This means that the community will have two less factories to pollute its air. If, as a result of this, the quality of the air is suitable, nothing further needs to be done.

If, however, the quality of the air still is below the desired level, the tax can be raised to $60 or $70 a ton. This might cause a third factory to install its own pollution equipment. If the air still is not clean enough, the community then could raise the tax again until the fourth factory decides to install scrubbers.

This tax approach, suggested by many economists, does not try to remove all pollution. It does, however, allow individual companies some freedom of choice. It also provides for some flexibility that legislated standards lack and may prevent some plants from closing entirely.

There always will be some firms that would rather pay the tax than clean up their own pollution. These firms, however, help fund the pollution clean-up campaign. This means that consumers will not have to fund the effort out of their income, sales, or property taxes.

Section Review

1. What is pollution? What is the major incentive for it?

2. What are two ways in which pollution can be controlled? What are the characteristics of each?

22.4 Using Resources Wisely

The resource challenge is central to the study of economics. Resources become scarce when their demand is greater than their supply. At times, this is due to the fact that resources are priced so low that they are used in a casual and inefficient manner. Other times, it is due to the fact that the resources have been "used up."

In a market economy such as the one in the United States, the price system plays a major role in the allocation of resources. It tells the people when resources are scarce. Then the price associated with the resources helps the decision-makers allocate them more wisely. For this reason, most economists who believe in a market economy tend to be optimistic about the future, especially if the price system is allowed to function and fulfill its role in the economy.

Whether or not other countries adjust to the resource challenge depends on the way in which they make their economic decisions. Those with command-type economies need vast quantities of information before they can make any decisions. This information then has to filter through layers of bureaucracy. Although economists do not always agree as to which system is better suited to deal with the problem of scarce resources, at present the market economies of the world are proving more able to cope with the crisis.

Section Review

1. Why is the demand for resources greater than their supply?

2. Why do free market economists tend to be optimistic about the future?

Chapter 22 Review

Summary

1. One of the major problems today is that the demand for many vital resources is outrunning the supply.

2. In 1973, the oil-producing countries placed an embargo on oil sales to the West, which led to energy shortages and higher oil prices.

3. In 1981, oil prices fell because of an oil glut caused by a recession, less demand for oil and gas, and the development of other sources of energy.

4. Three energy sources being used as alternatives to oil are solar power, hydroelectric power, and wind power.

5. The high price of oil led to increased interest in nonrenewable energy sources.

6. Other natural resources in short supply in many parts of the United States are water and land.

7. The United States does not suffer from a critical food shortage because of the price supports paid to farmers by the federal government.

8. In the United States, the problem of adequate food supply is one of distribution rather than production.

9. Another problem today is pollution, which can be controlled by legislated standards and tax incentives.

10. In a market economy, the price system tells people when resources are scarce and helps decision-makers allocate resources more wisely.

Building an Economic Vocabulary

subsistence	glut	aquifers	allotments
embargo	gasohol	target prices	pollution
spot market	deep gas	support prices	acid rain

Reviewing the Main Ideas

1. What is the relationship between population and the demand for resources?

2. What is the difference between renewable and nonrenewable energy sources?

3. What were the side effects of efforts in the 1960's to keep gas prices low to protect consumers? What happened when the prices rose?

4. What will happen to the price of water when some of the shallow water wells become useless? How will this affect agriculture?

5. How does the problem of adequate food supply in the United States differ from that in other countries?

6. What is the role of the price system in the allocation of resources in a market economy?

■ *Practicing Critical Thinking Skills*

1. Explain how the Laws of Demand and Supply apply to the resource challenge.

2. Do you think the federal government should continue to provide price supports to farmers? Defend your answer.

3. Discuss the advantages and disadvantages of using legislated standards and tax incentives to control pollution.

4. List ten ways in which Americans could use resources more wisely than they are at present.

■ *Applying Economic Understandings*

Placing Information in Order of Significance

Determining how important one piece of information is compared to others is an important skill when studying economics. To do this, another skill is automatically being performed—*placing information in order of significance,* or arranging it in order from the most important to the least important. The following guidelines will help you develop this skill.

1. Find the sentence that expresses the main idea. It is the most important. Without it, none of the other information has anything to which it can relate.

2. Determine which statements support the main idea. These are next in importance. They describe, explain, or give details about the main idea. To help find these statements, look for *signals*—words or phrases used to signal a supporting statement. Examples are: *the reasons for, the following characteristics,* and *for example.*

3. Determine what information is unimportant or *incidental,* giving details that may be interesting but not necessary to understand or support the main idea. This information is least important.

Read the following paragraph, each sentence of which is numbered and classified according to its order of significance.

(1) The costs of pollution to society are huge. *(Main idea; gives meaning to supporting statements)* (2) For example, the acid rain that falls in the industrial Northeast is stripping countless rivers and streams of aquatic life. *(Supporting statement; explains how pollution hurts society)* (3) Fertilizers and chemicals used by many farmers are entering the water supply and contaminating it. *(Supporting statement; explains how pollution hurts society)* (4) Tax incentives can be used to help solve the problem. *(Incidental; not needed to understand how pollution hurts society)*

For practice in this skill, use the guidelines to help you place the information found in any three paragraphs of Chapter 22 in order of significance.

Unit 7 Review

The Unit in Perspective

1. All countries today must be concerned about population, distribution of income, poverty, and resource depletion and pollution.

2. The rate at which population grows affects the economic growth of a country.

3. Income is not distributed equally among individuals and groups because of such factors as education, wealth, discrimination, ability, and monopoly power.

4. Poverty is a relative measure generally defined by a poverty level.

5. Over the years, the government of the United States has tried to combat poverty by instituting special programs, most of which are social welfare net programs.

6. Some approaches proposed to reduce poverty, such as the negative income tax and enterprise zones focus on ways to use the incentive of the market to help the needy.

7. Despite efforts to reduce poverty progress towards that goal remains slow.

8. Many vital resources are scarce today—even in the United States—chiefly because their demand is greater than their supply.

9. Recently, the high cost of oil has led to increased interest in alternative energy sources. These include solar, hydroelectric, and wind power; natural gas; shale oil; tar sands; coal; and nuclear power.

10. Other resources, such as water, land, and food, are being depleted without being replaced; are being polluted at a rapid rate; or are in short supply.

11. Pollution occurs in a market economy because it lowers the cost of production for individual firms. Pollution can be controlled by requiring it to be reduced or by changing the economic incentives that encourage pollution.

The Unit in Review

1. How is the population of the United States changing? How is it expected to change in the immediate future?

2. How is the distribution of income measured? How is it shown graphically?

3. What is the relationship between the distribution of income and poverty?

4. What are some steps taken in the past to combat poverty? What are some which can be taken in the future?

5. What relevance do Thomas Malthus' theories have to the major problems facing most countries today?

6. What resource problems are facing most countries today? What has caused them?

7. What effects do population, distribution of income, poverty, and the supply of resources have on economic growth?

8. What are the causes of pollution? What are two ways to control it?

■ *Building Consumer Skills*

Making a Household Budget

Almost every budget has a category which covers household expenses and includes everything from food to towels. The following exercise will help you buy wisely for a household on a weekly or monthly basis.

1. Make a list of the items you intend to buy. Ask yourself the following about each item: Why do I want this? Do I really need this? Can I afford this? Can I wait until this goes on sale? Cross out any items you do not need or you can wait to buy on sale.

2. Select the stores in which you will shop on the basis of convenience of location, price policy, quality of merchandise, and general reputation. Be familiar with a store before you buy anything in it. That way, you will know when a sale is really a sale, whether or not items are over priced, and if goods can be returned.

3. Look up each item in a consumer magazine or booklet. Such publications tell you what you can and cannot expect from a product and will help you determine the best buy for you.

4. When shopping, keep the following in mind:

   ● When buying food, always shop alone and with a list. Buy only what is on the list. Do not shop when you are hungry.

   ● Fancy packaging and a high price do not necessarily mean quality or convenience. Do not buy on the basis of brand name alone.

   ● Quality is relative. Buying the highest quality towels to be used only for special occasions is not really necessary, but buying them for everyday use for the next few years may be a savings in the long run.

The Value of Economics

Time and the human potential are the two most precious resources. Nothing else comes close. **Dr. Richard L. Lesher**

Epilogue

A FRAMEWORK FOR DECISION MAKING

As a science, economics is devoted to an analysis of the way in which people cope with the problem of scarcity. Because scarcity is a universal problem, the study of economics is important to everyone.

Through the study of economics, a person learns that choices must be made. He or she begins to discover that there are different ways to analyze a problem and that alternatives must be considered. The person also begins to see the need for decision-making tools that can help with choices.

In essence, then, when a person studies economics, he or she learns about ways that help to solve problems. In other words, economics provides a framework for decision making and helps a person become a better decision maker.

As the economist Kenneth Boulding pointed out, economics has evolved to the point where it is now a generalized theory of choice. When people study economics, it is important that they understand the way in which it helps them become better decision makers capable of making better choices.

ECONOMICS AS A SCIENCE. As a social science, economics is concerned with how people deal with scarcity. As a science, however, economics is not without some drawbacks. One is that it always will be a bit inexact. This is because it deals with people, and people are unpredictable at times. They may do one thing in one situation and something totally different in another situation. When people study economics, then, they really study themselves. They examine the ways in which they react to high prices, to low prices, to the needs of others, and to the ways in which others go about solving their problems.

A major part of economics is devoted to the description of the world around us. This includes the three different forms of business organizations—proprietorships, partnerships, and corporations. It also includes the labor market—the number of workers who belong to unions, the income received by labor, and the measures of employment and unemployment. Another thing into which economics delves is the motivational factors that make the economy work. In the case of a free enterprise economy like that of the United States, for example, the motivation is profit. The profit motive is the driving force that encourages functional institutions to bring resources and consumers together.

In short, the study of economic activity deals with more than a description. It is also concerned with the motivational factors that help people make decisions, with how things work, and with how things are. It is not concerned, however, with questions about how things should, or ought, to be.

Today, it is important that people have some knowledge of economics. With what is the study of economics concerned?

A REASONED APPROACH

Economic decision making requires a careful, reasoned approach to problem solving. The Joint Council on Economic Education, a national nonprofit organization dedicated to the improvement of economic literacy in the United States, recommends five steps to economic decision making. These are listed below.

1. *State the problem or issue.*
2. *Determine the personal or broad social goals to be obtained.*
3. *Consider the principal alternative means of achieving these goals.*
4. *Select the economic concepts needed to understand the problem and use them to appraise the merits of each alternative.*
5. *Decide which alternative best leads to the attainment of the most goals or the most important goals.*

These steps clearly show how important a systematic approach is when making decisions. They also illustrate how important it is to consider all approaches and alternatives to a problem.

DECISION MAKING TOOLS. To help in the decision making process, the economist may choose from a number of "tools." These include the decision making grid, supply and demand, marginal analysis, statistics, and formal models.

The decision making grid has become more important recently. It forces a person to state a problem, and then identify the range of alternative solutions and the criteria needed to evaluate alternatives. The grid forces a person to follow the "reasoned approach" outlined earlier.

Two other tools are supply and demand. The Law of Demand, for example, is nothing more than a broad generalization of the way people react to a range of prices for a certain product. When prices are high, consumers tend to buy less than they would otherwise. When prices are low, consumers tend to buy more than they would otherwise. The Law of Demand, then, simply reflects the way in which people tend to react to the "signals" supplied by the price system.

The same is true for supply. Producers tend to produce more of a product when the price is high and less when it is low. This behavior can be described as the Law of Supply. When supply is put together with demand, they explain the way prices are determined. They can even help explain the shortages and surpluses that may result if someone or something interferes with the price mechanism.

Another tool is marginal analysis. The study of economics shows that economists are more concerned with measures like total cost or total profit than with those like average cost or average profit. This is because people tend to make decisions "at the margin." A producer, for example, will be more likely to produce one more unit of output if he or she knows that the additional cost of production will be less than the revenue gained from the sale of the product. Before a consumer makes a decision, he or she will want to know if enough additional utility will be gained by giving up some income or other goods and services in exchange.

Most decisions really are made in this way. People simply want to know the additional or extra cost of making a decision. In economics, the word "marginal" is the same as "extra" or "additional." As a result, economists use the term marginal analysis to describe this kind of decision making.

Economic models are yet another tool of analysis. They can be simple supply and demand models of a market, circular flow diagrams, or elaborate formulations such as the output-expenditure model drawn up by Keynes. The advantage of a model is that it allows the economist to combine many factors in order to predict or explain outcomes.

Another tool is statistics. Economists compile measures of the overall performance of the economy in the form of GNP. They compile measures for the labor force in the form of unemployment and employment statistics. They even keep a record of progress over time by constructing price indices that can be used to remove the distortions of inflation. Even though statistics may be the easiest of the tools to understand, that does not make them any less important to the study of economics.

ALLOCATING SCARCE RESOURCES

Once it is understood that scarcity is the basic economic problem, the problem shifts to allocation. How, for example,

should the scarce resources of land, labor, and capital be allocated to satisfy competing wants and needs? The answer to this depends in part on the kind of economic system a society has chosen to use.

ROLE OF MARKETS.   In a free enterprise economy, like that of the United States, the basic guidance for the allocation of resources is provided by markets. The forces of supply and demand interact to establish prices in a market. The prices, in turn, act as the "signals," which cause producers and consumers to alter their spending decisions.

Prices, however, do more than just affect producing and spending decisions in a market. They also influence the allocation of resources across markets. In the 1950's and 1960's, for example, there was no market for synthetic fuels because the price of oil was so low. But when the price went up, there was a demand for alternative energy sources. Soon, markets developed for these products. It was the high price of oil that made other sources competitive. And as a result, land, labor, and capital shifted into the other markets where alternative energy sources were being developed.

The advantage of a market economy is that it adjusts to change gradually. As long as the forces of supply and demand are allowed to do their work, they will always be sending producers and consumers the signals that help them allocate their resources and adjust to change.

The drawback of a pure market is that it can be ruthlessly efficient. Only those who produce earn enough income to consume and provide for the necessities of life. In such an economy, there is very little room for the very old, the ill, or the incapacitated. For this reason, many economies, including that of the United States, have what is known as a modified market economy or modified free enterprise system.

Over the years, the role of government has grown to the point where it cares for some of the less fortunate. It also has other powers, including the right to make decisions about national defense and the military. In addition, government makes decisions on the allocation of output, especially in he area of social and welfare needs. Almost all of these decisions, however, are made through elected officials pledged to represent the people. Although all of the decisions may not be made by the markets, most people are more comfortable knowing that some basic protection has been provided for those who need it the most.

OTHER ECONOMIC SYSTEMS. Countries with other economic systems also face scarcity and make the decisions that affect allocation. Traditional economies, for example, provide evidence of the universal nature of economics.

Like other economies, traditional economies must deal with the problem of scar-

This craftsman lives in a traditional economy. How does a traditional economy differ from a command one?

city and make decisions about what, how, and for whom to produce. Beyond this, however, the study of the traditional economy loses interest. Decisions are made in a "traditional" manner—the same way they were made by parents, grandparents, and great-grandparents. As a result, traditional societies tend to be static with little growth or change taking place.

This is not the case, however, with command economies. Countries that have a strong central control over economic decision making have made great strides in brief periods of time. These strides, however, have been made at the cost of great sacrifice on the part of the people.

The Soviet Union, for example, went from one of the largest peasant economies in the world to a leading industrial power in a few generations. At the same time, however, the people had to make do with long hours, low pay, poor working conditions, and the virtual absence of consumer goods. Even so, success with industrialization has made the Soviet Union a growth model that has been followed by other countries.

Recently, there has been some question as to whether command-type economies like the Soviet Union and the Comecon countries can deliver on their promises. There are major problems involved in the complex task of coordinating all economic decisions through a central planning agency. For one, many central planners are too far removed from the factory floor to be aware of the importance of their decisions. For another, many factories have a hard time motivating workers to perform to the best of their abilities.

Then, too, growth means that more decisions must be made. It also means that the problem of communication becomes more complex. If the quality of the decision making is not satisfactory before the growth occurs, it probably will not be much better afterwards, or it may be worse.

Although command economies are capable of massive change over longer periods of time, they are somewhat resistant to gradual change. In both the Soviet Union and the People's Republic of China, large numbers of people were forced to live on huge state-owned collective farms in an effort to boost agricultural output. The central planners, however, are less able to cope with the problem of gradual change on a week-to-week or month-to-month basis. Small requests often get lost in the bureaucracy, and minor changes are often not made.

Command economies, then, tend to lurch along from one great plan to the next, while market economies tend to make their adjustments more gradually. Socialist economies, on the other hand, incorporate a mixture of market and command. The attractiveness of economies like those of Sweden, Denmark, and Finland seems to be due to the great many social and welfare services provided by the government. However, these economies also have to face the problem of scarcity. As it turns out, no country can afford to spend more than it has. This can be seen most vividly in Sweden today.

Societies, then, have organized themselves differently to cope with the problem of scarcity. Some have made progress while others have not. The fundamental problem, however, remains the same—how to most effectively use scarce resources to achieve maximum output.

SEARCH FOR STABILITY IN AN UNCERTAIN WORLD

It has been said that only two things are certain in this world—death and taxes.

This is just another way of saying that uncertainty has become a fact of life. In the field of economics, as elsewhere, a great deal of time and effort is devoted to the problems caused by uncertainty.

ECONOMIC GOALS. To a certain extent, the economic goals of most Americans are closely linked to the country's political goals. Freedom, for example, is just as highly valued in an economic sense as it is in a political sense. Workers value their right to choose for whom they work and to select whatever occupation they desire. Producers value their right to produce the goods and services they choose.

While these basic freedoms exist in a free enterprise economy like that of the United States, they are not possible in some other countries. In many command economies, for example, students are often given aptitude tests that determine the occupations they will be allowed to enter. In many of these same countries, the government owns the factories and the means of production, and there is no free enterprise.

Other broad economic and social goals such as efficiency, equity, security, full employment, price stability, and economic growth are also important. Collectively, the goals give people a way to gauge the performance of their economic system.

It is not always possible to achieve all of these economic goals at the same time. Some individuals, for example, may feel that high tax rates for one group, but not another, violate the concept of equality. Or a company may feel it has lost some freedom if it is forced to deal with a union. The union, on the other hand, may feel it is not being treated justly if it cannot negotiate with the employer.

At times, then, economic goals do conflict. The conflict can be resolved in the political arena by people casting their votes for the politicians of their choice.

Even if all the economic goals are not achieved, they are important because they provide the measuring stick by which the American people evaluate the performance of the economy. If the economy does not measure up to the goals the people have set, it can be modified. This, in fact, is exactly why there is a modified free enterprise economy in the United States today.

POLITICAL AND ECONOMIC STABILITY.

It is generally agreed that economic stability and growth are desirable. What must be kept in mind at the same time, however, is that economic and political stability are mutually dependent. It is not easy for a country to have a growing and healthy economy if it does not have a stable government. Foreign investors, for example, may shy away from countries that suffer revolutions or other forms of political turmoil.

The same is true in reverse. Even if a country has a relatively stable government, a weak economy can pose a threat

to the political system. A great deal of the current political unrest in Latin America, for example, can be traced to vast differences in the distribution of income. Many poor peasants become revolutionaries simply because the government in power has had a hand in taking land or other material goods from them or has looked the other way when such things happened. In the long run, the existence of a relatively strong and stable central government is threatened by the poverty and misery of the masses.

THE ROAD AHEAD

The road ahead may be bumpy because today's world is a dynamic one that is changing constantly. Nonetheless, that road need not be unfamiliar. The study of economics helps add structure to the complex and changing world. Economics provides the framework for reference so that analysis, explanation, and prediction can take place.

Because of this, the study of economics can help people cope with the uncertainty that lies ahead. Although people, problems, and sometimes even institutions come and go all the time, many of the underlying behaviors and relationships remain the same.

In the United States, economics and politics often go together. What are some common economic and political goals?

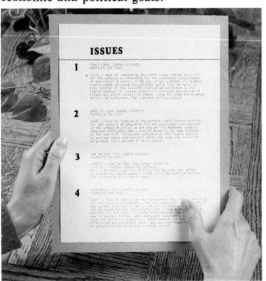

▊ Epilogue Review

1. To what is a major part of economics devoted?
2. What are the five steps to economic decision making?
3. How do decision making tools help the economist?
4. Why do economic goals sometimes conflict?
5. How are political and economic stability dependent on each other?

Life Skills

Consumer Guidelines

Budgeting

According to many financial planners, the best way to increase wealth is not through more income but through better use of the resources one already has. You can move toward better use of your resources by taking the time to plan your expenditures so that you can live within your means. This can be accomplished by making a **budget**—a plan that matches expenditures with income. Budgeting can help you manage your money better and prevent you from buying goods and services you do not really need or cannot afford.

The first step in setting up a budget is to obtain a **spreadsheet**—a large sheet of paper with columns for weeks and months and rows for different types of expenditures. If you cannot find one in your local office supply store, you can make your own. The next step is to decide whether you want to set up your budget on a weekly, monthly, or yearly basis. Most people set up annual budgets divided according to when they get paid. For example, if you get paid every two weeks, you might want to set up an annual budget with 26 bi-weekly columns. If you get paid monthly, you might prefer to set up an annual budget with 12 monthly columns.

The first row of your budget should consist of the income you expect to have for each weekly, bi-weekly, or monthly period. Be sure to record your **net income**—the income received after taxes have been taken out. The remainder of the rows should be used to list your expenditures by category. The number of categories will depend on your needs and your finances. Prioritize your expenditures, listing first those things you must pay, such as rent and utility bills. Make sure you have a category for miscellaneous expenditures to take care of the unexpected, such as a last-minute gift you might have to buy. Since you really cannot know how many unexpected expenditures you will have, allow five to ten percent of your net income for this category. Also, set up a category for repairs or maintenance of items you may own, such as a car. Such items are likely to be too large to absorb in the miscellaneous category. Lastly, keep in mind that it is more efficient and sometimes easier to spread larger expenditures across time. For example, your car insurance may be due every six months. Rather than try to budget the entire payment in one or two periods, set aside enough money each period so that you have the entire amount on hand when the bill arrives.

Monitor your budget as you go along to make sure that the amounts you have allotted for each category are reasonable. For example, you may discover after a month or so that you have not set aside enough for groceries. If you find that a category does not reflect your actual spending, adjust it. An important benefit of a budget is that it can show you where you need to increase or decrease your spending.

When you make your budget, remember that you are designing a system that will work for you. You must be comfortable with the budget you set up.

1. Why is making a budget important?
2. What are the steps involved in making a budget?
3. What does it mean to monitor a budget?

Buying Insurance

If you read newspapers or magazines, watch television, or listen to the radio, you have seen or heard many different advertisements for insurance. While you may not like the advertisements or agree with all their claims, their product is important. Almost everyone needs some kind of insurance. Your parents, for example, may have several types of insurance—insurance on their home to protect it in case of theft, fire, or natural disaster; insurance on their automobile to provide for them in case of accident or disability; insurance on their health to cover them if they are hospitalized or ill for a long time. The stores in which you shop may have insurance to protect them against employee theft or to cover customers hurt or injured while shopping. The doctor you see when you are ill, the school that you attend, and the city and state in which you live all carry some types of insurance.

There are some questions you—and every other consumer—must answer before buying any insurance—Why do I need it?; What kinds are there?; What kind(s) do I need?; Which companies have the best rates? The answers to some of these questions are simple. You need insurance to protect yourself. How much and what kind of insurance you need depends on your life style, your job, your age, and many other things. Basically, you need enough insurance to protect your belongings and potential income, but not so much that paying for it strains your budget.

There are six major types of insurance that you should consider—whole life, term, health, automobile, homeowners, and property liability.

Whole life insurance, sometimes called ordinary life insurance, pays money to your survivors in the event of your death. It also carries a provision for savings against which you can borrow. You may also collect the savings in one large sum when you retire. Although this type of insurance can be expensive, it offers a combination of coverage to those who cannot buy individual coverages separately.

Term insurance offers one type of coverage only—payment to your survivors in the event of your death. It is relatively inexpensive, with a $50,000 policy generally costing about $300 a year.

Health insurance covers medical and hospital bills if you become ill. Some health insurance policies also cover medication. A good policy covers approximately 80 percent of medical expenses.

Automobile insurance can provide several different kinds of coverage, including liability, collision, and term and health. **Liability** coverage protects you from claims and lawsuits if you cause an accident. **Collision** covers damage to your automobile if another vehicle hits it. Most people driving new cars want collision coverage. Most people driving olders cars worth only a few hundred dollars often find that it is not worthwhile.

Homeowner insurance covers a homeowner when his or her home or property has been damaged. Mortgage lenders generally insist that a homeowner carry this type of insurance until his or her mortgage has been paid in full.

Property liability insurance protects renters and homeowners against claims of negligence filed by others when an accident occurs on the renter's or homeowner's property. It will protect the home-owner or renter when, for example, a person who trips or falls on a broken step on the renter's or homeowner's property files or sues to collect damages for his or her injuries.

Deciding exactly what insurance to buy can be difficult and confusing. One reason for this is that different insurance companies often offer the same type of insurance under different names. This makes it hard for the consumer to know whether or not insurance agents representing different companies are talking about the same kind of policy. Another reason is that the product—coverage—is invisible. The consumer cannot tell how much the policy will pay until something happens for which he or she wants to collect payment.

There are, however, several things that will help you when buying insurance. First, keep in mind that **group policies**—policies offered to a group of people, generally by an employer or organization—tend to be less expensive than individual policies purchased from an insurance agent. Second, always consult more than one agent before buying a policy. Describe your needs carefully to each agent, and ask each to recommend a policy and provide a written list of benefits and estimate of costs. Inform each agent that you are consulting other agents and intend to compare costs and benefits before making any decision. Base your decision as to which policy to buy on the results of your comparison.

1. Why do consumers need insurance?
2. What are six major types of insurance?
3. What are some important things to consider when buying insurance?

Filing an Income Tax Form

If you work, you probably have to file income tax forms with the federal government and, in some cases, with the state and/or city in which you live or work. The first step in filing income tax forms is to fill out a withholding statement with your employer. The federal withholding form, known as a W-4, asks for such information as your name and address, social security number, marital status, and any special allowances for disabilities or dependents. This form is shown below. The purpose of the W-4 is to help your employer determine how much money to withhold from each of your paychecks. For this reason, it is important for you to complete the form properly. If you do not, your employer may not withhold enough money, and you will have to pay additional taxes.

Your pay stubs and the receipts for your expenditures are important records and should be kept together in a safe place. By law, in January of every year, you must receive from your employer a W-2 form, which summarizes your earnings for the year. Check the information on your pay stubs against that on the W-2 to make sure that it is correct. Some expenditures are tax deductible and will save you money by lowering your taxes. You must be able to prove,

Form **W-4** Department of the Treasury Internal Revenue Service	**Employee's Withholding Allowance Certificate** ▶ **For Privacy Act and Paperwork Reduction Act Notice, see instructions.**	OMB No. 1545-0010 **1987**
1 Type or print your full name		**2** Your social security number

Home address (number and street or rural route) City or town, state, and ZIP code	**3** Marital Status	☐ Single ☐ Married ☐ Married, but withhold at higher Single rate **Note:** *If married, but legally separated, or spouse is a nonresident alien, check the Single box.*

4 Total number of allowances you are claiming (from the Worksheet on page 3) . . . .

5 Additional amount, if any, you want deducted from each pay (see Step 4 on page 2) . . . . $

6 I claim exemption from withholding because (see Step 2 above and check boxes below that apply):

  a ☐ Last year I did not owe any Federal income tax and had a right to a full refund of **ALL** income tax withheld, **AND**

  b ☐ This year I do not expect to owe any Federal income tax and expect to have a right to a full refund of **ALL** income tax withheld. If both a and b apply, enter the year effective and "EXEMPT" here . . . . . ▶ Year 19

  c If you entered "EXEMPT" on line 6b, are you a full-time student? . . . . ☐Yes ☐No

Under penalties of perjury, I certify that I am entitled to the number of withholding allowances claimed on this certificate or, if claiming exemption from withholding, that I am entitled to claim the exempt status.

Employee's signature ▶   Date ▶   , 19

7 Employer's name and address **(Employer: Complete 7, 8, and 9 only if sending to IRS)**	**8** Office code	**9** Employer identification number

however, that you actually made the expenditures. Your proof is the receipts that you have saved.

Since tax laws change, it is important to be aware which expenditures are deductible. Depending on the current tax laws, these may include mortgage interest; medical bills and pharmaceutical expenses; child-care expenses; alimony payments; such charitable contributions as donations to your church or to such non-profit organizations as the United Way; such work-related expenses as union dues or uniforms; and uninsured losses from theft or natural disaster.

At the first of each year, the Internal Revenue Service sends out tax forms with detailed instructions on how to fill them out. If you do not receive the forms, or if you misplace or damage them, you can find the same forms at most post offices, public libraries, or banks. By following the instructions, you can complete the forms yourself. Or, if you prefer, you can have them filled out by a professional tax preparer. The fee for this service varies according to the complexity of the return and the amount of time it takes to prepare it. You generally must file the completed forms by midnight, April 15.

1. What is a W-4 form? What is its purpose?
2. In preparing to file an income tax form, why are receipts important?
3. What are some examples of tax deductible expenditures?

Maintaining a Checking Account

Checks have become so common today that they are considered one of the major components of the money supply, and most consumers find that a checking account is a convenience they must have. A person who has a checking account does not have to carry around large sums of cash. He or she can pay bills with a check, often through the mail. But having a checking account is one thing, and maintaining it properly is another. Almost anyone can open a checking account, but it takes special care to maintain it.

Checking accounts are not free, unless you are able to deposit—and not use—a minimum sum of money that generally varies from $500 to $1000. If you do not maintain the required minimum, you will have to pay both a monthly maintenance fee and an additional charge for new checks. Therefore, before opening a checking account, you must decide if you need it.

Once you decide to open a checking account, there are several things you should do to make sure that it is used effectively. First, order checks that have printed on them your full name, current address, and telephone number. Second, when you write checks, make sure that all figures and amounts are legible. Start writing on the extreme left, using all the space available so that no one can change the amount or add in extra. Be sure to date the checks correctly. Also be sure to sign them clearly and accurately. This will help bank tellers identify your signature and recognize forgeries. A sample check that incorporates these procedures is shown below. Third, immediately after writing a check, record in your checkbook

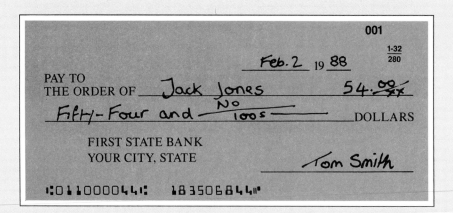

the date on which the check was written, to whom it was written, and the amount for which it was written.

For many people, the most difficult task involved in maintaining a checking account is balancing their checkbook. This should be done every month upon receiving a statement from the bank. The statement will tell you exactly which of your checks the bank has received and which of your deposits it has recorded. It will also tell you what the balance in your account is at the time the statement was issued. At the same time, the bank will also send you the cancelled checks listed in the statement. It is up to you to **reconcile** your account—make sure your balance agrees with the balance indicated by the bank.

The first step in reconciling your account is to take the checks returned to you by the bank and put them in numerical order. Next, in your checkbook, mark each check entry with an *X* or some other symbol to show that the check has been processed. As you do this, compare the amount of each check with the amount you recorded in your checkbook to make sure they match. Then, list the checks you wrote but that were not returned to you or deducted from your account. Total these amounts then add this total to the balance you have written in your checkbook. Subtract from this any fees or charges indicated on the bank statement, such as a monthly service charge or a charge for new checks, and compare this balance with the balance on the bank statement. If no mistakes were made, your balance and the one shown by the bank should match.

If the two balances do not match, you must go back and look for mistakes. Check to make sure that all your deposits and checks were recorded accurately and that no subtraction or addition errors were made. If the error does not show up, check the handwritten amount on each check against the computer code on the bottom of the check to see if the bank operator recorded it properly. If you still have not found the error, call your bank and discuss the problem with the appropriate person there. If you do not clear up the error immediately, it will carry over to the next month, making balancing your checkbook next month even more difficult. If the balance gets too far out of line, a check may **bounce**—be returned for insufficient funds—which will cost you a fee of $10 or $15. If a number of checks bounce, it could give you a bad credit rating.

If you follow the above guidelines, maintaining a checking account is not difficult. Most people agree that, despite the time and cost involved, having a checking account is worthwhile.

1. Why is having a checking account convenient for many consumers?
2. How do you balance a checkbook?
3. What does it mean for a check to bounce?

Preparing a Resumé

At one time or another, you probably will need to look for a job. One of the most critical parts of this process is preparing a resumé. A good resumé provides a brief, neatly typed history of your strengths, abilities, and accomplishments. Very often, whether or not a prospective employer decides to interview you depends on his or her reaction to your resumé.

Before you start writing your resumé, conduct an inventory of your strengths and weaknesses by asking yourself questions like these: What kinds of skills and talents do I have? What is my work history? How much formal education have I had? What were my grades and class standings? In what activities have I participated? What physical handicaps do I have that might limit my ability to work? What are my goals? Do I want full time or part-time employment? What kind of work do I want to do? What salary would I be willing to accept?

When you have answered these questions, organize the entries on your resumé. Begin with your name, address, and telephone number. This tells an employer where he or she can reach you. Then, indicate the position or kind of position you are seeking. Next, list all your relevant work experience, beginning with your most recent job. Include the dates of your employment, the names of the companies for which you worked, and the positions you held. Go next to your education, listing the schools you have attended. Potential employers are interested in your education and how you have performed in school.

Next, list any special honors or awards you have received and any activities in which you have been or are involved. Lastly, provide at least three references, all of whom know you well enough to vouch for your abilities or strengths. Do not use relatives as references, and do not use more than one or two teachers.

The illustration that follows is an example of a resumé. Keep in mind, however, that since a resumé should fit an individual's strengths and weaknesses, its format can vary.

1. Why is a resumé an important step in finding a job?
2. What kinds of questions should you ask yourself when preparing a resumé?
3. What kinds of things should you list on a resumé?

Bobby Little
4144 Valley Court
Cranston, Illinois 60505
(312) 676–2242

Position Desired:
Seeking part-time employment during the school year: Prefer to work one afternoon or evening per week plus one day of the weekend; willing to work full time during the summer.

Work Experience:
June 1986–Present: Part-time Cook, McDonald's, Inc., Cranston, Illinois
January 1986–May 1986: Part-time Stock Clerk, Brown's Hardware Store, Cranston, Illinois

Education:
Senior at Scott High School, Class of 1988, currently an honors student

Honors and Awards:
- First Place Medal (computer division), State of Illinois Science Fair, for project entitled "NYSE: The Stock Market Simulation," April, 1988
- Air Force Best Overall Project Award, State of Illinois Science Fair, April, 1988
- First Place, Computer Division, Blake County Science Fair, May, 1988
- Outstanding Physical Education/Health Student Award, Scott High School, Spring 1986

Special Interests
- Computers, strategy games, playing the guitar
- Member of Scott High School Chess Club (September 1986–May 1988)
- Member of Scott High School Spanish Club (September 1985–May 1988)

References:
Mr. Allen Williamson
Head, Department of Science
Scott High School
Cranston, Illinois 60505
(312) 676–3633

Mr. John Brown
Owner, Brown's Hardware Store
Cranston, Illinois 60505
(312) 622–3414

Mr. Richard Adams
McDonald's, Inc.
Cranston, Illinois 60505
(312) 676–8970

Rights of Consumers

How many of the following federal laws are you familiar with?

Consumer Leasing Act
Fair Credit Billing Act
Magnuson-Moss Warranty Act
Truth-in-Lending Act
Fair Credit Reporting Act
Federal Wage Garnishment Act
Fair Debt Collection Practices Act

The federal government has passed all of these acts in recent years to protect you, the consumer. If you do not know what protection they offer you, it would be well worth your while to look them up.

In addition to the help provided by the above acts, you have certain rights of which you should be aware so you can put them to use when necessary. The following are just a few things you should know.

1. If you receive merchandise you did not order through the mail and for which you are billed, you have the right to keep the merchandise without paying for it.

2. If you complain in writing about an error in a bill and the seller does not respond within two months, you have the right to keep up to $50 of the amount you stated was in error.

3. If a moving company does not pick up and deliver household goods at the agreed-upon time, you have the right to charge them for any motel and dining expenses you incur as a result.

4. If a mail-order company does not fill your paid order in 30 days, you have the right to demand your money back.

5. If you report in writing your lost or stolen credit card immediately, you are liable for only $50 worth of purchases not made by you.

6. If you are refused credit, insurance, or a job, you have the right to receive the name and address of the consumer reporting agency that provided the information on which the refusal was based.

7. If you are "bumped" from an airplane flight because the airline overbooked that flight, you have the right to a refund

for your fare as well as to a seat on another plane to take you to your destination.

8. If you are over 18 years of age, you have the right to see most school records and have them corrected if they are not accurate.

9. If you, as a consumer, go to Small Claims Court, you do not have to be represented by a lawyer.

10. If you buy something from a door-to-door salesperson, you have three days in which to change your mind about the purchase.

These are only a few of your specific rights as a consumer. In general, you have four basic rights. These were outlined in 1962 by President John F. Kennedy in a special message to Congress. According to President Kennedy, consumers have the right to safety, the right to be informed, the right to choose, and the right to be heard. These four rights protect you against goods and services that are dangerous to life, limb, and health, and against false or misleading advertising, inaccurate labeling, and deceptive practices. They also help provide you access to a variety of products at different prices and to facts that enable you to get full value for your money. In addition, they allow you to obtain legal redress of complaints and grievances when the market place fails.

Although knowing your rights is important, it is only part of the picture. Using those rights is the other part. Honest, well-based complaints should be voiced where they will do some good. Complaining to your best friend, boyfriend or girlfriend, or relatives may make you feel better, but it will not prevent the same thing from happening to someone else. Complain where it will do some good— to the store manager, the company president, or the board of directors. If this does not do any good, contact your local Better Business Bureau. If that fails, write or call the appropriate state or federal agency. These include the Federal Trade Commission, the Interstate Commerce Commission, the Office of Interstate Land Sales Registration, the Office of Consumer Affairs (all located in Washington, D.C.), and the Food and Drug Administration (located in Rockville, Maryland).

1. As a consumer, what are your rights if you receive merchandise through the mail that you did not order?

2. If you have been denied credit, what are your rights?

3. What are four basic rights of consumers?

Responsibilities of Consumers

Consumers have certain rights. At the same time, however, they also have certain responsibilities. These include the obligation to be honest, to supply correct information, to report harmful and dangerous goods, and to disclose instances of wrongful consumer dealings.

Being honest means not taking goods without paying for them and not tolerating such actions by others. Businesses work hard to produce goods and services for consumers. They compete with one another to offer their products at the lowest competitive prices. When someone **shoplifts**—steals goods on display at a store—all consumers are hurt because it forces stores to raise their prices to cover the cost of the goods they have lost.

Supplying correct information means being truthful when filling out product surveys. As part of the warranty on their goods, manufacturers often include a short questionnaire designed to collect information about the consumers who are most likely to buy their product. One reason they do this is to determine the best audience at which to target their advertising. Another reason is to compile and maintain a list of the individuals who buy their products in the event that, at a later date, those individuals have to be notified of a product defect or improvement.

Reporting harmful and dangerous goods means making manufacturers aware of the danger or potential danger of their product. A consumer may discover, for example, that a baby toy has sharp metal edges or that, after it has been used a few times, an electrical appliance develops a short circuit in its wiring. In many cases, manufacturers are unaware of problems with their products, and it is up to the consumer to make them aware by reporting problems to the appropriate company or agency as soon as possible. There are several agencies set up to investigate and deal with such complaints. In the case of automobiles, for example, the United States Department of Transportation maintains a toll-free "Auto Safety Hotline" for just this purpose.

Disclosing instances of wrongful consumer dealings means reporting experiences with such unfair practices as false or misleading advertising, faulty packaging, or overcharges for goods or services provided. Reporting such incidences can be accomplished by writing a letter of complaint to the manufacturer. Like the letter that follows, it should clearly identify the problem, be specific about the corrective action you want taken, and include all the necessary documentation.

If the manufacturer does not respond to your letter or resolve the problem to your satisfaction, it is up to you to contact other sources of help such as the Better Business Bureau or a media hotline.

Consumer responsibilities and rights are much like two sides of a coin—they go together with each supporting the other. When you fulfill your consumer responsibilities, you are helping other consumers as much as you are helping yourself.

1. How does shoplifting hurt consumers?
2. Why should consumers report harmful and dangerous goods to manufacturers?
3. What kinds of information does a letter of complaint contain?

Your Street Address
Your City, State, Zip Code
Date

Person in Charge
Company Name
Street Address
City, State, Zip Code

Dear _____:

On (date), I purchased (indicate name, serial number, model number or name) from (store name and location). Unfortunately, the product has not performed satisfactorily because (describe problem).

To solve this problem, I would appreciate (state the specific action or actions you want taken). Enclosed are copies (do not include originals) of my records (receipts, guarantees, warranties, cancelled check or charge slip, model and serial numbers, contracts, etc.).

I am looking forward to your reply and resolution of my problem. I will wait (reasonable time for action) before seeking third-party assistance. You may contact me at the above address or by telephone at (home and/or office number).

Sincerely,
(Your Name)

Borrowing Money

At one time or another, almost everyone buys the use of money, or borrows. In each case, the borrower assumes some risks. And, in each case, he or she has a "good" reason for borrowing. In truth, however, there are right reasons and wrong reasons for borrowing money. The wrong reasons include borrowing to buy something on impulse, to make you feel better because you are depressed, or to make you more important in someone else's eyes. They also include borrowing to gamble, to make a risky investment or to buy something that will be worn out or useless before it is paid for. It is just as wrong to borrow so you can live beyond your income or because you expect to get a raise, an inheritance, or win the lottery.

Being in a great deal of debt is dangerous and can lead to personal bankruptcy. If, however, you have a legitimate need to borrow money, there are some things to keep in mind.

1. Do not borrow so much that if you become ill or lose your job, you no longer will be financially stable.
2. Stagger your debts. Spread out your payments so they are not all due at the same time.

There are several places other than family or friends to which you can go for a loan—life insurance companies, savings institutions, credit unions, commercial banks, retail organizations, finance companies, pawnshops. Several types of loans are available to consumers including installment sales credit, installment cash credit, single lump sum credit, open-ended or revolving credit, and credit card loans.

Installment sales credit, the most common type of loan available, is generally taken out to buy such merchandise as household furniture or appliances. The consumer makes an initial deposit on the goods, and then agrees to pay the balance, plus interest and service charges, in equal installments over a period of time.

Installment cash credit is a direct cash loan often used for vacations, home improvements, or other personal expenses. No down payment is required, but the loan, plus interest and other charges, must be repaid in equal installments over a specified period of time.

Single lump sum credit is a direct cash loan that requires that the amount borrowed plus interest be repaid on a specified day.

Open-ended or **revolving credit** allows consumers to purchase goods and services from merchants on credit, often without a down payment. In some cases, the loan may have a provision that allows the entire balance to be repaid within 30 days without any interest charges. Monthly payments are required thereafter, with interest being computed on the outstanding balance.

Credit card loans are loans made through the use of a bank credit card. The payment plans for this type of loan vary widely. In some cases, annual fees are charged for use of the card, while in others, interest may be charged on the outstanding balance. In still others, the balance may have to be paid in full at the end of the month, or monthly installment payments may be made.

Regardless of the type of loan you obtain, you, as a consumer, are entitled by law to information about the cost of credit. First, the consumer is entitled to know the **finance charge**—the total dollar amount the credit will cost, including interest charged plus any carrying or service charge. Secondly, the borrower is entitled to know the **annual percentage rate (APR)**—the interest cost of the loan on a yearly basis. Since repayment schedules differ, the APR is your guide to the true cost of the loan.

No matter what type of loan you apply for, you must be a good credit risk. To determine this, the lender checks on character, ability to repay the loan and capital assets. If you can answer "yes" to the following questions, you probably would be considered creditable: Does your employment history show that you can keep a job? Is your job stable? Have you paid off your previous loans, including charge accounts, promptly and on schedule? Are your assets greater than your liabilities? Do you own your own home or have you lived in the same rented home for an extended period of time?

Before agreeing to lend anything, lenders will often check with a **credit bureau**—an agency that collects credit and other information on consumers to determine creditability. If your **credit history**—a record of debt and payment history—is not good or is in doubt, you probably will be denied credit. Thus, to maintain a good credit rating, debts should be paid on time.

Once your request for a loan is granted, you should check to make sure that the contract for the loan does not include the following:

1. An **add-on clause,** which allows the seller to keep title to an entire list of items until all payments on the loan have been completed.

2. A **balloon clause,** which makes the final payment larger than the other monthly payments.

3. An **acceleration clause,** which allows the lender to demand an immediate payment in full if one payment is not made.

1. What are some wrong reasons for borrowing?

2. What kinds of loans are available for consumers?

3. What is a credit rating? Why is it important to maintain a good one?

Paying for College

College costs have risen steadily in recent years. As a result, even families who have saved for years for their son's and daughter's education may find they do not have enough to pay all the costs. For parents on a tight budget, state colleges and universities and community colleges offer the most value because they generally cost up to 40 percent less than most private schools.

If you need financial aid, regardless of the reason, it is best to get started in your search in your junior year or early in your senior year of high school. Check with your guidance counselor about federal aids and state, military, ethnic, and fraternal grants. Generally, students whose family income is low are eligible for some aid even if their grades are low. Students from middle-income families, on the other hand, generally are eligible for less aid and then only if they have good grades. These students will have to rely more on subsidized student loans and special scholarships. Students from high-income families generally are not eligible for any aid at all.

In general, financial aid comes in three basic forms, no matter what the source may be—loans, which must be repaid; scholarships and grants, which need not be repaid; and jobs. Most big financial-aid sponsors give out their money through colleges. For this reason, the financial aid office of the college(s) of your choice is one of the first places to contact. Most colleges send out financial aid applications only upon request, so it is important to apply for forms ahead of time to file when you apply for admission. Missing the appointed deadline will reduce your chances for aid.

Basically, there are four major types of student loans. One is the National Direct Student Loan, which is granted only to needy students. The funds come from the federal government, but the students who receive them are chosen by individual colleges. The loan is interest-free while you are in school. Starting nine months to one year after graduation, you have ten years in which to repay the loan at low interest. To apply for this type of loan, contact the financial aid office at the college(s) of your choice.

A second type of loan is the Government Guaranteed Student Loan. This loan is made by financial institutions, which are guaranteed repayment by the federal government. While you are in school, the government pays the interest, which is generally 9 percent. Once you graduate, you have ten years for repayment. Like the National Direct Student Loan, this loan is granted to you rather than to your parents. To apply, contact financial institutions.

A third type of loan is a bank loan, which you or your parents will have to begin repaying while you are still in college. Although interest rates vary on this type of loan, they generally are higher than those on government loans. A fourth type of loan is the special student loan offered by colleges, civic and professional groups, and other organizations. The interest rates vary on these loans.

There are as many, or more, kinds of scholarships as there are loans. In most cases, income plays no part in eligibility. The following are just some of the kinds available.

1. National, state, and college merit scholarships, which are awarded on the basis of academic excellence.
2. Athletic scholarships, which are awarded to students who excel in a sport or sports.
3. Talent scholarships, which are awarded to students gifted in the arts.
4. Reserve Officers' Training Corps scholarships, which are awarded to students willing to spend four years in the armed forces after graduation.

More detailed information on scholarships can be found in *The A's and B's: Your Guide to Academic Scholarships*, which can be bought for $4.25 from Octameron Associates, P.O. Box 3437, Alexandria, Va. 22302. It is important to apply for every award for which you feel you may qualify. There is no limit on the number for which you can apply nor on the number you can receive.

Although grants also are available, they generally are for the needy only. For those who qualify, Pell Grants can be used at any accredited college, vocational schools, technical institutes, nursing schools, and the like. Grades play no role in eligibility.

The third basic kind of financial aid is in the form of a job. Several different programs fall into this category. One is the College Work-Study Program sponsored by the federal government. To be eligible, you must be a full-time student who would not be able to attend school without the job. Another program is cooperative education. Under this program, you work six months and go to school six months each year. What you earn on the job will pay your tuition.

These are just a few of the possibilities for financial aid. There are many more. The important things to remember are to start your investigation early, that you can borrow from more than one program, and that there are people and publications to help you.

1. If you need financial aid for college, when should you begin your search?
2. What are three forms of financial aid?
3. What kinds of scholarships are available?

Renting an Apartment

Everyone needs a place to live and renting also has some advantages. There is no large down payment nor cash outlay for taxes, major repairs, or maintenance. In addition, your commitment lasts only as long as your rental contract. This gives you more financial flexibility.

If you determine that your best course is to rent an apartment, it is important that you take time to make sure you choose wisely. Before you even begin to look for the apartment, ask yourself the following questions:

1. What would be the best location in terms of getting back and forth from work or school and convenience to shopping?
2. Do I want a furnished or unfurnished apartment?
3. How much space do I need to have adequate storage and be comfortable?
4. How much rent can I afford to pay? (Monthly rent plus related expenses should not be more than one week's take-home pay.)

You can try to find an apartment by yourself by consulting the classified section of newspapers or the bulletin board at work and by asking friends for recommendations. Or, for a fee, you can have a rental agent look for you. In either case, do not agree to rent an apartment until you have seen it for yourself. The best time to do this is during the evening or on the weekend when other tenants and neighbors are at home. That way, you will be able to tell how noisy or quiet the apartment and area are and what the neighbors are like. If possible, try to talk to some of the people in the neighborhood, apartment complex, or building to learn the advantages and disadvantages of moving into the area.

Inspect the apartment and the surrounding area carefully for the following:

1. Is the building well-built, well-maintained, and well-lit?
2. Is the apartment the right size? Does it have a convenient floor plan, enough wall space for your furniture, and adequate lighting and electrical outlets?
3. How many windows are there? Do they open and close easily? Are there screens and storm windows?
4. Is the apartment air-conditioned? Does it have its own heating and cooling controls?

5. Do major appliances such as a stove and refrigerator come with the apartment? If so, in what condition are they?

6. Is the apartment carpeted? Are there drapes, blinds, or shades for the windows?

7. Does the building have fire walls? Smoke alarms?

8. Are laundry equipment and storage facilities available?

9. Is there trash collection or disposal? Where? How often? By whom? Who pays for it?

10. What kind of burglary protection is there?

11. What are the parking facilities?

Once you have selected the apartment you want, you probably will have to sign a **lease,** a written agreement between you and the landlord that states the major terms of your occupancy. It generally includes a description of the rental property; the amount of rent to be paid and the dates on which it is due; how much deposit is required and what it covers and under what conditions it may be forfeited; and how long the lease is in force and under what conditions it may be renewed. The lease also should include the conditions under which the rent may be raised and by how much; who pays for specific utilities and repairs; what alterations you can make on the property; how much notice you must give before moving; whether or not you can rent the apartment to someone else; and whether or not children, pets, or roommates are allowed. Make sure the lease states that the landlord cannot enter the apartment in your absence without checking with you first. It is not uncommon for a landlord to enter an empty apartment to make repairs or to show it to a prospective tenant.

In addition to reading the lease carefully, there are several other things you should do before signing it. First, take an inspection tour with the landlord. Point out and write down all the damage you can see to walls, floors, appliances, and fixtures. Keep the original list for yourself, and send a copy via registered mail to the landlord to be attached to the lease. That way, you cannot be held responsible for damage done before you moved into the apartment. Second, check to see if a security deposit is required in addition to the rental deposit. If it is, determine the amount and when and under what conditions it will be returned. Insist that this information be included in the lease. Third, find out who pays for personal injury or loss of personal property due to the landlord's negligence. Finally, make sure all the blanks in the lease are filled in or crossed out and all verbal contracts you made with the landlord are included.

1. Before looking for an apartment, what kinds of questions should you ask yourself?

2. When is the best time to look for an apartment?

3. What is a lease? What does it include?

Consumer Protection Agencies

Competitive markets protect consumers. In a **purely competitive market**—one that has a large number of buyers and sellers, identical products, independent action by buyers and sellers, information about the products being sold, and freedom to enter or leave it—it is unlikely that dishonest or incompetent producers can take advantage of consumers. Thus, purely competitive markets help ensure low prices and high quality.

If, on the other hand, the market is dominated by imperfect competition, the consumer is at a disadvantage. There may not be enough producers to ensure competition. There may be too few products from which to choose. Or, the information about the products may be inadequate, preventing consumers from making wise choices.

To make up for differences in market conditions, legislation has been passed to protect consumers by making imperfect markets behave more like competitive ones. Various agencies have been set up by Congress to protect consumers. Some of these agencies serve as a clearinghouse for information, while others make sure that the information furnished is accurate and reliable. Still others ensure that the products perform as promised.

The following list provides the names and addresses of some agencies set up to protect consumers and the area of specialization of each.

Agencies

Assistant Staff Director
Commission on Civil Rights
1121 Vermont Avenue, N.W.
Room 500
Washington, D.C. 20425
(202) 376–8307

Office of the Secretary
Consumer Product Safety
  Commission
5401 Westbard Avenue
Bethesda, Md. 20207
(301) 492–6800
800–638–2772 (toll free)

For Problems with or Complaints About:

Discrimination on matters such as employment, housing, workman's compensation, or educational benefits if there is possible discrimination based on race, color, religion, sex, age, nationality, or physical handicap.

Accidents due to unsafe or dangerous consumer products, including toys, home appliances, playground equipment, and clothing.

Office of Consumer Affairs
Room 5725
Department of Commerce
Washington, D.C. 20230
(202) 377–5001

Sale or promotion of goods or
services that do not measure up
to advertised claims. Some
examples include retirement
land or homes in other states,
mail order items, insurance,
product warranties, home
entertainment equipment, and
recreation and travel.

Consumer Assistance and Small
  Business Office
Federal Communications
  Commission
1919 M Street, N.W.
Room 254
Washington, D.C. 20554
(202) 632–7000

Radio, television, telephone, or
other communications products
and services; interference with
the reception of the above
services caused by CB radios, or
other sources of disturbance.

Division of Consumer and
  Community Affairs
Federal Reserve Board
Washington, D.C. 20551
(202) 452–3946

Denial of credit, overcharging of
interest for consumer loans,
failure to disclose all interest
cost information on a consumer
installment loan.

Auto Safety Hotline
Department of Transportation
Washington, D.C. 20590
(202) 426–0123
800–424–9393 (toll free)

Automobile safety and product
failure, child and infant car
seats and restraint systems.

Federal Information Centers

If you have any questions about a service or agency in the federal government,
you may want to contact the Federal Information Center (FIC) nearest you. These
agencies are prepared to help consumers find needed information or to locate the
right agency for help with problems.

Alabama
Birmingham (205) 322–8591
Mobile (205) 438–1421

Alaska
Anchorage (907) 271–3650

Arizona
Phoenix (602) 261–3313

Arkansas
Little Rock (501) 378–6177

California
Los Angeles (213) 894–3800
Sacramento (916) 551–2380
San Diego (619) 293–6030
San Francisco (415) 556–6600
Santa Ana (714) 836–2386

Colorado
Colorado Springs (303) 471–9491
Denver (303) 236–7181
Pueblo (303) 544–9523

Connecticut
Hartford (203) 527–2617
New Haven (203) 624–4720

Florida
Ft. Lauderdale (305) 522–8531
Jacksonville (904) 354-4756
Miami (305) 350–4155
Orlando (305) 422–1800
St. Petersburg (813) 893–3495
Tampa (813) 229–7911
West Palm Beach (305) 833–7566

Georgia
Atlanta (404) 221–6891

Hawaii
Honolulu (808) 546–8620

Illinois
Chicago (312) 353–4242

Indiana
Gary (219) 883–4110
Indianapolis (317) 269–7373

Iowa
From all points in Iowa
(800) 532–1556 (toll free)

Kansas
From all points in Kansas
(800) 432–2934 (toll free)

Kentucky
Louisville (502) 582–6261

Louisiana
New Orleans (504) 589–6696

Maryland
Baltimore (301) 962–4980

Massachusetts
Boston (617) 223–7121

Michigan
Detroit (313) 226–7016
Grand Rapids (616) 451–2628

Minnesota
Minneapolis (612) 349–5333

Missouri
St. Louis (314) 425–4106
From elsewhere in Missouri
(800) 392–7711 (toll free)

Nebraska
Omaha (402) 221–3353
From elsewhere in Nebraska
(800) 642-8383 (toll free)

New Jersey
Newark (201) 645–3600
Trenton (609) 396–4400

New Mexico
Albuquerque (505) 766–3091

New York
Albany (518) 463–4421
Buffalo (716) 846–4010
New York (212) 264–4464
Rochester (716) 546–5075
Syracuse (315) 476–8545

North Carolina
Charlotte (704) 376–3600

Ohio
Akron (216) 375–5638
Cincinnati (513) 684–2801
Cleveland (216) 522–4040
Columbus (614) 221–1014
Dayton (513) 223–7377
Toledo (419) 241–3223

Oklahoma
Oklahoma City (405) 231–4868
Tulsa (918) 584–4193

Oregon
Portland (503) 221–2222

Pennsylvania
Philadelphia (215) 597–7042
Pittsburgh (412) 644–3456

Rhode Island
Providence (401) 331–5565

Tennessee
Chattanooga (615) 265–8231
Memphis (901) 521–3285
Nashville (615) 242–5056

Texas
Austin (512) 472–5494
Dallas (214) 767–8585
Fort Worth (817) 334–3624
Houston (713) 229–2552
San Antonio (512) 224–4471

Utah
Salt Lake City (801) 524–5353

Virginia
Norfolk (804) 441–3101
Richmond (804) 643–4928
Roanoke (703) 982–8591

Washington
Seattle (206) 442–0570
Tacoma (206) 383–5230

Wisconsin
Milwaukee (414) 271–2273

1. What is a purely competitive market? How does it work to a consumer's advantage?
2. What happens if the market is dominated by imperfect competition?
3. What action has Congress taken to make up for differences in market conditions?

Appendix

■ Atlas and Data Bank

The United States
The World
World, Population, 1983
World Population
World Population by Region
GNP Per Capita and Population Growth
Infant Mortality in the 16 Largest Developing Nations
Life Expectancy in the 16 Largest Developing Nations
U.S. Population, Present and Projected
U.S. Population by Race and Origin, 1980
U.S. Population by Age, 1970–2000
World GNP, 1983
World Gross National Product
Distribution of GNP Per Capita
GNP Per Capita Growth
Average GNP Per Capita

■ Suggested Readings
■ Glossary
■ Index
■ Photo Credits
■ Acknowledgments

ARCTIC OCEAN

GREENLAND
(DENMARK)

GREENLAND
SEA

NORWE
SEA

Point
Barrow

BEAUFORT
SEA

BAFFIN
BAY

JAN MAYEN
(NORWAY)

Arctic Circle

ALASKA
(U.S.)

Mackenzie R.

Great
Bear Lake

Yukon R.

Davis Strait

Denmark Strait

ICELAND

FAROE IS.
(DEN.)

NO

▲ Mt. McKinley
20,320 ft.
(6,193 m.)

Great
Slave Lake

HUDSON
BAY

Cape
Farvel

GULF OF
ALASKA

ROCKY MOUNTAINS

NORTH
AMERICA

LABRADOR
SEA

NORTH
SEA

UNITED
KINGDOM

DE
NET

Lake
Winnipeg

CANADA

Great Lakes

ATLANTIC

IRELAND

London

BEL

Cape Mendocino

GREAT
PLAINS

Missouri R.

Chicago

OCEAN

Paris

FRANC

UNITED STATES

APPALACHIAN MTNS.

New York

Cape Finisterre

SPAIN

Los Angeles

Mississippi R.

Cape Hatteras

AZORES IS.
(Port.)

PORTUGAL

30°

Tropic of Cancer

ATLAS
MOUNT
TU

CANARY IS.
(SP.)

MOROCCO

ALGERIA

HAWAIIAN IS.
(U.S.)

MEXICO

GULF OF
MEXICO

THE
BAHAMAS

TURKS AND
CAICOS IS. (U.K.)

WESTERN SAHARA
(MOR.)

SA
HA

Mexico City

CUBA

DOMINICAN
REPUBLIC

PUERTO RICO (U.S.)

Cape Blanc

MAURITANIA

MALI

JAMAICA

GUADELOUPE (FR.)

CAPE
VERDE

BELIZE

HONDURAS

HAITI

DOMINICA

Niger R.

PACIFIC

GUATEMALA

CARIBBEAN
SEA

MARTINIQUE (FR.)

SENEGAL

EL SALVADOR

NICARAGUA

ST. LUCIA

BARBADOS

GAMBIA

BUR.

COSTA RICA

TRINIDAD AND TOBAGO

GUINEA

GRA

PANAMA

VENEZUELA

GUYANA

SIERRA
LEONE

OCEAN

Equator

COLOMBIA

SURINAME

LIBERIA

IVORY
COAST

TOGO

BEN

GALÁPAGOS IS.
(EC.)

ECUADOR

AMAZON

FRENCH GUIANA
(FR.)

CAMERO

0°

Pariñas Point

BASIN

Amazon R.

Cape São
Roque

SÃO TOMÉ
AND PRÍNCIPE

PERU

SOUTH
AMERICA

BRAZIL

ANDES MOUNTAINS

BOLIVIA

MATO GROSSO
PLATEAU

Tropic of Capricorn

PARAGUAY

Paraná R.

Rio de Janeiro

ATLANTIC

GRAN
CHACO

São Paulo

30°

Mt. Aconcagua
22,834 ft.
(6,960 m.)

URUGUAY

OCEAN

CHILE

ARGENTINA

PAMPAS

Buenos Aires

West Longitude

Prime Meridian

THE WORLD

• World's most populous cities
— International boundary
--- Disputed boundary
··· Undefined boundary

0   1000   2000 Miles

0   1000   2000   Kilometers

Projection: Miller Cylindrical

FALKLAND IS.
(U.K.)

Strait of
Magellan

SOUTH
GEORGIA I.
(U.K.)

Cape Horn

Drake Passage

Antarctic Circle

60°

ANTARCTICA

Copyright © by Merrill Publishing Co.
A Bell & Howell Information Company
All rights reserved.

ARCTIC OCEAN

BARENTS SEA
KARA SEA
LAPTEV SEA
EAST SIBERIAN SEA

FRANZ JOSEF IS. (U.S.S.R.)
VALBARD IS. NORWAY)
Cape Zelaniya

INAVIA
FINLAND
EN
North Cape
Lake Ladoga
Leningrad
Moscow

EUROPEAN PLAINS
AND
EUROPE

CENTRAL
SIBERIA
SIBERIAN
PLATEAU

VERKHOYANSK RANGE

Bering Strait
60°
BERING SEA

SIBERIA
WEST
SIBERIAN
PLAIN
Ob R.
Yenisey R.
URAL MOUNTAINS
SOVIET UNION
ASIA
Volga R.
Lena R.
Lake Baykal
YABLONOVY RANGE
Amur R.
Cape Lopatka
KURIL IS. (U.S.S.R.)
SEA OF OKHOTSK

N. ROMANIA
Danube R.
30°
B. BUL.
GREECE
BLACK SEA
TURKEY
CASPIAN DEPRESSION
Aral Sea
MONGOLIA
ALTAY SHAN
GOBI DESERT
MANCHURIA
International Date Line

CYPRUS
RRANEAN SEA LEB.
ISR.
QATTARA DEPRESSION
VA
EGYPT
SYR.
JORDAN
IRAQ
Mt. Elbrus 18,510 ft. (5,642 m.)
CASPIAN SEA
Teheran
IRAN
PLATEAU OF IRAN
PLAINS OF TURAN
TAKLA MAKAN DESERT
TIAN SHAN
CHINA
Beijing Tianjin
Seoul N. KOR.
S. KOR.
SEA OF JAPAN
JAPAN
Tokyo
PACIFIC
30°

SAUDI ARABIA
QATAR
U.A.E.
AFGHANISTAN
PAKISTAN
Delhi
Karachi
HIMALAYAS
NEPAL
Ganges R.
BHU.
Mt. Everest 29,028 ft. (8,848 m.)
Chang Jiang (Yangtze R.)
Chongqing
Shanghai
EAST CHINA SEA
TAIWAN
Tropic of Cancer

OMAN
Cairo
Nile R.
SUDAN
YEMEN
P.D.R. YEMEN
Cape Asir
Bombay
INDIA
Calcutta
BANGL.
BURMA
LAOS
THAILAND
VIETNAM
HONG KONG (U.K.)
MACAO (PORT.)
SOUTH CHINA SEA
PHILIPPINE SEA
OCEAN

FRICA
C.A.R.
DJI.
ETHIOPIA
ETHIOPIAN HIGHLANDS
SOMALIA
ARABIAN SEA
BAY OF BENGAL
Cape Comorin
SRI LANKA
CAMB.
PHILIPPINES
TRUST TERR. OF THE PACIFIC IS. (U.S.)
Monday Sunday

Zaire R.
ONGO (ZAIRE)
BASIN
ZAIRE
RWA.
BU.
UGANDA
KENYA
Lake Victoria
Mt. Kilimanjaro 19,340 ft. (5,895 m.)
SEYCHELLES
MALDIVES
BRITISH INDIAN OCEAN TERR. (U.K.)
BRUNEI
MALAYSIA
INDONESIA
Jakarta
PAPUA NEW GUINEA
Cape York
SOLOMON IS.
KIRIBATI
CORAL SEA
VANUATU
TUVALU
Equator
0°

LA
ZAMBIA
MALAWI
COMOROS
COCOS IS. (AUSTL.)
TONGA
FIJI

TANZANIA
ZIMB.
BOTSWANA
MADAGASCAR
Mozambique Channel
MOZAMBIQUE
MAURITIUS
RÉUNION (FR.)
WESTERN PLATEAU
AUSTRALIA
GREAT DIVIDING RANGE
NEW CALEDONIA (FR.)
Tropic of Capricorn
30°

SOUTH AFRICA
SWA.
LESO.
Cape of Good Hope
INDIAN OCEAN
Sydney
Mt. Kosciusko 7,310 ft. (2,228 m.)
TASMAN SEA
NEW ZEALAND
30°

st Longitude
KERGUELEN IS. (FR.)
N

60°

Antarctic Circle

					SWA.	—Swaziland
ALB.	—Albania	CAMB.	—Cambodia	LEB.	—Lebanon	SWITZ.	—Switzerland
AUS.	—Austria	C.A.R.	—Central African Republic	LESO.	—Lesotho	SYR.	—Syria
BANGL.	—Bangladesh	CZECH.	—Czechoslovakia	NETH.	—Netherlands	U.A.E.	—United Arab Emirates
BEL.	—Belgium	DJI.	—Djibouti	N. KOR.	—North Korea	W. GER.	—West Germany
BHU.	—Bhutan	EQ. GUI.	—Equatorial Guinea	P.D.R.–YEMEN	—People's Democratic	YUGO.	—Yugoslavia
BU.	—Burundi	GHA.	—Ghana		Republic of Yemen	ZIMB.	—Zimbabwe
BUL.	—Bulgaria	HUN.	—Hungary	RWA.	—Rwanda		
BUR.	—Burkina	ISR.	—Israel	S. KOR.	—South Korea		

Figure A–1

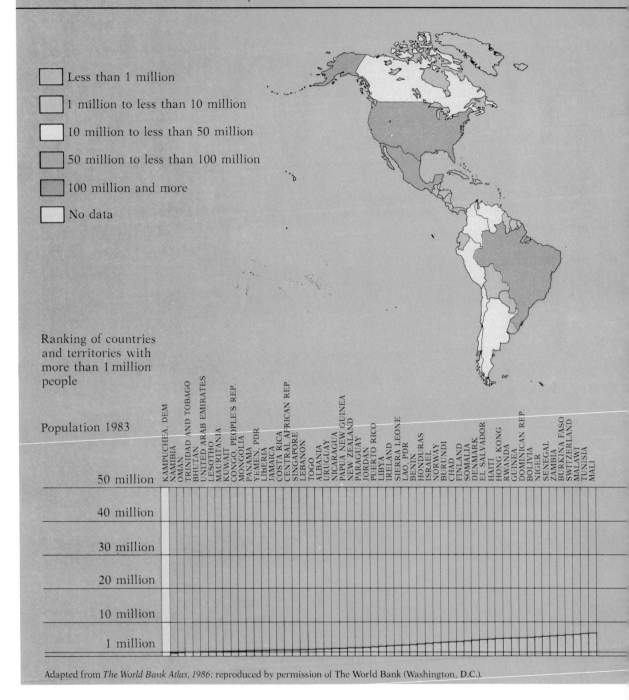

Adapted from *The World Bank Atlas, 1986;* reproduced by permission of The World Bank (Washington, D.C.).

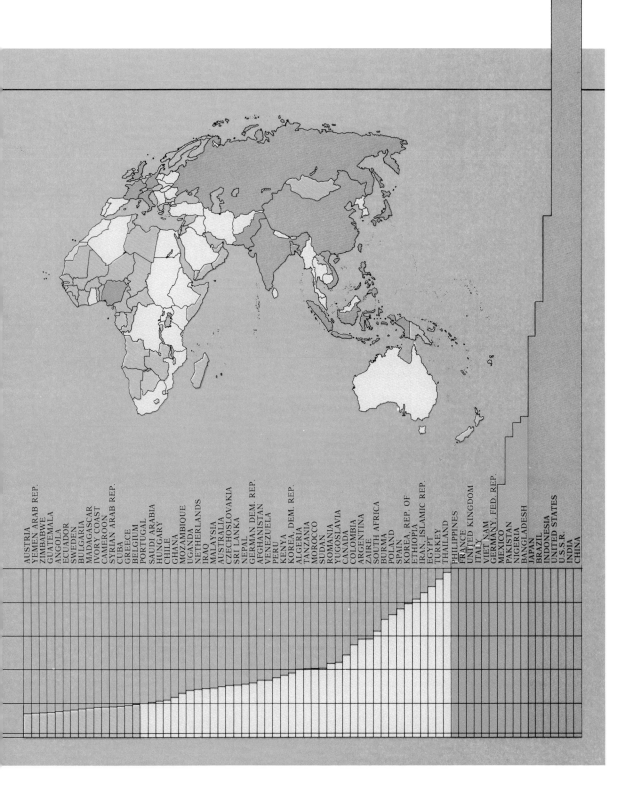

AUSTRIA
YEMEN ARAB REP.
ZIMBABWE
GUATEMALA
ANGOLA
ECUADOR
SWEDEN
BULGARIA
MADAGASCAR
IVORY COAST
CAMEROON
SYRIAN ARAB REP.
CUBA
GREECE
BELGIUM
PORTUGAL
SAUDI ARABIA
HUNGARY
CHILE
GHANA
MOZAMBIQUE
UGANDA
NETHERLANDS
IRAQ
MALAYSIA
AUSTRALIA
CZECHOSLOVAKIA
SRI LANKA
NEPAL
GERMAN DEM. REP.
AFGHANISTAN
VENEZUELA
PERU
KOREA, DEM. REP.
TANZANIA
ALGERIA
KENYA
MOROCCO
SUDAN
ROMANIA
YUGOSLAVIA
CANADA
COLOMBIA
ARGENTINA
ZAIRE
SOUTH AFRICA
BURMA
POLAND
SPAIN
KOREA, REP. OF
ETHIOPIA
IRAN, ISLAMIC REP.
EGYPT
TURKEY
THAILAND
PHILIPPINES
FRANCE
UNITED KINGDOM
ITALY
VIET NAM
GERMANY, FED. REP.
MEXICO
PAKISTAN
NIGERIA
BANGLADESH
JAPAN
BRAZIL
INDONESIA
UNITED STATES
U.S.S.R.
INDIA
CHINA

Table A–A

WORLD POPULATION, 1983, (IN THOUSANDS)

Afghanistan	n.a.	Greece	9840	Norway	4133
Albania	2841	Greenland	52	Oman	1131
Algeria	20,577	Grenada	91	Pacific Islands, Trust Terr.	141
American Samoa	34	Guadeloupe	318	Pakistan	89,729
Angola	8202	Guam	113	Panama	19,624
Antigua and Barbuda	78	Guatemala	7932	Papua New Guinea	3190
Argentina	29,627	Guinea	5830	Paraguay	3211
Australia	15,369	Guinea-Bissau	863	Peru	17,877
Austria	7549	Guyana	802	Philippines	52,055
Bahamas	222	Haiti	5300	Poland	36,571
Bahrain	391	Honduras	4093	Portugal	10,099
Bangladesh	95,497	Hong Kong	5313	Puerto Rico	3295
Barbados	253	Hungary	10,699	Qatar	281
Belgium	9856	Iceland	237	Reunion	523
Belize	153	India	733,248	Romania	22,553
Benin	3801	Indonesia	155,669	Rwanda	5674
Bermuda	58	Iran, Islamic Republic	42,503	Saint Christopher and Nevis	45
Bhutan	1187	Iraq	14,654	Saint Lucia	131
Bolivia	6034	Ireland	3508	Saint Vincent	107
Botswana	998	Isle of Man	68	Sao Tome and Principe	103
Brazil	129,662	Israel	4097	Saudi Arabia	10,421
Brunei	208	Italy	56,836	Senegal	6211
Bulgaria	8939	Ivory Coast	9472	Seychelles	64
Burkina Faso	6457	Jamaica	2258	Sierra Leone	3588
Burma	35,492	Japan	119,259	Singapore	2502
Burundi	4465	Jordan	3247	Solomon Islands	254
Cameroon	9562	Kampuchea, Dem.	n.a.	Somalia	5086
Canada	24,907	Kenya	18,902	South Africa	31,551
Cape Verde	315	Kiribati	60	Spain	38,228
Central African Republic	2470	Korea, Dem. People's Rep.	19,185	Sri Lanka	15,416
Chad	4789	Korea, Republic of	39,951	Sudan	20,807
Channel Islands	130	Kuwait	1672	Suriname	374
Chile	11,682	Lao PDR	3657	Swaziland	705
China	1,019,102	Lebanon	n.a.	Sweden	8331
Colombia	27,515	Lesotho	1451	Switzerland	6482
Comoros	368	Liberia	2057	Syrian Arab Republic	9606
Congo, People's Republic	1777	Libya	3447	Tanzania	20,771
Costa Rica	2379	Luxembourg	365	Thailand	49,169
Cuba	9782	Macao	304	Togo	2836
Cyprus	655	Madagascar	9452	Tonga	104
Czechoslovakia	15,415	Malawi	6626	Trinidad and Tobago	1149
Denmark	5114	Malaysia	14,863	Tunisia	6886
Djibouti	345	Maldives	168	Turkey	47,279
Dominica	74	Mali	7175	U.S.S.R.	272,500
Dominican Republic	5961	Malta	360	Uganda	13,881
Ecuador	8216	Martinique	311	United Arab Emirates	1206
Egypt	45,169	Mauritania	1629	United Kingdom	56,334
El Salvador	5232	Mauritius	993	United States	234,496
Equatorial Guinea	359	Mexico	75,011	Uruguay	2969
Ethiopia	40,900	Mongolia	1803	Vanuatu	127
Faeroe Islands	45	Montserrat	13	Venezuela	17,257
Fiji	670	Morocco	20,801	Viet Nam	58,538
Finland	4863	Mozambique	13,083	Virgin Islands (U.S.)	101
France	54,652	Namibia	1089	Western Samoa	161
French Guiana	77	Nepal	15,738	Yemen Arab Republic	7595
French Polynesia	156	Netherlands	14,362	Yemen, PDR	1974
Gabon	797	Netherlands Antilles	256	Yugoslavia	22,800
Gambia, The	697	New Caledonia	145	Zaire	29,671
German Dem. Republic	16,699	New Zealand	3203	Zambia	6259
Germany, Federal Republic	61,421	Nicaragua	2999	Zimbabwe	7856
Ghana	12,818	Niger	6062		
Gibraltar	30	Nigeria	93,642		

Adapted from *The World Bank Atlas*, 1986; reproduced by permission of The World Bank (Washington, D.C.).

WORLD POPULATION BY REGION AND SELECTED NATIONS, 1983

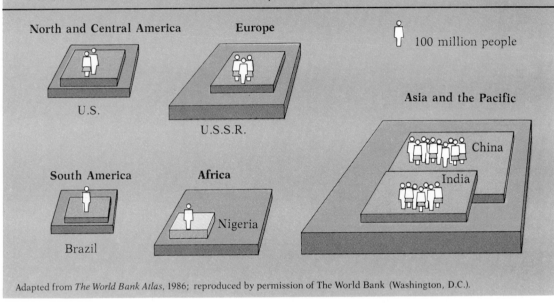

Adapted from *The World Bank Atlas*, 1986; reproduced by permission of The World Bank (Washington, D.C.).

Figure A-3

GNP PER CAPITA AND POPULATION GROWTH

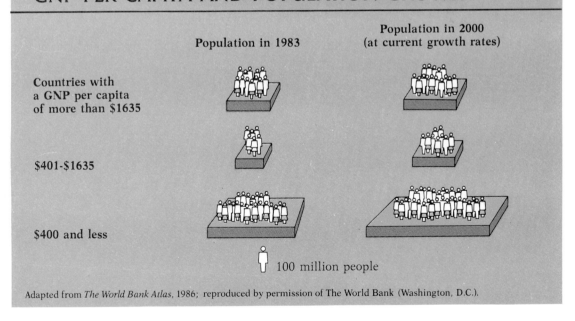

Adapted from *The World Bank Atlas*, 1986; reproduced by permission of The World Bank (Washington, D.C.).

Figure A–4

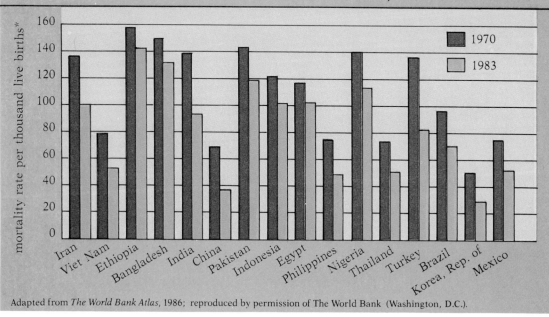

INFANT MORTALITY RATE IN 16 LARGEST DEVELOPING COUNTRIES, 1983

mortality rate per thousand live births*

1970
1983

Iran, Viet Nam, Ethiopia, Bangladesh, India, China, Pakistan, Indonesia, Egypt, Philippines, Nigeria, Thailand, Turkey, Brazil, Korea, Rep. of, Mexico

Adapted from *The World Bank Atlas*, 1986; reproduced by permission of The World Bank (Washington, D.C.).

Figure A–5

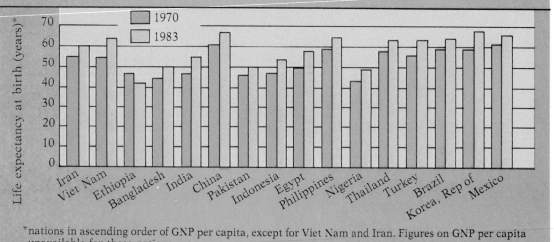

LIFE EXPECTANCY AT BIRTH IN 16 LARGEST DEVELOPING COUNTRIES

Life expectancy at birth (years)*

1970
1983

Iran, Viet Nam, Ethiopia, Bangladesh, India, China, Pakistan, Indonesia, Egypt, Philippines, Nigeria, Thailand, Turkey, Brazil, Korea, Rep of, Mexico

*nations in ascending order of GNP per capita, except for Viet Nam and Iran. Figures on GNP per capita unavailable for those nations.

Adapted from *The World Bank Atlas*, 1986; reproduced by permission of The World Bank (Washington, D.C.).

Figure A–6

UNITED STATES POPULATION, PRESENT AND PROJECTED

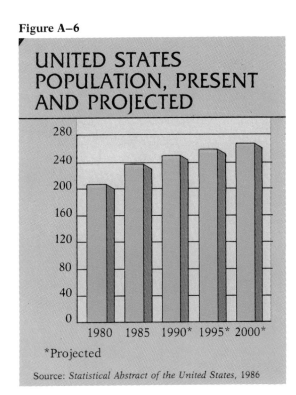

*Projected

Source: *Statistical Abstract of the United States, 1986*

Figure A–7

UNITED STATES POPULATION BY RACE AND ORIGIN, 1980

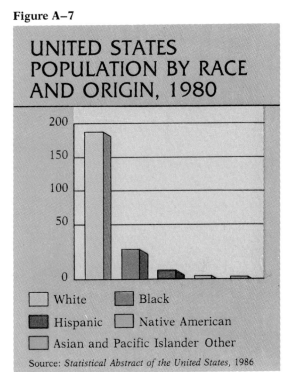

☐ White   ☐ Black
☐ Hispanic   ☐ Native American
☐ Asian and Pacific Islander   Other

Source: *Statistical Abstract of the United States, 1986*

Figure A–8

UNITED STATES POPULATION BY AGE, 1970-2000

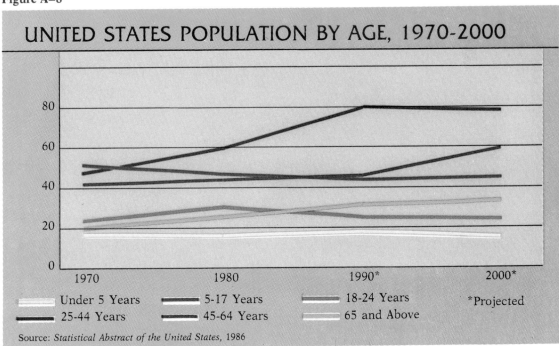

Under 5 Years   5-17 Years   18-24 Years   *Projected
25-44 Years   45-64 Years   65 and Above

Source: *Statistical Abstract of the United States, 1986*

WORLD GNP, 1983

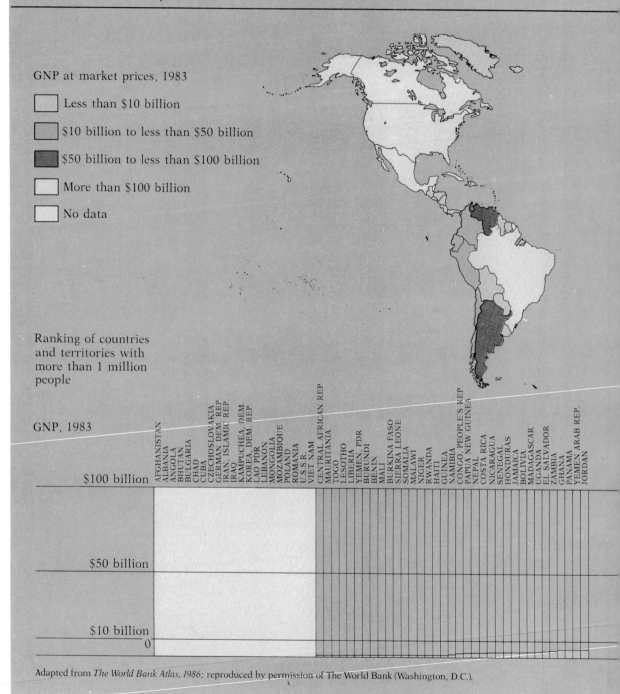

GNP at market prices, 1983

☐ Less than $10 billion

☐ $10 billion to less than $50 billion

■ $50 billion to less than $100 billion

☐ More than $100 billion

☐ No data

Ranking of countries
and territories with
more than 1 million
people

GNP, 1983

$100 billion

$50 billion

$10 billion
0

AFGHANISTAN
ALBANIA
ANGOLA
BHUTAN
BULGARIA
CHAD
CUBA
CZECHOSLOVAKIA
GERMAN DEM. REP.
IRAN, ISLAMIC REP.
IRAQ
KAMPUCHEA, DEM.
KOREA, DEM. REP.
LAO PDR
LEBANON
MONGOLIA
MOZAMBIQUE
POLAND
ROMANIA
U.S.S.R.
VIET NAM
CENTRAL AFRICAN REP.
MAURITANIA
TOGO
LESOTHO
LIBERIA
YEMEN, PDR
BURUNDI
BENIN
MALI
BURKINA FASO
SIERRA LEONE
SOMALIA
MALAWI
NIGER
RWANDA
HAITI
GUINEA
NAMIBIA
CONGO, PEOPLE'S REP.
PAPUA NEW GUINEA
NEPAL
COSTA RICA
NICARAGUA
SENEGAL
HONDURAS
JAMAICA
BOLIVIA
MADAGASCAR
UGANDA
EL SALVADOR
ZAMBIA
GHANA
PANAMA
YEMEN ARAB REP.
JORDAN

Adapted from *The World Bank Atlas, 1986;* reproduced by permission of The World Bank (Washington, D.C.).

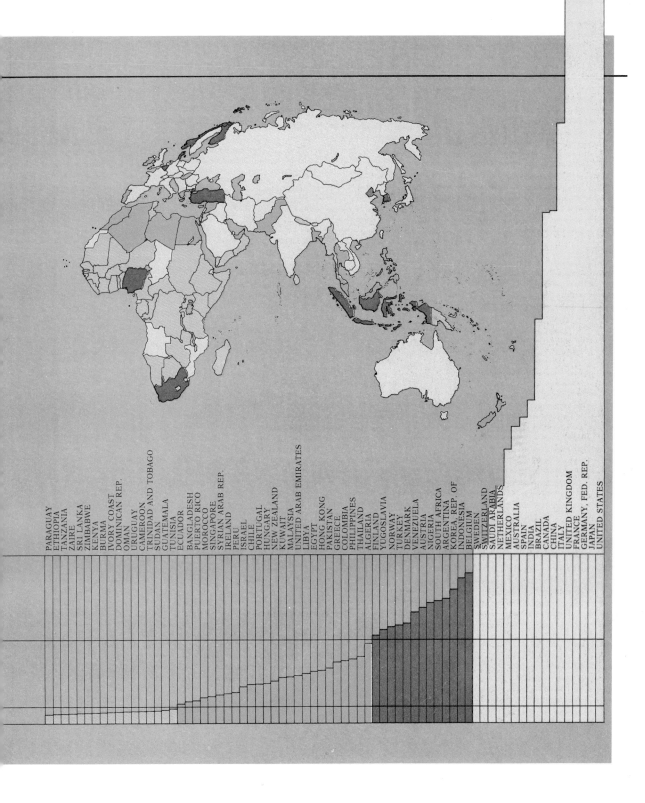

PARAGUAY
ETHIOPIA
TANZANIA
ZAIRE
SRI LANKA
ZIMBABWE
KENYA
BURMA
IVORY COAST
DOMINICAN REP.
OMAN
URUGUAY
CAMEROON
TRINIDAD AND TOBAGO
SUDAN
GUATEMALA
ECUADOR
TUNISIA
BANGLADESH
PUERTO RICO
MOROCCO
SINGAPORE
SYRIAN ARAB REP.
IRELAND
PERU
ISRAEL
CHILE
PORTUGAL
HUNGARY
NEW ZEALAND
KUWAIT
MALAYSIA
UNITED ARAB EMIRATES
LIBYA
EGYPT
HONG KONG
PAKISTAN
GREECE
COLOMBIA
PHILIPPINES
THAILAND
ALGERIA
YUGOSLAVIA
FINLAND
NORWAY
TURKEY
DENMARK
VENEZUELA
AUSTRIA
NIGERIA
SOUTH AFRICA
ARGENTINA
KOREA, REP. OF
INDONESIA
BELGIUM
SWEDEN
SWITZERLAND
SAUDI ARABIA
NETHERLANDS
MEXICO
AUSTRALIA
SPAIN
INDIA
BRAZIL
CANADA
CHINA
ITALY
UNITED KINGDOM
FRANCE
GERMANY, FED. REP.
JAPAN
UNITED STATES

Table A–B

WORLD GROSS NATIONAL PRODUCT

Country or territory	GNP at market prices		Country or territory	GNP at market prices	
	Millions of current U.S. dollars 1983	Real growth rate (percent) 1973-83		Millions of current U.S. dollars 1983	Real growth Rate (percent) 1973-83
Afghanistan	n.a.	n.a.	Egypt	31,320	9.1
Albania	n.a.	n.a.	El Salvador	3550	−0.2
Algeria	47,720	5.8	Equatorial Guinea	n.a.	n.a.
American Samoa	150	0.4	Ethiopia	4840	2.7
Angola	n.a.	n.a.	Faeroe Islands	500	4.5
Antigua and Barbuda	130	3.6	Fiji	1190	3.0
Argentina	74,340	−0.2	Finland	52,090	2.6
Australia	176,170	2.3	France	572,610	2.4
Austria	69,660	2.6	French Guiana	n.a.	n.a.
Bahamas	900	2.0	French Polynesia	1280	5.4
Bahrain	4,100	6.4	Gabon	2740	−3.4
Bangladesh	12,400	5.5	Gambia, The	200	2.3
Barbados	1,010	2.4	German Democratic Rep	n.a.	n.a.
Belgium	89,970	1.6	Germany, Federal Rep	700,450	2.1
Belize	170	5.6	Ghana	4080	−1.5
Benin	1110	5.3	Gibraltar	140	1.2
Bermuda	780	4.5	Greece	38,490	2.9
Bhutan	n.a.	n.a.	Greenland	400	1.7
Bolivia	2890	0.3	Grenada	80	2.6
Botswana	910	10.5	Guadeloupe	n.a.	n.a.
Brazil	241,910	4.4	Guam	730	−0.8
Brunei	4,270	3.5	Guatemala	8790	3.7
Bulgaria	n.a.	n.a.	Guinea	1,720	2.2
Burkina Faso,	1,170	3.7	Guinea-Bissau	160	2.1
Burma	6,460	5.9	Guyana	450	−1.0
Burundi	1,050	3.9	Haiti	1,560	3.0
Cameroon	7,840	6.8	Honduras	2,760	3.9
Canada	305,940	2.1	Hong Kong	32,240	9.3
Cape Verde	100	6.9	Hungary	22,960	5.3
Central African Republic	700	0.6	Iceland	2,430	2.1
Chad	n.a.	n.a.	India	192,940	4.2
Channel Islands	1,440	0.8	Indonesia	86,900	6.8
Chile	22,080	2.2	Iran, Islamic Republic	n.a.	n.a.
China	306,060	6.1	Iraq	n.a.	n.a.
Colombia	38,740	4.1	Ireland	17,490	2.2
Comoros	n.a.	n.a.	Isle of Man	410	0.9
Congo, People's Republic	2,170	7.6	Israel	21,580	3.1
Costa Rica	2,540	2.4	Italy	363,100	2.1
Cuba	n.a.	n.a.	Ivory Coast	6,700	4.5
Cyprus	2,400	n.a.	Jamaica	2,860	−2.3
Czechoslovakia	n.a.	n.a.	Japan	1,204,330	4.2
Denmark	59,020	1.5	Jordan	4,220	10.9
Djibouti	n.a.	n.a.	Kampuchea, Dem.	n.a.	n.a.
Dominica	70	1.0	Kenya	6,430	4.7
Dominican Republic	6,910	3.5	Kiribati	30	−11.2
Ecuador	11,670	5.0	Korea, Democratic People's Rep.	n.a.	n.a.
Korea, Republic of	80,280	7.0			

Adapted from *The World Bank Atlas*, 1986; reproduced by permission of The World Bank (Washington, D.C.).

Country or territory	GNP at market prices Millions of current U.S. dollars 1983	Real growth rate (percent) 1973-83	Country or territory	GNP at market prices Millions of current U.S. dollars 1983	Real growth Rate (percent) 1973-83
Kuwait	27,080	8.4	Saint Christopher and Nevis	60	1.3
Lao PDR	n.a.	n.a.	Saint Lucia	140	5.3
Lebanon	n.a.	n.a.	Saint Vincent	90	4.0
Lesotho	810	6.4	Sao Tome and Principe	40	2.3
Liberia	990	2.0	Saudi Arabia	127,330	9.2
Libya	29,170	3.6	Senegal	2,730	2.4
Luxembourg	5,330	3.5	Seychelles	160	4.3
Macao	n.a	n.a.	Sierra Leone	1,180	1.7
Madagascar	2,930	0.0	Singapore	16,650	8.0
Malawi	1,390	4.1	Solomon Islands	n.a.	n.a.
Malaysia	27,720	7.2	Somalia	1,270	2.5
Maldives	n.a.	n.a.	South Africa	73,160	2.8
Mali	1,110	4.3	Spain	182,350	1.7
Malta	1,250	9.7	Sri Lanka	5,130	5.2
Martinique	1,320	n.a.	Sudan	8,250	5.8
Mauritania	780	2.4	Suriname	1,270	3.8
Mauritius	1,150	3.6	Swaziland	610	3.2
Mexico	163,510	5.0	Sweden	103,640	1.0
Mongolia	n.a.	n.a.	Switzerland	105,300	0.8
Montserrat	30	5.1	Syrian Arab Republic	17,190	8.0
Morocco	15,750	4.5	Tanzania	4,900	2.6
Mozambique	n.a.	n.a.	Thailand	40,380	6.3
Namibia	1,820	4.1	Togo	790	2.2
Nepal	2,480	3.1	Tonga	n.a.	n.a.
Netherlands	141,730	1.4	Trinidad and Tobago	7,850	5.1
Netherlands Antilles	n.a.	n.a.	Tunisia	8,920	5.9
New Caledonia	960	0.1	Turkey	58,860	3.5
New Zealand	24,690	0.6	U.S.S.R.	n.a.	n.a.
Nicaragua	2,630	−1.3	Uganda	3,050	−2.1
Niger	1,460	5.3	United Arab Emirates	28,660	11.6
Nigeria	71,710	1.5	United Kingdom	517,110	1.0
Norway	57,820	3.4	United States	3,300,560	2.4
Oman	7,050	9.4	Uruguay	7,340	2.5
Pacific Islands, Trust Terr.	150	1.1	Vanuatu	n.a.	n.a.
Pakistan	34,710	6.2	Venezuela	66,020	2.4
Panama	4,140	4.8	Viet Nam	n.a.	n.a.
Papua New Guinea	2,430	1.3	Virgin Islands (U.S.)	850	1.9
Paraguay	4,250	8.5	Western Samoa	n.a.	n.a.
Peru	18,590	1.3	Yemen Arab Republic	4,170	7.4
Philippines	39,270	5.3	Yemen, PDR	1,020	7.4
Poland	n.a.	n.a.	Yugoslavia	56,820	4.4
Portugal	22,490	2.6	Zaire	5,040	−0.6
Puerto Rico	12,530	1.2	Zambia	3,620	0.6
Qatar	5,950	−3.1	Zimbabwe	5,800	3.5
Reunion	2,050	1.7			
Romania	n.a.	n.a.			
Rwanda	1,550	5.7			

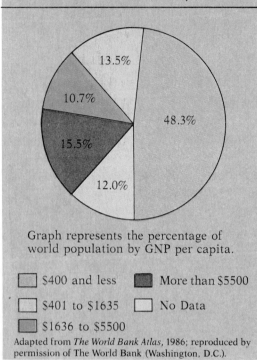

DISTRIBUTION OF GNP PER CAPITA, 1983

13.5%

10.7%

15.5%

12.0%

48.3%

Graph represents the percentage of world population by GNP per capita.

☐ $400 and less
☐ $401 to $1635
☐ $1636 to $5500
☐ More than $5500
☐ No Data

Adapted from *The World Bank Atlas*, 1986; reproduced by permission of The World Bank (Washington, D.C.).

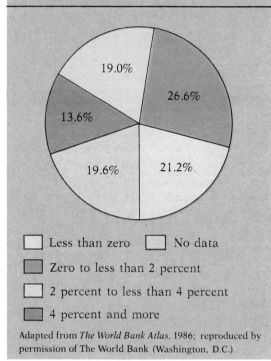

GNP PER CAPITA GROWTH RATE, 1983

19.0%

26.6%

13.6%

19.6%

21.2%

☐ Less than zero
☐ Zero to less than 2 percent
☐ 2 percent to less than 4 percent
☐ 4 percent and more
☐ No data

Adapted from *The World Bank Atlas*, 1986; reproduced by permission of The World Bank (Washington, D.C.).

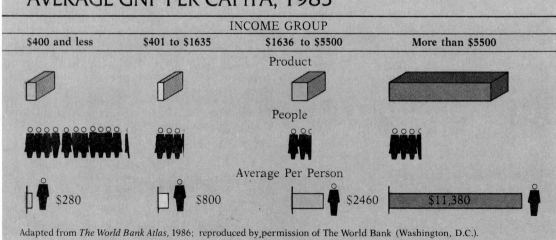

AVERAGE GNP PER CAPITA, 1983

INCOME GROUP

$400 and less	$401 to $1635	$1636 to $5500	More than $5500

Product

People

Average Per Person

$280 $800 $2460 $11,380

Adapted from *The World Bank Atlas*, 1986; reproduced by permission of The World Bank (Washington, D.C.).

Suggested Readings

NON-FICTION

Allen, William R. *Midnight Economist: Choices, Prices, and Public Policy.* New York: Playboy Press, 1981.

Asimov, Isaac. *Earth: Our Crowded Spaceship.* New York: Fawcett Book Group, 1978.

Brooks, Thomas R. *Picket Lines and Bargaining Tables: Organized Labor Comes of Age, 1935–1955,* Crosscurrents of the Twentieth Century Series. New York: Grosset & Dunlap, Inc., 1968.

Brown, Susan L., et al. *The Incredible Bread Machine.* Pasadena, California: Ward Ritchie Press, 1975.

Ehrlich, Paul R. *The End of Affluence.* New York: Ballantine Books, 1974.

Ellis, Edward Robb. *A Nation in Torment: The Great American Depression, 1929–1939,* Capricorn Books–Giant Series. New York: G.P. Putnam's Sons, 1972.

Friedman, Milton. *Capitalism and Freedom.* Chicago: Univ. of Chicago Press, 1963.

Friedman, Milton and Rose. *Free to Choose: A Personal Statement.* New York: Avon Books, 1981.

Galbraith, John Kenneth. *Money: Whence It Comes, Where It Went.* New York: Bantam Books, Inc., 1976.

Galbraith, John Kenneth. *The Affluent Society.* New York: New American Library, 1978.

Galbraith, John Kenneth. *The Great Crash, 1929.* Boston: Houghton Mifflin Co., 1979.

Galbraith, John Kenneth and Nicole Salinger. *Almost Everyone's Guide to Economics.* New York: Bantam Books, Inc., 1979.

Harrington, Michael. *The New American Poverty.* New York: Holt, Rinehart, and Winston, Inc., 1984.

Heilbroner, Robert L. *Beyond Boom and Crash.* New York: W.W. Norton & Co., Inc., 1978.

Heilbroner, Robert L. and Thurow Lester. *Five Economic Challenges.* Englewood Cliffs: Prentice-Hall, 1981.

Iacocca, Lee. *Iacocca, An Autobiography.* New York: Bantam Books, 1984.

Lacy, Robert. *Ford: The Men and the Machine.* Boston: Little, Brown, and Company, 1986.

Lekachman, Robert. *The Age of Keynes.* New York: McGraw-Hill Books Co., 1975.

Meltzer, Milton. *Bread and Roses: The Struggle of American Labor, 1865–1915.* New York: New American Library, 1977.

Naisbitt, John. *Megatrends: Ten New Directions Transforming Our Lives.* New York: Warner Books, Inc., 1982.

North, Douglas C. and Roger Leroy Miller. *The Economics of Public Issues.* New York: Harper and Row, 1983.

Passell, Peter. *How to Read the Financial Pages.* New York: Warner Books Inc., 1986.

Peters, Thomas J. and Robert H. Waterman, Jr. *In Search of Excellence. Lessons from America's Best Run Companies.* New York: Harper and Row, 1982.

Reich, Robert B. *The Next American Frontier.* New York: Times Books, 1981.

Schumacher, E.F. *Small is Beautiful.* New York: Harper and Row, 1973.

Sowell, Thomas. *Markets and Minorities.* New York: Basic Books, 1981.

Stein, Herbert. *Presidential Economics.* New York: Simon and Schuster, 1984.

Stockman, David. *The Triumph of Politics.* New York: Harper and Row, 1986.

Terkel, Louis (Studs). *Hard Times: An Oral History of the Great Depression in America.* New York: Pantheon Books, 1970.

Ward, Barbara, *Progress for a Small Planet.* New York: W.W. Norton & Co., Inc., 1979.

Ward, Barbara. *The Rich Nations and the Poor Nations.* New York: W.W. Norton & Co., Inc., 1962.

FICTION

Anderson, Sherwood. *Windy Macpherson's Son.* Chicago: Univ. of Chicago Press, 1965. Midwesterner's rise to success as a Chicago financier after the Spanish-American War.

Backer, George. *Appearance of a Man.* New York: Random House, Inc., 1966. The career of a Wall Street broker ends in the crash of 1929.

Dos Passos, John. *Midcentury.* New York: Pocket Books, Inc., 1962. A documentary of the American labor movement and the growth of the big unions.

Hawley, Cameron. *Executive Suite.* New York: Popular Library, Inc., 1977. The struggle among a company's vice presidents for the top position.

Howells, William D. *The Rise of Silas Lapham,* Norton Critical Edition Series. New York: W. W. Norton & Co., Inc., 1981. One of the earliest books about American business, focusing on a Boston paint merchant's efforts to become a member of Beacon Hill society.

Jevons, Marshall. *Murder at the Margin.* New York: Thomas Horton and Daughters, 1978.

Kern, Alfred. *Made In U.S.A.* Boston: Houghton Mifflin Co., 1966. Portrait of a union leader's rise to the top.

Marquand, John P. *Sincerely, Willis Wayde.* Boston: Little, Brown & Co., 1955. A successful industrialist's rise from 1900 to the 1940's.

Martin, William. *Back Bay.* New York: Pocket Books, Inc., 1981. Adventure focusing on a New England family of merchants and traders.

Norris, Frank. *Tower in the West.* New York: Harper and Brothers, 1957. American social and economic life from the 1920's to World War II, revolving around the people living in a St. Louis skyscraper-hotel.

Powell, Richard. *Don Quixote, U.S.A.* New York: Charles Scribner's Sons, 1966. Comic adventures of a Peace Corps volunteer on a Caribbean island.

Sayles, John. *Union Dues.* New York: Pocket Books, Inc., 1978. Working his way to Boston as a day laborer, a West Virginia coal miner follows his runaway son.

Schiffman, Ruth. *Turning the Corner.* New York: Dial Press, 1981. The life of a high school senior in Forgetown, Pennsylvania, during the Great Depression.

Simmons, Herbert. *Man Walking on Eggshells.* Boston: Houghton Mifflin Co., 1962. The economic and social struggles of a black family from 1927 to the 1960's.

Wilson, Sloan. *The Man in the Gray Flannel Suit.* Cambridge, Mass.: Robert Bentley, Inc., 1980. The problems and pressures of business executives.

Wolfson, Murray and Vincent Buranelli. *In the Long Run We Are All Dead.* New York: St. Martin's Press, 1984.

Glossary

A

Ability-to-Pay Principle of Taxation belief that taxes should be paid according to level of income regardless of benefits received (p. 215)

absolute advantage country's ability to produce more of a product than another country (p. 440)

accelerated depreciation use of depreciation over a shorter than normal period of time to reduce taxes (p. 229)

accelerator change in investment spending caused by a change in consumption spending (p. 419)

acid rain pollution in the form of acid rain mixed with rain (p. 542)

agency shop arrangement under which non-union workers must pay union dues (p. 190)

aggregate demand total demand by all sectors of the economy (p. 354)

aggregate supply total amount of goods and services produced in one year (p. 349)

agricultural banks banks with more than one-quarter of their loans and investments in the agricultural sector (p. 294)

allotments quotas limiting farm acreage that can be used for some crops (p. 541)

American Stock Exchange (AMEX) association that handles the purchase and sale of corporate stocks; second largest stock market in the United States (p. 335)

annual percentage rate (APR) true interest cost of a loan (p. 573)

annually balanced budget budget with expenditures equal to revenue (p. 257)

appropriations bill legislation earmarking money for certain expenditures (p. 242)

aquifers porous rock formations that hold underground water (p. 538)

assets property, possessions, and claims on others that are owned by individuals, businesses, or governments (p. 284)

automatic stabilizer income-boosting policy that automatically comes into play when the economy is weak (p. 419)

automation production with machinery and equipment rather than people (p. 401)

B

balance of payments accounting summary of funds earned from exports and spent on imports (p. 447)

balance sheet listing showing assets, liabilities, and net worth at a given point in time (p. 284)

balanced budget budget in which revenue equals expenditures (p. 241)

Balanced Budget and Emergency Deficit Control Act 1985 law requiring a balanced federal budget by 1991; also known as Gramm-Rudman-Hollings (p. 259)

balloon clause makes final payment on debt more than twice the regular payment (p. 573)

bank holding companies companies that hold stock of and control one or more banks (p. 309)

bankers acceptance money market item that promises payment by a bank (p. 337)

bankruptcy condition of being unable to pay bills; insolvency (p. 58)

barometric price leadership price announcements by a company that are usually regarded as trend-setting (p. 164)

barter economy moneyless economy that has to rely on trade and exchange (p. 271)

base year year used as a point of comparison in a price index or other statistical series (p. 204)

Benefit Principle of Taxation belief that taxes should be paid according to benefits received regardless of level of income (p. 214)

Better Business Bureau business sponsored non-profit organization providing information to consumers about local companies (p. 67)

bill consolidation loan consumer loan made to pay off all outstanding debts (p. 334)

black market illegal market where a wide variety of goods are available (p. 476)

blue-collar workers wage-earners in factories and similar jobs (p. 518)

board of directors representatives elected by common shareholders to set policies and goals and to hire professional managers of a corporation (p. 55)

bonds formal promises to repay borrowed money (p. 56)

bourgeoisie Marxist term for capitalists (p. 464)

boycott protest in the form of a refusal to buy, including attempts to convince others to do the same (p. 185)

break-even point amount of output needed if the firm is to recover its costs; production where total cost equals total revenue (p. 145)

budget itemized summary of probable expenditures for a given period (p. 558)

bullion heavy bars of precious metal, usually gold or silver (p. 275)

business cycles periodic changes in real GNP with recession and expansion (p. 381)

business fluctuations erratic movements of real GNP over time (p. 381)

business organization economic institution that produces in hopes of earning a profit (p. 48)

C

capital tools, factories, machines used in production; factor of production (p. 17)

capital consumption allowances depreciation in the national income accounts (p. 361)

capital flight transport of currency, foreign exchange, or other monetary wealth out of a country (p. 497)

capital good manufactured tool or equipment used in production; factor of production (p. 13)

capital market market where money is loaned for more than one year (p. 337)

capital-intensive production method using more capital than labor (p. 480)

capital-to-labor ratio average amount of capital available per worker (p. 375)

capitalism economic system in which the means of production are privately owned (p. 34)

capitalists land and factory owners who hire labor for production; bourgeoisie (p. 464)

cartel group of producers acting together to control the price of a good (p. 496)

cash surrender value refund on premium of an insurance policy when canceled (p. 330)

center of population point that represents the hypothetical "center of balance" of the U.S. population (p. 513)

central bank central banking institution where bankers bank; the Federal Reserve System in the United States (p. 284)

certificates of deposit (CD's) receipts certifying that funds have been loaned to a financial institution (p. 332)

Chamber of Commerce non-profit organization of local businesses whose purpose is to promote common interests (p. 67)

change in demand shift of the demand curve; new and different amounts of output demanded at every price (p. 103)

change in quantity demanded change in amount people will buy as a result of a price change; movement along the demand curve (p. 103)

change in quantity supplied change in amount offered for sale in response to a change in price; movement along the supply curve (p. 125)

change in supply   different amount offered at each and every possible price in the market; shift of the supply curve (p. 126)

charter   written government permission allowing a corporation to be formed (p. 54)

civilian labor force   part of the population over 16 years old and working, or actively looking for work (p. 181)

Clayton Antitrust Act   1914 law passed to outlaw price discrimination (p. 92)

closed shop   illegal arrangement under which workers must join a union before they can be hired (p. 190)

co-op   cooperative association (p. 63)

coin   metallic component of a nation's money supply (p. 277)

collateral   security given to guarantee repayment of a loan or obligation (p. 294)

collective bargaining   process during which labor and management discuss pay, benefits, and working conditions (p. 65)

collective farms   farms controlled and partially owned by the state but worked by families who share in the profits (p. 471)

collectivize   force common ownership of the means of production (p. 468)

collision insurance   policy covering damage to vehicles in an accident (p. 571)

collusion   agreements, usually illegal, among producers to fix prices, limit output, or divide markets (p. 164)

Comecon   Council for Mutual Economic Assistance made up of Poland, East Germany, Czechoslovakia, Hungary, Romania, and Bulgaria (p. 475)

command economy   society where a central authority makes most major economic decisions (p. 28)

commercial banks   financial institutions that accept deposits, issue checks, and make short-term loans (p. 279)

commercial paper   unsecured short-term debt obligations issued by companies (p. 337)

commodity money   money that has utility apart from its use as money (p. 273)

common stock   ownership shares in a corporation that allows owners to vote for board of directors, but has last claim on dividends and assets (p. 55)

communism   economic and political system characterized by common ownership of the means of production and the absence of social class (p. 461)

company unions   unions organized, supported, and sometimes even controlled by the employer (p. 185)

comparable worth   doctrine stating that pay should be based on degree of difficulty rather than type of work performed (p. 201)

comparative advantage   country's ability to produce a product relatively more efficiently than another country (p. 440)

complements   goods that increase the usefulness or value of other goods (p. 105)

Comptroller of the Currency   Federally appointed official who supervises the National Banking System (p. 281)

compulsory arbitration   situation requiring labor and management to use a mediator to reach a binding settlement (p. 191)

conglomerate   firm with four or more businesses producing unrelated products, none of which is responsible for a majority of its sales (p. 61)

conspicuous consumption   consumption for the purpose of impressing others with wealth, status, or position (p. 15)

constant dollars   dollar measure adjusted to remove distortions of inflation; same as real dollars (p. 204)

consumer cooperative   nonprofit association that buys consumer products for its members at below-retail prices (p. 63)

consumer good   tangible economic product used by consumers to satisfy wants and needs (p. 13)

consumer price index   statistical series used to measure changes in the prices of consumer products (p. 365)

consumer sovereignty   doctrine that the consumer rules the market (p. 15)

consumers those who use economic products to satisfy wants and needs (p. 15)

consumption act of using up goods and services to satisfy wants and needs (p. 15)

Continental Currency paper money issued by the Continental Congress in 1775 (p. 274)

cooperative nonprofit association of people that works to benefit members' welfare; co-op (p. 63)

copyright exclusive claim of an author or artist to his or her work (p. 89)

corporate income tax tax on profits paid by corporations to government (p. 222)

corporation form of businesses recognized as a separate legal entity with all the rights and responsibilities of an individual (p. 54)

craft union union of workers who have a common skill or share the same kind of work; same as a trade union (p. 184)

credit bureau agency that compiles credit histories of consumers and makes them available to merchants (p. 565)

credit history consumer's record of borrowings and repayments (p. 565)

credit union service cooperative that accepts deposits from, and makes loans to, members at favorable rates (p. 64)

creditor person or business to whom money is owed (p. 293)

creeping inflation barely noticeable rise in the price (p. 404)

crowding-out effect growing inability of private investors to secure funds because of high interest rates caused by heavy government borrowing (p. 255)

crude birth rate number of live births per 1000 population (p. 499)

currency paper currency part of a nation's money supply (p. 277)

current GNP GNP measured in inflation-distorted dollars; nominal GNP (p. 365)

customs duty tax on imported goods (p. 223)

customs union group of countries with no tariffs among themselves and uniform tariffs to non-members (p. 495)

cyclical unemployment unemployment due to swings in the business cycle (p. 400)

cyclically balanced budget budget balanced over the course of the business cycle (p. 259)

D

deep gas natural gas located 15,000 feet or more below the surface (p. 537)

deficit spending situation where expenditures exceed revenues (p. 249)

deflation decline in the general price level (p. 403)

demand willingness to purchase representing desire and ability to satisfy a want or need; same as effective demand (p. 12)

demand curve downward-sloping curve showing quantity demanded at each possible price in the market; graphical representation of the demand schedule (p. 102)

demand deposits funds on deposit that can be withdrawn (p. 278)

demand elasticity response of change in the quantity demanded to a change in price (p. 108)

demand schedule table that shows the quantity demanded at every possible price in the market (p. 101)

demand-side economics policies that emphasize the stimulation of total demand; Keynesian economics (p. 417)

Depository Institutions Deregulation and Monetary Control Act 1980 law allowing more competition among financial institutions (p. 290)

depreciation gradual wear and tear on equipment during production (p. 136)

depression severe drop in real GNP with very high unemployment (p. 382)

depression script money issued by towns and municipalities in the 1930's (p. 384)

deregulation relaxation of government regulations on business (p. 421)

devaluation lowering of the gold backing of a country's currency (p. 452)

discomfort index series representing the sum of the inflation and the unemployment rates; misery index (p. 410)

discount rate interest rate the FED charges to member banks when they borrow; a tool of monetary policy (p. 315)

discount window FED teller window where member banks arrange for loans (p. 315)

disposable personal income (DI) income of the household sector after taxes (p. 362)

distribution of income allocation of income among families, individuals (p. 514)

dividend quarterly profit payments to the owners of a corporation (p. 55)

Dow Jones Industrial Average stock index that gauges the NYSE performance (p. 336)

dual banking system system under which banks can secure a charter from federal or state governments (p. 282)

E

easy money policy action to expand the money supply and lower the price of credit (p. 311)

econometric model model used to predict changes in prices, employment, and GNP (p. 388)

economic institutions people and organizations that represent or use productive resources to satisfy wants and needs of producers and consumers (p. 47)

economic model simplified model of the world using assumptions about the likely behavior of people and businesses (p. 151)

economic products relatively scarce goods and services that are useful and transferable to others (p. 12)

Economic Recovery Tax Act 1981 law designed to stimulate the economy by lowering taxes for people and firms (p. 229)

economic system organized way a society provides for the production and distribution of goods and services for its people (p. 27)

economics study of how people can best use scarce resources to satisfy unlimited wants (p. 9)

economy of scale efficient production resulting from a larger plant size (p. 90)

effective demand desire to have or own, based on ability and willingness to pay; same as demand (p. 99)

elastic relatively large change in quantity demanded or supplied caused by a small change in price (p. 108)

electronic banking transactions made with computer terminals, telephones, or remote tellers (p. 288)

embargo prohibition of the export or import of a product (p. 532)

employed persons people working at least one hour a week for pay or at least 15 hours a week for no pay in a family business (p. 396)

employment rate ratio of persons working to the total number in the civilian labor force (p. 396)

energy banks banks with more than one-quarter of their loans and investments in energy-related businesses (p. 294)

enterprise zones depressed areas where government regulations have been suspended to attract industry (p. 524)

entitlements state and federal programs that provide economic, health, and other assistance to qualifying people (p. 419)

entrepreneur person who takes a financial risk to establish or maintain a business enterprise (p. 36)

equilibrium price price where the quantity brought to market is equal to the amount purchased; price that leaves neither a shortage nor a surplus (p. 151)

equilibrium wage rate rate at which there is neither a surplus nor an excess demand for labor (p. 196)

equity ownership, usually in a business enterprise; stock certificates (p. 284)

estate tax tax levied on the estate of a deceased person (p. 223)

Eurodollars United States dollar deposits in banks in other countries (p. 337)

European Common Market association of European countries with no tariff barriers among themselves and a uniform tariff for non-members (p. 496)

excess reserves bank cash or FED deposits not needed to back customer deposits (p. 311)

excise tax tax levied on the manufacture or sale of selected items (p. 223)

expansion period of growth of real GNP; period following a recession (p. 382)

expropriation government confiscation of privately owned goods (p. 494)

external debt debt a country owes to other banks and countries (p. 497)

F

fact-finding agreement between union and management to have a neutral third party collect facts about a dispute and present non-binding recommendations (p. 191)

factor markets markets where the factors of production are bought and sold (p. 79)

factors of production land, labor, and capital used to produce goods and services (p. 16)

family two or more people related by blood, marriage, or adoption living in a household (p. 356)

FED see "Federal Reserve System"

federal budget annual budget of the federal government that projects revenues, expenditures, and deficits (p. 241)

federal debt total money owed to investors by the federal government (p. 250)

Federal Deposit Insurance Corporation (FDIC) governmental agency that insures deposits in commercial banks (p. 290)

Federal Reserve Notes modern paper currency issued by the FED (p. 309)

Federal Reserve System privately owned, publicly controlled, central bank of the United States (p. 277)

Federal Savings and Loan Insurance Corporation (FSLIC) government agency that insures deposits in savings and loans; similar to the FDIC (p. 328)

fiat money something declared to be money by order of the government (p. 273)

FICA Federal Insurance Contributions Act; law that provides for the collection of Social Security funds (p. 219)

finance charge total dollar cost of borrowed money including service charges, fees, and interest (p. 565)

finance company firm that makes loans to consumers and buys installment contracts from retailers who sell on credit (p. 334)

financial assets receipts or documents indicating that a loan or deposit has been made; CD's, mortgages, bonds (p. 327)

financial capital money used to buy tools and equipment (p. 17)

financial system system of savers, investors, and financial institutions working together to transfer savings dollars to investors (p. 326)

fiscal policy use of spending and taxing measures to achieve desired economic results (p. 417)

fiscal year annual planning period used by governments and businesses, may be different from the calendar year (p. 242)

Five-Year Plan long-range plan used by most Communist countries to develop agriculture and industry (p. 468)

fixed cost cost of production that does not change as output changes (p. 136)

fixed exchange rates system under which the prices of foreign currencies are set and do not vary (p. 450)

fixed income income that does not adjust to changes in the level of prices (p. 41)

flexible exchange rates system under which supply and demand set foreign exchange rates; floating exchange rates (p. 452)

floating exchange rates see flexible exchange rates (p. 452)

food stamps government-issued coupons that can be exchanged for food (p. 520)

foreign exchange another nation's currency (p. 450)

foreign exchange futures foreign currencies bought or sold in the future at rates agreed upon today (p. 453)

foreign exchange market market where foreign currencies are traded (p. 450)

foreign exchange rate price of a country's currency in terms of another (p. 450)

fractional reserve system system under which banks must set aside a portion of every deposit (p. 311)

franchise exclusive right to produce or sell a certain product in an area or region (p. 86)

free enterprise economy market economy in which individuals and businesses have the freedom to operate for a profit with limited government intervention; same as private enterprise economy (p. 22)

free products relatively plentiful and abundant products that have little or no scarcity value (p. 13)

free traders those in favor of unrestricted trade between nations (p. 445)

free-trade area group of countries with reduced or no trade barriers among themselves but without a common tariff for non-members (p. 496)

frictional unemployment unemployment due to workers changing jobs or waiting to take new ones (p. 399)

fringe benefits benefits received by employees in addition to wages and salaries (p. 52)

full employment lowest unemployment rate thought possible in the economy (p. 402)

full-employment budget budget constructed under the assumption that people are fully employed (p. 259)

futures contracts for delivery of goods at a future date at prices agreed upon today (p. 337)

futures market market where futures contracts are bought and sold (p. 338)

G

galloping inflation rapid inflation, as high as 300 percent annually (p. 404)

gasohol gasoline with 10 percent grain alcohol content (p. 535)

General Agreement on Tariffs and Trade (GATT) international agreement to lower tariffs and other trade barriers (p. 449)

general partnership most common form of a partnership where all partners have unlimited liability (p. 52)

geographic monopoly market situation in which a firm can act as a monopolist because of its location or the small size of the market (p. 88)

gift tax tax levied on wealth transferred in the form of a gift (p. 223)

giveback wages and fringe benefits given up by workers when union contracts are renegotiated (p. 203)

glut considerable oversupply (p. 533)

GNP gap difference between potential and actual GNP (p. 409)

GNP in constant dollars GNP with inflation removed; real GNP (p. 365)

gold certificates paper currency backed by gold in late 1800's and early 1900's (p. 301)

gold standard mechanism providing for exchange of paper currency into gold (p. 301)

good tangible economic product used to satisfy wants and needs (p. 13)

Gosplan central economic planning agency of the Soviet economy (p. 29)

government monopoly monopoly created and/or owned by the government (p. 89)

grant-in-aid transfer payment from one level of government to another (p. 240)

Great Depression worst economic decline in United States history beginning in 1929 and lasting until 1933 (p. 186)

Great Leap Forward China's second Five-Year Plan begun in 1958 (p. 476)

greenbacks money used in 1862 to finance Civil War; United States notes (p. 301)

grievance procedure contractual provision that outlines the way future grievance issues will be resolved (p. 190)

gross national product (GNP) total dollar value of all final goods and services produced annually by an economy (p. 251)

gross private domestic investment
investment sector spending in the output-expenditure model (p. 357)

group policy   insurance policy offered to groups of individuals such as employees at a business (p. 571)

growth triangle   table showing annual rates of growth between dates (p. 380)

H

homeowner insurance   policy covering damage from accidents occurring on policyholder's property (p. 561)

horizontal merger   joining of two or more companies involved in the same type of business (p. 61)

household   all individuals who reside together in a house, apartment, or separate place of residence; basic unit of the consumer sector (p. 354)

hyperinflation   extreme increase in inflation that can threaten confidence in the money supply (p. 404)

I

immediate period   extreme short run; period so short that firms cannot adjust variable inputs used in production (p. 157)

imperfect competition   market structure where pure competition is not present; monopoly, oligopoly, or monopolistic competition (p. 82)

implicit GNP price deflator   index used to measure price changes in GNP (p. 365)

incidence of a tax   place where the final burden of a tax falls (p. 227)

income effect   change in amount purchased when a consumer's real income changes as a result of a change in the price of that item (p. 103)

inconvertible fiat money standard
monetary system in which money cannot be converted into gold or silver on demand (p. 303)

incorporate   legal steps taken to form a corporation (p. 54)

independent pricing   pricing policy that ignores desires of other producers in the industry (p. 166)

independent unions   labor unions not affiliated with the AFL-CIO (p. 189)

index of leading indicators   index used to predict business cycle turning points (p. 388)

indexing   adjustment of tax brackets to keep abreast of inflation; (p. 231)

indirect business taxes   licenses, taxes, and other fees a firm pays in order to do business (p. 361)

individual income tax   tax levied on wages, salaries, and other labor income (p. 218)

industrial union   labor union made up of workers in a given industry regardless of the types of jobs they perform (p. 184)

industry   collectively, all firms engaged in producing a certain product (p. 157)

inelastic   relatively small change in quantity demanded or supplied caused by a large change in price (p. 109)

infant industries argument   belief that trade should be restricted to protect new industries (p. 445)

inferior goods   cheap food items for low-income families whose consumption appears to be contrary to the Law of Demand (p. 116)

inflated dollars   dollar measures distorted by inflation (p. 407)

inflation   rise in the general price level (p. 41)

injunction   court order issued to prevent a company or union from taking action during disputes (p. 192)

insider trading   illegal activity involving the purchase or sale of stock based on knowledge not available to the investing public (p. 339)

installment cash credit   consumer cash loan requiring periodic repayment of principal and interest (p. 572)

installment sales credit   consumer loan for household items requiring down payment at time of purchase and periodic payments thereafter (p. 572)

intangible personal property ownership rights to property as opposed to the property itself; includes stocks, bank accounts, mortgages (p. 225)

interest money paid for the use of borrowed funds (p. 56)

intergovernmental revenues money one level of government receives from another level of government (p. 223)

intermediate products goods that become components of other goods (p. 350)

International Monetary Fund (IMF) international agency that helps stabilize exchange rates and facilitate trade (p. 454)

inventory extra supplies of goods held in reserve to meet demand (p. 52)

investment tax credit (ITC) reduction of tax liability based on the purchase price of tools or equipment (p. 229)

J

jurisdictional dispute disagreement as to which party should perform a certain kind of task (p. 189)

K

Keynesian economics policies that emphasize the stimulation of total demand; demand-side economics (p. 417)

L

labor human abilities and effort used in production; a factor of production (p. 16)

labor mobility ability and willingness of workers to move from one area to another in search of work (p. 199)

labor productivity measure of goods produced per worker; measure of efficiency in production (p. 376)

labor union association of workers that promotes and defends pay and other job-related interests of its members (p. 64)

labor-intensive production method using more labor than capital (p. 477)

Laffer Curve economic model relating tax rates to tax collections (p. 422)

laissez faire principle what government should not interfere with business activity (p. 78)

land natural resources and other "gifts of nature" used in production; a factor of production (p. 16)

Law of Demand economic rule that states that more will be demanded at lower prices and less at higher prices (p. 103)

Law of Supply principle that states that more will be brought to market at high prices and less at lower ones (p. 125)

Law of Variable Proportions economic principle which holds that total output will change in response to a change in a single variable input when all other inputs are held constant (p. 129)

legal tender any substance declared to be money by government decree (p. 300)

less-developed countries (LDC's) poor countries with low per capita GNP (p. 485)

liabilities legal obligations or debts owed to others (p. 284)

life expectancy estimate of the number of years a person is expected to survive (p. 499)

limited liability requirement that an owner's responsibility for the debts of a business is limited to the owner's investment; applies to corporations and limited partners in a partnership (p. 54)

limited life situation in which a firm ceases to exist when the owner(s) sell, leave, or new ones join; applies mainly to partnerships and sole proprietorships (p. 54)

limited partnership form of partnership where one or more partners contribute financial capital but seldom participate in management decisions (p. 52)

liquidity ease with which an asset can be converted to cash (p. 286)

lockout refusal by management to allow workers to enter a plant to work (p. 185)

long run period long enough for producers to change amount of fixed and variable inputs used in manufacturing (p. 157)

Lorenz Curve curve that shows the variance between the equal and the actual distribution of income (p. 515)

loss leader item sold below cost to attract customers (p. 160)

M

macroeconomics theory that deals with the decision making of groups of individuals, businesses, or governments (p. 354)

margin requirement minimum percentage payment required when stock is purchased from a broker (p. 316)

marginal analysis decision making that evaluates the extra cost of doing something against the extra benefits to be gained (p. 144)

marginal cost extra cost of producing one more unit of output (p. 138)

marginal product extra output due to the addition of one more unit of input (p. 133)

marginal revenue extra revenue from the sale of one more unit of output (p. 142)

marginal utility extra utility or satisfaction gained from the consumption of an additional unit of a product (p. 106)

market meeting place or other means whereby buyers and sellers can get together (p. 31)

market basket hypothetical collection of goods and services typical of purchases made by some group (p. 364)

market economy economic system in which supply, demand, and the price system help people make decisions and allocate resources (p. 31)

market equilibrium condition of price stability where quantity demanded equals quantity supplied (p. 150)

market structure market classification according to number and size of firms, type of product, and type of competition (p. 79)

Marxists followers of the theories and teachings of Karl Marx (p. 463)

maturity life or length of a loan (p. 254)

measure of value common denominator with which to measure value; one of the functions of money (p. 272)

mediation process involving a neutral third party to resolve a dispute (p. 191)

Medicaid medical insurance program administered jointly by the federal and state governments for low-income people (p. 245)

Medicare federal health program for senior citizens, regardless of income (p. 245)

medium of exchange money or other commodity generally accepted in exchange for goods and services; one of the three functions of money (p. 272)

member banks commercial banks that are members of the FED (p. 303)

merger the joining of two or more companies, sometimes by takeover, to form a single business enterprise (p. 59)

microeconomics economic theory dealing with decision making by individual people, businesses, or other units (p. 354)

minimum wage lowest legal wage that can be paid to most workers (p. 204)

misery index series representing the sum of the inflation and the unemployment rates; discomfort index (p. 410)

modified private-enterprise economy economic system based on free enterprise with some government involvement (p. 43)

modified union shop arrangement under which workers have the option to join a union but do not have to do so to keep their jobs (p. 190)

monetarism school of thought that emphasizes the controlled growth of the money supply as a cure for inflation and economic instability (p. 423)

monetary policy actions by the Federal Reserve System to control the availability and cost of credit (p. 311)

monetary standard mechanism designed to keep the money supply useful and reliable; a gold standard (p. 299)

monetary unit country's basic currency component (p. 276)

monetize the debt expansion of the money supply to offset government borrowings and keep interest rates stable (p. 319)

money medium of exchange, a measure of value, and a store of value (p. 272)

money market market where money is loaned for one year or less (p. 337)

money market funds pool of funds collected from small investors and loaned at competitive rates to large investors (p. 289)

money market instruments loan certificates or receipts with maturities of one year or less; CD's, Treasury bills (p. 337)

money market mutual shares large-denomination accounts with money market mutual funds subject to check withdrawal (p. 278)

monopolistic competition market structure in which firms produce a differentiated product yet have all other characteristics of pure competition (p. 84)

monopoly market structure in which output is supplied by a single seller; form of imperfect competition (p. 86)

moral suasion use of persuasion by the FED to influence credit decisions of member banks (p. 315)

most favored nation clause provision allowing a third country to enjoy trade benefits granted to others (p. 449)

multinational corporation that produces and sells without regard to national boundaries and whose business activities are located in several countries (p. 62)

multiplier change in total income caused by change in investment spending (p. 418)

mutual fund company that sells stock in itself and uses the proceeds to invest in securities (p. 332)

mutual savings bank non-bank financial institution wholly owned by its depositors who share the earnings (p. 328)

N

national bank notes paper currency issued by the National Banking System and backed by U.S. government bonds (p. 301)

National Banking System system in which banks receive federal charters and are members of the FED (p. 281)

national banks commercial banks chartered by the federal government (p. 281)

national income (NI) measure of the country's total income (p. 361)

national income accounting accounting records measuring the overall performance of the economy (p. 349)

National Labor Relations Act (NLRA) 1935 law defining unfair labor practices by employers and giving workers the right to bargain collectively (p. 186)

natural monopoly market situation in which one firm exists because competition may not be desirable or even possible (p. 86)

need basic requirement for survival; food, clothing and/or shelter (p. 11)

negative income tax tax system substituting cash payments for welfare programs (p. 522)

net export of goods and services balance of exports over imports (p. 358)

net national product (NPP) total net output; GNP less depreciation (p. 358)

net worth what is left after liabilities are substracted from assets (p. 284)

New Economic Policy (NEP) Soviet policy put into effect in 1921 to restore capitalism on a temporary basis (p. 468)

New York Stock Exchange (NYSE) association that handles the purchase and sale of corporate stocks; largest stock market in the United States (p. 335)

nominal GNP GNP in current, or inflation-distorted dollars; current GNP (p. 365)

non-bank depository institutions institutions other than commercial banks that receive deposits and make loans (p. 327)

non-market transactions economic activity such as housework that does not take place in the market (p. 352)

non-price competition form of competition involving the advertising of a product's appearance, quality and design, rather than its price (p. 162)

noncompeting labor grades broad groups of unskilled, semiskilled, skilled, and professional workers who do not compete with one another (p. 193)

nonprofit organizations economic institutions operating not for financial gain (p. 48)

Norris-LaGuardia Act 1932 law keeping federal courts out of union labor disputes (p. 186)

NOW account Negotiable Order of Withdrawal; interest-bearing checking accounts issued by banks, savings and loans (p. 278)

O

oligopoly market structure where output is produced by a few large firms (p. 84)

OPEC nations members of the Organization of Petroleum Exporting Countries (p. 495)

open market operations purchase or sale of government securities by the FED to change the money supply and affect the price of credit; tool of monetary policy (p. 313)

open-ended credit authorization allowing consumer credit purchases up to a limited amount; revolving credit (p. 572)

opportunity cost goods, services, or time given up because one choice is made rather than another (p. 18)

output-expenditure model macroeconomic model describing the consumption of GNP by sectors; $GNP = C + I + G + F$ (p. 357)

over-the-counter market (O-T-C) informal system of security dealers who buy and sell stocks not listed on organized exchanges (p. 335)

overhead broad category of fixed costs; includes interest, rent, taxes and executive salaries (p. 136)

P

paradox of value apparent contradiction between the high value of a non-necessity and the low value of a necessity (p. 14)

paradoxical demand curve demand curve not showing the usual price-quantity relationships; upward-sloping curve (p. 116)

partnership business organizations owned by two or more people (p. 52)

patent exclusive right to any new art, machine, item of manufacture, or improvement thereof (p. 89)

payroll withholding system system that automatically deducts income taxes from paychecks on a regular basis (p. 218)

peak point where real GNP stops growing and starts to decline (p. 381)

pension retirement allowance (p. 332)

pension fund fund collecting contributions to be distributed later as retirement, old-age, or disability allowances (p. 333)

personal consumption expenditures household sector spending on consumer goods and services (p. 357)

personal income (PI) individual and household income before taxes (p. 361)

personal liability insurance policy protecting against personal liability from an accident (p. 571)

picket demonstration before a place of business to express dissatisfaction with company actions (p. 185)

piecework payment system under which workers are paid according to the number of "pieces" of output produced (p. 472)

pollution spoilage of the environment with poisonous or noxious materials (p. 542)

population density number of people living per square mile of land area (p. 502)

population tree figure showing the distribution of population by age and sex in a given year (p. 514)

poverty level official minimum income needed for bare necessities (p. 519)

preferred stock non-voting ownership shares in a corporation that has first claim on dividends and, in the case of liquidation, assets (p. 56)

premium purchase price of a life insurance policy (p. 330)

price discrimination illegal practice of charging different prices to customers for the same good or service (p. 93)

price index statistical series used to measure inflation or remove its distortions from other measures (p. 364)

price leadership independent pricing decisions made by a leading firm on a regular basis that results in generally uniform industry-wide prices (p. 164)

price maker firm that has enough market power to set the price for its output; usually refers to a monopolist (p. 166)

price taker firm with no ability to influence market price of its product; refers to a perfect competitor (p. 166)

price war fierce price competition between sellers, sometimes to the point where price is below the cost of the product (p. 165)

price-fixing agreement, usually illegal, among producers to establish a uniform price for a product (p. 85)

prime rate interest rate banks charge to their best customers (p. 318)

primitive equilibrium first stage of economic development during which the economy is static (p. 488)

principal amount of money borrowed when getting a loan or issuing a bond; basis upon which interest is computed (p. 56)

Principle of Diminishing Marginal Utility doctrine that people receive less and less satisfaction for every additional unit of a product consumed (p. 108)

Principle of Diminishing Returns law that states that additional units of input add less and less to total product; Stage II of the production function (p. 133)

private enterprise economy market economy where the means of production are owned by private citizens; free enterprise economy (p. 79)

private property right of private citizens to own and control their property, including the factors of production (p. 35)

private sector that part of the economy made up of individuals and privately owned businesses (p. 237)

problem bank list Federal Deposit Insurance Corporation list of troubled banks requiring close FDIC attention (p. 292)

producer cooperative nonprofit cooperative organization that secures a market for the output of its members (p. 64)

producer price index series used to measure changes in prices of raw materials and other producer goods; formerly the wholesale price index (p. 365)

product competition non-price competition that emphasizes product quality rather than price (p. 162)

product differentiation differences, real or imaginary, among competing products within an industry (p. 84)

product markets markets where economic products are bought and sold (p. 79)

production combining the factors of production to create goods and services (p. 17)

production function concept that relates total input to increasing amounts of inputs; illustrates the Law of Variable Proportions (p. 130)

production possibilities frontier graph representing various combinations of maximum output when all resources are fully employed (p. 20)

productivity efficiency with which resources are used in production (p. 376)

professional association affiliations of professional workers from specialized occupations (p. 66)

professional labor workers with high-level technical and managerial skills (p. 193)

profit income remaining after all costs involved in the production and/or sale of a good or service have been met (p. 37)

profit motive urge or desire to engage in business activity for gain; driving force for improvement in a market economy (p. 37)

profit-maximizing quantity of output amount of output that maximizes profits; output level where marginal revenue equals marginal cost (p. 144)

progressive tax tax where the percentage of income paid in tax rises as income goes up (p. 215)

proletariat Marxist term for workers with no capital goods of their own (p. 463)

promotional competition non-price competition based on product promotion (p. 162)

property tax tax levied on assessed value of real and personal property (p. 224)

proportional tax tax where percentage of income paid in tax is the same regardless of the level of income (p. 215)

protectionists those favoring quotas and tariffs to protect domestic industries (p. 445)

protective tariff tariff levied on imports to protect domestic producers (p. 443)

proxy ballot that allows the representative of a shareholder to vote in corporate matters (p. 56)

public goods goods and services provided by the government and collectively consumed by many individuals (p. 237)

public sector that part of the economy made up of federal, state, and local governments (p. 237)

public utilities companies providing essential services to consumers and are subject to some governmental regulations (p. 68)

pure competition market structure in which a large number of buyers and sellers deal with exactly the same economic product, all producers are too small to influence price, and it is relatively easy for new firms to enter the industry (p. 81)

Q

quantity supplied amount brought to market at a given price; a point on the supply curve (p. 125)

quantity theory of money theory that the growth of the money supply affects the rate of inflation in the long run (p. 318)

quota absolute limit on the number of goods allowed into a country (p. 443)

R

rationing system that distributes limited amounts of a product to everyone (p. 153)

raw materials unrefined natural resources used in the productive process (p. 132)

Reaganomics President Ronald Reagan's supply-side policies (p. 420)

real dollars dollar measure adjusted to remove distortions of price changes; same as constant dollars (p. 204)

real estate investment trust (REIT) financial organization that channels funds to the home-building industry (p. 333)

real GNP GNP with inflation removed; GNP in constant dollars (p. 365)

real GNP per capita real GNP divided by population (p. 378)

real property wealth in the form of real estate and permanent attachments to land and buildings (p. 225)

rebate partial refund of purchase price of a product made after the sale (p. 170)

recession phase of the business cycle during which real GNP declines (p. 381)

Reciprocal Trade Agreements Act 1934 law empowering the government to lower tariffs if other nations reciprocate (p. 447)

regressive tax tax where percentage of income paid in tax goes down as income goes up (p. 216)

Regulation Q federal requirement in effect until April, 1986, that capped the maximum interest paid on savings accounts (p. 290)

Regulation Z provision that extends truth-in-lending disclosures to individuals and businesses (p. 309)

renewable resources natural resources that can be renewed for future use (p. 374)

required reserves dollar amounts set aside by law to back a deposit (p. 285)

reserve requirement rule that a certain percent of every deposit be set aside for pro-

tection of the depositor; one of the tools of monetary policy (p. 285)

retained earnings business profits kept for investment purposes; undistributed corporate profits (p. 361)

revenue tariff tax on imported goods to raise revenue (p. 443)

revolving credit authorization allowing a consumer to buy goods on credit without prior approval; open-ended credit (p. 572)

right-to-work laws state legislation outlawing union shops (p. 190)

run on the bank sudden rush of withdrawals by depositors who anticipate possible bank failure (p. 291)

S

sales tax general tax levied on a product at the time of sale (p. 223)

sanctity of contract right of individuals and businesses to make agreements and contracts enforceable by law (p. 36)

saving absence of spending that frees goods and services for use in other investments (p. 39)

savings funds made available by savers for investors to use (p. 325)

savings and loan association non-bank financial institution that accepts deposits and makes mortgage loans (p. 327)

savings bond small denomination, non-transferable, and registered debt obligations of the U.S. government (p. 255)

savings deposits interest-earning deposits that can be withdrawn without prior notice (p. 279)

scarcity fundamental economic problem resulting from a combination of scarce resources and people's virtually unlimited wants and needs (p. 6)

seasonal unemployment unemployment due to conditions that prevail during certain seasons of the year (p. 401)

secondhand sales sales of products that are not new (p. 350)

securities collective name for bonds, notes, and stock certificates (p. 334)

securities exchanges organized markets where stocks are bought and sold (p. 334)

securities market market where corporate and government securities are traded (p. 334)

seizure temporary government takeover of a company to keep it running during a labor-management dispute (p. 192)

selective credit controls powers vested in the FED to control credit conditions in selective markets (p. 316)

semiskilled labor workers with enough ability to run simple machines (p. 193)

seniority amount of time a worker has been on a job; practice of rewarding workers according to length of service (p. 196)

service work or labor performed for someone (p. 13)

service cooperative nonprofit association of consumers that secures services for the benefit of its members (p. 63)

share drafts checkable-type accounts issued by credit unions (p. 330)

shareholders businesses or individuals who own shares of stock in a corporation; same as stockholders (p. 55)

short run production period long enough to allow producers to change amount of variable inputs used in production (p. 157)

shortage condition in which the quantity demanded is greater than the quantity supplied at a given price (p. 150)

silver certificates currency first issued in 1886 and backed by silver dollars (p. 301)

skilled labor workers who can operate complex equipment and require little supervision (p. 193)

Social Security federal program that covers many disability and retirement needs for most workers (p. 41)

social welfare net programs government programs that provide support for the poor (p. 520)

socialism economic system in which government owns some means of production and has a hand in distribution of output (p. 462)

sole proprietorship form of business organization owned and operated by one person (p. 49)

Solidarity underground Polish labor union (p. 476)

special drawing right (SDR) reserve account used by the International Monetary Fund to settle trade balances (p. 455)

spot market market where commodities are traded for cash; market where contracts are written for delivery in the present as opposed to a future market (p. 533)

stages of production three phases—increasing, diminishing, and negative—of the production function (p. 133)

Standard and Poor's 500 stock performance index based on 500 NYSE stocks (p. 337)

standard of living quality of life based on kind and amount of material goods owned (p. 371)

state banks banks that receive permission to operate from the state in which they reside (p. 280)

state farms large farms in the Soviet Union owned and operated by government (p. 471)

stock ownership shares of a corporation; common and preferred stock (p. 55)

stockbroker individual who buys and sells stocks for others (p. 336)

stockholders owners of shares of corporate stock; shareholders (p. 55)

store of value property of money that permits a person to store purchasing power until needed; a function of money (p. 272)

storming Soviet practice of rushing production at month's end to fill quotas (p. 472)

strike organized work stoppages by union workers (p. 185)

structural unemployment unemployment due to fundamental, underlying changes in the economy (p. 399)

subsidies transfer payments made to certain groups to bolster income (p. 240)

subsistence state in which just enough is produced for survival (p. 529)

substitutes goods or services that can be used in place of others (p. 105)

substitution effect change in quantity demanded of a product due to its use as a substitute for other products when the price of that product changes (p. 103)

Supplemental Security Income (SSI) federal aid program that makes cash payments to elderly who are blind or disabled (p. 520)

supply array of quantities that would be produced and offered for sale at each and every possible market price (p. 123)

supply curve graphic representation of the quantities produced at each and every price in the market (p. 124)

supply elasticity responsiveness of a change in quantity supplied to a change in price (p. 127)

supply schedule listing showing the quantity produced at each and every possible price in the market (p. 124)

supply-side economics policies focusing on stimulation of total production (p. 420)

surcharge additional charge added to other charges already in place; (p. 217)

surplus leftover output resulting from too much production and too little demand at a given price (p. 150)

surplus value Marxist term for the difference between a worker's pay and the value of his or her output (p. 464)

T

takeoff second stage of economic development where growth and change begins (p. 490)

tangible personal property items of wealth not permanently attached to land or buildings (p. 225)

tariff tax (p. 443)

tax assessor person who examines property to determine its tax value (p. 226)

tax base total amount of taxable income and property in an area (p. 372)

tax loopholes missing information or exceptions in the tax law that permit businesses and individuals to avoid taxes (p. 216)

tax neutral outcome of tax revision that does not affect total collections (p. 216)

tax return annual report filed with the local, state, or federal government detailing income earned and taxes owed (p. 218)

tax-exempt free from tax (p. 333)

technological monopoloy market condition allowing a firm to act as a monopolist because it owns or controls manufacturing methods or other technologies (p. 88)

technological unemployment lack of employment caused by automation and new production techniques (p. 401)

theory of negotiated wages explanation of wage based on influence of organized labor and collective bargaining (p. 196)

theory of production the combination of inputs to get outputs (p. 128)

Third World developing countries not aligned with a superpower (p. 485)

tight money policy actions designed to slow the growth of money and increase the price of credit (p. 311)

time deposits interest-earning deposits that cannot be withdrawn without prior notice (p. 279)

total cost variable plus fixed costs; all costs associated with production (p. 137)

total product total output or total production of a business firm (p. 132)

total revenue total receipts; price of goods sold times quantity sold (p. 142)

trade deficit deficit in the balance of payments (p. 447)

trade union union of workers who have a common skill or share the same kind of work; craft union (p. 184)

trade-weighted value of the U.S. dollar index of U.S. dollar strength against foreign currencies (p. 455)

traditional economy society in which economic decisions are made according to habit, custom, or tradition (p. 28)

traditional theory of wage determination explanation of wage rates that relies on the forces of supply and demand (p. 195)

transfer payment financial assistance provided by government for which nothing is received in return (p. 240)

treasury bills short-term federal debt used to borrow money from the private sector; part of the national debt (p. 254)

treasury bonds long-term federal debt used to borrow money from the private sector; part of the national debt (p. 254)

Treasury coin notes currency first issued by the U.S. Treasury in 1890 (p. 301)

trend line growth path of the economy if not affected by periods of expansion and recession (p. 382)

trough bottom of the business cycle; point where real GNP stops going down and turns up (p. 381)

trusts combinations of corporations to insure uniform behavior, usually price fixing or other agreements, to restrict competition (p. 92)

truth-in-lending legal requirement that lenders provide consumers with certain basic information about loans (p. 309)

two-tier wage system wage policy that pays newer workers a lower wage than others already on the job (p. 204)

U

underground economy economic activity that is not reported because it is illegal or because of tax-dodging (p. 352)

undistributed corporate profits profits not paid out; retained earnings (p. 361)

unemployed persons people who have made an attempt to find a job within the past month, but are still unemployed (p. 395)

unemployment condition of not having a job (p. 395)

unemployment insurance government program providing payments to the unemployed; an automatic stabilizer (p. 419)

unemployment rate   ratio of the unemployed to total persons in the civilian labor force (p. 395)

union shop   arrangement under which workers must join a union shortly after being hired (p. 190)

unit elastic   proportional change in quantity demanded or supplied in response to a given change in price (p. 111)

United States notes   paper currency issued by the federal government in 1862 to finance the Civil War; greenbacks (p. 300)

unlimited liability   requirement that owners are personally and fully responsible for all business debts; applies to sole proprietorships and partnerships (p. 50)

unlimited life   situation in which the legal entity of a business is not affected by changes of ownership; applies only to the corporation (p. 58)

unrelated individuals   persons who live alone or with non-relatives (p. 354)

unskilled labor   workers not trained to run machines and equipment (p. 193)

user fee   fee paid for the use of a product; form of benefit tax (p. 231)

usury laws   state regulations that put a ceiling on the interest charged on certain types of loans (p. 290)

utility   ability or capacity of a good or service to be useful and give satisfaction to someone (p. 14)

V

value   worth of a good or service as determined by the market (p. 14)

value added tax (VAT)   tax placed on the value added at every stage in the production process (p. 229)

variable cost   production expense that varies as the level of output changes; labor, raw materials, energy (p. 137)

vertical merger   joining together of companies that engage in successive stages of production or marketing (p. 61)

voluntary arbitration   agreement by labor and management to place a dispute before a third party for a binding settlement (p. 191)

voluntary exchange   act of buying or selling without involvement of others (p. 34)

W

wage rate   prevailing amount of pay for a particular type of job (p. 195)

wage-price controls   laws that make it illegal to raise prices or wages (p. 423)

wampum   shell money used by native Americans in the colonial period (p. 273)

want   way of expressing or communicating a need (p. 11)

wealth   tangible goods that have value and can be owned (p. 15)

white-collar workers   employees in professional fields who generally receive salaries (p. 518)

whole life   form of insurance with both a savings and a death benefit; ordinary life insurance (p. 560)

wildcat banks   name given to fraudulent banks located in remote and inaccessible areas during the early 1800's (p. 300)

workfare   program requiring welfare recipients to perform community-service work in exchange for benefits received (p. 523)

World Bank   international agency that makes loans to developing countries; International Bank for Reconstruction and Development (p. 495)

Z

zero-population growth   state of equilibrium in which population size does not change (p. 499)

Index

production: 17; basic decisions of society re: 7–8, 28–29, 31, 83; cost of, 134–40, 143–45, 158, 166–67; factors of, 16–18, 20–22, 128–33, 374–76; stages of, 133–34
productivity 127, 128–36, 163, 376–78
professional associations 47, 66
profit: 37–38; maximization of, 142, 143–45, 158; and sales maximization hypothesis, 143
profit motive 36–38
property: private, 35–36, 461–62, 466, 467; real, 225; tangible and intangible personal, 225–26
protectionism 445–47; vs. free trade, 448; tariffs, 443
psychic income 198
public sector of economy 237, 238
public utilities 68, 90–91, 248
purchasing power, effects of federal debt on 254, 257

R

rationing 153–55
raw materials: 132; and cost efficiency, 134–36; of developing nations, 488; variable inputs of, in production, 157
Reagan, Ronald, President 192, 216, 249, 255, 259
Reaganomics 420–21, 422–23, 426
real estate agent 87
Real Estate Investment Trust (REIT) 333–34
recession 381, 383; average length of, 386; deflation of early 1920's, 403; Marxist view of, 464; of 1981, 407; predicting, 388; post WW II, 384, 386, 428
Reciprocal Trade Agreements Act 447–49
recreation, state and local expenditures for 248
religion, and economic development 501–2
rents 355

reserves, bank, required by law 285, 311–13
resources, natural: allocation of 90, 170, 261, 372, 545, 553, 555; nonrenewable, 536–37; population and, 529; renewable 374, 534–36; shortages, 499–500. See also raw materials
resumé 566–67
retailers offering financial services 290
returns: diminishing, 133–34; increasing, 133; negative, 134
revenue, business: marginal, 142–45; total, 142
Ricardo, David 83, 355
right-to-work laws 190, 203
Rivlin, Alice M. 241
roads and highways: construction programs, 240; state and local expenditures for, 246–48
Russia 467, 468. See also Union of Soviet Socialist Republics

S

sales clerk 141
sales maximization hypothesis 143
Samuelson, Paul 91
Saudi Arabia 310, 495, 496
saving 39–40, 375–76
savings 325; in command economy, 492; in market economy, 325–26, 491–92
savings accounts 279
savings bonds 255
savings and loan associations 327–28, 329, 340
Say, John Baptiste 135
scarcity 6–7, 14, 551, 553–55
securities 334; government, 255–56, 313–15; market for, 334–37
Securities and Exchange Commission (SEC) 58, 94
security, economic 40–41
seizure 191, 192
services 13, 15, 16.
sewer and sanitation services 215, 248

Sherman Antitrust Act of 1890 92, 185
shortages, and prices 150, 151
silver certificates 301
silver coins 301
silver futures 338–39
size of business, and cost efficiency 90–91
Smith, Adam 33, 83, 135
Smoot-Hawley Tariff 447
socialism 462, 463, 467
Social Security 41, 68, 219–22, 242, 260, 420
social services in Sweden 478
social welfare-net programs 419–20, 520; federal expenditures for, 245–260; federal vs. state role in providing, 525; negative income tax as alternative, 524
society: choices of, 7–8; economic and social goals of, 40–42; ethical judgments of, 11; tax system as tool to promote goals of, 218; unstable economy and, 390–91, 415; values of, and economy, 51, 501–2
sole proprietorship 49–52
Soviet Union 467–74, 554–55. See also Union of Soviet Socialist Republics
Sowell, Thomas 517
specialization, as key to trade 437, 441–42
stabilizers, automatic 419–20, 422
Stalin, Joseph 468
Standard and Poor's 500 337
standard of living 371–72
state government expenditures of, 246–49; federal control vs., 525; social services, 520, 523, 525
statistician 331, 521
statistics, federal government: importance, 352–53; shortcomings of, 351–52, 427; national income accounting, 349–50, 358
stock 55, 56; margin requirement for, 316; prices of, 336–37
stock market 335–37; as expression of investors'

Photo Credits

Pages 2–3, Mitchel L. Osborne; 4, Don Smetzer/Click Chicago; 6, Cobalt Productions; 8, Zimmerman/Alpha; 9, University of Colorado at Boulder; 12 (l) Gerard Photography, (r) File Photo; 14, Larry Hamill; 16, National Coal Association; 18, Doug Martin; 19, Charles Zirkle; 26, Commercial Image; 29, Marvin J. Wolf/FPG; 32, John Huehnergarth; 33, The Granger Collection/New York; 36, Pictures Unlimited; 37, (t) Reprinted by permission/Tribune Media Service, (b) Johnson Publishing; 39, Tony Freeman; 41, Allen Zak; 46, Mike Penney; 48 (l) Doug Martin, (r) Hickson-Bender; 50, Universal Press Syndicate, © 1984. Reprinted with permission. All rights reserved; 51, Historical Pictures Service, Inc.; 64, National 4–H Council; 53, Apple Computer, Inc.; 57, Doug Martin; 65, Communications Workers of America; 66, Fred Ward/Black Star; 67, Cobalt Productions; 68, File Photo; 74–75, Cameramann International; 76, © Leverett Bradley/After Image, Inc.; 78, Norma Morrison; 83, The Granger Collection, New York; 85, Milt Priggee/Dayton Journal Herald; 87, Allen Zak; 88, C.P. Houston; 91, Wide World Photos, Inc.; 92, Library of Congress; 98, Bob Daemmrich; 100, Howard DeCruyenaere; 105, S.L. Craig/Bruce Coleman, Inc.; 107, Historical Pictures Service, Inc.; 109, Hodgins in New York Daily News; 112, Larry Hamill; 116, American Red Cross; 117, Courtesy Whirlpool; 118, Cameramann International; 122, © Don Klumpp/The Image Bank; 124, Cobalt Productions; 129, Robert Weber; 130, Cobalt Productions; 132, Werner Stoy/Camera Hawaii; 135, Historical Pictures Service, Inc.; 137, Eric Hoffhines; 139, 140, Latent Image; 141, Hickson-Bender; 143, Ulli Steltzer/Princeton University; 148, Howard DeCruyenaere; 154, Vince Streano/After Image, Inc.; 155, Wide World Photos, Inc., (inset) Cobalt Productions; 159, Cobalt Productions; 161 (l) From *The Wall Street Journal*/Permission by Cartoon Features Syndicate, (r) Cobalt Productions; 163, Historical Pictures Service, Inc.; 165, Bill Nation/Sygma; 169 (l) Tony Freeman, (r) Mary Messenger; 178–179, U.A.W. Solidarity; 180, O. Franken/Sygma; 182, The Granger Collection, New York; 186, The Archives of Labor & Urban Affairs/Wayne State University; 188, Wide World Photos, Inc.; 191, The Archives of Labor & Urban Affairs/Wayne State University; 193 (l) Nippon Electric Company, (r) Eric Hoffhines; 197, Walter E. Williams; 200, Don Klumpp/Don Klumpp Productions; 202 (l) Debbie Dean, (r) Eric Hoffhines; 210, Bob Daemmrich; 214 (l) Cobalt Productions, (r) Allen Zak; 217, © 1986 by Herblock in *The Washington Post*; 222, Marc Pokemoner/Click Chicago; 226, © Shepard Sherbell/Picture Group; 232, PHOTRI; 236, Cobalt Productions; 239, 241, Wide World Photos, Inc.; 244 (r) Doug Martin, (l) Cobalt Productions; 249, Universal Press Syndicate, © 1981. Reprinted with permission. All rights reserved.; 254, The Jeff Stahler Collection, The Ohio State University, Library for Communication and Graphic Arts; 255, Cobalt Productions; 258, File Photo; 260, Cynthia Johnson/Gamma-Liaison; 268-269, Frank Fisher/After Image, Inc.; 270, Cameramann International; 272, Reprinted by permission News America Syndicate; 274, The Granger Collection, New York; 276, Historical Pictures Service, Inc.; 279, Elaine Comer; 281, The Granger Collection, New York; 283, Cobalt Productions; 286, Chick Young/King Features Syndicate; 287, Wide World Photos, Inc.; 289, Pictures Unlimited; 292, Cobalt Productions; 298, Bob Daemmrich; 300, Eric Hoffhines; 306, Diana Walker/Gamma-Liaison; 315, Cobalt Productions; 316, Dennis Brack/Black Star; 319, Jefferson Communications, Inc.; 324, Pictures Unlimited; 328, FlexPhoto; 331, Doug Martin; 332, Latent Image; 333, Doug Martin; 335, R.M. Smythe Co., Inc.; 338, Larry Downing/Woodfin Camp & Associates; 340, Charles Zirkle/The Image Broker; 346–347, © Barrie Rokeach/The Image Bank; 348, Commercial Image; 350, Joseph Nettis/Photo Researchers, Inc.; 353, Frank Oberle/After Image, Inc.; 354 Lorenz, © 1982/*The New Yorker Magazine*; 355, The Granger Collection/New York; 356 (l) George Kufrin/Click Chicago, (r) Ohio Agriculture Research & Development Center; 362, By permission of Bill Mauldin & Wil-Jo Associates; 370, Peter Pearson/Click Chicago; 372, Ronald Greer/Click Chicago; 373, Cobalt Production; 375, Doug Martin; 377, John T. Bledsoe/U.S. News & World Report; 387, United Features Syndicate; 390, Cartoon Features Syndicate; 394, © Eugene Richards/Magnum Photos, Inc.; 396, Randy Taylor/Sygma; 398, Wide World Photos, Inc.; 399, Cameramann International; 400, Brian Parker/Tom Stack & Associates; 401 (l) Stevenson © 1977/*The New Yorker Magazine*, (r) Sepp Seitz/Woodfin Camp & Associates; 404, King Features Syndicate; 408, Doug Hoke; 414, Terry Arthur/The White House; 416, Dany Krist/Uniphoto; 418, Tom Stack/Tom Stack & Associates; 419, Cobalt Productions; 428, Reprinted by permission of Tribune Company Syndicate, Inc.; 431, Universal Press Syndicate, © 1984. Reprinted with permission. All rights reserved.; 434–435, Travel Pix/FPG; 436, Cameramann International; 440, J.P. Laffont/Sygma; 441, University of Chicago; 442, Martin Rodgers/Woodfin Camp & Associates; 444, Pressen Bild/PhotoReporters; 445, Reprinted by permission Newspaper Enterprise Association, Inc.; 446, Martin A. Levick/Black Star; 450, Allan Zak; 454, John Troha/Black Star; 460, Tom Zetterstrom/Rainbow;

464, Karen Des Jardin/Gamma-Liaison; 465, The Granger Collection, New York; 466, FPG; 470, Tass from Sovfoto; 473, Chicago Tribune/New York News Syndicate; 477, Hiroji Kubota/Magnum; 479, Joseph Rodriguez/Black Star; 480 (l) Martin Rodgers/Uniphoto, (r) Wide World Photos, Inc.; 484, Toby Molenaar/Woodfin Camp & Associates; 489, McAllister Denver/Uniphoto; 490, Clyde/FPG; 492, Robert Nickelsberg/Gamma-Liaison; 493, David Perry; 497, P. Vauhty/Sygma; 498, Susan Meiselas/Magnum; 501, The Granger Collection/New York; 503, Cameramann International; 508–509, Paola Koch/Photo Researchers, Inc.; 510, Larry Day Photography; 517, Wide World Photos, Inc.; 519, J.P. Laffont/Sygma; 521, Latent Image; 522, Doug Martin; 523, Morrie Turner, © 1983, Field Enterprises, Inc.; 528, Dennis Brack/Black Star; 530, The Granger Collection/New York; 531, Henry Bureau/Sygma; 534, Universal Press Syndicate, Reprinted with permission. All rights reserved.; 536, Alex Gotfryd; 538, Jim Pickerell; 539, James N. Westwater; 540, Bob Bliss; 542, 543, Susan Marguart; 544, Doug Martin; 550, Commercial Image; 552, Allen Zak; 555, Shostal Associates; 557, Pictures Unlimited.

Acknowledgments

We would like to acknowledge the following: **p. 60,** "FTC Takes the Fizz Out of Two Soft-Drink Mergers," reprinted from *U.S. News & World Report* issue of June 30, 1986, Copyright 1986, U.S. News & World Report; **p. 154,** "Cattle Contracts Fall Due to Woes of Edwin L. Cox," reprinted by *The Wall Street Journal* © Dow Jones and Co., 1986, all rights reserved *World Rights in the English Language; **p. 198,** "Money Isn't Everything," excerpted from *U.S. News & World Report* issue of June 23, 1986, Copyright 1986, *U.S. News & World Report;* **p. 293,** "Most Bank Failures Since Depression," reprinted from the *Kentucky Post* issue of November 8, 1986; **p. 310,** "The Case of the Missing Billions," excerpted from *U.S. News & World Report* issue of March 3, 1986, Copyright 1986, U.S. News & World Report; **p. 336,** "New York Stock Exchange, The Dow Jones Averages," reprinted by *The Wall Street Journal* © Dow Jones and Co., 1986, all rights reserved *World Rights in the English Language; **p. 385,** "Economic Index Rose 0.6% in October/Leading Indicators (graph)," reprinted by *The Wall Street Journal* © Dow Jones and Co., 1986, all rights reserved *World Rights in the English Language; **p. 405,** "When Inflation Rate is 116,000%, Prices Change by the Hour," reprinted by *The Wall Street Journal* © Dow Jones and Co., 1986, all rights reserved *World Rights in the English Language; **p. 451,** "Foreign Exchange," reprinted by *The Wall Street Journal* © Dow Jones and Co., 1986, all rights reserved *World Rights in the English Language; **p. 525,** "Poverty Levels," reprinted by *The Wall Street Journal* © Dow Jones and Co., 1986, all rights reserved *World Rights in the English Language; **p. 533,** "Even $18-a-Barrel Oil Won't Halt Plunging U.S. Output," reprinted by *The Wall Street Journal* © Dow Jones and Co., 1986, all rights reserved *World Rights in the English Language; **pp. 486–487, 586–590, 592–596,** adapted from *The World Bank Atlas* 1986; reproduced by permission of The World Bank (Washington, D.C.).